NATIONAL *Sciences*
ACADEMIES *Engineering*
Medicine

NATIONAL
ACADEMIES
PRESS
Washington, DC

Reducing Intergenerational Poverty

Greg J. Duncan, Jennifer Appleton Gootman, Priyanka Nalamada, *Editors*

Committee on Policies and Programs to Reduce Intergenerational Poverty

Board on Children, Youth, and Families

Committee on National Statistics

Division of Behavioral and Social Sciences and Education

Consensus Study Report

NATIONAL ACADEMIES PRESS 500 Fifth Street, NW Washington, DC 20001

This activity was supported by contracts between the National Academy of Sciences and the Administration for Children and Families, a division of the U.S. Department of Health and Human Services (75ACF121C00093), Bainum Family Foundation (7608), Doris Duke Foundation (2021249), Foundation for Child Development (NAS 03-2021), National Academy of Sciences W.K. Kellogg Fund, Russell Sage Foundation (2104-31166), and W.K. Kellogg Foundation (P-6000158-2021). Support for the work of the Board on Children, Youth, and Families is provided by the Robert Wood Johnson Foundation (79846). Any opinions, findings, conclusions, or recommendations expressed in this publication do not necessarily reflect the views of any organization or agency that provided support for the project.

International Standard Book Number-13: 978-0-309-70366-6
International Standard Book Number-10: 0-309-70366-2
Digital Object Identifier: https://doi.org/10.17226/27058
Library of Congress Control Number: 2023952320

This publication is available from the National Academies Press, 500 Fifth Street, NW, Keck 360, Washington, DC 20001; (800) 624-6242 or (202) 334-3313; http://www.nap.edu.

Copyright 2024 by the National Academy of Sciences. National Academies of Sciences, Engineering, and Medicine and National Academies Press and the graphical logos for each are all trademarks of the National Academy of Sciences. All rights reserved.

Printed in the United States of America.

Suggested citation: National Academies of Sciences, Engineering, and Medicine. 2024. *Reducing Intergenerational Poverty*. Washington, DC: The National Academies Press. https://doi.org/10.17226/27058.

The **National Academy of Sciences** was established in 1863 by an Act of Congress, signed by President Lincoln, as a private, nongovernmental institution to advise the nation on issues related to science and technology. Members are elected by their peers for outstanding contributions to research. Dr. Marcia McNutt is president.

The **National Academy of Engineering** was established in 1964 under the charter of the National Academy of Sciences to bring the practices of engineering to advising the nation. Members are elected by their peers for extraordinary contributions to engineering. Dr. John L. Anderson is president.

The **National Academy of Medicine** (formerly the Institute of Medicine) was established in 1970 under the charter of the National Academy of Sciences to advise the nation on medical and health issues. Members are elected by their peers for distinguished contributions to medicine and health. Dr. Victor J. Dzau is president.

The three Academies work together as the **National Academies of Sciences, Engineering, and Medicine** to provide independent, objective analysis and advice to the nation and conduct other activities to solve complex problems and inform public policy decisions. The National Academies also encourage education and research, recognize outstanding contributions to knowledge, and increase public understanding in matters of science, engineering, and medicine.

Learn more about the National Academies of Sciences, Engineering, and Medicine at **www.nationalacademies.org**.

Consensus Study Reports published by the National Academies of Sciences, Engineering, and Medicine document the evidence-based consensus on the study's statement of task by an authoring committee of experts. Reports typically include findings, conclusions, and recommendations based on information gathered by the committee and the committee's deliberations. Each report has been subjected to a rigorous and independent peer-review process and it represents the position of the National Academies on the statement of task.

Proceedings published by the National Academies of Sciences, Engineering, and Medicine chronicle the presentations and discussions at a workshop, symposium, or other event convened by the National Academies. The statements and opinions contained in proceedings are those of the participants and are not endorsed by other participants, the planning committee, or the National Academies.

Rapid Expert Consultations published by the National Academies of Sciences, Engineering, and Medicine are authored by subject-matter experts on narrowly focused topics that can be supported by a body of evidence. The discussions contained in rapid expert consultations are considered those of the authors and do not contain policy recommendations. Rapid expert consultations are reviewed by the institution before release.

For information about other products and activities of the National Academies, please visit www.nationalacademies.org/about/whatwedo.

COMMITTEE ON POLICIES AND PROGRAMS TO REDUCE INTERGENERATIONAL POVERTY

GREG J. DUNCAN (Chair), University of California, Irvine
FENABA R. ADDO, University of North Carolina, Chapel Hill
ANNA AIZER, Brown University
MARGARET R. BURCHINAL, University of Virginia
RAJ CHETTY, Harvard University
STEPHANIE A. FRYBERG, University of Michigan
HARRY J. HOLZER, Georgetown University
VONNIE C. MCLOYD, University of Michigan
KIMBERLY G. MONTEZ, Wake Forest School of Medicine
AISHA D. NYANDORO, Springboard to Opportunities
MARY E. PATTILLO, Northwestern University
JESSE ROTHSTEIN, University of California, Berkeley
MICHAEL R. STRAIN, American Enterprise Institute
STEPHEN J. TREJO, University of Texas at Austin

Study Staff

JENNIFER APPLETON GOOTMAN, *Study Director* (from March 2022)
SUZANNE LE MENESTREL, *Study Director* (until January 2022)
PRIYANKA NALAMADA, *Program Officer*
BRIANA SMITH, *Senior Program Assistant* (from July 2022)
MARISSA GLOVER, *Senior Program Assistant* (until July 2022)
CONNIE CITRO, *Senior Scholar*
EMILY P. BACKES, *Deputy Board Director*

Consultant

RITA HAMAD, James C. Puffer American Board of Family Medicine / National Academy of Medicine Fellow, Harvard School of Public Health

BOARD ON CHILDREN, YOUTH, AND FAMILIES

JONATHAN TODRES (*Chair*), Georgia State University College of Law
RICHARD F. CATALANO, JR., University of Washington School of Social Work
TAMMY CHANG, University of Michigan
DIMITRI A. CHRISTAKIS, Seattle Children's Research Institute, University of Washington
ANDREA GONZALEZ, McMaster University
NANCY E. HILL, Harvard University
CHARLES HOMER, Economic Mobility Pathways
MARGARET KUKLINSKI, University of Washington
MICHAEL C. LU, UC Berkeley School of Public Health
STEPHANIE J. MONROE, Wrenwood Group
STEPHEN RUSSELL, The University of Texas at Austin
NISHA SACHDEV, Premnas Partners, Washington, DC
JANE WALDFOGEL, Columbia University School of Social Work
JOANNA L. WILLIAMS, Rutgers University

Staff

NATACHA BLAIN, *Senior Board Director*
EMILY P. BACKES, *Deputy Board Director*

COMMITTEE ON NATIONAL STATISTICS

KATHARINE G. ABRAHAM (*Chair*), University of Maryland, College Park
MICK P. COUPER, Institute for Social Research, University of Michigan
DIANA FARRELL, JPMorgan Chase Institute
ROBERT M. GOERGE, Chapin Hall at the University of Chicago
ERICA GROSHEN, School of Industrial and Labor Relations, Cornell University
DANIEL E. HO, Stanford Law School and Stanford Institute for Economic Policy Research
HILARY HOYNES, Goldman School of Public Policy and Department of Economics, University of California, Berkeley
DANIEL KIFER, Department of Computer Science, The Pennsylvania State University
SHARON LOHR, School of Mathematical and Statistical Sciences, Arizona State University, *Emeritus*
NELA RICHARDSON, ADP Research Institute
C. MATTHEW SNIPP, School of the Humanities and Sciences, Stanford University
ELIZABETH A. STUART, Department of Mental Health, Johns Hopkins Bloomberg School of Public Health

Staff

MELISSA CHIU, *Director*
BRIAN HARRIS-KOJETIN, *Senior Scholar*
CONSTANCE F. CITRO, *Senior Scholar*

Reviewers

This Consensus Study Report was reviewed in draft form by individuals chosen for their diverse perspectives and technical expertise. The purpose of this independent review is to provide candid and critical comments that will assist the National Academies of Sciences, Engineering, and Medicine in making each published report as sound as possible and to ensure that it meets the institutional standards for quality, objectivity, evidence, and responsiveness to the study charge. The review comments and draft manuscript remain confidential to protect the integrity of the deliberative process.

We thank the following individuals for their review of this report:

RICHARD V. BURKHAUSER, Cornell University
RONALD F. FERGUSON, Harvard University
VIVIAN L. GADSDEN, University of Pennsylvania
CHARLES J. HOMER, Economic Mobility Pathways
KATHERINE MAGNUSON, University of Wisconsin–Madison
CYNTHIA S. OSBORNE, Vanderbilt University
STEVEN RAPHAEL, University of California, Berkeley
H. LUKE SHAEFER, University of Michigan
C. MATTHEW SNIPP, Stanford University
FLORENCIA TORCHE, Stanford University

Although the reviewers listed above provided many constructive comments and suggestions, they were not asked to endorse the conclusions or recommendations of this report, nor did they see the final draft before its release. The review of this report was overseen by **KENNETH A. DODGE,** Duke University, and **SHERRY GLIED,** New York University. They were responsible for making certain that an independent examination of this report was carried out in accordance with the standards of the National Academies and that all review comments were carefully considered. Responsibility for the final content rests entirely with the authoring committee and the National Academies.

Acknowledgments

An ad hoc consensus study committee of the National Academies of Sciences, Engineering, and Medicine was convened to analyze the evidence on key determinants of intergenerational poverty and the effectiveness of programs designed to address those determinants in order to identify policies and programs with the potential to reduce long-term, intergenerational poverty.

The committee thanks the sponsors of this study for their support: the Administration for Children and Families, a division of the U.S. Department of Health and Human Services, the Bainum Family Foundation, the Doris Duke Foundation, the Foundation for Child Development, the National Academy of Sciences W.K. Kellogg Fund, the Russell Sage Foundation, and the W.K. Kellogg Foundation.

This report would not have been possible without the contributions of many people. Special thanks go to the members of the committee, who dedicated extensive time, expertise, and energy to the drafting of the report. The committee also thanks the members of the staff of the National Academies for their significant contributions to the report: Jennifer Appleton Gootman, Priyanka Nalamada, Emily Backes, and Briana Smith, as well as Suzanne LeMenestral and Marissa Glover, who both contributed to the early stages of working with the committee.

The committee is also grateful to Javed Kahn, Pamella Atayi, and Lisa Alston for their administrative and financial assistance on this project. From the Office of Reports and Communication of the Division of Behavioral and Social Sciences and Education (DBASSE), Kirsten Sampson Snyder, Viola Horek, Douglas Sprunger, and Meredith Fender shepherded the report through the review and the production process and assisted with its communication and dissemination. Hannah Fuller and Megan Lowry, of the Office of News and Public Information, and Sandra McDermin and Julie Eubank, of the Office of Congressional and Government Affairs, were instrumental in the release and promotion of the report. The committee also thanks Clair Woolley of the National Academies Press and Bea Porter of DBASSE for their assistance with the production of the final report; Anne Marie Houppert, in the National Academies research library, for her assistance with fact checking and literature searches; as well as Connie Citro and Alix Beatty, National Academies staff, for their skillful writing and editing contributions.

Many individuals volunteered significant time and effort to address and educate the committee during our information gathering sessions. Their willingness to share their perspectives, research, and personal experiences was essential to the committee's work. We thank: Megan Bang, Northwestern University; Jill Duerr Berrick, University of California, Berkeley; Cheryl Crazy Bull, American Indian College Fund; Matt Gregg, Federal Reserve Bank of Minneapolis; Brenda Jones Harden, University of Maryland; Anna Haskins, University of Notre Dame; Joe Hobot, American Indian OIC; Kevin Killer, Oglala Sioux Tribe; Judith LeBlanc, Native Organizers Alliance and Parents; Jens Ludwig, The University of Chicago; Susan Mangold, Juvenile Law Center; Leslie Paik, Arizona State University; Steven Raphael, University of California, Berkeley; Beth Redbird, Northwestern University; Emilia Simeonova, Johns Hopkins University; C. Matt Snipp, Stanford University; Karina L. Walters, University of Washington; Bruce Western, Columbia University; and the parents, caregivers, organizational representatives, and policy experts who participated in our listening sessions.

The committee thanks the researchers who conducted original analyses and prepared commissioned papers: Lawrence M. Berger, Sophie Collyer, Brenda Jones Harden, Margaret Thomas, Jane Waldfogel, Chris Wimer; as well as the staff at Ascend, Aspen Institute, for organizing and shepherding the committee's listening sessions: Marjorie Sims and Andrea Camp. The committee also thanks the following individuals for their contributions to this study and the final report: Nicholas Ainsworth, Dorothy Duncan, Jonathan Fisher, Abby Hiller, David Johnson, Zachary Parolin, and Austen Zheng.

Throughout the project, Natacha Blain, director of the Board on Children, Youth, and Families, Carlotta Arthur and Patti Simon, executive director and associate executive director of DBASSE, alongside Mary Ellen O'Connell and Monica Feit, the then executive director and deputy executive director of DBASSE, provided valuable oversight and guidance.

Greg J. Duncan, *Chair*
Committee on Policies and Programs to
Reduce Intergenerational Poverty

Contents

Acronyms	xxvii
Summary	1
1 Introduction	21

    STUDY APPROACH, 23
    ORGANIZATION OF THE REPORT, 25
    DEFINING INTERGENERATIONAL POVERTY, 26
    ORGANIZING OUR DISCUSSION OF DRIVERS AND
        INTERVENTIONS, 28
    APPLYING A RACIAL/ETHNIC LENS IN ASSESSING
        THE EVIDENCE, 28
    CRITERIA FOR SELECTING PROGRAM AND POLICY
        INTERVENTIONS, 30
        Strength of the Research Evidence, 30
        Magnitude of Impacts and Costs of Policies and
            Programs, 36
        Possible Behavioral Responses to Policies and
            Programs, 36
        Policy Conclusions, 37
        Political Feasibility, 37
        Considering Combinations of Programs, 37

2   A Demographic Portrait of Intergenerational Child Poverty   39
     MEASURING INTERGENERATIONAL POVERTY, 39
     THE DEMOGRAPHICS OF INTERGENERATIONAL
        POVERTY, 41
     A BROADER LOOK AT INTERGENERATIONAL INCOME
        MOBILITY ACROSS GROUPS, 47
     INTERGENERATIONAL INCOME MOBILITY AMONG
        CHILDREN OF IMMIGRANTS, 49
     THE GEOGRAPHIC DISTRIBUTION OF
        INTERGENERATIONAL POVERTY, 51
     INTERGENERATIONAL MOBILITY: TRENDS AND
        COMPARISONS WITH OTHER COUNTIES, 55
        Trends in U.S. Intergenerational Mobility, 55
     INTERGENERATIONAL MOBILITY IN THE UNITED
        STATES VERSUS OTHER COUNTRIES, 58

3   Racial Disparities in Intergenerational Poverty   61
     DEFINING DISPARITY, INEQUALITY, DISCRIMINATION,
        AND STRUCTURAL RACISM, 62
     HISTORICAL ROOTS OF RACIAL DISPARITIES IN
        INTERGENERATIONAL MOBILITY, 62
     CONTEMPORARY DRIVERS OF RACIAL DISPARITY
        IN INTERGENERATIONAL POVERTY, 63
        Education, 66
        Health, 70
        Wages and Employment, 72
        Housing and Neighborhood Environments, 75
        Crime, Victimization, and Criminal Justice, 79
        Child Welfare System, 81
     SOME IMPLICATIONS FOR PROGRAM AND POLICY
        INTERVENTIONS, 83

4   Children's Education   87
     HOW EDUCATION AFFECTS THE ECONOMIC
        MOBILITY OF CHILDREN, 89
     ACHIEVEMENT AND ATTAINMENT DIFFERENCES
        ACROSS RACIAL AND ETHNIC GROUPS, 91
     EARLY-LIFE EDUCATION, CARE, AND PARENTING, 93
     ELEMENTARY AND SECONDARY EDUCATION, 96
     POSTSECONDARY EDUCATION, 99
     CAREER TRAINING, 101

EDUCATION INTERVENTIONS, 101
  K-12 Policy and Program Ideas Based on Direct Evidence, 102
  K-12 Policy and Program Ideas Based on Indirect
    Evidence, 103
  Postsecondary Education Policy and Program Ideas Based
    on Direct Evidence, 104
  Postsecondary Education Policy and Program Ideas Based on
    Indirect Evidence, 105
  Career Training Policy and Program Ideas Based on
    Direct Evidence, 106

5 Child and Maternal Health   109
  HEALTH DIFFERENCES ACROSS INCOME, RACIAL,
    AND ETHNIC GROUPS, 110
  HOW HEALTH AFFECTS THE ECONOMIC MOBILITY
    OF CHILDREN, 113
  ACCESS TO HEALTH CARE: FAMILY PLANNING,
    MEDICAID, INDIAN HEALTH SERVICES, AND
    MENTAL HEALTH SERVICES, 115
    Access to Family Planning Services, 115
    Health Insurance Coverage During Pregnancy and
      Childhood Through Medicaid, 116
    Access to Publicly Provided Health Care via the Indian
      Health Service (IHS), 118
    Access to Mental Health Care, 120
  ENVIRONMENTAL INFLUENCES AS A DRIVER:
    POLLUTION, STRESS, AND VIOLENCE, 122
    Pollution, 122
    Increased Stress in Utero and During Childhood, 125
    Greater Exposure to Violence, Especially Gun Violence, 127
  NUTRITION AND FOOD INSECURITY AS A DRIVER, 129
  INTERVENTIONS INVOLVING CHILDREN'S HEALTH, 133
    Increasing Access to Health Care Based on Direct
      Evidence, 133
    Improving the Environment Based on Direct Evidence, 134
    Improving Nutrition Based on Direct Evidence, 135
  HEALTH INTERVENTIONS BASED ON INDIRECT
    EVIDENCE, 135
    Increasing Access to Medical Care Among Native
      American Families, 135
    Increasing Access to Mental Health Care, 136
    Reducing Child Exposure to Pollution, 137
    Increasing Child Nutrition via WIC, 137

6	**Children's Family Income, Wealth, and Parental Employment**	139

TRENDS IN INCOME AND EARNINGS, 140
    Family Income and Child Poverty, 140
    International Comparisons of Child Poverty Rates, 142
    Trends in Earnings and Employment, 144
    Causes of Labor Market Trends, 144
    Causes of Unequal Employment and Earnings by Gender and Race, 148
DO FAMILY INCOME, PARENTAL EMPLOYMENT, AND EARNINGS DURING CHILDHOOD DRIVE INTERGENERATIONAL POVERTY?, 151
    Childhood Poverty and Intergenerational Outcomes, 151
    Parental Employment and Intergenerational Outcomes, 155
    Increased Access to Work-Based Safety-Net Benefits, 156
WEALTH AND INTERGENERATIONAL POVERTY, 158
    Household Wealth and Intergenerational Outcomes, 159
INTERVENTIONS INVOLVING CHILDREN'S FAMILY INCOME AND WEALTH AND PARENTAL EMPLOYMENT, 162
    Policy and Program Ideas Based on Direct Evidence, 162
    Policy and Program Ideas Based on Indirect Evidence, 165

7	**Children's Family Structure**	167

TRENDS IN FAMILY STRUCTURE, 167
FAMILY STRUCTURE AND INTERGENERATIONAL CHILD WELL-BEING, 171
DOES FAMILY STRUCTURE AFFECT INTERGENERATIONAL MOBILITY?, 172
    Neighborhood Differences in Family Structure, 173
    Incarceration and Family Structure Differences, 173
FAMILY STRUCTURE INTERVENTIONS, 174

8	**Children's Housing and Neighborhood Environments**	175

HOUSING AS A DRIVER OF INTERGENERATIONAL POVERTY, 175
    Housing Quality, 176
    Housing Crowding, 178
    Housing Stability and Tenure, 178
    Housing Affordability, 180
    Homelessness, 182
NEIGHBORHOODS AS A DRIVER OF INTERGENERATIONAL POVERTY, 183

HOUSING AND NEIGHBORHOOD INTERVENTIONS, 187
  Policy and Program Ideas Based on Direct Evidence, 188
  Policy and Program Ideas Based on Indirect Evidence, 190

9 Neighborhood Crime and the Criminal Justice System — 191
  VICTIMIZATION AND EXPOSURE TO VIOLENCE AS
    A DRIVER OF INTERGENERATIONAL POVERTY, 192
    Exposure to Neighborhood Violence, 192
    Predictors of Neighborhood Violence, 194
    Crime Prevention Strategies, 195
  YOUTH OFFENDING AND THE CRIMINAL JUSTICE
    SYSTEM AS DRIVERS OF INTERGENERATIONAL
    POVERTY, 196
    Causes of Youth Offending, 199
    High-Frequency Police Encounters and Excessive Use
      of Force, 200
    Youth Confinement, 201
    Parent and Caregiver Interaction with the Criminal
      Justice System: Incarceration, Fines, and Fees, 204
  INTERVENTIONS INVOLVING NEIGHBORHOOD CRIME
    AND CRIMINAL JUSTICE, 205
    Policy and Program Ideas Based on Direct Evidence, 206
    Policy and Program Ideas Based on Indirect Evidence, 208

10 Child Maltreatment — 209
  WHICH CHILDREN ARE INVOLVED WITH THE CHILD
    WELFARE SYSTEM?, 209
  CHILD MALTREATMENT AND CHILD WELFARE
    SYSTEM INVOLVEMENT AS DRIVERS OF
    INTERGENERATIONAL POVERTY, 211
    Adult Correlates of Childhood Maltreatment, 211
    Consequences of Involvement with Child Protective
      Services, 212
    Out-of-Home Care (Foster Care), 213
    Factors Leading to Child Welfare Involvement, 215
  INTERVENTIONS REDUCING CHILD MALTREATMENT, 219

11 Research and Data Needs for Understanding and Ameliorating
  Intergenerational Poverty — 221
  PRIORITIES FOR FUTURE RESEARCH, 225
  RESEARCH FUNDING PRINCIPLES AND GUIDANCE, 226
    Principles, 226
    Other Guidance, 230

CREATING A FEDERAL DATA INFRASTRUCTURE
   FOR RESEARCH USE, 232
   Data Sources and Linkage Possibilities for Economic
      Resources, 233
   Promising Developments, 238
   Remaining Challenges for Economic Opportunity
      Research, 241
CONCLUSIONS AND RECOMMENDATIONS ON
   RESEARCH AND DATA NEEDS, 244
   Experiments and Long-Term Follow-Ups, 244
   A Federal Data Infrastructure for Research Use, 245

APPENDIX A Biosketches 247

APPENDIX B Perspectives on Intergenerational Poverty 257
   PUBLIC INFORMATION GATHERING SESSIONS, 258
      Perspectives on Native American Communities, 258
      Perspectives on Children Involved with the Child Welfare
         and Justice Systems, 259
   CLOSED LISTENING SESSIONS, 259
      Parent and Caregiver Perspectives, 259
      Public Policy Perspectives, 262
      Rural Community Perspectives, 262
      Alaskan Native and Pacific Islander Community
         Perspectives, 263
      Latino Community Perspectives, 264

APPENDIX C Appendices to Chapters 265
   APPENDIX TO CHAPTER 2, 265
      Contemporary Measures of Mobility by Subgroup and
         Area Based on Tax Data, 265
      Comparisons with Studies Based on the Panel Study of
         Income Dynamics, 267
      Translating Percentiles of the Adjusted Gross Income (AGI)
         Distribution to Incomes Relative to the Poverty Line, 271
      Historical Trends in Absolute Mobility, 286
   APPENDIX TO CHAPTER 3, 289
      Patterns of Intergenerational Mobility by Race and
         Gender, 289
      Defining Disparity, Inequality, Discrimination, and
         Structural Racism, 292

Historical Roots of Racial Disparities in Intergenerational Mobility, 296
Contemporary Drivers of Racial Disparities in Intergenerational Poverty, 309

APPENDIX TO CHAPTER 4, 325
Early Childhood Interventions, 325
Early Care and Education (ECE), 328
Possible Explanations for Discrepant Findings on Long-Term ECE Impacts, 333
Transforming Model Programs into At-Scale Public Programs, 334
Targeting Recipients of ECE Services, 334
To What Extent Subsequent Experiences Support Initial Gains, 335
Changes in Instructional Focus Over Time, 336
Quality Improvement Systems, 337
Child Care Subsidies, 337
K–12 Education, 338
Postsecondary Education, 345
Career Education, 348

APPENDIX TO CHAPTER 5, 353
Inadequacy of Funding for the Indian Health Service (IHS), 353
Mental Health, 353
Pollution, 355
Nutrition and Food Insecurity, 355
Paid Family and Medical Leave, 357

APPENDIX TO CHAPTER 6, 359
Impacts of the Earned Income Tax Credit on Child Outcomes, 359
Wealth, 360
Background Section for Interventions, 363

APPENDIX TO CHAPTER 8, 374
Evidence on Housing Assistance for Intergenerational Mobility, 374

APPENDIX TO CHAPTER 9, 378
Trends in Crime and Incarceration: Causes and Policy Implications, 378
Direct-Evidence Interventions, 383
Indirect-Evidence Interventions, 387

APPENDIX TO CHAPTER 10, 390
   Descriptive Studies of the Possible Consequences of CPS
      Involvement, 390
   Descriptive Studies of the Possible Consequences of Foster Care
      Placement, 391
   Background Sections for Interventions, 393
APPENDIX TO CHAPTER 11, 399
   Report Conclusions About Drivers of Intergenerational
      Poverty, 399

REFERENCES   **411**

Boxes, Figures, and Tables

BOXES

1-1 Statement of Task, 24
1-2 How Much Child Poverty Is There?, 27
1-3 Standards of Evidence Used in Identifying Program and Policy Ideas: Strong Direct Evidence, Promising Direct Evidence, Indirect Evidence, and Other Evidence, 35

3-1 Key Terms and Concepts, 64
3-2 Direct-Evidence Interventions in Chapters 4 Through 10 That Have Been Shown to be Effective for Reducing Intergenerational Poverty Among Black or Latino Children, 86

5-1 Federal Food Programs Serving Children, 132

9-1 Useful Definitions, 198

11-1 Research Priorities to Ameliorate Intergenerational Poverty and Facilitate Socioeconomic Mobility, by Domain, 228
11-2 Mixed Methods and Interdisciplinary Teams in the Moving to Opportunity (MTO) Residential Mobility Experiment, 231
11-3 Data on Health, Education, and Criminal Justice, 234
11-4 Enhancing Panel Surveys for Intergenerational Poverty Research, 236
11-5 Data Linkage Projects at the U.S. Census Bureau, 239

11-6 Relevant Legislation and Statements of Support for Linked Data for Evidence, 240

C-3-1 History of Land Dispossession and the Sauk Tribe, 298
C-3-2 Labor Exploitation Through Sharecropping, 302

FIGURES

S-1 Intergenerational persistence of low-income status, by racial and ethnic group, 4
S-2 Fraction of intergenerationally low-income people in different racial and ethnic groups, 5
S-3 Intergenerational mobility, by racial and ethnic group, 6

1-1 Direct and indirect evidence of a policy change on long-run, intergenerational outcomes, 31

2-1 Percent of low-income children who are also low-income in adult by racial group and type of poverty measure, 42
2-2 Intergenerational low-income persistence, by racial and ethnic group, 43
2-3 Fraction of children with low income in both childhood and adulthood, by racial and ethnic groups, 44
2-4 Intergenerational earnings and household income mobility for sons, 45
2-5 Intergenerational earnings and household income mobility for daughters, 46
2-6 Intergenerational mobility, by race/ethnicity, 48
2-7 Average income rank of sons with low-income parents, by father's country of origin, 50
2-8 Geographic distribution of children with parents in the bottom income quintile who reach the top three income quintiles, 53
2-9 Age-35 household income of children of low-income parents in the New York City area, 54
2-10 Percent of children earning more than their parents, by birth cohort and parental income percentile, 57

3-1 How air pollution across America reflects racist policy from the 1930s, 77

4-1 Employment rates for 25- to 34-year-olds in 2019, by education and sex, 88
4-2 Median annual earnings for 25- to 34-year-old workers in 2019, by education, 90

4-3	8th grade reading proficiency rates, by race/ethnicity, 1998–2019, 92
4-4	College enrollment and bachelor of arts (BA)+ attainment rates, by race/ethnicity, 94
5-1	Adult health and early childhood income status, for individuals born between 1968 and 1975, 111
5-2	Health of children living in poverty vs. other children, 2001–2005, 112
5-3	Maternal and infant health disparities by race/ethnicity, 113
5-4	Average suicide rate per 100,000 among children and adolescents, ages 0–19, by race/ethnicity, 2010-2020, 119
5-5	Annual death rates for the four most common causes of death in the United States among children and adolescents, ages 1–19, 1999–2020, 128
5-6	Food insecurity among children, by race and ethnicity of household head, 2008–2021, 130
6-1	Average U.S. household income of children in the bottom, middle, and top income quintiles, 1967–2019, 141
6-2	Child poverty in the United States and four other anglophone countries, 2016, 143
6-3	Average real wages in the United States for the 10th, 50th, and 90th percentiles, 1973–2019, 145
6-4	Median usual weekly earnings of full-time wage and salary workers by race/ethnicity and sex, 4th quarter 2022 averages, 149
6-5	Employment-to-population ratios by race and gender, November 2022, 150
6-6	Median net worth of U.S. families in 2019, 159
6-7	Earned Income Tax Credit (EITC) expansion options, 164
7-1	Percent of children living with married parents and in other arrangements, 1980–2019, 168
7-2	Percent of children living with married parents, by race/ethnicity and education, 2019, 169
7-3	Supplemental Poverty Measure (SPM) child poverty rates by family composition, 2019, 170
8-1	Inadequate housing by poverty status and race/ethnicity, 177
8-2	Homeownership rates based on household income as a percent of area median by race/ethnicity, 2019, 180

8-3   Housing cost burden, by tenure, income, and race/ethnicity, 2020, 181
8-4   Children living in high-poverty areas by race and ethnicity in the United States, 2017–2021, 185

9-1   Violent crime victimization rates (per 1,000) in 2019, by income, age, and race/ethnicity, 193
9-2   Juvenile overall and violent crime arrest rates (per 1,000) in 2018, by race/ethnicity, 197
9-3   Number of confined youth by type of facility in 2019, 202
9-4   Number of youth in long-term secure facilities/detention in 2019 by offense category, 203

10-1 Rates of substantiated maltreatment of children ages 0–17 by selected characteristics, 2008–2020, 210

C-2-1 Intergenerational mobility based on several measures of economic status, by race/ethnicity, 273
C-2-2 Average income-to-needs of children by percentile of the adjusted gross income distribution for children under age 18, 276
C-2-3 Adjusted gross income and income-to-needs distribution of children under 18 by tax-unit dependency status, 281
C-2-4 Average income-to-needs of children by percentile of the adjusted gross income distribution, including and excluding minor filers, 282

C-3-1 Incarceration rates by race from 1880 to 1950, 311
C-3-2 Rate of youth confined in juvenile residential placement facilities per 100,000 by race/ethnicity, 2019, 312

C-9-1 U.S. violent crime rate per 100,000 from 1960–2021, 378
C-9-2 Incarceration rates by race, age, and education from 1960–2010, 380
C-9-3 Rate of juvenile confinement by race/ethnicity, 1997–2019, 381

TABLES

S-1   Program and Policy Ideas Linked by Direct Evidence to Reductions in Intergenerational Poverty, 18

8-1   Families Without Housing by Race/Ethnicity, 2020, 182

11-1	Programs and Policies Linked by Direct Evidence to Reductions in Intergenerational Poverty, 223
C-2-1	Intergenerational poverty statistics based on adjusted gross income (AGI) data in tax records, 269
C-2-2	Intergenerational poverty statistics based on data from the Panel Study of Income Dynamics, 270
C-2-3	Intergenerational income mobility statistics based on data from the Internal Revenue Service (IRS) and Panel Study of Income Dynamics (PSID), 272
C-2-4	Average income-to-needs by percentile of the adjusted gross income (AGI) distribution, children under age 18, 277
C-2-5	Average income-to-needs by percentile of the adjusted gross income (AGI) distribution when minor filers are included, 283
C-3-1	Interventions in chapters 4 through 10 that have been shown to be effective for Black, Latino, or Native American children and families, 319
C-4-1	Ratio of statistically significant ($p < .10$) treatment impacts to outcomes examined in the HomVee literature review, 327
C-4-2	Ratio of statistically significant ($p < .10$) treatment impacts averaged over the two cohorts on outcomes examined in the Puma et al. (2012) Head Start Impact Study, 331
C-4-3	Sector-based training program models, 350
C-11-1	Internal Revenue Service (IRS)/Social Security Administration (SSA) tax forms and data elements for accurate measurement of family income over time—available to the Census Bureau and additional items needed for data linkage, 407
C-11-2	Nontaxable benefit records for accurate measurement of family income over time: Records available to the Census Bureau and additional records needed for data linkage, 409

Acronyms

ABC–Infant	Attachment and Biobehavioral Catch-up–Infant
ACA	Affordable Care Act
ACLU	American Civil Liberties Union
ACS	the American Community Survey
AFDC	Aid to Families with Dependent Children
AGI	adjusted gross income
AI	artificial intelligence
AMI	area median income
AOS	American Opportunity Study
ARPA	American Rescue Plan Act
ASAP	Accelerated Study in Associates Program
BAM	Becoming a Man
BLLs	blood lead levels
BLS	Bureau of Labor Statistics
CAA	Clean Air Act
CBT	congitive behavioral therapy
CDAs	child development accounts
CDC	Centers for Disease Control and Prevention
CID	Comprehensive Income Dataset
CIPSEA	Confidential Information Protection and Statistical Efficiency Act
CJARS	Criminal Justice Administrative Records System
CMTO	Creating Moves to Opportunity program

CPS	Child Protective Services
CPS ASEC	Current Population Survey Annual Social and Economic Supplement
CTC	Child Tax Credit
CTE	career and technical education
DCDL	Decennial Census Digitization and Linkage
ECE	early care and education
EEO	Equal Employment Opportunity
EITC	Earned Income Tax Credit
EPA	Environmental Protection Agency
FDA	Food and Drug Administration
FERPA	Family Educational Rights and Privacy Act
FHA	Federal Housing Authority
FMR	Fair Market Rents
FPL	Federal Poverty Line
FSOVA	Family Stability and Opportunity Vouchers Act
FSRDC	Federal Statistical Research Data Center
HANDS	Health Access Nurturing Development Services
HCV	housing choice vouchers
HFA®	Healthy Families America®
HOLC	Home Owners' Loan Corporation
HRS	Health and Retirement Study
HSIS	Head Start Impact Study
HUD	Department of Housing and Urban Development
IHS	Indian Health Service
IRS	Internal Revenue Service
IT	Information Technology
K–12	kindergarten through grade 12
LIHTC	Low-Income Housing Tax Credit program
MSI	minority-serving institution
MTO	Moving to Opportunity
NCHS	National Center for Health Statistics
NFP®	Nurse-Family Partnership®

ODRs	office discipline referrals
OECD	Organization for Economic Cooperation and Development
OJJDP	Office of Juvenile Justice and Delinquency Prevention
OMB	Office of Management and Budget
PBIS	Positive Behaioral Interventions and Supports
PCEPI	Personal Consumption Expenditures Price Index
PM	particulate matter
PRO Act	Protecting the Right to Organize Act
PSID	Panel Study of Income Dynamics
RCT	randomized controlled trial
REO	Reentry Employment Opportunities
SAMHSA	Substance Abuse and Mental Health Services Administration
SBHC	school-based health center
SES	socioeconomic status
SIPP	Survey of Income and Program Participation
SLDS	Statewide Longitudinal Data Systems
SNAP	Supplemental Nutrition Assistance Program
SPM	Supplemental Poverty Measure
SSI	Supplemental Security Income
STEM	science, technology, engineering, and mathematics
TNAF	Temporary Assistance to Needy Families
TRI	Toxic Release Inventory
Triple P	Positive Parenting Program
USDA	United States Department of Agriculture
WIC	Special Supplemental Nutrition Program for Women, Infants and Children

Summary

Capable and responsible adults are the foundation of any well-functioning and prosperous society. Yet low-income families struggle to offer their children the same advantages and necessities that better-off families can offer. As a result, throughout their childhoods children living in families with low incomes face an array of challenges that place them at much higher risk of experiencing poverty in adulthood as compared with other children.

The costs of perpetuating this cycle of economic disadvantage fall not only on low-income individuals and families themselves, but also on society as a whole. Poverty reduces overall economic output and places increased burdens on the educational, criminal justice, and health care systems. Understanding the causes of intergenerational poverty and implementing policies and programs to reduce it would yield a high payoff for children and for the entire nation.

The United States has made remarkable progress in reducing child poverty in recent decades, with the most comprehensive measure of child poverty used by the Census Bureau showing dramatic declines through 2021 but then increasing sharply in 2022 (Current Population Survey, 2023; National Academies of Sciences, Engineering, and Medicine [National Academies], 2019a). But these data do not speak directly to the issue of *intergenerational* poverty—the chances that children who grow up in low-income families are themselves in low-income households as adults. Concerns over the threat to the United States' economic future posed by intergenerational poverty led Congress to include in the Consolidated

Appropriations Act of 2021 a provision directing the National Academies to conduct a comprehensive study of intergenerational child poverty in the United States that would:[1]

- Identify key drivers of long-term, intergenerational poverty;
- Evaluate the racial and ethnic disparities and structural factors that help perpetuate intergenerational poverty;
- Identify evidence-based policies and programs that have the potential to significantly reduce the effects of the key drivers of intergenerational poverty; and
- Identify key, high-priority gaps in the data and research needed to develop effective policies for reducing intergenerational poverty in the United States.

To meet this charge, the Board on Children, Youth, and Families of the National Academies convened an ad hoc committee with wide-ranging expertise across economics, education, medicine, sociology, social psychology, public health, and developmental psychology, and with subject area expertise in structural racism, labor markets, intergenerational mobility, minority populations, immigration, policy development, and community-based empowerment work. The committee reviewed research literature and a commissioned paper and held public sessions focused on Native American communities, the child welfare system, and the justice system. The committee also held closed listening sessions with low-income parents and caregivers,[2] federal-level public policy experts, and community-based service providers with perspectives on poverty in rural areas, among Alaskan Native and Native Hawaiian communities, and among Latino[3] communities. These sessions were held with subsets of committee members and were organized as small group discussions with organizational leaders supporting communities that the committee had identified as being inadequately represented in its public sessions and in the evidence base.

---

[1] The committee's full Statement of Task is listed in Chapter 1, Box 1-1.

[2] Parents and caregivers involved in these listening sessions were primarily Black American individuals from southern urban areas.

[3] The report uses the terms "Latino," "Black," "White," "Native American," and "Asian" in identifying these racial and ethnic groups. The term "Latino" is used in this report as an ethnonym of "Hispanic" and is referring collectively to the inhabitants of the United States who are of Spanish or Latin American ancestry. The term "Native American" is being used to be inclusive of Indigenous populations in the United States, including Alaska Natives. The term "Asian" is being used to be inclusive of a person having origins in any of the original peoples of the Far East, Southeast Asia, or the Indian subcontinent.

INTERGENERATIONAL MOBILITY AND POVERTY PERSISTENCE

The committee defined intergenerational poverty as a situation in which children who grow up in families with incomes below the poverty line are themselves poor as adults. It is a substantial problem in the United States. Among U.S. children born around 1980 who grew up in households with incomes below or near the poverty line, 34% were living in low-income households when they were in their 30s.[4] In other words, one-third of children living in low-income households also had low household incomes in adulthood, which is twice the 17% rate found among adults in their 30s who did not grow up in low-income households.

Intergenerational economic disadvantage disproportionately affects Black and Native American families. As shown in Figure S-1, only 17% of Asian children living in households with incomes below or near the poverty line were poor in adulthood, compared with 29% of poor White children and 25% of Latino children. However, close to half (46%) of Native American children and over one-third (37%) of Black children who grew up in low-income families had low incomes in adulthood.

Despite the higher rates of low-income persistence among Black and Native American children, the largest share (40%) of persistently low-income children is White (Figure S-2). More than one-third are (34%) Black, 19% are Latino, and Native American and Asian children account for 2% each.

The flip side of intergenerational persistence is upward mobility out of a low-income childhood, and here also Black and Native American families fare worst. One can think of economic status as rungs on a 100-step ladder, with the lowest rungs corresponding to the lowest incomes, the highest rungs representing the highest incomes, and each individual rung representing one percentile of the income distribution. On average, White children who grew up in low-income families—with incomes on the 10th rung of the ladder in the 1980s and 1990s—were able to climb their way to the 41st rung by the time they were in their 30s (Figure S-3). Asian children rose higher up the ladder (53rd rung) than White children, while Latino children did only slightly worse (39th rung) than White children.

In contrast, Black and Native American children who grew up in the same economic circumstances—the 10th rung of the parental income ladder—on average climbed only as far as the 28th rung by the time they were in their

---

[4] As detailed in Chapter 2, a similar study based on different data and an income cutoff corresponding to the U.S. Official Poverty Measure threshold found that 29% of children growing up in poor households were themselves poor at age 30. This Summary uses the terms "poverty" and "low income" to denote economic disadvantage, depending on the income concept used in the cited research.

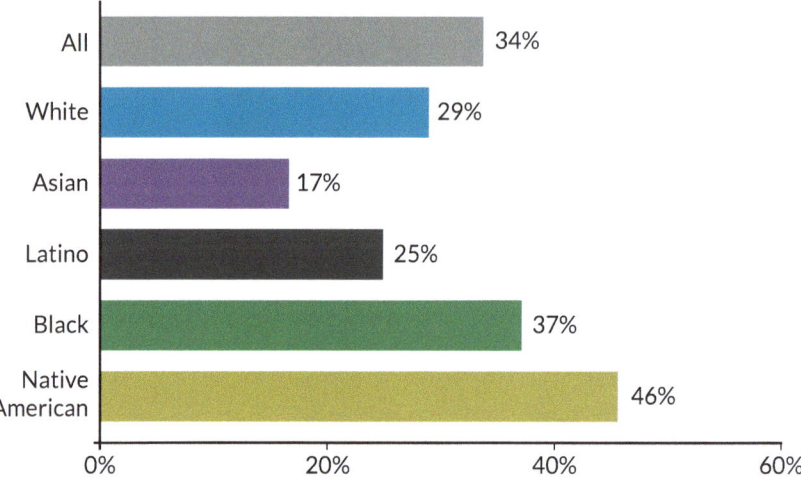

FIGURE S-1 Intergenerational persistence of low-income status, by racial and ethnic group.
NOTES: This figure shows the share of children with parents in the bottom income quintile, who remained in the bottom income quintile in adulthood. Child income is measured as mean household adjusted gross income (AGI) in 2014–2015, and parent income is measured as mean household AGI in 1994–2000. Children were born between 1978 and 1983.
SOURCE: Data from Chetty et al. (2020).

30s—13 rungs below White children. These racial and ethnic gaps persist for children whether they started out on the 20th or even the 50th rung. Comparable data on intergenerational mobility in wealth for Black and White children show even larger gaps favoring White children. The size and consistency of these gaps across the entire distribution of parental household income point to the importance of developing and implementing large-scale, effective policies and programs to ameliorate them.

KEY DRIVERS OF INTERGENERATIONAL POVERTY

The committee examined the drivers of intergenerational poverty and mobility for all children as well as the factors that moderate these drivers (e.g., histories, practices, contexts, and structural factors) and limit the intergenerational mobility of both Black and Native American children. It focused on seven specific domains:

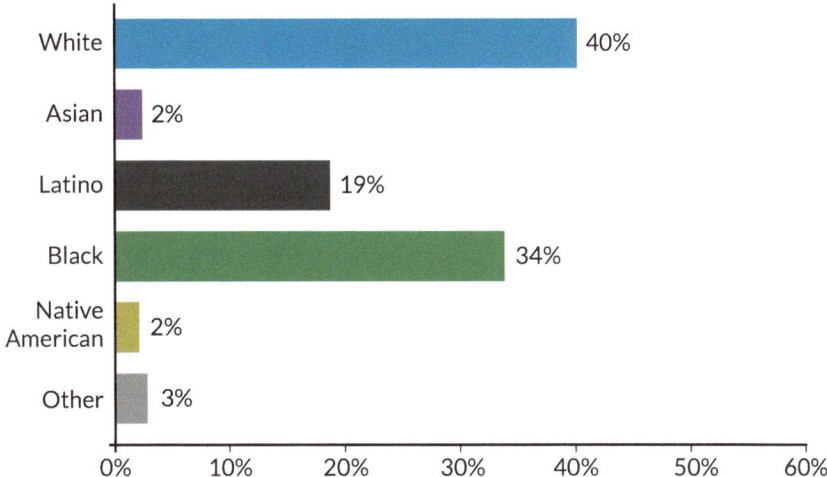

FIGURE S-2 Fraction of intergenerationally low-income people in different racial and ethnic groups.
NOTES: This figure shows the racial/ethnic composition of children with parents in the bottom income quintile who remained in the bottom income quintile in adulthood. Child income is measured as mean household adjusted gross income (AGI) in 2014–2015, and parent income is measured as mean household AGI in 1994–2000. Children were born between 1978 and 1983.
SOURCE: Data from Chetty et al. (2020).

Children's Education and the Educational System[5]

By imparting skills and other capacities valued by employers, the U.S. education system—including early education, K–12, and postsecondary schooling, as well as career training—is a key driver of upward intergenerational mobility for many children, including low-income children. However, low-income children start school with lower levels of academic and social skills than other children, on average, and these average gaps do not close as they progress through school. Large gaps in school achievement and completed schooling also persist across racial and ethnic subgroups.

---

[5] Adapted from Conclusions in Chapter 4.

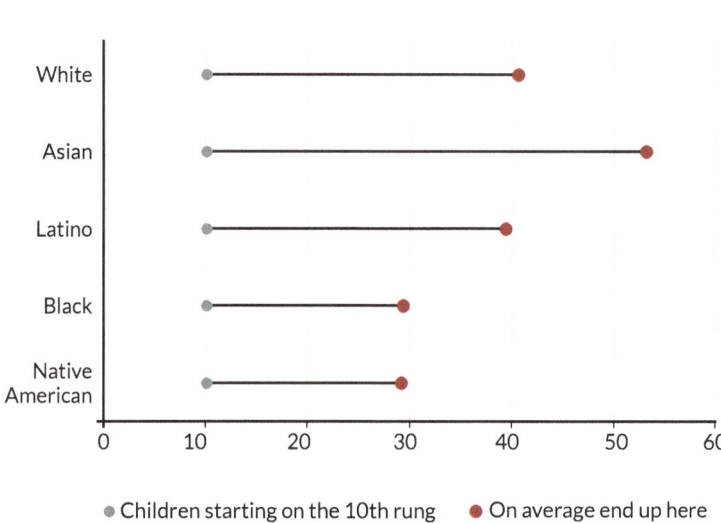

FIGURE S-3 Intergenerational mobility, by racial and ethnic group.
NOTES: This figure shows the mean household income percentile of children with parents at the 10th income percentile. Child income is measured as mean household adjusted gross income (AGI) in 2014–2015, and parent income is measured as mean household AGI in 1994–2000. Children were born between 1978 and 1983.
SOURCE: Data from Chetty et al. (2020).

Child Health and the Health Care System[6]

Children in low-income families have worse health than other children, a disparity that begins at birth and increases as children grow older. Improving the health of low-income children improves their future educational attainment, employment, and earnings while reducing their reliance on public assistance. Three important mechanisms for improving child health and other outcomes are access to family planning services, health insurance coverage in pregnancy and childhood, and food and nutrition programs. A child's environment (including pollution, stress, and violence) also has a profound impact on health and development during childhood and on the longer-run economic outcomes that lead to intergenerational poverty.

---

[6] Adapted from Conclusions in Chapter 5.

Family Income and Wealth and Parental Earnings and Employment[7]

Low wages, earnings, and income among low-income families risk perpetuating the cycle of economic disadvantage, in part by leaving low-income parents unable to provide their children with proper nutrition, access to medical care, and enrichment and learning activities, along with a host of other factors that might promote intergenerational mobility. Evidence suggests that safety net programs during childhood and adolescence can improve children's educational and labor market attainment, as well as their physical health, in adulthood. Studies covering policy changes over the past 25 years provide the strongest evidence for the beneficial intergenerational impacts of expanding the Earned Income Tax Credit (EITC). In the absence of changes in household income, changes in parental employment alone do not have consistent positive or negative effects on children's development.

Family Structure[8]

Over the past 50 years, single-parent families have become much more prevalent, but largely among parents who lack 2- or 4-year college degrees. The committee finds a strong association between growing up in a single-parent family and childhood poverty. The links between family structure during childhood and adult poverty (i.e., the transmission of poverty intergenerationally) suggest a causal effect.

Housing, Residential Mobility, and Neighborhood Conditions[9]

The places where children live—their homes and neighborhoods—are foundational for their health, education, and development. Consistent correlational evidence has linked intergenerational poverty with high lead levels, homelessness, overcrowding, moving frequently, and high housing costs relative to family income in childhood. Stronger evidence links improvements in low-income children's long-term economic, educational, and health outcomes to moving to less disadvantaged neighborhoods.

Neighborhood Safety and the Criminal Justice System[10]

Crime affects children in two ways—through victimization and through involvement with the criminal justice system, whether the crime episode

---
[7] Adapted from Conclusions in Chapter 6.
[8] Adapted from Conclusions in Chapter 7.
[9] Adapted from Conclusions in Chapter 8.
[10] Adapted from Conclusions in Chapter 9.

involved them directly or involved a member of their family. Low-income and younger people are most likely to report being victims of crime in their neighborhoods and schools. Gun violence is now the leading cause of death among American children, with the highest rates among low-income, Black, and Native American children. Exposure to violence in childhood can have lasting adverse effects on children's health, well-being, and achievement.

At the same time, despite generally declining rates of crime in recent decades, increases in incarceration rates (with small drops in recent years) disproportionately affect children in families with low incomes, with negative consequences for their healthy development and long-term economic success. Children in low-income families are more likely than other children to have a close relative who is or has been incarcerated, and they themselves are more likely to be involved in the juvenile justice system or to be incarcerated as adults. Experiencing juvenile detention has been linked to less completed schooling and more adult crime.

Child Maltreatment and the Child Welfare System[11]

Children who experience abuse, neglect, and/or involvement with child welfare systems have worse outcomes in adulthood than their peers who have not been maltreated or involved in the child welfare system. Furthermore, income and poverty are highly correlated with child maltreatment and child welfare system involvement. While there is a dearth of definitive causal evidence on the effects of the various components of the child welfare system on eventual adult poverty, research does point to some promising approaches to preventing child maltreatment in the first place.

RACIAL DISPARITIES AND STRUCTURAL FACTORS THAT CONTRIBUTE TO THESE DRIVERS[12]

The challenges that Black and Native American families face in propelling their children into socioeconomic security result from contemporary and historical disparities, discrimination, and structural racism. Behaviors and choices can also have major causal impacts on intergenerational mobility. Many factors influence the behaviors and choices of, and therefore the outcomes for, Black and Native American individuals, including the experiences of historical violence, oppression, and marginalization. This history has shaped contemporary racial disparities in education, health, the labor market, housing, the criminal legal system, and child maltreatment.

---

[11] Adapted from Conclusions in Chapter 10.
[12] Adapted from Conclusions in Chapter 3.

Taken together, these factors have been crucial in shaping contemporary determinants of intergenerational poverty. The evidentiary base is strongest for Black-White disparities; additional research is needed on the causes and correlates of intergenerational poverty among Native American individuals. Given these persistent intergenerational disparities, improving outcomes for Black people and Native Americans will likely require some race consciousness in our policies and their implementation to ensure that impacts are as positive as possible for these marginalized groups.

Education Disparities

Despite decades of improving educational outcomes among Black and Native American individuals, achievement and attainment gaps remain. Forced assimilation, an absence of culturally relevant instruction, school segregation by race and class, and disproportionate punishment create learning environments that do not foster educational achievement and attainment. The most rigorous contemporary causal evidence points to the negative long-term effects of harsh school discipline.

Health and Health Care Disparities

A history of unethical medical experimentation, contemporary implicit bias among health care professionals, high uninsurance rates among Native American individuals, and greater exposure to chronic stress, racism, and environmental toxins all have a negative impact on the health of low-income Black and Native American children, reducing their chances of upward mobility.

Employment and Earnings Disparities

Even after improvements in their relative earnings over time, Black workers still have lower average earnings, face less predictable work hours and less stable employment, and reside disproportionately in states where the relatively low federal minimum wage is binding. Some of these differences can be attributed to their lower educational achievement and attainment, as well as lower labor force participation rates. At the same time, audit studies document the ongoing prevalence of racial discrimination against Black workers.

Housing Disparities

Despite recent reductions in race-based residential segregation, the long history of redlining in the United States is still affecting people's lives in the form of higher poverty rates, lower life expectancy, higher rates of chronic disease, greater exposure to pollution, and lower rates of upward mobility, among other outcomes. Discrimination against Black house seekers and renters is correlated with greater residential segregation and with larger Black-White gaps in intergenerational income mobility. Black and Native American children are significantly more likely to grow up in high-poverty neighborhoods, which is also correlated with lower intergenerational mobility.

Criminal Justice System Disparities

Substantial evidence documents racial disparities in both the commission of violent crime and victimization as well as in arrests, charging, convictions, sentencing, incarceration, and community supervision. Black and Native American youth experience disproportionate punishment in the juvenile justice system. Community violence poses a significant risk to health and well-being for Black, Native American, and low-income communities, while disproportionate system involvement and incarceration negatively affect young people's later employment and earnings.

Child Maltreatment and Welfare-System Involvement Disparities

Black and Native American children have the highest rates of child maltreatment and are more likely to be referred to child welfare services. Such exposures correlate with worse educational and employment outcomes in early adulthood.

EVIDENCE-BASED POLICIES AND PROGRAMS TO REDUCE INTERGENERATIONAL POVERTY

The committee sought to identify evidence-based policies and programs for low-income children that could reduce their chances of remaining low-income as adults. We identified three types of policies: (1) those that target children directly, such as higher-quality or expanded education and health services; (2) those that target families, such as income support or residential mobility policies and programs; and (3) those that target neighborhoods, such as neighborhood policing programs.

The committee reviewed evidence on both the short- and the longer-run impacts of these policies. In some cases, evaluators have been able to estimate impacts on intergenerational poverty by tracking the adult outcomes of children who were and were not affected by the policy change or intervention years or even decades before. The committee decided to highlight policy and program ideas whose effectiveness is supported by this kind of *direct* intergenerational evidence (see Table S-1 for a summary of these policy and program ideas). Moreover, the committee developed rules for using the strength of the supporting evidence to distinguish between policies and programs supported by "strong" versus "promising" direct evidence.

The committee also reviewed policy and program ideas supported by *indirect* evidence. For example, if a program evaluation establishes effectiveness based on shorter-run outcomes such as school test scores rather than adult outcomes, that would be considered indirect evidence. Most of the details on programs supported by indirect evidence appear in Appendix C. We note that because our filter was designed to include only studies that offered rigorous long-run causal evidence, it is likely that many effective policies and programs that have not yet been evaluated for long-run effectiveness are not included in our list of highlighted policies.

The committee found direct evidence of success in reducing intergenerational poverty for five of the seven key drivers: education; health; income and parental employment; housing; and crime.

Education Interventions

Evidence for the value of *early care and education programs*, including parenting support programs such as home visiting, is mixed. Well-studied model programs implemented in the 1960s and 1970s generated impressive benefits that persisted well into adulthood. However, evidence on more recent programs is too weak and contradictory to identify profitable incremental federal investments in the early education area.

At the *elementary* and *secondary* education levels, too many low-income students attend schools with crumbling infrastructure and have inexperienced or poorly qualified teachers as well as curricula unlikely to prepare them for college. Recent studies have shown that increases in school funding directed at under-resourced districts are effective in promoting both higher student achievement and higher rates of completed schooling, so the committee proposes that policy makers consider increasing federal funding for school districts with the highest concentrations of low-income students.

Causal evidence also points to the positive effects of Black teachers on the high school graduation and college enrollment of Black students and the positive effects of Ethnic Studies course-taking for high school graduation, which suggests supporting efforts that increase teacher workforce and curricular diversity. Conversely, exclusionary school discipline increases students' chances of dropping out of high school and criminal justice contact in young adulthood, and it also reduces their college enrollment rates. Policy makers should consider the development and evaluation of positive behavioral and alternative disciplinary interventions.

With respect to *postsecondary education*, the strongest evidence was for the programs to increase attendance and completion among low-income students. Specifically, programs designed to increase enrollment, improve relevant instruction and support services, and give students incentives to enroll in higher-value institutions and programs of study all show promise. The primary ways to accomplish these goals are through carefully targeted financial aid programs and increased funding for proven support services for low-income students (such as tutoring and case management).

Strong evaluation research on *career training programs* also points to promising approaches, including career and technical education pathways beginning in high school as well as sectoral training programs for youth and adults that develop occupational skills valued by employers in key growing sectors of the labor market.

Child Health Interventions

Child health interventions that appear likely to reduce intergenerational poverty include federal programs that have funded family planning and Medicaid services, including medical services provided by the Indian Health Service. Strong evidence also links reductions in pollution to improvement in child health and future earnings. Finally, although the strongest evidence on the long-term impacts of child nutrition is based on historical data, more recent evidence links nutrition programs in childhood to medium-term outcomes such as health in early adolescence.

Family Income, Wealth, and Parental Employment Interventions

Evaluations of expansions of the EITC have produced strong direct evidence that intergenerational poverty can be reduced through earnings subsidies that increase both family income and parental employment during childhood and adolescence.

Family Structure Interventions

While two-parent family structures may protect families against intergenerational poverty, the committee could not identify proven policies and programs that promote such structures.

Housing, Residential Mobility, and Neighborhood Interventions

Emerging evidence suggests that programs to stimulate housing production and neighborhood improvement may hold considerable promise. The strongest causal evidence supports housing choice vouchers coupled with assistance moving to low-poverty neighborhoods.

Neighborhood Safety, Prevention, and the Criminal Justice System Interventions

A diverse array of interventions to address violence and victimization show promise, as do interventions addressing the ways the criminal justice system affects youth outcomes and intergenerational mobility. One approach is interventions designed to reduce future juvenile offending by means of investments in child human capital, reducing children's exposure to lead, and scaling-up successful therapeutic interventions. Another approach is to strengthen communities by reducing violent crime, victimization, and gun violence, for example through effective policing strategies, such as expanding police presence and supporting community policing in high-crime neighborhoods.

Child Maltreatment and the Child Welfare System Interventions

Research has identified a number of promising programs focused on reducing the risk of child maltreatment. Evaluation evidence on the longer-run impacts of these programs is too weak to identify profitable incremental federal investments in the child maltreatment area.

Reducing Racial Disparities

Racial disparities are relevant to virtually any intervention aimed at reducing intergenerational poverty, so the committee also looked for evidence about programs specifically designed to reduce them. The committee was unable to identify long-term evaluations of programs that would specifically address racial disparities in intergenerational poverty. It did, however, find that a number of the programs listed in Table S-1 would disproportionately benefit Black children (see Table C-3-1). These include increasing K–12 school funding, having more Black teachers, reducing harsh school discipline, strengthening financial aid and student support programs in postsecondary education, establishing career training programs, expanding Medicaid access, reducing pollution, funding nutrition programs, expanding the EITC, reducing juvenile incarceration, supporting therapeutic programs such as Becoming a Man, engaging in vacant lot abatement, and policing in high-crime neighborhoods. It also found direct evidence of programs that promoted the intergenerational mobility of Latino children: funding nutrition programs, reducing harsh school discipline, and offering Ethnic Studies courses.

CROSS-CUTTING POLICY AND PROGRAM ISSUES

The committee also considered how the seven drivers of intergenerational poverty—and the interventions that might address them—might be interrelated. It identified several cross-cutting issues.

First, it recognized that interventions designed to address any one driver might have spillover effects for other drivers. For example:

- Health interventions early in life, including access to family planning services and health insurance coverage in pregnancy and childhood, have been shown to improve children's educational attainment, employment, and earnings as well as employment outcomes for mothers.
- Increases in school funding have been linked not only to improved educational and labor market outcomes for children, but also to reductions in juvenile and adult crime.
- Reductions in lead exposure have been linked to long-run improvements in educational, criminal, and health outcomes.
- Reductions in harsh school discipline have been linked with higher educational achievement and attainment, lower usage of safety net programs, and reduced involvement in the criminal legal system later in life.

Second, the committee found that some important issues that arose in our listening sessions did not fit neatly into just one of the seven intervention domains. A prominent example is the struggle many families face in securing high-quality early care and education (ECE), particularly for their youngest children, in order to enter or remain in the labor market or secure additional schooling. The lack of affordable ECE can interfere with the effectiveness of many programs designed to address intergenerational poverty. Children themselves need ECE that promotes their health, safety, and school readiness. Reliable ECE is also important for parents because steady employment requires affordable and reliable ECE. The Child Care and Development Block Grant program has provided subsidies to many low-income working mothers, and while it has been shown to promote parental employment, it has been less successful at promoting children's school readiness. Finding affordable approaches to promoting both parental employment and children's school readiness is a key policy research priority.

A third cross-cutting issue, which was also stressed by community members in our listening sessions, is the need to ensure equitable and ready access to programs. Unnecessarily burdensome administrative procedures discourage families from receiving benefits for which they are eligible.

Burdensome requirements can also interfere with parents' ability to secure steady employment.

A final cross-cutting issue, which was raised in the committee's statement of task, is related to children's ages: Are incremental investments in a particular childhood stage (preschool, middle childhood, or adolescence) consistently more effective than investments in other stages? A look at Table S-1 shows that this is not the case; promising investments were identified in all childhood stages.

PROGRAM COMBINATIONS THAT REDUCE INTERGENERATIONAL POVERTY

The committee's charge also included a request to identify combinations of federal policy investments that could reduce intergenerational poverty persistence. Given the high standard of evidence the committee adopted, this task proved difficult because virtually all of the policy and program evaluation literature focuses on individual policies, rather than on combinations of such policies. Nevertheless, the report does speculate on the efficacy of some program combinations—in particular those combining work incentives, income supplementation, and ECE support. It also concludes that studies of the effectiveness of program combinations are urgently needed.

RESEARCH AND DATA NEEDED FOR UNDERSTANDING AND REDUCING INTERGENERATIONAL POVERTY

Although the committee was able to identify a number of policies and programs that appeared to be effective in reducing intergenerational poverty, it lacked high-quality evidence on the intergenerational impacts of many other promising programs. This is sobering but not surprising, given the expense and difficulty of scaling up promising interventions identified in controlled experiments, the length of time required to see the effects of interventions on intergenerational poverty, the difficulties of assembling data for historical, retrospective analysis, and the costs of obtaining adequate sample sizes for the populations most at risk of intergenerational poverty, especially Native Americans.

The committee therefore offers recommendations to funders concerning the highest priorities for research related to intergenerational poverty, and to federal agencies responsible for collecting the data researchers need to analyze the likely impacts of promising policies and programs.

Research Funding Guidance

Research aimed at identifying proven programs for boosting every child's chances to succeed should conform to the following three principles:

1. Prioritize strong research designs that provide causal estimates of long-term program impacts.
2. Set aside funding not only for rigorous small-scale experiments, but also for replications and long-term follow-ups of promising programs at scale.
3. Fund research arms for specific communities at highest risk.

The committee suggests, in addition, that new research and ongoing surveys, both cross-sectional and longitudinal, add samples of high-risk population groups to the extent feasible, gather detailed information about race and ethnicity, and include questions about where respondents were born and grew up. Finally, the committee notes the potential utility in evaluation research of involving members of the communities under study, understanding the implementation challenges, and adding mixed-method and interdisciplinary approaches to the research designs.

Creating a Federal Data Infrastructure for Research Use

Existing census, survey, and administrative data—linked for families over time and across subject domains, including income, wealth, demographics, health, and education, and with appropriate confidentiality protection—would be invaluable for cost-effective research on intergenerational mobility. At present, much of the data for studying intergenerational poverty and related topics are controlled by various federal and state agencies and are difficult to link or use for academic research or policy evaluation. Recent efforts to ameliorate this situation include the Foundations for Evidence-based Policymaking Act of 2018, which presumes access to federal data by statistical agencies for evidence-building; supportive reports of the Commission on Evidence-based Policymaking and other organizations; and innovative projects at the Census Bureau and other agencies to build linked datasets.

To address the significant limitations on researcher access to linked datasets, which include technical and feasibility issues, the need to balance privacy protection appropriately against data accuracy, and legal barriers:

Recommendation 11-1: The Chief Statistician at the Office of Management and Budget (OMB), to facilitate research on economic opportunity, intergenerational poverty, and related topics, should:
- Work within OMB and with relevant agencies and congressional committees to amend the Foundations for Evidence-based Policymaking Act to:
  - include a presumption of secure access to confidential data for academic research and policy evaluation, explicitly superseding provisions in U.S.C. Titles 26 and 13, which require research to benefit the Internal Revenue Service (IRS) and the Census Bureau, respectively;
  - provide secure access for statistical use, academic research, and policy evaluation to records of state benefit programs that receive federal funds (e.g., the Supplemental Nutrition Assistance Program);
  - require federal agencies with custody of confidential datasets to use a risk-utility framework for determining appropriate privacy protection methods for their data; and
  - impose penalties on researchers and other data users for willful, harmful disclosure of confidential data, similar to the penalties imposed on statistical agency staff;
- Work with the IRS Statistics of Income Division and the Census Bureau to expand the tax items available to the Census Bureau under regulation 6103(j)(1)-1 for research use;
- Work within OMB and with relevant agencies and congressional committees to secure sustained funding for data linkage projects, Federal Statistical Research Data Centers, and technical capacity in the states to share records to support cost-effective research on intergenerational poverty, economic opportunity, and related topics; and
- Work with relevant agencies to establish guidelines for consent and data storage that will facilitate the re-use of survey and intervention data, linked to subsequent administrative records, for long-term follow-up and for studies not yet anticipated at the time of the original study.

TABLE S-1 Program and Policy Ideas Linked by Direct Evidence to Reductions in Intergenerational Poverty

Driver	Program or policy idea (* indicates that the supporting evidence was particularly strong)
Education	
• Early childhood	None identified in recent research
• K–12 education	Increase K–12 school spending in the poorest districts* Increase teacher workforce diversity* Reduce exclusionary school discipline* Increase access to Ethnic Studies courses
• Postsecondary education	Expand effective financial aid programs for low-income students* Increase campus supports (such as tutoring and case management)*
• Career training	Expand high-quality career and technical education programs in high school* Expand sectoral training programs for adults and youth*
Child and Maternal Health	
• Family planning	Increase funding for Title X family planning programs* Ensure that Medicaid beneficiaries have access to family planning services*
• Health insurance	Expand access to Medicaid with continuous 12-month eligibility and 12-month post-partum coverage* Expand access to Indian Health Services for all eligible mothers and children
• Pollution reduction	Support the U.S. Environmental Protection Agency to work with local partners to adopt and expand efficient methods of monitoring outdoor and—especially in schools—indoor air quality
• Nutrition	Remove the 5-year waiting period of Supplemental Nutrition Assistance Program (SNAP) eligibility for legal permanent resident parents* Eliminate the proration of SNAP benefits for citizen children with undocumented parents
Family Income, Wealth, and Employment	
• Work-based income support	Expand the Earned Income Tax Credit by increasing payments along some or all portions of the schedule and possibly by providing a credit to families with no earnings*
Family Structure	
	None identified by research to date

TABLE S-1 Continued

Driver	Program or policy idea (* indicates that the supporting evidence was particularly strong)
Housing and Neighborhoods	
• Residential mobility	Expand coverage of the Housing Choice Voucher program and couple it with customized counseling and case management services to facilitate moves to low-poverty neighborhoods
Neighborhood Crime and the Criminal Justice System	
• Juvenile incarceration	Use juvenile confinement only for youth who pose a serious and immediate threat to public safety*
• Child investment strategies	Improve school quality and reduce lead exposure in ways identified in the education and health categories* Scale up evidence-based therapeutic interventions such as the Becoming a Man program
• Strengthen communities to reduce violent crime and victimization	Scale up programs that abate vacant lots and abandoned homes* Increase grants to community-based organizations*
• Policing strategies	Expand funding for policing in high-crime neighborhoods* Expand use of effective strategies like community policing*
• Gun safety	Improve gun safety in ways that pass constitutional review* Promote child access prevention laws and restrictions on right-to-carry laws, limit access to guns by domestic abusers* Promote sentencing add-ons for violence involving firearms*
Child Maltreatment	
	None identified by research to date
Racial Disparities	
	A number of the policies and programs listed above have been shown to be effective for Black children and families (See Table C-3-1)*

NOTES: "*" indicates that the program's or policy's impact on intergenerational poverty is supported by random-assignment evaluation evidence that has been replicated across several sites or by compelling quasi-experimental evidence based on national or multi-state data or a scaled-up program. Table entries without an "*" represent programs or policies for which the evidence has not been replicated or the policy has not been scaled up.

1

Introduction

Children are the future of every society. The more they live in economically secure, nurturing families, are healthy, receive high-quality education, and are otherwise supported to achieve their potential as adults, the better off that society as a whole will be. Over the past decade, an average of about 10 million U.S. children (14% of all children) lived in families with incomes below the poverty line.[1] These children face a multitude of disadvantages that, taken together, ensure that they will not have the same opportunities to achieve adult success as will children from more advantaged backgrounds. Abundant research has shown that children living in households in poverty are more likely than their more affluent peers to struggle in school and to suffer from poor health and other problems (National Academies of Sciences, Engineering, and Medicine [National Academies], 2019a, Ch. 3). Children living in economic poverty for most of their childhood are more likely to remain poor as they become adults and have children of their own.

Researchers have estimated that the societal costs associated with children growing up in economic poverty—for example, the costs of reduced adult productivity and increased costs of crime and health care—amount to 4.0% to 5.4% of U.S. Gross Domestic Product annually (National Academies, 2019a). This is roughly $1 trillion per year when applied to the current size of the U.S. economy. Children who remain poor into

---

[1] These data are based on Census data compiled over the period from 2012 to 2021 using the Supplemental Poverty Measure.

adulthood—that is, those who experience intergenerational poverty—risk transmitting their poverty status and its costs to their own children as well.

Intergenerational poverty is not only a burden for these families and the U.S. economy, but also a rebuke to the American ideal of upward mobility for every generation and to the dream of all American parents that their children will have the chance to prosper. The perpetuation of intergenerational poverty among children who happen to be born into low-income families is also fundamentally unfair, going against the widely agreed-upon moral imperative that all children should have equal opportunities for success.

Recent research documenting the scope of child poverty and its intergenerational transmission in America today provides reasons for both optimism and pessimism. The most comprehensive measure of child poverty used by the Census Bureau shows dramatic declines over the past several decades (National Academies, 2019a; U.S. Census Bureau, 2022). And the most comprehensive study of intergenerational economic disadvantage finds that nearly 40% of children who grew up on the bottom rungs of the economic ladder were well above that level when they reached their 30s (Chetty et al., 2020), although one-third of those children remained low income as adults.[2] International comparisons of intergenerational mobility based on an absolute income standard for parents and children show similar patterns in the United States and Canada. In the United Kingdom and Scandinavian countries, in contrast, rates of intergenerational mobility are much higher than in the United States (Manduca et al., 2020).

Most striking in the U.S. data are differences in these intergenerational mobility rates across children in different racial and ethnic groups. Broadly speaking, rates of intergenerational poverty persistence are relatively similar for White, Latino, Asian, and immigrant children, but much higher for native-born Black and, especially, Native American children.[3]

A congressionally mandated National Academies study committee—the Committee on Building an Agenda to Reduce the Number of Children in Poverty by Half in 10 Years—produced a report on short-term strategies for reducing the number of children living in poverty in the United States

---

[2] The "bottom rungs" refers to children growing up with family incomes in the bottom quintile of the distribution, and "well above" is defined as incomes in the top three quintiles of the adult income distribution when they were in their 30s. See Chapter 2 for details.

[3] The report uses the terms "Latino," "Black," "White," "Native American," and "Asian" in identifying these racial and ethnic groups. The term "Latino" is used in this report as an ethnonym of "Hispanic" and refers collectively to the inhabitants of the United States who are of Spanish or Latin American ancestry. The term "Native American" is used to be inclusive of Indigenous populations in the United States, including Alaska Natives. The term "Asian" is used to be inclusive of persons having origins in any of the original peoples of the Far East, Southeast Asia, or the Indian subcontinent.

(National Academies, 2019a). However, because that report focused on immediate poverty reduction, it did not attempt to identify policies and programs directed at children or their families that have been shown to be effective in reducing the likelihood that the children will grow up to be poor in adulthood.

In response to a second congressional mandate, and with support from the Administration for Children and Families, a division of the U.S. Department of Health and Human Services, the Bainum Foundation, the Doris Duke Foundation, the Foundation for Child Development, the National Academy of Sciences W.K. Kellogg Fund, the Russell Sage Foundation, and the W.K. Kellogg Foundation, the National Academies undertook a study to examine the drivers of long-term intergenerational poverty and identify policies and programs with the potential to reduce it. The Committee on Policies and Programs to Reduce Intergenerational Poverty was appointed to carry out this charge. The committee includes 14 members with disciplinary expertise in economics, education, medicine, sociology, social psychology, public health, and developmental psychology, and with subject area expertise in structural racism, labor markets, intergenerational mobility, minority populations, immigration, policy development, and community-based empowerment work.

The principal elements of the congressional charge were to identify key drivers of long-term, intergenerational poverty, including the racial disparities and structural factors that contribute to this cycle; to assess existing research on the effects on intergenerational poverty of major assistance, education, and other intervention programs; and, most important, to identify evidence-based policies and programs that have the potential to significantly reduce the effects of the key drivers of intergenerational poverty. Finally, the committee was asked to identify high-priority gaps in the data and research needed to help develop effective policies for reducing intergenerational poverty in the United States. The full text of the charge is shown in Box 1-1.

STUDY APPROACH

The committee proceeded on complementary tracks in responding to its charge. First, it conducted a review of the scientific literature related to intergenerational poverty and economic mobility. The committee supplemented this literature review with a commissioned paper on child welfare and special tabulations on child poverty based on data from the U.S. Census Bureau.

To broaden its understanding of the causes and impacts of poverty, the committee convened two public sessions and six closed listening sessions with key stakeholders. In these sessions the committee heard from

> **BOX 1-1**
> **Statement of Task**
>
> An ad hoc committee of the National Academies of Sciences, Engineering, and Medicine will identify policies and programs with the potential to reduce long-term, intergenerational poverty. This study is designed to complement and will build on the findings, conclusions, and recommendations in the recent Congressionally mandated report, *A Roadmap to Reducing Child Poverty*. The committee will apply a racial/ethnic disparities lens in analyzing the literature on key determinants of entrenched poverty and the evidence on the effectiveness of programs designed to address those determinants. It will assess the implications of that analysis for policy and make recommendations to guide future federal investments in long-term measures to reduce intergenerational poverty.
>
> Specifically, the committee will:
> 1. Briefly assess the available research documenting the correlates and causes of the perpetuation of poverty from childhood into adulthood. The committee will evaluate the racial disparities and structural factors that contribute to this cycle. Based on that review of evidence, the committee will identify key drivers of long-term, intergenerational poverty.
> 2. Assess existing research on the effects of major assistance, intervention, and education programs on intergenerational poverty. Based on the available evidence, the committee may assess relevant programs in the United States and other industrialized countries (such as the United Kingdom, Canada, and Ireland) and may consider both well-established programs and innovative ideas developed at the state or local level or in other countries that have the potential to be scaled up for use nationwide. In reviewing the literature, the committee will:

parents and caregivers;[4] researchers with expertise in the child welfare and justice systems; community leaders and researchers with expertise on Native American communities; community-based service providers serving rural areas, Alaskan Native and Native Hawaiian communities, and Latino communities; and federal-level public policy experts. A summary of these sessions is included in Appendix B. While the participants in these information-gathering sessions were not selected to be representative and do not reflect the full range of perspectives or experiences of those affected by intergenerational poverty, they provided the committee with important contextual information and key narratives for understanding the lived experience of families at risk of intergenerational poverty. These discussions served as a backdrop for the committee's review and assessment of the

---

[4] Parents and caregivers involved in these listening sessions were primarily Black American individuals from southern urban areas.

> i. consider impacts on intergenerational poverty, if possible as defined by the Supplemental Poverty Measure;
> ii. consider the distribution of poverty-reducing impacts across demographic groups (as defined by such characteristics as race and ethnicity, rural or urban location, immigrant status, age of parent, and age of child); and
> iii. consider behavioral responses to these programs that may influence their poverty-reducing effects (for example, the Earned Income Tax Credit creates incentives to increase parental earnings).
> 3. Identify policies and programs that have the potential to significantly reduce the effects of the key drivers of long-term, intergenerational poverty identified in question 1 above and for which there is strong evidence that they will reduce multi-generational poverty. The committee will consider expansions to existing federal programs as well as the possibility of developing new programs. The committee's review will include analyses of program costs, benefits, and efficacy. The committee may directly compare programs with one another to determine which efforts make the most efficient use of funds and hold the greatest promise to end intergenerational poverty. In the case of programs identified as having strong potential to reduce intergenerational poverty, the committee will provide analysis in a way that will allow federal policy makers to identify and assess potential combinations of policy investments that can best meet their policy objectives. To the extent possible, the committee will also identify combinations of programs that may result in synergies or redundancies, in terms of either the programs' effects or the populations targeted.
> 4. Identify key, high-priority gaps in the research needed to help develop effective policies for reducing intergenerational poverty in the United States.

available empirical literature, as well as for its deliberations on "best bet" policies and programs for reducing intergenerational poverty. Appendix B provides more detail on key themes and quotes from those sessions.

ORGANIZATION OF THE REPORT

This report of the committee's response to the charge describes its findings about the drivers of intergenerational poverty and conclusions regarding "best bet" policies that the committee judged worthy of consideration by policy makers and in public policy discussions. It has been divided into a set of relatively short chapters and a set of appendices that provide additional details to support the claims and analyses discussed in the main report. The committee urges interested readers to consult these appendices to gain a more complete picture of its work.

Chapters 2 and 3 offer contextual background: Chapter 2 is a demographic portrait of intergenerational poverty and income mobility in the United States, and Chapter 3 is an overview of the historical and contemporary experiences of Black and Native American people in the United States and the enduring effects of their disparate treatment. Chapters 4 through 10 present the committee's findings and conclusions from the research on seven primary drivers of intergenerational poverty: children's education, children's health, parental income, family structure, housing and neighborhoods, crime and criminal justice, and child maltreatment. Chapter 11 briefly summarizes what the committee has learned and identifies the gaps in the data and research needed to develop effective policies for reducing intergenerational poverty in the United States that the committee regards as most pressing.

DEFINING INTERGENERATIONAL POVERTY

The Statement of Task explicitly instructs the committee to use an economic definition of intergenerational poverty: the Supplemental Poverty Measure (SPM). As explained in Chapter 2, the SPM defines poverty by comparing an individual's household income with a poverty threshold that varies with household size and local cost of living. Poverty thresholds ranged between $25,000 and $30,000 for two-adult, two-child families in 2020 (Fox & Burns, 2021). Children and all other family members in households with incomes below the relevant threshold are considered poor.[5] Using the SPM, which includes noncash sources of income, the U.S. Census Bureau estimates that 12.4% of U.S. children lived in families with incomes below the poverty line in 2022 (Shrider & Creamer, 2023; Box 1-2).

The Census Bureau first began issuing SPM-based poverty estimates in 2011, and prior to that time there was only limited work extending SPM-based estimates (Burkhauser et al., 2023). As the committee assessed the evidence concerning patterns of intergenerational poverty and policies and programs that might reduce it, it found no estimates of the SPM poverty status in adulthood of individuals who, as children, lived in household with incomes below the SPM-based poverty line. The committee turned to other income and mobility measures, for example looking at the share of children with families in the bottom fifth of the income distribution who remained in that income quintile as adults or who moved into a higher quintile. The committee also expanded its conception of economic success, or lack of it,

---

[5] The SPM differs from the Official Poverty Measure in a number of ways, most notably in that it includes "in-kind" sources of income such as tax credits and benefits from programs such as the Supplemental Nutrition Assistance Program (SNAP; formerly Food Stamps) and because it is adjusted for the local cost of living.

> **BOX 1-2**
> **How Much Child Poverty Is There?**
>
> Using a poverty measure (the SPM) that includes noncash sources of income, the U.S. Census Bureau estimates that 12.4% of U.S. children lived in families with incomes below the poverty line in 2022 (Shrider & Creamer, 2023). This poverty rate is nearly half its level in 2013. And this recent decline is on top of a 10 percentage-point decline in SPM-based poverty between 1967 and 2013 (National Academies, 2019a, Figure 2-11). These rapid declines in child poverty may lead some to raise the question of whether the United States is on the cusp of eliminating child poverty, and perhaps intergenerational poverty as well.
>
> The committee's view is that, despite these welcome reductions in child poverty, both current and intergenerational poverty remain urgent national problems. The primary reason is that single-year poverty rates fluctuate with policy changes and macroeconomic conditions. Child poverty rates in 2021 were only 5.2%, but that low rate can be attributed to pandemic relief policies, such as the expansion of the Child Tax Credit to very-low-income parents.
>
> Moreover, many children not classified as in poverty are nevertheless living in families with incomes not far above the poverty line. Drawing the line at 150% of the current SPM poverty thresholds increases the number of children in low-income families by 60%.
>
> SOURCE: Committee generated.

in adulthood to include strong correlates of family income, such as earnings from employment, level of schooling completed, health status, and involvement as an adult with the criminal justice system.

Most of the poverty standards used by the U.S. government are based on an *absolute* income standard that is adjusted for inflation and family size but little else. A broader set of measures conceives of economic position in a *relative* sense—where parental families and adult children are on the economic ladder relative to other families and adult children. Most parents hope that their children will do better than they have done by climbing up to the middle or even upper rungs of the economic ladder in adulthood (discussed in more detail in Chapter 2). These hopes are based on the relative economic position attained by their children. Much of the data in this report on intergenerational mobility has been compiled using a ladder-based relative standard; however, both relative and absolute conceptions of poverty were relevant in the committee's search for evidence-based policies and programs that would reduce intergenerational poverty.

ORGANIZING OUR DISCUSSION OF DRIVERS AND INTERVENTIONS

The committee is asked to identify key drivers of long-term, intergenerational poverty and then identify policies and programs that have the potential to significantly reduce the effects of those drivers. In organizing its discussion of drivers and interventions, the committee found it useful to classify the many factors that influence the developmental trajectories of children living in households below the poverty line into seven domains:

1. The educational system—early childhood through higher education;
2. The health care system—health services for children of all ages and for their parents, especially during pregnancy;
3. Family income and wealth as well as parental earnings and employment, including the labor market for low-skilled workers;
4. Family structure;
5. Housing, residential mobility, and neighborhood conditions;
6. Neighborhood safety and the criminal justice system, particularly the juvenile justice system; and
7. The child welfare system.

Drivers and interventions within each of these domains are presented in separate chapters (Chapters 4 through 10).

APPLYING A RACIAL/ETHNIC LENS IN ASSESSING THE EVIDENCE

The Statement of Task directs the committee to "apply a racial/ethnic disparities lens" in assessing the evidence on the determinants of and solutions to intergenerational poverty, and to "evaluate the racial disparities and structural factors that contribute to this cycle." The importance of applying a racial disparities lens is highlighted in the research reviewed in Chapter 2, which shows that Black and Native American people are much more likely than White Americans to experience intergenerational poverty and downward economic mobility.

Several members of the committee have expertise in the study of race and racism, as did some of the invited scholars and community members who participated in the listening sessions. In discussing how to interpret this mandate, members of the committee expressed differing and sometimes competing views. Some argued that applying a racial lens requires calling into question the basic premise that intergenerational poverty is the overarching problem that needs to be solved. The low-income parents the committee heard from—most of whom were non-White—emphasized the importance of noneconomic factors, such as family stability, health, culture, personal growth, and community. The Native American scholars and leaders stressed that it is crucial to start from "an Indigenous framework," which requires an "understanding of being in relationship," and a different sense of time in which one is "able to see ourselves in seven generations, the way our ancestors saw us seven generations ago."

The committee recognizes the limitations of a narrower economic concept of poverty that would not reflect cultural, family, and community experiences or aspects of community and individual wealth that extend beyond income. Nevertheless, intergenerational poverty, as specified in the committee's congressional charge, demonstrably affects children's lifetime health and welfare in measurable ways, so the committee decided to use an economic concept of poverty as the main framework for its analysis.

Applying a racial/ethnic lens also caused the committee to think carefully about the standards of evidence and sources of knowledge, or what researchers call "epistemology," that are accepted in different spheres of investigation (Collins, 2002). The committee engaged in spirited debates about what constitutes rigorous social science evidence. These discussions are not unique to this committee's work. Experts on race and racism have long challenged the dominance of quantitative methods and the assumptions that underlie them (e.g., Zuberi & Bonilla-Silva, 2008). Many also challenge the view that only experimental and quasi-experimental quantitative research can reliably explain observed social phenomena and support the development of effective intervention strategies (Krieger & Smith, 2016; Kvangraven, 2020). This debate is ongoing and unresolved, and the committee opted to focus on quantitative evidence, ideally from randomized trials or other study designs that support causal inference, as its primary epistemology.

The committee's use of both the term "race" and the contemporary labels of racial categorization within the United States should not be read as attributing any biological facts about or inherent characteristics of groups who have been racialized as White, Black, or Native American (National Academies, 2023). These categories are not direct measures of "cultural, social, biological, and economic processes" (Zuberi, 2001, p. 142). Instead, the signifier of "race" most commonly used in the social sciences imperfectly encodes the impacts of centuries of legal, social, economic, cultural, and biological processes of racialization.

The committee provides a citation-rich narration of this racialization of Black and Native American people in the United States as well as a review of continuing practices of disparate treatment and their impacts on intergenerational mobility in Chapter 3 and its appendix. Also, in Chapter 3 and throughout the report, we describe empirical trends and patterns in education, health, households, crime and incarceration, and the labor market that often reveal stark differences by race. Finally, when possible, the committee assessed how various interventions have shown varying levels of effectiveness among different racial groups.

CRITERIA FOR SELECTING PROGRAM AND POLICY INTERVENTIONS

The committee examined research studies across the seven domains and used several criteria to identify policies and programs directed at children currently living in poverty that show strong evidence of reducing those children's chances of being poor as adults. Within each of the seven domains, the committee cast a wide net for programs or policies that might reduce intergenerational poverty, both overall and among children in certain racial and ethnic minority groups. Some interventions, such as higher-quality or expanded education and health services, target children directly. Other programs, such as income support or residential mobility policies and programs, target families. Still others, such as neighborhood policing programs, target the neighborhoods where children grow up. Each of these types of programs has a potential role in targeting intergenerational poverty. Across these kinds of policies and programs, the committee used the following considerations to select the most promising:

- Strength of the research and evaluation evidence;
- Magnitude of impacts relative to costs; and
- Possible behavioral responses to policies and programs.

Strength of the Research Evidence

The most important criteria for selecting policies and programs were the nature and strength of the relevant research and evaluation evidence. Specifically, the committee considered the type of evidence, whether it was direct or indirect, and its historical timing.

Type of Evidence

The committee weighed a variety of views about the types of evidence that would satisfy the call for "strong" evidence in the Statement of Task. Mindful of the fact that policies and programs are intended to bring about change in the family, schooling, health care, or other environments in which children are reared, the committee opted to prioritize evidence from random-assignment program evaluations and methodologically strong natural experiments (studies that have examined the impacts on children and their families of unanticipated changes in the timing and structure of policies). These methods are based on a comparison of the likely long-run consequences for children in both the *presence* and the *absence* of the policy or program. Random assignment to a program or policy versus "business as usual" conditions come closest to providing the needed comparison. High-quality quasi-experimental studies approximate random assignment conditions. Almost all of our featured policy and program ideas for reducing intergenerational poverty are supported by this kind of evidence.

In assessing the effectiveness of certain policies and programs, the committee was divided on the question of how to interpret and weigh evidence from correlational studies and qualitative studies about the lived experiences of the children and families who stood to benefit from those under consideration. It decided to feature these kinds of considerations in its discussion of policy and program implementation but not in its identification decision of featured programs and policy ideas supported by strong evidence.

Direct Evidence Policies and Programs

The committee reviewed both direct and indirect evidence on policies and programs that might reduce intergenerational poverty (Figure 1-1). It chose to feature program and policy ideas supported by *direct* long-term evidence, which requires that evaluations track the children into adulthood who were or were not affected by the childhood policy change or intervention. In contrast, *indirect* evidence on policies and programs comes from coupling shorter-run evidence on program effectiveness with other kinds of information on longitudinal linkages between these short-term outcomes and intergenerational outcomes. The difference between direct evidence and indirect evidence is discussed in more detail below.

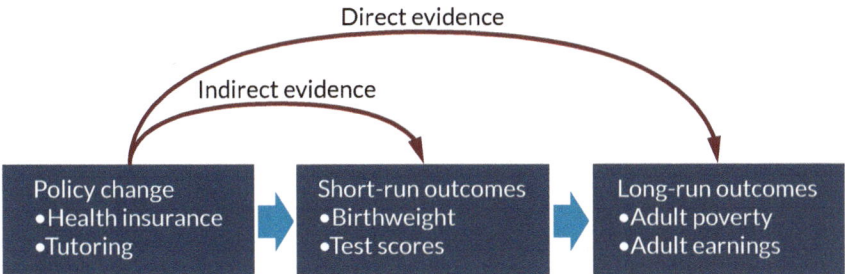

FIGURE 1-1 Direct and indirect evidence of the effects of a policy change on long-run, intergenerational outcomes.
SOURCE: Committee generated.

Direct evidence supporting a program or policy idea comes from an evaluation study that tracks children or youth involved in the program long enough to be able to observe outcomes—typically completed schooling[6] or earnings but also adult health and involvement in the criminal justice system—that are closely correlated with adult poverty status. The committee considered direct evidence on program evaluations to be "strong" if it was based on a program that had already been scaled up to serve large numbers of children or youth or if positive results had been independently replicated at two or more sites. It judged evidence on policy evaluations to be particularly strong if it was based on a methodologically strong study using national or multi-state data.

Moreover, to be recognized by the committee as having long-term effects, a policy has to include a developmental channel. In other words, exposure to the policy during childhood would reduce the likelihood that a child would be poor as an adult, independent of any direct effect of an ongoing policy after the child reaches adulthood. For example, an income transfer policy would be judged to reduce intergenerational poverty only if it would result in a lower level of poverty among adults who were exposed to the policy during childhood even if that policy were no longer in place when those individuals were adults.

Programs supported by strong direct evidence include a number of high-quality youth occupational training programs that target high-demand sectors of the economy, such as IT and health care, and require and reward specific occupational skills (Katz et al., 2022.) As detailed in Chapter 4, random-assignment evaluations of a number of these programs have shown that they can boost earnings for up to 10 years beyond the end of the programs.

Recent work on state expansions of the Earned Income Tax Credit (EITC) provides another good example of strong direct evidence of the intergenerational effects of a certain policy. As explained in Chapter 6, Bastian and Michelmore (2018) found causal links between the timing and generosity of the state EITC supplements and children's completed schooling, employment, and earnings in early adulthood. Other EITC-focused studies reviewed in Chapter 6 have found complementary state EITC impacts on children's birthweight, test scores, behavior problems, and food insecurity. Overall, the evidence supporting further expansions of the EITC appears to be robustly positive. In other cases, direct evidence gathered on the impacts of policies and programs is less robust. A methodologically strong study

---

[6] We considered high school graduation as a close correlate of adult poverty because it serves as a gateway for additional training and more than 80% of adults with a high school diploma but no additional formal schooling had household incomes above the poverty line (Semega & Koller, 2021).

of the impacts of ninth-grade enrollment in Ethnic Studies courses showed improved rates of high school graduation and engagement of students in a large urban school district (Bonilla et al., 2021), but studies attempting to replicate these results in other districts are still in progress. This direct evidence is therefore considered "promising" rather than "strong" for the purposes of this report (see below).

Indirect Evidence Policies and Programs

Indirect evidence comes from coupling shorter-run evidence on program effectiveness with other kinds of information on longitudinal linkages between these shorter-run outcomes and intergenerational outcomes. For example, suppose that a health insurance reform is shown to be highly effective at reducing the number of low-birthweight births. Since other studies have shown that, on average, low birthweight is associated with worse adult labor market and health outcomes, one might conclude that the health insurance policy will indirectly reduce intergenerational poverty. Or suppose that rigorous evaluations of high-intensity tutoring programs produce convincing evidence that these programs boost achievement test scores for the next year or two. Because test scores in childhood and adolescence are associated with higher earnings in adulthood, one might conclude that these kinds of tutoring programs are likely to reduce intergenerational poverty. Unfortunately, many programs that have shown encouraging short-run effects on outcomes such as test scores have not yielded enduring benefits.[7] Because such short-term effects may disappear in the long run, the committee decided that although it was important to consider such indirect chains of evidence, they did not constitute strong evidence.

Historical Timing of the Evidence

It was also important to the committee to consider the historical context in which the reviewed policies and programs were implemented. The only reason evaluators of the famous Perry Preschool program have been able to track outcomes through age 54 is that the program was in operation in the 1960s. Policies and programs begun in the past 20 years cannot possibly have generated such long-run evidence.

But long-run evidence suffers from a changing-context problem. In the case of Perry, the conditions facing the children who were studied and their families were vastly different from the conditions for children today

---

[7] Recent methodological work (Athey et al., 2019) has attempted to provide rigorous ways of using program impacts on short-run outcomes to estimate intergenerational impacts, but the committee judged that these methods were not yet reliable enough to feature in its report.

(Duncan & Magnuson, 2013). Safety-net programs such as the Supplemental Nutrition Assistance Program (SNAP), Medicaid, and the EITC have been introduced and expanded during the intervening years. Expressed in 2021 dollars, annual federal expenditures on children rose more than sixfold, from $800 per child in 1970 to $5,270 in 2019 (Lou et al., 2022). Home environments have improved as well. The education levels of low-income mothers of preschool-age children have risen dramatically since the 1960s, while family sizes have fallen, which means that the quality and quantity of parental care for children in the comparison group are likely to have increased substantially. Moreover, low-income mothers today spend much more on enrichment goods such as books and toys, and have more access to center-based child care (Bassok et al., 2016; Duncan & Murnane, 2014). All of these changes raise the bar for current policies and programs. to demonstrate effectiveness, which makes it more difficult to identify the policies and programs that, if instituted today, would be likely to result in reduced intergenerational poverty several decades from now.

When are cohorts "recent enough" that counterfactual conditions are sufficiently similar to those facing today's children? The committee drew the line at the year 1990, so even if policies and programs run prior to that year demonstrated intergenerational impacts, we required more recent evidence of effectiveness before including a program in our featured list of direct-evidence programs. For example, a large body of literature documents the health benefits for children of environmental changes wrought by the 1970 Clean Air Act (see Chapter 5). But the committee also looked for more recent evidence, finding it in evaluations of the child health impacts of the 1990 amendments to the 1970 Clean Air Act. The recent evidence increased the committee's confidence that additional steps to improve environmental quality would also improve child health and reduce intergenerational poverty.

We also considered evidence to be direct if strong post-1990 evidence of impacts on pre-adult mediators was coupled with strong pre-1990 evidence on long-run adult impacts in the same domain. East (2018) provides an example with evidence of substantial SNAP impacts based on program changes in the period 1996–2003 on improvements in child health between ages 6 and 16. This post-1990 evidence, coupled with the Hoynes et al. (2016) evidence on adult health impacts from the pre-1990 Food Stamp program roll-out, was judged by the committee to be strong evidence in support of a policy idea involving expansions to the SNAP programs. Taken together, these rules regarding direct and indirect evidence seemed to the committee to strike a reasonable balance between the need for evidence on intergenerational impacts and the challenge of evolving counterfactual conditions.

Our 1990 cutoff interacts with the childhood timing of an intervention in ways that reduce our chances of finding direct evidence supporting early childhood interventions. Because our standards for direct evidence require documented impacts in late adolescence or adulthood, an early childhood intervention instituted in, say, 2010 would have no chance of documenting impacts on adolescent or adult outcomes. In contrast, an occupational training program for teenagers implemented in 2010 would be able to follow its participants well into their 20s and early 30s. This is important to bear in mind when considering our list of policies and programs supported by direct evidence.

Strength of the Research Evidence: A Summary

The committee built into its classification of policies and programs considerations of historical timing, distinctions between direct and indirect evidence, and the categorization of direct evidence as "strong" or merely

---

**BOX 1-3
Standards of Evidence Used in Identifying Program and Policy Ideas: Strong Direct Evidence, Promising Direct Evidence, Indirect Evidence, and Other Evidence**

Direct evidence – evaluation studies based on random-assignment or compelling quasi-experimental methods linking recent (post-1990) implementations of a childhood or adolescent program or policy to improvements in adult correlates of poverty status (such as completed schooling or earnings). Policies and programs supported by direct evidence are featured in this report.
- Direct evidence is considered **strong** if random-assignment evaluation evidence has been replicated across several sites or if quasi-experimental evidence is based on national or multi-state data or a scaled-up program.
- Direct evidence is considered **promising** if it is limited to program or policy implementation in a single site or jurisdiction.

Indirect evidence – evaluation studies based on random-assignment or compelling quasi-experimental methods linking recent (post-1990) implementations of a childhood program or policy to improvement in childhood or adolescent correlates of poverty status in adulthood (such as birthweight or test scores).

Other evidence considered – evidence from correlational and qualitative studies, as well as random-assignment and quasi-experimental studies of policies and programs implemented prior to 1990, was also considered.

SOURCE: Committee generated.

"promising" (Box 1-3). The report highlights policy and program ideas for which strong direct evidence, based on evaluations of relatively recent policy or program implementations, is available. It also discusses policy and program ideas supported by what it considers to be promising direct evidence, plus indirect evidence. Most of the details about indirect-evidence studies are provided in Appendix C.

In distinguishing among these evidence standards, the committee does not mean to imply that the highlighted programs that are based on direct evidence are necessarily more effective than the others. The distinction refers only to the nature of the evidence—direct or indirect—from the available evaluation studies.

The relative paucity of direct-evidence policy and program ideas was disappointing to the committee and points to the need for policy evaluation studies with intergenerational scope as well as enhanced data infrastructure that would make it easier to conduct such studies. These topics are discussed in Chapter 11, which covers research and data needs.

Magnitude of Impacts and Costs of Policies and Programs

With respect to assessing program costs, benefits, and efficacy, the committee recognized the advantages of a benefit/cost approach. However, it is difficult to translate the information provided in many of the policy and program evaluations into quantitative measures of program benefits and costs. Wherever it was possible based on available information, we discuss program cost information, including in estimates of the costs of the policy and program interventions and in discussions of how program impacts varied across different racial and ethnic groups.

Possible Behavioral Responses to Policies and Programs

The committee's charge included a directive to assess possible behavioral responses to policies and programs. When the research literature includes information on behavioral responses, the report notes this in its policy and program descriptions. The responses studied are primarily labor supply responses—in other words, to find out whether the availability of a government benefit affects how much low-income people choose to work. In some cases, as with parental employment, these behavioral responses, and their consequences for children's development, are important channels by which the policy in question might affect intergenerational poverty. Unfortunately, so few evaluations provided estimates of possible behavioral responses that we were unable to incorporate these considerations into our selection of "best bet" policy and program ideas.

Policy Conclusions

The committee used its direct-evidence criterion to identify policies and programs that have the strongest likelihood of reducing intergenerational poverty and presents the findings as conclusions about "best bets." That is, we identified those policies and programs we judged most worthy of consideration by policy makers and in public policy discussions. But, like its predecessor at the National Academies, the *Roadmap to Reducing Child Poverty* committee, our committee did not attempt to reach consensus on policy recommendations. We believe that those judgments require weighing not only evidence on effectiveness within and across domains, but also normative judgments about the kinds of policies that governments should and should not pursue.

Political Feasibility

All National Academies consensus committees are instructed to base conclusions and recommendations on the evidence. The committee interpreted this to mean a focus on the effects of policies, and not on the likelihood of their being enacted. It did not attempt to address the political feasibility of potential interventions.

Considering Combinations of Programs

The statement of task also instructed the committee to "identify combinations of programs that may result in synergies or redundancies, in terms of either the programs' effects or the populations targeted." As described below, we found it necessary to categorize evidence into specific domains (e.g., education, health) in part because policy making typically occurs within these kinds of siloes. For example, safety-net policies focused on income operate through the tax system and are administered by the Internal Revenue Service, while nutrition-focused programs are administered by the U.S. Department of Agriculture. However, both in listening sessions with low-income families and in reviewing the research, the committee found clear evidence of the multifaceted nature of poverty. Families struggling financially are often the same families that have limited access to high-quality health care, education, and neighborhoods, and that have increased negative interactions with the criminal justice and child welfare systems. It is therefore likely that programs in each domain will be more effective if delivery could be coordinated for the families needing multiple types of support. For example, attempts to increase employment among parents with young children may backfire if there is limited availability of high-quality child care. However, there is very little available evidence about the precise nature of these program interactions. Thus, our discussion mostly considers interventions in isolation, though it does note (and values) potential cross-domain effects of the interventions.

A related cross-cutting theme was the administrative barriers to participation in the safety net programs featured in this report. Because of the siloed nature of policy making, low-income families are often forced to complete multiple redundant and complex applications, such as for SNAP, Women, Infants and Children, and the EITC, some of which require in-person interviews. This often results in low take-up of these programs among eligible families. To support the evaluation and implementation of combined programs called for in the statement of task, and more fundamentally to increase take-up of these programs to maximize their poverty-alleviating benefits, efforts are needed to streamline program applications with the end user in mind. Given the limited nature of evidence on the impact such interventions have on intergenerational poverty, evaluations of any such efforts are needed.

Some important issues spanned multiple domains. For example, child care needs and policies arise in discussions of education, health, parental earnings, family structure, and child welfare. In this report we discuss them primarily in the education chapter (Chapter 4), although we note cross-domain effects elsewhere. Other prominent cross-cutting issues are lead exposure and air quality, both of which are discussed in the health chapter (Chapter 5), and parental employment, which is discussed in the family income chapter (Chapter 6).

2

A Demographic Portrait of Intergenerational Child Poverty

The committee was charged with identifying policies and programs that have the potential to reduce intergenerational poverty. To provide useful background information, this chapter describes the demographic structure of intergenerational mobility out of low-income status in the United States. Here the committee was aided by the availability of population-wide data that track individuals from the years when they were still living with their parents as children until they were well into their 30s and had families and careers of their own. With these data, the committee could identify the subset of individuals who were living in low-income households during childhood and then track their economic trajectories into adulthood. And because the data cover the entire population, they can describe the intergenerational fortunes of different racial and ethnic groups as well as the trajectories of children of immigrants from all parts of the globe. The chapter then turns to geographic differences in mobility out of a low-income childhood across the United States—shedding light on the geographic correlates of intergenerational poverty—and examines how the structure of intergenerational mobility has changed over time.

MEASURING INTERGENERATIONAL POVERTY

Intergenerational poverty can be defined as a situation in which children who have grown up in families in poverty are themselves living in poverty during their adult years. Given our Statement of Task, our ideal estimates of this status would be based on the Supplemental Poverty Measure

(SPM).[1] Recent counts of SPM-based childhood poverty are readily accessible because the Census Bureau issues an annual report on U.S. children with household incomes below the SPM-based poverty line (e.g., Shrider & Creamer, 2023). Over the decade preceding the COVID-19 pandemic, these child poverty rates averaged 14.9%, although they fell to 5.2% in 2021 in response to generous pandemic cash assistance programs and rose again to 12.2% in 2022 when these programs ended. These figures represent a likely upward bound on the prevalence of intergenerational poverty, because not all children who are poor during their childhood years will also be poor in adulthood.

It will be at least two decades before we can know how many of the children in these 2021 poverty counts are also poor in adulthood. What we can do now is observe intergenerational mobility out of poverty for past cohorts of children and then make educated guesses about the future economic position of current cohorts. But this is complicated by the absence of data on SPM-based poverty for past cohorts. In fact, the committee's review of evidence on patterns of intergenerational poverty and policies and programs that might reduce it produced only one limited study using an SPM-type measure of the poverty status in adulthood of individuals who, as children, lived in household with incomes below an SPM-type poverty line (Parolin et al., 2022; see Appendix C-2).

Most of our data on intergenerational poverty and mobility come from a much larger study that provides a wealth of population-wide information about intergenerational mobility out of low-income status defined by income reported on Internal Revenue Service tax (IRS) forms rather than SPM-based poverty (Chetty et al., 2020).[2] These data allow us to focus on children with low-income parents—defined as parents with incomes in the bottom 20% of the income distribution for the full population of children. We are most interested in what fraction of these children remained in low-income status in their 30s and how these fractions vary across groups defined by race and ethnicity. We also show counterpart calculations in Parolin et al. (2022), which are based on data from the Panel Study of

---

[1] The SPM provides the most comprehensive measure of poverty. Specifically, it compares household income with a set of poverty thresholds, which ranged between $25,000 and $30,000 for two-adult, two-child families in 2020 for the SPM (Fox & Burns, 2021). Children and all other family members in households with incomes below the corresponding threshold are considered poor. The SPM differs from the Official Poverty Measure in a number of ways, most notably in that it includes "in-kind" sources of income such as tax credits and benefits from programs such as the Supplemental Nutrition Assistance Program (SNAP; formerly Food Stamps). Because some "in-kind" income sources such as SNAP payments may not be completely substitutable with cash income, there is more ambiguity with the household income component of the SPM than the official poverty measure poverty measure. See Chapter 6.

[2] Our methods using these data are detailed in Appendix C: Chapter 2; and in Chetty et al. (2020).

Income Dynamics (PSID) and a measure of economic status that is much closer to the SPM poverty definition that what can be constructed from IRS data. Case counts for these PSID-based data are much lower than those in the IRS data, permitting subgroup comparisons only between White and Black children.

A disadvantage of an IRS-based approach is that a "bottom fifth" definition of poverty is somewhat arbitrary and is relative—it will always be the case that 20% of the population is low income by this definition, even though we have already seen that, using the SPM poverty measure, poverty rates have fallen substantially in recent years. Another drawback is that tax records do not measure some of the household resources that are relevant for defining "poverty," in particular because they exclude government transfers. To address this last issue, we provide data from Parolin et al. (2022) and from other intergenerational studies based on more complete income measurements. Based on data presented in Appendix C: Chapter 2, we also describe the correspondence between our measures of household income and measures of income used to define the SPM based on the Current Population Survey.[3] Because the Chetty et al. (2020) 20th percentile threshold does not correspond to any conventional poverty thresholds used in the United States, we refer to it as a marker of "low-income status" rather than poverty.

We also use IRS-based data on intergenerational economic status at the individual level, based on each child's eventual earnings between ages 31 and 37. In this case, we focus on the same group of children as before—those whose parental income was in the bottom quintile. But instead of measuring economic status in adulthood by household income, we use the individuals' own earnings. This approach reveals some noteworthy gender differences in adult earnings for certain racial and ethnic groups and provides a more nuanced portrait of intergenerational mobility than one based only on household income.

THE DEMOGRAPHICS OF INTERGENERATIONAL POVERTY

Focusing on U.S. children born around 1980 who grew up in low-income families, the committee found that, depending on the measure, between 29% and 34% of them were living in low-income families when they were adults (Figure 2-1). In other words, around one-third of all children

---

[3] The appendix tables show that the majority of children growing up in families with parents' income below the 20th percentile of the parental adjusted gross income (AGI) distribution grow up in poverty as measured by the SPM; however, many children whose parents are in the bottom 20% are still above the poverty line, because they receive transfers or have other household members whose earnings place them above that line.

raised in low-income families also lived in a low-income household in adulthood. The 34% rate based on tax data is twice as high as the 17% rate found among children who did not grow up in such families.

Figure 2-1 also shows immobility estimates separately for Black and White children—the only two groups large enough to support reliable estimates in the Parolin et al. (2022) data. In both datasets, remaining in low-income status in adulthood is considerably more likely for Black than White children.

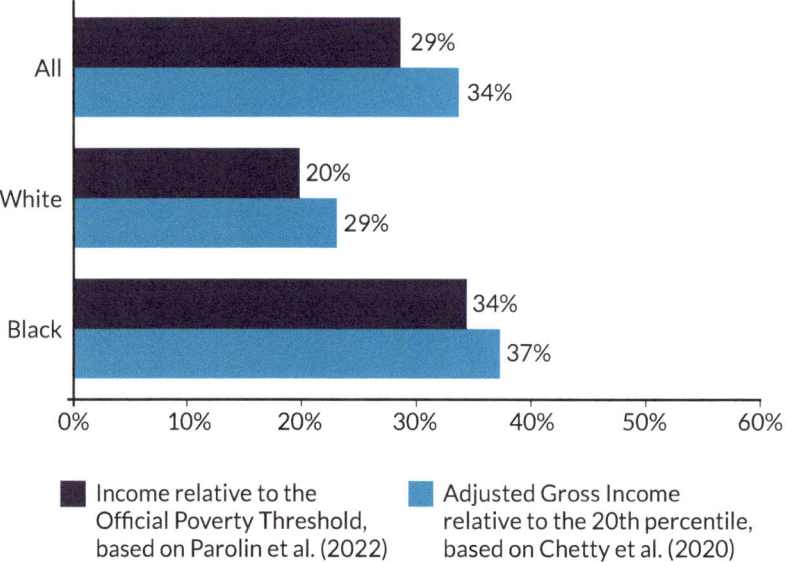

FIGURE 2-1 Percent of low-income children who are also low-income in adulthood, by racial group and type of poverty measure.
NOTES: This figure shows the percentage of children with low family incomes in childhood who also have low incomes in adulthood based on both absolute and relative measures of low-income status. Absolute poverty data come from the PSID; absolute poverty is measured by whether cash plus in-kind income is below the Official Poverty Measure threshold between ages 0 and 10 (childhood) or at age 30 (adulthood). Children in the PSID analysis were born between 1965 and 1994. Relative poverty data come from IRS tax records; relative poverty is measured by whether average AGI between 1994 and 2000 is in the bottom 20% of the AGI distribution between ages 0 and 18 (childhood) or by whether AGI between 2015 and 2016 is in the bottom 20% of the AGI distribution between ages 31 and 39 (adulthood). Children in the IRS analysis were born between 1978 and 1983.
SOURCE: Data from Parolin et al. (2022), based on data from the PSID and Chetty et al. (2020), based on data from the IRS.

Because the Chetty et al. (2020) data are based on all tax records, they support a much more detailed comparative look at intergenerational persistence across population subgroups. Figure 2-2 shows that the 29% rate of intergenerational low-income persistence for White children is similar to the 25% rate for Latino children, while Asian children raised in poor families have a considerably lower rate of low-income persistence (17%). In contrast, nearly half (46%) of Native American children and 37% of Black children who grow up in low-income households remain poor in adulthood.[4]

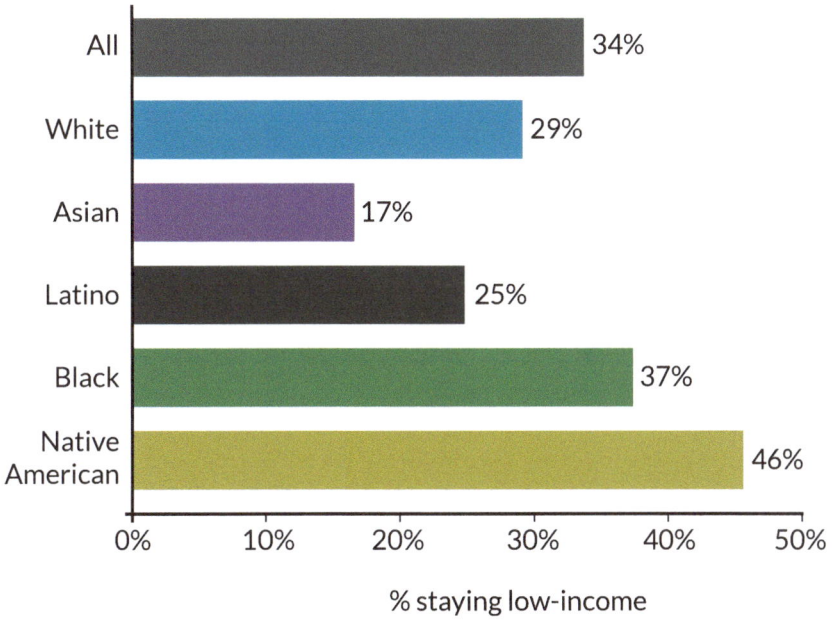

FIGURE 2-2 Intergenerational low-income persistence, by racial and ethnic group.
NOTES: This figure shows the percentage of children with parents in the bottom income quintile who remained in the bottom income quintile in adulthood, by racial/ethnic group. Child income is measured as mean household income in 2014–2015, and parent income is measured as mean household income in 1994–2000. Children were born between 1978 and 1983.
SOURCE: Data from Chetty et al. (2020).

---

[4] To provide an idea of what kind of economic status corresponds to the 20th percentile of the distribution of adjusted gross income (AGI), we used the Current Population Survey to rank children by both AGI and income/needs based on the SPM needs standard. The 20th percentile of the AGI distribution for parents corresponds to an income that is 36% above the poverty line—an income of about $37,500 for a family of four (in 2022 dollars). See Appendix C: Chapter 2 for more details on the comparison of data from these two sources.

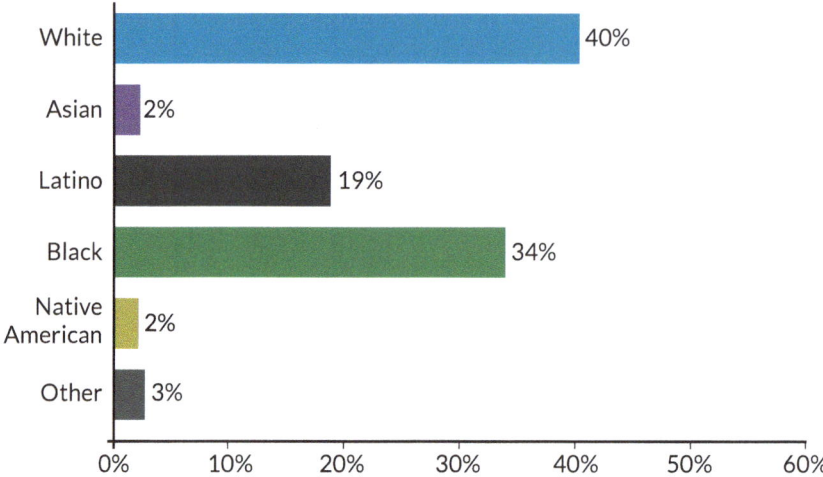

FIGURE 2-3 Fraction of children with low income in both childhood and adulthood, by racial and ethnic group.
NOTES: This figure shows the race/ethnicity of children with parents in the bottom income quintile who remained in the bottom income quintile in adulthood. Child income is measured as mean household income in 2014–2015, and parent income is measured as mean household income in 1994–2000. Children were born between 1978 and 1983.
SOURCE: Data from Chetty et al. (2020).

Despite the higher rates of low-income persistence among Black and Native American children, White children make up the largest share (40%) of children with persistently low economic status (as defined by the 20th income percentile; Figure 2-3). One-third of persistently low-income children (34%) are Black, 19% are Latino, and Native American and Asian children account for 2% each.

Measuring adult economic success by individual earnings rather than family income allows us to differentiate between patterns for males and females. In contrast to the focus on low-income persistence in prior figures, Figure 2-4 shows rates of upward mobility for male children using both adult earnings and household income, defined as earnings or household income in the top 60% of their respective distributions. As before, all the data presented in this figure are for children born between 1978 and 1983 and with parental family incomes below the 20th percentile while they were growing up. The lighter-colored bars show fractions of males with adult earnings in 2014 and 2015 above the 60th percentile of the adult earning distribution, while the darker bars show those with household incomes above the 60th percentile, but in the case of Figure 2-4 only for males.

For males, there appears to be more intergenerational mobility in earnings than in household income. This stems, in part, from the fact that males' earnings in adulthood are being compared with the full distribution of earnings across both males and females. Since men generally have higher labor force participation rates and earn more than women, their mobility into the top three earnings quintiles exceeds that of women. Slightly more than half of White, Asian, and Latino men have adult earnings that place them in the top 60% of the overall earnings distribution, while the corresponding rates for Black and Native American men are considerably lower. A comparison of the earnings and household income results in Figure 2-4 shows broadly similar patterns across groups.

In the case of daughters, there is a notable difference between the relative rates of household income mobility and earnings mobility for Black individuals and White individuals (Figure 2-5). Black and White women who have grown up in low-income households have identical (39%) rates

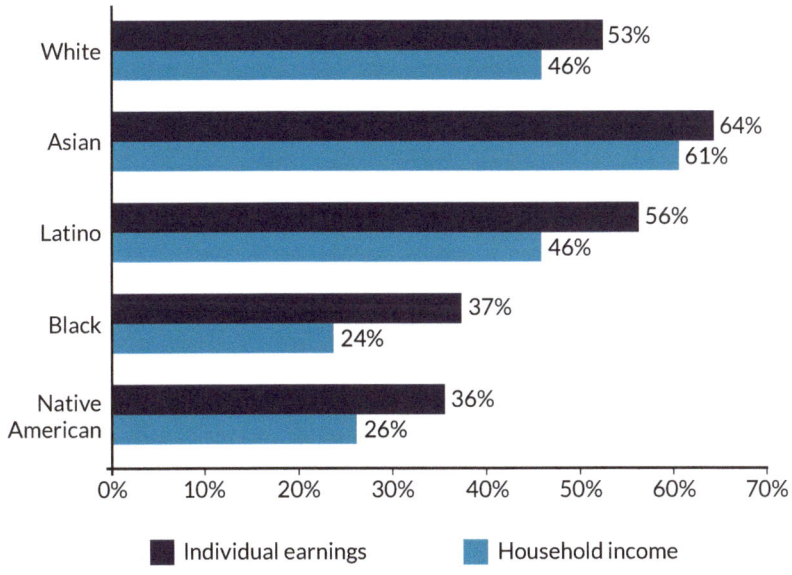

FIGURE 2-4 Intergenerational earnings and household income mobility for sons.
NOTES: The figure shows the fraction of male children growing up in households with AGI in the bottom 20% of the AGI distribution whose individual earnings and household incomes in adulthood (ages 31–37) placed them in the top three quintiles of the adult earnings and household AGI distributions. Children were born between 1978 and 1983.
SOURCE: Data from Chetty et al. (2020).

of earnings mobility but very different (26% vs. 47%) rates of household income mobility. As detailed in Chapter 7, this is probably due to the fact that Black women are more likely than White women to live in single-parent families, and thus also to be the primary earners in their families. In the case of both earnings (30%) and household income (28%), Native American women have roughly the same low rates of intergenerational mobility for both household income and earnings.

> *Conclusion 2-1: As measured by household income, rates of intergenerational persistence in low-income status in the United States differ starkly by race/ethnicity. The lowest rates are found for Asian children, followed by White and Latino children. In contrast, persistence rates are very high for Black and Native American children. When adult economic success is measured using individual earnings rather than household income, mobility patterns are generally similar. Black women*

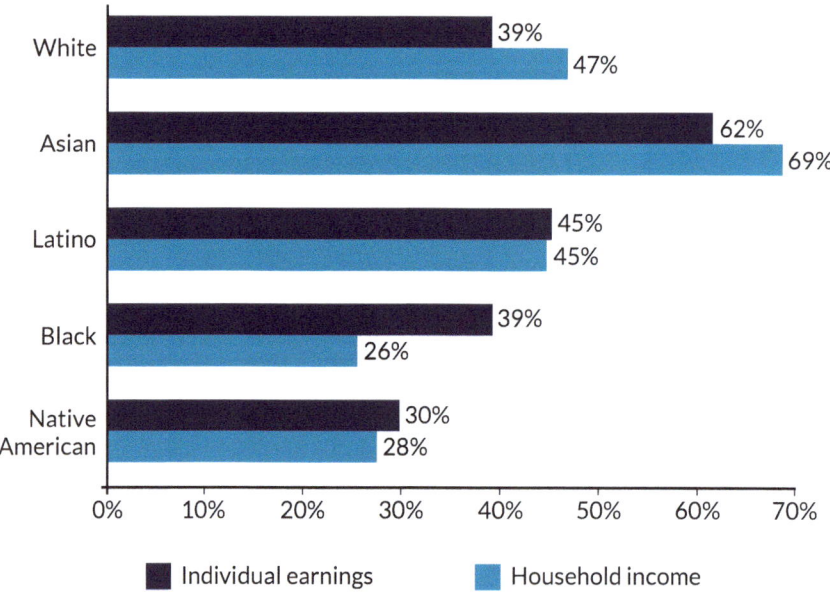

FIGURE 2-5 Intergenerational earnings and household income mobility for daughters.
NOTES: The figure shows the fraction of female children growing up in households with AGI in the bottom 20% of the AGI distribution whose individual earnings and household incomes in adulthood (ages 31–37) placed them in the top three quintiles of the adult earnings and household AGI distributions. Children were born between 1978 and 1983.
SOURCE: Data from Chetty et al. (2020).

who grew up in low-income households are an exception; their earnings in adulthood are just as high, on average, as those of White women who grew up in similar economic circumstances. This reflects the greater likelihood that they are the primary earners in their families.

A BROADER LOOK AT INTERGENERATIONAL INCOME MOBILITY ACROSS GROUPS

For a more comprehensive look at intergenerational mobility across groups, it is useful to think of economic status as rungs on a 100-step ladder, with the lowest rungs corresponding to the lowest incomes and the highest rungs representing the highest incomes. Each rung corresponds to a percentile in the income distribution. In the case of intergenerational mobility, there are two ladders—one showing the family income rank of children throughout childhood and the other showing the family income rank of those children in adulthood (ages 30–39).

The top five lines in Figure 2-6 show mobility patterns for children with very low childhood family incomes—on the 10th rung (percentile) of the income ladder. The topmost line shows considerable mobility in the case of White children, whose adult income, on average, reached the 41st rung. Asian children who grew up with 10th-rung income levels rose even higher, on average to the 53rd rung. Latino children's average upward mobility (39th rung) nearly matched that of White children. In sharp contrast, both Black and Native American children starting out on the 10th rung ended up at the 29th rung—12 rungs lower than White children.[5]

What about intergenerational economic mobility from other starting points? The second set of lines in Figure 2-6 shows average mobility for children in the five racial/ethnic groups who all started out with family incomes across childhood placing them on the 50th rung—the middle position in the childhood income distribution. The 10-rung gap persists for children starting out at the middle of the income distribution (the 50th rung), with White children advancing about 4 rungs and both Black and Native American children losing ground and falling back to the 39th and 41st rungs, respectively. Looking across the top and bottom sets of lines, it appears that if Black and Native American children were to match the average economic position of White adults who started out on the 10th rung as children, they had to have grown up in families with incomes above the middle (50th) rung.

---

[5] As detailed in Appendix C-2, Fisher and Johnson (2023) provide counterpart data from the PSID based on measures of income, consumption and wealth. Upward mobility from the 10th percentile is several rungs lower in PSID than IRS income data, but consumption and wealth-based destination rungs are more similar to IRS results.

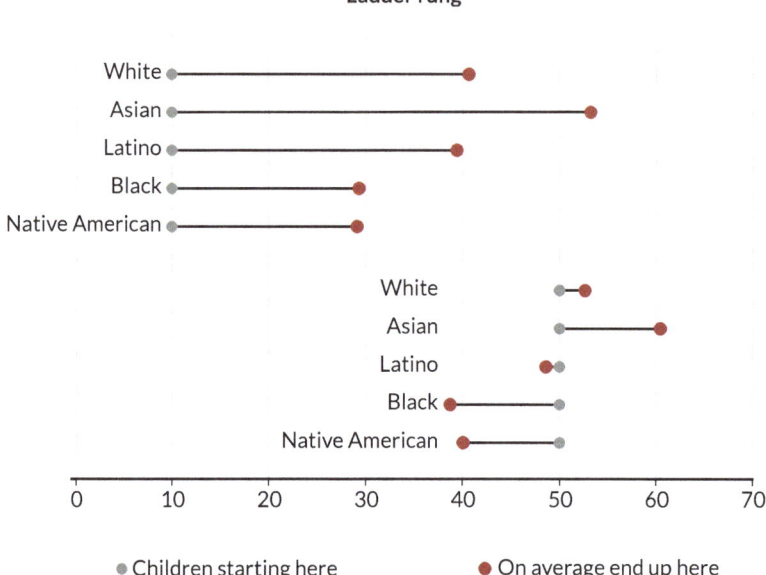

FIGURE 2-6 Intergenerational mobility, by race/ethnicity.
NOTES: This figure shows the mean income percentile of children with parents at the 10th and 50th income percentiles. Child income is measured as mean AGI income in 2014–2015, and parent income is measured as mean AGI income in 1994–2000. Children were born between 1978 and 1983.
SOURCE: Data from Chetty et al. (2020).

These differences reinforce the importance of applying a racial/ethnic disparities lens in analyzing key determinants of entrenched intergenerational economic disadvantage. As a result, Chapter 3 examines the histories, practices, and contexts that limit the intergenerational mobility of both Black and Native American children.

Conclusion 2-2: Racial/ethnic disparities are an enduring feature of the intergenerational trajectories of children, with Black and Native American children experiencing much less upward mobility than White children growing up in the same economic circumstances.

INTERGENERATIONAL INCOME MOBILITY AMONG CHILDREN OF IMMIGRANTS

Immigrants come to the United States with a wide range of human capital and labor market skills. Compared with the U.S.-born, foreign-born individuals disproportionately have either very high or very low levels of educational attainment (Card, 2005). Immigrants are more likely than U.S. natives to hold a graduate or professional degree, while at the same time, particularly if they come from poorer countries, they are far more likely than natives to have completed fewer than 12 years of schooling. Not only do many immigrants from less developed countries arrive with only a few years of relatively low-quality schooling, many also lack proficiency in English. These factors limit the labor market opportunities and earnings of low-skilled immigrants (Duncan & Trejo, 2012).

Because of the large share of immigrants with low skills, average earnings are substantially lower for foreign-born workers than for their U.S.-born counterparts (Card, 2005). Not surprisingly, the poverty rate tends to be higher for immigrants than for those born in the United States. In 2018, for example, the poverty rate was 14.6% for the foreign-born compared with 12.9% for the U.S.-born (Budman et al., 2020).[6] As a result, children of immigrants are more likely than children of natives to grow up in poverty.

Nevertheless, children of immigrants tend to experience remarkable socioeconomic progress. On average, they acquire more education and have higher earnings in adulthood than do children of the U.S.-born (Abramitzky et al., 2021; Card, 2005). Children of immigrants enjoy larger economic gains relative to their parents than do U.S.-born children (Abramitzky et al., 2021; Chetty et al., 2020), and this is particularly true of children who grew up in poverty. In other words, among children raised in poor households, children of immigrants are substantially more likely than children of non-immigrants to escape poverty as adults.

Figure 2-7, taken from Abramitzky et al. (2021), illustrates this finding. As in the case of our earlier figures, the analysis is based on data from Chetty et al. (2020) using tax records and census information to link the incomes of millions of parental households with the incomes of their adult children. For sons whose parental households between 1994 and 2000 ranked at the 25th percentile of the income distribution (i.e., families near the bottom of the distribution), the figure reports the average rank of the sons' household incomes when they were ages 31 to 37. Figure 2-7 reports this information both for children of U.S.-born parents (the red bar in the

---

[6] These statistics are based on the Official Poverty Measure rather than the alternative poverty measure (SPM) that is primarily used in this report.

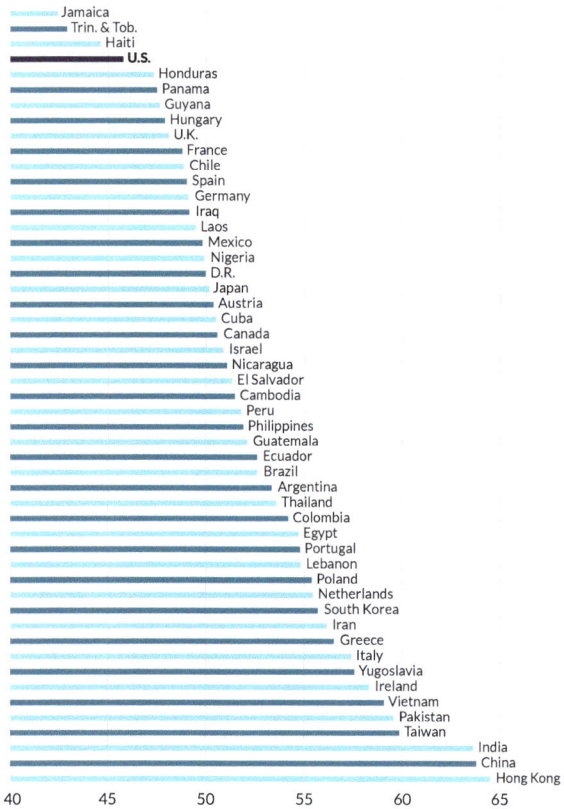

FIGURE 2-7 Average income rank of sons with low-income parents, by father's country of origin.
NOTES: This figure is adapted from Figure 3C of Abramitzky et al. (2021). It shows the mean income percentile of sons with parents at the 25th income percentile, by father's country of origin. Child income is measured as mean income in 2014–2015, and parent income is measured as mean household income in 1994–2000. Children were born between 1978 and 1983.
SOURCE: Data from Abramitzky et al. (2021), Figure 3C.

figure) and separately for children of immigrants by country of origin (the gray bars).

The figure documents extraordinary intergenerational mobility among children of poor immigrants. On average, sons of U.S.-born parents who grew up in households at the 25th percentile of the income distribution climbed more than 20 rungs to the 46th percentile in adulthood. But most sons of immigrants who grew up in similarly low-income households did considerably better as adults. Sons of parents from almost every country of origin—countries both rich and poor—experienced greater intergenerational mobility, on average, than did sons of U.S.-born parents. Abramitzky et al. (2021) find a similar pattern of results when looking at daughters rather than sons.

Why do children of immigrants experience these larger intergenerational advances? Part of the difference seems to be rooted in the fact that immigrants are more likely to settle in areas that offer their children better opportunities for upward mobility (Abramitzky et al., 2021). Also worth noting is that in many cases, the earnings of immigrants from poorer countries do not reflect the full potential of these individuals, who did not typically grow up speaking English or attending U.S. schools. Their children, however, enjoy these advantages and the economic gains associated with them (Abramitzky et al., 2021; Bleakley & Chin, 2004, 2008, 2010).

Conclusion 2-3: Children of immigrants from almost every country of origin—rich and poor nations alike—experience greater intergenerational mobility than children of U.S.-born parents. This immigrant advantage is larger for children from lower-income households, and to a large extent it reflects the fact that immigrants are more likely to settle in areas that offer their children better opportunities for upward mobility.

THE GEOGRAPHIC DISTRIBUTION OF INTERGENERATIONAL POVERTY

Rates of intergenerational economic disadvantage differ greatly from one part of the country to another, and even from one neighborhood to another in some cities. Figure 2-8 shows national patterns of intergenerational mobility in the United States. Constructed from anonymized adult tax records for more than 10 million children born between 1980 and 1982, it shows the average likelihood that children with parents in the bottom quintile of the income distribution will be in one of the top three quintiles in adulthood (Chetty et al., 2014a). Children are assigned to commuting zones based on the location of their parents, and their household incomes are measured in 2011–2012, when they are approximately age 30.

The blue parts of the map represent commuting zones in which children from the bottom quintile are more likely to reach one of the top three quintiles; the red areas represent places where such intergenerational mobility is less likely. The persistence of intergenerational economic disadvantage varies substantially across regions. Low-income children who grow up in the deepest-blue areas, such as the Great Plains, are about twice as likely to rise in the income distribution as otherwise comparable children growing up in parts of the Southeast and Midwest.

Although the red areas in Figure 2-8 overlap substantially with areas with concentrations of Black children, Chetty et al. (2020) show that, even among White populations, mobility is lower in the Southeast and areas with larger Black populations more generally.

Variation among nearby census tracts is also evident. A broad range of outcomes can be found in both rural and metropolitan areas; indeed, low-income children in neighboring areas may experience vastly different life trajectories. Chetty et al. (2018) use a dataset similar to that used to construct Figure 2-8 to measure intergenerational mobility for each census tract in the United States. Their estimates show that the geographic distribution of intergenerational economic disadvantage within communities in the United States is far from uniform. Some areas offer opportunities on par with some of the most upwardly mobile countries in the world, while in nearby areas intergenerational economic disadvantage is much more persistent. Figure 2-9 provides an illustrative example by plotting upward mobility by census tract in New York City (analogous data for other cities are available in Chetty et al.'s Opportunity Atlas at www.opportunityatlas.org). Here the measure of upward mobility is the predicted income of children raised in families at the 25th percentile of the national income distribution, a measure that can be estimated more precisely at the census tract level than the probability of remaining in or rising out of low-income status for the subset of children who start out in the bottom quintile.

Several studies have demonstrated that the variations shown in Figures 2-8 and 2-9 are driven largely by the causal effects of place, rather than by differences in the types of people living in different places (Chetty et al., 2016; Chetty & Hendren, 2018; Chyn, 2018; Chyn et al., 2023). This argues for examining place-focused policies such as investing in the economic development of low-opportunity areas and in approaches to increase children's upward mobility in those areas.

Race remains a factor as well. The geographic distribution of intergenerational poverty in each location varies by race, with one racial group experiencing good outcomes while other groups may not. Consistent with Figures 2-1 and 2-3, Chetty et al. (2020) show that, on average, Black children and Native American children in the United States have much lower rates of upward mobility (and higher rates of downward mobility) than White Americans. But these researchers go on to demonstrate that the gaps often persist *within* neighborhoods. In 99% of U.S. census tracts, Black boys have lower average incomes in adulthood than White boys. Therefore, to paint an accurate portrait of the geographic distribution of intergenerational poverty, it is necessary to take into account how economic mobility varies across places and across racial and ethnic subgroups.

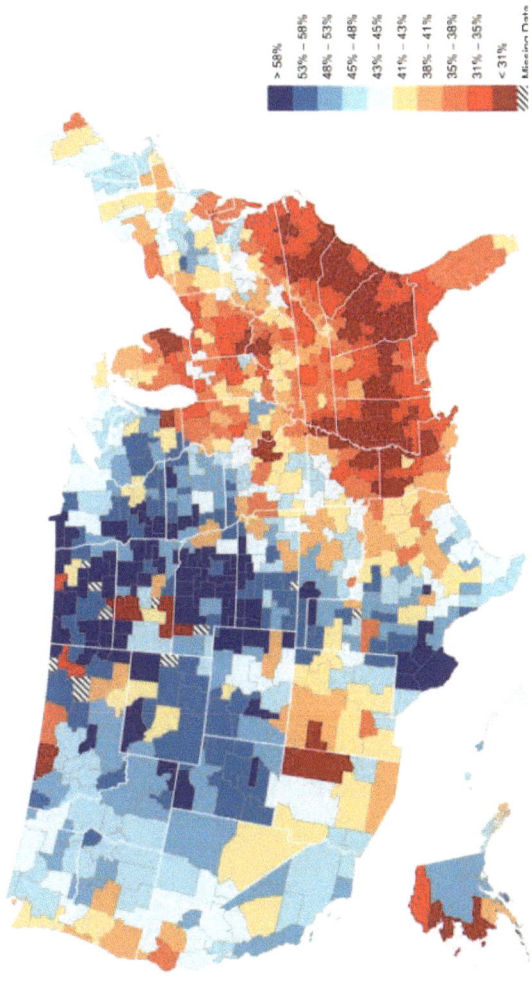

FIGURE 2-8 Geographic distribution of children with parents in the bottom income quintile who reach the top three income quintiles.
NOTES: This map shows the share of children with parents in the bottom income quintile who reached the top three income quintiles in adulthood, by commuting zone. Child income is measured as mean AGI household income in 2011–2012, and parent income is measured as mean AGI household income in 1996–2000. Children are from the 1980–1982 birth cohorts and are assigned to the commuting zones where they grew up.
SOURCE: Data from Chetty et al. (2014a).

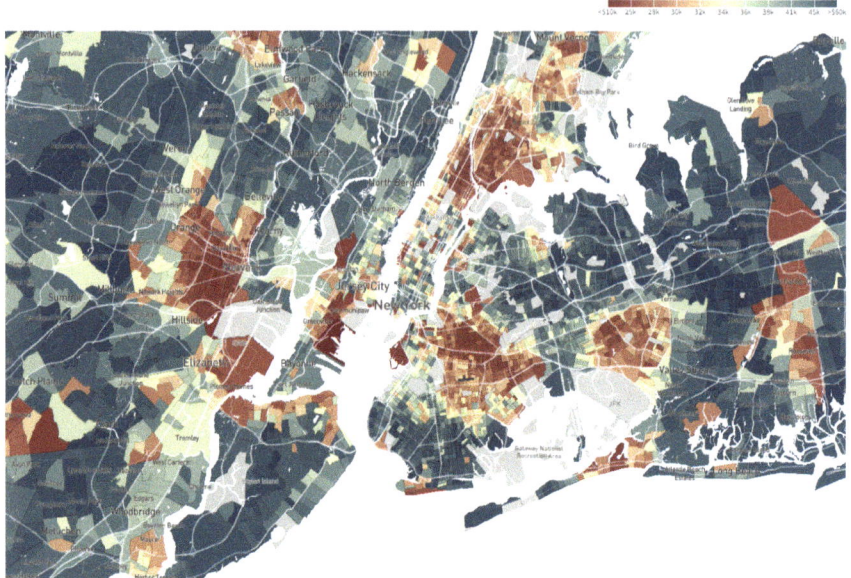

FIGURE 2-9 Age-35 household income of children of low-income parents in the New York City area.
NOTES: This map shows the mean household income of children with parents at the 25th income percentile, by census tract in the New York City area. Child income is measured as mean AGI household income in 2014–2015, and parent income is measured as mean AGI household income in 1994–2000. Children are from the 1978–1983 birth cohorts and are assigned to the census tracts where they grew up.
SOURCE: Image generated from https://www.opportunityatlas.org/ for Chetty et al. (2018).

Motivated by this finding, a rich literature has emerged using geographic variation to understand what factors explain differences in intergenerational mobility across areas. Studies have found several systematic predictors of differences in mobility, from poverty rates and school quality to the degree of inequality and historical factors such as redlining and Jim Crow laws (see Chapter 3).

The demographic characteristics of neighborhoods also show strong correlations with levels of upward mobility. Living in an area with a larger concentration of Black residents is associated with lower intergenerational mobility for both Black individuals and White individuals. One of the strongest predictors of differences in mobility across areas is the neighborhood fraction of children living with single parents. This correlation was nearly as strong for children growing up in married-parent families as for children growing up in single-parent families. However, because this is merely a correlation, it does not mean that changes in neighborhood family structure will necessarily cause changes in intergenerational mobility. In fact, Chetty et al. (2014a) find evidence that some of this correlation can be explained by the fact that family structure is associated with an area's degree of income inequality.

"Economic connectedness" is another strong predictor. Chetty et al. (2022) examine a measure of social capital constructed from Facebook friendships among low- and high-income individuals. They find that "economic connectedness"—as measured by the share of a person's Facebook friends from higher social strata—is among the strongest predictors to date of upward intergenerational income mobility. In fact, they find that it can explain several of the other correlations discussed above, such as the link between mobility and poverty rates, racial demographics, and income inequality. For example, areas where poverty is more concentrated tend to have fewer social connections between low- and high-income people, and this can explain (in a predictive sense) why higher poverty is associated with lower mobility.

Conclusion 2-4: Children's chances of growing up and escaping low-income status vary substantially depending on where they live. At both a broad regional level and within community boundaries, there are areas where low-income children tend to grow up and join the middle class, as well as areas where generations are more likely to remain mired in poverty. The spatial patterns of economic mobility vary by racial/ethnic group; nonetheless, disparities in economic mobility between Black and White children persist even within neighborhoods.

INTERGENERATIONAL MOBILITY: TRENDS AND COMPARISONS WITH OTHER COUNTRIES

Regardless of whether the amounts of intergenerational mobility out of low-income status shown in Figures 2-1 and 2-3 are perceived to be large or small, it is useful to examine how mobility rates have changed over time and how they compare in the United States and other countries.

Trends in U.S. Intergenerational Mobility

A number of economic and demographic changes over the past 75 years have created strong headwinds for children who grew up in poverty and have sought to do better economically than their parents. Economic growth was much stronger before the mid-1970s than it has been since. Moreover, as detailed in Chapter 6, high-income families have experienced far more growth since the mid-1970s than low-income families. Much of this differential growth can be attributed to increasing rewards for workers with college degrees relative to those whose schooling came to an end in high school. Some of the lower growth in family income is due to an increasing prevalence of single-parent families among the less educated.

Data presented thus far have shed light on the intergenerational mobility of children born around 1980. What about children born 20 or 40 years earlier? In the United States, intergenerational data spanning multiple cohorts are scarce. Although our decennial census counts the entire U.S. population every 10 years, there is no easy way of linking the data for a child in, say, the 1940 or 1950 census to the data gathered for that same child 30 or 40 years later. Chetty et al. (2020) matched the relevant data with the censuses starting in 2000, but no one has yet done so with prior cohorts.

Concentrating on children born in the first half of the 20th century, Jácome et al. (2021) find clear evidence of increasing intergenerational mobility. In contrast, for more recent cohorts, decreasing mobility is evident in some but not all measures. Davis and Mazumder (2022) take advantage of two large Bureau of Labor Statistics surveys covering cohorts born around 1950 and cohorts born in the early 1960s. They describe mobility patterns for all of the children in these birth cohorts, making no distinction between children born into low- and higher-income families. As did a number of other intergenerational studies they review, they find considerable decreases in intergenerational mobility between their two cohorts. They also show that declining mobility can be attributed, in part, to increasing returns to education beginning in the late 1970s, a factor that drives up mobility rates for middle- and upper-middle-income children relative to low-income children, as well as to the increasing prevalence of single-parent families, which leads to more persistent intergenerational disadvantage among lower-income children.

As described in Appendix C: Chapter 2, Chetty et al. (2017) take a different approach that enables them to describe mobility patterns for birth cohorts going back to 1940. Their data provide answers to a simple question: How many children born in a given year (e.g., 1940, 1970) will grow up to enjoy a family income that exceeds that of their parents? To adjust for the fact that family incomes tend to grow with time, both parent and child household incomes are measured when earners are around age 30. Figure 2-10 shows their results for birth cohorts every 10 years, beginning

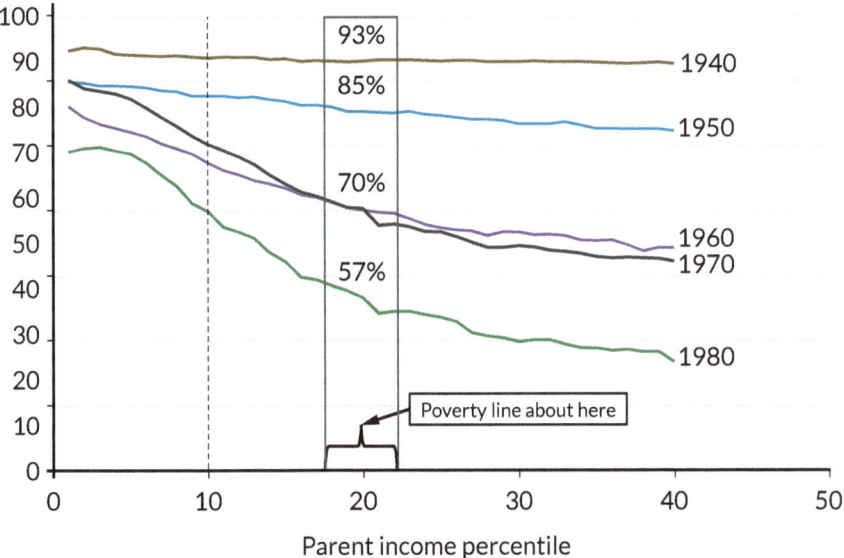

FIGURE 2-10 Percent of children earning more than their parents, by birth cohort and parental income percentile.
NOTES: This figure shows the share of children earning more than their parents, by child birth cohort and parental income percentile. This measure is calculated using children's and parents' marginal income distributions estimated using the Current Population Survey and decennial U.S. Census for the 1940–1984 birth cohorts, and a rank-rank copula estimated using tax records for the 1980–1982 birth cohorts, which is then applied to all cohorts from 1940 to 1984. See Appendix C: Chapter 2 for more details.
SOURCE: Data from Chetty et al. (2017).

in 1940. It further breaks down the chances of upward mobility separately by parental income percentile.[7]

Declining intergenerational mobility is quite apparent in the figure. Among children born in 1940 to families at the 20th percentile of the income distribution, almost all (93%) were found to have higher incomes in adulthood than their parents did. This fraction drops steadily in later cohorts; for the 1980 birth cohort, it is estimated to be only slightly more

---

[7] Because AGI and the SPM are not perfectly aligned, lower-income parental income percentiles contain a mix of households above and below the poverty line. At the 20th percentile of AGI, for the years we consider, the average SPM poverty rate was 29.1%, meaning that roughly 3 out of 10 households were living in poverty. For the same years, at the 10th percentile of AGI, the average SPM poverty rate was 68.3%.

than half (57%).[8] At the 10th percentile there is a similar decline across birth cohorts, although among this group the share of children born in 1980 who went on to have higher incomes in adulthood than their parents is substantially higher, at roughly 70%. Similar patterns of decline are observed in other industrialized countries for children born in the second half of the 20th century (Berman, 2022).

Seeking an explanation for the trends, Chetty et al. (2017) estimate what the trends would have been in a "higher growth" scenario in which the economy had grown as fast in recent decades as in past decades, and a "more broadly shared growth" scenario in which the benefits of the growth that did occur were equally shared across the income distribution. They find that both conditions matter. Higher growth would have reduced the decline in absolute mobility by about a third, while more broadly shared growth would have reduced the decline in absolute mobility by about two-thirds of what actually occurred. In this sense, changes in inequality—particularly the relative stagnation of wages at the bottom of the income distribution in the United States over the past 40 years—are central to understanding the decline of absolute upward mobility.

INTERGENERATIONAL MOBILITY IN THE UNITED STATES VERSUS OTHER COUNTRIES

We conclude our portrait with an international comparison. Do U.S. children have an easier or more difficult time surpassing their parents' economic fortunes than children in other countries? More specifically, given that the Chetty et al. (2017) study, described above, finds that about half of U.S. children born in 1980 do better than their parents, what are the counterpart fractions in other countries?

Studies based on income comparisons between parents and children have found that the U.S. mobility rate of 50% is similar to that of Canada (Ostrovsky, 2017), lower than Germany's 70% rate (Bönke et al., 2019; Stockhausen, 2018), and considerably smaller than Sweden's 77% rate (Liss et al., 2019). A recent and more comprehensive study (Manduca et al., 2020) found quite high mobility across most Scandinavian countries and in the United Kingdom and confirmed the lower rates in the United States and Canada.

---

[8] Although the pattern of declining mobility is clear in the Chetty et al. (2017) analysis, the exact numbers are less certain. A key technical question is how to adjust for cost-of-living differences, a contentious issue among economists. Chetty et al. (2020) show that alternative inflation measures can generate estimates of the overall fraction of, for example, children born in 1980 who are doing better than their parents that range from around 50% to a little over 70%.

Conclusion 2-5: After declining over the past 75 years, the fraction of children doing better than their parents is now lower in the United States than in most other industrialized countries. The most likely cause is that gains from economic growth have been disproportionately enjoyed by higher-income families, which has made it even more difficult for those at the bottom rungs of the income distribution to work their way up.

3

Racial Disparities in Intergenerational Poverty

While progress toward socioeconomic parity has occurred between White people and Black and Native American people in some domains, such as in high school graduation rates, residential integration, and poverty rates, in other domains gaps have been persistent or even widened. And despite whatever progress has been made, the previous chapter documents stark differences in intergenerational mobility for Black American and Native American children relative to other groups, even for children born between 1978 and 1983—more than a decade after the civil rights legislation of the mid-1960s. Chapter 2 provides two striking examples:

- Much higher fractions of low-income Black (37%) and Native American (46%) children are also low income in adulthood, as compared with low-income White children (29%).
- Both Black and Native American children with middle-class (50th rung) family incomes in childhood attain lower rungs of economic status in adulthood than White children who were low-income (10th rung) in childhood.

This chapter examines the histories, practices, and contexts that limit the intergenerational mobility of both Black and Native American children. These patterns are also gendered, as is discussed further in Appendix C: Chapter 3. The evidence presented in this chapter points to historical and contemporary racism as a driving factor in intergenerational economic outcomes. For example, in comparison with other advanced countries, the United States has a relatively weak social safety net, which limits the resources available for reducing intergenerational poverty. This weak welfare state is due in part to greater racial polarization in the United States and racist stereotypes of non-White people (Alesina et al., 2001; Fox, 2012). Many mechanisms of structural racism can be found in an array of institutional arrangements and public policy choices of the past and present (e.g., Baker, 2022), although the magnitude of the effects of such choices is unknown. Because racial disparities in intergenerational poverty were, in part, a product of past policy choices, future policy choices may help to reduce current and future disparities.

DEFINING DISPARITY, INEQUALITY, DISCRIMINATION, AND STRUCTURAL RACISM

Because this chapter discusses disparities and inequalities among racialized groups, it is vital to clarify what is meant by "racial inequality," "racial disparity," "racial discrimination," and "structural racism." Box 3-1 provides a list of brief definitions of these terms, and Appendix C: Chapter 3 offers a more in-depth discussion. It is also important to note that race can interact with gender, sexual orientation, religion, socioeconomic status, and disability in ways that compound inequality (Crenshaw et al., 2015; Harris, 2000; Nanda, 2019a).

HISTORICAL ROOTS OF RACIAL DISPARITIES IN INTERGENERATIONAL MOBILITY

To elaborate on structural racism and its link to intergenerational poverty, the persistent racial and ethnic disparities in upward mobility that are documented in this report can be better understood when placed in historical context. The report focuses on the historical experiences of Native Americans and Black Americans, given the persistence of intergenerational poverty in these populations (see Chapter 2). Though other racial and ethnic minorities in the United States have been impacted by structural racism, the duration, depth, and breadth of anti-Black and anti-Native racism are distinct.

Native Americans and Black Americans stand out as groups subjected to centuries of structural racism rooted in beliefs about White supremacy. Among the most severe forms of historical structural racism that set Black and Native Americans on a course of socioeconomic disadvantage are (a) forced migration and land theft; (b) chattel slavery and labor exploitation (Kiernan, 2007; Saito, 2020); and (c) forced assimilation and legalized racial discrimination imposed by racially oppressive institutions. While land theft is paramount for Native American people and slavery for Black people, it is important to note that Native American people were also enslaved

(Johnson, 2017; Reséndez, 2016; Trafzer & Hyer, 1999), and Black people have experienced both historical and contemporary theft (Atuahene & Berry, 2018; Immergluck et al., 2020; McMillan & Chakraborty, 2016; T. Mitchell, 2005). These primary histories and their long-term effects are discussed in depth in Appendix C: Chapter 3.

These forms of structural racism were means of economic exploitation that enriched White individuals and deprived generations of Black and Native Americans of economic assets, including income, wealth, and land ownership, as well as the correlated human capital, such as educational attainment and occupational skills, that are necessary for upward mobility and that they otherwise stood to gain (Desmond, 2021; Dubois, 1998). Native and Black Americans experience myriad other forms of theft, extraction, loss, and appropriation, both historically and in the present, from paying higher property taxes for similar public goods (Avenancio-León & Howard, 2022), to bearing a greater parking ticket burden (Brazil, 2020), to being the revenue-generating "mascot" for sports teams (Black, 2002; Fryberg et al., 2008). Whether historical or contemporary, the disproportionate rates of intergenerational poverty among Black people and Native Americans are due in part to their disproportionate subjection to impoverishment.

CONTEMPORARY DRIVERS OF RACIAL DISPARITY IN INTERGENERATIONAL POVERTY

The historical context described above and in Appendix C: Chapter 3 sets the stage for understanding contemporary intergenerational poverty in the United States and its relationship to Black and Native American communities. Black and Native American children and families face more challenging conditions rooted in a racialized distribution of resources and social processes of racial exclusion in the United States that have compounded over time. Today those processes manifest as inadequate access to health care and to well-funded, quality schools; greater exposure to crime, violence, and harm from the criminal justice system; housing insecurity and exposure to toxins; and lower family incomes, wealth, and neighborhood resources (National Academies, 2018).

Given this history and contemporary context, the question of how to address racial inequality thus looms large. The social determinants of health framework, which is widely accepted in the scientific literature today, is an instructive example. This framework is used to understand racial inequalities in the unequal risk of poor health outcomes, the lack of access to health care, and differential treatment by health care providers. Adult health is influenced by an individual's health-related behaviors and choices, but the factors that influence the behaviors and choices of Black and Native American individuals include the experiences of historical violence,

> **BOX 3-1**
> **Key Terms and Concepts**
>
> **Racial Disparities**
> Racial disparities are group-based average differences in outcomes. Chapter 2 and the opening section of this chapter documented the disparities between White people and Black and Native American people in rates of intergenerational economic mobility. Racial disparities are also evident in the key life experiences that are relevant for upward mobility, such as exposure to environmental toxins, residence in high-poverty neighborhoods, and attendance at schools with college-preparatory curricula. The cumulative and intersecting nature of these disparate exposures over the life course partly explains higher rates of intergenerational poverty. The word "gaps" is often used interchangeably with disparities.
>
> **Racial Inequality**
> Racial inequality refers to group-based differential treatment or access to valued resources that are rooted in law and public policy as well as in individual behavior and institutional practices National Academies, 2022b, pp. 1–7). Racial inequalities can result from multiple sources, including both historic and contemporary oppression, structural racism, and prejudice, whether intended or not. Racial inequality is a more comprehensive term than racial disparities because it recognizes that disparities occur across multiple domains and multiple outcomes. While the term may sometimes be used as synonymous with racial disparities to mean group-based differences in a particular domain or outcome, it is more often used to describe differences at a more macro level. For example, there might be *racial disparities* in access to preschool, and *racial inequality* in the educational system.
>
> **Racial Discrimination**
> An important part of racial discrimination is differential treatment on the basis of race that disadvantages a racial group (National Research Council, 2004, p. 4). This type of discrimination can reflect either animus toward specific racial groups, which economists call "taste-based" discrimination, or else what some social scientists call

oppression, and marginalization (National Academies, 2017d, 2021). Public health researchers understand that to varying degrees, health outcomes for these groups are a product of a racially stratified society rooted in historical and material conditions that remain salient in the health care system itself (Jones, 2002). Improving health outcomes for Black and Native American individuals means fixing the constituent pieces of an unequal society.

A logic similar to that of the social determinants of health framework pertains to intergenerational poverty. Identifying the structural mechanisms that drive racial inequality can help ensure that the policy or practice solutions are designed at an appropriate institutional or systemic level. To that end, this section describes the systems and social drivers—education, health,

statistical discrimination, a situation in which the discriminator possesses too little information about the characteristics of an individual and instead makes assumptions about the individual based on group-based stereotypes regarding, for example, skills or criminal behavior. Both racial animus–based and stereotype-based discrimination are illegal in the United States. Recent labor market evidence (e.g., Cordoba et al., 2021; Hurst et al., 2021) suggests there has been a decline in racial animus but growing statistical discrimination, although audit studies show no decline in employment discrimination since at least 1989 (Quillian et al., 2017). Regardless of its origin and nature, discrimination is relevant for intergenerational poverty because it excludes Black people and Native Americans from access to contexts that enhance opportunities or exposes them to situations that reduce opportunity.

Structural Racism

Structural racism refers to a system in which public policies, institutional practices, cultural representations, and other systems work in often reinforcing ways to maintain or compound racial inequalities (National Academies, 2022b, pp. 1–7). Thus, structural racism goes beyond mere patterns (disparities) or treatment (discrimination) to capture how rules, routines, and assumptions of U.S. law, institutions, norms, ideologies, policies, and technologies create disadvantages and advantages for people and groups based on how they are racialized in society. Structural racism can be historical or contemporary. Federal acquiescence to local segregationist laws and practices, which resulted in the near exclusion of Black World War II veterans from the benefits of the GI Bill, is an example of historical structural racism (Delmont, 2022). Historical structural racism affects the stocks of assets, skills, exposures, and opportunities—e.g., college degrees and home equity—that compound with families over generations into the present. A contemporary illustration of structural racism is how ostensibly race-neutral artificial intelligence algorithms may incorporate racial biases and inequalities from the real world to produce racially disparate outcomes when applied (Benjamin, 2019; Noble, 2018; Obermeyer et al., 2019). The qualities of being "built in" and often obscured are hallmarks of structural racism.

housing and neighborhood resources, child welfare, criminal justice, and income and employment—that perpetuate racial disparities in intergenerational poverty today.

Throughout each section, we discuss the patterns and experiences for both Black and Native American individuals when possible. However, much of the research on racial disparities uses a Black-White paradigm. Native American people are often left out of reported data, given their small overall population numbers, and even when there are available data they are often left out of analyses. Chapter 11 on future priorities for research and data collection discusses this issue in further detail.

Education

While educational attainment and skills have dramatically improved over time among Black and Native American children, and while racial disparities have declined in magnitude in some areas, disparities in access to educational opportunity are still deep and enduring characteristics of the American education system. Education can play a powerful role in undoing intergenerational poverty, as it promotes the development of the knowledge and skills that will allow children to be successful in the labor market, but the progress here remains far too limited. (See Chapter 4.)

For Native Americans, for example, there is a history of the U.S. government using education as a tool for colonization and forced assimilation. Throughout much of the 20th century, in the name of education, Native children were taken from their families, placed in federally controlled boarding schools, and punished for "speaking or acting Indian" (Adams, 1995). As a result, for generations, getting an education has been a metaphor for assimilation or "becoming White" (Deloria, 1999; Deyhle & Swisher, 1997; Elliott-Groves & Fryberg, 2019; Ogbu & Davis, 2003). Although most tribal nations and Native individuals today recognize that education is essential for socioeconomic success, the path toward attaining an education is replete with structural and social barriers.

When a Native American child enters kindergarten, compared with other American children, they are often behind in reading, mathematics, and fine motor skills (Snyder & Dillow, 2011). This result is largely due to the lack of early childhood education and the preponderance of economic and social struggles in the home. Native American children have lower preschool enrollment rates (44%) than White children (49%).[1] Disparities continue throughout the life course: Compared with other ethnic groups, Native students ages 3–17 are more likely to be identified as having a learning disability and as needing special education intervention services (U.S. Census Bureau, 2012). Native students have the highest dropout rates of any ethnic group in the United States. Recent statistics from the Bureau of Indian Affairs show that 29% to 36% of all Native American students drop out of school, mostly between the 7th and 12th grades. In the 12 states with the largest populations of Native American students, these numbers are even higher, with less than 50% of Native American students graduating from high school, compared with 71.4% of all students in those states (Faircloth & Tippeconic, 2010). These high school graduation rates are the lowest among American students.

---

[1] See https://www.diversitydatakids.org/research-library/data-visualization/neighborhood-preschool-enrollment-patterns-raceethnicity

The same patterns apply to college completion. The 6-year graduation rate for Native American students from 4-year degree-granting institutions is 39%, compared with 74% for Asian American students and 64% for White students (National Center for Education Statistics, 2019). These outcomes do not constitute a snapshot of one generation of Native students but rather reflect a history of distrust stemming, in large part, from the physical and social abuses experienced during the boarding school era (late 1800s to the mid-1900s) that constitute an intergenerational trauma passed down from one generation to the next (Adams, 1995; A. Smith, 2007) and the lack of cultural fit for Native American students in mainstream educational institutions (Fryberg & Markus, 2007; Fryberg et al., 2013, 2018).

Native American students who attend schools in which Natives are more than one-quarter of total enrollment reported more serious problems with absenteeism, tardiness, low family involvement, and low expectations than other schools (Devoe & Darling-Churchill, 2008). One potential reason for these differences is the landscape of social representation in the schools, that is, the ideas and images available. Shear et al. (2015, Table 3) found that 87% of state-level U.S. history standards portray Native people in pre-1900 contexts. In high Native contexts, this bias in the curriculum may be more salient (Fryberg & Leavitt, 2014; Lomawaima & McCarty, 2006). Beyond the curriculum, Native American students rarely see members of their group represented as primary or secondary teachers (0.5% are Native American), as college students (1% are Native American), or as professors (0.5% are Native American; Coopersmith, 2009; Snyder et al., 2009). The lack of self-relevant social representations in education subtly conveys to Native students that they do not belong and cannot be successful in these educational contexts (Fryberg & Eason, 2017; Fryberg & Townsend, 2008; Gay & Howard, 2000; Ladson-Billings, 1995).

Similar disparities in treatment and outcomes are evident for Black children. As described further in Chapter 4, Black students entering kindergarten are about half a year behind their White counterparts in early math achievement, with gaps apparent in kindergarten-entry literacy as well. These differences in learning continue throughout the educational process and through school completion (Kuhfeld et al., 2020; Paschall et al., 2018; Reardon, 2021). One explanation is that teachers' expectations for their students differ based on students' race and ethnicity. Lower expectations have harmful effects on actual achievement (Jussim & Harber, 2005), and White teachers have lower expectations of Black students than they do of White students (Gershenson et al., 2016; Papageorge et al., 2020).

Also meriting attention is access to high-quality, well-funded schools and the school environment itself. After years of progress toward racial desegregation, on some measures pre-K-to-12 schools have become increasingly segregated by class and race (An & Gamoran, 2009; Reardon

& Owens, 2014; Reardon et al., 2021). Most school districts reflect the demographic and socioeconomic compositions of their neighborhoods, and Black and Native American children are more likely than White children to live in high-poverty areas (National Academies, 2019a). School assignment policies that send all (or many) children from a high-poverty neighborhood or community to the same school create schools with high concentrations of children living in poverty. Schools serving children from low-income families tend to have fewer material resources (e.g., books, libraries, classrooms), fewer course offerings, and fewer experienced teachers. The educational opportunities available to students attending these schools are not of the same quality as those in schools in more affluent areas (Monarrez & Chien, 2021). These trends pose increasing challenges for school systems that serve large numbers of non-White students, which all too often are the same school systems that have fewer economic resources in the first place.

School discipline is relevant as well. Black and Native American students are disproportionately subjected to harsh in-school discipline, which threatens students' well-being and learning (Beland & Kim, 2016; Gregory et al., 2017; Nowicki, 2018). Disparities in punishment appear at the very earliest ages. In preschool, Black and Native American toddlers are suspended at rates 2.5 and 1.5 times higher, respectively, than their representation in the preschool population, and Black preschoolers are overrepresented among expelled children by a factor of 2 (U.S. Department of Education Office for Civil Rights, 2021a). In K–12 settings, Black and Native American youth are also at higher risk of being referred to law enforcement and being arrested at school (Brown, 2014; U.S Department of Education Office for Civil Rights, 2021b).

Studies show that such disparities are not always due to children's behavior but rather are sometimes due to between-school differences in punishment cultures and to the differential labeling of behaviors of Black and White children and ensuing punishments (Gilliam et al., 2016; Goff et al., 2014; Okonofua & Eberhardt, 2015; Owens & McLanahan, 2020; Sabol et al., 2022; Skiba et al., 2014), and higher rates of racial bias at the community level (Riddle & Sinclair, 2019). For example, Okonofua and Eberhardt (2015) found that when presented with identical descriptions of student behavior, teachers viewed two minimal infractions as more troubling and deserving of harsher punishment when committed by a Black student than by a White student. At the same time, students in classrooms with higher shares of Black, Native American, and Latino peers report a greater likelihood that classroom misbehavior slows down learning and experience greater pressure to misbehave (Ferguson, 2016). Okonofua et al. (2016) hypothesize that there is a negatively reinforcing causal loop from disproportionate punishment to poor student behavior, whereby racially stigmatized students experience a lack of belonging, delinquent labeling, and perceived unfair treatment, which increases their misbehavior. Field-tested randomized controlled experiments show that increasing teachers' use of "empathic discipline" (Okonofua et al., 2016) and improving Black students' identity self-affirmations (Borman et al., 2022) and sense of belonging, inclusion, and growth (Goyer et al., 2019) all decrease exclusionary discipline against Black students.

Exclusionary school discipline leads to lost learning days (Losen & Martinez, 2020). The U.S. Department of Education reports that students lost more than 11 million days of school owing to out-of-school suspensions in 2017–2018, with this burden falling disproportionately on Black and Native American students (and also falling disproportionately on boys). The Civil Rights Project at the University of California, Los Angeles reports (using 2015–2016 data) that "Black students lost 103 days per 100 students enrolled, which is 82 more than the 21 days their White peers lost due to out-of-school suspensions." Native American students lost 54 days per 100 students enrolled (Losen & Martinez, 2020)

Correlational and quasi-experimental studies show that school discipline is negatively related to standardized test scores and high school and college graduation and is positively correlated with involvement in the criminal legal system (Bacher-Hicks et al., 2019; Chu & Ready, 2018; Mittleman, 2018; Rose et al., 2022; Rosenbaum, 2020; Wolf & Kupchik, 2017). Raffaele Mendez (2003) found that unequal treatment based on race and other characteristics results in disparate outcomes for children, as out-of-school suspensions are highly predictive of future involvement with the criminal justice system and reduced educational achievement. Using integrated administrative data from the state of Oregon linking school discipline with adult outcomes, Davison et al. (2022) found that:

> approximately 30% of the gap between Black and White young adult criminal justice outcomes, SNAP participation, and bachelor's degree (BA) receipt can be traced back to inequalities in school discipline, and that just accounting for out-of-school suspensions for insubordination reduces the Black-White disparity by approximately 10% (Davison et al., 2022, p. 233).

In sum, large gaps in school achievement and completed schooling persist across racial and ethnic subgroups, posing a key challenge for policy makers seeking to reduce intergenerational poverty and pointing to the importance of education-related interventions, which will be discussed in Chapter 4.

Health

Child physical and mental health is an important driver of intergenerational mobility, as will be examined in Chapter 5. Children born to mothers with lower socioeconomic status in the United States are born in worse health than other children, and this disparity increases as they age (Case et al., 2002), culminating in a strong relationship between childhood poverty and adult health as well as adult income given the link between health and income. Inequalities in health derive largely from unequal risk of poor health outcomes (through environmental influences on health and nutrition and food insecurity), lack of access to health care, and differential treatment by health care providers. For example, a study of the desegregation of hospitals after the 1964 Civil Rights Act demonstrated sharp declines in Black infant mortality, demonstrating how the lack of appropriate maternity care to Black women had resulted in the deaths of Black newborns (Almond et al., 2006). Using a social determinants of health framework, public health researchers hypothesize that these inequalities are all, to varying degrees, outcomes of a racially stratified society and are rooted in historical and material conditions that remain salient in the health care system itself (Jones, 2002).

Historically, science and medicine have reinforced White racial superiority to justify and perpetuate disparate treatment of individuals. Examples of racism in science and medicine that have engendered Black people's mistrust of the medical system include the eugenics movement of the 1900s, which resulted in the forced sterilization of Black women; and the use of tissue from Henrietta Lacks (a Black woman with cervical cancer) to create cell lines for scientific research without her permission. The effects of the "Tuskegee Study of Untreated Syphilis in the Negro Black Male," in which Black men were deliberately not treated for syphilis despite effective available treatment in order to study the natural course of the disease in Black men is perhaps most well-documented. Alsan and Wanamaker (2018) compared older Black men to other demographic groups, before and after the information about the Tuskegee study was revealed, and in varying proximity to the Tuskegee study's victims. They found that the public disclosure of the study in 1972 was associated with increases in medical mistrust and mortality and decreases in both outpatient and inpatient physician interactions for older Black men, with the largest effects found for Black men living in closest geographic proximity to Tuskegee. They estimate that life expectancy fell for Black men by up to 1.5 years in response to the disclosure, accounting for approximately 35% of the 1980 life expectancy gap between Black and White men (Alsan & Wanamaker, 2018).

Implicit bias has also been shown to be prevalent in health care (FitzGerald & Hurst, 2017; Hall et al., 2015) and to result in disparate outcomes among individuals of different races. For example, some research suggests that Black women are less likely than their White counterparts to receive an epidural during childbirth because of providers' beliefs about the relationship between race and pain tolerance, as well as poor communication in racially discordant provider-patient relationships (National Academies, 2021). Research has also shown that providers perceive Black individuals as less likely than White individuals to adhere to medical advice, a perception that contributes to poor communication and care (Laws et al., 2014; Van Ryn & Burke, 2000). These experiences of implicit bias can lead to mistrust and avoidance of the system, thus exacerbating health disparities (Chaturvedi & Gabriel, 2020).

Lack of access to health care also affects the health of Black and Native American people. Native Americans experience very high uninsured rates; the Centers for Disease Control and Prevention reports that 28.6% of Native Americans under age 65 are uninsured (Assistant Secretary for Planning and Evaluation, 2023). Although the Indian Health Service provides medical care, funding is adequate to meet the needs of only about half of those eligible for services, and staff shortages are persistent (Chapter 5). Black individuals under age 65 have an uninsurance rate (11.5%) that is roughly 60% higher than the uninsurance rate for White individuals (7.5%; Artiga et al., 2020). A landmark study demonstrated that even after accounting for socioeconomic factors, race and ethnicity remained significant predictors in access to and the quality of health care received (Institute of Medicine, 2003).

Racism impacts health through environmental influences, including greater exposure to and experiences of trauma and chronic stress (Giscombé & Lobel, 2005; Nuru-Jeter et al., 2009), environmental toxins, and violence. Stress, for example, has been associated with poor health in multiple arenas, including mental health (Paradies et al., 2015), sleep (Slopen et al., 2016), obesity (Bernardo et al., 2017), hypertension (Dolezsar et al., 2014), and cardiovascular disease (Lewis et al., 2014). In addition to the actual experience of discrimination, just the threat of discrimination—and its associated hypervigilance—can harm a person's health. Chronic exposure to racism and discrimination leads to dysregulation of stress hormones and to epigenetic modifications, in which environmental influences regulate gene expression without changing genetic sequences (Seeman & Crimmins, 2001; Seeman et al., 2014). It also leads to "weathering," that is, premature aging at the cellular level (Geronimus et al., 2006). These biological changes are associated with chronic disease in childhood, such as asthma and obesity, and poor cardiovascular outcomes in adulthood, which affect future economic prospects (McEwen & Seeman, 1999; McEwen & Stellar 1993; Shonkoff et al., 2009).

In sum, Black and Native American children continue to experience worse health than their White counterparts, and drivers of worse health among Black and Native American children include those related to access to health care, environmental influences including pollution and community violence, and nutrition, as well as differential treatment by health care providers. Improving the health of Black and Native American children living in low-income households is therefore a key lever for reducing intergenerational poverty, as improvements in child health have been shown to improve economic status in adulthood (see Chapter 5).

Wages and Employment

The persistence of economic immobility has defined Black Americans' relationship to labor and the labor market throughout much of U.S. history (Collins & Wanamaker, 2022; also see Appendix C: Chapter 3, where this issue is discussed in detail). Black people's relationship to the labor market can be divided into at least three distinct periods: (1) slavery to emancipation, (2) emancipation to the Civil Rights Act of 1964, and (3) post-Civil Rights Act to the present. In both the first and second periods, racist and discriminatory employment practices were legally sanctioned, protected, or ignored.

In the third (contemporary) period, explicit discrimination based on race and ethnicity is illegal. Yet despite declines in Black-White wage and employment gaps, significant disparities remain (Bayer & Charles, 2018). Black workers receive lower average earnings, face less predictable work hours, experience less overall employment stability, and reside disproportionately in states where the relatively low federal minimum wage is binding (Hardy & Logan, 2020). They also tend to be concentrated in low-skilled or disappearing occupations (Meschede et al., 2019; Smith, 2002), resulting in their overrepresentation among low-income populations (National Academies, 2019a).

One explanation of these disparate outcomes is racial discrimination in the labor market—affecting who gets an interview as well as who gets hired. Evidence from audit and correspondence studies indicates that White applicants are more likely than Black applicants with the same education and employment qualifications to receive employer call-backs (Bertrand & Mullainathan, 2004; Neumark, 2012; Pager, 2003) and job offers (Quillian et al., 2020b). These employment patterns are present in entry-level positions (Agan & Starr, 2018; Pager, 2008), among the college-educated (Gaddis, 2015), and among those with advanced degrees (Reeves, 2014). Experimentally identified discrimination against Black applicants may be of either the taste (i.e., based on racial animus) or statistical kind, although Bertrand and Mullainathan (2004, p. 1010) note that both models "struggle to explain" their findings in full.

A weakness of this research is that audit studies cannot be used directly to measure the role of discrimination in generating observed outcome disparities in wages or employment rates. In an essay reviewing the field, Neumark (2018, p. 855) states that "very few [audit] studies have tried to capture wage outcomes, and none have done so convincingly." Other studies, however, suggest that employment discrimination identified in audit studies translates into wage gaps (Lanning, 2013), as do higher levels of White racial prejudice in an area (Charles & Guryan, 2008). And in the related field of housing-discrimination audit studies, Christensen et al. (2021, p. 7) find that "differential treatment identified in the correspondence study predicts...the probability of a subsequent lease by a renter from the same [racial] group." In other words, housing discrimination identified against Black auditors is related to a lower probability that a Black person ultimately lives in the audited housing unit. This study offers a model for research matching employment audits to hiring and wage outcomes for the same jobs.

Racial disparities in employment and earnings can also be attributed in part to gaps in educational attainment, achievement, and skills between Black and White Americans. As discussed in the previous section on education, such gaps are in part the result of unequal treatment and access in educational institutions. The relative contribution of cognitive and non-cognitive skills and education to the employment and wage gap is a topic of long-standing scholarly debate (Carneiro et al., 2005; Darity & Mason, 1998; Elder & Zhou, 2021; Neal & Johnson, 1996; Rodgers & Spriggs, 1996; Tomaskovic-Devey et al., 2005), and often depends on how the education controls are specified and the specific outcome of interest. For example, Thompson (2021, p. 20) reports that the "contribution of human capital to differences in the earnings of Black and white men grew steadily over the past 50 years," whereas Cajner et al. (2017) find that differences in observable characteristics have consistently explained very little of the Black-White employment gap over a similar time period, and Coleman (2003) reports a wider wage gap controlling for skill. Importantly, achievement and education gaps now favor women relative to men in all racial groups (Reeves, 2022) and may help explain why intergenerational poverty is more pronounced for Black men than for Black women when measured by individual earnings. Other important considerations such as union density and wage structures are also important for explaining racial earnings gaps (Bayer & Charles, 2018). As is discussed further in Chapter 4, improving education and skills for low-income Black and Native American children is likely to increase their adult wages and decrease their intergenerational poverty.

Labor market segmentation may also explain racial disparities in employment. Black workers are more likely to be employed in less stable jobs, with less regular work, and with more precarious work hours. For instance, while Black people make up 12.1% of the labor force, they make up 25.9% of temporary workers earning 40% less for the same jobs as permanent workers in the same position (Wilson, 2020). Racialized wage gaps also manifest along gender lines. In 2017, the median annual earnings for full-time Black women workers was 21% lower than for White women and 39% lower than for White men, reflecting the over-representation of Black women in low-wage service and sub-minimum wage jobs (Banks, 2019).

Black workers tend to fare worse in the labor market, independent of macroeconomic conditions, though they suffer more during downturns and benefit relatively more during tight labor markets. During the economy recovery following the COVID-19 pandemic, unemployment rates have declined, yet racial disparities remain. As of July 2022, the unemployment rate of Black workers was 6.0%, compared with 3.9% for Latino workers and 3.1% for White workers (U.S. Bureau of Labor Statistics [BLS], 2021). In April 2020, when the COVID-19 pandemic raged, the unemployment rate of Black Americans reached 16.6%, compared with 12.8% for White Americans (Fairlie et al., 2021). More than 6 in 10 Black adults with a 2019 household income of less than $35,000 reported losing labor income in 2020 (Sanchez Cumming & Kopparam, 2021). In late 2009, during the peak of the Great Recession (2007–2009), unemployment for Black workers was 14.8%, significantly higher than the White unemployment rate of 8.5% (BLS, 2010).

Differences in labor force participation rates—particularly among men (Binder & Bound, 2019; Eberstadt, 2016; Thompson, 2021)—also contribute to racial disparities in earnings and household income. In 2021, according to data on adult men from the BLS (2023), Latino men (75.4%) were more likely to participate in the labor force than men of other races, and Black men (63.5%) were the least likely, with White men (67.9%) and Native American men (66.2%) between the two. In contrast, among adult women, Black women (58.8%) were more likely to participate in the labor force than were Latina women (55.8%), White women (55.4%), and Native American women (55%). The BLS data overstate labor force participation among Black men because they do not include incarcerated populations (Pettit, 2014) and there is evidence of underreporting of those not incarcerated (Holzer, 2021). Measured progress between White men and Black men in relative earnings becomes much more limited when the lower labor force of the latter, especially among the incarcerated, is taken into account (Bayer & Charles, 2018).

Important racial disparities can be found not only among workers but also among business owners and entrepreneurs. Black-owned businesses comprise about 9% of privately owned businesses in the United States and are overwhelmingly newly founded or started (Fairlie & Robb,

2010; M'Balou Camara et al., 2019). These businesses are denied loans at 2.5 times the rate of White-owned businesses (Cavalluzzo & Wolken, 2005). Black-White differences in loan denials are largest at the top end of the wealth distribution (Ards & Myers, 2001). In one study, only 56% of minority-owned businesses were approved for financing, compared with 73% of White-owned firms (de Zeeuw, 2019). In addition to loan denials, Black-owned firms are more likely to be charged higher interest rates despite clean credit histories and creditworthiness (Ards & Myers, 2001; Blanchflower et al., 2003). Disparities in the source and amount of start-up capital may mean the difference between success or failure.

In sum, disparities in both employment and earnings remain between White individuals and Black individuals. Given that persistently low family incomes and employment are an important driver of intergenerational poverty, policies that increase parental incomes and employment may increase intergenerational mobility (and will be discussed in Chapter 6).

Housing and Neighborhood Environments

Housing represents a bundle of possible inputs—such as access to good schools, parks, safety, doctors and health care, and commercial offerings—that affect family well-being and can promote or hinder mobility out of poverty. Despite a reduction in Black-White residential segregation in recent decades (Logan & Stults, 2022), Black Americans have experienced systematic exclusion from places that promote upward mobility and have instead been concentrated in places with various forms of toxicity. Additionally, the rise in segregation by socioeconomic status (Reardon & Bischoff, 2011) means that Black and Native American families living below the poverty line suffer a double blow, which limits the upward mobility of their children over time.

After the Great Depression, the federal government came to play a greater role in housing policy, replicating and intensifying the discrimination already present in the private housing market (see Appendix C: Chapter 3). Government programs were a source of wealth accumulation and upward mobility for White families, while excluding Black families from homeownership and its wealth-generating potential (Katznelson, 2005; Radford, 2008; Taylor, 2019). The Federal Housing Administration and the Veterans Administration insured approximately half of all mortgages for single-family homes and small buildings by the 1950s (Fishback et al., 2022, p. 25), yet "between 1945 and 1959, less than two percent of all federally insured home loans went to African Americans" (Hanchett, 2000, p. 166). To insure private mortgages, the federal government developed standardized appraisal systems that regarded Black neighborhoods as high-risk (Fishback et al., 2022; Stuart, 2003). The rating system color-coded sections of cities in green, blue, yellow, and, for the lowest category, red. The term redlining refers to the systematic denial of mortgage loans based on these federal guidelines, which were steeped in racial, ethnic, and antiurban biases (Jackson 1985; Rothstein, 2017, see Appendix C: Chapter 3). Exclusion from mortgage markets reduced housing wealth in redlined areas (Xu, 2022), and exposed Black neighborhoods to predatory private lenders like contract sellers, who siphoned off the income and wealth of Black individuals (Dubois Cook Center, 2019; Satter, 2009). Family wealth—or its lack—is an important determinant of children's outcomes (Conley, 1999; Moulton et al., 2021; Orr, 2003; Pfeffer, 2011), and thus discrimination against Black people in the housing market reverberates across generations (Oliver & Shapiro, 1997; Pfeffer & Killewald, 2018).

Research shows the long arm of redlining reaching into the present. Aaronson et al. (2021b) compare areas along actual and potential Home Owners' Loan Corporation (HOLC) boundaries and show that the HOLC appraisal ratings in the early 20th century impact the long-term socioeconomic outcomes of children born in the 1970s and 80s. In particular, children in the lower-graded areas were in lower household-income rankings at age 29 and were less likely than other children to move toward the top of the income distribution as adults. Today, historically redlined neighborhoods have lower homeownership rates and lower home values (Aaronson et al., 2021a,b), higher poverty rates, lower life expectancy, higher rates of chronic disease (National Community Reinvestment Coalition, 2020), higher rates of preterm births (Krieger et al., 2020), less health-promoting tree cover and green space (Hoffman et al., 2020; Nardone et al., 2021; Schinasi et al., 2022), and higher incidence of emergency room visits for asthma (Nardone et al., 2020). Lane et al. (2022) find that historically redlined areas are disproportionately occupied by non-White residents today and have greater exposure to pollution. Figure 3-1 shows these patterns clearly for the city of Oakland, California. Exposure to pollution has negative effects on children's health and long-term outcomes, as discussed above and in Chapter 5. This is an area that has been positively impacted by policy, namely the Clean Air Act of 1970, which has reduced racial disparities in such exposure (Currie, 2023).

Redlining and the association of Black residents with risk did not end in the 1930s. Appraisal manuals explicitly called for lower appraised values in racially mixed neighborhoods up until at least 1977 (Kuebler, 2012; Yinger, 1995), and private appraisal practices continue to disadvantage Black home buyers today (Freddie Mac, 2022; Howell & Korver-Glenn, 2021; Perry et al., 2018). In the decades leading up to the housing crisis of 2007, Black neighborhoods and households were disproportionately targeted by lenders and banks to receive subprime loans, no matter their socioeconomic status and despite other indicators of creditworthiness (Bayer et al., 2018; Faber,

FIGURE 3-1 How air pollution reflects racist policy from the 1930s. SOURCE: Zhong and Popovitch (2022).

2013; Hwang et al., 2015; Institute on Race and Poverty, 2009; Massey et al., 2016; Rugh & Massey, 2010; Steil et al., 2018). Scholars have referred to these practices as "predatory inclusion" (Taylor, 2019).

Targeting Black neighborhoods for lower appraisals or subprime loans is possible in part because of enduring patterns of racial residential segregation. The causes of that segregation are manifold, including historical and contemporary "preferences," racial steering and discrimination by real estate agents and landlords, White flight, and anti-Black prejudice (Boustan, 2010; Card et al., 2008; Charles, 2006; Christensen et al., 2021; Flage, 2018; Krysan & Crowder, 2017; Massey & Lundy, 2001; Rugh & Massey, 2014). While residential segregation between Black and White Americans has declined steadily since about 1970, it remains higher than for any other racial or ethnic group. Given current trends, Black-White residential segregation will not dip into what social scientists consider to be low levels until the year 2080 (Rugh & Massey, 2014, p. 213).

The most recent national audit study using matched pairs of houseseekers found declines in discrimination against Black people compared with previous decades, but it also found continued practices of racial steering of Black testers into neighborhoods with higher poverty rates, lower school test scores, higher rates of violent crime, and greater exposure to air toxins (Christensen & Timmins, 2022; Turner et al., 2013). Christensen et al. (2021) conducted the largest correspondence study of racial discrimination in the rental market to date. They found that apartment seekers with Black-identified names were 9.3% less likely than White renters to receive a response. Further, they show that greater housing market discrimination is correlated with greater residential segregation and with larger White-Black gaps in intergenerational income mobility. Likewise, Black boys who grow up in areas with less racial bias, as measured by Google searches for racial epithets and on-line implicit bias tests, have higher incomes in adulthood (Chetty et al., 2020). Past and current racial residential discrimination and segregation are correlated with lower rates of intergenerational mobility (Andrews et al., 2017; Chetty et al., 2014; Christensen et al., 2021; Derenoncourt, 2022).

Patterns of racial residential segregation increase Black people's exposure to high poverty neighborhoods (Ananat, 2011; Christensen & Timmins, 2022; Massey & Denton, 1993; Quillian, 2012). Roughly 30% of Black and Native American children, compared with 4% of non-Hispanic White children, live in neighborhoods where 30% or more of the residents have incomes below the poverty line (Annie E. Casey Foundation, 2019a,b). Just as the intergenerational experience of poverty is higher among Black people, so is the intergenerational exposure to neighborhoods experiencing poverty (Sharkey, 2013). Growing up in high-poverty neighborhoods, and in counties with greater concentrated poverty and racial segregation, is correlated with lower intergenerational mobility (Chetty & Hendren, 2015, 2018). As such it is a key policy lever, which will be described in greater detail in Chapter 8.

Crime, Victimization, and Criminal Justice

There is substantial contemporary evidence of racial disparities not only in the commission of violent crime and victimization but also across the criminal legal system in arrests, charging, convictions, sentencing, incarceration, and community supervision (Alesina & La Ferrara, 2014; Alexander, 2010; Arnold et al., 2018; Feigenberg & Miller, 2021; Franklin, 2013; Stewart et al., 2022; Weaver et al., 2019; for reviews and compilations of this research see Arya & Rolnick, 2008; Balko, 2020; Du, 2021; Hinton et al., 2018; Kurlychek & Johnson, 2019; National Academies, 2022b; National Research Council, 2014; Nielsen & Silverman, 2009; Redner-Vera & Wang, 2022). Black and Native American youth also experience disproportionate punishment in the juvenile justice system (Development Services Group, 2016; National Research Council, 2013; Rovner, 2016). An analysis of juvenile incarceration in 2019 shows that the rate of confinement for Black and Native American youth is higher than the rates of confinement for White, Latino, and Asian youth combined (Wang, 2021).

At the same time, community violence poses a significant risk to health and well-being for Black, Native American, and low-income communities, as is discussed in Chapter 9. Black and Native American youth are more likely to be homicide victims than White youth, but rates of other kinds of violent victimization are more comparable (Hullenaar & Ruback, 2020). Black and Native youth also witness more community-level violence (Kravitz-Wirtz et al., 2022; Office of Juvenile Justice and Delinquency Prevention, 2016). Data from the Federal Bureau of Investigation's Uniform Crime Reports (Federal Bureau of Investigations, 2019) also show racial disparities in the commission of violent crime—particularly robberies and homicide. For instance, in 2019, Black people committed over half of reported homicides in which the race of the perpetrator was known, despite being just 13% of the U.S. population. Although some analysts have been critical of these data and suggest racial bias (e.g., Hinton, 2016), the National Crime Victimization Survey shows similar over-representation of Black assailants (Carson, 2021). Chapter 9 shows that reducing crime and exposure to violence are important strategies for reducing intergenerational poverty.

A recent National Academies committee was charged with understanding these racial disparities in criminal involvement and criminal justice processing. The resulting report concludes that "Racially inscribed inequalities, especially disadvantage, explain most of the dramatic differences in crime across racialized areas. These same disadvantaged contexts also contribute to racial disparities in criminal justice contacts, further compounding inequality" (National Academies, 2022b, p. 137). In other words, racial disparities in criminal offending and criminal justice contact emerge within the broader histories of structural racism and racial inequality in the important domains of education, health, neighborhoods, and labor markets, which is documented in this chapter. As the aforementioned report argues: "Racial inequality can drive disparities in both crime and [criminal justice] system involvement; racial differences in criminal victimization, offending, and incarceration can further exacerbate racial inequality in socioeconomic life (National Academies, 2022b, p. 1)."

It is important to note that the process of *criminalization* is often excluded from such analysis of offending and criminal behavior. The term "criminalization" acknowledges that conduct designated as "crimes" is necessarily a product of societal efforts to label, enforce, surveil, and punish. Criminalization refers to how the law, the police, and court officials classify and act upon some kinds of conduct, but not others, as criminal. Social norms, prejudices, and power relations at a given point in time can influence this process, potentially codifying and locking in definitions of crime that have a disproportionate impact on Black and Native American people (Lacey & Zedner, 2017; Lacey et al., 2018). For example, the Bureau of Indian Affairs created criminal codes and reservation court systems that criminalized traditional religious and cultural activities that the U.S. government sought to eradicate in its campaign to forcibly assimilate Native Americans (Ross, 2010).

A wide range of evidence points to the negative effects of criminal conviction and incarceration, which disproportionately affect Black and Native Americans, on later employment and earnings. Field studies, for example, find that employment outcomes after incarceration are worse for Black youth and men compared with White youth and men (Sullivan, 1989; Western & Sirois, 2019). Consistent with these findings, Pager (2007; Pager et al., 2009) also finds that the stigma of a criminal record in the labor market is larger for Black job-seekers than for White ones. Monetary sanctions and court-ordered fees resulting from contact with the criminal justice system can also impact socioeconomic outcomes. A randomized controlled trial in a misdemeanor court in Oklahoma showed that court fines and fees led to warrants for nonpayment, debts in collection, and state garnishment of tax refunds (Pager et al., 2022). Studies show that these sanctions are both disproportionately imposed on and are associated with the adverse treatment of Black Americans by police and other officials (Bing et al., 2022; Shoub et al., 2021). Finally, punishment in one generation reverberates in the next through worse child and young-adult health, educational attainment and achievement, socioeconomic and psychological adjustment, and behavior

(Finlay et al., 2022; Haskins et al., 2018; Heard-Garris et al., 2018; Shaw, 2019; Wakefield & Wildeman, 2013).

In sum, racial inequality in crime, victimization, and criminal justice system involvement contributes to disproportionate rates of intergenerational poverty among Black and Native Americans. Interventions that address both violence and victimization as well as how the criminal justice system affects youth outcomes and, ultimately, intergenerational mobility are discussed in detail in Chapter 9.

Child Welfare System

Involvement with the child welfare system is also marked by pronounced racial inequalities (e.g., see H. Kim et al., 2017). Research suggests that associations between maltreatment or child welfare involvement and later outcomes do vary by race/ethnicity. For example, in a large study of children in Mississippi (n = 30,000), Yoon et al. (2021) documented that children who experienced maltreatment had worse educational outcomes than those who had not, specifically in grade retention and chronic absenteeism. Black male children who were maltreated had worse educational outcomes compared with similar White males or Black or White females. Further, Mersky and Topitzes (2010) analyzed data from the Chicago Longitudinal Study, which included 1,539 children from economically disadvantaged backgrounds, 93% of whom were Black. They found that children with substantiated reports of maltreatment had an increased likelihood of adverse education and employment outcomes during early adulthood (18–24 years), such as lower high school graduation rates (54% vs. 37%), less employment or college attendance (53% vs. 41%), and increased history of arrest (36% vs. 48%).

The strong relation between family poverty and race/ethnicity in the United States, especially among the child population (National Academies, 2019a; Thiede et al., 2021), also has implications for maltreatment and child welfare involvement. It may be challenging to differentiate child maltreatment and neglect from the common sequalae of poverty (e.g., food insecurity, lack of child care), and thus the child welfare system risks sweeping in families—particularly Black and Native American families—just for being low income.

A strong evidentiary base exists on the overrepresentation of Black children in the child welfare system. Specifically, Black children are more likely than their White counterparts to be referred to the child welfare system regarding suspected maltreatment (Administration for Children and Families, 2022a; Drake et al., 2011; Putnam-Hornstein et al., 2013) and to be substantiated for maltreatment (Administration for Children and Families, 2022a; Drake et al., 2011; Putnam-Hornstein et al., 2013). According to the most recent federal data, Black children have the second highest maltreatment victimization rate, at 13.2 per 1,000 children of the same race or ethnicity (Administration for Children and Families, 2022a). The limited rigorous data on children from Native populations (American Indian/Alaska Native) suggest that they have the highest rate of maltreatment at 15.5 per 1,000 children of the same race or ethnicity (Administration of Children and Families, 2022a; Wulczyn, 2020).

These disparities have been attributed to elevated risks among non-White families (Barth et al., 2020, 2022; Drake et al., 2011) as well as structural racism internal and external to the child welfare system (e.g., increased community surveillance, biased decision making), and policies of removal of Native American children (Boyd, 2014; Detlaff & Boyd, 2022). Both these explanations can be considered in the context of poverty. Specifically, Black and Native American families are more likely to experience the poverty-related risks identified previously, such as mental health challenges, substance use, and criminal justice system involvement (Birckhead, 2012; Jones Harden & Slopen, 2022; Wadsworth et al., 2016). They are also more likely to reside in neighborhoods with higher concentrations of poverty and experience the adverse neighborhood conditions that characterize these communities (Jones Harden & Slopen, 2022; Molina et al., 2012; Quillian, 2012), including child maltreatment (Coulton et al., 2007; Maguire-Jack et al., 2022).

Scholars have attempted to disentangle the influences of race and poverty on child welfare system involvement. For example, in a population-based study, Putnam-Hornstein et al. (2013) documented that Black children were more than twice as likely as other children to experience child maltreatment referral and substantiation, as well as foster care placement prior to age 5. However, when the authors adjusted for the contribution of socioeconomic factors, they found that Black children with low socioeconomic status (SES) were less likely to be referred, substantiated, and enter foster care than White children from similar SES backgrounds.

In sum, these disparities point to the need for policies and programs that can reduce child maltreatment and child welfare system involvement in order to address intergenerational poverty. Such interventions are discussed in Chapter 10.

> *Conclusion 3-1: The challenges that Black and Native American families face in propelling their children into socioeconomic security result from contemporary and historical disparities, discrimination, and structural racism. Behaviors and choices can also have major causal impacts on intergenerational mobility. Many factors influence the behaviors and choices of Black and Native Americans, including the experiences of historical violence, oppression, and marginalization manifested through*

mechanisms of contemporary structural racism. These factors are crucial in shaping the relevant determinants of poverty over generations.

SOME IMPLICATIONS FOR PROGRAM AND POLICY INTERVENTIONS

The most obvious policy implication of the prevalence of racism in all its forms, even today, is that there is a need to end racism and counter the persistent effects of past discrimination. Nevertheless, there are few direct policy mechanisms available for achieving this goal, outside the existing body of federal and state antidiscrimination laws in employment, housing, and other realms. Improving outcomes for Black people and Native Americans will likely require some race consciousness in our policies and their implementation to ensure that their impacts are as positive as possible for these marginalized groups.

Race consciousness requires marshalling data to understand racial disparities and the policies and practices that contribute to it. For example, the U.S. Treasury Department (2021) is "examining the tax system through a racial equity lens," as facilitated by the Executive Order on Advancing Racial Equity and Support for Underserved Communities Through the Federal Government (White House, 2021). As discussed in Chapter 4, Black teachers can have a positive long-term impact on Black students, so race consciousness may also be important for workforce policies. Race-targeted policies may result from race conscious data gathering. For example, responding to the underrepresentation of Black and Native American (and Latino) students from universities, race-targeted affirmative action in university admissions and employment (for government contractors) can help achieve more racial equity and has done so relatively successfully (Holzer & Neumark, 2000; Long & Bateman, 2020).[2]

Race consciousness and targeting in policy making is politically contentious. But policies such as Texas's Top Ten Percent Rule, which targets the highest achieving high school students rather than race, have been shown to "pull in" larger concentrations of Black and Hispanic into higher-quality Texas universities than White students and, in the case of Black students, disproportionately increase their college graduation rates as well (Black et al., 2023). In the labor market, the 1966 Fair Labor Standards Act, a race-conscious policy that extended minimum-wage laws to previously uncovered workers in agriculture and service employment, where Black people

---

[2] In June 2023, the Supreme Court issued a ruling to restrict affirmative action that will present challenges to efforts to diversify the nation's colleges and universities (National Academies, 2023).

were over-represented, had the effect of reducing the Black-White earnings gap significantly (Derenoncourt & Montialoux, 2021).

Even race-neutral efforts to reduce poverty can have disproportionately beneficial effects. An analysis by the Center on Budget and Policy Priorities (Trisi & Saenz, 2021) concludes that "economic security programs have become more effective at reducing poverty and racial disparities over the last 5 decades" (p. 2) and that "economic security programs reduce gaps in child poverty by race and ethnicity by nearly half" (p. 9). The National Academies report *A Roadmap to Reducing Child Poverty* (2019a, Table 5-1) lists several programs that disproportionately reduce Black child poverty (the report did not highlight Native American children), including the Earned Income Tax Credit, child care subsidies, housing vouchers, and a universal child allowance. Other research shows causal evidence that expanded Medicaid coverage has disproportionately positive impacts on Black children's long-term health outcomes and suggestive evidence on positive impacts on educational outcomes (Miller & Wherry, 2019; Wherry & Meyer, 2016; Wherry et al., 2018). Similarly, another race-neutral policy, the Clean Air Act of 1970 and its National Ambient Air Quality Standards has contributed significantly to the narrowing of Black-White disparities in exposure to particulate matter (Currie et al., 2023). Reducing school suspensions is another race-neutral way to disproportionately benefit the long-term outcomes of Black students (Bacher-Hicks et al., 2019). While these policies and programs are promising for reducing various disparities, there is less direct causal evidence on interventions that will improve intergenerational mobility for Black and Native American individuals.

In the chapters that follow, we identify a set of policies and programs for reducing intergenerational poverty that are supported by direct evidence on intergenerational impacts. There are notably few interventions for which there is direct evidence of intergenerational impacts specifically on Black and Latino Americans, and none assessing impacts on Native Americans. As discussed elsewhere, there are relatively few studies that are able to measure direct intergenerational impacts at all, and those often rely on small samples. Subsetting these studies to examine effects specifically for Black or Latino families leaves even smaller samples.

A common pattern is that an intervention yields a measurable, statistically significant effect on the overall population, but that the estimated effect on the Black or Latino subpopulation is imprecisely measured and not statistically significant. This can be so even when the estimate of the effect on the subpopulation is equal to or larger than the full-population effect, simply because the subpopulation effect is less precisely measured. In this case, the appropriate conclusion is not that the intervention does not work for Black or Latino families, but rather that we do not have enough data to distinguish the effects on these families from the overall positive effect.

Still, there is some promising evidence that the subgroup effects of the interventions we identify elsewhere have direct intergenerational effects. These are detailed in Appendix C, Table C-3-1, and are summarized in Box 3-2 in the case of interventions that have been found to have statistically significant effects in samples (or subsamples) that consist primarily of Black or Latino families. Where the subgroup effects are not significant, they are not included here. As noted, this should not be taken as evidence that the programs do not work for members of those subgroups.

The implications of our findings above for research are clear and extremely important. Because rigorous analysis of structural racism is a fairly recent phenomenon, a great deal remains to be done. Developing more consensus on how to define, measure, and test its effects—especially in the contemporary context—is a necessary first step. Then, testing and evaluating innovative and targeted policies and programs can also address the lack of rigorous evidence on how to improve upward mobility for those who have suffered from both poverty and racism.

BOX 3-2
Direct-Evidence Interventions in Chapters 4 Through 10 That Have Been Shown to Be Effective for Reducing Intergenerational Poverty Among Black or Latino Children

Education
   K–12 education: Increased K–12 school spending in the poorest districts benefits Black students. Having Black teachers benefits Black students. Reducing harsh school discipline benefits Black and Latino students, especially males. Ethnic Studies course-taking benefits Latino students.
   Postsecondary education: Some programs that expand effective financial aid programs for low-income students and increase campus supports (such as tutoring and case management) benefit Black students.
   Career training: Expanding high-quality career and technical education programs in high school and sectoral training programs for adults and youth increases the later earnings of Black youth and young adults.

Child and Maternal Health
   Health insurance: Access to Medicaid improves the life expectancy of Black children.
   Pollution reduction: Some pollution reduction policies increase the adult work hours and earnings of Black children and have reduced racial gaps in exposure to pollution by 60%.
   Nutrition: Expanding SNAP access for legal permanent resident parents and eliminating proration for citizen children of undocumented parents would improve intergenerational health for Latino children.

Family Income, Employment, and Wealth
   Work-based income support: State supplements to the Earned Income Tax Credit generate generally positive effects on educational attainment and earnings of Black children.

Neighborhood Crime and the Criminal Justice System
   Juvenile incarceration: Reducing juvenile detentions and incarcerations promotes school completion and reduces adult crime among Black youth.
   Child investment strategies: Scaling-up evidence-based therapeutic interventions such as the Becoming a Man program improves youth outcomes for Black males.
   Strengthening communities to reduce violent crime and victimization: Scaling up programs that abate vacant lots and abandoned homes reduces crime in majority-Black neighborhoods.
   Policing strategies: Expanding funding for policing in high-crime neighborhoods reduces homicides among the Black population.

SOURCE: Appendix Table C-3-1; Chapters 4, 5, 6, and 9.

4

Children's Education

Education plays a vital role in human development and national prosperity. It is central to citizenship and supports human flourishing in many ways, including the development of the knowledge and skills that will allow children to be successful in the labor market. Earnings from work have been crucial in allowing past generations of families to avoid intergenerational poverty, and that will remain true in the future. Over the last 50 years, earned income consistently lifted the non-work-related incomes of between 70% and 75% of families above the Supplemental Poverty Measure–based poverty line (National Academies of Sciences, Engineering, and Medicine [National Academies], 2019a, Figure 4-1). Building children's earning capacities is key for enabling them to avoid poverty in adulthood.

Evidence reviewed in this chapter shows that educational outcomes such as years of completed schooling have a strong causal connection with higher earnings and other important measures of life success and well-being, and thus with the ability of children to rise out of poverty when they are adults. There is also a strong association between student achievement—as measured by test scores—and labor market outcomes, although in this case it is more difficult to show a causal connection. Thus, educational institutions that help children from families in poverty to complete more schooling and, perhaps, achieve higher test scores have the potential to dramatically reduce the intergenerational transmission of poverty.

However, the education system is not always as successful as it might be at delivering these educational outcomes. Children who grow up in families in poverty are systematically exposed to lower-quality educational experiences and resources than children from wealthier families. This, in

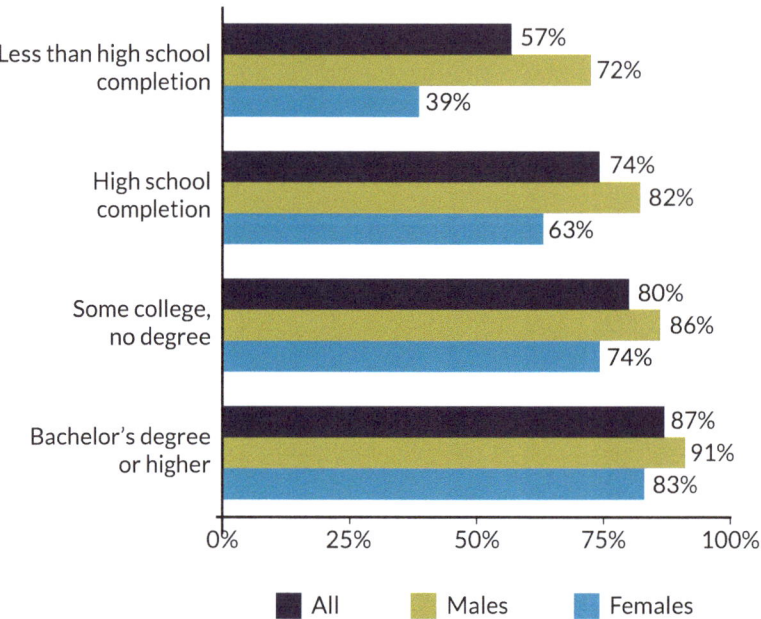

FIGURE 4-1 Employment rates for 25- to 34-year-olds in 2019, by education and sex.
SOURCE: Data from DeBrey et al. (2021), Tables 501.50, 501.60, and 501.70.

turn, leads to lower levels of achievement, completed schooling, and earnings in adulthood. Resource and achievement gaps are also apparent across children of different races and ethnicities.

Fortunately, recent educational research and evaluation work points to promising ways to increase the chances that children growing up in low-income families will enter the labor market with the skills needed to keep their family incomes well above the poverty threshold.

This chapter begins by reviewing evidence on the importance of education for children's eventual economic success. It then considers, in turn, four components of the educational process: child care and early education programs for young children; elementary and secondary school; postsecondary education; and, for some, career training. While the chapter focuses on the importance of children's educational experiences for their development, there is a less direct channel that may be even more important in the long run: Educational successes in one generation may affect children of the next generation by influencing parenting practices, helping parents to provide enriching home environments and in other ways support their children's educational experiences (e.g., Currie & Moretti, 2003).

HOW EDUCATION AFFECTS THE ECONOMIC MOBILITY OF CHILDREN

The skills that people bring to the labor market are a key determinant of success at finding sufficient employment and earnings to lift themselves and their families above the poverty line. Autor (2019) documents the increasing bifurcation of work in industrialized countries over the past 50 years into occupations that require high levels of education and pay high wages, on the one hand, and low-education occupations that pay relatively little—and often leave workers and their families in poverty—on the other. Traditional midlevel jobs that require only a high school education but pay well are less and less available, and workers who might have secured these jobs in the past are now largely relegated to lower-wage jobs that do not pay enough to lift a family above the poverty line.

Most workers who acquire the skills needed for professional, managerial, and technical jobs do so through formal postsecondary schooling. Workers with college degrees are much more likely to be employed than those with less education, and when they are employed they earn substantially more. Employment rates among 25–34-year-olds in 2019 were 30 percentage points higher (87% vs. 57%) for workers with college degrees than for workers who had not finished high school (Figure 4-1). And while employment rates are generally higher for men than women, both groups show the same pattern of increased employment with higher levels of completed schooling.

Earnings, too, increase steadily with additional years of education: College graduates earn twice as much as high school dropouts and 50% more than workers with high school diplomas but no additional education (Figure 4-2). Autor (2014) shows that even after accounting for tuition costs and the time value of money, college graduates can expect to earn between $500,000 and $800,000 (in 2022 dollars) more than high school graduates over the course of their careers.

Decades of rigorous labor economics research demonstrate that these earnings advantages are not simply reflections of other differences between graduates and nongraduates. Instead, they largely reflect the labor market rewards generated by the knowledge and skills that students gain as they complete more schooling (Card & Giuliano, 1999). On average, each additional year of education causes subsequent earnings to increase by 7% to 12%. Educational credentials can signal persistence, conscientiousness, and other noncognitive traits to employers (as argued, for example, by Caplan, 2018). But the rewards to completed schooling reflect more than credentialism; even a year or two of college, without a degree, raises employment and earnings over what someone would obtain with just a high school diploma. Moreover, the benefits of education are not confined to the labor

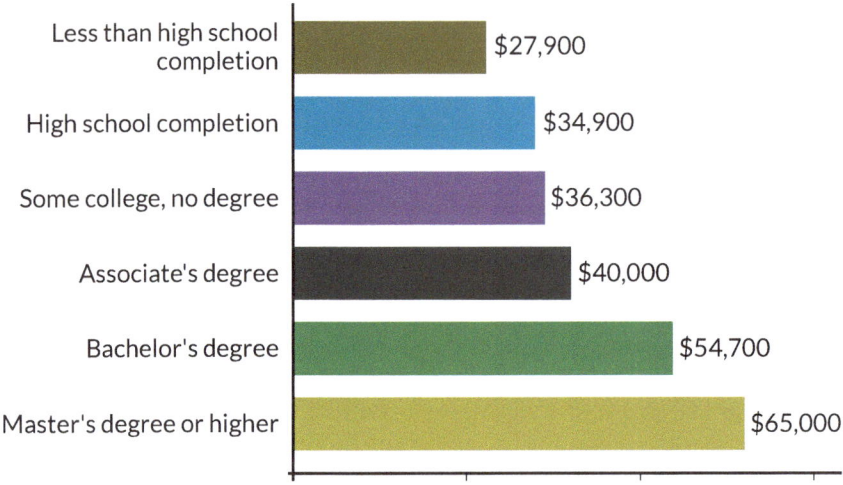

FIGURE 4-2 Median annual earnings for 25- to 34-year-old workers in 2019, by education.
SOURCE: Data from U.S. Department of Commerce, Census Bureau, Current Population Survey, Annual Social and Economic Supplement, 1996–2020, Table 502.30.

market—research has also shown that additional years of education reduce criminal behavior (Lochner, 2020) and improve health (Galama et al., 2018; Hamad et al., 2018) and parenting (Currie & Moretti, 2003).

Labor market success appears to depend not only on completed years of schooling, but also on the skills acquired during time spent in school. Many studies have documented associations between test scores, even as early as kindergarten (Chetty et al., 2011), and labor market success. Associations between earnings and high school reading and math test scores appear to be just as strong for men as for women, and they predict earnings as late as age 50 (Watts, 2020).

The labor market rewards for education and skills have grown in magnitude over the past four decades, as documented in Chapter 6. This appears to be partly because technological change and globalization have increased the productivity of highly educated or highly skilled workers, and partly because of the rising monopoly power of employers in the labor market and the weakening of institutions (such as unions and minimum wage statutes) that traditionally protect workers from such power. For an individual child, educational attainment—in whatever form—is more important than ever for escaping poverty in adulthood, and it is a major driver of intergenerational poverty and mobility.

While a college education is an important path out of poverty, other paths are available to workers without college degrees. These often involve acquiring occupational skills in high-demand industries (such as health care, advanced manufacturing, information technology, construction, and transportation/distribution logistics) that allow workers to earn more than their counterparts without these skills. Such skills can be attained in high school career and technical education (CTE) and in work-based learning programs; in various certificate programs in community (or for-profit) colleges, whether or not they are for-credit programs; and in high-quality sector-based training programs, as noted below.[1]

ACHIEVEMENT AND ATTAINMENT DIFFERENCES ACROSS RACIAL AND ETHNIC GROUPS

Given the importance of achievement and years of completed schooling for reducing intergenerational poverty, it is alarming to see large gaps on those measures between income, racial, and ethnic groups. Looking at the reading and math scores of children who entered kindergarten in 2010, Reardon and Portilla (2016) found that children from low-income (10th percentile) families were more than a year behind children from high-income (90th percentile) families. Black and Latino students entering kindergarten were about half a year behind their White counterparts in early math achievement (separate data on Native Americans were not available). In the case of kindergarten-entry literacy skills, Latino students again lagged behind their White classmates by about half a year, with a somewhat smaller gap for Black students. Achievement gaps that become evident in kindergarten tend to remain relatively stable or grow slightly after second grade (Kuhfeld et al., 2020; Paschall et al., 2018; Reardon, 2021).

The National Assessment of Educational Progress has tracked reading and math proficiency for decades. Figure 4-3 shows the fractions of 8th graders of different races and ethnicities judged to be proficient in reading; similar patterns appear in 4th grade and in both 8th and 4th grades for math achievement.

Although proficiency rates have increased somewhat for most groups, the rates themselves are very low—generally around 20% for low-income

---

[1] On average, for-credit community college credentials generate higher labor market rewards than not-for-credit credentials, although both can earn a labor market premium (Baum et al., 2020). Credentials from for-profit colleges also generate lower returns, on average, than those from colleges in the public nonprofit sector (Cellini & Turner, 2019).

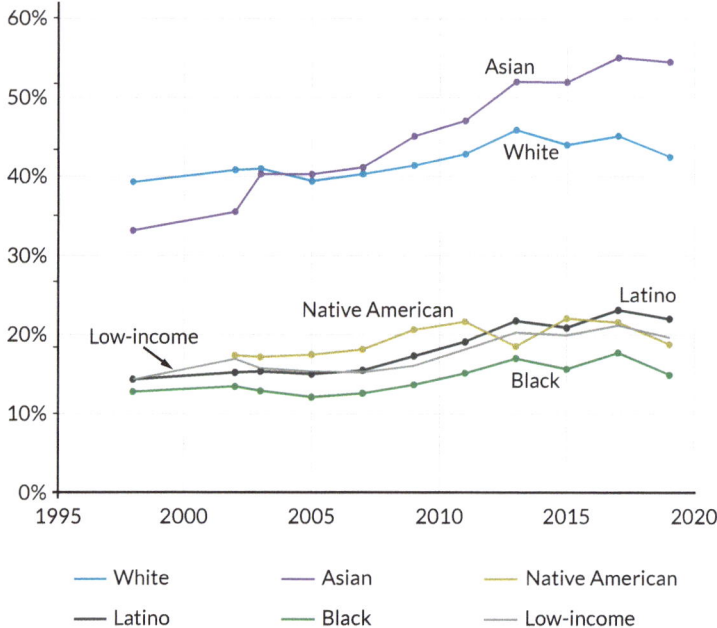

FIGURE 4-3 8th grade reading proficiency rates, by race/ethnicity, 1998–2019. SOURCE: Data from National Assessment of Education Progress. https://www.nationsreportcard.gov/ndecore/xplore/NDE

students and for Black, Latino, and Native American/Alaska Native students. Asian students are the only group with proficiency rates above 50%.

These early and persistent achievement differences are no doubt largely due to the differences between the childhood environments experienced by children from more and less affluent families. Higher-income families are able to provide safer and more nurturing home environments and tend to have different parenting styles (Bassok et al., 2016; Phillips et al., 1998). There are racial and socioeconomic differences in exposure to a range of influences that affect cognition and learning—for example, Sampson et al. (2008) and Currie et al. (2014) document racial differences in exposure to violence and pollution (see also Chapters 5 and 9). Higher-income families are also able to invest more in supporting their children's education, spending an average of $8,000 more annually than lower-income families on educational enrichments such as books, computers, high-quality child care, summer camps, and private schooling (Kaushal et al., 2011). All of these differences contribute to kindergarten-entry achievement gaps across racial/ethnic groups, as well as to differences in learning throughout the educational process. The differences in out-of-school environments make it very difficult for public schools to equalize educational opportunities across groups.

Importantly, gaps in out-of-school environments tend to accompany gaps in the quality of K–12 schools. While many states have modified their school funding systems in recent years to ensure that schools serving low-income students are as well funded as those serving high-income students, other states have not (Lafortune et al., 2018). Moreover, schools serving low-income students face higher costs (for safety, remedial education, special education, students' basic needs, and so on), so even equal funding cannot equalize the quality of educational inputs (Duncombe & Yinger, 2005). By nearly any metric, average school quality is lower at schools serving high-poverty populations. As a result, while in principle the formal education system could help to close preexisting gaps, it often seems to magnify them instead (Chetty et al., 2023; Hashim et al., 2023; Reardon, 2011).

Given achievement gaps throughout K–12, it is unsurprising to see parallel gaps in completed schooling. The top panel of Figure 4-4 shows rates of fall college enrollment among previous spring high school graduates, while the bottom panel shows the fractions of all young adults (defined here as people between ages 25 and 29) holding college or advanced degrees as of 2019. Greater than 70% of Asian young adults had completed college, compared with 45% of White, 29% of Black, and 21% of Latino young adults and 14% of young adults in the Native American category. It is encouraging to note that among Black and Latino people as well as White people, these rates were more than 10 percentage points higher than they had been two decades earlier (earlier data are unavailable for Asian people). In the case of Native American people, however, the rates were lower in 2019 than in 2000.

Conclusion 4-1: By imparting skills and other capacities valued by employers, the education system is a key driver of upward intergenerational mobility for low-income children. Large gaps in school achievement and completed schooling persist across socioeconomic, racial, and ethnic subgroups, pose a key challenge for policy makers seeking to reduce intergenerational poverty, and underscore the importance of education-related interventions.

EARLY-LIFE EDUCATION, CARE, AND PARENTING

The early years of life lay the groundwork for a child's healthy cognitive and behavioral development (Knudsen et al., 2006). From the time of conception, early development is a complex interplay between the child's genetic blueprint and the early experiences that are essential for subsequent learning and development (Shonkoff, 2010). Children thrive when they are

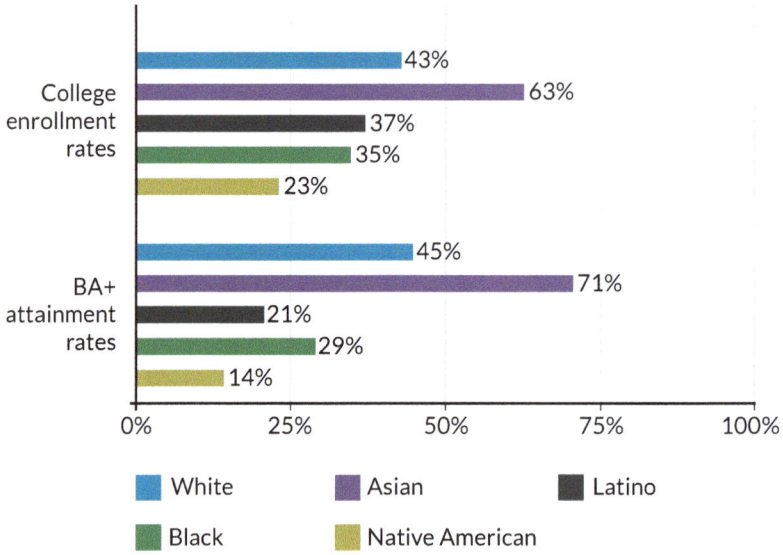

FIGURE 4-4 College enrollment and bachelor of arts (BA)+ attainment rates, by race/ethnicity.
NOTES: The top panel shows the share of new high school graduates who are enrolled in college the following fall. The bottom panel shows the share of 25–29-year-olds who had BAs.
SOURCE: Graduation rates are for 2019 and are taken from the Digest of Education Statistics, 2019, Table 104.20. Enrollment rates are for 18-24-year-olds in 2015 and are taken from Musu-Gillette et al. (2017), Figure 18.2.

well nourished, protected from disease and violence (see Chapter 5 for more details regarding health), and have caregivers who are responsive to their needs and provide them with learning opportunities from birth onwards (Black et al., 2017). Extensive evidence documents the importance of responsive and stimulating caregiving during a child's first 5 years, as social and academic skills are developing (Shonkoff, 2010). The importance of these early experiences appears to be universal, but their impacts vary and depend on the family's culture (Rogoff, 2003).

Early childhood educational programs can enhance children's early development (Black et al., 2017; Shonkoff, 2010). Early care and education programs in which caregivers form responsive and supportive relationships with the children in their care and provide stimulating and engaging learning opportunities promote healthy development (Hamre & Pianta, 2010).

Children from impoverished families experience lower-quality community-based early childhood education; however, programs like Head Start and public pre-kindergarten have been funded by federal, state, and local governments to ensure access to higher-quality programs for low-income children (Kraus-Friedman et al., 2020; Zigler & Styfco, 2010). In theory, these programs should provide children with the skills they need to succeed in school (Bailey, 2021; Deming, 2009; Garces et al., 2002; García et al., 2021).

Similarly, home-visiting programs promote infant and child health, foster educational development, and help prevent child abuse and neglect by arranging for trained professionals or paraprofessionals to pay regular visits to parents, typically mothers, and to provide coaching on parenting issues (Duncan et al., 2023). The home visitors offer a wide variety of supports, ranging from facilitating access to public services and modeling positive behavior management to addressing discipline issues to promoting stimulating learning activities and interactions (Office of Planning, Research and Evaluation, 2021). Some of these programs have demonstrated long-term impacts (Olds et al., 1997, 1998).

In light of such compelling evidence, early childhood education programs are widely regarded as one of the most effective means to promote success in school for low-income children (Heckman, 2011). Despite the proven potential of these kinds of programs, however, for reasons detailed in Appendix C: Chapter 4, the committee was unable to propose expansions of existing programs or new programs that would meet the evidentiary standards the committee has set for itself. There were two reasons for this: First, many of the programs that showed long-term benefits, such as the Perry Preschool Project, Abecedarian Project, and Nurse Family Partnership programs, were designed and run by researchers. Scaling up demonstration programs to serve hundreds of thousands of children and families, in the face of relentless pressures to cut costs, can significantly dilute program quality. Indeed, the classroom experiences in programs like Head Start, which in the early years showed long-term impacts (e.g., Bailey, 2021), are quite different from classroom experiences in today's programs (Markowitz & Ansari, 2020).

Second, the families of children not selected into these programs (including Head Start in its early years) faced much worse conditions than do the families of children today who do not participate in such programs. During those early years, safety-net programs like Food Stamps and Medicaid were not yet universally available, center-based child care choices were more limited, and parental schooling levels and spending on children's "enrichment goods" were much lower than they are now (Duncan et al.,

2014). It was therefore much easier for early programs to demonstrate long-run effectiveness.

Because of the ambiguity of the evidence, the committee was unable to identify the best ways to expand early childhood education and home visitation programs in order to reduce intergenerational poverty. While it is certainly possible that expanding or reforming our current patchwork of early childhood and home visitation programs would reduce intergenerational poverty, we do not know enough about how to do so in a manner that is very likely to generate long-run benefits.

ELEMENTARY AND SECONDARY EDUCATION

Educational quality can be measured in many ways, but at the most basic level it reflects the extent to which students are receiving instruction that matches their skill level, supports and is responsive to their needs, and helps them advance to the next level of proficiency. This is difficult to do in crumbling buildings (Lafortune & Schonholzer, 2022), with teachers who are poorly qualified or inexperienced (Goe, 2007), or in overcrowded classrooms (Krueger, 1999). Children in households living in poverty are more likely than more affluent children to attend struggling public schools that repeatedly fail to meet accountability standards, are burdened by crumbling physical infrastructure and high levels of violence, and are staffed with less experienced, lower-quality teachers (Kozol, 1991, 2005; Lankford et al., 2002). These schools have fewer enrichment courses, are often unable to offer even the minimum courses needed to prepare their students for four-year colleges, and provide far fewer extracurricular activities.

Moreover, even if instruction is expertly delivered in an up-to-date facility by excellent teachers, students will struggle to learn if they are unstably housed, lack regular and appropriate meals or adequate medical, dental, or vision care, or are threatened by crime and violence on their way to and from school (Rothstein, 2004). Many of these barriers to learning are outside the purview of traditional education, although recent movements to follow a "community schools" model or establish school-based health centers, as well as other expansions of the usual school mission, have attempted to broaden that purview to address students' multiple needs (Maier et al., 2017). All these challenges are much more difficult to address in schools serving high concentrations of children in poverty. Persistently high levels of neighborhood and school economic and racial segregation therefore represent a real barrier to student progress.

If schools are to provide a high-quality educational environment, they need adequate funding. Traditionally, low-income schools have had fewer resources than schools serving wealthier students, despite their students' greater needs. Many states have reformed their school finance systems to ensure that funding in low-income districts equals or even exceeds that in higher-income districts, although others have not. Several recent studies of these reforms show that directing more funding to low-income schools raises students' test scores in the short run (Jackson & Mackevicius, 2021; Lafortune et al., 2018) as well as boosting their longer-run earnings and health (Jackson et al., 2016; Rothstein & Schanzenbach, 2022). Other studies show shorter-term positive impacts of spending on capital improvements (Lafortune & Schonholzer, 2022); however, longer-term impact estimates for these kinds of investments are not yet available.

Of course, funding is closely related to school segregation. Predominantly non-White schools tend to have less funding, fewer resources, and less skilled teachers (Bischoff & Owens, 2019; Elder et al., 2021). The Supreme Court's landmark *Brown v. Board of Education* decision and subsequent court orders resulted in the desegregation of school districts around the country, which led to slow but substantial racial integration throughout the United States (Orfield et al., 2016; Reardon & Owens, 2014; Reardon & Yun, 2003; Reardon et al., 2012). One set of studies using national data compared the educational and occupational attainment of students enrolled before and after courts issued desegregation orders in the 1960s and 1970s, and it found that the resulting desegregation improved educational and occupational attainment among Black adults (Johnson, 2011; Johnson & Nazaryan, 2019). Specifically, each additional year after court-ordered desegregation led to a 1.8-percentage-point increase in the likelihood of high school graduation, and the average effects of 5 years of exposure to court-ordered school desegregation led to about a 15% increase in wages. This study used the same comparisons to examine the ways in which schools may have changed in response to the court orders and found two potential mechanisms: increased per-pupil spending and reduced class sizes. However, Supreme Court decisions since 1991 have made it easier for school districts to be released from prior court orders to desegregate, and they provide limited guidance on maintaining integration after those orders are lifted. This, coupled with rising income inequality and residential segregation, has contributed to school segregation levels that are, by many measures, as high as they were before the school desegregation movement began (Reardon & Owens, 2014; Reardon et al., 2012).

Context, school composition, and funding are obviously important. In addition, students will learn more when instruction is more effectively delivered. Efforts to identify the active ingredients of school quality have had mixed success, however. Some "structural" factors that are easy to measure and screen for, such as teacher experience and educational credentials, fail to show consistent links with student achievement (e.g., Papay & Kraft, 2015). However, smaller class sizes in the early grades—which are closely related to school resources—have been linked to better outcomes (Chetty et al., 2011; Krueger, 1999), and recruiting science, technology, engineering, and mathematics (STEM)-trained college graduates to teach math and science classes has been shown to correlate with better student grades and test scores in these subjects (Backes et al., 2018).

The No Child Left Behind Act of 2001 refocused federal education policy to hold schools accountable for student performance, and some evidence indicates that this accountability had modest but positive impacts on student outcomes. A related movement has been the rapid growth of charter schools, which provide alternatives to public schools that can test different instructional or organizational strategies. Evidence indicates that on average, charter schools are neither better nor worse at promoting student achievement (CREDO, 2013) than conventional public schools. However, a subset of charter schools known as "no excuses" schools have been found to have substantial positive effects on students' test scores and 4-year college enrollment, relative to traditional public-school alternatives (Angrist et al., 2016). This is particularly important because these types of charter schools disproportionately serve low-income urban students, use a very different educational model (more school time, drilling, testing, and emphasis on behavior) than is typically found in schools serving middle- and upper-class students.

Both charter and traditional public schools have tested several new strategies for increasing student learning, many of which show promise. For example, rigorous evaluations have been conducted of tutoring programs that provide for frequent one-on-one or small-group interactions with struggling students (e.g., Fryer et al., 2016). Although these programs are generally too new to have demonstrated long-term impacts, early evidence of short-run impacts is promising, suggesting that personalizing instruction to students' specific skills and needs may be beneficial.

The nature of the match between students and their teachers may also matter for student learning. Causal evidence shows that having a Black elementary school teacher has positive effects on high school graduation and 2-year college enrollment for low-income Black boys—a population of particular interest in this report (Gershenson et al., 2022). These effects appear to be generated by some combination of role modeling, fewer disciplinary actions, and higher teacher expectations (Gershenson et al., 2016; Lindsay & Hart, 2017). Moreover, a recent study found that enrollment in Ethnic Studies courses improved rates of high school graduation and engagement, and may also increase college enrollment (Bonilla et al., 2021). These courses focus on social justice, anti-racism, stereotypes, and social movements in U.S. history led by people from various racial and ethnic minority groups, spanning the period from the late eighteenth century to the 1970s.

The content of course offerings and the labor market skills they can impart to students also appear to be significant. For students who might not go directly from high school to college, CTE in high schools offers an alternative path to better jobs over time, although it can also divert students—particularly low-income students and students of color—from a path toward traditional college enrollment. Many young adults who begin full-time work after completing their schooling return to take advantage of vocational training and adult programs, often through community colleges, that provide job skills outside of a traditional academic setting. Evidence indicates that these programs, when implemented well, can also increase earnings (Brunner et al., 2021; Hemelt et al., 2021).

As seen in the case of charter schools, school policies beyond direct instruction can have large impacts on student outcomes. Research shows that harsh school discipline, such as suspensions and expulsions, leads to long-term negative outcomes for children. One study, for example, found that students who were randomly assigned to schools with higher suspension rates were more likely to be arrested or incarcerated as adults, more likely to drop out of high school, and less likely to attend a 4-year college. The effects on arrest and incarceration were substantially larger for Black, Latino, and male students, and especially for Black and Latino males (Bacher-Hicks et al., 2019; also see Chu and Ready, 2018). No studies have examined the long-term effects of interventions to reduce harsh school discipline; however, Appendix C: Chapter 4 discusses some promising strategies with documented shorter-run beneficial impacts.

POSTSECONDARY EDUCATION

Although the bottom panel of Figure 4-4 (above) shows widely disparate rates of college completion across racial/ethnic groups, the top panel shows that the rates of fall college enrollment across different groups of recent high school graduates are more similar. Thus, Figure 4-4 points to a key challenge in seeking to reduce intergenerational poverty through postsecondary education: Many of those who enroll fail to graduate with 4-year degrees.

An important factor underlying differences in enrollment rates is success in secondary school. One recent study found, for example, that Black students are more likely to enroll in college than are White students with similar family backgrounds and prior academic performance (Ciocca & DiPrete, 2018).

Two-year colleges offer a wide range of associate degrees and certificates (along with noncredit programs), many of which have significant labor market value (Backes et al., 2015; Holzer & Baum, 2017). But they can also be complicated institutions for students to navigate, and they often provide too little structure or guidance (Bailey et al., 2015; Holzer & Xu, 2021; Scott-Clayton, 2011). Students need to not only make many high-stakes academic decisions (major or program, classes to take each term, whether to transfer, and if so, where), but also navigate a wide range of needlessly complex processes (transferring credits if they take classes at more than one institution, navigating financial aid, arranging for parking, obtaining support services). These challenges are not intellectually or academically important, but failing to complete them can mean not being able to continue in a program.

Among those who aspire to earn a bachelor of arts degree, students starting at 2-year rather than 4-year institutions are less likely to complete their studies. More general differences in postsecondary success are driven by a range of factors, including weaker academic preparation, as a result of having attended lower-quality K–12 schools; a lack of family financial resources and the necessary information for choosing the institution that best suits their needs; the need to work full-time while attending college, making it very difficult to be a full-time student; a lack of social capital and guidance on accessing available resources or studying effectively; and a lack of support services at their current institutions (Baum & McPherson, 2022; Holzer & Baum, 2017). Low-income students of color may face cultural and social barriers at predominately White institutions. All these factors lead to higher dropout rates, lower grades, and a lower probability of success in majors leading to highly compensated employment (Bleemer & Mehta, 2021). It should be noted, however, that minority-serving institutions (MSIs) offer culturally relevant support and encouragement, and there is evidence that they are more successful than non-MSIs at facilitating upward mobility for low-income students of color (Espinosa et al., 2018; National Academies, 2019b).

Cost is another important barrier for low-income students as they seek access to colleges in general and to high-quality colleges in particular. The National Center for Education Statistics (2019) finds that in 2015–2016, the average out-of-pocket net price for a full-time, low-income student was $7,100 per year, which constitutes 70% of the total income of a very low-income family of three. The primary federal program designed to make college more affordable is the Pell Grant, which offers funding of up to $6,495 (in 2022 dollars) to students from lower- and moderate-income families. Although the research evidence on Pell grants is mixed, substantial increases in the value of these grants have generated notable increases in degree attainment (Denning et al., 2019; Dynarski et al., 2022b). Other recent evidence (Angrist et al., 2022) shows that generous and well-targeted financial aid, especially when it allows higher-achieving low-income students to enter 4-year programs to which they would otherwise lack access, can substantially increase the rates of bachelor of arts attainment.

CAREER TRAINING

Much of our K–12 schooling system is oriented toward providing students with skills and other capacities that will enable them to attend and graduate from 4-year postsecondary universities. At the same time, there are many well-paying industry-specific occupations that do not require a bachelor's degree, are in strong local demand, and offer opportunities for advancement. Placing students from disadvantaged backgrounds into these jobs can help to reduce the likelihood that they will remain mired in persistent intergenerational poverty. So too can educational opportunities aimed at enabling adults to participate in retraining for these jobs in mid-career.

Community colleges can provide some of the needed training through traditional degree programs. But so too can other kinds of training-related interventions, and strong evaluation evidence points to a number of promising approaches. The first consists of CTE pathways in high schools. The second involves sectoral programs that provide occupational skills training resulting in credentials that are valued by prospective employers in local labor markets.

While evidence on training programs in general is mixed, there is clear evidence that high-quality training programs that target certain high-demand sectors of the economy that need particular occupational skills can generate strong labor market returns (Katz et al., 2022). Sometimes these programs (such as Project Quest, which provides training in health care occupations) are offered at community colleges, while others (such as Per Scholas for Information Technology training) use other providers. Completing these programs can take anywhere from 6 months to 2 years, and they can cost between $5,000 and $12,000. But the best of these programs are clearly cost-effective.

Conclusion 4-2: The vast U.S. education system is a potentially important factor in enabling individuals to escape from poverty. However, it fails to equalize educational opportunities for students across socioeconomic and racial/ethnic groups. Research points to many possible ways to improve the quality of educational experiences offered to students in K–12 and postsecondary school settings, to create high-quality job training programs, and to prepare young people for the labor market.

EDUCATION INTERVENTIONS

There are many possible interventions for promoting child and youth learning in educational settings as well as encouraging young people to complete more years of education. Our discussion of such interventions is presented in the same order as above: K–12 schooling; postsecondary schooling; and career training, with many of the details relegated to Appendix C: Chapter 4. For reasons discussed above, the committee does not offer policy and program ideas for the early childhood period.

Where possible, we structure the policy and program ideas in a way that enables us to provide a rough estimate of their costs. Smaller or larger scale versions of the policies or programs would reduce or increase these cost estimates accordingly. As discussed in Chapter 1, we characterize the evidence on some of the programs or policies as "strong" and denote them with an "*." This indicates that the program's or policy's impact on intergenerational poverty is supported by random-assignment evaluation evidence that has been replicated across several sites or by compelling quasi-experimental evidence based on national or multi-state data or a scaled-up program.

K–12 Policy and Program Ideas Based on Direct Evidence

K–12 Spending in Low-Income School Districts

Recent impact studies have found that directing increased school funding at under-resourced districts improves both student achievement and rates of completed schooling, both of which have been linked to reductions in intergenerational poverty (Jackson & Mackevicius, 2021). This argues in favor of increasing federal funding for school districts with the highest concentrations of low-income students (details in Appendix C: Chapter 4):

- **Increase K–12 school spending in the lowest-resourced districts.** Increase annual spending by $1,000 per pupil in the 20% of districts with the lowest average family incomes. These districts serve one-third of free and reduced-price lunch (a proxy for poverty) students in the country. The committee estimated that this would cost $15 billion, with the assumption that states would use some of this money (or their own money that this would supplement) for other purposes.

Racial disparities are relevant for virtually any intervention aimed at reducing intergenerational poverty, so the committee looked for evidence about types of programs specifically designed to reduce them. It found three related to K–12 schooling that passed the committee's direct evidence test:

- **Increase teacher workforce diversity,** based on strong evidence of the positive effects of Black teachers on the high school graduation and college enrollment of Black students.

- **Reduce exclusionary school discipline practices**, based on strong evidence that such exclusionary school discipline increases students' chances of dropping out of high school and their contact with the criminal justice system in young adulthood and reduces their college enrollment.
- **Increase access to Ethnic Studies** courses, based on strong evidence of the positive effect of Ethnic Studies course-taking for high school graduation.

The evidence supporting these three policy areas is detailed in Appendix C: Chapter 4. The committee was unable to identify specific evidence-based ways of implementing them, nor could it determine how responsibilities for funding and implementing these policies should be allocated across federal, state, and school district entities responsible for public education. That said, the committee felt that the strength of the direct evidence supporting these policies warranted bringing them to the attention of policymakers.

K–12 Policy and Program Ideas Based on Indirect Evidence

A complementary approach to improving K–12 education outcomes is to focus on specific educational practices and policies that school districts could adopt, given additional resources, to achieve their educational goals. The federal government has little control over the spending decisions of states and districts. This can be a virtue, as local policy makers are often in the best position to judge local needs. In any event, because the education system is constantly evolving, evidence of long-term effects of specific practices or policies is scarce. That said, a number of promising educational strategies have proved effective in promoting short- to medium-run gains in student achievement (evidence is detailed in Appendix C: Chapter 4):

- *Introduce or expand high-dosage tutoring* for struggling students, with educated young adults serving as tutors and following carefully crafted instructional plans;
- *Improve teacher quality, focusing on teachers of Black, Latino, and Native American students.* This might be done, for example, through university programs that encourage and facilitate the certification of STEM undergraduate majors and Black, Latino, and Native American undergraduates as public-school teachers;
- *Reduce class sizes*, particularly in the early grades; and
- *Expand high-quality ("no excuses") charter schools.*

Other curricular programs are still in the earlier stages of the evidence life cycle; there is only short-run evidence of the effectiveness of pilot programs that have not yet been implemented or studied at scale. This category includes small high schools, double-dose algebra courses, and reading curricula that emphasize phonics for early readers. Again, the committee reviews several of these programs in Appendix C: Chapter 4.

Last, there is strong evidence that integrating schools by race/ethnicity, and probably by socioeconomic status (SES) as well, brings both short-run benefits in achievement and attainment and long-run improvements in adult life outcomes for Black students and low-SES students. As pointed out above, with the decline in court-ordered desegregation plans, schools are as segregated now as they were before the desegregation movement. Reversing this trend is a complex challenge, affected by both logistical hurdles and a complex legal environment. The committee is unaware of specific interventions that have been shown to be effective at increasing integration and that could be implemented at the federal level. Nevertheless, this is an important issue, and the committee believes that continued experimentation in this area (e.g., via changes in local school assignment processes) might yield evidence that could lead to meaningful reductions in intergenerational poverty.

Postsecondary Education Policy and Program Ideas Based on Direct Evidence

Interventions to improve postsecondary attendance and completion for low-income students can focus on the *demand* side, or institutions of higher education; as well as the *supply* side, or the students. Interventions focused on higher education might pursue three different goals:

1. Increasing the fraction of students who attend college, through both demand-side changes that make it less expensive for colleges to enroll low-income students and supply-side interventions that provide incentives for students or further financial support to attend college;
2. Improving instruction and student support services at institutions with large low-SES enrollments by providing additional resources to raise completion rates; and
3. Incentivizing students to enroll at higher-value institutions and in higher-value programs of study within institutions.

They include these interventions:

- **Increase federal funding for higher education by $10 billion annually for supply-side programs like financial aid that targets low-SES students (while limiting crowding-out of state and local funding).** For instance, spending $10 billion on college scholarships (with

$5 billion each spent on community and 4-year programs) could support an extra one million full-time community college students per year (spread evenly across two or three yearly cohorts at an annual cost of $5,000 per year) and a half million for 4-year programs (also spread evenly across yearly cohorts at a cost of about $10,000 per year).
- **Increase federal funding by $8 billion to $10 billion a year for institutional supports to improve completion rates among low-income students.** Spending an additional $8 billion on proven student support programs (with $4 billion for community colleges and $4 billion for 4-year programs) would cover a half million community college students.

Postsecondary Education Policy and Program Ideas Based on Indirect Evidence

Other approaches to help achieve the three broad goals defined above—but with less rigorous research support to date—could include these:

- *Increase maximum Pell awards*, with limits imposed on states or institutions regarding offsetting these increases with other cuts in aid;
- *Provide matching federal funds for state higher education allocations*, conditional on a maximum tuition threshold and a minimum level of low-SES enrollment;
- *Expand support for MSIs*, which currently raise attainment of college degrees but to a lesser degree earnings;
- *Simplify financial aid applications*, which are intrusive and difficult for students and their parents to complete, by limiting the information required to that already collected by the IRS;
- *Adjust federal aid formulas and the Integrated Postsecondary Education Data System data on specific colleges and programs to provide more information to students applying for admission* (for instance, on their "expected family contributions" before they apply to college and on required grade point averages in specific institutions if they wish to major in certain fields);
- *Target aid to programs with high labor market value*—through grants to institutions that provide such programs; and
- *Expand "Gainful Employment" regulations* to limit the eligibility for receiving federal student financial aid to attend institutions or programs that show poor outcomes in their graduates' post-program earnings and debt-to-income ratios.

Career Training Policy and Program Ideas Based on Direct Evidence

Much of the evaluation research concerning career training programs is based on random assignment, which provides strong, direct evidence on a number of promising approaches to career education and training. The first area of research involves CTE pathways in high schools. The second includes sectoral programs that provide occupational skills training leading to credentials that are valued by prospective employers in local labor markets.

High School Career and Technical Education

- **Provide (through reforms of the federal Perkins Act and by allocating additional funds) both formula and competitive funding for states and localities to expand high-quality career and technical education.** Three models of CTE can be prioritized: (1) Career Academies, which provide education and training focused on a specific high-demand economic sector (such as health care, IT, or finance) within comprehensive high schools; (2) technical high schools, or newer approaches (like Innovation Pathways in Massachusetts) to create programs similar to technical high schools within comprehensive schools; and (3) Grade 9–14 pathways, modeled after P-Tech, which would combine work-based learning and work experience with rigorous academics.

Postsecondary Sectoral Training Programs

"Sectoral programs" train people for well-paying jobs in specific industries and occupations that do not require a bachelor's or associate's degree for which there is strong local demand and that offer opportunities for advancement. The programs that the committee discussed scaling up combine intensive screening, career readiness services, specific occupational skills training that yields credentials valued by prospective employers, and post-training counseling in the interest of maximizing job retention and advancement.

Several such programs—including Year Up (for youth), Per Scholas (for youth or adults), and Project Quest (all for community college students)—have been evaluated using rigorous methods and found to be effective. The estimated impacts of these programs on earnings are generally large and persist over time. In the interest of reducing intergenerational poverty, the committee discussed scaling up sectoral programs that have proven impacts for youth:

- **Offer sectoral training for youth.** Offer scaled-up versions of Year Up, Per Scholas, and other proven sectoral training programs to 250,000 youth each year who come from low-income families and appear unlikely to earn postsecondary credentials. This would cost roughly $7.5 billion annually.

In addition, the committee suggests considering the following, which would help low-income youth indirectly by raising the incomes in their households (while providing models of labor market success and information on how to achieve success):

- **Offer sectoral training for low-income parents.** Each year, offer scaled-up versions of Project Quest, Per Scholas, and other proven sectoral training programs to one million low-income adults with children, which would indirectly reduce intergenerational poverty by raising the incomes of parents and households. This would cost roughly $10 billion annually.

5

Child and Maternal Health

Child health is an important driver of intergenerational mobility. Children whose families live in poverty experience worse health early in life than children growing up in higher-income families, and this disparity worsens as they age. Better health in childhood promotes greater educational attainment and leads to better health in adulthood, both of which are important determinants of earnings—a key driver of mobility out of poverty.

Evidence reviewed in this chapter demonstrates that child health has a strong causal connection with future earnings. Moreover, the United States has seen significant reductions both in child mortality, an important measure of child health, and in the association between income and child health (called the income "gradient"), particularly in the case of child mortality (Currie & Schwandt, 2016). Multiple public programs have contributed to these improvements, underscoring the effectiveness of public investments in child health. However, the United States continues to be characterized by higher child mortality rates than other high-income countries, and the income-based gaps in child health, although smaller than they used to be, remain large, suggesting scope for additional investments.

In its investigation of the role child health plays in intergenerational poverty and whether further public investments in child health can effectively increase intergenerational mobility, this chapter begins with a discussion of differences in child health across incomes and racial/ethnic groups. It then presents evidence on the importance of child health as a key determinant of adult earnings. In so doing, the chapter is organized around three main determinants of child health: access to medical care (i.e., family planning services, health insurance coverage, mental health care, and public care providers such as school-based clinics and the Indian Health Services; environmental influences, including pollution, stress and violence; and nutrition.

After presenting the evidence regarding the importance of the three factors, we discuss promising interventions for which there is evidence of direct impacts on both child health and future earnings.

HEALTH DIFFERENCES ACROSS INCOME, RACIAL, AND ETHNIC GROUPS

Children growing up in households with incomes below the poverty line are born in worse health than other children. This disparity in health increases as they age (Case et al., 2002), culminating in a strong relationship between childhood poverty and adult health (Figure 5-1). In the United States, adults who spent their early childhoods in low-income families are nearly three times more likely than those from higher-income families to rate their adult health as "fair" or "poor" and four times more likely to report health-related restrictions on their daily activities. They are also 30% more likely to have been born with low birthweight, and they report more psychological distress in adulthood.

The links to adult health begin in childhood. Children living in poverty are twice as likely as other children to be hospitalized, miss 22% more school because of sickness, are 18% more likely to have asthma, and are 33% more likely to have a mental health condition (Figure 5-2). They are also 3.5 times more likely to have high blood lead levels (Braveman et al., 2010; Larson & Halfon, 2010; Wood, 2003) and suffer worse oral health (Seirawan et al., 2012). While these disparities in child health by parental income are present in other developed nations, they are more pronounced in the United States (Chen et al., 2016).

There are important racial/ethnic differences in child health as well. The rate of preterm and low-birthweight births is 50% higher among Black families relative to White families and 30% higher for Native American families (Figure 5-3). Significant disparities are also observed for maternal mortality and for infant and child mortality. In particular, Black and Native American children have considerably higher mortality than all other groups in every age category (infancy, childhood, and adolescence). These disparities in child health are apparent across a range of other measures, including prevalence of asthma and limitations on amount of play, which are similar for Latino and White children but 50% higher for Black children (Mehta et al., 2013). Interestingly, Black and Latino children with asthma are much more likely than White children to visit the emergency room, a result that

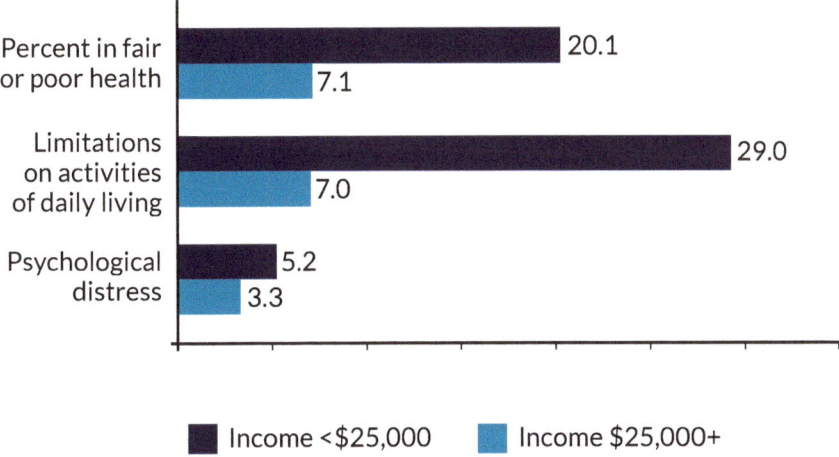

FIGURE 5-1 Adult health and early childhood income status, for individuals born between 1968 and 1975.
NOTES: Income is measured between the prenatal year and age 2 and is expressed in 2010 dollars. Adult health responses are averaged between ages 30 and 41. Percent in fair or poor health is based on a subjective health rating scale asking respondents whether their current health is excellent, very good, good, poor, or fair. Limitations on activities is measured by the Activity of Daily Living scale and multiplied by 100. Psychological distress is measured by the Kessler Screening Scale for Psychological Distress. All differences are $p < .001$.
SOURCE: Data from Ziol-Guest et al. (2012), based on data from the Panel Study of Income Dynamics.

is consistent with racial/ethnic differences in the prevalence and severity of this condition but also in access to care. One measure along which Black children fare better than White or Latino youth, and much better than Native American youth, is suicide, as discussed later, though rates of suicide among Black youth have recently grown more quickly.[1] These racial/ethnic differences in child health translate into adult disparities in health, with significant labor market consequences. Differences in income across racial groups contribute to, but cannot fully explain, these racial/ethnic disparities in health and suggest that poverty alleviation efforts alone will not close these gaps.

---

[1] It is important to note that health outcomes for American Indian children are often difficult to measure for multiple reasons, as detailed elsewhere (Stratford, 2018).

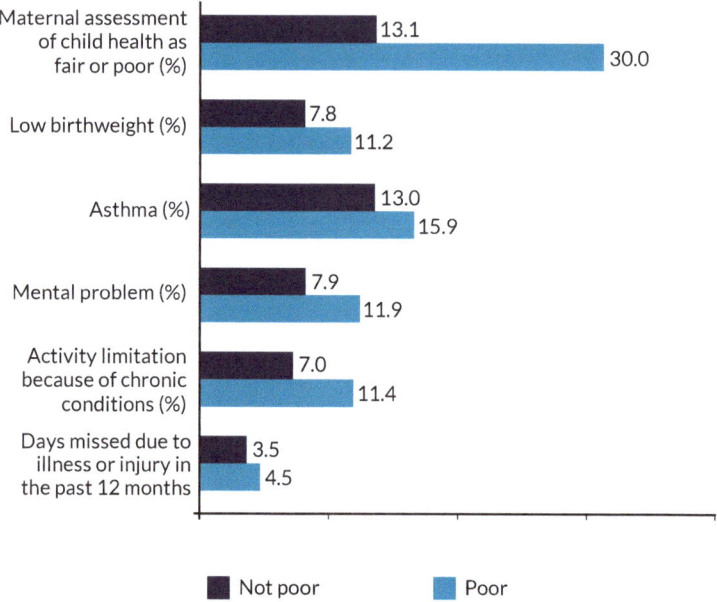

FIGURE 5-2 Health of children living in poverty vs. other children, 2001–2005.
NOTES: Low birthweight is defined as birthweight of less than 2,500 grams (or 5.5 pounds). "Mental problem" includes learning disability, developmental delay, Down syndrome, and autism. "Poverty" is measured by the Official Poverty Measure.
SOURCE: Data from Currie (2009), based on data reported in the National Health Interview Survey 2001–2005.

Sources of the observed racial and ethnic disparities in child health beyond income include exposure to pollution and violence, as well as access to high-quality medical care. Regarding the former, a history of residential segregation by race has resulted in Black children being more likely to live in highly polluted areas (Jbaily et al., 2022; Kodros, 2022; Woo et al., 2019). Regarding disparate access to high-quality medical care, there are multiple causes. Child health insurance coverage does not differ appreciably for Black and White children, largely because of the Medicaid program. Rates of uninsurance are much higher for the Native American and Latino population.[2] Other important sources of disparate access to medical care include differences in geographic access, distrust of the medical system based on past injustices, and racial discordance between patient and provider (Alsan & Wannamkaer, 2018; Alsan et al., 2019). Programs

---

[2] Native American and Latino children have rates of uninsurance that are 13.3% and 8.6%, respectively, compared with 5.4% overall as of 2021 (U.S. Census Bureau, 2022).

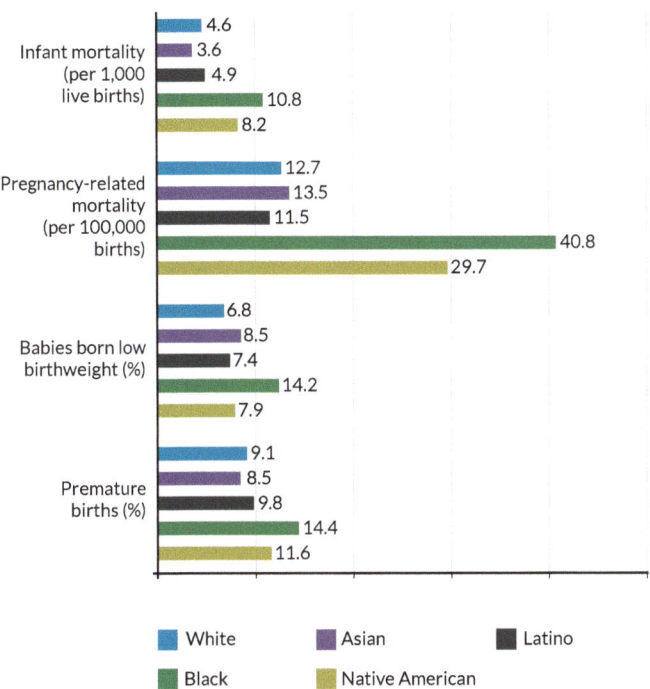

FIGURE 5-3 Maternal and infant health disparities by race/ethnicity.
NOTES: Infant mortality statistics are from 2018. Maternal mortality statistics are from 2007 to 2016. Both rates of low birthweight and premature births are from 2020. Infant mortality is defined as the death of an infant before their first birthday. Low birthweight is defined as birthweight of less than 2,500 grams (or 5.5 pounds). Premature birth is defined as birth prior to 37 weeks gestation.
SOURCE: Kaiser Family Foundation (2023).

and policies that fail to address such sources are unlikely to eliminate racial/ethnic gaps in child health.

HOW HEALTH AFFECTS THE ECONOMIC MOBILITY OF CHILDREN

There are many reasons why child health might vary with parental income that would not necessarily imply the causal relationship needed to establish that health is a driver of intergenerational poverty. To isolate the causal impact of parental income on child health, researchers have relied upon natural experiments, including changes in policy that can raise or lower family income, keeping all other characteristics constant. For example, work based on expansions in tax credits to low-income working families through the Earned Income Tax Credit (EITC) show that this increase in family income during pregnancy significantly improved newborn health (Hoynes et al., 2015). Taking advantage of variation in the earned income of workers between strong and weak labor markets, researchers have found that an additional dollar in earnings yields greater gains in child health at lower levels of family income (Doyle et al., 2007).

Where might these connections between family income and child health come from? A direct route runs from child health to adult health, which in turn affects future earnings via disability, employment, and wages. That is, healthy children grow up to become healthy adults who are more productive in the labor market, generating greater earnings and reducing reliance on public programs. Evidence for this is based on comparisons of siblings (who share the same family and neighborhood environment) showing that less healthy siblings are more likely to grow up to be unhealthy adults and to work less, earn less, and have less income (J. Smith, 2007, 2009; Stephens & Toohey, 2022). Other evidence relies on expansions to Medicaid, the public health insurance program for low-income families in the United States, which improved access to medical care but kept other family characteristics unchanged. Not only did Medicaid expansions improve child health (Currie & Gruber, 1997), but also the effects were long-lasting, reducing adult disability and improved earnings in adulthood (Brown et al., 2020).[3]

An indirect route is based on the facts that child health can affect cognitive development and schooling, which in turn also affect adult earnings. This evidence is likewise based on sibling comparisons and Medicaid expansions. An example of the former includes a comparison of twin siblings born in Norway between 1967 and 1997 documenting that the twin with higher birthweight (an important marker of prenatal health) grew up to score higher on IQ tests, complete more schooling, and earn more than their lower-weight twin (Black et al., 2007). Other work has confirmed this relationship in U.S. data (Conley & Bennett, 2000, 2001; Royer, 2009). The above-mentioned Medicaid expansions have also been shown to improve educational attainment.

Why does parental income matter for child health? One channel, alluded to above, is access to health insurance and medical care, which is lower for families living in poverty. But there are other ways in which parental income affects child health. Child, and ultimately adult, health is a function of the child's health at birth, and all subsequent adverse "shocks"

---

[3] Medicaid expansions for families have also been found to improve financial well-being by reducing medical debt, which has led to reduced borrowing and even evictions (Allen et al., 2019; Baicker et al., 2013; Hu et al., 2018).

to and investments in the child's health (Currie, 2009). Shocks might include exposure to pollution, food insecurity, stress, and violence, all of which are more common for families living below poverty. There is also evidence that, conditional on an exposure or medical condition, income is protective (Case et al., 2002; Currie & Stabile, 2003). In other words, poverty magnifies the adverse impacts of such shocks on child health. This can also be true even when children have access to medical care. As an example, in an RCT for cancer treatment at a major cancer institute where children received equivalent, high-quality medical care, 5-year survival rates were significantly lower for children from neighborhoods with high poverty rates (Bona et al., 2021). Though the subject of ongoing work, the researchers have hypothesized that this disparity is likely attributable to a combination of worse underlying health prior to diagnosis and treatment, greater barriers to treatment adherence, or increased stress among the families experiencing poverty.

ACCESS TO HEALTH CARE: FAMILY PLANNING, MEDICAID, INDIAN HEALTH SERVICES, AND MENTAL HEALTH SERVICES

Access to Family Planning Services

Low-income families currently have the highest fertility rates, the lowest use of contraception, and the highest unmet need for family planning services. Eighteen percent of sexually active low-income women (below 200% of the Federal Poverty Line [FPL]) report that they are not using contraception even though they are not trying to conceive, compared with 14% nationally (Frederiksen, 2021). This finding is consistent with that of unintended pregnancies, which are higher among women who are adolescents, low-income, racial/ethnic minorities, or single. Those with unintended pregnancies have delayed prenatal care access and have higher rates of preterm birth, an important marker of newborn health with long-term consequences (Haider et al., 2013).

The causal research on the impact of access to family planning services has established that family planning services improve the short- and long-term outcomes of affected families. Bailey (2013) estimates the impact of Title X, the federal legislation in the 1970s that increased financial access to family planning services for low-income mothers, on the long-term outcomes of mothers and their children. To do so, she takes advantage of the roll-out of Title X across counties and over time by comparing the outcomes of families that gain local access to Title X before others. She finds that within a given county, children born after the roll-out of Title X were more likely to complete high school and college, had 2% higher earnings as adults, and were 7.4% less likely to live in families with incomes below the poverty line than children born before roll-out (Bailey et al., 2019).

This reduction in poverty caused by access to family planning services operates in part through improved economic outcomes for mothers. Women who gained legal access to family planning services in their early childbearing years earned 5% to 11% more per year in their mid-40s than those who did not (Bailey et al., 2012). In other more recent work comparing the outcomes of women who sought an abortion just before reaching the gestational limit for legal abortion with those who just exceeded the gestational limit (and therefore did not receive an abortion), researchers have found that those denied an abortion experience a large increase in financial distress that persists for at least 10 years (Miller et al., 2023).

Access to family planning services also leads to delays in childbearing and reductions in teen parenting. Severe funding cuts to the family planning program in Texas in 2011–2013 led to a 3.4% increase in the teen birth rate, or 2,200 additional teen births over 4 years (Packham, 2017). Estimating the impact of teen parenting on child outcomes is complicated by the fact that teen mothers tend to be drawn from the most disadvantaged families. To address this, researchers have relied on "sister comparisons," comparing the children of sisters, one of whom gave birth as a teen and one who did not. Unfortunately, U.S. data for this kind of analysis is largely inadequate due to the small sample sizes of surveys and a lack of long-term follow-up information. Exploiting the wealth of administrative data available in Scandinavian countries such as Norway that enable such an analysis, researchers have found that compared with the child of a sister who delayed childbearing, a child born to a teenaged mother completes fewer years of schooling and has lower long-term earnings (Aizer et al., 2022).

Health Insurance Coverage During Pregnancy and Childhood Through Medicaid

A major source of health insurance for low-income families is the Medicaid program, a means-tested public health insurance program that is funded via a combination of federal and state funds. Medicaid has expanded significantly over time since its establishment in 1966 as part of the War on Poverty.[4] Medicaid covered 17.5 million children in 1995, and by

---

[4] In 1966, when Medicaid was founded, the program covered only those families enrolled in the Aid to Families with Dependent Children (AFDC) program. Between 1985 and 1990, Medicaid expanded eligibility to low-income pregnant women and children who were not enrolled in AFDC. In 1997, as part of the State Children's Health Insurance Program, states could further expand Medicaid eligibility, and finally the 2014 Affordable Care Act (ACA) further increased Medicaid eligibility in those states that opted into the ACA.

2019 this number had doubled to 36 million. Medicaid is a major source of coverage for pregnancy, covering 42% of all births in 2019.

Pregnancy and Post-Partum Care

Even with Medicaid expansions, women with lower socioeconomic status are still significantly less likely to have continuous health insurance for their pregnancies (Admon et al., 2021). If one considers preconception and post-partum coverage as well, only 40% of low-income pregnant women have continuous coverage over this period. This lack of continuous coverage during pregnancy is due to significant churn in the Medicaid program combined with post-partum coverage being limited to only 2 months. Recent legislation made permanent the 12-month extended post-partum coverage option provided by the American Rescue Plan Act in 2021 and utilized by 23 states. Although the option is too new to generate evidence on long-term outcomes, evaluation of the program in Texas suggests it improved access to care, especially contraceptive, preventive, and behavioral health services, and reduced short-interval pregnancies in the first year (Wang et al., 2022).

Childhood

Historic expansions in eligibility for the Medicaid program among children have contributed to significant declines in rates of uninsurance for low-income children over time. For children with household incomes below the poverty line, the share with health insurance rose from 60% in 1987 to 85% by 2012 (Buchmuller et al., 2016). Despite the large expansions in Medicaid, there are still disparities in child health insurance coverage by income, race, and ethnicity.

Children below 250% of the FPL have an uninsurance rate of 7.7%, compared with 3.8% for those above 250% of the FPL. Broken down by race and ethnicity, uninsurance rates are much higher for Native American (13.8%) and Latino children (9.2%) than they are for White and Black children.

Among children who lack health insurance, two-thirds are eligible for Medicaid but not enrolled, suggesting that efforts to increase health insurance coverage by targeting the already eligible and simplifying enrollment and re-enrollment processes are likely to be highly effective. Indeed, increases in the uninsurance rate of low-income children between 2018 and 2020 have been linked to changes in federal guidance that increased administrative requirements for reenrollment (Arbogast et al., 2022). Other work has identified administrative barriers as important in explaining low take-up of public programs, including health insurance (Aizer, 2007; Herd

& Moynihan, 2019; Sugar et al., 2021). Finally, work showing that among children eligible for Medicaid, those whose parents are also eligible are more likely to be enrolled, which suggests that parental ineligibility for Medicaid also contributes to lack of child take-up (Dubay & Kenney, 2003).

A large body of rigorous research links Medicaid expansions in pregnancy and childhood with better health at birth and throughout childhood and even improved future labor market outcomes. To establish this, researchers have taken advantage of the roll-out of Medicaid expansions for pregnant women and children in the late 1980s and early 1990s. The federal government increased Medicaid eligibility levels, but states had discretion in the timing of these expansions as well as the size of the expansion. Examining this variation in the timing of the Medicaid expansions across the states, researchers have linked expanded Medicaid eligibility to improved birthweight and child health (Currie & Gruber, 1996a, 1996b). Given the established causal relationship between newborn health and future economic outcomes, it is not surprising that researchers have also linked these Medicaid expansions in childhood to higher school attainment and earnings later in life (Brown et al., 2020). Expanding Medicaid access to older children is also beneficial: childhood Medicaid expansions reduced the mortality of Black children ages 15–18 by 13% to 20% (Wherry & Meyer, 2016). Recent research has established further intergenerational effects: Access to Medicaid in-utero improves the newborn health of the next generation (East et al., forthcoming).[5]

Lacking continuous coverage including preconception and post-partum is associated with worse health outcomes for new mothers and their children, including maternal deaths, one-third of which occur in the post-partum period (Johnston et al., 2021). Medicaid expansions through the ACA are associated with lower maternal mortality, with the effects concentrated among non-Latino Black mothers and in later maternal deaths (Eliason, 2020).

Access to Publicly Provided Health Care via the Indian Health Service (IHS)

Native American children experience the worst health along many measures and are more likely to be uninsured than the rest of the U.S. population. Infant mortality, for example, was 60% higher for the Native

---

[5] Medicaid was introduced in the late 1960s and early 1970s and disproportionately improved the health of low-income mothers and children. Subsequent Medicaid expansions have been shown to have reduced disability and receipt of disability transfers and mortality (Goodman Bacon, 2021).

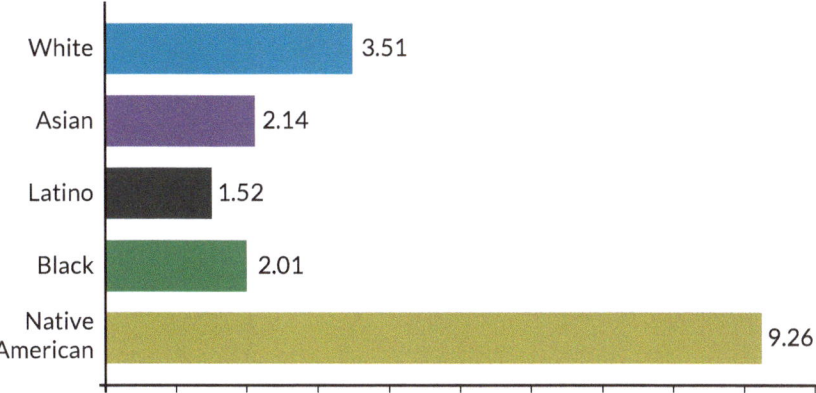

FIGURE 5-4 Average suicide rate per 100,000 among children and adolescents, ages 0–19, by race/ethnicity, 2010–2020.
SOURCE: Centers for Disease Control and Prevention (2023).

American population than it was for the United States overall. Youth suicide is also highest among this group (see Figure 5-4). Access to health care likely contributes to this disparity, as Native American children are more than twice as likely to be uninsured (14%) as U.S. children overall (Roygardner et al., 2019). Native American children are unique in that they are also served by the IHS, a direct provider of health care services.[6] However, according to the U.S. Department of Human Health and Services:

> Funding for IHS addresses only an estimated 48.6% of the health care needs of Native American children and has historically been subject to year-by-year discretionary allocations from Congress, which creates substantial long-term uncertainty in funding and makes it challenging to maintain and modernize needed health care infrastructure (Office of the Assistant Secretary for Planning and Evaluation, 2022, p. 1).

Given the growing body of research linking access to medical care during childhood and the prenatal period to children's long-term health

---

[6] Not all Native Americans are eligible for services from the IHS. Out of every 5.7 Native Americans, 2.7 are eligible. They include those who reside in geographic areas covered by the IHS.

and economic status, the inability to adequately serve all eligible Native American children likely contributes to the intergenerational poverty of the Native American populations.

Access to Mental Health Care

One in five young people in the United States has a mental health disorder that will persist into adulthood, with mental illnesses that emerge before adulthood costing 10 times more than those emerge later in life (Lee et al., 2014). The five most common mental health disorders emerging in childhood and adolescence are attention deficit hyperactive disorder, conduct disorder, anxiety and mood disorders, schizophrenia, and substance use disorder. Mental health conditions are more prevalent among children with family incomes persistently below the poverty line and with children making transitions into poverty (Fitzimons et al., 2017; Wadsworth & Achenbach, 2005). Moreover, mental health conditions are an important predictor of adult earnings. Multiple studies have linked attention deficit hyperactive disorder and other mental health conditions in childhood with worse adult economic outcomes, including employment, earnings, and welfare use (Currie et al., 2010; Fletcher, 2014; Smith & Smith, 2010).

Between 2016 and 2020, anxiety, depression, and behavior and conduct problems increased among children (Lebrun-Harris et al., 2022), with a pronounced increase in depression, suicidal thoughts, and substance use during the COVID-19 pandemic (Mayne et al., 2021). It is important to note that these increases were largely the continuation of an alarming trend in rising rates of depression, suicide, and substance use among adolescents in the United States. In contrast to declines in child and youth mortality more generally, youth suicide rates have increased significantly over time for all racial/ethnic groups, with higher increases among Native American and White youth. Importantly, the method of suicide has shifted to include more use of firearms, which are deadlier.

Substance use disorders, such as the use of marijuana and alcohol, and overdoses among teens also increased during the pandemic (FAIR Health, 2021; Romm et al., 2022). Substance use can have long-term consequences as both the frequency and quantity of substance use during adolescence are strongly associated with a risk of heavy use and misuse in adulthood (Moss et al., 2014; Windle & Zucker, 2010). Substance use during adolescence and young adulthood is associated with neurocognitive and psychological impairment and increased risk for academic underachievement, chronic physical disease, and poor mental health outcomes (Atherton et al., 2016; M. Kim et al., 2017), which in turn lead to adult disabilities.

Mental health conditions are more highly predictive of school outcomes than physical health conditions (Currie & Stabile, 2006). This is also true for outcomes related to employment, marriage, and income in adulthood, with some estimates suggesting that childhood mental health conditions are associated with a 28% decline in earnings at age 50 (Goodman et al., 2011). Adolescents with serious mental health disorders or substance use disorders have seven times greater risk of criminal justice encounters (Prince & Wald, 2018). However, establishing a causal link is complicated by confounding factors.

Some of the strongest evidence of a causal link between mental health and important medium- and longer-term outcomes emerged from two studies based on natural experiments. Examining the timing of school shootings and comparing short- and long-term outcomes of children exposed to a school shooting with similar children living nearby but not directly exposed, researchers established that fatal school shootings result in an immediate increase in prescriptions to treat depression and anxiety that persists over time (Rosin Slater et al., 2020). Using this same setting, researchers have in turn linked this to reduced high school graduation, college enrollment and completion, and earnings and employment at ages 24–26 (Cabral et al., 2021). Together, these two studies point to a causal link between mental health in adolescence and future educational and economic outcomes. Though low-income children are not more likely to be exposed to a school shooting, they are more likely to be exposed to violence and to have mental health conditions. We draw upon the research on school shootings in order to highlight the likely causal relationship between low-income children's greater exposure to violence, mental health conditions, and worse future economic outcomes.

Conversely, a separate study linked treatment for depression in adolescence with positive schooling outcomes. A natural experiment caused by a 2004 Food and Drug Administration (FDA) decision to issue warnings on antidepressive medications for teenagers provides evidence on long-term academic impacts of adolescent treatment of depression with selective serotonin reuptake inhibitors. The FDA warning resulted in a significant drop in the use of antidepressants among teenagers, which in turn resulted in a significant decline in school outcomes among those affected (Busch et al., 2014).

Treatment for mental health conditions can be effective (see Appendix for more details), but despite this, many children fail to receive treatment for mental health disorders. A 2016 survey covering 50,000 children in the United States found that of those with a mental health disorder, nearly half did not receive needed treatment from a mental health professional, with significant variation across the United States (Whitney & Peterson, 2019). Surveys suggest that lack of treatment stems from a combination of internal (e.g., limited mental health knowledge, perceived stigma) and external (e.g., costs and the availability of mental health providers) causes (Radez et al., 2021). With 35% of the U.S. population living in an area with a shortage of mental health professionals, it is unsurprising that adolescents often have to wait 1 to 3 months for an appointment with a provider of adolescent psychiatric care (Steinman et al., 2015), with greater barriers to access for racial/ethnic minority individuals (Cook et al., 2016).

Conclusion 5-1: Improving the health of children experiencing poverty has been shown to improve economic status in adulthood as measured by future educational attainment, employment, earnings, and reduced reliance on public assistance. Two important mechanisms include access to family planning services and health insurance coverage in pregnancy and childhood, both of which are key to improving the short- and long-term health and economic outcomes of children. Yet many low-income families are still without health insurance coverage or access to family planning services. This is due in part to administrative barriers that reduce child Medicaid enrollment, the fact that Medicaid coverage for pregnancy often ends 2 months post-partem, an Indian Health Service that serves only half the eligible population, and declines in funding for Title X over time. For access to mental health, additional barriers include lack of providers.

ENVIRONMENTAL INFLUENCES AS A DRIVER: POLLUTION, STRESS, AND VIOLENCE

Pollution

A strong causal link has been established between child health and exposure to pollution, particularly during the in-utero period, based on both epidemiological and quasi-experimental methods (Currie et al., 2011b). More recently, this research has been extended to show causal impacts of childhood exposure to pollution on adult outcomes and even the health of the next generation (Colmer & Voorheis, 2022; Isen et al., 2017). Pollutants that have been the subject of the most study include air pollution (particulate matter [PM] 2.5) and lead. While other pollutants may exert a strong impact on child health, there is less research establishing this connection, in part due to limitations in the number and kind of pollutants that are regularly measured and monitored.[7]

---

[7] For example, the Toxic Release Inventory (TRI) requires firms to disclose their use and emissions of listed chemicals. The lists have grown sharply over time as additional research establishes their negative impact on health.

Due in large part to federal action, childhood exposure to pollution (both air pollution and lead) has declined considerably over time. As overall pollution has fallen, so too have income and racial disparities in exposure to pollution, though disparities remain (Bell & Ebisu, 2012; Currie et al., 2023; Jbaily al., 2022; Liu et al., 2015). The major sources of pollution are stationary sources, such as power plants, refineries, and industrial facilities, and mobile sources, such as cars, buses, and planes, which pollute areas near major roadways, along with residual lead (and other toxins) that remains in the environment. Low-income and racial/ethnic minority families have historically been (and continue to be) exposed to more pollution due to the high degree of residential segregation by income and race in the United States, and the concentration of polluting sources in low-income, high racial/ethnic minority neighborhoods (Alexander & Currie, 2017; Teye et al., 2021). For example, children living in more racially segregated cities are exposed to twice the pollution, as measured by fine particulate matter (PM 2.5), than those in less segregated cities, and this difference increases to tenfold when one considers exposure to more toxic metals (Kodros et al., 2022).

Multiple federal policy efforts have been shown to have effectively reduced pollution and improved child health. These include the Clean Air Act (CAA) of 1970 and its 1990 amendments, the federal ban of lead from gasoline and paint, which dramatically reduced the amount of lead in the environment in the decade between 1976 and 1986, and the federal cleanup of Superfund sites, abandoned hazardous waste sites. We discuss the evidence linking each of these policy efforts to reduced pollution and to important short- and long-term outcomes for children. We follow this with a discussion of the evidence on other sources of pollution that are more common and widespread, such as automobile exhaust.

The CAA and its amendments dramatically reduced exposure to particulate matter by roughly 70% between 1970 and 1990.[8] Researchers have linked the CAA and its amendments to important short- and long-term outcomes for children. To do so, they took advantage of variation across local areas in whether they were subject to the new CAA rules regarding acceptable pollution levels. Those areas subject to the new pollution limits saw dramatic declines in air pollution levels after the CAA, while those already "in attainment" (i.e., within the new limit for pollution levels) saw no to little appreciable decline in pollution. Reductions in pollution induced

---

[8] In 1990, the Environmental Protection Agency (EPA) estimated that between 1970 and 1990, "Americans received 20 dollars of value in reduced risk of death, illness and other adverse effects for every one dollar spent to control air pollution" (EPA, 1996). It is estimated that the CAA amendments of 1990 prevented more than 230,000 early deaths (mostly adult deaths) and reduced the number of lost school days by 5.4 million by 2020.

by the CAA were found to improve infant health (Chay and Greenstone, 2003a, 2003b) as measured by infant mortality. More recently, researchers have linked the CAA to long-term outcomes. Children born after the CAA in areas that saw a steep decline in air pollution were found to have increased employment and earnings at age 30, driven in part by reductions in those with earnings in the bottom of the distribution, consistent with declines in disability (Isen et al., 2017, for the 1970 CAA and Colmer et al., 2022, for the 1990 amendments).

Lead is another major source of pollution that has been found to negatively affect child development, with long-term consequences. Recent research has taken advantage of naturally occurring variation in exposure to lead—as a result of federal and local policies that have sought to reduce exposure—to generate causal impacts. It has found that providing incentives to landlords to remediate lead in homes reduced children's blood lead levels and increased child test scores in reading and math, especially among low-income and racial/ethnic minority households (Aizer et al., 2018). Moreover, work shows that remediating lead paint in homes increases their value (Billings & Schnepel, 2017). Examining variation in exposure to lead over time due to the de-leading of gasoline, by federal mandate, which disproportionately reduced lead levels in children living near roadways, researchers have documented reduced in-school disciplinary infractions, juvenile detention, and adult crime (Aizer & Currie, 2019; Groqvist et al., 2020), important predictors of adult earnings.

However, air pollution and toxic chemicals including lead are still present in the environment. For example, PM 2.5 (fine particulate matter that poses the greatest risk to health), while declining continuously between 1970 and 2016, increased by nearly 6% between 2016 and 2018 (Clay et al., 2021). Likewise, lead, while continuing to decline, still remains in the environment. It is present in water because of lead drinking pipes, is concentrated in the air and the soil near roadways, and remains in homes built before 1978. As a result, low-income and racial/ethnic minority children who are more likely to live near roads and in older homes are still more likely to be exposed to air pollution and other toxic substances including lead than their more advantaged counterparts.

A third area where federal policy has reduced exposure to pollution is the Superfund program. The program, established in 1980, allocates resources to abating the most hazardous sites in the United States. Twenty-one million Americans, 7% of all children under the age of 5, were living within a mile of a Superfund site as of 2020. This population is disproportionately living in poverty and is disproportionately Black and Latino (EPA, 2020). Research has linked Superfund clean-up with improved infant health and student test scores (Currie et al., 2011a; Persico et al., 2020), as discussed in Appendix C: Chapter 5. Other long-term benefits are likely but have not yet been the subject of research.

Other sources of pollution that are more common and generally below federally determined limits (e.g., automobile exhaust, pollution from coal-fired plants, release of toxic chemicals from manufacturing facilities) have also been linked to important outcomes in children, both short- and medium-term. The installation of EZ-pass tolls on New Jersey and Pennsylvania highways significantly reduced exhaust and air pollution around toll plazas. Researchers linked this decline in pollution with improved infant health, as measured by an 11% and 12% reduction in prematurity and low birthweight, respectively (Currie & Walker, 2011). Public transportation is another important source of pollution for urban populations. A recent study estimated the impact of EPA transit bus emissions standards on infant health. Examining EPA requirements that new buses meet increasingly lower PM thresholds, Ngo (2017) took advantage of variation in bus fleet vintage over the period 1990–2009 in New York City to estimate the impact of proximity to pollutants on infant health. Mothers exposed to the oldest buses gave birth to newborns nearly 100 grams lighter. Still other research, using quasi-random variation induced by declines in coal-based energy production over time and across areas, has linked pollution with child test scores (Gilraine & Zheng, 2022). Given the similar magnitudes of the short-run impacts of the CAA of 1970 and these more common sources of pollution today, it is reasonable to assume they likely have similar long-term consequences given the link between newborn health, child school performance, and long-term outcomes. However, this has not yet been directly established.

Finally, children in families living below poverty and Black children are more likely to live near one of the 300,000 facilities that emit toxic chemicals, known as toxic release inventory sites (Perlin et al., 1999). There is research linking childhood exposure to toxic chemicals at these sites to short-term and (though more preliminarily) to long-term outcomes, including educational attainment and wages. This evidence is discussed in Appendix C: Chapter 5.

Increased Stress in Utero and During Childhood

Lower-income families are exposed to more stressful events than other families, and repeated exposure to stress can result in a greater allostatic role, the physiological response to the body's neuroendocrine response to stress (Taylor & Seeman, 1999). This can result in the development of maladaptive behaviors and adverse physical and mental health outcomes in childhood (McLoyd, 1997, 1998). Over time, this can make the child more vulnerable to future stressors (Boyce et al., 2021; Shonkoff & Garner, 2012;

Taylor et al., 1997). Stress can affect children indirectly as well, through parental exposure to stress. Parental stress can harm children either by changing parental behavior or through "prenatal programming," the process by which exposure to environmental influences in utero can affect fetal development, with long-term implications for health and development. In this chapter we focus on in-utero exposure to stress and its impact on offspring outcomes not because it is more important than childhood exposure, but because the finite nature of the in-utero period makes it easier to control for potential confounding, enabling causal inference.

In animal studies, experimental exposure in utero to elevated levels of stress and the stress hormone cortisol leads to worse outcomes for offspring (Harris & Seckl, 2011). Evidence of a causal impact of in-utero stress on child outcomes is new and somewhat mixed, with some work finding negative effects on cognitive development, mental health, and educational attainment (Aizer et al., 2016b; Persson & Rossin-Slater, 2018; Torche, 2018), and another study finding no effect (Black et al., 2016). These studies are based on sibling comparisons in which one sibling is exposed to high levels of maternal stress in-utero and the other is not. There is causal evidence that income transfers via the EITC reduce maternal stress (Evans & Garthwaite, 2014), underscoring the role that poverty and income can play in perpetuating elevated stress in families experiencing poverty.

Researchers have identified racism and discrimination as additional sources of stress faced by Black, Latino and Native American families in the United States (Collins et al., 2014; Nam et al., 2022; Paradies et al., 2015; Sawyer et al., 2012). This has been confirmed in lab experiments in which human subjects are brought into a lab and some are subjected to racist stimuli, which generates a heightened physiological stress response, including increased blood pressure and heart rate, relative to control subjects who are not subjected to the stimuli (e.g., Sawyer et al., 2012). Researchers have long hypothesized that higher rates of stress from racial discrimination may explain the worse child and maternal health outcomes experienced by Black mothers that cannot be explained by differences in income and education (see Braveman et al., 2021).

Establishing a causal link is challenging, as it is difficult to isolate the impact of stress from the stressor itself. Recent work has sought to do so using a somewhat idiosyncratic source of stress: formal complaints of excessive police force in women's neighborhoods. Black women living in neighborhoods with excessive-use-of-force complaints are 1.2 times as likely to have a preterm birth and 1.4 times as likely to develop cardiovascular disease as women in the same neighborhood before and after an incident, or neighborhoods with otherwise equivalent levels of neighborhood disadvantage and crime. The negative effects for Black women were larger and more precise than those for White women. These results are unchanged when one limits comparisons to two births to the same mother at different points in time, further reducing the possibility of confounding (Freedman et al., 2022). This finding is consistent with discrimination resulting in greater stress and worse health among Black families. While this has not yet been linked with long-term outcomes of the child, indirect evidence suggests that it likely will have long-term consequences given the relationship between newborn health and long-term outcomes.

Underlying sources of stress in the lives of low-income and racial/ethnic minority families include uncertainty, income volatility, victimization, and discrimination, among others. Policies and interventions that promote stability and reduce discrimination have the potential to reduce stress and improve health, particularly newborn health, an important determinant of adult economic outcomes.[9] So too do policies that reduce violence and victimization, as discussed briefly below and in greater detail in the chapter on neighborhood crime.

Greater Exposure to Violence, Especially Gun Violence

Children living in poverty are more likely to be exposed to violence in their communities and their homes (Sedlak et al., 2010). Being a victim of violence affects child health directly through increased mortality and morbidity. Firearm-related injury has risen significantly over time and is now the primary cause of death among children in the United States, surpassing motor vehicle accidents and accounting for 20% of all child deaths (Figure 5-5). There are significant disparities by income and race. Youth in counties with the highest poverty rates had firearm-related mortality rates that were nearly five times higher than those living in counties with the lowest poverty rates (Barrett et al., 2022) and Black children experienced rates of firearm-related deaths (12 per 100,000) that were nearly six times higher than the rates among White children and three times higher than those among Native American children in 2021 (Kaiser Family Foundation, 2022).

Evidence shows that even indirect exposure to neighborhood or family violence (i.e., witnessing or knowing victims of violence) can result in significant long-term harm related to physical and mental health, problem behaviors, and poor academic performance and educational attainment (for reviews see Osofsky, 1999; Rivara et al., 2019; Sharkey, 2018; for more evidence see Bor et al., 2018, and Chapter 9). Perhaps the best evidence of a causal impact of exposure to gun violence on children's long-term outcomes is the work linking school shootings to short-term mental health outcomes

---

[9] Practitioners and researchers have developed interventions to reduce the stress response in affected families. However, the evidence linking such interventions to the short- or long-term social and economic outcomes of children is not yet sufficiently developed.

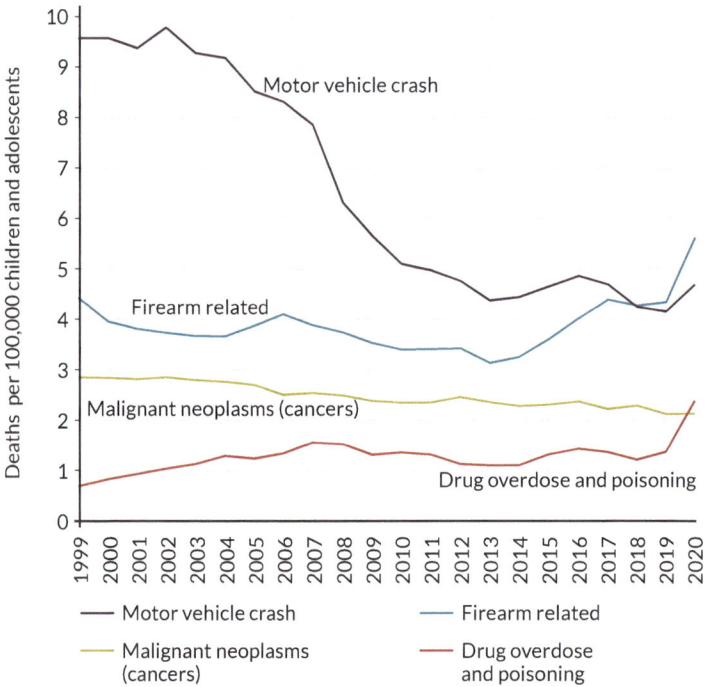

FIGURE 5-5 Annual death rates for the four most common causes of death in the United States among children and adolescents, ages 1–19, 1999–2020.
NOTE: Death rates are reported per 100,000.
SOURCE: Adapted from Goldstick et al. (2022) using data from the Centers for Disease Control and Prevention (n.d.).

and long-term economic outcomes. That research addresses confounding in exposure to violence by examining the timing of school shootings and comparing children living closest to the affected schools, and therefore exposed, with those living slightly further away and therefore similar but not exposed themselves (Cabral et al., 2021; Rosin Slater et al., 2020).

To the extent that exposure to violence leads to premature death as well as stress to those indirectly exposed, thereby contributing to intergenerational poverty, we discuss interventions to reduce violence in Chapter 9, which discusses crime and the criminal justice system.

Conclusion 5-2: A child's environment (pollution, stress, and violence) exerts a strong influence on child health and development, with long-term economic consequences. Federal regulation of pollution has led to significant improvements in infant and child health and, ultimately, adult income. Due in large part to federal action, disparities in exposure to pollution by income, race, and ethnicity have declined significantly over time. While child mortality has been falling over time, firearm-related violence is on the rise and is now the leading cause of death among all children in the United States, with significant disparities by income, race, and ethnicity. Direct exposure to violence or victimization resulting in premature death and disability, as well as indirect exposure resulting in increased stress, anxiety, and depression with long-term consequences, both contribute to the intergenerational persistence of poverty.

NUTRITION AND FOOD INSECURITY AS A DRIVER

Adequate nutrition during infancy and early childhood (first 1,000 days), the most critical and rapid time for neuronal proliferation, is essential for growth, health, and development for children to reach their fullest potential as adults (Schwarzenberg et al., 2018). Malnutrition, which includes both undernutrition, or the inadequate provision or intake of micro- and/or macronutrients, and overweight or obesity, or the provision/intake of excessive calories, both lead to unhealthy nutritional status.

Many low-income communities and racial/ethnic minority individuals are more likely than others to experience food insecurity, meaning a lack of adequate access to affordable, high-quality, nutritious food (Coleman-Jensen et al., 2022). Food insecurity is defined by the U.S. Department of Agriculture (USDA) as "a household-level economic and social condition of limited or uncertain access to adequate food" and is monitored through regular household surveys by the USDA (2021). Children living in households experiencing food insecurity might not have food insecurity themselves, as parents often compensate. Though household food insecurity has fallen for all groups over time (see Figure 5-6), it is still the case that children in poverty are twice as likely (28% vs. 14%) to live in a household that has experienced food insecurity. As compared with White children, Black children are 3.5 times more likely and Latino children almost 3 times more likely to live in a household that has experienced food insecurity.

Food insecurity during childhood is associated with worse physical health (Gunderson & Kreider, 2009; Thomas et al., 2019) and mental health (McIntyre et al., 2013), lower academic achievement in childhood (Jyoti et al., 2005), and worse psychological distress and physical health during adulthood (Fertig, 2019). Although the evidence linking food insecurity to overweight and obesity is clear for adults, the evidence for the association in children is mixed (St. Pierre et al., 2022). It is important

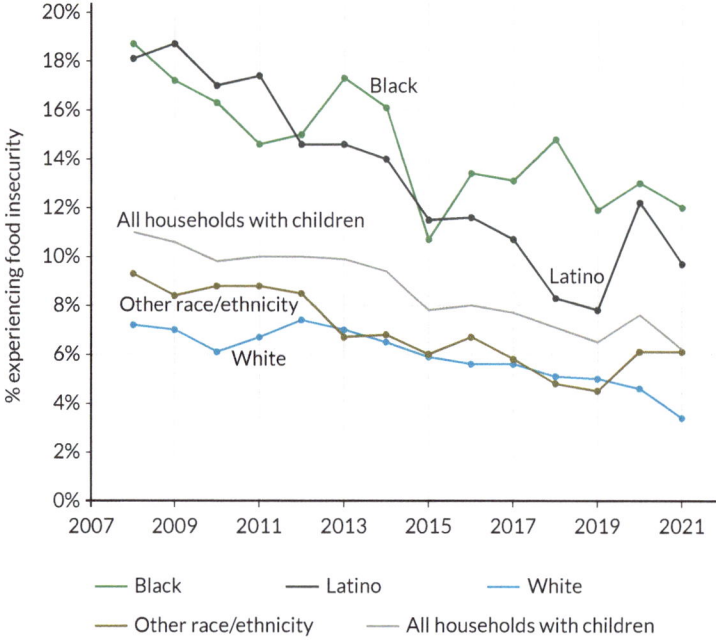

FIGURE 5-6 Food insecurity among children, by race and ethnicity of household head, 2008–2021.
SOURCE: Calculated by USDA, Economic Research Service, using Current Population Survey Food Insecurity Supplement data. https://www.ers.usda.gov/topics/food-nutrition-assistance/food-security-in-the-u-s/interactive-charts-and-highlights/#disability

to note that most of this evidence is based on comparisons of children in food-secure and -insecure households controlling for family background characteristics.

To establish the causal impact of nutrition in utero and during childhood on short- and long-term outcomes, researchers have taken advantage of policy changes that increased low-income families' access to federal nutrition programs (see Box 5-1 for a description of the main programs). Examining the initial roll-out of the federal Supplemental Nutrition Assistance Program (SNAP) during the 1960s and 1970s, researchers have compared the short- and long-term outcomes of children born before and after SNAP became available in their county of birth. The staggered nature of the roll-out allows researchers to compare the long-term outcomes of children born in the same county before and after SNAP became available but also compare those born in same the year but in different counties, one with SNAP and one not yet with SNAP. Researchers have found that SNAP availability led to improvements in newborn health, improved child outcomes, reductions in poverty, reductions in criminal activity, and improved economic and health outcomes in adulthood (Almond et al., 2011; M. Bailey et al., 2020; Barr & Smith, 2023; Hoynes & Schanzenbach, 2015; Hoynes et al., 2011, 2016). This body of research did not determine the comparative role of SNAP's nutritional and general economic supplementation.[10]

One might be concerned, however, that evidence on the long-term benefits of SNAP availability based on the 1960s and 1970s might not generalize to the experience of children in a more recent setting. The current nutritional status of children may differ, and the impact of the creation of the SNAP program may be larger than the impact of marginal increases in SNAP benefit levels. One way to assess this is to compare results for child and adult health based on the roll-out of SNAP in the 1960s and 1970s with evidence from a more recent period. A study based on the period 1996–2003, during which the state of California first eliminated and then restored SNAP eligibility for immigrant parents, shows moderate medium-term effects associated with increases in SNAP benefit levels that are very similar to the effect sizes from the historic roll-out of SNAP (East, 2018; see Appendix C: Chapter 5 for details). This evidence suggests that SNAP benefits today are likely to have similar long-term positive benefits for children as they did in the 1970s.

The Special Supplemental Nutrition Program for Women, Infants and Children (WIC), the other major federal food program for children, is also associated with better nutrition, dietary intake, food security, and health, including birth outcomes. To estimate a causal impact of WIC receipt during pregnancy on newborn health, Currie and Rajani (2015) compared the health of newborns born to the same mother who received WIC for one pregnancy but not the other. In this way, Currie and Rajani controlled for underlying differences in mothers who did and did not use WIC but could otherwise bias estimated effects. She documents significant improvements in newborn health under WIC, as measured by birthweight. This is an important finding given that birthweight is causally associated with educational attainment and later economic outcomes (Black et al., 2007; Royer, 2009).

Despite the positive impact of federal nutrition programs on children, many pregnant individuals and children do not benefit from them. There are two main reasons: lack of take-up among the eligible (relevant for WIC, less

---

[10] The issue of the "fungibility" of resources from cash and in-kind programs is a general one. In the SNAP studies cited above, we do not know whether cash payments equal in value to the SNAP payments would have generated the same benefits for children. Similar issues arise with housing vouchers (Jacob et al., 2015) and the Medicaid program benefits reviewed above.

> **BOX 5-1**
> **Federal Food Programs Serving Children**
>
> The Supplemental Nutrition Assistance Program (SNAP), formerly known as "food stamps," is a federal program that provides nutrition benefits to low-income individuals and families below 130% of the Federal Poverty Level (FPL) that are used at participating stores to purchase food. The maximum monthly benefit for a family of four in 2023 is $939. One in five children received SNAP benefits in 2017.
>   The Special Supplemental Nutrition Program for Women, Infants, and Children (WIC) provides nutritious foods to supplement the diets of low-income pregnant and lactating individuals as well as infants and children up to age 5 who are at nutritional risk, and also provides information on healthy eating and referrals to health care. Families with incomes below 100% or 185% of the FPL (depending on the state) are eligible for WIC. WIC serves half of all infants in the United States, but take-up falls as children age, declining from 98% to 26% from infancy to age 4.
>   The National School Lunch Program provides free lunches to children in families below 130% of the FPL and reduced-cost lunch to children between 130% and 185% of the FPL. In the fiscal year 2020, the program provided 2.46 billion free or reduced-price lunches to school children.

so for SNAP), and reduced eligibility in the immigrant population (more relevant for SNAP), as discussed in Appendix C: Chapter 5.

One thing that does not appear to influence child nutrition among low-income families is geographic proximity to high-quality, nutritious foods (i.e., the problem of "food deserts"). While low-income families are more likely to live in food deserts, their nutrition does not improve when high-quality supermarkets enter the local market or when they move to "healthier" neighborhoods (Allcott et al., 2019).

Conclusion 5-3: Today, children living in poverty are still more likely to reside in households that experience food and nutrition insecurity than their better-off counterparts. Evidence from the introduction of the Supplemental Nutrition Assistance Program (SNAP) program in the 1960s and 1970s suggests that food supplements for children in low-income families, both in utero and during childhood, can contribute to intergenerational mobility, improving child health and ultimately future adult health and earnings. Evidence on the impact of SNAP from a more recent period shows similar effects on child health, at least in the short to medium term, suggesting that long-term outcomes of enhancing child nutrition today may be similarly effective in promoting intergenerational mobility. Barriers to take-up in the Supplemental Nutrition

Program for Women, Infants, and Children program eligibility among immigrant families limit the ability of children in the United States to benefit from federal nutrition programs.

INTERVENTIONS INVOLVING CHILDREN'S HEALTH

Our discussion of potential mechanisms focuses on child health interventions for which there is strong direct evidence that they will improve adult earnings and increase mobility. These include the family planning and Medicaid interventions. With regard to pollution, there is direct evidence that reductions in pollution improve child health and future earnings, but many of the current sources of pollution differ from historical sources on which the direct evidence is based, influencing the types of interventions we explore. Finally, the direct evidence on child nutrition is based on historical data, the roll-out of the food stamp program in the 1960s. There is no evidence from more recent time periods of effects of nutrition programs in childhood on adult earnings, but the evidence on medium-term effects of nutrition programs in more recent periods are similar in magnitude to the medium-term effects of the historical program, suggesting that longer-term effects are also likely to be similar.

As discussed in Chapter 1, we characterize the direct evidence for some of the programs or policies as "strong" and denote them with an "*." This indicates that the program's or policy's impact on intergenerational poverty is supported by random-assignment evaluation evidence that has been replicated across several sites or by compelling quasi-experimental evidence based on national or multi-state data or a scaled-up program. We also considered evidence to be direct if strong post-1990 evidence of impacts on pre-adult mediators is coupled with strong pre-1990 evidence on long-run adult impacts in the same domain.

Increasing Access to Health Care Based on Direct Evidence

Family Planning

The main sources of funding for family planning are private health insurance, Medicaid, and the Title X Family Planning program. Recently, low-income families' access to family planning services has declined due to changes in both public programs. Given the strong causal evidence linking mothers' access to family planning services to improvements in their children's long-term outcomes, including teen childbearing, the committee developed the following ideas to increase access to family planning services among low-income families:

- **Increase funding for Title X family planning programs** from its current level of $286 million per year to at least $500 million per year. Were Title X funds to have increased with inflation since the program's inception in the 1970s, funding today would be slightly more than $1 billion. However, the significant increases in Medicaid coverage since Title X's inception suggest that more modest funding for the program is needed to maintain access.
- **Ensure that Medicaid beneficiaries have access to family planning services.** Because all Medicaid beneficiaries are eligible for family planning services from any willing qualified provider, the Centers for Medicare & Medicaid Services (CMS) could ensure that these requirements are being met in all states.

Medicaid

Strong direct evidence has shown that Medicaid expansions during the prenatal period and childhood lead to better health, greater educational attainment, and higher earnings later in life. With 2.8 million children currently eligible for Medicaid but uninsured, enrolling those already eligible through outreach and continuous enrollment requirements is the most effective way to increase health insurance coverage for low-income families (Kaiser Family Foundation, 2024). The committee developed the following ideas to increase Medicaid enrollment among low-income women and children:

- **Expand access to Medicaid with continuous 12-month eligibility and 12-month post-partum coverage** even if the family experiences a temporary change in income during the year.
- **Make the federal continuous eligibility requirements following pregnancy from 60 days to 12 months mandatory instead of optional.** The annual cost of this nationwide was estimated at $466 million in Fiscal Year 2022, increasing to $786 million by Fiscal Year 2030 (Congressional Budget Office, 2020).

Improving the Environment Based on Direct Evidence

Reducing Maternal and Child Exposure to Pollution

Strong direct evidence has shown improvements in child health and increases in adult earnings stemming from the 1970 CAA and its 1990 amendments, as well as the de-leading of gasoline and paint. The current challenges to reducing children's exposure to pollution, going forward, include the increasingly local phenomenon of pollution, the EPA's inability to monitor very local and common pollution sources, the high levels of indoor air pollution that are not monitored by the EPA, and climate change, which is disproportionately affecting low-income communities and communities of color (EPA, 2022). To address this, the committee developed the following ideas:

- The EPA could work with local communities to develop and maintain more local monitoring of air quality using less expensive technologies.
- The federal government, through the CDC and EPA, could provide information and resources to state and local governments to encourage the most efficient lead monitoring and abatement activities and provide appropriate funding.

Reducing Gun Violence

Direct-evidence studies have established that gun violence is both a crime issue and a health issue. That evidence and interventions to address are detailed in Chapter 9.

Improving Nutrition Based on Direct Evidence

Supplemental Nutrition Assistance Program

Numerous studies have shown that the SNAP programs promote intergenerational mobility out of poverty. Changes to several federal policies could address these gaps in coverage and increase food security among low-income children:

- **To increase food security for children, remove the 5-year waiting period of SNAP eligibility for legal permanent-resident parents.**
- **To ensure that all children are adequately covered, eliminate the proration of SNAP benefits for children with undocumented parents.**

HEALTH INTERVENTIONS BASED ON INDIRECT EVIDENCE

Increasing Access to Medical Care Among Native American Families

There is no direct evidence linking the IHS to adult poverty, However, the direct evidence on Medicaid likely applies to IHS as both operate by increasing access to medical care. In order to meet the considerable unmet health care needs of Native American children, there is a need to increase funding for the IHS to levels that would adequately support the provision of services to all eligible children:

- To provide care to all mothers and children eligible for IHS services, *increase federal funding to eliminate the funding gap for direct health care services*. In 2018, that gap was estimated to cost approximately $7.8 billion.

Increasing Access to Mental Health Care

Given the established link between child mental health and reduced educational and labor market outcomes and the evidence showing significant barriers to receiving care among youth, the CDC could pilot multiple ways to increase child and adolescent access to mental health care, including these:

- *Establish and/or expand school-based health clinics* so that they include more mental health providers.
- *Pilot telehealth access for children and youth in underserved areas.*

As noted previously, barriers to youth receiving mental health care include the constrained supply of mental health providers, which can result in either a lack of willing providers or, even if providers are available, long wait times. To increase the number of mental health and substance use disorder providers available to serve youth, the federal government could consider the following:

- *Increase funding for physician residency and fellowship positions in psychiatry and expand Medicare's Health Professional Shortage Area bonus program* to attract more mental health providers to underserved areas.
- *Expand funding for pediatric mental health integration and support mental health care telehealth access programs.*
- The Government Accountability Office could be directed to *report on Medicaid payment rates for mental health services compared with medical and surgical services across multiple states and, if justified, raise payment rates for the former.*

Reducing Child Exposure to Pollution

Resources provided to the CDC and the EPA would enable agencies to:

- *Develop guidelines and recommendations for schools to follow based on their needs and resources to increase the monitoring of air quality in indoor settings and reduce indoor air pollution*, particularly in schools. Partnerships could be established between the CDC and the EPA, the states, and local schools, so that air filtration systems are installed/improved as indicated.[11]
- *Issue more stringent EPA regulations of air pollution from vehicles, especially public transportation in dense areas.*
- *Strengthen EPA monitoring of Toxic Release Inventory (TRI) sites and consider regulating them to reduce children's exposure to toxic chemicals.*

Increasing Child Nutrition via WIC

Several steps could be taken to increase WIC enrollment among low-income women and children and eligibility for children who do not yet have access to school meals:

- Infant certification could be extended to 2 years to prevent churn and increase participation rates within the first 1,000 days. The cost estimate is $380 million.
- Adjunctive eligibility could be allowed for infants, children, and pregnant and post-partum individuals in households that participate in CHIP, Head Start, Early Head Start, or the Food Distribution Program on Indian Reservations. The committee was unable to develop a cost estimate for this policy change.
- Remote services could be provided, including virtual appointments through telephone and video conferencing, as well as remote benefits issuance. Based on COVID-19 changes to WIC rules, the committee estimates the additional cost of continuing remote services to be $53.8 million.

---

[11] Gilraine (2023) shows that air filtrations in schools reduced pollution and led to a 0.20 standard deviation increase in test scores. While this has not yet been linked with long-term outcomes, the evidence linking outdoor air pollution to greater mobility likely generalizes to the indoor setting.

6

Children's Family Income, Wealth, and Parental Employment

Family economic resources and parental employment during childhood play an important role in shaping the family, schooling, and neighborhood contexts where children develop. These contexts, in turn, are key for children's academic skills, health, and opportunities to secure good jobs when they become adults. Persistently low levels of family income, wealth, and employment may therefore be important drivers of intergenerational poverty, while policies that increase parental incomes, wealth, and employment may increase intergenerational mobility.

In assessing the role of family economic factors as a driver of intergenerational poverty, we begin with data on trends in U.S. incomes and wages and comparisons of the extent of child poverty in the United States and other industrialized Anglophone countries. Employment rates and earnings for lower-skilled workers in general—and for the women and people of color in this group in particular—remain lower than for other populations, despite wage growth for the bottom quintile in the late 2010s and early 2020s and supplementation from the work-based safety net. Moreover, gaps between workers and families at the bottom (and middle) of the income distribution and workers and families in the top tier grew substantially.

We then provide a brief review of the literature on the correlational and causal connections between children's household income, parental employment, and well-being in adulthood. With regard to household income, we point out that the introduction of safety net programs such as the Supplemental Nutrition Assistance Program (SNAP; formerly known as Food Stamps) and more recent changes in the Earned Income Tax Credit (EITC) appear to have reduced intergenerational poverty. However, the intergenerational impacts of further expanding safety-net benefits are less certain, especially if doing so does not also increase parental employment. Furthermore, rigorous evidence suggests that increased parental employment improves child outcomes only when it also raises family incomes. Evidence on the causal impact of wealth on intergenerational poverty is suggestive, but does not support strong conclusions.

Given direct evidence linking reductions in intergenerational poverty to programs that increase both family income and parental employment, the committee outlines several possible expansions of the EITC (perhaps accompanied by other changes in tax credits) that appear to be most likely to reduce intergenerational poverty. We then list a number of other program and policy ideas that are supported by indirect evidence.

TRENDS IN INCOME AND EARNINGS

Family Income and Child Poverty

To determine the extent to which family income is associated with intergenerational poverty, it is important to examine how intergenerational mobility is affected by both the absolute *levels* of family income and earnings and the degree of income and earnings *inequality* between low- and higher-skilled parents. Poverty persistence across generations would seem to relate most closely to the absolute levels of children's family income, in both childhood and adulthood. However, as reviewed in Chapter 2, evidence on trends in intergenerational mobility presented in Chetty et al. (2017) shows that while trends in national income play an important role, an even more significant factor is how the gains from economic growth are shared between families at the top and bottom of the income distribution. Accordingly, we will focus on the absolute levels of income and earnings as well as on inequality.

Trends in children's family income can best be illustrated by showing the evolution of the average household incomes of children whose families are in the bottom, middle, and top of the income distribution. Figure 6-1 provides this information for 1967–2019, using data from the U.S. Census Bureau. The income data include both the usual sources of cash income, such as earnings, and in-kind income sources including tax credits and payments from programs such as SNAP.[1] The average annual household

---

[1] Dollars of cash and in-kind income received in different years are adjusted for inflation using the Personal Consumption Expenditures Price Index (PCEPI). Inflation measured by the PCEPI over this period is more modest than when measured using another popular inflation adjustment, the CPI-U-RS, and thus inflation-adjusted measures increased more (or fell by less) than they would if we used the CPI-U-RS. Another possible adjustment for these kinds of income comparisons is for family sizes, which were considerably larger in the 1960s and 1970s than they are today. As noted in Chapter 5, cash and in-kind sources of transfer income, and the programs that provide them, may affect total household resources in the same ways.

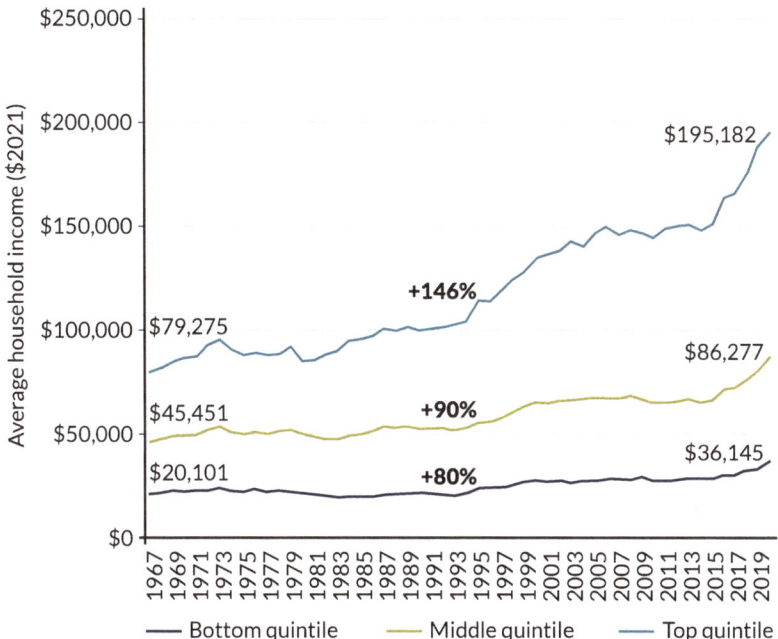

FIGURE 6-1 Average U.S. household income of children in the bottom, middle, and top income quintiles, 1967–2019.

NOTES: Figure 6-1 shows the average household incomes for children in the bottom, middle, and top income quintile. Household income includes all post-tax cash income and in-kind resources counted under the Supplemental Poverty Measure with the exception of nondiscretionary expenses. Adjustment to $2021 are made using the PCEPI. Due to higher rates of nonresponse to survey questions about income and resources at the top and bottom end of the income distribution, and to changes in the U.S. Census Bureau's top-coding procedure across time (Bollinger et al., 2018), we do not include households in the top or bottom 2.5% of the distribution when producing within-quintile averages in the top and bottom quintiles, respectively. See Appendix C: Chapter 6 for a discussion of the sensitivity of the results to this decision.

SOURCE: Data for 1967–2009 produced with the Historical Supplemental Poverty Measure Data series (Wimer et al., 2022) and the Annual Social and Economic Supplement to the Current Population Survey (CPS-ASEC) data from IPUMS-CPS (2022). Results for 2010 to 2020 produced with the CPS-ASEC data from IPUMS-CPS (2022). Income adjusted to $2021 using the PCEPI, produced by the U.S. Bureau of Economic Analysis and retrieved from FRED, Federal Reserve Bank of St. Louis.

incomes of children in the bottom quintile increased during this period by 80%, from about $20,000 to $36,000. For children in the middle of the income distribution, the increase amounted to more than $40,000, but the percentage change (+90%) was only a little larger than the increase for low-income children. Both absolute (+$116,000) and relative (+146%) household income increases were largest for children in families at the top of the distribution.

The near doubling of household incomes at the bottom end of the distribution over the past half century has significantly reduced child poverty. Using an Supplemental Poverty Measure (SPM)-based poverty measure, National Academies (2019a; Figure S-2) found that child poverty rates fell by 45% between 1967 and 2016. The U.S. Census Bureau documents further declines through 2020, although it still counted 9.7% of children as living in poverty in 2020 (Shrider and Creamer, 2023). Pandemic programs such as the expansion of the Child Tax Credit (CTC) produced a dramatic further reduction in the nation's child poverty rate—from 9.7% to 5.2%—between 2020 and 2021. However, the CTC expansion and other income-based pandemic programs ended in December 2021 and the SPM-based child poverty more than doubled to 12.4% in 2022 (Shrider & Creamer, 2023).

International Comparisons of Child Poverty Rates

The income gaps among children living in low-income, middle-class, and affluent families are larger in the United States than in other industrialized Anglophone countries. This is most evident in international comparisons of child poverty provided by the Organization for Economic Cooperation and Development (OECD), which typically use a poverty line defined by a certain fraction—often 50%—of each country's median income. In the case of the United States, median household income was about $68,000 in 2020. A poverty line based on 50% of median income would thus be $34,000, so any child living in a household with income below that amount would be counted as poor. In contrast to the poverty threshold approach to tracking poverty in the United States, these international comparisons rely on a *relative* definition of poverty based on the fraction of families whose income is low relative to overall income in the country.[2]

---

[2] National Academies (2019a) also provides international data on *absolute* child poverty, which involve translating the poverty thresholds in the United States, measured in dollars, into comparable thresholds based on other countries' currencies. Countries with the lowest per capita income will tend to have higher child poverty rates using absolute (rather than relative) poverty measure. As a result, relative to the United States, absolute child poverty is found to be higher in the United Kingdom and lower in other Anglophone countries. U.S. child poverty rates for 2021 are likely to compare more favorably to other countries because of the resources provided to low-income families through the CTC expansion and other pandemic relief measures.

Estimates of child poverty defined in this way for the United States and four English-speaking comparison countries are shown in Figure 6-2. At 20.9%, the rate of child poverty is much higher in the United States than in these peer countries—more than twice as high as in Ireland and more than 5 percentage points higher than in Canada, the country with the second-highest child poverty rate. More detailed analyses trace most of these differences to the much lower fractions of gross domestic product spent on safety-net programs such as child allowances in the United States relative to the comparison countries (National Academies, 2019a, Chapter 4).

Conclusion 6-1: When tax credits, Supplemental Nutrition Assistance Program benefits, and other noncash sources are counted as part of income, the family incomes of children on the bottom rungs of the income distribution have nearly doubled over the past 40 years, and rates of child poverty have been cut in half. The family incomes of children on the middle rungs have grown a bit faster, while those of children on the top rungs have grown much faster. Child poverty in the United States is considerably higher than in other Anglophone countries when poverty is measured by relative income position.

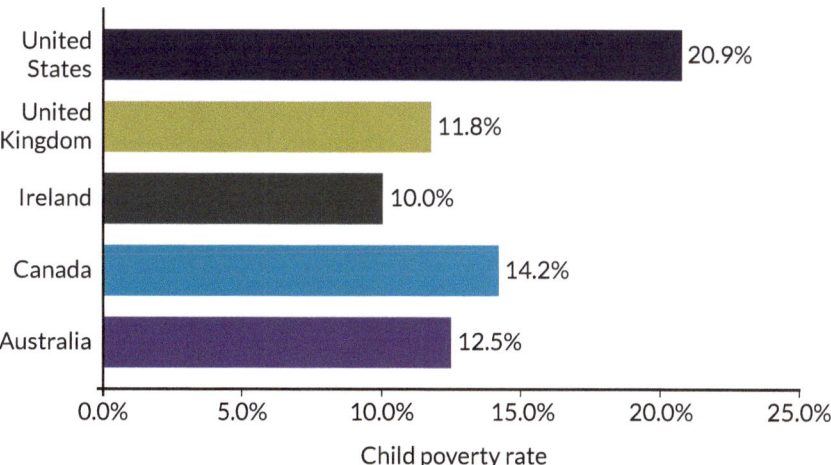

FIGURE 6-2 Child poverty in the United States and four other anglophone countries, 2016.
NOTES: Poverty is measured by the Organization for Economic Cooperation and Development-50 poverty rate, which is defined as 50% below each country's median income. All data are for 2016, the most recent year available.
SOURCE: Data from OECD Stats, https://stats.oecd.org/

Trends in Earnings and Employment

Parents' employment has always been and remains one of the most important means of avoiding intergenerational poverty. Over the last 50 years, earned income alone lifted the incomes of between 70% and 75% of children above the poverty line (National Academies, 2019a, Figure 4-1). Like family incomes, the earnings of low- and middle-skilled workers have risen more slowly than the earnings of higher-skilled workers (Figure 6-3).[3] Between 1973 and 2019, the average hourly earnings for workers at the 10th and 50th percentiles grew by about 25%. Worker wages at the 90th percentile grew by more than twice that amount. The gaps between the earnings of workers in these various groups are generally larger in the United States than in most other industrial countries, and for the most part they have grown more quickly here than elsewhere over the past four decades (Bourguignon, 2022).

Causes of Labor Market Trends

To design effective policies to raise parental earnings among those living below poverty, it is important to understand the causes of low levels of employment and earnings and their impact on inequality. Although scholars continue to debate these causes, they point to three sets of factors in the U.S. labor market:

- Competitive market forces, like technological change and globalization, that have favored higher-skilled workers much more than their lower-skilled counterparts;
- Structural problems in labor markets, such as the fact that firms have more access to labor market information than workers do and the often-high costs to workers of changing jobs, both of which can increase the relative power of employers and lead to lower wages for workers; and
- Weakening laws and institutions, leading to stagnant federal minimum wages and a smaller share of workers who are union members.[4]

---

[3] The wage data presented in this chapter end in 2019—just before the onset of the COVID-19 pandemic. The committee judged that it was too soon to interpret wage trends during COVID, given high inflation and large fluctuations in unemployment.

[4] These three factors help explain why less of the nation's productivity growth in recent decades has gone to less-educated U.S. workers than to highly-educated workers and employers, compared with the period right after World War II. Rising health care costs also help account for a growing gap between worker earnings and productivity (Saez & Zucman, 2019); and U.S. productivity growth has also slowed over time, and this slowdown still contributes to the lower earnings growth of all workers (Stansbury & Summers, 2017).

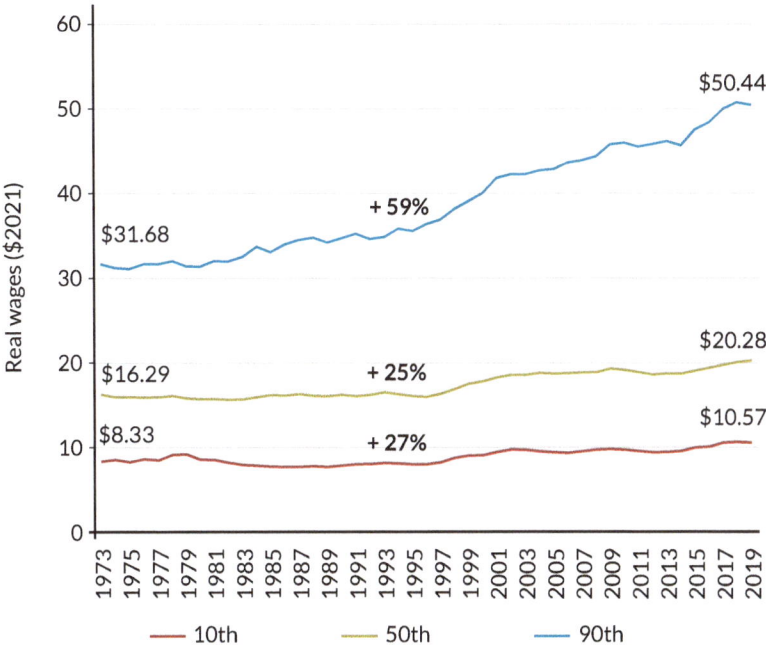

FIGURE 6-3 Average real wages in the United States for the 10th, 50th, and 90th percentiles, 1973–2019.
NOTE: Average hourly wages are reported for those who are 16 years or older and are adjusted to $2021 by the PCEPI.
SOURCE: Data from Economic Policy Institute (2022a).

Technological Change and Globalization

Many economists believe that technological changes in the digital era (and earlier) are behind the increasing gap between low- and higher-skilled workers, since many of these changes have favored and rewarded workers with college degrees more than less-skilled workers. Technological changes—and globalization—have restructured the labor market by reducing the amount of "routine" work required by middle- and high-wage jobs. Today jobs in the middle of the wage distribution—in technical aspects of health care or in advanced manufacturing or information technology, for example—usually require some postsecondary skills and credentials, making it much harder for many low-income workers to secure them (Holzer,

2015; Strain, 2020). Increasingly, the labor market also rewards a range of socioemotional skills—such as interpersonal skills and the ability to communicate and work in teams (Orrell, 2021).

Globalization in its many forms—including an expansion of trade in goods and services, as well as immigration—probably reinforces this trend, as good-paying jobs for workers without college degrees in durable manufacturing and other industries have become scarcer as a result of automation and foreign competition (Autor et al., 2008). Labor-market changes favoring higher-skilled workers have laid the groundwork for the impressive successes of a number of career training programs and form the basis for career training policies considered in Chapter 4.

The labor market that children in families living below poverty will enter will continue to evolve, as new forms of robotics and artificial intelligence (AI) become established throughout the economy. Whether the same skills will continue to be compensated well over time remains quite uncertain, as AI gains the ability to perform a much wider range of tasks that have previously required human capabilities (Autor, 2022). Workers will need a solid base of general skills—often referred to as 21st century skills (National Research Council, 2012)—if they are to adapt to changes in the specific skills that the labor market demands and rewards at a given time and place.

Structural Problems in Labor Markets

A second set of explanations for low wages and labor-market inequality focuses on non-competitive forces in the U.S. labor market, which give employers power to set lower wages than they could if the labor market were fully competitive.[5] The importance of these factors is reflected in the substantial difference between the earnings of apparently comparable workers who are employed by different firms. Many, but not all, firms have aggressively cut wages, particularly for less-educated workers. At the other end of the spectrum are firms that choose to pay above-market wages and create "good jobs" by investing heavily in worker skills and performance (Osterman, 2018; Ton, 2014). Indeed, high-wage firms can create a "public good" by raising worker productivity and wages. Economists argue that public goods might merit public support (e.g., in this case subsidies or technical assistance)—although there is little evidence to date on the effectiveness of strategies to encourage the creation of "good jobs."

---

[5] Economists refer to the power employers have to lower wages when they face limited competition for workers as "monopsony power." Monopsony can have many causes, ranging from a literal market concentration of employers (e.g., in company towns) to frictions in the job search process or anti-competitive collusion among employers through tools such as non-compete agreements (Card, 2022; Nunn & Hunt, 2021).

Weakening Laws and Institutions

A third set of explanations involves institutional factors, including legislation, that may have slowed wage growth over time, particularly for workers without college degrees. Historically, labor unions have helped to balance power in the labor market and enabled workers to bargain effectively with their employers. Recent studies indicate that unions have increased members' wages by about 10% to 20% (Farber et al., 2018). However, the prevalence of unions in the United States has declined precipitously. Today only 11.6% of U.S. workers represented by unions (Macpherson & Hirsch, 2021), as compared with 30% of U.S. workers in the 1950s and the current average of 33.1% in countries belonging to the OECD (2019). U.S. unionization is increasingly concentrated in the public sector with only 7.0% of private-sector workers represented by unions. Given the relatively high wage rates of unionized workers, the relevance of unions for the economic status of parents who would otherwise be experiencing poverty remains subject to debate, since it has always been very difficult for unskilled workers in the bottom decile or quintile of earnings in the United States to unionize (Hirsch, 1980).

Legislatively mandated minimum wages have failed to keep pace with the cost of living, contributing to wage stagnation among lower-skilled workers in general and workers of color in particular (Brown & Hamermesh, 2019; Derenoncourt & Montialoux, 2021). The 2022 federal minimum wage was $7.25 per hour, its lowest value in real terms (using the personal consumptions expenditure inflation index) since 2007 (and, before that, since 1996).[6] By setting minimum wages above the federal level, a number of states and some cities have offset this decline to some extent, although many U.S. jobs are in states and localities that have not raised the statutory minimum above the federal level.[7]

Economists continue to debate whether higher minimum wages reduce employment among the youngest and least-educated workers—and if so, by how much (Burkhauser et al., 2023; Cengiz et al., 2019). Some evidence (Clemens & Strain, 2021; Sorkin, 2015) suggests that minimum wage increases have larger long-run negative effects, and that large increases are particularly problematic, although there is disagreement about these conclusions as well. Economists also disagree about the extent to which higher minimum wages can reduce poverty.

---

[6] Using the Consumer Price Index to measure inflation, the real value of the minimum wage is now at its lowest level since the 1950s.

[7] In 2022, more than 30 states raised their minimum wages above the federal statutory level of $7.25, as have several major cities (New York, NY, Los Angeles, CA, Seattle, WA, San Francisco, CA, Washington, DC, and many others).

Conclusion 6-2: Low wages among less-educated workers (including lower-skilled workers who are parents) over the last several decades in the United States can be attributed largely to three factors: competitive market forces, such as technological change and globalization, which have increased skill requirements for middle-class jobs; structural problems, as limited information for employees and the costs associated with changing jobs have strengthened the bargaining power of employers and reduced the power of employees; and weakening laws and institutions, such as federal minimum wages and unionization.

Causes of Unequal Employment and Earnings by Gender and Race

Both wage levels and employment rates show important differences by gender and by race. Figure 6-4 shows the median wages of full-time wage and salary workers by race and gender, while Figure 6-5 presents employment rates for these groups. They show that:

- Median wages among Black and Latino workers are well below the wages of White workers, and this holds true for both men and women. At the same time, wages for women are below men's wages for all subgroups.
- Employment among women continues to lag behind that of men within each racial group.
- Employment of Black men lags substantially behind that of other men.[8]

While the wages and employment rates of women relative to men improved greatly during the second half of the 20th century, progress largely slowed or ceased after 2000 (Blau & Kahn, 2017). Many economists believe that the conflicting demands of employment and caregiving responsibilities contribute to this persistent gender gap (Black et al., 2017; Goldin, 2021). This is a particular challenge for low-wage women, since the cost of child care relative to their wages can be very high (Borowsky et al., 2022).

---

[8] Figure 6-5 shows employment rates for the "noninstitutional" population, which excludes inmates. In 2018, 1.5% of Black men were incarcerated—a rate that was twice as high as for Latino men and five times as high as the White rate. https://www.pewresearch.org/fact-tank/2020/05/06/share-of-black-white-hispanic-americans-in-prison-2018-vs-2006/. Low-income Black men in the population are also significantly undercounted. As a result, the official employment counts for Black men are biased upwards, and racial employment and labor-force gaps are actually wider than those shown in Figure 6-5 (Holzer, 2021).

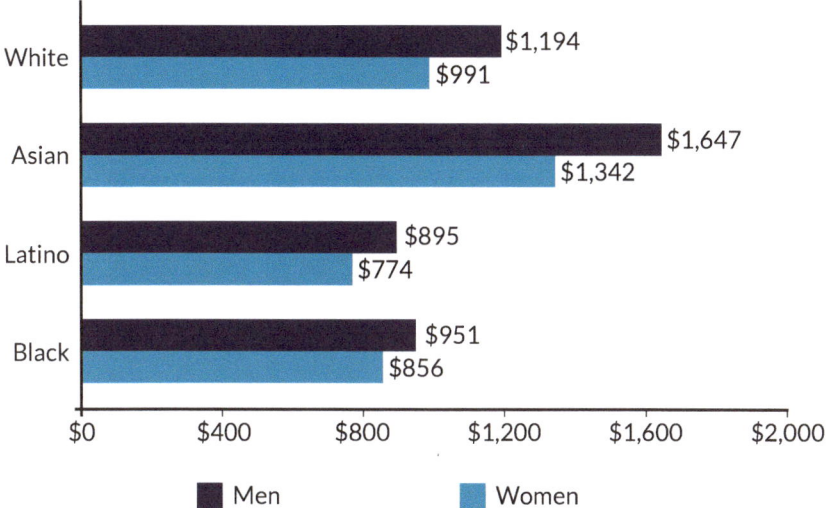

FIGURE 6-4 Median usual weekly earnings of full-time wage and salary workers by race/ethnicity and sex, 4th quarter 2022 averages.
NOTES: Data are for wage and salary workers ages 16 and older. Persons whose ethnicity is identified as Hispanic or Latino may be of any race. Data on Native American and Alaska Natives are not reported.
SOURCE: Data from the U.S. Bureau of Labor Statistics (2023).

Policies that increase maternal employment could have deleterious effects on child development if parents are unable to secure high-quality child care. Rigorous evidence shows that expansions of the federal Child Care and Development Fund's child care subsidies prior to the revision of that program in 2014 increased maternal employment, but also may have worsened child development outcomes (Herbst & Tekin, 2010; see also Baker et al., 2019, and Chapter 4). The 2014 revisions expanded access to higher quality child care, but whether they have improved child outcomes remains uncertain (Johnson & Ryan, 2015). Increasing the generosity of child and dependent care tax credit payments to low-income parents may also increase employment, although the impacts of those types of increases have not been studied.

Substantial disparities in both employment and earnings remain between White workers and both Black and Latino workers, at least partly because of discrimination (Charles & Guryan, 2008; see also Chapter 3).

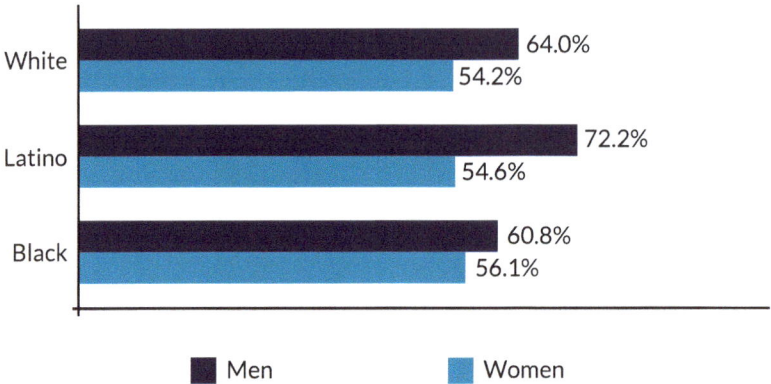

FIGURE 6-5 Employment-to-population ratios by race and gender, November 2022.
NOTE: Data show the share of the civilian noninstitutional population ages 16 and older who are employed.
SOURCE: Data from Economic Policy Institute (2022b).

Owing to low employment and labor force participation rates, the annual earnings of Black men are lower than those of White men (Bayer & Charles, 2018; Holzer, 2021)—especially in the case of previously incarcerated people. The lower employment rates and earnings of Black men reentering the labor market after incarceration reflect their lower skills and work experience, but also their lack of access to social networks that might help them get jobs and, as confirmed in a number of rigorous studies, clear discrimination by employers (Holzer et al., 2003; Pager, 2003). Employers tend to fear poor work performance or even criminal conduct, even when the risks of recidivism are very low (Bushway et al., 2022). However, tight labor markets are known to reduce discrimination against people of color (Holzer et al., 2006) and vulnerable workers, including those with criminal records or disabilities (Shambaugh & Strain, 2021).

Conclusion 6-3: Earnings and employment gaps by gender, especially among less-educated women, can probably be attributed in part to difficulties securing affordable and high-quality child care. Gaps by race, especially between Black and other groups of men, reflect differences in skill and experience, but also reflect discrimination and other barriers to employment. Discriminatory barriers appear to be especially severe for previously incarcerated men, particularly Black men.

DO FAMILY INCOME, PARENTAL EMPLOYMENT, AND EARNINGS DURING CHILDHOOD DRIVE INTERGENERATIONAL POVERTY?

Childhood Poverty and Intergenerational Outcomes

A child growing up below the poverty line experiences worse outcomes, on average, than a child from a nonpoor family in virtually every dimension. In its review of the relevant literature, the National Academies' 2019 report, *A Roadmap to Reducing Child Poverty,* documented worse outcomes for children in poverty ranging from physical and mental health to completed schooling and from labor market success to risky behaviors and delinquency (National Academies, 2019a). But the largely correlational evidence on which that conclusion is based does not prove that policy-driven increases in the family incomes of children who are in households living below poverty would reduce intergenerational poverty. Income-based childhood poverty is associated with a cluster of other disadvantages for children, including low levels of parental education and living with a single parent (Currie et al., 2013). Are the differences between the life chances of children living in poverty and other children a product of differences in childhood economic resources per se, or do they stem from these other, correlated conditions?

It is easy to think of reasons why income itself matters. Families with higher incomes are better able to meet their children's basic needs and to invest in goods and services for their families, such as toys and books that provide cognitive stimulation as well as higher-quality nonparental child care and enrichment activities. Moreover, higher incomes may allow parents to reduce or restructure their work hours to spend more time interacting with their children (Becker, 1991). A complementary "stress" perspective focuses on possible links between economic hardship and parental psychological distress. Psychological distress can spill over into couple relationships and can trigger harsher, inconsistent, and more detached parenting (Brody et al., 1994; Conger et al., 1994). Such lower-quality parenting may, in turn, harm children's cognitive and socioemotional development (Conger et al., 2002; McLoyd, 1990).

Causal Studies

The National Academies (2019a) poverty report moved beyond the correlational literature to focus its attention on studies that attempted to estimate the causal impacts of childhood poverty on children. It considered studies of poverty impacts on both short- and longer-run outcomes, as well as studies of programs such as Food Stamps (now SNAP) and Medicaid that were introduced decades ago. The report's overall conclusion was that

> (t)he weight of the causal evidence indicates that income poverty itself causes negative child outcomes, especially when it begins in early childhood and/or persists throughout a large share of a child's life. Many programs that alleviate poverty either directly, by providing income transfers, or indirectly, by providing food, housing, or medical care, have been shown to improve child well-being (National Academies, 2019a, p. 89).

Of particular interest for the current report is the subset of studies that provide causal evidence regarding intergenerational poverty; for example, those that link poverty in childhood to children's adult economic well-being. One example is the Aizer et al. (2016a) study of the Mother's Pension Program, which was rolled out during the first three decades of the 20th century. The study found that receipt of benefits in childhood led to an increase in completed schooling and earnings and improvements in adult health. A more recent example is the Hoynes et al. (2016) evaluation of the county-based roll-out of the Food Stamp program in the 1960s and 1970s, which linked the timing of the availability of Food Stamps during childhood to a strong correlate of adult economic status: adult cardiovascular health. It found that the availability of Food Stamps prior to conception or surrounding birth was associated with substantially lower rates of cardiovascular symptoms in adulthood than when Food Stamps first became available later in childhood or in adolescence.

Both the Aizer et al. (2016a) and the Hoynes et al. (2016) studies provide strong evidence that cash or near-cash programs can reduce intergenerational poverty. In both cases, however, the program benefits were first provided five or more decades ago—at a time when the economic conditions faced by low-income families were far worse than they are today. Those conditions set a much lower bar for improvement than was the case in the more recent past or would be today.

An example of more recent research on the intergenerational impacts of safety net policies is Barr et al.'s (2022) study of the availability of child tax credits like the EITC and CTC very early in life. They took advantage of the fact that the families of children born just before January 1 received the tax credits for the baby (which averaged $1,300) for virtually all the child's first year of life, whereas families of children born just after January 1 were not eligible for the extra year of tax credit until the final (18th) year of the child's eligibility. In this case, the total amount of tax credits received for the two groups is the same, but the first group received the extra benefits when the children were infants rather than adolescents. Using data on children born during the 1980s and 1990s, the study found small but statistically significant adult earnings advantages for the early-receipt group. This study reinforces the conclusions of the Hoynes et al. (2016) food stamp study by highlighting the importance of income in the early years of life. Barr et al. (2022) repeated their analyses using data from school records in North Carolina for children born in the 1990s. Here again they found positive impacts for the extra income in the first year of life, specifically on a number of achievement score and behavioral outcomes.

Studies Focused on the Intergenerational Impacts of the EITC

Yet another group of studies has taken advantage of the fact that, beginning in the mid-1990s, many states enacted supplements to federal EITC payments (which are the same regardless of where recipients live). Using this information, Bastian and Michelmore (2018) found causal links between the timing and generosity of the state EITC supplement and children's completed schooling, employment, and earnings in early adulthood. Specifically, each additional $1,000 of state EITC availability during adolescence was associated with a 4.2% increase in children's completing college, a 1.0% increase in their employment, and a 2.2% increase in their early-adult earnings. In contrast to the Barr et al. (2022) tax credit study and the Hoynes et al. study of the roll-out of the Food Stamp program, Bastian and Michelmore (2018) found that EITC-induced income increases in adolescence were more potent predictors of children's adult outcomes than were income increases earlier in childhood.

As described in Appendix C: Chapter 6, other EITC studies based on variation in cross-time or cross-state payment generosity have found impacts on childhood correlates of adult well-being: children's test scores (Dahl & Lochner, 2012), behavior problems (Hamad & Rehkopf, 2016), college enrollment (Manoli & Turner, 2014), birthweight (Hoynes et al., 2015), and food insecurity (Batra & Hamad, 2021). EITC-based studies generally show both short-run and intergenerational impacts for children, but they differ in their conclusions as to whether effects are larger for EITC payments received while young or later in childhood. Some EITC-based studies suggest that the benefits of the EITC to families and children may be larger for Black individuals than other recipients. For example, Komro et al. (2019) and Batra et al. (2022) found larger effects of state and federal EITC benefits for birth outcomes among Black mothers. Racial/ethnic differences in the literature linking EITC receipt to adult outcomes have not been reported.

When looking at this EITC evidence, it is important to bear in mind that the program creates powerful work incentives for most recipients, and research has shown that it does in fact increase employment among poor single mothers (Nichols & Rothstein, 2016; Schanzenbach & Strain, 2021). The program's simultaneous impacts on both household income and parental employment make it difficult to determine just how much of the program's beneficial impact on children comes from its boost to household resources and how much from an increase in parental employment or work hours.

Other Noteworthy Causal Studies of the Intergenerational Impacts of Income Supplementation

Among the relatively few recent studies of the possible intergenerational benefits of increases in family income, in the absence of increases in employment, is the Jacob et al. (2015) comparison of children in families that won the lottery to receive Section 8 housing vouchers in Chicago with children in families that lost that lottery. These researchers found virtually no differences between the two groups in educational achievement and attainment, criminal involvement, or health care utilization, even in the case of children who were very young at the time of the lottery.

Other researchers have taken advantage of actual lotteries that are structured to pay out large prizes in installments over many years, thus creating random variation in household income between lottery winners and losers. Cesarini et al. (2017) find that Swedish lottery wins lead to more health care utilization by winners' children but have no effect on academic performance. Bulman et al. (2021) examine impacts of lottery wins on college attendance in the United States. Impacts are modest at best and no larger for children in low- than those in high-income families, even when the money was won when the children were young. This suggests no more than a modest role for pure income supplementation, at least with regard to promoting college attendance.

Other studies provide more support for causal impacts of income supplementation. In particular, using data on children from western North Carolina with an oversample of Cherokee Indians, Akee et al. (2010) and Akee et al. (2018) find that unexpected income increases from the distribution of casino winnings to Cherokee youth and their parents reduce symptoms of both behavioral and emotional disorders and also increase the probability that the Cherokee youth would graduate from high school.[9] The

---

[9] The strength of the evidence of income effects on completed schooling is weakened by the fact that the structure of payouts to youth required that they earn high school degrees prior to age 21.

intergenerational evidence on income supplementation does not allow for unambiguous conclusions; EITC-based studies suggest that children benefit when income supplementation is coupled with increases in parental employment, but they may or may not benefit from pure income supplementation.

A different interpretation of the evidence concludes that children may benefit more when parents perceive that the income supplementation is intended for their children. The CTC clearly encourages that perception, and qualitative accounts of parents who receive the EITC also suggest that many believe that EITC dollars are "kids' money" that should be disproportionately directed toward children's consumption needs (Sykes et al., 2015). Emerging evidence from a clinical trial of a monthly cash supplement labeled "4MyBaby" indicates that parents allocate a much larger fraction of the cash supplement, relative to other income sources, to child-related expenditures such as books and toys (Gennetian et al., 2022). Messaged connections between income supplementation and child expenditures are weaker in the case of lotteries and assistance from programs providing Housing Choice Vouchers.

Conclusion 6-4: Evidence suggests that income transfer programs during childhood and adolescence have the potential to improve children's educational and labor market attainment, as well as their physical health, in adulthood. Studies examining policy changes over the past 30 years provide the strongest evidence for intergenerational impacts of expansions of the Earned Income Tax Credit, which increases both employment and income.

Parental Employment and Intergenerational Outcomes

As noted above, programs like the EITC increase both family incomes and parental employment, and it is unclear which effect is responsible for its beneficial impacts on children. Studies of the effect of incomes on intergenerational poverty are reviewed above. Here, we focus on parental employment. Higher levels of parental employment might reduce intergenerational poverty by

- Increasing childhood access to public benefits from the work-based safety net,
- Creating positive parental role models and social networks that boost the future employment and earnings of children, and
- Increasing neighborhood employment or earnings, thereby perhaps expanding children's access to job networks and role models.

These are reviewed in turn.

Increased Access to Work-Based Safety-Net Benefits

Because so much of the U.S. safety net is tied to work, increasing employment and earnings among parents living below poverty may also increase family income by increasing the family's access to benefits from programs such as the federal EITC and state supplements to that program. As shown above, strong evidence links parental receipt of the EITC to improved child outcomes and children's earnings in adulthood, presumably through some combination of increased parental income, employment, and earnings (during the EITC's phase-in range of income).[10] On the other hand, employment-based benefits are, by design, not provided to low-income families whose members are unable or unwilling to work, which can limit the intergenerational mobility of children growing up in these families.

Role Modeling

Parental employment might benefit children by creating positive role models or by expanding parents' social networks in ways that improve their children's access to better jobs. On the other hand, children's development, especially in the case of young children, might be compromised if children are placed in substandard child care or if the often-erratic work schedules of parents provide less continuity at home and limits the time parents can spend interacting with their children. While there is very little evidence on the mechanisms of role modeling and social networks, the possible benefits or harms to children from parental employment *per se* have been studied for years. On balance, this literature shows neither strong benefits nor harm to children from parental employment.

---

[10] Barr et al. (2022) show impacts of the EITC on children's earnings in adulthood that are larger than can be attributed solely to increases in parental employment. On the other hand, Dahl and Lochner (2012) estimate education gains that are larger than can be attributed to earnings and income increases alone. Some policy makers consider the EITC and other work-based public benefits (like subsidized child care) to be preferable to unconditional cash assistance to the poor, which can reduce the work effort of parents. The estimated wage and income elasticities of labor supply in the United States suggest that employment will rise when the wages of the poor are subsidized, but fall if these subsidies are replaced with unconditional cash transfers, including child tax credits. Corinth et al. (2021) argue that the CTC expansion of 2021 would be likely to substantially reduce maternal employment. Using similar methods but different assumptions about the magnitude of wage elasticities, Goldin et al. (2021) estimate a much smaller labor supply response. Ananat (2022) showed very small, if any, negative effects on employment rates associated with the increases in the CTC of 2021, though a permanent increase in the CTC might have larger employment effects than the temporary 2021 credit; and Baker et al. (2021) find virtually no negative effects of child allowances on maternal employment in Canada.

Some of the most rigorous evidence on the effects of parental employment comes from random-assignment evaluations of state welfare reforms made during the 1990s. Some reforms increased maternal employment, but because benefits were reduced dollar-for-dollar as earnings increased, they did not raise family income. Others boosted both maternal employment and family income. There was no evidence from the first set that income-neutral increases in maternal employment either hurt or helped children's school achievement. Consistent with the EITC-based evidence reviewed above, however, the second set of reforms—which increased both work and family income—produced positive benefits for children, at least in the short run (Duncan et al., 2011). Schildberg-Horisch (2016) provides a more general review of the literature and concludes that most studies fail to find any effect of maternal employment *per se*—positive or negative—on a child's short- or long-term educational attainment.

Some evidence suggests that parental employment may have different impacts on child outcomes by child gender and that a mother's employment very early in the life of a child can have negative impacts on the child (Hill et al., 2005). Furthermore, involuntary employment loss among mothers and fathers may have different impacts on children: Mothers spend more time with their children after losing a job, which offsets the negative effects of their lost income. In contrast, loss of employment does not appear to induce fathers to spend more time with their children or to improve child outcomes (Lindo et al., 2013; Page et al., 2016).

Neighborhood Employment Effects

As discussed in Chapters 2 and 8, increasing parental employment at the neighborhood level might benefit children in the ways suggested by Wilson (1987, 1996)—perhaps through peer effects on behavior as well as through social networks. Correlational evidence shows positive associations between neighborhood employment and the mobility of children later in life (Chetty & Hendren, 2018; Chetty et al., 2016), but there has been no rigorous research on this question.

Conclusion 6-5: Higher parental earnings and employment among low-income families can potentially reduce intergenerational poverty by raising family income, increasing access to the Earned Income Tax Credit (EITC) and other safety-net benefits, and—at both the family and neighborhood levels—providing positive role models and access to good jobs through social networks. Interventions such as the EITC that promote employment and increase income improve children's long-run outcomes; interventions that promote employment in the absence of increased income do not appear to improve child outcomes; and evidence on whether income supplementation alone improves long-term child outcomes is inconclusive, with some studies showing positive effects and others showing no improvement.

WEALTH AND INTERGENERATIONAL POVERTY

Wealth and income are distinct from one another, and each may play an independent role in the perpetuation or alleviation of intergenerational poverty. A common economic measure of wealth is net worth, which is the sum of a household's financial assets (e.g., savings) and nonfinancial assets (e.g., housing equity) minus the sum of all debts or liabilities. In other words, net worth is a point-in-time accounting of assets and liabilities. In contrast, household income refers to the flow of economic resources received by a household over some period, typically a calendar year. Elderly-couple households often have relatively modest annual incomes but may have accumulated substantial net worth, particularly if they have owned a house in an area with rapidly rising housing prices. The families of children, particularly young children with parents in the early stages of adulthood, often have both modest incomes and low (or even negative) net worth, when total debt surpasses total assets, for example if they have accumulated debt to finance their postsecondary education.

Black and Latino families have much less wealth, on average, than White families (Figure 6-6). In the case of Black families, some of these differences may be traced to discriminatory policies like redlining that prevented the accumulation of wealth among Black people (Chapter 3). Black households hold less than 3% of the nation's wealth, despite constituting 14% of the nation's population. Their wealth position is also more fragile. Moreover, they are significantly less able to transfer an improved wealth position to their children (Pfeffer & Killewald, 2019). Kerman and Wong (2021) also show that distressed sales of homes, often associated with unstable household income, contribute significantly to the gap in housing wealth between Black and White families.

In the short term, wealth can buffer families against unexpected events such as unemployment, whereas wealth accumulated over the life course can provide economic security in older age or be passed on to children. In the case of intergenerational poverty, low-income families with higher net worth may be able to use their wealth to pay for their children's education or provide a more stable, safer, or healthier environment for them as they grow up; this, in turn, might reduce the children's chances of being low

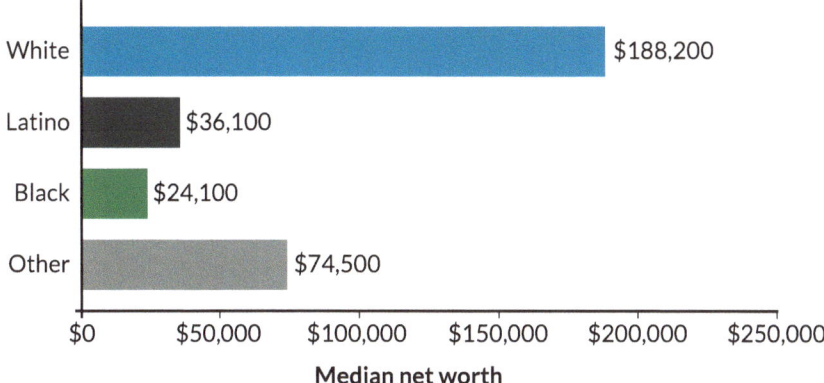

FIGURE 6-6 Median net worth of U.S. families in 2019.
SOURCE: Data from Federal Reserve Board, 2019 Survey of Consumer Finances. https://www.federalreserve.gov/econres/scfindex.htm

income in adulthood. By the same token, wealth-augmenting interventions such as "baby bonds" (described below) might help parents overcome financial obstacles that stand in the way of their children's success.

Because surveys rarely ask about wealth and its components, wealth is rarely included in discussions of child poverty. Income and wealth are often presumed to be highly correlated, and a low-income household is also assumed to be a wealth-poor household. Using a definition of "net-worth poverty" defined as possessing assets worth just one-fourth of the federal poverty line and data from the Surveys of Consumer Finances, Gibson-Davis et al. (2021) find that three times as many households with children are in poverty when it is defined by net worth rather than income, and that the fraction of households that are in poverty based on both net worth *and* income is considerably higher among Black (16%) and Latino (14%) households with children than White households (5%).

Household Wealth and Intergenerational Outcomes

Correlational Studies

Parental wealth or its components are highly predictive of child outcomes, based on a number of correlational studies. Most studies focus on postsecondary schooling outcomes, since parents may use their financial resources to help their children attend postsecondary institutions, contribute to meeting college expenses, and incur debt on behalf of their children (Hotz et al., 2021). This may be a contributing factor explaining why college attainment has also become increasingly unequal, as children from higher-net-worth families are more likely to attend college and graduate with 4-year degrees (Pfeffer, 2018). In an international context, Karagiannaki (2017) in Britain as well as Hällsten and Pfeffer (2017) in Sweden found similar relationships when they examined parental wealth and adult child educational and labor outcomes.

The amount that parents are able to save for their children's college is positively associated with household income. About one-third of households with less than $35,000 in total annual income reported saving for college; this was true of almost all (91%) households making more than $150,000 (Black & Huelsman, 2012). Parental wealth is associated with increased college enrollment and attendance (Conley, 2001; Doren & Grodsky, 2016; Williams et al., 2009), choosing a 4-year selective college over a 4-year nonselective one (Jez, 2014), and with less undergraduate student debt (Addo et al., 2016; Jackson & Reynolds, 2013). Parental savings earmarked for higher education are associated with increases in attendance (Charles et al., 2007) and college retention (Elliott & Beverly, 2011), as well as reductions in the child's education debt (Elliott et al., 2014).

Children from wealthier families are more likely to attend college and complete their degrees (Conley, 1999; Jackson & Reynolds, 2013). It is also very common in the United States for parents to provide financial transfers to their children for educational purposes, which are facilitated by greater familial wealth (Taylor & Meschede, 2018). When wealth was disaggregated, liquid assets predicted the likelihood of college graduation (Zhan & Sherradan, 2011), and unsecured debt was negatively associated with graduating (Nam & Huang, 2009; Yeung & Conley, 2008; Zhan & Sherradan, 2011).

Fewer studies focus on links between parental wealth and child labor outcomes in adulthood. Toney and Robertson (2021) connect familial wealth to children's income returns and document a positive correlation between parental and grandparental wealth and younger generations' income levels. Fox (2016) found heterogeneous associations between parental wealth and income mobility among Black and White households, with increasing upward income mobility for low-income White families but not low-income Black families.

Causal Studies

Evaluating the likely impacts of wealth interventions requires an understanding of the causal relationship between parental wealth and child outcomes. Causal studies are typically based on the effects of wealth changes that are beyond the control of individual households. One approach is to relate changes in local housing market values to child outcomes. Lovenheim (2011) and Lovenheim and Reynolds (2013) took this approach, focusing on the consequences of housing market–induced changes in parental wealth a few years before children would be expected to start college. Lovenheim (2011) found that students from low- and middle-income families were more likely to attend college when families experienced gains in housing wealth. An additional $10,000 of housing equity increased college attendance by 6 percentage points. It was also associated with families selecting higher-quality schools, and children graduating with a 4-year degree. Lovenheim and Reynolds (2013) found that an increase in home equity is associated with sending children to flagship universities over non-flagship schools. Using a similar causal-modeling approach, Hotz et al. (2021) found that greater housing equity increased college attendance and completion, but did not reduce children's student debt. Cooper and Luengo-Prado (2015) found that parental wealth increases children's labor income when they become adults.

Because lotteries can be thought of as a wealth transfer paid in monthly or annual installments, the aforementioned Bulman et al. (2021) study of lottery-winning households is relevant to the discussion of the effects of wealth and income. As discussed above, it found no more than weak linkages to college attendance among children of low-income parents, and it failed to generate strong support for a wealth-effect hypothesis.

While these studies come closer to estimating causal relationships, there are reasons to be concerned about whether the results for lottery winners or homeowners generalize to low-income families. All told, the literature offers no strong evidence as to whether increases in the wealth of low-income families might be expected to reduce intergenerational poverty.

> *Conclusion 6-6: Controlling for income, family wealth is strongly correlated with children's adult outcomes. There is mixed evidence on the causal impact of wealth transfers on children's long-run outcomes. Black families, having significantly less wealth than White families, are more likely to be both income- and wealth-poor, and more likely to experience downward intergenerational wealth mobility. No causal studies have examined differential wealth impacts by race.*

INTERVENTIONS INVOLVING CHILDREN'S FAMILY INCOME AND WEALTH AND PARENTAL EMPLOYMENT

The committee's key task is to use the evidence reviewed above to identify income- and employment-based policies and programs with the potential to reduce intergenerational poverty. As explained in Chapter 1, we characterize the evidence on some of the programs or policies as "strong" and denote them with an "*." This indicates that the program's or policy's impact on intergenerational poverty is supported by random-assignment evaluation evidence that has been replicated across several sites or by compelling quasi-experimental evidence based on national or multi-state data or a scaled-up program. In this case, the evidence supporting all three of our direct-evidence policy ideas was judged to be "strong."

However, this section also lists policy and program ideas for which supporting evidence is indirect and therefore less certain.

Policy and Program Ideas Based on Direct Evidence

Expanding the Earned Income Tax Credit

The committee's review of the literature on the intergenerational impacts of policy-induced changes in children's family income and wealth, as well as parental employment, reveals several promising approaches, but few have been proven to be effective. The strongest direct evidence on the likely intergenerational effects for children is found for programs that increase both family income and parental employment during childhood and adolescence. This leads us to consider potential expansions to tax credits that would produce such increases. The policy research literature does not tell us from which income levels increases are most effective at reducing intergenerational poverty, nor does it identify the most powerful combinations of increased income and employment for enhancing intergenerational mobility. Accordingly, we present three options for reforms with different features. All are presented as modifications to the EITC program, although it would also be possible to link such reforms to other tax credits (such as the CTC). The first option scales up the existing EITC proportionally. The second concentrates the expansion among very low earners. The third adjusts the credit to provide income to nonworkers while still strengthening the incentive to work that is a key feature of the current EITC.

- **EITC Option 1: Expand the EITC by increasing payments by 40% across the entire schedule, keeping the current range of the phase-out region.** This option is the most straightforward because it would simply increase the amounts of existing credits by 40%. It is illustrated in the upper-left panel of Figure 6-7 for the example of a single mother with two children and detailed in Appendix C: Chapter 6. This EITC reform was also included as "EITC #2" in the National Academies (2019a) report. That report estimated the annual cost of this EITC expansion to be $20.4 billion and predicted that it would increase employment among low-income adults by 548,000 and reduce short-run poverty among children by 15%.

- **EITC Option 2: Expand the Earned Income Tax Credit by increasing payments along the phase-in and flat portions of the EITC schedule.** This less expensive ($8.5 billion annually) option would increase the phase-in rate and thus expand the incentive to work, while increasing resources available to the lowest-income families with earnings. A version of this idea is also included as "EITC #1" in the National Academies (2019a) report. There is a real-world precedent: California supplements the federal EITC with a payment schedule of this type. If this option is implemented, the policy will need to be designed to address low take-up among low-income filers, since those below the IRS filing threshold often forgo filing taxes (Hamad et al., 2022), and the administrative burdens of filing may therefore limit the access of the lowest-income families that need the benefit the most.

- **EITC Option 3: Increase generosity throughout the schedule, as in Option 1, but also make available an annual credit of $1,000 per child to families without earnings, phasing this out as earnings approach the first threshold.** A key feature of this policy is that it is available to families without work, which are entirely left out of both the EITC as it currently stands and the first two options. These families tend to have the lowest level of resources, and a transfer to such families was a feature of the 2021 CTC expansion. In this option, the maximum credit is increased sufficiently to ensure that the incentive to work is greater than in the status quo. As for Option 2, the committee considered policy design that could facilitate the access of low-income earners and those with zero income who are not required to file taxes. The precise cost of Option 3 is unknown, although it would be considerably more expensive than either Option 1 or Option 2.

164

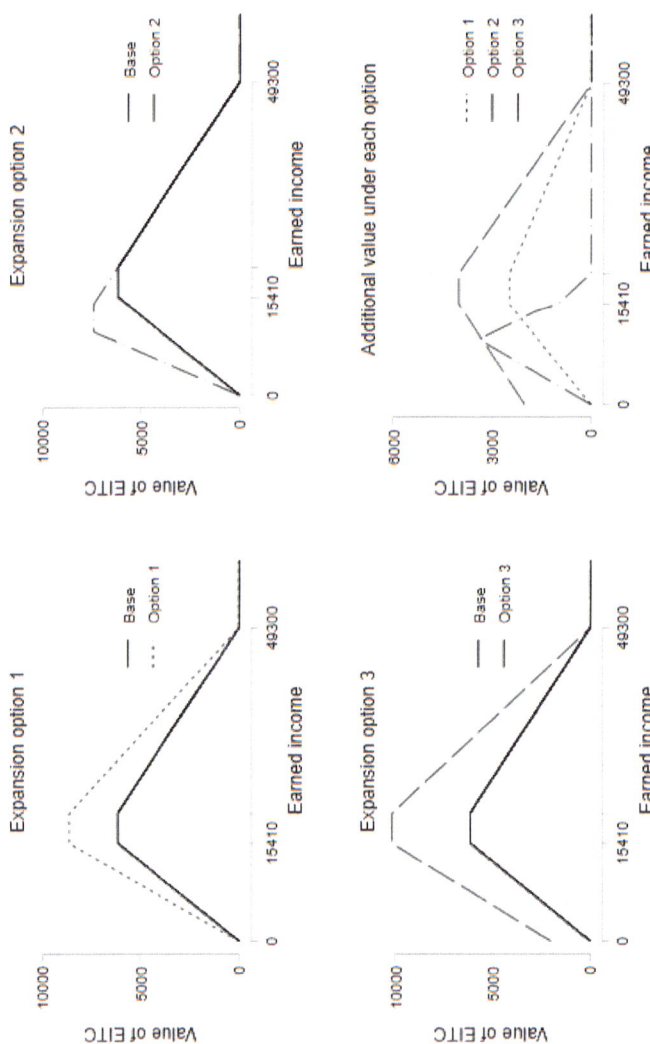

FIGURE 6-7 EITC expansion options.
SOURCE: Based on committee-created simulations under different policy options for structuring an EITC expansion.

Policy and Program Ideas Based on Indirect Evidence

A number of additional policy and program ideas are supported by indirect evidence, though not by direct evidence. They are listed here, with details provided in Appendix C: Chapter 6.

Combining Expansions of the EITC with Other Programs

To increase the stability of monthly incomes for low-income families with children, the EITC expansion could be combined with other programs. As detailed in Appendix C: Chapter 6, three possible options are as follows:

- *Combine an expansion of the EITC with expanding coverage of the Child Care and Development Fund block grant* to help address the problem of a mismatch between the timing of child care expenses and EITC receipt during a child's first year of life.
- *Combine an expansion of the EITC with expanding coverage of the Child Care and Development Fund block grant* to provide more generous and timely reimbursement for the child care expenses of low-income parents.
- *Combine an expansion of the EITC with expanding coverage of the Child Care and Development Fund block grant* along the lines of what was implemented temporarily for the 2021 tax year.

Steps to Address Low Wages

The education chapter (Chapter 4) spells out several policy ideas for addressing wage stagnation among low-skilled workers by improving the education and labor market skills of parents in poverty. These include broadening supports for low-income students at community colleges and expanding sector-based training. All these policy ideas are supported by direct evidence on intergenerational effectiveness. Other approaches to reduce inequities associated with growing employer market power and weakening worker institutions, all of which rely on indirect evidence, include these:

- *Increase the federal minimum wage* to $11 per hour or to $15 per hour, in 2023 inflation-adjusted dollars.
- *Encourage the expansion of union representation in the labor force.*
- *Assist and incentivize the creation by private employers of more good jobs.*

To improve labor market opportunities for people of color living below poverty (including those who have been formerly incarcerated):

Improve disadvantaged workers' access to more or better jobs.

Steps to Increase the Labor Force Participation of Young Mothers

Improving the labor market opportunities of low-income mothers could be accomplished with two policy approaches, which were also included above in the EITC section:

- *Expand coverage of the Child Development Block Grant.*
- *Restructure the Child and Dependent Care Tax Credit* to provide more generous and timely reimbursement for the child care expenses of low-income parents.

Steps to Increase the Wealth of Low-Income Households

Attempts to increase the wealth of low-income households and improve the short-term outcomes of these families and longer-term outcomes of their children have focused on encouraging the accumulation of savings, for example through child development accounts, and the acquisition of assets, such as by becoming a homeowner (see Appendix C: Chapter 6). To raise wealth among low-income households, especially those of color, the committee views baby bonds as promising:

- *Create baby bonds for children born in the United States*, with the value of the bonds determined by the family's income and net worth at the time of the child's birth and targeting families with incomes below the SPM poverty thresholds and total net worth in the bottom quintile of the U.S. net worth distribution.

7

Children's Family Structure

Trends in child poverty over the past half century have been shaped by a number of demographic changes (National Academies, 2019a, Chapter 4). Increases in both educational attainment and employment among low-income mothers, coupled with reductions in teen births, have lowered the child poverty rate. At the same time, the declining share of children living with married parents has led to an increase in child poverty. Much less is known about the impact of these demographic factors on the subject of this report—intergenerational poverty.

For several reasons, this chapter focuses on family structure as a possible driver of intergenerational poverty. First, significant changes have taken place in the structure of families with lower levels of schooling and in Black families. Second, there has been voluminous research linking family structure during childhood to intergenerational outcomes such as completed schooling. And third, some recent research suggests that family structure at the neighborhood level might influence intergenerational outcomes, independently of the structure of children's immediate families.

TRENDS IN FAMILY STRUCTURE

The share of children living in homes with married parents has fallen considerably over the past five decades, dropping from 77% in 1980 to 63% four decades later (Figure 7-1). Most of the decline had occurred by the turn of the millennium. Increases in family structures characterized by unpartnered mothers, cohabiting parents, or more complex arrangements

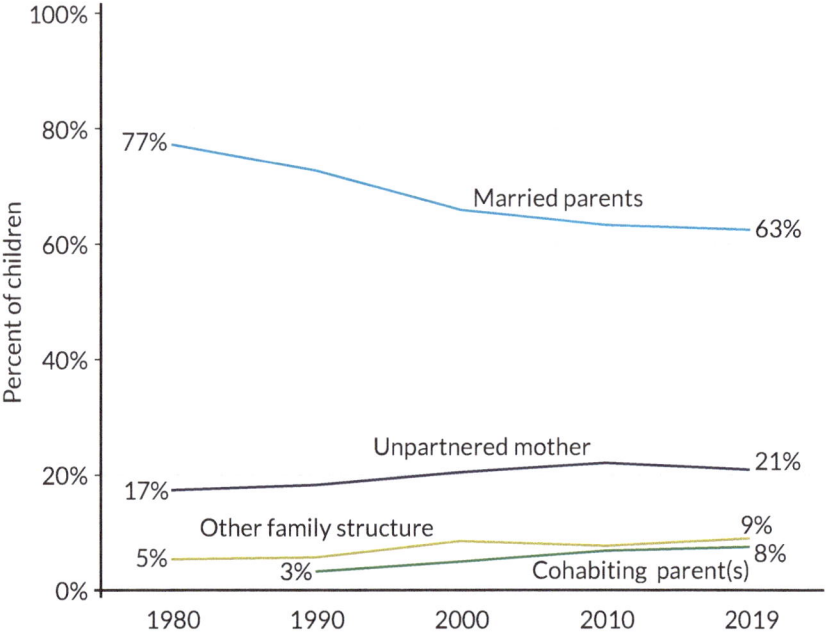

FIGURE 7-1 Percent of children living with married parents and in other arrangements, 1980–2019.
NOTES: A *married-parent* family is defined as a living arrangement in which the child's mother and father are married and present in the home, a mother and her married spouse are present in the home, or a father and his married spouse are present in the home. This includes biological parents, step-parents, adoptive parents, and both same- and opposite-sex married couples. An *unpartnered-mother* household is defined as one in which a mother is present in the household, but no other parental figure is present in the household. A *cohabiting parent(s)* household is defined as one in which a child's mother or father and an unmarried partner are present in the household.
SOURCE: Adapted from Figure 1 in Kearney (2022) and based on data from the American Community Survey.

have all contributed to a decline in the fraction of children living with married parents.

Family structures differ markedly by race/ethnicity and education levels. The dark bars in Figure 7-2 show that in 2019, the largest proportions of children living with both married parents could be found among Asian children (88%), followed by White (77%) and Hispanic (62%) children, while only 38% of Black children were living with married parents (Kearney, 2022). All these fractions are considerably lower than they had been four decades earlier. In the case of White, Hispanic, and Black children, rates of married-parent family structures were all more than 10 percentage points higher in 1980 than in 2019.

Rates of married-parent family structures are also markedly different across maternal education levels. Figure 7-2 shows differences between mothers with college degrees and mothers who had not completed high school; more complete data can be found in Kearney (2022). Rates of married-parent family structures are 28 percentage points higher for White college graduates than White high school dropouts. Corresponding differences amount to 17 percentage points for Hispanic children, 30 percentage points for Black children, and 9 percentage points for Asian children.

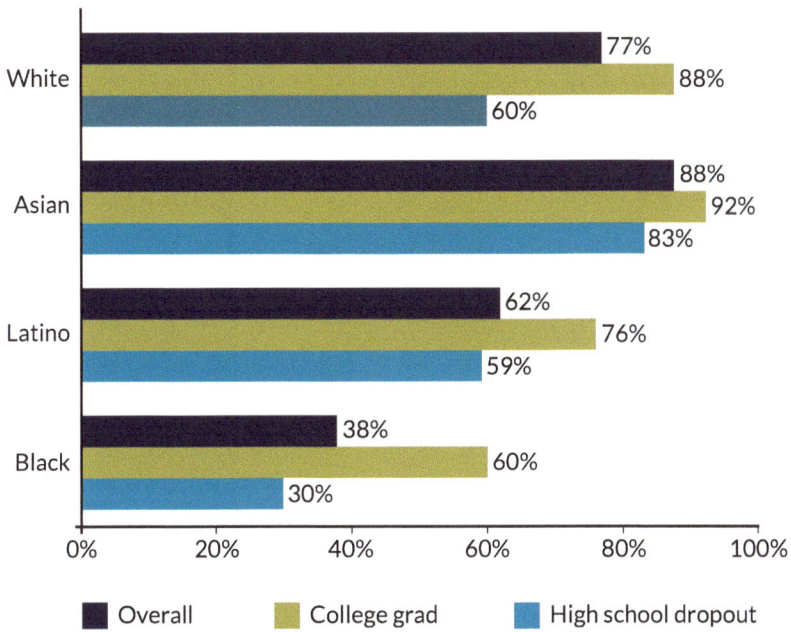

FIGURE 7-2 Percent of children living with married parents, by race/ethnicity and education, 2019.
NOTES: A *married-parent* family is defined as a living arrangement in which the child's mother and father are married and present in the home, a mother and her married spouse are present in the home, or a father and his married spouse are present in the home. This includes biological parents, step-parents, adoptive parents, and both same- and opposite-sex married couples.
SOURCE: Adapted from Figure 4 in Kearney (2022) and based on data from the American Community Survey.

Children reared in single-parent homes are much more likely than other children to be living in poverty. In 2019, 8% of children living in homes with married parents had family incomes below the Supplemental Poverty Measure (SPM) poverty line, compared with more than a quarter of children living with single mothers (Figure 7-3). It is important to note that, at least in the United States, what seems to matter is that parents are married and not merely cohabiting, as marriage tends to be associated with greater stability. Among nonmarried, cohabiting couples, the probabilities of family dissolution before a child turns 12 for parents with a high school education or less, some college, or a bachelor's degree or more were 41%, 45%, and 49%, respectively, between 2006 and 2010. For married parents, those probabilities were 26%, 27%, and 18% (Strain et al., 2022).

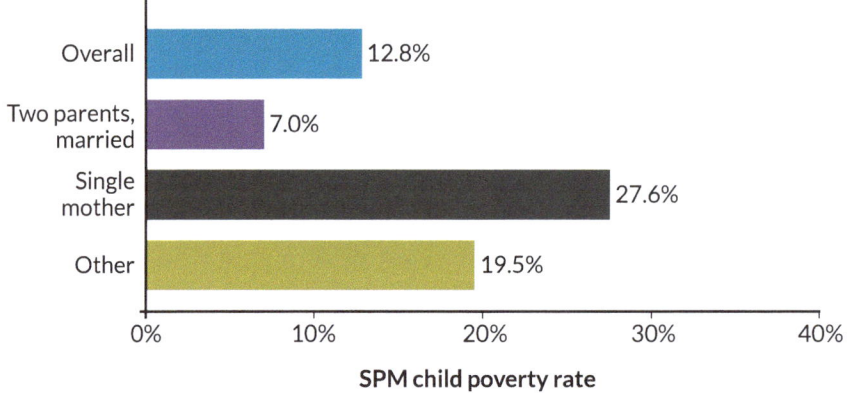

FIGURE 7-3 SPM child poverty rates by family composition, 2019.
NOTES: SPM poverty rates apply to the calendar year 2019 as reported in the March 2020 Current Population Survey. Estimates produced with the Census Bureau's public-use weights, which adjust for survey nonresponse related to the COVID-19 pandemic. See Rothbaum and Bee (2021) for additional details regarding these weights. We identified the marital status of children's parents by linking them to their parents and then determining their parents' marital status. "Two-parent, married" includes children living with both of their parents who are married to each other. "Single mother" includes children living with their mother, and their mother is neither married nor cohabiting. Children in all other family types are in the "other" category.
SOURCE: Data from the Annual Social and Economic Supplement to the Current Population Survey data from IPUMS-CPS (2022).

FAMILY STRUCTURE AND INTERGENERATIONAL CHILD WELL-BEING

Many studies have found that children growing up in families with two married parents tend to fare better during both childhood and adulthood. Children raised in married-parent homes earn higher grades and are less likely to be suspended from school (Autor et al., 2016; Kearney & Levine, 2017; Tillman, 2007). Living in a married-parent home is positively associated with completing high school and both attending and graduating from college (Kearney & Levine, 2017). These correlates are all linked to skill acquisition, which itself is associated with better adult economic outcomes.

In their study of intergenerational outcomes, Lopoo and DeLeire (2014) found that children growing up in stable married households completed 1.6 more years of schooling than other children. In addition, they found that these children's adult family incomes were $52,000 higher than those of children in families with never-married parents. Differences in these intergenerational outcomes were smaller, yet still notable, when children in stable married families were compared with children who were born into married-couple families but experienced marital dissolution while they were growing up. Indeed, the effects of divorce may offer a window into the benefits of marriage. Gruber (2004) found that adults who, as children, experienced the easing of legal requirements for divorce were less well educated, had lower family incomes, separated from a partner more often, and were at higher risk of suicide than those who had grown up in areas that had maintained stricter divorce laws.

An obvious possible reason why married-parent family structure is associated with better child outcomes is that having two adults in the home means twice as many potential income earners relative to single-parent families. Hastings and Schneider (2021) find this pattern of income differences in the Consumer Expenditure Survey data and go on to show that families with married parents spend nearly twice as much on enrichment goods and services (e.g., daycare centers, private-school tuition, lessons, and other extra-curricular activities) for their children than either cohabiting or single parents. Family income accounted for virtually all of these expenditure differences between married and single parents but, interestingly, for only about half of the differences between married and cohabiting parents.

Chen et al. (2009) found that wages and educational attainment (among other outcomes) are negatively associated with growing up in a single-mother household. When they control for income, the association between growing up in a single-mother household and later-life outcomes of youth falls by one-third to one-half. On the other hand, conditional on parent income, Chetty et al. (2020) find little association between children's adult earnings and their parents' marital status.

If parental family income explains most of the associations between family structure and intergenerational outcomes, this does not imply that differences in child outcomes would disappear if families without two married parents in the home were simply given more money. Factors associated with a married, two-parent family structure, such as stability, a nurturing home environment, health insurance coverage, home ownership, and paternal involvement, may have independent effects on intergenerational mobility (Ribar, 2015). Marriage increases the likelihood that these factors will be present in the home. Even after holding them constant, however, Ribar (2015) found a direct positive association between child well-being and marriage. Children growing up in a two-parent home may also enjoy substantially more time with a parent (Hamermesh, 2022), which could complement parental financial investments (Lundberg & Pollak, 2014).

DOES FAMILY STRUCTURE AFFECT INTERGENERATIONAL MOBILITY?

Associations between family structure and longer-run outcomes, even after adjustments for income and other demographic differences, do not prove that family structure itself is the active ingredient. Estimating the causal effect of marriage on child outcomes, including intergenerational poverty, is notoriously difficult because the true causes may lie in unmeasured differences across family types, rather than in family structure itself.

In their review of the evidence on the effects of a father's absence, McLanahan et al. (2013) report that the most rigorous studies tend to show detrimental impacts on child outcomes, although the impacts are smaller than those suggested by correlational studies. They argue that the most convincing evidence of impacts concerns high school graduation and adult mental health. The review by Kearney and Levine (2017) observed that while no study yields truly convincing causal evidence, the persistence of impacts across so many different kinds of studies is, in their words, "strongly suggestive of a causal relationship."

A notable recent working paper by Pope et al. (forthcoming) uses data from U.S. Census and tax records to compare siblings who experience a parental divorce at different ages to estimate the effect of the duration of living in a post-divorce household on children's adult outcomes. These researchers find that the changes in family structure associated with divorce lead to reductions in adult earnings and college attendance and increases in teen births and incarceration. Exposure to divorce prior to age 11 is associated with a reduction of greater than 6% in children's family income in adulthood. In addition, Pope et al. (forthcoming) find larger effects for children who experience a divorce at younger ages and children of low-income families.

Neighborhood Differences in Family Structure

Thus far, we have concentrated on the structure of a child's immediate family. As described in Chapter 2, however, the Chetty et al. (2014) correlational study of intergenerational mobility finds lower mobility for low-income children in neighborhood areas with a large fraction of single parents in the neighborhood. Family structure appears to operate independently at the family and neighborhood levels; for example, children of single parents have higher rates of upward intergenerational mobility if they grow up in a neighborhood with fewer single-parent households. Importantly, this study also controls for household income.

Chetty et al. (2020) find that these neighborhood effects are particularly strong for Black males. While differences in family characteristics explain little of the Black-White income gap across generations, there is a striking association between Black father presence in neighborhood and second-generation outcomes for Black males. Although not a causal study, the specific nature of these correlations rules out broad mechanisms that would affect both genders and races (such as differences in the quality of schools). Instead, it points to channels that affect Black boys in particular, such as mentoring by Black male role models in the community or differences in the way Black men are treated by their peers and adults in areas where Black fathers are involved in their children's households.

Incarceration and Family Structure Differences

A possible cause of trends toward single-parent family structures is the striking increase in incarceration over the last quarter of the 20th century (National Research Council, 2014; Wilson & Neckerman, 1986). Lopoo and Western (2005) found sharply lower rates of first marriage among individuals who have been incarcerated, and they observed that negative associations between incarceration and marriage are stronger for White men than for either Hispanic or Black men. However, simulations based on their correlational evidence show that marriage rates for Black men would change very little in the absence of incarceration. This is consistent with the analyses of Schneider et al. (2018), which finds that prior incarceration accounts for only about 8% of the decline in marriage rates among Black men. The more general conclusion of Lopoo and Western (2005) is that men at risk of imprisonment are very unlikely to marry, whether or not they are actually incarcerated.

Conclusion 7-1: Single-parent families have become much more prevalent over the past 50 years, though largely among parents who lack community college or 4-year college degrees. Rising rates of incarceration account for some but not most of these trends. There is a strong association between growing up in a single-parent family and low-income status in adulthood. Evidence on causal links between growing up in a single-parent family and being poor as an adult is strongly suggestive.

FAMILY STRUCTURE INTERVENTIONS

A number of social policies might influence the decisions that teens and adults make about family composition, but recent reviews conclude that the existing literature on marriage incentives and disincentives provides little reason to believe that current social policies have had a substantial impact (e.g., National Academies, 2019a, Chapter 7).

An alternative approach to promoting married, two-parent families is to develop interventions that are specifically intended to increase the share of children living in two-parent households (Haskins, 2015). An ambitious attempt to develop and evaluate a number of such programs was undertaken during the George W. Bush administration, but recent reviews have concluded that all failed to boost marriage rates or improve longer-run child well-being (National Academies, 2019a, Chapter 7). A recent meta-analysis of clinical trials of a broader range of education programs designed to improve couple relationships showed modest but statistically significant impacts on relationship skills and quality, but not on the key family-structure outcome: the stability of the relationship (Hawkins et al., 2022). These results do not prove that couple relationship programs are without value—but simply that we have not yet discovered a program model that, if scaled up, is actually effective at promoting married, two-parent families.

Conclusion 7-2: While it appears that married, two-parent family structures may, in fact, reduce intergenerational poverty, we lack direct evidence of policies and programs that are capable of promoting such structures.

8

Children's Housing and Neighborhood Environments

The places where children live are strong correlates of their own poverty later in life. Both the homes and the broader neighborhoods in which they live, learn, and grow can provide stability, safety, and opportunity to enable children to thrive. Alternatively, they can present obstacles and risks to their healthy development and socioeconomic futures. This chapter begins with a discussion of research in the housing field and then turns to the research on neighborhoods. Each respective section describes the housing and neighborhood conditions for low-income families and reviews the evidence on how housing and neighborhood factors are linked with intergenerational poverty. The final section provides evidence on specific interventions targeting these factors. The role of neighborhood crime and crime-related interventions are covered in Chapter 9.

HOUSING AS A DRIVER OF INTERGENERATIONAL POVERTY

School-age children spend a majority of their time on activities (including sleep) within their families' housing unit (Hall & Nielsen, 2020). That housing is a foundational environment for their health, education, and development, and a strong correlate of their long-term outcomes. *Housing* here refers to the physical unit itself—the walls, the systems, the stairs, the windows—and the ways families occupy, use, pay for, and change housing. Children in low-income families experience considerably more housing problems than children in higher-income families. In this section, we review the evidence on five key dimensions of these housing problems, from the most micro level of housing quality to the more global issue of homelessness, which is the product of many factors related to housing.

Housing quality is the factor most closely linked with children's outcomes, representing the physical character and maintenance of the housing unit. *Housing crowding* refers to the number of people within a housing unit, which is relevant for things such as noise levels and study spaces. *Housing stability and tenure* are tightly related, since homeowners tend to move less frequently than renters, and frequent moves can be disruptive. *Housing affordability* affects the availability of household financial resources to pay for children's development. Finally, a lack of housing, or *homelessness*, reflects critical housing needs that make other investments in children more difficult. While there are consistent findings about the importance of these factors for children's long-term outcomes, much of the research on housing is correlational in nature.

Housing Quality

Low-income households are more likely to experience "inadequate housing," defined by the federal government as housing "with severe or moderate physical problems, including plumbing and heating deficiencies; rodent and cockroach infestations; and structural issues such as cracks and holes in walls and ceilings, water leaks, broken windows, and crumbling foundations"[1] (Lew, 2016; U.S. Department of Housing and Urban Development, 2014). Figure 8-1 shows the distribution of those experiencing inadequate housing by poverty status and race/ethnicity. Households with cash incomes below the official poverty line are more than twice as likely as nonpoor households to experience inadequate housing, and Native American, Black, and Latino households are disadvantaged relative to White households. Homeownership, which we discuss in greater detail below, is related to better housing quality (Haurin et al., 2002). Exposure to household and environmental toxins (e.g., mold, asbestos, dust mites, lead, smoke, heavy metals, nitrogen dioxide, fine particulate matter) is also greater for low-income and racial/ethnic minority groups (Adamkiewicz et al., 2011; Hauptman et al., 2021; Vivier et al., 2011). Further evidence on lead exposure and its effects is provided in the neighborhood section below and in Chapter 5, which covers children's health.

Housing quality is positively correlated both with children's health and with cognitive and social development (e.g., Barros et al., 2018; Coley

---

[1] For full typology, see American Housing Survey, 2019, Appendix A: Subject Definitions, and Table Index, A-15-16 (U.S. Department of Housing and Urban Development and U.S. Census Bureau). https://www2.census.gov/programs-surveys/ahs/2019/2019%20AHS%20Definitions.pdf

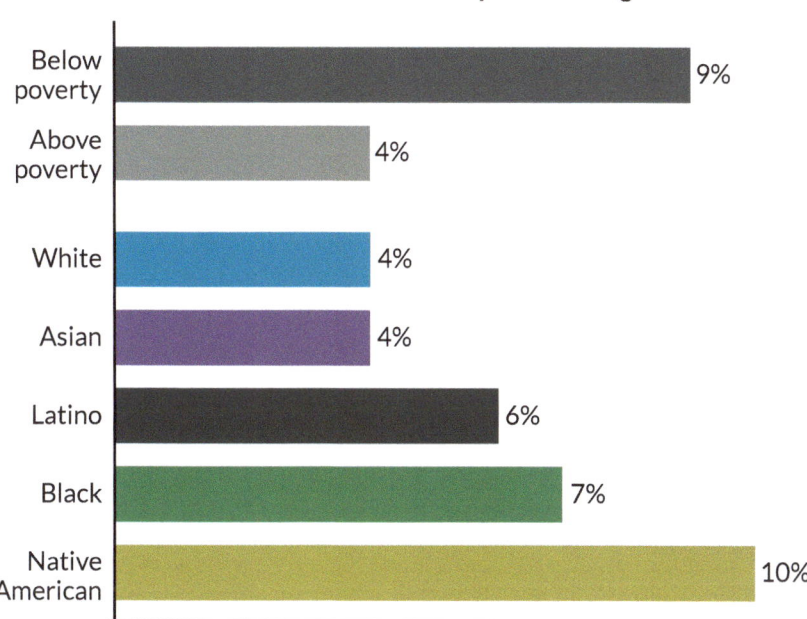

FIGURE 8-1 Inadequate housing by poverty status and race/ethnicity.
NOTES: See text for the definition of inadequate housing according to the U.S. Department of Housing and Urban Development. Poverty is measured with the Official Poverty Measure.
SOURCE: Data from U.S. Census Bureau, American Housing Survey, 2019. https://www.census.gov/programs-surveys/ahs/data/interactive/ahstablecreator.html?s_areas=00000&s_year=2021&s_tablename=TABLE1&s_bygroup1=1&s_bygroup2=1&s_filtergroup1=1&s_filtergroup2=1

et al., 2013; Dunn, 2020; Leventhal & Newman, 2010). Exposure to household lead, pollutants, and allergens harms children's health and development (Huang et al., 2021; Maciag et al., 2022; and see Chapter 5). The "Healthy homes" policy and grant initiatives at the Department of Housing and Urban Development (HUD), the Centers for Disease Control and Prevention, and the U.S. Department of Agriculture all recognize the relationship between household quality indicators and children's well-being. Researchers and healthy housing advocates have identified a number of interventions—such as air filters, education on pollutants, remediation, and smoking bans—that can improve children's health (Butz et al., 2011; Morgan et al., 2004; National Center for Healthy Housing, 2009; Reddy et al., 2017). However, there are no studies that establish a direct causal link from housing quality during childhood to adult socioeconomic outcomes, and the indirect pathways are based on correlational studies.

Housing Crowding

Moving from the unit itself to the density of people who reside within it, research on household crowding hypothesizes that in a given household, more people per room increases the household's stress and interrupts children's study, sleep, and play. *Crowding* is frequently defined as more than one person per room or per bedroom (Blake et al., 2007). Household crowding is more common among low-income and non-White households (Cross, 2018; Kunesh, 2021; Mateyka, 2015). Longitudinal studies have found negative short-term (Solari & Mare, 2012) and long-term (Conley, 2001; Lopoo & London, 2016) impacts of household crowding on educational attainment and on youth criminal convictions (Blau et al., 2019). Similarly, living with extended kin and non-kin adults during childhood is associated with lower high school graduation and college attendance rates (Harvey, 2020). However, sensitivity to ethno-racial diversity in household composition is important. Native American, Asian, Black, and Latino households are more likely than White households to be multigenerational and to include extended kin, and these arrangements may be beneficial for other outcomes (Cross, 2018).

Housing Stability and Tenure

The evidence suggests that housing stability—or low residential mobility—improves children's long-term outcomes. According to the Joint Center for Housing Studies, "Low-income Americans are more likely to move…, with 14% of people in the bottom income quartile moving between 2017 and 2018, compared with 11% of those in the top income quartile" (Frost, 2020, p. 1). Frequent moves harm children's educational attainment, health, and delinquency in short- and long-term studies (Metzger et al., 2015; Schmidt et al., 2018; Simsek et al., 2021). A large-scale population study in Norway using sibling fixed-effects models found weak but significant effects of residential moves on dropping out of high school, lower adult incomes, and early parenthood (Tønnessen et al., 2016).

Evictions are one driver of housing instability that has been shown to harm children and their families. Each year, there are six eviction filings nationally for every 100 renting households (Eviction Lab, 2018), and rates are higher among female-headed households, families with children, and Black and Latino families (Desmond, 2014; Desmond & Gershenson, 2017; Desmond et al., 2013). Families experiencing an eviction order are at higher risk of homelessness, and have reduced earnings and consumption (Collinson et al., 2019; 2022). Studies have shown that evictions increase the odds of losing Medicaid coverage, with subsequent disruptions in health care access (Schwartz et al., 2022). They have also found that exposure to evictions *in utero* is associated with higher rates of preterm birth and low birthweight among infants (Khadka et al., 2020), and that greater neighborhood-level eviction rates are associated with higher rates of child maltreatment, particularly among older children (Bullinger & Fong, 2021). Families that are already vulnerable—for example, because of a child with special health needs—are more likely to be evicted (Schwartz et al., 2021). Conversely, during the COVID-19 pandemic state policies that protected renters from eviction were associated with improvements in renters' mental health (Leifheit et al., 2021). While these studies do not establish causation, they suggest an important relationship between housing instability and negative impacts on children that have been shown to worsen later adult outcomes.

Home ownership, in contrast, increases residential stability, including for low-income families (Kull et al., 2016). This may be one explanation for the correlational research that finds positive short-term (Cordes et al., 2023) and long-term effects on children of living in an owned home (Aarland et al., 2021; Blau et al., 2019; Galster et al., 2007; Harkness & Newman, 2003; Rostad et al., 2019), although some research finds that differences may be due to selection into home ownership and are thus weaker than previously estimated (Cordes et al., 2023; Holupka & Newman, 2012). For low-income White families, home ownership seems to be beneficial for children's outcomes, but this does not hold true for Black families (Holupka & Newman, 2012). It should also be noted that low-income homeowners are more likely to exit from home ownership than higher-income homeowners (Herbert & Belsky, 2008), thereby losing whatever benefits home ownership may have conferred on their children.

There are sizable disparities in home ownership rates by income and race/ethnicity (Figure 8-2). Households of all races with incomes below 50% of area median income (AMI) have lower home ownership rates than their counterparts further up the income distribution. Notably, White households with incomes below 50% of AMI are just as likely to be homeowners as Black households earning between 80% and 120% of AMI. Racial disparities in asset ownership and housing wealth may explain racial gaps in intergenerational mobility (Fox, 2016; Toney & Robertson, 2022), a topic explored further in Chapter 6. While there is some evidence to support home ownership as a housing intervention (as opposed to an asset intervention) to improve low-income children's outcomes, there is no strong causal evidence. Indeed, the relevant operating mechanisms may be residential stability and housing and neighborhood quality, rather than ownership *per*

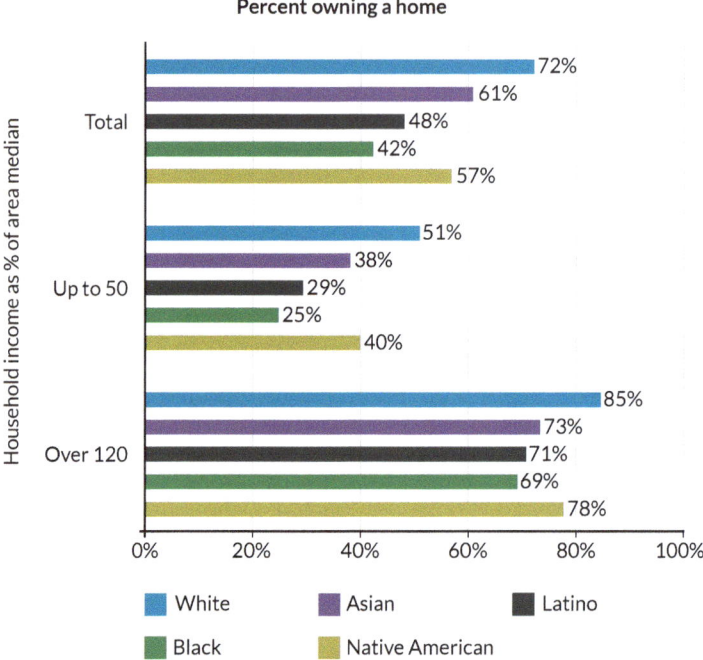

FIGURE 8-2 Homeownership rates based on household income as a percent of area median by race/ethnicity, 2019.
NOTE: White, Asian, Black, and Native American householders are non-Latino. Latino householders may be of any race(s).
SOURCE: Data adapted from Figure 18 of Joint Center for Housing Studies of Harvard University (2022) with the original source using data from the U.S. Census Bureau, 2019 American Community Survey 1-Year Estimates. https://www.jchs.harvard.edu/sites/default/files/interactive-item/files/Harvard_JCHS_State_Nations_Housing_Figures_1.pptx

se. Furthermore, there are significant financial risks of homeownership for low-income households that may lead to greater stress and more residential moves for families (Bostic & Lee, 2008; Tyuse & Birkenmaier, 2006; Wainer & Zabel, 2020).

Housing Affordability

Low-income households are less likely than high-income households to be able to afford their housing. The standard measure of affordability is "housing cost burden," or the condition of paying more than 30% (or 50%, defined as severe housing cost burden) of gross income toward housing. Figure 8-3 shows housing cost burdens for 2020 by income, home ownership

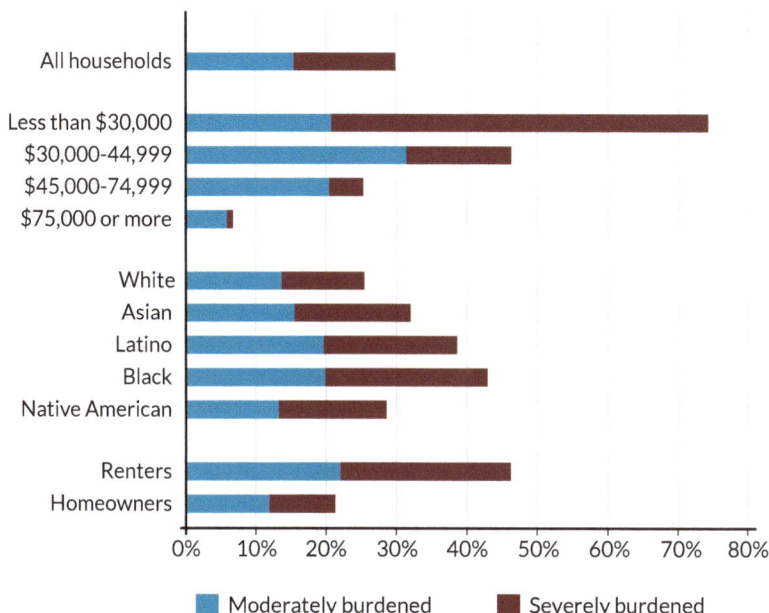

FIGURE 8-3 Housing cost burden, by tenure, income, and race/ethnicity, 2020.
NOTES: Moderately cost-burdened households pay greater than 30% and up to 50% of their household income for housing. Severely cost-burdened households pay greater than 50% of their household income for housing. White, Asian, Black, and Native American householders are non-Latino. Latino householders may be of any race(s).
SOURCE: Data from Joint Center for Housing Studies of Harvard University (2022) with the original source using data from the U.S. Census Bureau, 2019 & 2020 Experimental American Community Survey 1-Year Estimates. https://www.jchs.harvard.edu/sites/default/files/interactive-item/files/Harvard_JCHS_State_Nations_Housing_2022_Appendix_Tables_0.xlsx

status, and race/ethnicity. Renters are more burdened than owners, low-income households are more burdened than higher-income households, and Black, Latino, and Asian households are more burdened than White households. Native American households experience slightly higher rates of housing cost burden than White households, but this fact is accompanied by significantly higher rates of overcrowding and lower housing quality in tribal areas (U.S. Department of Housing and Urban Development, 2017). Greater than 70% of households earning less than $30,000 a year pay more than 30% of their income toward rent or mortgages, and roughly half pay more than 50% of their income.

Limited research has been done on the direct impacts of housing affordability (without housing assistance) on short-run child outcomes (Holme,

2022), and to our knowledge no research has been done on later-life outcomes. Using propensity score matching and instrumental variable techniques, Newman and Holupka (2014) found an inverted U-shaped pattern for the effects of housing cost burden on children's cognitive outcomes. That is, as housing becomes more expensive relative to families' resources, children's math and reading scores improve, but then they decline as housing cost burden exceeds 30% to 40%. Newman and Holupka (2015) find a similar inverted-U relationship between housing cost burden and parental investments in child enrichment. In other words, very low-cost and very high-cost housing relative to income seems to be associated with poor short-term child educational performance. The negative effect of low-cost housing may be due to the correlation of such housing with poor housing quality. Housing unaffordability may also contribute to other housing-related factors that affect children's long-term outcomes, such as housing quality and stability (Holme, 2022). We found no studies on the direct relationship between housing costs and intergenerational poverty.

Homelessness

Being without housing entirely is the most severe form of housing deprivation. The 2020 Annual Homeless Assessment Report (U.S. Department of Housing and Urban Development, 2021) estimates the population living in unhoused families with children to be 171,575, or 30% of the total population without housing. This represents a decline from a peak of over 240,000 people in unhoused families with children in 2010. All non-White groups, with the exception of Asian Americans, are overrepresented among unhoused families relative to their proportion of the total U.S. population (see Table 8-1). Native American and Pacific Islander families

TABLE 8-1 Families Without Housing, by Race/ethnicity, 2020

Race or Ethnicity	Unhoused Families (%)	U.S. Population (%)	Ratio
White	35.0	75.8	0.5
Asian	1.1	6.1	0.2
Latino	29.2	18.9	1.5
Black	53.1	13.6	3.9
Native American	2.3	0.3	7.7
Pacific Islander	2.1	0.3	7.3
Multiple Race	6.5	2.9	2.2

NOTE: Racial categories include Latino people in both columns.
SOURCE: Data from U.S. Department of Housing and Urban Development (2021); U.S. Census Bureau (2023).

are overrepresented by a factor of more than seven. Point-in-time counts of people without any form of shelter underestimate the total number of families in precarious housing situations or who may experience homelessness over the course of the year. For example, the U.S. Department of Education reports that over the course of the 2019–2020 school year, 52,307 enrolled school children were unsheltered, 146,769 lived in shelters or other transitional housing, and 991,300 lived doubled-up with other families (National Center for Homeless Education, 2021, Table 3).

Correlational studies find negative effects of being unhoused during childhood on children's education and health (Perlman & Fantuzzo, 2010; Sandel et al., 2018) and on high school graduation, adult employment, and the likelihood of being stably housed as an adult (Bassuk et al., 2014; Cobb-Clark & Zhu, 2017; Parpouchi et al., 2021). Most studies cannot distinguish between the unique effect of being unhoused from the general effect of growing up in a poor household (Buckner, 2008). However, an experimental policy treatment showed that giving unhoused families permanent housing reduced homelessness, food insecurity, the number of schools that children attended, school absences, and child behavior problems (Gubits et al., 2018). Many of these measures are correlated with later adult outcomes. For example, childhood food insecurity is related to poorer adult outcomes (see Chapter 5 for more detail), and school mobility correlates with lower educational attainment, lower occupational prestige, and greater likelihood of arrest in adulthood (Herbers et al., 2013). Hence, there is indirect evidence that reducing homelessness in childhood would increase the likelihood of upward mobility. Permanent housing subsidies have been shown in a randomized controlled trial (RCT) study to reduce family homelessness (Gubits et al., 2018); accordingly, we discuss housing choice vouchers later as an intervention to interrupt this pathway of intergenerational poverty.

Conclusion 8-1: The evidence on the effects of housing on intergenerational poverty is nearly all correlational or drawn from longitudinal panel surveys. The most consistent correlational evidence is on the effects of housing quality on children's short-term outcomes, with the strongest evidence on the long-term effects of lead exposure. There is also correlational evidence on the negative effects of homelessness, overcrowding, residential mobility, and very low or high housing costs on children's short and long-term outcomes.

NEIGHBORHOODS AS A DRIVER OF INTERGENERATIONAL POVERTY

As discussed in Chapters 2 and 3, the neighborhood environments of low-income children and non-White children differ significantly from those of high-income and White children and are an important correlate of intergenerational mobility. Residential segregation by income has increased since at least the 1980s (Logan et al., 2020; Reardon et al., 2018), particularly among families with children (Owens, 2016). This means that struggling and affluent families are more likely to live in separate neighborhoods and more likely to live close to families of a similar socioeconomic status now than in the past.

The racial residential segregation of Black and White people has declined steadily since about the 1970s, but it is still high in many large cities. Residential segregation between Latino and White households has remained steady or increased slightly in some areas (Elbers, 2021; Logan, 2013). Because of residential segregation by both race and class, poverty is disproportionately concentrated in the neighborhoods in which non-White families and children live. Black and Native American children are more than seven times as likely and Latino children more than four times as likely as White children to live in neighborhoods with poverty rates of 30% or more (see Figure 8-4). The child poverty rate on Native American reservations was 42% in 2010 (Akee & Taylor, 2014). Children who grow up in high-poverty neighborhoods have worse adult outcomes than children living in low-poverty neighborhoods (Chetty et al., 2016).

Children in families with incomes below poverty and children living in low-income neighborhoods are disproportionately exposed to lead through air pollution, soil-based lead, leaded water pipes, and lead paint and dust in older housing structures (Hauptman et al., 2021; Vivier et al., 2011). Children in families below poverty experience greater negative cognitive and physiological effects from living in census tracts where the risk of lead is high (Marshall et al., 2020). As discussed in more detail in the chapters on health (Chapter 5) and crime and criminal justice (Chapter 9), childhood lead exposure is linked with greater delinquency in adolescence and young adulthood (Aizer & Currie, 2019; Manduca & Sampson, 2019; Wright et al., 2008) and with lower adult IQ, higher rates of teenage pregnancy, and declines in occupational status and income relative to parents (Reuben et al., 2017; Zhang et al., 2013; also see Boyle et al., 2021; Manduca & Sampson, 2021). While the magnitude of the impact seems to be the same for Black, White, and Latino children, the levels of exposure are much higher for Black and Latino children (Manduca & Sampson, 2021). More research on household and environmental exposures in Native American communities is needed (Barros et al., 2018).

Concentrated poverty also increases young people's exposure to violence, which is negatively correlated with children's educational, labor market, and delinquency outcomes (Beland & Kim, 2016; Burdick-Will

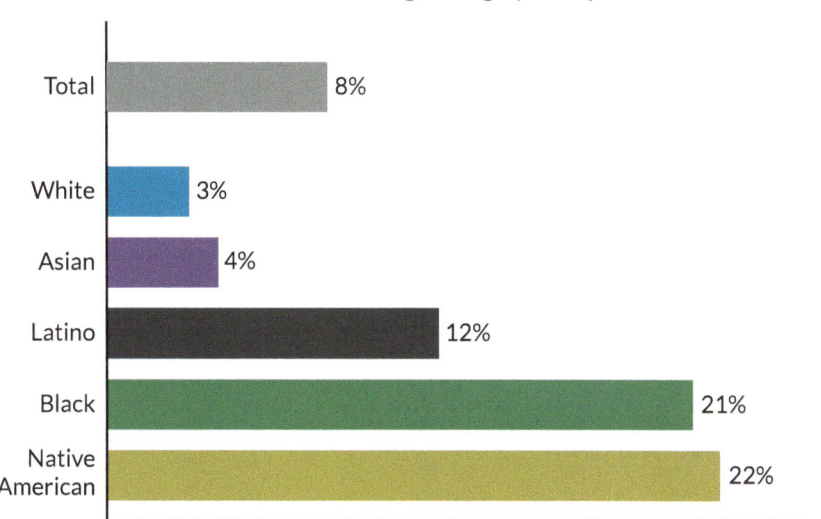

FIGURE 8-4 Children living in high-poverty areas by race and ethnicity in the United States, 2017–2021.
NOTE: *High-poverty area* is defined as living in a census tract with 30% or more of the population having an income below the federal Official Poverty Measure thresholds.
SOURCE: Data from Kids Count Data Center (2023) with the original source using data from the U.S. Census Bureau, 2006–2010 to 2017–2021 American Community Survey 5-year data. https://datacenter.kidscount.org/data/tables/7753-children-living-in-high-poverty-areas-by-race-and-ethnicity#detailed/1/any/false/2454,2026,1983, 1692,1691,1607,1572,1485,1376,1201/10,11,9,12,1,185,13/14943,14942

et al., 2021; Eitle & Turner, 2002; Nader et al., 1990; Sharkey, 2010) and reduces intergenerational mobility (Chetty et al., 2014; Sharkey & Torrats-Espinosa, 2017). We review this literature more fully in Chapter 9.

Experimental and quasi-experimental evidence demonstrates that exposure to "better neighborhoods" during childhood has a significant association with children's outcomes in adulthood. But what is a better neighborhood? Experimental interventions to improve the physical quality of neighborhoods show that beautifying vacant lots and fixing abandoned homes significantly reduce crime rates (see Chapter 9). Just as housing quality seems to matter, so does the physical quality of the neighborhood. However, understanding which aspects of neighborhoods matter most—e.g., poverty levels, crime rates, labor markets, or residential segregation that decreases resources for racial/ethnic minorities in particular—is challenging, as these factors are often highly correlated. As discussed in Chapter 2, a literature has emerged using geographic variation and following families that move across neighborhoods to understand what factors explain differences in intergenerational mobility across areas (Chetty, 2014; Chetty et al., 2020, 2022). Studies have found several systematic predictors of differences in intergenerational mobility, such as poverty rates, school quality, the degree of inequality, the fraction of children living with single parents, connectedness to high-income people, and historical factors such as redlining and Jim Crow laws. Because many of these factors can be interrelated, most studies therefore consider a single dimension of neighborhood disadvantage—often neighborhood poverty—or examine a composite measure of a few facets of disadvantage.

Much of the experimental evidence on the importance of neighborhood factors comes from HUD's Moving to Opportunity (MTO) experiment, which began in the 1990s and has since been revisited by numerous researchers using contemporaneous data to measure participants' long-run outcomes along a range of dimensions. This work has revealed that some of the children who moved to lower-poverty neighborhoods as part of MTO experienced positive effects not only on their average earnings and educational prospects (Chetty et al., 2016), but also on their physical and mental health as well (Pollack et al., 2021). Importantly, it was young children in particular whose long-run outcomes improved after they moved, suggesting that the age prior to adolescence may be a key point to intervene on the children's neighborhood environment; similar benefits were not observed for older children or adults in this study.

These results have been replicated in many quasi-experimental and observational studies of children who move across areas at different ages using larger samples. Using de-identified tax records covering more than five million children whose families moved across counties between 1996 and 2012, Chetty et al. (2016) showed that, on average, children whose families move to a better neighborhood have better outcomes, and the beneficial effect increases as the amount of time they spend growing up in the better area increases. This pattern holds for a range of outcomes including earnings, college attendance, incarceration rates, and teenage birth rates. Similar findings were documented for children who moved out of severely distressed public housing projects in Chicago (Chyn, 2018).

Analogous exposure effects on educational and economic outcomes have been shown in datasets covering movers in international settings, including Australia, Canada, and Denmark (Deutscher, 2020; Faurschou, 2018; Laliberté, 2021). Researchers have observed similar patterns for health. A series of studies examined the effects of quasi-randomly assigned neighborhoods of arrival among refugee children and adults in Denmark and Sweden (Foverskov et al., 2022a,b; Hamad et al., 2020; White et al., 2016) and found that relatively more disadvantaged neighborhoods were associated with poorer long-run physical and mental health outcomes.

Yet despite the importance of high-opportunity neighborhoods for children's prospects of achieving upward mobility, the vast majority of low-income families in the United States, including those that receive housing assistance, live in neighborhoods with relatively low rates of intergenerational economic mobility (see Figures 2-8 and 2-9 in Chapter 2; Mazzara & Knudsen, 2019; Metzger, 2014). A recent randomized experiment conducted in Seattle showed that families stayed in low-opportunity neighborhoods largely because of barriers that impede residential choice, such as limited time and resources to search for housing, challenges in communicating with landlords, and a lack of information about neighborhood opportunities (Bergman et al., 2019).

Some interventions aimed at increasing neighborhood opportunity and reducing residential segregation have proved effective at helping low-income families access better neighborhoods regardless of their racial background (Bergman et al., 2019). Nevertheless, Native, Black, and Latino families currently disproportionately live in high-poverty, low-opportunity neighborhoods. Recent quasi-experimental work has demonstrated the adverse effects of residential segregation on intergenerational mobility, academic achievement, and teenage birth rates (Chyn et al., 2022). Expanding access to high-opportunity neighborhoods therefore has the potential to narrow racial disparities, although this will not eliminate them entirely, because disparities persist even within higher-opportunity neighborhoods (Chetty et al., 2020).

Conclusion 8-2: Strong evidence shows improvements in low-income children's long-term economic, educational, and health outcomes when they move to less disadvantaged neighborhoods. Less is known regarding which characteristics of neighborhoods foster upward mobility.

HOUSING AND NEIGHBORHOOD INTERVENTIONS

The main public policies that address housing problems and neighborhood characteristics involve housing assistance. Housing assistance can be in many forms, such as subsidies for the construction and maintenance of housing units, which result in lower rents for low-income households, or vouchers issued to low-income households who use them in the private rental market to pay the difference between the asking rent (up to a certain threshold) and what they can afford, which is set at roughly 30% of their gross income. Housing assistance may improve low-income children's outcomes as adults by freeing up parental income for investments in children, by improving housing quality and stability, and by reducing homelessness. Access to neighborhoods that promote upward mobility also requires being able to afford the often-higher costs of housing in such neighborhoods.

We first discuss the intervention of housing choice vouchers (HCVs) *with supports for moving to low-poverty neighborhoods*, for which promising causal evidence of direct effects on long-term outcomes is available. Then we discuss housing choice vouchers *alone*, which shows promising evidence for improving children's outcomes in the short term, specifically for unhoused families, but mixed evidence for addressing intergenerational poverty. (In Appendix C: Chapter 8, we give additional information on HCVs alone and housing assistance beyond vouchers, and we discuss the limited evidence on the effects of housing production, neighborhood improvement, and targeted initiatives for Native American families. Neighborhood interventions associated with reductions in neighborhood crime are reviewed in Chapter 9.)

As discussed in Chapter 1, we characterize the evidence on some of the programs or policies as "strong" and denote them with an "*." In the case of our direct-evidence HCV program idea, the evidence is "promising" but not "strong" because this program has not been scaled up and tested in other cities.

Policy and Program Ideas Based on Direct Evidence

Enhancing the Housing Choice Voucher Program

The HCV program allows low-income households to lease an apartment in the private market using subsidy funds allocated by the federal government to the local public housing authority. The HCV program ensures that households pay no more than 30% of their income toward housing costs. The evidence that an enhanced version of the HCV program generates positive later-life outcomes for children is robust. Specifically, pairing the HCV program with enhanced and customized mobility services is a key evidence-based intervention for increasing mobility out of poverty. The Family Stability and Opportunity Vouchers Act (FSOVA) is one example of bipartisan, evidence-based legislation aimed at this goal. Originally introduced in 2019, and reintroduced in 2021, the FSOVA bill would expand rental assistance to 500,000 families with young children. In addition to providing a 25% increase over the current 2.2 million families served annually in the HCV program, the bill also includes provisions aimed at bolstering low-income families' access to higher-opportunity neighborhoods. The legislation would provide families with access to customized counseling and case management services designed to overcome barriers to residential choice. It would also provide housing authorities with new resources to engage landlords in the HCV program and to partner with community-based supports to support the moving process. Additionally, the FSOVA bill includes provisions for voucher programs to reduce administrative burdens and to employ "small-area fair market rents"[2] to align vouchers with the cost of living in specific neighborhoods.

The FSOVA bill is built on evidence of positive outcomes that result from opportunity moves. Its design was based on research-backed practices from the Creating Moves to Opportunity (CMTO) program, a housing mobility intervention in the Seattle area (Bergman et al., 2019). Run as an RCT, CMTO showed that it was barriers, not preferences, that caused the majority of HCV participants to reside in low-opportunity areas. The CMTO program, which provided customized services to families along with flexible financial assistance, resulted in a dramatic increase in opportunity moves: 53% of families assigned to receive CMTO services moved to high-opportunity areas, as compared with 15% of families in the control group (who also received a voucher but without additional supports). The annual program cost was $2,700 per family—an amount that would be offset by anticipated lifetime earnings increases and other positive outcomes among participants who moved to high-opportunity neighborhoods. The elements included in the FSOVA bill, such as a streamlined search process, landlord mediation, and customized support from housing navigators are all based on program elements shown to be effective in CMTO.

Although expanding enhanced voucher assistance meets the committee's criteria for being supported by direct evidence, it is not yet supported by evidence that has been replicated across several sites. As explained in Chapter 1, we therefore characterize its supporting evidence as "promising" rather than "strong."

- **Expand and enhance choice-based residential mobility assistance.** Expand the housing choice voucher program's rental assistance to an additional 500,000 families with young children (at an estimated cost of $5 billion) and couple it with customized counseling and case management services to facilitate low-income families' access to higher-opportunity neighborhoods.

---

[2] Small Area Fair Market Rents are Fair Market Rents (FMR) calculated for ZIP Codes within metropolitan areas. The use of Small Area FMRs is expected to give HCV tenants access to areas of high opportunity and lower poverty areas by providing a subsidy that is adequate to cover rents in those areas, thereby reducing the number of voucher families that reside in areas of high poverty concentration. https://www.huduser.gov/portal/datasets/fmr/smallarea/index.html; https://www.hudexchange.info/programs/public-housing/small-area-fair-market-rents/

Policy and Program Ideas Based on Indirect Evidence

Expanding the Housing Choice Voucher Program Alone

Expanding the HCV program alone is supported by both correlational and indirect evidence on the potential to reduce intergenerational poverty. Currently, housing subsidy programs reach less than 25% of income-eligible households. In the mid-2010s, an estimated 6.5 million households were on waitlists for public or voucher housing (Collinson et al., 2019). Nationally, families who received vouchers had spent nearly 2.5 years on a waitlist (Acosta & Gartland, 2021). Of the 16 million currently unserved households, 5.2 million are families with children. Collyer et al. (2020) estimated that the total cost to make the HCV program an entitlement would be roughly $96.7 billion, or $74.5 billion above current funding. Since families with children comprise roughly a third of currently unserved households (Gartland, 2022), prioritizing them would cost roughly $24.6 billion.

- *Expand the HCV program to serve all eligible families with children.* Such an expansion would build on substantial correlational research and an RCT intervention with unhoused families that show positive long-term outcomes for children.

Most correlational evidence on the efficacy of the HCV alone for improving long-term outcomes for children in households below poverty is positive (e.g., Pollakowski et al., 2022; see Appendix C: Chapter 8). However, a study based on an HCV lottery in Chicago and a multicity random assignment voucher study found no long-term impacts on a host of child educational outcomes (Jacob et al., 2015; Wood et al., 2008). Still, for unhoused families in an RCT intervention, permanent housing subsidies like vouchers improved children's behavioral outcomes and increased school stability (Gubits et al., 2018), both of which are correlated with later adult outcomes. Therefore, there is causal evidence for the indirect effects of vouchers on intergenerational mobility, specifically for homeless families. We discuss the potential role of housing assistance in reducing intergenerational poverty further in Appendix C: Chapter 8.

9

Neighborhood Crime and the Criminal Justice System

Crime and the criminal justice system both play important but complicated roles in hampering the ability of children raised in poverty to escape poverty as adults. On the one hand, low-income youth are especially likely to report being victims of crime in their neighborhoods and schools, and research has shown that victimization in childhood can harm children's health, well-being, and achievement, with lasting consequences.

On the other hand, changes in policing tactics and increases in incarceration since the late 1970s (with small declines in recent years), despite declining crime rates for much of this period, have also disproportionately involved low-income children and families, with negative consequences for their development and long-term economic success (National Research Council et al., 2014; New York Civil Liberties Union, 2013).

In evaluating whether crime and the criminal justice system are key drivers of intergenerational poverty, this chapter begins by reviewing evidence on how these factors affect the well-being, development, and intergenerational mobility of children, devoting particular attention to disparities by race and ethnicity. Given the strong potential for confounding—that is, the possibility that the relationship with intergenerational poverty can be explained by other factors that are correlated with crime, victimization, and criminal justice involvement—the committee was careful to rely on evidence that points to a causal relationship.

The first part of this chapter is organized into two sections. In the first, we discuss victimization and exposure to violence as a driver of the intergenerational persistence of poverty. In the second, we discuss how youth crime and the criminal justice system itself contribute to worse economic outcomes for poor youth. The last section of the chapter suggests policies and programs that might limit harmful youth interactions with the criminal justice system and reduce child victimization and violence more generally. The committee confines its discussion of ways to reduce the disruptive nature of adult and caregiver interaction with the criminal justice system to Appendix C: Chapter 9, owing to the more speculative nature of the interventions considered by the committee.

VICTIMIZATION AND EXPOSURE TO VIOLENCE AS A DRIVER OF INTERGENERATIONAL POVERTY

Low-income and younger people are much more likely than higher-income and older people to report being victims of crime in their neighborhoods and schools (Figure 9-1; Nowicki, 2020; Kearney et al., 2014). Since the mid-1990s, sharp declines in crime, especially violent crime (Federal Bureau of Investigation, 2019), have reduced victimization among low-income children, improving their prospects for healthy development and future economic success. But violent crime has been rising again since 2014, though it remains far below the levels of earlier decades.[1]

Gun violence is now the leading cause of death among children in the United States (see Chapter 5 for more detail), surpassing motor vehicle accidents.[2] Rates of gun violence are highest in low-income communities and in Black, Latino, and Native American communities (Barrett et al., 2021).[3] The premature deaths of low-income children obviously impede upward mobility. More generally, crime victimization is strongly correlated with future depression, anxiety, and post-traumatic stress disorder (Kilpatrick & Acierno, 2003; Simons et al., 2002), all of which can adversely affect healthy child and adolescent development.

Exposure to Neighborhood Violence

Beyond direct victimization, children's exposure to violence and violent crime in their neighborhoods is traumatic and can have a negative effect on their development, reducing future educational attainment and earnings (Nader et al., 1990; Sharkey, 2010). Sharkey and Torrats-Espinosa (2017) show that in the case of adolescents growing up in low-income families,

---

[1] Reported violent crimes fell from 1.9 million in 1992 (the peak) to 1.15 million in 2014 (the nadir), then increased to 1.3 million in 2021 (Federal Bureau of Investigation, 2019).

[2] Two-thirds of the fatalities from gun violence among 15- to 24-year-olds between 2007 and 2016 were homicides; the remaining third were suicides.

[3] Over a 9-year period ending in 2016, there were 34,000 more firearm deaths among 15–24-year-olds in the poorest counties in the United States than in the richest counties.

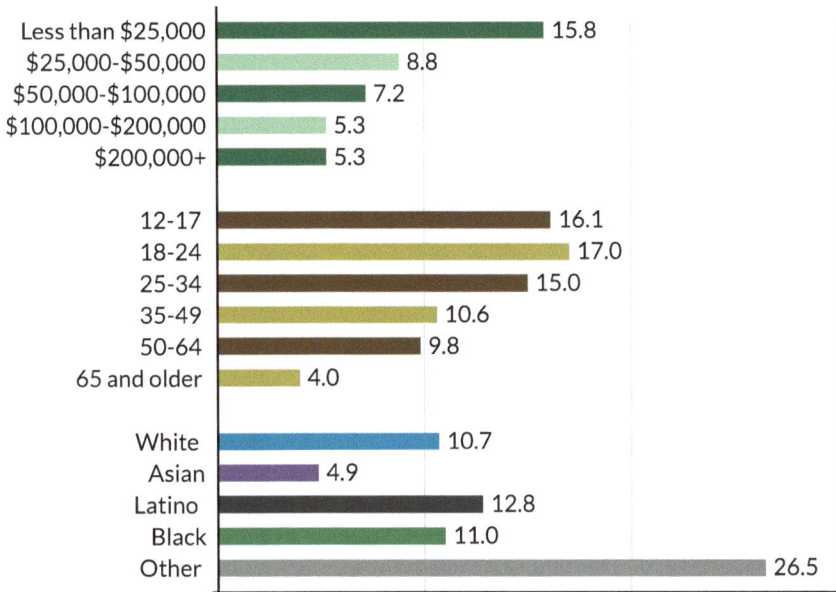

FIGURE 9-1 Violent crime victimization rates (per 1,000) in 2019, by income, age, and race/ethnicity.
NOTES: Figures are the proportion of a group reporting being a victim of a violent crime in 2019. Income data are on crimes reported to police. Age and race/ethnicity data are based on survey reports. Income refers to the household income levels of the victims.
SOURCE: Data from the Supplemental Statistical Tables of the Bureau of Justice Statistics' Criminal Victimization, 2020 (Morgan & Thompson, 2020).

lower exposure to neighborhood crime during adolescence increases intergenerational mobility as measured by their family-income ranking at age 26 (also see Chetty et al., 2014).

Estimating the causal impact of exposure to violence on future outcomes is complicated by the fact that crime tends to be concentrated in neighborhoods characterized by high poverty and racial segregation, factors that can independently worsen children's trajectories. To address this problem, researchers have taken advantage of the timing of violent incidents in a neighborhood and compared the outcomes of children before and after a violent incident. Such research shows that exposure to community violence just before an assessment negatively affects children's sleep patterns and stress responses (Heissel et al., 2018) and reduces their attention and impulse control (Sharkey et al., 2012). Other studies linking exposure to violence with medium-term outcomes have found that exposure to violence increases the likelihood of school dropout (Burdick-Will et al., 2021), increases the risk of offending in young adulthood (Eitle & Turner, 2002), and reduces performance on standardized tests, especially for Black students (Schwartz et al., 2022; Sharkey, 2010; Sharkey et al., 2014).

Some of the strongest evidence on the relationship between exposure to violence and future outcomes comes from school shootings. Such shootings are largely random and uncorrelated with underlying characteristics of the neighborhood or of the students. This allows researchers to estimate the impact of exposure to violence independent of underlying neighborhood or student characteristics. Comparing the outcomes of affected youth with outcomes of nearby similar youth who were not directly exposed to school shootings, researchers have documented negative effects of fatal school shootings on mental health and long-term economic outcomes, including reduced educational attainment and earnings at age 26 (Cabral et al., 2022; Rossin-Slater et al., 2020).

Predictors of Neighborhood Violence

What is known about the predictors of neighborhood violence? Concentrated poverty and racial segregation both contribute to higher rates of violent crime (Cox et al., 2022; Peterson & Krivo, 2010). Historical efforts to segregate Black families through the red-lining maps drawn by the Home Owners Loan Corporation in the 1930s predict both racial segregation and high rates of neighborhood violence today (Mehranbod et al., 2022; Chapters 3 and 8). Research suggests that underinvestment in the community and policing are also highly predictive (Love, 2021). We discuss each of these issues in turn.

Community-level physical disorder, as evidenced by dilapidated buildings, trash, graffiti, and vacant lots, is strongly correlated with crime (Branas et al., 2012; Chen & Rafail, 2022; O'Shea, 2006; Wei et al., 2005). Branas et al. (2018) found causal evidence for this link: In a randomized controlled trial in Philadelphia, some vacant lots were cleaned up and improved, while control lots were left untouched. Over a three-year period, the intervention resulted in significant declines in overall crime and a 29% reduction in violent crime in the low-income neighborhoods where the vacant lots were improved. Other work (Kondo et al., 2016; South et al., 2021) supports these findings, with South et al. (2021) finding impacts on homicide.

Strong correlational research finds a connection between public and private investments and local crime rates. Velez et al. (2012) examined nearly 30 years of home mortgage lending, crime, and demographic data for neighborhoods in the city of Seattle. They found a negative correlation between mortgage investments (i.e., loans per housing unit and total dollars invested) and violent crime in the subsequent two years (and no relationship between violent crime rates and later mortgage investments), net of other neighborhood factors. Focusing on public investments, Shrider and Ramey (2018) used 10 years of data, also from Seattle, on the Neighborhood Matching Fund program, which supports community-building or physical improvement efforts by local organizations. They found that such investments have a direct effect on reducing violent crime in disadvantaged neighborhoods, and indirectly reduce crime by increasing private mortgage investments.

Civic engagement is another important predictor of neighborhood crime. Sharkey et al. (2017) used changes in the presence of nonprofits across cities and over time to estimate the impact of the establishment of nonprofits on crime. Using 20 years of data in 264 U.S. cities, they found that "10 additional organizations focusing on crime and community life in a city with 100,000 residents leads to a 9-percent reduction in the murder rate, a 6-percent reduction in the violent crime rate, and a 4-percent reduction in the property crime rate" (p. 1215).

Crime Prevention Strategies

Police officers reduce crime, and especially homicide and other violent crime, although the estimated effects vary considerably across settings (Chalfin & McCrary, 2017).[4] Estimating a causal impact of police on crime is complicated by the fact that areas with more crime often expand their police force in response. The strongest evidence of causal impacts of police on crime can be derived from sudden increases in funding made possible by the federal allocation of grants to local precincts to hire more police officers (e.g., Evans & Owens, 2007). The effects of an expanded police force vary across racial groups, with disproportionate gains and costs for the Black population (Chalfin et al., 2022). While 10 additional police officers result in one fewer homicide overall, the estimated per capita reduction is twice as large for Black victims as for White victims.

At the same time, the costs of additional police are also disproportionately borne by the Black population, who are more likely to be arrested for "quality of life" infractions such as liquor-law violation and drug possession when the police force increases in size. Policing tactics, not just police manpower, are important in reducing violent crime. More focused interventions such as hot-spot policing, problem-oriented policing, and proactive and disorder policing all generate greater reductions in crime than less discriminate strategies (Chalfin & McCrary, 2017; MacDonald et al., 2016; National Academies, 2018).

---

[4] The estimated elasticities range from -0.1 to -2, meaning a 10% increase in police personnel reduces crime by 1% to 20%, depending on the study.

As to community policing, recent reviews of the evidence by the Center on Evidence-Based Crime Policy and, especially, a review of experimental studies by Gill et al. (2014), find small negative effects of community policing on violent crime and larger positive effects on citizen satisfaction, perceived disorder, and police legitimacy.

Gun safety regulations can also reduce homicides and firearm-related injuries. Studies evaluating this relationship typically rely upon changes in laws across states and over time to estimate causal effects. Specifically, by examining changes in violence before and after a change in gun safety law within a state and comparing those changes with trends in otherwise similar states that did not change the law, researchers limit the effect of secular trends in violence or differences across states in estimated effects. A review by Cook and Donohue (2017) of gun safety regulation and its impact on violent crime, and more focused work by Donohue et al. (2022) on "right to carry" laws, both found a causal link between an increase in homicides and an expansion of local right-to-carry laws, and also that limiting domestic abusers' access to guns and imposing sentencing add-ons for violence involving guns appear to be effective in reducing gun violence. Child-access prevention laws can reduce non-fatal gun injuries, and the effects are larger when the law covers older children (DeSimone et al., 2013).

Conclusion 9-1: Crime victimization and exposure have negative consequences for children's development and long-term economic outcomes. Gun violence is now the leading cause of death among American children. Low-income, Black, and Native American youth are more likely to have these exposures. Rigorous research shows that neighborhood violent crime can be reduced through community investments and engagement, certain kinds of policing, and gun safety regulations.

YOUTH OFFENDING AND THE CRIMINAL JUSTICE SYSTEM AS DRIVERS OF INTERGENERATIONAL POVERTY

The incarcerated population is overwhelmingly poor and less educated, so it is not surprising that childhood poverty is a strong predictor of future incarceration (Looney & Turner, 2018). There are also significant racial/ethnic disparities: Even conditional on income or education, Black men are twice as likely as White men to have been incarcerated by age 30 (National Research Council et al., 2014). This affects children in two ways: indirectly through adult involvement (including caregiver involvement) in the criminal justice system, and directly through juvenile involvement in the system.

Recent estimates suggest that 1 child in 5 has a biological parent or caregiver who has been convicted of a felony, and 1 in 10 has a parent or caregiver who has served time in prison (Finlay et al., 2021). Parent and caregiver interaction with the criminal justice system can affect children in multiple ways, for example by placing additional strain and stress on the household, increasing financial insecurity, and resulting in the removal of an adult (or even a child through foster care) from the household.

Youth involvement in the criminal justice system also varies considerably by income and race; low-income children and Black and Native American children are much more likely to be arrested and detained (Figure 9-2 shows racial differences in arrest rates for all crimes and violent crimes only). Evidence reviewed below supports a causal link between family income and juvenile involvement in the criminal justice system. In the case of links between criminal justice involvement and children's economic outcomes in adulthood, the research reviewed below has shown that juvenile detention and incarceration are associated with worse educational outcomes and

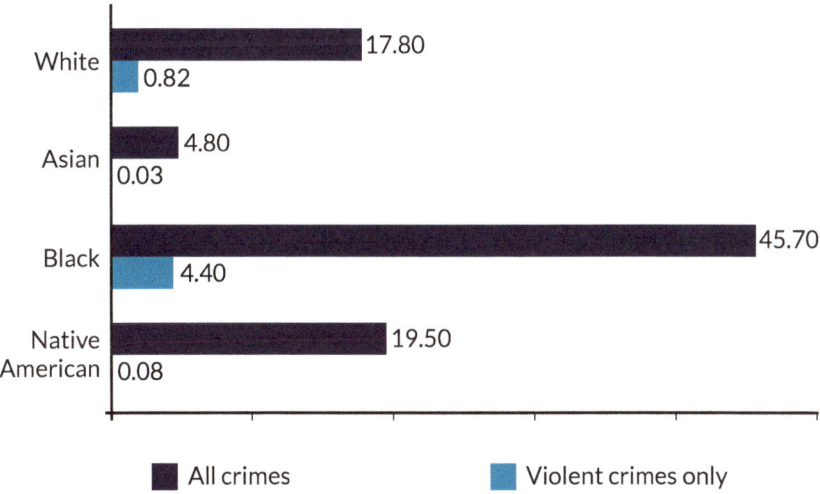

FIGURE 9-2 Juvenile overall and violent crime arrest rates (per 1,000) in 2018, by race/ethnicity.
NOTES: Figures are arrest rates per 1,000 10–17-year-olds in the resident population. *Violent crime* includes murder and nonnegligent manslaughter, forcible rape, robbery, and aggravated assault.
SOURCE: Data from OJJDP Statistical Briefing Book. https://www.ojjdp.gov/ojstatbb/special_topics/qa11501.asp?qaDate=2018

increased involvement with the criminal justice system in adulthood, with negative implications for earnings later in life (Aizer & Doyle, 2015; Baron et al., 2023).

There are many reasons why poor youth are more likely to be involved in the criminal justice system. Some relate to criminal justice policy and practices that target low-income communities and populations, but others relate to differences in youth behavior. Regarding the latter, research has found that schooling and educational attainment, exposure to the environmental toxin lead, household income, and the development of socioemotional skills all play important roles in youth offending. Each of these factors is described briefly below. We follow this with a discussion of the effects of the criminal justice system on low-income youth, and especially youth of color, and how the system itself perpetuates intergenerational poverty. We focus on three aspects of the criminal justice system. These include high-frequency police encounters and excessive use of force, juvenile detention and incarceration, and adult interaction (including caregiver interaction) with the criminal justice system.

BOX 9-1
Useful Definitions

Confinement: Detention or incarceration in secure facilities.

Detention: The temporary holding of individuals accused of crime awaiting an adjudication hearing, disposition, or commitment placement.

Disposition: A sentence or punishment.

Incarceration: The long-term confinement of convicted and sentenced offenders.

Juvenile delinquency: The violation of a law of the United States committed by a person prior to his 18th birthday which would have been a crime if committed by an adult.

Status offenses: Noncriminal offenses only applicable to children, such as being truant, running away from home, possessing alcohol or cigarettes.

Technical violation: No crime or arrest, but failure to follow the rules and conditions of probation.

Violent crime: Crimes of violence include rape, robbery, assault, and murder.

SOURCE: Committee generated.

Causes of Youth Offending

Evidence suggests a causal connection between higher quantity and quality of schooling and the committing of fewer crimes. Studies taking advantage of the fact that states have raised their school-leaving age (the age at which a student can legally stop attending high school) at different times have found that children who are legally required to remain in school longer are less likely to commit crimes and/or to be subsequently incarcerated than children who do not face legal constraints (Lochner & Moretti, 2004, for the United States; Machin et al., 2011, for the United Kingdom).

School financing reforms that have increased school spending overall and disproportionately among low-income school districts have also been shown to reduce future offending: A 10% increase in school funding is associated with a 15% reduction in the probability of children in that school district being arrested by age 30 (Baron et al., 2022b). A recent study of North Carolina's Smart Start early childhood grants also found links to reductions in later youth crime but as pointed out in Chapter 4, these findings might not generalize (Anders et al., 2023).

Reductions in childhood exposure to lead and lead poisoning have also played an important role in the declines in youth crime since the mid-1990s. Children are especially vulnerable to lead exposure because they absorb more lead than adults, and the neurological effects of exposure (including cognitive declines and aggressive behavior) are more consequential in developing brains. The removal of lead from gasoline and paint in the United States in the 1970s and 1980s eliminated two major sources of lead from the environment, and a decline in the incidence of childhood lead poisoning soon followed. Recent work has taken advantage of the timing of these regulations, combined with spatial variation in exposure to lead, to estimate a causal impact of lead on crime. One research strategy focuses on proximity to roads: Children who lived closer to roads before lead was removed from gasoline had higher blood lead levels (BLLs) than those who lived farther away, but as lead was eliminated, these differences declined significantly. These differential declines in child BLLs were then found to be linked with declines in school suspensions, juvenile detention, and adult incarceration (Aizer & Currie, 2019; Grönqvist et al., 2020). Once children are exposed to lead, evidence suggests, providing additional services to those children with elevated levels can be effective in improving outcomes, including reducing arrest rates (Billings & Schnepel, 2018).

Interventions can be effective in changing young people's decision-making skills and self-control, which in turn can affect their criminal behavior. Using cognitive behavioral therapeutic techniques, researchers conducted a random-assignment evaluation of an intervention designed to encourage youth to consider alternative responses to a provocation. They found that the intervention, called Becoming a Man (BAM), reduced arrests overall by 35% and arrests for violent crimes by 50%, and it increased high school graduation rates by 19% (Heller et al., 2017).

Finally, family income in adolescence has been shown to have a direct causal impact on criminal activity in some settings. As reviewed in Chapter 6, some families took advantage of the openings of casinos on Native American reservations, which resulted in regular government transfers of casino profits to eligible Tribal members, whether or not they were employed in the casinos. This immediately increased family income for the children residing in Native American families, but not other children. Researchers documented that a $4,000 increase in casino-based transfers reduced criminal offending at age 16 by 22% (Akee et al., 2010).

A second income-based study took advantage of the fact that the federal Supplemental Security Income (SSI) program, which provides cash transfers to low-income children with a disability, introduced a new policy requiring children born after a certain date to be recertified at their 18th birthday. This resulted in a large number of children losing this benefit at age 18. Researchers found individuals who lost their SSI benefits were much more likely to be arrested for property crime, but not violent crime, than those who were born before the cut-off date and did not lose their benefits (Deshpande & Mueller-Smith, 2022).

Random-assignment evaluations have also shown that summer employment programs for youth reduce arrests, although they do not improve educational or employment outcomes. The differences in arrests largely disappear after 4 years (Davis & Heller, 2020).

High-Frequency Police Encounters and Excessive Use of Force

As noted above, policing can reduce violent crime, but aggressive policing that results in high-frequency interactions with community members (i.e., stop-and-frisk) has been shown to harm child development.[5] Legewie and Fagan (2019) studied the impact of a New York Police Department strategy of saturating high-crime areas with additional police officers instructed to engage in aggressive, order-maintenance policing. Exploiting the quasi-random timing of the roll-out of the strategy across precincts, the authors document that test scores for Black male youth fell after the strategy was rolled out in their neighborhood, consistent with the finding that greater exposure to aggressive policing hurts school performance. They found no corresponding effect for Black girls or Latino students.

---

[5] In New York City alone, stop-and-frisk (also known as Terry stops) increased from 100,000 stops per year in 2002 to nearly 700,000 by 2011, after which it was outlawed (https://www.prisonpolicy.org/blog/2016/05/16/stop-frisk-ineffective/).

A complementary working paper by Bacher-Hicks and de la Campa (2020) examines the impact of stop-and-frisk policing tactics in New York City. The authors took advantage of the quasi-random assignment or transfer of commanding officers across precincts. They found that the departure of a commanding officer who is more likely to employ stop-and-frisk tactics from a precinct causes a decrease in stop-and-frisk and an increase in educational attainment (high school and college completion) among the young people who were most likely to have been exposed to stop-and-frisk policies under the old regime.

Aggressive policing can also have a negative indirect effect on children and youth who may not be targets themselves but are nonetheless exposed to such tactics. Ang (2021) examined the impact of 627 officer-involved killings on the educational attainment and psychological well-being of 700,000 students in Los Angeles. Ang found that in the days following an officer-involved killing, absenteeism increases and student average GPA falls as much as 0.08 standard deviations in the following semester. In the long run, students exposed to an officer-involved killing in the 9th grade are 3.5% less likely to graduate from high school and 2.5% less likely to enroll in college.

Youth Confinement

Juvenile crime and confinement have fallen by two-thirds over the past 30 years, and the most dramatic declines have occurred for White, Black, Latino, and Native American youth (see Appendix C: Chapter 9). Despite these declines, youth are still incarcerated in the United States at rates far higher than in all other developed democratic countries and many developing countries (Nowak, 2019). The dramatic decline in youth confinement appears to be driven by the declines in crime, and not by changes in the probability of confinement conditional on a juvenile court case, a probability that has held steady at 29% since 2005 (Annie E. Casey Foundation, 2021). Moreover, while among all young people involvement in the criminal justice system has declined, Black, Latino, and Native American youth are still significantly more likely than their White counterparts to be arrested, referred to court, and placed in out-of-home facilities after adjudication (Office of Juvenile Justice and Delinquency Prevention, 2022).

Most confined youth have not been convicted of a violent crime. Figure 9-3 shows that there were roughly 48,000 young people confined to a facility in 2019, including 16,858 youth in detention centers awaiting trial or sentencing; that is, without a conviction. Of those in detention (data not shown), roughly 4,000 had been charged with status offenses—which are behaviors that are not law violations for adults—or technical violations, and more than 6,000 had been charged with nonviolent offenses (property,

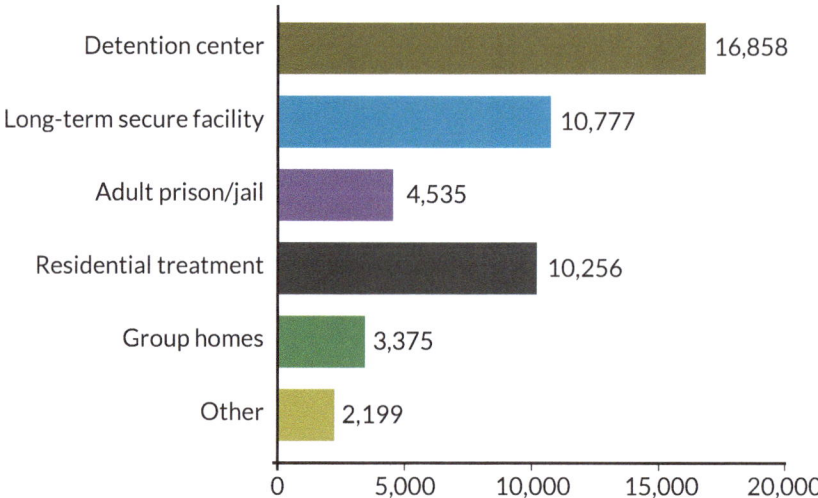

FIGURE 9-3 Number of confined youth by type of facility in 2019.
SOURCE: Adapted from the Prison Policy Initiative's "Youth Confinement: The Whole Pie 2019" (Sawyer, 2019). https://www.prisonpolicy.org/reports/youth2019.html

drug, public order violations; Sawyer, 2019). Combining youth in detention centers and in long-term secure facilities, Figure 9-4 shows that over half had been charged with or convicted of nonviolent offenses, a pattern that is even more pronounced in residential treatment centers and group homes (Sawyer, 2019).

Detaining or incarcerating juveniles for even short periods results in significant human capital costs for them. Research relying on variations in the sentencing propensities (strictness) of different judges, coupled with the random assignment of youth defendants to judges, shows that youth accused of either nonviolent or violent offenses are significantly more likely to graduate from high school and less likely to be arrested or incarcerated as an adult if they are not detained (Aizer & Doyle, 2015; Baron et al., 2023).[6]

---

[6] Aizer and Doyle (2015) study this in the context of detention of any kind in Illinois; and Baron et al. (2023) study this in the context of pretrial detention in Michigan. Effects are similar across the two studies; however, the results from Baron et al. (2023) are precise for violent offenders as well as nonviolent offenders, while the estimated results from Aizer and Doyle are precise only for nonviolent offenders. The estimated magnitudes are similar for both violent and nonviolent offenders.

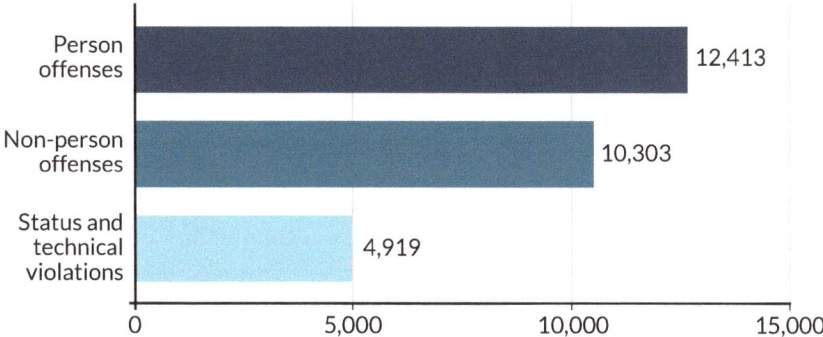

FIGURE 9-4 Number of youth in long-term secure facilities/detention in 2019 by offense category.
SOURCE: Adapted from the Prison Policy Initiative's "Youth Confinement: The Whole Pie 2019" (Sawyer, 2019). https://www.prisonpolicy.org/reports/youth2019.html

Juvenile incarceration has also been found to harm mental and physical health (Barnert et al., 2016; see Development Services, Inc., 2017, for a review), both of which are strong predictors of adult economic outcomes and future well-being more generally (see Chapter 5 for more detail). One might argue that although detention appears to increase recidivism among those detained, it might reduce juvenile offending through a deterrence effect, justifying a role for juvenile detention in reducing crime and victimization. Among adults, the evidence for the deterrent effect of incarceration is weak (Chalfin & McCrary, 2017). In the case of young people, a large body of research has examined differences in reoffending among those who face different sanctions, based on adult court transfer laws, and has found modest differences (Redding, 2010). Lee and McCrary (2017) studied offending around the time of an individual's 18th birthday, when sanctions increase immediately, and found a very small reduction.

In addition, fines and fees levied against juveniles may have negative long-term consequences. All 50 states allow juvenile courts to require restitution, although the types of fines and fees may vary, including fees for supervision, evaluation, testing, detention, and court costs (Smith et al., 2022). Descriptive studies show that fines and fees place a significant financial burden on youth and families, especially low-income and Black, Latino, and Native American families, who have disproportionate contact with the criminal justice system (Feierman et al., 2016; Paik & Packard,

2019; Policy Advocacy Clinic, 2017). Piquero and Jennings (2017) found that owing fines, fees, and restitution, as well as the total amounts owed, is correlated with an increase in the likelihood of recidivism among juveniles during the 2-year period following adjudication. Further research is needed to determine whether this reduces intergenerational mobility.

Finally, realigning costs and incentives for incarcerating juveniles more generally so that the localities responsible for sentencing decisions bear the costs of incarceration would lead to greater accountability and, evidence suggests, lower costs, and no increase in crime (Ouss, 2020).

Parent and Caregiver Interaction with the Criminal Justice System: Incarceration, Fines, and Fees

Parent and caregiver incarceration as well as their court fines and fees reduce household resources available for investment in children. In addition to lowering children's future earnings (Looney & Turner, 2018; Mueller-Smith, 2015), caregiver incarceration is an adverse childhood experience that is associated with increased stress and worse socioeconomic outcomes (Metzler et al., 2017).

Through fines and fees, interaction with the court system increases household debt. The share of prisoners with court fines and sanctions increased from 25% in 1991 to 66% in 2006. As of 2006, the most recent year for which a comprehensive figure is available, an estimated 10 million people had debts of more than $50 billion as a result of their involvement in the criminal justice system; that figure is likely to be higher today (Harris et al., 2010, 2022).[7] Fines and fees create a special burden for poor defendants who have difficulty complying with financial sanctions to avoid further penalties (Friedman & Pattillo, 2019). Recent evidence from a randomized control trial in misdemeanor court in Oklahoma County showed that court fines and fees led to warrants for nonpayment, debts in collection, and state garnishment of tax refunds (Pager et al., 2022).

Research has not yet established whether fines and fees affect the intergenerational mobility of children growing up in low-income families, nor is the evidence regarding the impact of parental incarceration on child outcomes entirely consistent (see Appendix C: Chapter 9). However, it is

---

[7] Many legal infractions are punished through the imposition of fines. Courts can require defendants to pay fees for services and for their court-appointed lawyer (43 states), and they can charge room and board for time in prison (41 states). Failure to pay can result in imprisonment. Since 2008, every state has increased its reliance on fees and fines to raise revenue (see Hayes & Barnhorst, 2020, for an overview and citations).

known that both disproportionately affect the poor and further reduce household resources available for investment in children.

Conclusion 9-2: While reductions in crime and victimization clearly benefit children, some efforts to reduce crime also have the potential to harm them. Aggressive policing has been linked to worse educational outcomes for youth, especially Black and Latino youth. Juvenile detention lowers the rate of high school completion and increases the likelihood of incarceration in adulthood. Declines in juvenile offending, stemming in part from increased investment in children's education and health, have lowered juvenile detention rates, although significant disparities by race and income remain. Finally, the rise in adult incarceration has increased the number of low-income children with parents/caregivers under supervision, reducing household earnings and increasing household debt. As a result, fewer resources are available to invest in children.

INTERVENTIONS INVOLVING NEIGHBORHOOD CRIME AND CRIMINAL JUSTICE

The committee identified a number of evidence-based interventions that address violence and victimization as well as the ways in which the criminal justice system affects youth outcomes and, ultimately, intergenerational mobility. As in other chapters, the committee highlights policies and programs for which direct evidence has established connections with correlates of intergenerational poverty in adulthood—earnings, educational attainment, and incarceration. As discussed in Chapter 1, we characterize the evidence on some of these programs or policies as "strong" and denote them with an "*." This indicates that the program's or policy's impact on intergenerational poverty is supported by random-assignment evaluation evidence that has been replicated across several sites or by compelling quasi-experimental evidence based on national or multistate data or a scaled-up program.

Policies and programs linked to child and adolescent mortality are also included here (and in Chapter 5, which focuses on health outcomes). Appendix C: Chapter 9 provides details on the interventions listed here. Interventions supported by indirect evidence; that is, those with possible, but not proven, impacts on intergenerational poverty, are briefly listed here and detailed in Appendix C: Chapter 9.

Policy and Program Ideas Based on Direct Evidence

Reducing Juvenile Confinement: Detention and Incarceration

Given the strong evidence linking juvenile detention for even short periods of time to lower high school graduation rates and increases in adult incarceration; the extremely high annual costs of detention (between $85,000 and over $500,000, depending on the state); and the effectiveness of alternatives to incarceration and detention, such as electronic monitoring, community supports, and Intensive Supervision Probation, the committee's consensus, consistent with previous National Academies reports,[8] was that:

- **Use juvenile confinement only for youth who pose a serious and immediate threat to public safety.** Restoring funding for the Office of Juvenile Justice and Delinquency Prevention, which has declined from $565 million in 2002 to $360 million in 2022, to its previous real level ($932 million in current dollars) would provide resources to states and localities to incentivize the use of non-secure settings for juveniles.

Providing incentives to state and local governments to reduce reliance on juvenile detention will likely lead to disproportionate mobility benefits for Black and Native American youth. It is important that any steps taken to reduce juvenile confinement be accompanied by efforts to monitor their possible effects on neighborhood crime levels.

Reducing Offending via Investments in Children

An alternative set of policies can lower the rate of juvenile detention indirectly by reducing future offending. These involve investments in children's human capital. Policies that have been shown to affect future offending include reducing exposure to lead, which is known to impair cognitive functioning and increase aggression, thereby improving educational outcomes, and influencing behavior through mentorship and other therapeutic interventions. Interventions to reduce lead are discussed in the health chapter; possible ways to boost educational attainment are discussed in the education chapter.

---

[8] The 2013 National Academies report, *Reforming Juvenile Justice: A Developmental Approach*, states: "To be clear, secure institutional confinement sometimes has a place in juvenile justice policy, but it should be used only for youth who pose a serious and immediate threat to public safety" (p. 123). A follow-up 2014 National Academies report, *Implementing Juvenile Justice Reform: The Federal Role*, established seven principles for the federal role in juvenile justice policy, one of which was "Confinement Only When Necessary for Public Safety."

In addition, the committee identified a promising therapeutic intervention that has been experimentally evaluated in one site and shown in several evaluations to significantly reduce arrests, especially for violent crime, and increase high school graduation rates. Details about our calculations are provided in Appendix C.

- **Scale up the BAM program to serve more of the at-risk population.** Providing a curriculum based on cognitive behavioral therapeutic approaches, the BAM program is estimated to cost $1,850 per participant per year. The committee considered funding BAM so that it can serve more of the population of at-risk adolescent boys, which is estimated to range between 300,000 and 500,000 annually. Serving 10% of the at-risk population (40,000) would cost a total of $720 million.

Reducing Victimization and Crime

Given the links between community-level physical disorder and crime, it is encouraging that several approaches appear to be successful in reducing disorder and crime. With details in Appendix C: Chapter 9, the committee considered scaling-up two of them.

- **Scale up successful programs that remediate vacant lots and abandoned homes.** A reasonable approach would be to appropriate $10 million per year over 10 years for a competitive grants process targeted at the 50 cities or jurisdictions with the highest rates of violent crime.
- **Improve and increase federal grants to community-based organizations.** Maintaining funding for nonprofit organizations at American Rescue Plan levels would support such community organizations.

Although policing has been shown to lower crime, especially homicides, and can be an effective means of reducing premature death and victimization, for any efforts to increase or enhance policing to reduce crime it is important to consider the potential for negative impacts of aggressive policing and frequent stops and searches of low-income and particularly minority youth. This leads us to suggest:

- **Expand funding for policing in high-crime neighborhoods and use of effective strategies like community policing.** This increased funding could be allocated toward: (a) putting more police on the streets in high-crime cities and neighborhoods; (b) providing technical assistance for local police to implement cost-effective "proactive" policing tactics that target areas of high violence, while also strengthening the practice of community policing and reducing/eliminating illegal or excessive force; and (c) funding cost-effective efforts to reduce youth violence by building stronger communities and training local residents to de-escalate violent situations.

Reducing Gun-Related Fatalities Among Children and Youth

Fatalities related to firearms are now the leading cause of death among children in the United States. The premature death of low-income children is a measure of extreme immobility. To reduce such fatalities, along with exposure to crime and violence, the committee explored a menu of proven interventions:

- Reduce access to guns in ways that pass constitutional review; promote child access prevention laws, restrictions on right-to-carry laws, limited guns access for domestic abusers, and sentencing add-ons for violence involving firearms.

Policy and Program Ideas Based on Indirect Evidence

As detailed in Appendix C: Chapter 9, a number of additional interventions may be promising avenues for increasing intergenerational mobility by reducing crime and the footprint of the criminal justice system, but still lack strong evidence of their effectiveness.

Ways for courts to reduce the negative impact of caregiver involvement in the criminal justice system:

- *Consider the best interest of the child* in pre-trial detention and sentencing decisions.
- *Consider financial obligations* to children in setting court fees and fines.

Promising programs to support at-risk youth:
- The *Choose to Change program* targets at risk youth and provides at-risk youth with community-based therapy and individualized support.
- *Mentoring programs* can reduce delinquent behavior and juvenile justice system involvement among youth.
- *Restorative justice programs* focus on the rehabilitation of offenders through reconciliation with victims and the community at large.
- *Eliminating fines and fees* for juveniles can reduce financial burdens.
- The *mental health* and *gun safety* interventions in Chapter 5 have the potential to reduce school shootings.

10

Child Maltreatment

Children who experience maltreatment and become involved with the child welfare system are at elevated risk for intergenerational poverty. This chapter provides a demographic overview of maltreatment and child welfare involvement and reviews the correlational evidence linking childhood maltreatment and child welfare involvement to adult poverty-related outcomes. It then reviews what is known about the factors that place children at risk of maltreatment and involvement with the child welfare system. Finally, it evaluates the evidence on effective policies and programs to reduce child maltreatment and child welfare system involvement and on their potential for reducing intergenerational poverty.

WHICH CHILDREN ARE INVOLVED WITH THE CHILD WELFARE SYSTEM?

Involvement with the child welfare system is surprisingly common in the United States. In 2020, the most recent year for which federal data are available (Administration for Children and Families, 2022a), approximately 7.2 million children were reported to child protective services (CPS), and of these about 3.1 million children were investigated or assessed by CPS. These children received foster care services in only about 3% (113,000) of these cases. In thinking about the causes of maltreatment and possible approaches to address it, it is important to bear in mind that most (more than three-quarters) of these investigated cases involved neglect, while the remaining quarter involved some form of alleged abuse—physical, sexual, or psychological.

Expressing the scope of child maltreatment in another way, each year the child welfare system substantiates maltreatment for just under 1% of U.S. children ages 0–17. As shown in Figure 10-1, this overall maltreatment rate has changed relatively little since 2008. But the figure also shows very different rates across racial/ethnic groups, with the highest rates among Black and Native American children and the lowest rates among Asian children. Subgroup rates have changed only in the case of Native American children and, in their cases rates have risen in the last 10 years and now exceed rates for Black children.

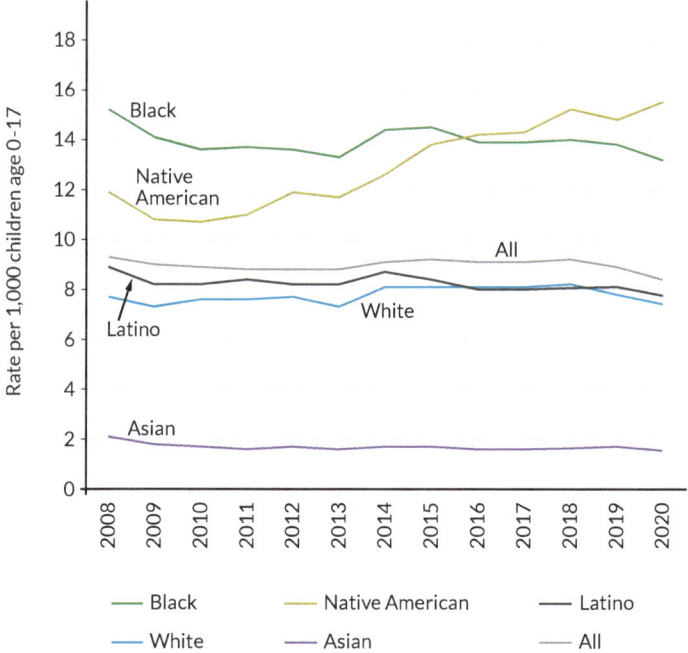

FIGURE 10-1 Rates of substantiated maltreatment of children ages 0–17 by selected characteristics, 2008–2020.
NOTES: Children are ages 0–17. The data in this table show rates of maltreatment based on investigations and assessments by CPS that found the child to be a victim of one or more types of maltreatment. The decrease in the rate of victims in 2020 is due in part to the decrease in the number of screened-in referrals during the March through June period. Additional technical notes are available in the annual reports titled *Child Maltreatment*. These reports are available at https://www.acf.hhs.gov/cb/data-research/child-maltreatment.
SOURCE: Data from Administration for Children and Families, National Child Abuse and Neglect Data System, as reported in Childstats.gov

These kinds of single-year estimates understate the childhood-wide risk of maltreatment. Wildeman et al. (2014) use data from 2011 and estimate that 12.5% of U.S. children will be involved with a confirmed case of maltreatment by 18 years of age. These rates are considerably higher for Black (20.9%), Native American (14.5%),[1] and Latino children (13.0%) than for White (10.7%) or Asian/Pacific Islander (3.8%) children. The risk for childhood maltreatment is highest in the first few years of life.[2]

Disparities by race and ethnicity are strongly correlated with subgroup differences in exposure to poverty and hardship (Eckenrode et al., 2014; Kim & Drake, 2018; Pelton, 2015; Putnam-Hornstein et al., 2021; Thomas & Waldfogel, 2022). Empirical evidence suggests that persistent racial/ethnic bias among actors within the child welfare system may expose Black, Native American, and Latino children to a greater risk of child welfare involvement (Dettlaff et al., 2011; Font et al., 2012).

Most children who are involved with the child welfare system disproportionately grow up in low-income families and are at elevated risk of poverty and other adverse outcomes in adulthood (Bunting et al., 2018; Currie & Widom, 2010; Mersky & Topitzes, 2010). Hence, they are a group at high risk of intergenerational poverty.

CHILD MALTREATMENT AND CHILD WELFARE SYSTEM INVOLVEMENT AS DRIVERS OF INTERGENERATIONAL POVERTY

Adult Correlates of Childhood Maltreatment

A large literature provides descriptive evidence that children who are maltreated (abused, neglected, or in other ways brought to the attention of the child welfare system) fare worse than their non-maltreated or non-child welfare-involved peers. Studies attempt to address selection by controlling for observable characteristics, which leaves open the possibility that outcome differences are partly or entirely caused by unobserved characteristics (Child Welfare Information Gateway, 2019).

---

[1] The childhood-wide risk estimates for Native American children are based on relatively small sample sizes, which may account for their different relative ranking in the single-year and childhood-wide estimates.

[2] Higher still are the estimates of the childhood-wide chance (37.4% overall) of *any* involvement with the welfare system, which can include cases reported to CPS but not substantiated by an investigation (H. Kim et al., 2017). Racial differences in estimates of lifetime involvement are also substantial. For example, half (53%) of Black children have at least some involvement, whether substantiated or not, with the child welfare system during their childhoods. At 32%, the rate of involvement is also elevated for Latino children. Rates for White (28%), Native American (23%) and Asian/Pacific Islander (10%) children are smaller.

In general, these descriptive studies consistently find that childhood abuse or neglect is predictive of poorer adult outcomes (see Appendix C: Chapter 10 for a more complete review). For example, Bunting et al. (2018) concluded that maltreatment in childhood is related to adverse economic outcomes, such as economic inactivity and income reductions, beyond the contribution of correlated poverty-related risk factors such as maternal education and welfare receipt during childhood. Examining intergenerational income mobility and child maltreatment, Bullinger et al. (2022) found that children residing in counties with lower child maltreatment report rates had a higher chance of intergenerational income mobility than those in counties with higher maltreatment rates. Zielinski (2009) found that adults who had experienced maltreatment as children had lower incomes, elevated utilization of Medicaid, and higher rates of unemployment than those without childhood maltreatment experiences. Notably, adults who had histories of multiple types of maltreatment were three times as likely as those who had not experienced maltreatment to live in poverty.

Consequences of Involvement with Child Protective Services

Only a few studies have used more rigorous methods to compare maltreated children with other children who are most similar to them. For example, Currie and Tekin (2012), using propensity score matching and twin comparisons, found that children who self-reported having been abused or neglected were much more likely to be involved in crime as adults than their non-abused or neglected counterparts. Currie and Widom (2010) used a case-control design and found that children who were substantiated by CPS to have been abused or neglected had lower levels of education, employment, earnings, and assets as adults. Although the methods used in these two studies are stronger than those used in purely correlational studies, at best their results should be considered suggestive of possible causal impacts. Moreover, neither of these studies (particularly Currie & Widom, 2010) was able to separate effects of maltreatment from effects of CPS involvement. For the same reasons that it is challenging to separate maltreatment effects from CPS involvement, it is also difficult to separate the effects of different degrees of CPS involvement. For example, estimating the effect of referral to CPS separate from the impact of substantiation of an allegation is complicated by the fact that substantiation likely involves more severe maltreatment. One exception to this is the decision to remove children from the home, for which there is causal evidence, which we summarize below.

Out-of-Home Care (Foster Care)

Among children with a substantiated case of maltreatment, roughly 3% receive foster care services involving relatives (kinship care), unrelated foster parents, or congregate care. Although they make up only a small share of those who experience maltreatment or child welfare involvement, foster care children are a very important group, as their families tend to be the most disadvantaged and the children themselves tend to face numerous challenges in adulthood.[3]

There is a large descriptive literature on children who are removed from their homes and placed into some form of out-of-home care. In general, children placed in congregate care fare worse than those placed with families through foster care (Lee et al., 2011). However, as with research on the more general child welfare population, the challenge in this research is to estimate the causal effects of out-of-home placement as distinct from the effects of factors that precipitated the placement. For that reason, a review of descriptive studies is provided in Appendix C: Chapter 10.

The strongest studies of the causal impacts of foster-care placements have used variation in the propensity of CPS investigators to remove children from their parental homes to identify the causal effect of out-of-home placement on later outcomes. In these studies, case assignment to investigators is generally based on their availability rather than characteristics of the case, so variation in investigators' propensities for out-of-home placements can be leveraged to identify causal impacts of the placements themselves. At the same time, it is important to note that these studies provide evidence about the effect placement has on a child who is at the margin between being removed and not being removed, but they are not informative as to the effect of placement on children whose circumstances at home are so severe that they would prompt placement regardless of the individual investigator or judge.

Taken together, these studies yield a mixed picture on whether out-of-home placements lead to better or worse child outcomes. Doyle (2007, 2008), who originated this method, find detrimental impacts. Specifically, using data from Illinois he found that removal from home between ages 5 and 13 leads to increased delinquency and arrests and reduced labor force participation.

Other studies have found beneficial impacts. Bald et al. (2022) use the investigator method with administrative data from Rhode Island to study outcomes for children who were investigated by CPS before age six. They find that removal leads to significantly higher test scores (an average gain

---

[3] Another important, and very disadvantaged, group is youth who are involved with both the child welfare and juvenile justice systems, who may be placed out of home by both systems (Herz et al., 2012; Hirsch et al., 2018).

of 1.4 standard deviations in math and reading) and significantly reduced grade repetition (an average reduction of 42.6 percentage points) for girls, with no significant effects for boys.[4] The same authors also examine outcomes for children removed at age 6 or later and, in contrast with their results for children removed at younger ages, find no significant effects for girls or boys, with some nonsignificant negative results on educational outcomes for boys.

Baron and Gross (2022) use the investigator method with administrative data from Michigan to study the effect removal has on involvement in crime. They found that foster care placement reduced adult arrests, convictions, and incarceration. Gross and Baron (2022), in a similar study, find that foster care placement led to improved safety and educational outcomes.

Impact studies based on investigator case assignment draw data from only three states and from different time periods, which is an important limitation if the effects of removal vary by state and time. For example, the likelihood that a child will be removed in a given state and period may vary considerably by factors such as whether there has been a recent high-profile child welfare case (e.g., a death), whether the state is under court mandate(s) or supervision, and the capacity, service availability, and quality of preventive and child welfare system services available, potentially including the size and composition of out-of-home placement slots.

More generally, it is probably overly simplistic to estimate a single effect of removal, since the effects on well-being likely vary by the types and quality of services provided, severity of maltreatment experienced, and length, stability, and type of out-of-home placement, as well as child and provider characteristics. Unfortunately, these issues have not been subject to rigorous examination. In addition, it is possible that the impact of out-of-home placement may differ by race and ethnicity if, for example, thresholds for removal (chronicity and/or severity of exposure to maltreatment), services received, types or quality of placements, or the "match" with placement settings and contexts (e.g., neighborhoods, schools) differ by race and ethnicity. Nevertheless, the empirical research to date has not established the extent to which the effects of removal vary by race and ethnicity. Doyle (2007, 2008) provides separate estimates for Black and Latino youth, but these constitute the bulk of his sample and thus, unsurprisingly, the estimates are similar to those for the full sample.

Conclusion 10-1: Children who have been maltreated and (or) involved with child welfare are at elevated risk of intergenerational poverty.

---

[4] A disadvantage of the investigator-based method is that it can lead to very large confidence intervals for its estimates. This is the case with Bald et al.'s (2022) estimates of impacts on achievement and grade retention.

However, high-quality research provides mixed evidence on the effects of foster care (occurring in only 3% of all child welfare cases) on subsequent outcomes in adolescence and adulthood and almost no evidence regarding the impact of child protective services more generally.

Factors Leading to Child Welfare Involvement

While the literature on the intergenerational impacts of child maltreatment is inconclusive, a parallel literature on the causes of child welfare involvement is more definitive and points to a number of policy approaches that appear successful in reducing involvement. The text portion of this chapter highlights four of the most promising policy-related approaches—income support, Medicaid, nutrition programs, and some community-focused prevention policies. Appendix C: Chapter 10 reviews the literature on four additional possible policy approaches: minimum wages, cash welfare programs, home visitation programs, and early care and education programs.

Parental Income and Employment

An extensive literature has documented that income and poverty are highly correlated with child maltreatment and child welfare system involvement. Indeed, across advanced industrialized countries, low income and poverty are the strongest and most consistent risk factors for child maltreatment and child welfare system involvement, and these relationships are particularly strong with respect to child neglect (Berger & Waldfogel, 2011). A growing body of research, predominantly from the United States, suggests that relatively modest increases in income, particularly among lower-income families, can lead to substantial reductions in child welfare system involvement (Font & Maguire-Jack, 2020b).

Cancian et al. (2013) capitalize on a policy experiment in Wisconsin in 1997–1998, which randomized families receiving Temporary Assistance for Needy Families into two groups, one of which received greater child support benefits and one of which received less. The differences in child support received between the two groups were modest, ranging between $101 and $180 per year. Despite this modest difference in income, the study found that families with more child support income were about 10%, or 2 percentage points, less likely to have a substantiated report of child maltreatment over the course of 2 years. A potential problem with an income-based interpretation of these results is that child support receipt may signal differential willingness or ability of fathers to be involved with their children. A review of the impacts of another major welfare program—Aid to Families with Dependent Children—is provided in Appendix C: Chapter 10.

Other research has capitalized on natural experiments in which policy benefits differ over time and place, providing exogenous sources of variation in families' income. Berger et al. (2017) draw on state-level differences in the generosity of Earned Income Tax Credit (EITC) benefits and find that $1,000 in additional income was associated with an 8% to 10% (0.58 to 0.70 percentage point) lower rate of child welfare contact and a 3% to 4% (1.0 to 1.2 percentage point) lower rate of parental behaviors proxying child neglect.

Klevens et al. (2017) use state-level variation in EITC payments between 1995 and 2013 to examine impacts on rates of hospital admissions for pediatric abusive head trauma. They find that states with a refundable EITC had 3.1 fewer hospital admissions for pediatric abusive head trauma per 100,000 children than states without a refundable EITC, but they found no difference in such hospital admissions between states with only a nonrefundable EITC and states without an EITC. Kovski et al. (2022) find that $1,000 in additional income available to families from EITC and Child Tax Credit benefits led to a 5% lower state-level rate of child maltreatment investigations in the short term.

Research on the effects of economic support policies (and income) on child maltreatment has not explicitly examined heterogeneity by race/ethnicity. However, given that populations of color, and Black and Native American populations in particular, are disproportionately likely to have both low family incomes and be involved in the child welfare system-involved, economic support policies have the potential to disproportionately benefit these groups and, thereby, to reduce racial/ethnic disparities in child maltreatment and child welfare system involvement. Pac et al. (2023), using estimates of the causal effect of income on child maltreatment, estimate that reducing child poverty by 40% to 46% by applying the policy proposals provided in National Academies (2019a) would result in 11% to 20% fewer child maltreatment investigations. Because these policies have greater poverty-reducing impacts on Black and Latino children, Pac et al. estimates suggest that the effects on children's involvement in the child welfare system would be two to three times larger among Black and Latino children than White children (Native American children were not separately analyzed).

Medicaid

Whether expanded access to health care through public programs for low-income families is likely to increase, decrease, or have no effect on reported child maltreatment or child welfare system involvement is theoretically ambiguous. Because health care providers are required to report cases of possible child maltreatment, greater family interactions with them may result in increased reports to CPS.

At the same time, greater access to health care for children and (potentially) parents may result in decreased child maltreatment and/or CPS involvement for several reasons. First, such access may reduce parental stress about their own or their children's health care needs and the cost thereof, including by reducing out-of-pocket medical expenditures and medical debt. Second, to the extent that parents access treatment for their own health and mental health needs, they may be better equipped to provide safe and consistent care for their children. Third, to the extent that children's health and mental health needs are treated (early), they may be easier to parent and thereby be less likely to experience maltreatment. Fourth, health care providers may serve as a referral source to other programs spanning parenting behaviors, child development, and food and nutrition, which may help reduce a family's likelihood of maltreatment or child welfare system contact. As a result, access to low-cost or free health care may help families meet their children's health and mental health needs and, potentially, developmental and material needs as well, which may result in better care for children and a decreased probability of being reported for child abuse or neglect.

Three methodologically strong studies have taken advantage of geographic variation in the Medicaid expansions enabled under the Affordable Care Act. In a county-level analysis of California, Pac (2019) finds that expanded access to Medicaid was associated with an 11% reduction in physical abuse investigations but no differences in overall investigations or investigations for other types of maltreatment. Brown et al. (2019) use data from 2010 to 2016 on the state-by-state expansions of the Affordable Care Act and find an 11% decrease in neglect investigations in Medicaid-expansion states relative to non-expansion states in the post-expansion period, but no effect on abuse investigations. Finally, McGinty et al. (2022) find that state Medicaid expansions were associated with reductions in neglect investigations of 13% for 0–5-year-olds, 15% for 6–12-year-olds, and 16% for 13–17-year-olds, although they find no effects for physical abuse. Together, these studies suggest a potential causal relationship between Medicaid access and reductions in child welfare investigations, for neglect, but not necessarily abuse.

Food and Nutrition Programs

The committee identified three rigorous studies examining the impact of food and nutrition programs on child maltreatment. Two focus on the Supplemental Nutrition Assistance Program (SNAP); the third considers both SNAP and the Special Supplemental Nutrition Program for Women, Infants and Children (WIC). Johnson-Motoyama et al. (2022) use variation in the number of state SNAP income generosity policies in effect (broad-based community eligibility, excluding child support received from income calculation, providing transitional SNAP benefits for families leaving cash welfare, simplified reporting of changes in household circumstances) to examine the effects of SNAP policy generosity and caseload size (participation) on child maltreatment rates across states and over the 2004–2016 time period. Results indicate that the effect on maltreatment of each additional income generosity policy and of a 5% increase in SNAP caseload size are similar in magnitude, with each resulting in an 8% to 9% reduction in child maltreatment investigations, 9% to 10% reduction in substantiation cases of maltreatment, and 9% to 15% reduction in foster care placements.

Bullinger et al. (2021) leverage within-monthly group variation by Census block in proximity to a SNAP-authorized retailer to estimate monthly within-Census block group changes in child maltreatment rates in Connecticut between 2011–2015. They find that, in large rural locales, each additional SNAP-authorized retailer in a Census block group is associated with a 4% decrease in maltreatment reports and an 11% decrease in maltreatment substantiations.

In their investigation of the effects of both SNAP and WIC participation on child maltreatment, Lee and Mackey-Bilaver (2007) compare siblings using individual-level administrative data on Medicaid-enrolled children in Illinois. They find that participation in SNAP only, WIC only, and both programs is associated with reductions in substantiated child maltreatment of 7%, 11%, and 9%, respectively.

Community-focused Prevention Programs

Several large-scale community-focused interventions have been launched in recent decades aimed at improving parenting and family functioning and reducing child maltreatment. Such programs typically include both universal (community-level) and targeted components, such that particularly at-risk families have opportunities to engage in more intensive services than their less at-risk counterparts. That is, they tend to offer a continuum of interventions intended to address the needs of particular subgroups of families through direct service provision and/or by assisting families to access existing programs and services (Berger & Font, 2015). Such programs are difficult to evaluate rigorously, and the evidence on their efficacy is quite limited. Moreover, they tend to be difficult to implement and sustain, as well as relatively expensive.

A notable exception, however, is the Positive Parenting Program (Triple P), which has been implemented in a growing number of communities and has been subject to the most rigorous evaluation of such programs to date. A summary of impact evaluations is available from the California

Evidence-Based Clearinghouse for Child Welfare.[5] An example is Prinz et al. (2009), an evaluation of Triple P in 18 counties that were randomly assigned to either Triple P implementation or services as usual. The evaluation found that, 2 years after implementation, Triple P counties experienced substantial reductions in substantiated child maltreatment, out-of-home placements, and hospital and emergency room admissions for child maltreatment-related reasons. In a more recent quasi-experimental study, Schilling et al. (2020) compare county-level child welfare and hospital discharge data in North Carolina for 34 counties that implemented Triple P and 66 counties that did not, for the period 2008–2015. Results indicate that implementation was associated with a 4% reduction in county-level child welfare investigations and a 7% decrease in foster care placements. The study found no effects on hospital admissions for child maltreatment-related reasons.

Conclusion 10-2: Causal evidence on factors leading to maltreatment and child welfare involvement is limited, although most evidence points to household economic hardship as elevating the risk of child welfare involvement and to income support and income-support policies reducing risk for child welfare involvement. Evidence on the likely favorable impacts of Medicaid and food and nutrition program eligibility is also relatively strong.

INTERVENTIONS REDUCING CHILD MALTREATMENT

Evidence on prevention policies and programs offers some promising avenues for reducing the number of child maltreatment cases reported to or substantiated by child welfare services. On the other hand, the literature on the longer-run causal impacts of the various elements of the child welfare system on poverty in adulthood is not strong enough to identify the changes to the system that would reduce intergenerational poverty. This leads us to consider the following promising prevention approaches as indirect approaches to reducing intergenerational poverty:

- The most consistent evidence of causal effects on reduced child maltreatment is for *direct income transfers to low-income families*.
- Consistent evidence of reductions in child maltreatment is also found in strong studies of the impacts of the *recent Medicaid expansions* occasioned by the Affordable Care Act.

---

[5] For more information see https://www.cebc4cw.org/

- Expansions of eligibility and benefit levels in *food and nutrition programs* such as SNAP and WIC have also been linked with reductions in child maltreatment.
- Some *community-level interventions* such as the Triple P appear to be promising approaches for reducing child maltreatment.

11

Research and Data Needs for Understanding and Ameliorating Intergenerational Poverty

Based on its review of the literature, the committee outlined the scope of intergenerational poverty in the United States. It found that many children growing up in low-income households experience some degree of upward mobility. At least two-thirds are not living in low-income households in adulthood, and some enjoyed standards of living well above any definition of poverty. But one in three children are still low-income when they become adults, and the chance of having low income in adulthood is much higher for a child raised in a low-income than more affluent household.

Regardless of the data source or the definition of poverty, the committee found that racial/ethnic disparities are an enduring feature of the intergenerational trajectories of children, with Black and Native American children experiencing much less upward mobility than White children growing up in the same economic circumstances. The size and consistency of these gaps underscore the importance of understanding the causes of racial/ethnic disparities (Chapter 3), as well as developing and implementing large-scale, effective policies and programs to ameliorate intergenerational poverty.

The committee reviewed research on potentially important drivers of intergenerational poverty in the following domains: children's education and the educational system; child health and the health care system; family income and wealth and parental earnings and employment; family structure; housing, residential mobility, and neighborhood conditions; neighborhood safety and the criminal justice system; and child maltreatment and the child welfare system (see Chapters 4–10 for the committee's assessment of the evidence and Appendix C: Chapter 11 for the conclusions regarding these drivers). It found that abundant correlational evidence established the potential importance of each of these domains for perpetuating or alleviating intergenerational poverty persistence. But definitive causal evidence quantifying the relative importance of each of these domains was often lacking, which pointed to a number of steps that could strengthen the evidence base.

The committee's primary assignment was to identify evidence-based policies and programs directed at children living in poverty today that would reduce those children's chances of being poor when they become adults. In operationalizing the definition of "evidence-based," the committee decided to highlight incremental policy and program ideas whose effectiveness is supported by *direct* intergenerational evidence—studies that offered rigorous long-run causal evidence (see Table 11-1 for the committee's list of policy and program ideas that met this standard of evidence).

The committee found a lack of high-quality evidence on the intergenerational impacts of many other promising programs. It emphasizes that this should not be taken to mean that most of those other programs are ineffective—only that their intergenerational impacts have not been assessed. This fact is sobering but not surprising, given the expense and difficulty of scaling up promising interventions identified in controlled experiments, the length of time required to see the effects of interventions on intergenerational poverty, the difficulties of assembling data for historical, retrospective analysis, and the costs of obtaining an adequate sample size for populations most at risk of intergenerational poverty, especially Native Americans.

Another noteworthy consequence of the committee's high standard of evidence is that because studies that met it focused on individual policies, the committee was unable to identify evidence-based combinations of federal policy investments that could reduce intergenerational poverty persistence. The report notes a number of instances where combining programs might generate more benefits than the individual programs taken by themselves, but here too the evidence does not support confident conclusions.

In this chapter, the committee offers general principles to guide private and public funding organizations in supporting needed research on intergenerational poverty. It then addresses the need for a federal infrastructure of census, survey, and administrative records data that can be linked, going forward and backward in time, and accessed for research and policy analysis purposes. These purposes would include analyzing trends in intergenerational poverty, overall and for population subgroups, and estimating the likely effects of policies and programs intended to foster intergenerational mobility for all children. As with all research data, it is vital to ensure that administrative and survey data be made available to the research and policy evaluation community in ways that respect respondents and protect the confidentiality of their data. At present, substantial barriers impede access

TABLE 11-1 Program and Policy Ideas Linked by Direct Evidence to Reductions in Intergenerational Poverty

Driver		Program or policy idea (* indicates that the supporting evidence was particularly strong)
Education		
	• Early childhood	None identified in recent research
	• K–12 education	Increase K–12 school spending in the poorest districts* Increase teacher workforce diversity* Reduce exclusionary school discipline* Increase access to Ethnic Studies courses
	• Postsecondary education	Expand effective financial aid programs for low-income students* Increase campus supports (such as tutoring and case management)*
	• Career training	Expand high-quality career and technical education programs in high school* Expand sectoral training programs for adults and youth*
Child and Maternal Health		
	• Family planning	Increase funding for Title X family planning programs* Ensure that Medicaid beneficiaries have access to family planning services*
	• Health insurance	Expand access to Medicaid with continuous 12-month eligibility and 12-month post-partum coverage* Expand access to Indian Health Services for all eligible mothers and children
	• Pollution reduction	Support the EPA to work with local partners to adopt and expand efficient methods of monitoring outdoor and—especially in schools—indoor air quality
	• Nutrition	Remove the 5-year waiting period of Supplemental Nutrition Assistance Program (SNAP) eligibility for legal permanent-resident parents* Eliminate the proration of SNAP benefits for citizen children with undocumented parents
Family Income, Wealth, and Employment		
	• Work-based income support	Expand the Earned Income Tax Credit by increasing payments along some or all portions of the schedule and possibly by providing a credit to families with no earnings*
Family Structure		
		None identified by research to date

(continued)

TABLE 11-1 Continued

Driver	Program or policy idea (* indicates that the supporting evidence was particularly strong)
Housing and Neighborhoods	
• Residential mobility	Expand coverage of the Housing Choice Voucher program and couple it with customized counseling and case management services to facilitate moves to low-poverty neighborhoods
Neighborhood Crime and the Criminal Justice System	
• Juvenile incarceration	Use juvenile confinement only for youth who pose a serious and immediate threat to public safety*
• Child investment strategies	Improve school quality and reduce lead exposure in ways identified in the education and health categories* Scale up evidence-based therapeutic interventions such as the Becoming a Man program
• Strengthen communities to reduce violent crime and victimization	Scale up programs that abate vacant lots and abandoned homes* Increase grants to community-based organizations*
• Policing strategies	Expand funding for policing in high-crime neighborhoods* Expand use of effective strategies like community policing*
• Gun safety	Improve gun safety in ways that pass constitutional review* Promote child access prevention laws and restrictions on right-to-carry laws, limit access to guns by domestic abusers* Promote sentencing add-ons for violence involving firearms*
Child Maltreatment	
	None identified by research to date
Racial Disparities	
	A number of the policies and programs listed above have been shown to be effective for Black children and families (See Table C-3-1)*

NOTES: "*" indicates that the program's or policy's impact on intergenerational poverty is supported by random-assignment evaluation evidence that has been replicated across several sites or by compelling quasi-experimental evidence based on national or multi-state data or a scaled-up program. Table entries without an "*" represent programs or policies for which the evidence has not been replicated or the policy has not been scaled up.

to federal data for evidence building use. The chapter ends with the committee's conclusions and recommendations to meet research and data needs.

PRIORITIES FOR FUTURE RESEARCH

This report has prioritized drawing lessons from strong causal research on drivers of intergenerational poverty and on policies and programs that might reduce it. The most obvious examples of strong causal research designs are studies modeled after clinical trials, which either randomly assign children or families to a policy or program or take advantage of some kind of lottery process that randomly offers opportunities to participate in the program or policy. The Head Start Impact Study is an example of explicit random assignment (Puma et al., 2012). However, most clinical trial–type studies are almost never conducted or followed up at the scale needed to establish that an intervention will be effective in a variety of settings and for all population groups.

Most of the available causal research on intergenerational poverty is "quasi-experimental," examining in retrospect the consequences for children of naturally occurring policy changes that were rolled out over time and across well-defined geographic areas. When matched to long-run administrative or survey data, these quasi-experimental data enable researchers to compare the longer-run outcomes of children to identify those who benefited from the program. A prominent example is Hoynes et al. (2016), which took advantage of the slow county-by-county roll-out of the Food Stamp Program in the 1960s and 1970s. Using longitudinal survey data from the Panel Study of Income Dynamics, the researchers found that the adult cardiovascular health of children born in counties already offering the Food Stamp Program was much better relative to children who were born at the same time but grew up in counties that did not offer food stamps until they had entered school.

Bailey et al. (2020) also analyzed the county-level roll-out of the Head Start Program, comparing long-run outcomes for children residing in Head Start counties and those in other counties using census and Social Security data. Aizer and Doyle (2015) took advantage of the fact that court cases are randomly assigned to judges who differ in their tendency to detain or incarcerate youth defendants. They matched defendants to administrative data on their adult labor-market and criminal behavior to study the impacts of juvenile detention and incarceration on adult crime and labor market success.

These examples illustrate the importance of facilitating several kinds of research by providing the necessary data—these examples illustrate the importance of facilitating policy research by supporting long-run follow-ups of random-assignment studies as well as providing administrative and survey data that can be used to study the impacts of policies and programs that are implemented in ways that create "natural experiments" for policy researchers. Supporting more of these kinds of exemplary studies and expanding their capacity to inform policy, however, poses a variety of challenges for researchers and their funders:

- The costs and difficulties of scaling up promising interventions identified in controlled experiments;
- The length of time required to see the effects of interventions on future intergenerational poverty, which means that researchers could have to wait 20 or more years for results;
- The difficulty of anticipating what policies and interventions will be of interest decades in the future;
- The costs of adequate sample size for population groups of interest (e.g., most surveys and evaluation studies are not able to support reliable analyses for Native Americans); and
- The difficulties of and barriers to accessing and linking the most useful data, which often come from federal, state, and local administrative records, for evaluating the impacts of past program and policy changes.

A central goal for research policy should be to reduce barriers to developing better evidence about drivers and policies impacting intergenerational poverty. This chapter discusses several ways to do this. To help target resources for research that could lead to effective policies, we list in Box 11-1 important research priorities for each of the domains we cover.

RESEARCH FUNDING PRINCIPLES AND GUIDANCE

Principles

In an effort to identify proven programs for boosting every child's chance to succeed, the committee proposes three broad principles for research funding. These principles apply both to evaluations of the effectiveness of past policy and program changes and to prospective research—that is, research where previous experimentation has not been done or has failed to identify promising programs and where retrospective research is impossible.

The committee also hopes that funding organizations, public and private, will support the construction and use of linked administrative and survey data that could support more extensive retrospective and prospective research (see next section). Moreover, the committee hopes that funding organizations will work together to provide the level of support that is necessary for effective research and policy assessment aimed at reducing intergenerational poverty, particularly among high-risk population groups.

The committee's research funding principles apply to evaluations of the effectiveness of past policy and program changes (Principle 1); prospective research (Principle 2); and focusing on populations in need (Principle 3).

- **Principle 1: Prioritize strong research designs that provide causal estimates of program impacts.** This report has prioritized drawing lessons from strong causal research on drivers of intergenerational poverty and on policies and programs that might reduce it. This is because methodological research has repeatedly shown that correlational techniques such as propensity score matching can often (but not always) provide badly biased estimates of program impacts (Cook et al., 2008; LaLonde, 1986).[1]
- **Principle 2: For prospective research, set aside funding for rigorous, small-scale experiments, but also for replications, scaled-up evaluations, and long-term follow-ups of promising programs.** Research portfolios on ameliorating intergenerational poverty in one or more domains should, as a matter of course, contain three broad funding components. The first would fund careful, smaller-scale, and shorter-term experimental evaluations of potentially promising program models. The second component would provide funding to replicate those programs that show promise in the experimental phase across diverse populations and at scale. The third component would fund the investigation of longer-run impacts of as many programs as possible that have shown promise in the experimental and replication arms of the research, using a combination of administrative data and surveys for follow-up purposes. So that outcomes can subsequently be tracked using administrative and survey data, researchers conducting shorter-term evaluations should secure and maintain the necessary permissions enabling them to track participants using administrative or survey data later on. In all these steps, protecting the identity of research subjects is of the utmost importance.
- **Principle 3: Fund research arms for specific communities.** Research portfolios should focus on population groups and communities at highest risk of intergenerational poverty, not only to target scarce research dollars as effectively as possible, but also to help people

---

[1] Heckman et al. (1999) established some conditions under which nonexperimental evaluations of job training programs can come close to generating similar results to experimental evaluations. However, in many other kinds of evaluations, no such conditions have been established.

BOX 11-1
Research Priorities to Ameliorate Intergenerational Poverty and Facilitate Socioeconomic Mobility, by Domain

Racial Disparities
- Conduct research to quantify structural racism in such domains as neighborhood, workplace, health care, and others, using standardized measures.
- Conduct quasi-experimental policy and intervention studies that prioritize data and research designs that provide separate impact estimates by race and ethnicity.
- Develop and expand interventions and evaluations aimed at decreasing intergenerational poverty among Black and Native American people, while prioritizing community control and input.

Education
- Carry out longer-run follow-ups of promising interventions, such as the highest-quality state pre-K programs and high-quality tutoring programs.
- Examine home-visiting programs to determine which ones best promote short- and longer-term developmental outcomes for different groups children.
- Expand the definition of "high-quality" early care and education to include teaching practices recommended by expert researchers and teachers, such as limiting whole group instruction and promoting multi-turn teacher-child conversations.
- Assess whether early childhood education programs with the recommended practices described above generate positive medium- and longer-term impacts.
- Evaluate, at scale, promising scholarship and support programs that seek to improve low-income students' access to higher education and to increase their success after enrollment.
- Evaluate sector-based training programs at scale, especially at community colleges.
- Design and evaluate the long-term impacts of interventions to reduce harsh school discipline and racial disparities in harsh school discipline.

Child and Maternal Health
- Conduct rigorous evaluations of the longer-run impacts of programs based in schools, clinics, community care settings, and primary care providers addressing children and youth's mental health needs.
- Conduct rigorous research around the most effective gun safety measures to reduce youth firearm-related injury and death, the leading cause of death among U.S. children.

- Conduct rigorous research on the prevalence and effects of air pollution—indoors and communitywide—on child health and wellbeing.
- Conduct long-term evaluations of nutritional and other child health interventions.

Family Income, Wealth, and Parental Employment
- Evaluate the long-run effects of federal assistance programs (e.g., SNAP, NSLP, LIHEAP, SSI), including strategies to reduce administrative burden to increase take-up.
- Evaluate promising programs at scale that attempt to promote high-wage jobs and ensure that low-income people have access to them (e.g., Good Jobs Challenge, Good Jobs Initiative).
- Evaluate the medium- and long-term effects of regular unconditional payments for children (e.g., the expanded refundable Child Tax Credit that was in effect in 2021).

Family Structure
- Evaluate potentially promising strategies for promoting two-parent family structures.

Housing and Neighborhood Environments
- Conduct long-term follow-ups (15–20 years) of broad-based housing vouchers and the Low Income Housing Tax Credit.
- Include small grants for remediation of toxic environments in programs to improve housing quality and monitor long-term child outcomes of remediation.

Neighborhood Safety and the Criminal Justice System
- Evaluate promising crime-prevention programs at scale, such as Becoming a Man, community policing, and others.
- Evaluate long-term impacts of supportive alternatives to juvenile arrest and detention.

Child Welfare System
- Conduct rigorous evaluations of policies and programs to reduce stigma and administrative burden and provide integrated services to families and children in the system to identify the most promising policies and practices for subsequent scaling up and long-term assessment.

NOTES: LIHEAP = Low Income Home Energy Assistance Program; NSLP = National School Lunch Program; SNAP = Supplemental Nutrition Assistance Program; SSI = Supplemental Security Income.

most in need. Evidence presented in Chapters 2 and 3 shows that intergenerational poverty is much more prevalent in some communities and population groups than others, in particular among Black and Native American children and youth. But high-risk subgroups can also be found among Asian, Latino, and White communities, as well as in other groups. Community-based strategies for developing tailored interventions are important (see below), but so are replication studies of programs that have proved successful in the context of other communities. Funding for these priorities should be responsive to Executive Order 13985 (January 20, 2021) on "Advancing Racial Equity and Support for Underserved Communities Through the Federal Government."[2]

Other Guidance

Experiments and quasi-experiments have the potential to deliver convincing estimates of policy and program impacts for the populations studied, in the context in which the interventions and their sequelae unfold. As valuable as this is, there are a number of ways to enhance these designs:

- Supplement the "black box" information emerging from experimental studies with *information about the active ingredients driving the effects*. Information on drivers can come from observational studies of program features and implementation quality, and from mixed-method designs involving open-ended interviews with participating families describing how they experienced the policies and programs (Weisner, 2005).
- Enrich evaluation studies with *multidisciplinary and diverse research and implementation teams*. Economics, sociology, cultural anthropology, psychology, and subject matter expertise in the particular domain (e.g., education, health care) and program evaluation all have something to contribute, especially since the causes and effects of intergenerational poverty span so many domains. If the research and implementation team lack diversity in their perspectives and backgrounds, miscommunication with the communities being studied and failure to take account of important control variables can undermine the validity of experiments and long-term follow-up studies. See Box 11-2 for how the Moving to

---

[2] https://www.whitehouse.gov/briefing-room/presidential-actions/2021/01/20/executive-order-advancing-racial-equity-and-support-for-underserved-communities-through-the-federal-government/

Opportunity experiment benefited from a mixed-method, multidisciplinary approach.

- *Involve the communities under study and seek their input even before the research gets under way.* Since people whose families have been poor for generations are vulnerable and perhaps also suspicious of researchers, it is imperative, in ethical and practical terms, for research on intergenerational poverty to work with the communities involved. The committee's listening sessions with Native American families, low-income families, and others underscored this point. Communication needs to be a two-way street—ideally, it will result in the informed participation of community members and also help the research team identify changes that will make the research design most effective in the given setting. Communication also needs to continue throughout the study—whether during initial experiments or during longer-term follow-ups.

BOX 11-2
Mixed Methods and Interdisciplinary Teams in the Moving to Opportunity (MTO) Residential Mobility Experiment

In the mid-1990s, the U.S. Department of Housing and Urban Development (HUD) launched MTO to test whether families living in public housing projects in high-poverty neighborhoods of five large inner cities could improve their lives and the lives of their children by offering them housing vouchers that enabled them to move to lower-poverty neighborhoods. The original conception was that the program would improve the long-term housing, employment, and educational achievements of the families participating in the program.

Shortly after the program began, HUD invited proposals for researchers to conduct intensive studies at each of the five sites to learn more about the early operation of the program. Qualitative work in the Boston site found that the most salient issues motivating interest in the program were not related to employment or children's education. Instead, concerns over neighborhood safety and the perceived effects of neighborhood crime on mental health dominated many of these conversations (Kling et al., 2001). This led the larger evaluation team to gather a great deal of information regarding the mental and physical health of participants and their families and to bring a preeminent mental health researcher onto the project leadership team. Subsequent evaluations found important impacts on mental and physical health and very few impacts on employment and educational outcomes (Ludwig et al., 2011).

CREATING A FEDERAL DATA INFRASTRUCTURE FOR RESEARCH USE

Through censuses, ongoing surveys, and forms used in program administration (e.g., income tax forms), the federal government regularly collects data on a broad set of social and economic characteristics that can support research and policy analysis relevant to intergenerational poverty and economic mobility (see Chapter 2 for examples of relevant research). State governments, too, keep useful program administrative records. The data are controlled by different agencies, however. For this and other reasons, the data are often difficult to link or to use for evidence building, whether performed in universities, private research organizations, governmental agencies that are not the data custodians, or cross-organization research teams.

Removing the barriers to data linking and putting research and policy evaluation uses on the same footing as custodial agency uses of linkable datasets would allow researchers to monitor longer-run outcomes of promising interventions and initiatives from controlled experiments and replication research. Researchers could also analyze natural experiments, monitor trends, and assess the effects of changes in government programs, such as the expanded Child Tax Credit that was provided to families in 2021 and then allowed to expire. Such research could be conducted retrospectively (as in Hoynes et al., 2016) or prospectively. Moreover, in the case of prospective research, the use of linked datasets would be much more cost-effective than original data collection.

The recently proposed student loan debt forgiveness plan provides another example of how data linkages across agencies could facilitate analysis of the impacts of policies on economic well-being, both now and in the future. Currently, there is no direct way to estimate the incidence of student loan forgiveness by students' own income, family income, or other demographic characteristics like race, nor whether and how student debt impacts intergenerational mobility out of poverty. If data from the Department of Education's National Student Loan Data System[3] could be linked to Internal Revenue Service (IRS) income data and Census Bureau demographic data, it would be a straightforward matter to determine who in the population would benefit from student loan forgiveness. While all the individual datasets currently exist, they exist in isolation, they are not easily linked, and their use is restricted to a narrowly defined set of purposes.

In this section we discuss available data, including federal censuses and surveys and tax and other administrative records, and the opportunities and challenges for linkages, using as our prime example the domain of economic

---

[3] National Student Loan Data System-Catalog. https://catalog.data.gov/dataset/national-student-loan-data-system

resources (income, assets, debts, employment). There are important data sources and linkage possibilities for other domains as well, including health, education, and criminal justice, which we summarize in Box 11-3. We also list potential enhancements to existing panel surveys for intergenerational poverty analysis in Box 11-4.

Data Sources and Linkage Possibilities for Economic Resources

Federal Censuses and Surveys

Since 1940, the U.S. Census Bureau has collected data on household and family income and employment in censuses and surveys, including what is now known as the Current Population Survey Annual Social and Economic Supplement (CPS ASEC), the American Community Survey (ACS), and the Survey of Income and Program Participation (SIPP). Because they gather a wide range of contextual variables, including race/ethnicity, educational attainment, and occupation, which allows for the examination of disparities among population groups, these surveys facilitate the assessment of economic well-being both at a given point in time and across time. However, on their own they do not provide an adequate platform for analysis of intergenerational poverty or mobility. Income reporting in surveys has become substantially less complete over the decades, and data on wealth are not sufficiently detailed. Furthermore, while these surveys support repeated cross-sectional (time-series) analyses, they do not provide linked longitudinal data on individuals and families, with the exception of short periods in the CPS ASEC and SIPP.

Tax Data

Painting an accurate picture of economic resources for U.S. households over time requires IRS tax data, linked for families across years, as well as relevant survey and other administrative data. IRS data are highly sensitive, and access to them, including for program administration and other legal purposes, is tightly constrained by Title 26, Section 6103, of the U.S. Code, *Confidentiality and disclosure of [tax] returns and return information*. Section 6103(a) states that, generally, "return information shall be confidential." Nowhere is there a provision for research or policy analysis uses of tax data, except for specific purposes by specific agencies.

Several departments and agencies have limited access to IRS data for statistical purposes under Section 6103(j), including the Department of Commerce, for which the rule reads as follows:

BOX 11-3
Data on Health, Education, and Criminal Justice

Health Data

Birth and death records going back to 1938 contain relevant information, such as birthweight and cause of death, for analyzing the effects of health on economic wellbeing. These records are owned by vital registration areas (the 50 states, the District of Columbia, New York City, and the territories), and each area determines who can use them, for what purposes, and at what cost. They are available going back to 1968 for linkage projects at the National Center for Health Statistics (NCHS) but only after a lag, at a cost, and within the NCHS secure data center.[a]

Medicare and Medicaid claims records, available to the Census Bureau and researchers (in the case of Medicaid with significant lags), are another potentially useful source of information on health conditions and treatments among poor populations. The Health and Retirement Study (HRS) regularly links Medicare and Medicaid claims records and Social Security and Veterans Administration records with responses from survey participants who have consented to the linkage.[b] While the HRS is not designed for analysis of intergenerational poverty, as it follows only about 20,000 couples and people living alone aged 50 and older, the HRS illustrates what can be done with linkages to medical claims and beneficiary records accessed in a secure online environment (see also Box 11-4).[c]

Local data on children's health can contribute to experiments and projects that scale up promising interventions at specific sites. Public health databases may include information on child blood levels, and hospital inpatient and emergency department records may provide useful data. Because children are relatively healthy (as compared with older adults, for example), access to administrative records is vital for meaningful analyses of the determinants and consequences of child health.

Education Data

Many states have built detailed Statewide Longitudinal Data Systems (SLDS) that follow school children at least through high school and in some instances through college and into the labor market.[d] These data could be invaluable for intergenerational poverty research. However, each state has its own arrangements for use, and interpretations of the Family Educational Rights and Privacy Act (FERPA) at present make it difficult for researchers to link the SLDS to other data except for state-commissioned projects.[e]

Criminal Justice Data

The involvement, through incarceration or parole, of people in poverty with the criminal justice system severely constrains their families' current and future economic well-being. The Bureau of Justice Statistics, beginning in 2008, developed a system to collect records from all state and federal criminal justice agencies to track recidivism, which linked with other data could potentially provide useful information for intergenerational poverty research.[f] The Criminal Justice Administrative Records System (CJARS), begun in 2016, is another potentially useful data system for such research. At the University of Michigan, CJARS collects longitudinal electronic records from criminal justice agencies and harmonizes these records to track a criminal episode across all stages of the system. At the Census Bureau, harmonized criminal justice records can be linked anonymously at the person-level with extensive social, demographic, and economic information from national survey and administrative records. At present, CJARS has records from 35 states, with longitudinal records covering 68% of U.S. population.[g]

SOURCE: Committee generated.
NOTES: [a]See National Vital Statistics System - Health, United States (https://www.cdc.gov/nchs/hus/sources-definitions/nvss.htm) and Research Data Center Homepage (https://www.cdc.gov/rdc/). [b]Available Restricted Data Products, Health and Retirement Study (umich.edu). It also has links for some respondents to 1940 census data—see Box 11.4 (https://hrs.isr.umich.edu/data-products/restricted-data/available-products). [c]See, e.g., Davis et al. (2022), *Time to Dementia Diagnosis by Race: A Retrospective Cohort Study*, which identifies lags in diagnosis for Black Americans. [d]Statewide Longitudinal Data Systems Grant Program – "About the SLDS Grant Program" (ed.gov). https://nces.ed.gov/programs/slds/about_SLDS.asp. [e]Family Educational Rights and Privacy Act (FERPA) (https://www2.ed.gov/policy/gen/guid/fpco/ferpa/index.html); see also National Research Council (2009) (https://nap.nationalacademies.org/catalog/12514/protecting-student-records-and-facilitating-education-research-a-workshop-summary) [f]National Recidivism and Reentry Data Program, Bureau of Justice Statistics (ojp.gov). https://bjs.ojp.gov/recidivism-program [g]Criminal Justice Administrative Records System (cjars.org).

> **BOX 11-4**
> **Enhancing Panel Surveys for Intergenerational Poverty Research**
>
> Several long-running panel surveys have contributed to understanding long-term poverty, including the Panel Study of Income Dynamics (PSID), the National Longitudinal Surveys of Youth, and the National Longitudinal Study of Adolescent to Adult Health. For cost and feasibility reasons, panel surveys generally have relatively small overall sample sizes. Yet there are opportunities, outlined below, to enhance their ability to identify areas for targeted research and follow-up of policy and program interventions that could ameliorate intergenerational poverty.
>
> **Increasing Samples for High-Risk Groups**
> To respond to the Equitable Data Working Group's report, issued in April 2022, which calls (p. 6) for more "disaggregated statistical estimates . . . for understanding potential disparities in life experiences and outcomes across demographic groups," panel surveys would need to find cost-effective ways to increase sample size for groups most at risk of intergenerational poverty. Panel surveys could gather some of their information from administrative data records or possibly cut back on sample subgroups at the higher end of the income and wealth continuum. Funders could also support small additional samples of high-risk groups in several surveys, with results pooled for greater statistical reliability.
>
> **Adding Questions on Respondents' Place of Birth and Childhood**
> Adding questions to panel surveys (and repeated cross-section surveys named in the text) on where the respondent was born and grew up would increase their value

(j) Statistical use
(1) Department of Commerce
   Upon request in writing by the Secretary of Commerce, the Secretary [of Treasury] shall furnish—
   (A) such returns, or return information reflected thereon, to officers and employees of the Bureau of the Census, and
   (B) such return information reflected on returns of corporations to officers and employees of the Bureau of Economic Analysis, as the Secretary may prescribe by regulation for the purpose of, but only to the extent necessary in, the structuring of censuses and national economic accounts and conducting related statistical activities authorized by law (Confidentiality and Disclosure of Returns and Return Information, 1979).

for intergenerational poverty research. Indeed, the PSID and several other panel surveys, including the Health and Retirement Survey, not only have survey information about respondents' childhoods, but also undertook a project to link public 1940 census records to respondents who were alive at the time. The 1940 census provides a wealth of detail for linked respondents' families and neighborhoods.[a]

Obtaining Additional Detail on Race and Ethnicity

It would be useful for panel surveys to gather additional details regarding identity beyond the standard race and ethnicity (Hispanic or Latino) categories—for example by asking about membership in specific Asian groups or American Indian tribes or about White or Black origins. The U.S. Office of Management and Budget issued a *Federal Register Notice* on January 27, 2023, which proposes as the new federal standard a detailed combined question in which Hispanic or Latino would be a race/ethnicity category and a new category would be added for Middle Eastern and North African.[b]

SOURCE: Committee generated.
NOTES: [a]Censuses are opened to the public 72 years after completion—the 1950 census forms were released in 2022 and are now being digitized—and it will be valuable to be able to link future surveys back to them. Surveys with adequate locating information can be linked to more recent censuses, not yet public, inside secure Census Bureau computing facilities. [b]Federal Register: Initial Proposals for Updating U.S. Office of Management and Budget's Race and Ethnicity Statistical Standards. https://www.federalregister.gov/documents/2023/01/27/2023-01635/initial-proposals-for-updating-ombs-race-and-ethnicity-statistical-standards?et_rid=35386254&et_cid=4581739

Research and policy analysis access to the IRS information available to the Census Bureau (comprising many but far from all items, as spelled out in regulation 6103(j)(1)-1)[4] is provided through the network of Federal Statistical Research Data Centers (FSRDCs) that the Census Bureau operates for the federal statistical system. Research proposals must undergo a lengthy review process by both the Census Bureau and the IRS and be justified in terms of utility to both agencies, and outputs must clear high hurdles for confidentiality protection. In addition, many of the institutions that house research data centers charge researchers for a "seat."[5] The Statistics of Income program of the IRS has its own small program of research access to tax data (which must be carried out at IRS facilities when individual

---

[4] Appendix C: Chapter 11, Table 11-1 documents types of IRS data available and not available to the Census Bureau under regulation 6103(j)(1)-1.

[5] Federal Statistical Research Data Centers (census.gov). https://www.census.gov/about/adrm/fsrdc.html

records are analyzed), and approved research must serve the purposes of tax administration.[6]

Administrative Data on Other Sources of Economic Support

Gaining a comprehensive picture of available economic resources requires access to administrative records from programs that provide nontaxable benefits to families. These include such income support programs as the Supplemental Nutrition Assistance Program (SNAP), the National School Lunch Program, housing subsidies, the Low Income Home Energy Assistance Program, the Supplemental Security Income program, and others. Many of these records are held by the states, only some of which provide access to the Census Bureau or other agencies for statistical purposes (see Appendix C: Chapter 11, Table 11-2).

A complete picture also requires records on major assets and debts, such as financial assets (savings, checking, securities), home equity, retirement equity, education tax-deferred accounts, and health insurance coverage on the asset side, along with debts for mortgages, credit cards, student loans, and medical care on the debit side. Tax returns provide or can be used to infer some of these items, and surveys ask about some of them, but additional sources are needed to obtain a complete picture—for example, records from the National Student Loan Data System.[7]

Promising Developments

Data Linkage Projects

Several statistical agencies are engaged in linkage efforts to help understand economic mobility and child outcomes that can foster mobility. For example, the National Center for Health Statistics has linked 20 years of data (1999–2018) from the National Health Interview Survey and the National Health and Nutrition Examination Survey with HUD records on major housing assistance programs.[8] Over a dozen research reports have already benefited from the linked data[9]—see, for example, Fenelon et al.

---

[6] SOI Tax Stats - Joint Statistical Research Program | Internal Revenue Service (irs.gov). https://www.irs.gov/statistics/soi-tax-stats-joint-statistical-research-program

[7] The Federal Reserve Board's Survey of Consumer Finances provides comprehensive estimates of income and wealth but is small in sample size, is conducted only every 3 years, and cannot be linked with other datasets because it includes a sample of high-income households from tax returns, which cannot be used for any other purpose.

[8] NCHS Data Linkage - HUD Administrative Data (cdc.gov); see also NCHS Linked Data Table (cdc.gov).

[9] Linked NCHS-HUD Citations List (cdc.gov).

(2018), who found that children living in public housing have better mental health outcomes than a control group (no effect appears for children whose families use housing vouchers). Three linkage projects at the Census Bureau are particularly promising for retrospective and prospective research on intergenerational poverty owing to their content and time span: the American Opportunity Study (AOS), which is supported by the Decennial Census Digitization and Linkage (DCDL) project; the Comprehensive Income Dataset (CID); and the Opportunity Atlas (see Box 11-5). There are also important efforts that take advantage of data that the states maintain

---

BOX 11-5
Data Linkage Projects at the U.S. Census Bureau

The AOS is an ongoing effort at the Census Bureau in collaboration with researchers at Opportunity Insights, the University of Michigan, and Stanford University to link the 1960–2020 censuses and ACS, thereby transforming cross-sectional data into longitudinal data representing the full U.S. population over the last 70 years. This panel can be continuously refreshed as additional census and ACS data become available and serve as a spine on which to append tax records, earnings reports, and program records. The Census Bureau, the National Academies, Opportunity Insights, and several foundations funded the infrastructure for the AOS. The DCDL project is linking the 1960–1990 censuses, which is the last component to be completed for the AOS (see https://www.census.gov/programs-surveys/dcdl.html).

The CID is a foundation-funded project of Bruce Meyer et al. at the University of Chicago working with the Census Bureau to combine surveys, tax records, and federal and state benefit program records. The goal is to overcome inaccuracies in basic understanding of economic well-being. To date, the CID project has linked tax records and 12 sources of federal and state administrative program data with the CPS ASEC, the ACS, and the SIPP, and has produced new research on extreme poverty and homelessness. The intention is to extend the dataset back in time for two decades and to update it continuously going forward (Corinth & Meyer, 2021; see also the CID website at https://cid.harris.uchicago.edu).

The Opportunity Atlas is a collaborative, foundation-funded effort by Opportunity Insights in cooperation with the Census Bureau to construct a small-area (census tract level) linked dataset for analyzing the economic mobility of children born between 1978 and 1983. The atlas, which is built from the 2000 and 2010 decennial censuses linked to tax returns and the 2005–2015 ACS, contains estimates of children's outcomes in adulthood, including earnings and incarceration (see The Opportunity Atlas website at https://www.opportunityatlas.org/).

SOURCE: Committee generated.

that are not available at the federal level—for example, the Texas Education Research Consortium has linked K–12 and higher education records to children's later labor market outcomes, and the California Policy Lab has linked a range of state-level data covering education, safety net participation, and criminal justice involvement.

Legislation, Regulations, and Other Support

There is growing recognition that research and policy analysis using linked survey and administrative data is key to advancing knowledge in many areas, including intergenerational mobility and poverty. New legislation—the Foundations for Evidence-Based Policymaking Act of 2018 (Foundations Act)—and reports of commissions that led to and were established by the Foundations Act represent important steps forward (see Box 11-6). Reports of the National Academies' Committee on National Statistics (National Academies, 2017a,c, 2022a) stress the need for "blended

---

BOX 11-6
Relevant Legislation and Statements of
Support for Linked Data for Evidence

The U.S. Commission on Evidence-Based Policymaking, chartered in March 2016 by the Evidence-Based Policymaking Commission Act (P.L. 114-140), in its final report envisioned "a future in which rigorous evidence is created efficiently, as a routine part of government operations, and used to construct effective public policy" (Commission on Evidence-Based Policymaking, 2017, p. 1). The report's 22 recommendations address four areas: modifying federal laws to facilitate data use; establishing a National Secure Data Service (NSDS, which would not store data, but instead link and return privacy-protected data to the requesting users); instituting processes to improve data access and transparency; and designating leadership positions to support evidence generation and use in government.

The Foundations for Evidence-based Policymaking Act of 2018 (Foundations Act) enacted almost half of the commission's recommendations. Title III contains important provisions for linking data to analyze economic mobility over time: It incorporated the Confidential Information Protection and Statistical Efficiency Act (CIPSEA), originally enacted in 2002 (CIPSEA enables researchers to become sworn agents of a statistical agency to gain access to confidential data in an FSRDC); codified Statistical Policy Directive No. 1 on the responsibilities of statistical agencies to produce relevant, objective data; added the presumption that statistical agencies may, on request, obtain federal data for evidence-building; expanded secure access to CIPSEA data assets; required a standard data application process for researchers to use confidential data; and charged the U.S. Office of Management and Budget (OMB) to coordinate statistical

data" to improve the timeliness, relevance, quality, and granularity of federal statistics and data for evidence-building. The value of research access to confidential datasets through the FSRDC network was shown in a recent study that took advantage of the natural experiment afforded by the rollout of FSRDC sites throughout the country (Nagaraj & Tranchero, 2023).

Remaining Challenges for Economic Opportunity Research

Significant technical, privacy, feasibility, and legal challenges must be overcome to achieve the vision outlined above. These are outlined next.

Technical Challenges

The Census Bureau has developed robust linking software, which performs very well for people with Social Security Numbers or Taxpayer Identification Numbers and reasonably well using date of birth and name

---

agencies' confidentiality and disclosure policies. The chief statistician's office in OMB is to issue regulations for these provisions, which will be key for researcher access to linked data.

The Advisory Committee on Data for Evidence Building (ACDEB), chartered by Title I of the Foundations Act, in its interim report (ACDEB, 2021) supported the concept of an NSDS and urged OMB to produce guidance and regulations on the presumption of accessibility for statistical agencies, expansion of access to CIPSEA datasets, the responsibilities for statistical agencies, how agencies should implement "open data by default," and interagency and intergovernmental data-sharing responsibilities. ACDEB's final report (2022) focused on establishing the NSDS. It recommended that funding in the CHIPS Act of 2022 (Section 10375) for the National Science Foundation to pilot the NSDS be assigned to National Science Foundation's America's DataHub Consortium; that the NSDS be a legally recognized entity owned by the federal government and operated by a contractor; that the NSDS facilitate analysis by researchers of data assets hosted by affiliated organizations, including federal, state, territorial, local, and tribal governments, nonprofits, and other organizations; that NSDS core functions be funded by Congress; and that it develop a mixed funding model to include federal, state, private-sector, and user support.

NOTES: The full text of the Foundations Act is at PUBL435.PS (congress.gov); Implementing the Foundations for Evidence-Based Policymaking Act at the U.S. Department of Health and Human Services, is a good summary. The ACDEB interim and final reports and other information are available at Advisory Committee on Data for Evidence Building, U.S. Bureau of Economic Analysis. See also America's DataHub Consortium: Seeing—and understanding—the entire elephant, National Science Foundation.
SOURCE: Committee generated.

as the linking variables. It misses some people, however, particularly immigrants and low-income individuals. Moreover, linking errors have not been well studied. Other technical issues include the handling of data gaps and inconsistencies.

Privacy Protection

Threats to privacy and the unauthorized disclosure of information collected under a pledge of confidentiality (e.g., tax and census data) have increased over the decades. New methods are under development to reinforce protection against disclosure, including algorithms that satisfy differential concepts of privacy and facilitate multiparty computing. These methods are in their infancy, however, in terms of feasibility and their ability to preserve accuracy. In fact, there is evidence that the Census Bureau's implementation of differentially private algorithms and deletion of previously available data in the 2020 census products has adversely affected data users out of proportion to the gains in privacy protection.[10] In contrast, the Year 2 Advisory Committee on Data for Evidence Building (2022) report concludes that:

> (1) disclosure risk is on a continuum and is not binary, (2) not all data are equally sensitive, (3) there is shared responsibility between the statistical agency and users for protecting and not disclosing or re-identifying data, and (4) there is a need to protect good faith actors (i.e., data providers and users who take all precautions appropriate for known risks; 2022, p. 34).

The report also explicitly recommends (p. 28) a risk-utility framework for balancing data utility with disclosure risks in determining appropriate levels of privacy protection for federal data assets (see also Hotz et al., 2022).

Feasibility

The Census Bureau is currently the locus for relevant linkage projects, such as the DCDL. However, it has no specific appropriations for such work and thus requires significant funding from foundations and other sources. The Foundations Act and the ACDEB reports clearly envision the NSDS as the future locus of linkage work. However, the NSDS is just getting under way through America's DataHub Consortium at the National Science Foundation, and it has no guarantee of a sustained funding stream nor that the Census Bureau or the IRS will make their confidential data available to it.

---

[10] See letter from Steering Committee, Federal-State Cooperative for Population Estimates, and signatories (2022, August 1) to Census Bureau director Robert Santos. FSCPE-SC-LetterToDirectorSantos-8-22-22.pdf (cornell.edu).

Whichever agency handles linking, access to linked data for research and policy analysis would presumably continue in the FSRDC network. The current processes for securing approval and operating the centers leave much to be desired; they are neither timely nor efficient, and they require resources if researchers are to get started, let alone complete their analyses.[11] It is hard to imagine the centers, as currently operated and resourced, scaling up to handle much additional load, particularly given the need for enhanced privacy protection, which requires significant agency staff time.

Legal Challenges

Despite undoubted advances in normalizing the use of linked datasets for research and evidence building, significant legal gaps remain. Titles 13 and 26 still restrict the use of census and IRS data to projects that will benefit the Census Bureau and tax administration, respectively. Moreover, IRS regulation 6103(j)(1)-1 omits important tax return data from the list of items available to the Census Bureau. Similarly, laws governing other federal agencies, such as the Social Security Administration, and state laws make it difficult to combine data from multiple sources. No law includes an affirmative presumption of research access.

Another challenge is the absence of any legal provision, except for the authorizing legislation for the Institute of Education Sciences, which houses NCES, that places the onus for privacy protection on data users (including researchers) as well as agency staff.[12] Imposing substantial penalties on users as well as agency staff for disclosing confidential information, as the Year 2 ACDEB report endorses (see above), should help statistical agencies strike a reasonable balance between disclosure protection and data usability.

The chief statistician's office in the OMB is the relevant locus for facilitating the drafting of legislation, regulations, and guidance that would make it easier to link federal and state census, survey, and administrative program records. Such linkage capabilities would allow for monitoring and

---

[11] The single sign-on system for researcher access to confidential data, mandated in the Foundations Act, is operational through the University of Michigan, but its functionality is limited to assisting researchers to locate data files of interest. The proposal and approval process for gaining access to files for research has not yet been streamlined. See Standard Application Process to access federal confidential data – National Science Foundation invites comments on process, common form—EconSpark (https://www.aeaweb.org/forum/2997/standard-application-process-federal-confidential-comments).

[12] The language is in the Education Sciences Reform Act of 2002, Section 183, parts c and d (see National Center for Education Statistics [2019], Restricted-Use Data Procedures Manual, App. D).

valuable research on long-term economic mobility in the United States and in certain population groups and geographic areas.

CONCLUSIONS AND RECOMMENDATIONS ON RESEARCH AND DATA NEEDS

Experiments and Long-Term Follow-Ups

Conclusion 11-1: In many domains, such as education, there is a lack of strong causal evidence about the effects of policies and programs on intergenerational poverty at the needed scale. Sometimes this is because careful research has failed to establish long-term effects. More often, the issue is a lack of data that would support estimates of long-run program impacts.

Conclusion 11-2: For many reasons, it is difficult to conduct research on intergenerational poverty and effective policies and programs to reduce it. Owing to the scale of effort required, it is suggested that funding organizations (public and private) consider joint grantmaking and the adoption of the following funding principles and research best practices to maximize the likelihood of achieving valid results:

- *Funding principles: (a) prioritize strong research designs that provide causal estimates of program impacts, (b) set aside funding, not only for rigorous, small-scale experiments, but also for replications and long-term follow-ups of promising programs and (c) fund research arms for specific communities that are at highest risk of intergenerational poverty (e.g., American Indians on tribal lands, rural Black people).*
- *Evaluation research can often be enhanced by (a) the use of mixed research methods (qualitative, quantitative including rigorous controlled experiments) to ensure to the extent possible that all relevant attitudes, behaviors, and outcomes are addressed; (b) multidisciplinary and diverse research and implementation teams to facilitate communication with the communities being studied and ensure that experiments include important control variables; and (c) the incorporation of community input through long-term, two-way dialogue to gain informed participation of community members throughout the life of a study and to tailor the research design for maximum effectiveness in the particular setting.*

A Federal Data Infrastructure for Research Use

Conclusion 11-3: Existing census, survey, and administrative data linked for families over time and across subject domains—income, wealth, demographics, health, education, and others—can facilitate cost-effective research and evidence building on intergenerational poverty and socioeconomic mobility, looking both backward and forward in time. The research and policy analysis community needs timely, cost-efficient access to linked datasets with appropriate confidentiality protection.

Conclusion 11-4: At present, data for studying intergenerational poverty and related topics are controlled by a variety of federal and state agencies and are difficult to link or use for research or policy evaluation. Recent developments designed to ameliorate this situation include the Foundations for Evidence-based Policymaking Act of 2018, which presumes access to federal data by statistical agencies for evidence-building and calls for a streamlined process for researcher access to such data; supportive reports of the Commission on Evidence-based Policymaking and other organizations; and innovative projects at the Census Bureau and other agencies aimed at building linked datasets.

Conclusion 11-5: Significant challenges remain for access to linked datasets for analysis of intergenerational poverty and related topics. They include technical issues related to constructing and evaluating linked datasets; technical and policy issues regarding new methods of privacy protection and their effects on data accuracy; making access feasible in terms of cost, timeliness, and adequate budgets for the agencies linking the data; and legal barriers (e.g., research and evaluation must be justified in terms of agency benefits).

Recommendation 11-1—To facilitate research and evidence building on economic opportunity, intergenerational poverty, and related topics, the Chief Statistician at the Office of Management and Budget (OMB) should:

- Work within OMB and with relevant agencies and congressional committees to amend the Foundations for Evidence-based Policymaking Act to:
    - include a presumption of secure access to confidential data for research and policy evaluation, explicitly superseding provisions in U.S.C. Titles 26 and 13, which require research to benefit the Internal Revenue Service (IRS) and the Census Bureau, respectively;

- o provide secure access for statistical use, research, and policy evaluation to records of state benefit programs that receive federal funds (e.g., the Supplemental Nutrition Assistance Program);
- o require federal agencies with custody of confidential datasets to use a risk-utility framework for determining appropriate privacy protection methods for their data; and
- o impose penalties on researchers and other data users for willful, harmful disclosure of confidential data, similar to the penalties imposed on statistical agency staff;
- Work with the IRS Statistics of Income Division and the Census Bureau to expand the tax items available to the Census Bureau under regulation 6103(j)(1)-1 for research use;
- Work within OMB and with relevant agencies and congressional committees to secure sustained funding for data linkage projects, Federal Statistical Research Data Centers, and technical capacity in the states to share records to support cost-effective research and policy analysis on intergenerational poverty, economic opportunity, and related topics; and
- Work with relevant agencies to establish guidelines for consent and data storage that will facilitate the re-use of survey and intervention data, linked to subsequent administrative records, for long-term follow-up and for studies not yet anticipated at the time of the original study.

Appendix A

Biosketches

COMMITTEE MEMBERS

GREG J. DUNCAN (*Chair*) holds the title of distinguished professor in the School of Education at the University of California, Irvine. His recent work has focused on estimating the role of school-entry skills and behaviors on later school achievement and attainment and the effects of increasing income inequality on schools and children's life chances. Duncan is part of a team conducting a random-assignment trial assessing impacts of income supplements on the cognitive development of infants born to poor mothers in four diverse U.S. communities. He was elected to the National Academy of Sciences in 2010 and chaired the National Academies of Sciences, Engineering, and Medicine consensus committee Building an Agenda to Reduce the Number of Children in Poverty by Half in 10 Years. Duncan received his Ph.D. in economics from the University of Michigan.

FENABA R. ADDO is an associate professor of public policy at the University of North Carolina-Chapel Hill, where she is also an affiliate of the Carolina Population Center. She is also a faculty affiliate of the Institute for Research on Poverty and Samuel Dubois Cook Center for Social Equity, and is a research fellow with the Institute for Economic Equity at the Federal Reserve Bank of St. Louis. Addo is an applied social scientist whose work spans the fields of social demography, economics, and policy analysis. Her research program examines the causes and consequences of debt and racial wealth inequality with a focus on family and relationships and higher education. Addo is the co-author of *A Dream Defaulted: The*

Student Debt Crisis Among Black Borrowers with Jason Houle. She holds a B.S. in economics from Duke University and a Ph.D. in policy analysis and management from Cornell University.

ANNA AIZER is the Maurice R. Greenberg professor of economics at Brown University, co-director of the National Bureau of Economic Research Program on Children, and editor of *The Journal of Human Resources*. The focus of her work is the intergenerational transmission of economic status. Aizer previously served on the National Academies Committee on the Neurobiological and Socio-behavioral Science of Adolescent Development and its Applications. She received her M.S. in public health from Harvard University and her Ph.D. in economics from the University of California, Los Angeles.

MARGARET R. BURCHINAL is a research professor in the School of Education and Human Development at the University of Virginia. Her research examines the role early childhood education plays in children's learning and development. Burchinal served as the lead statistician for landmark early education studies, including the Abecedarian Project, the National Institute of Child Health and Human Development Study (NICHD) of Early Child and Youth Development, and the Family Life Project and evaluations of major early childhood policy initiatives. She has authored or co-authored over 150 peer-reviewed articles, served on review panels for the Maternal and Child Health Bureau, Institute of Education Sciences, and NICHD, as an associate editor for *Child Development* and *Early Childhood Research Quarterly*, and is a board member for the William T. Grant Foundation and the American Educational Research Association's Research Board. Previously Burchinal served on the National Research Council Committee on Developmental Outcomes and Assessment for Young Children, Early Care and Education Workshop, and Leading Educational Indicators Workshop. She holds a Ph.D. in quantitative psychology from the University of North Carolina.

RAJ CHETTY is the William A. Ackman professor of economics at Harvard University. He is also the director of Opportunity Insights (formerly the Equality of Opportunity Project), which uses "big data" to understand how to give children from disadvantaged backgrounds better chances of succeeding. Chetty's research combines empirical evidence and economic theory to help design more effective government policies. His work on topics ranging from tax policy and unemployment insurance to education and affordable housing has been widely cited in academia, media outlets, and Congressional testimony. Chetty has received numerous awards for his research, including a MacArthur "Genius" fellowship and the John Bates

Clark medal. Before joining the faculty at Harvard, he was a professor at the University of California, Berkeley and Stanford University. Chetty received his Ph.D. from Harvard University.

STEPHANIE A. FRYBERG is the university diversity and social transformation professor of psychology and founding director of the Research for Indigenous Social Action and Equity Center at the University of Michigan. Her research expertise focuses on how social representations of race, culture, and social class influence the development of self, psychological well-being, and educational attainment as well as on how to design interventions that reconfigure spaces to improve outcomes for racial minority and low-income students. Fryberg testified before the U.S. Senate Committee on Indian Affairs regarding the impact of racist stereotypes on Indigenous people, served as lead psychologist on an Amicus Brief for *Harjo v. Pro-Football*, served as an expert witness in the *Keepseagle v. U.S. Department of Agriculture* class action lawsuit, and provided testimony to the Spotted Bear and Soboleff Congressional Committee on Native Children. Fryberg has received many awards for her work, including the Society for the Psychological Study of Social Issues' Louise Kidder Early Career Award and Society for the Psychological Study of Social Issues Service Award, among others. She is past president of the Society for the Psychological Study of Social Issues (Division 9 of the American Psychological Association). Her research has been funded by the National Science Foundation, Mellon Foundation, Gates Foundation, Raikes Foundation, Yidan Foundation, Doris Duke Charitable Foundation, and New Venture Fund. Fryberg received her B.A. from Kenyon College and both her M.A. and Ph.D. in psychology from Stanford University.

HARRY J. HOLZER is the John LaFarge Jr. S.J. professor of public policy at Georgetown University, a nonresident senior fellow at the Brookings Institution, and an institute fellow at the American Institutes for Research. He is a former chief economist for the U.S. Department of Labor and a former professor of economics at Michigan State University. Holzer was a founding faculty director of the Georgetown Center on Poverty and Inequality. He is also an affiliate of the Institute for Research on Poverty at the University of Wisconsin-Madison, and of the Stanford Institute on Poverty and Inequality. Holzer has authored or edited several books and journal articles, mostly on disadvantaged American workers and their employers, as well as on education and workforce issues and labor market policy. He received his B.A. from Harvard University and his Ph.D. in economics from Harvard University.

VONNIE C. MCLOYD is the Ewart A. C. Thomas Collegiate professor of psychology at the University of Michigan—Ann Arbor. As a developmental psychologist, she studies the role of maternal psychological distress, parenting behavior, and family relations as mediators of the links between economic stress and socioemotional development during childhood and adolescence, and factors that moderate these links. McLoyd also examines the extent to which family processes and sociocultural factors (e.g., racial-ethnic identity, racial socialization) protect youth's socioemotional adjustment from adversities such as neighborhood violence, peer victimization, and perceived racial discrimination. Her scholarly work has been recognized by many awards from the Society for Research in Child Development, the American Psychological Association, and the MacArthur Foundation, among others. Previously, McLoyd was the associate editor of *Child Development* and *American Psychologist*, past president of the Society for Research on Adolescence, and president-elect of the Society for Research in Child Development. She was a member of the National Academies of Sciences, Engineering, and Medicine's consensus committee on Building an Agenda to Reduce the Number of Children in Poverty by Half in 10 Years. McLoyd received a Ph.D. in developmental psychology from the University of Michigan and post-doctoral training at Stanford University.

KIMBERLY G. MONTEZ is associate professor of pediatrics, associate program director of the Pediatric Resident Program, vice chair for Justice, Equity, Diversity, Inclusion in Pediatrics, and an associate director of the Maya Angelou Center for Health Equity at the Wake Forest University School of Medicine. She is a health services researcher with a focus on the social drivers of health, health equity promotion among under-resourced populations, and diversity and inclusion in pediatrics. Montez serves in leadership positions for the American Academy of Pediatrics (AAP), is lead author on multiple AAP policy statements and technical reports, including Poverty and Child Health, and has received the AAP Health Equity Award. Her advocacy work has been featured in news outlets, radio shows, and podcasts, including for the National Public Radio show and NBC Nightly News. Montez is also an associate editor for the journal *Pediatrics*. She received her undergraduate degree from Yale University, her medical degree from the Stanford School of Medicine, and her master's degree from the Harvard School of Public Health.

AISHA D. NYANDORO is the founding chief executive officer of Springboard to Opportunities, a Jackson, Mississippi, nonprofit that uses a "radically resident-driven" approach to end generational poverty. She created the Magnolia Mother's Trust, which is now the country's longest-running guaranteed income program, and the only one in the world to focus on

Black women. In addition to leading Springboard's community work and growing the Magnolia Mother's Trust, Nyandoro is focused on shifting gendered and racialized narratives around poverty and deservedness, while also working to show how the success of the Trust can be scaled nationally through policies like the expanded Child Tax Credit and a federal guaranteed income. Her expertise on economic, racial, and gender justice issues is regularly featured in outlets including *The Washington Post*, Amanpour & Company, *Essence* Magazine, NBC Nightly News, and CNN. Nyandoro is a TEDx speaker and a fellow of the W.K. Kellogg Foundation Community Leadership Network and Ascend at the Aspen Institute. She holds a B.A. from Tennessee State University and an M.A. and Ph.D. from Michigan State University.

MARY E. PATTILLO is the Harold Washington professor of sociology and Black studies, and chair of the Black Studies Department, at Northwestern University. Her areas of research include race and inequality, housing, urban politics, poverty, education, criminal legal studies, and Black communities. Pattillo is the author of two award-winning books—*Black Picket Fences: Privilege and Peril among the Black Middle Class* and *Black on the Block: The Politics of Race and Class in the City*; she also is co-editor of *Imprisoning America: The Social Effects of Mass Incarceration* and co-editor of a two-issue volume on monetary sanctions in the criminal legal system. Pattillo has won grants and fellowships from the Ford, Fulbright, Spencer, and MacArthur Foundations, among others. She is a member of the American Academy of Arts and Sciences and the American Academy of Political & Social Science. She is a trustee of the William T. Grant Foundation and Chicago Appleseed Center for Fair Courts and was a founding board member of Urban Prep Charter Academies in Chicago. Pattillo holds a B.A. in urban studies from Columbia University and an M.A. and Ph.D. in sociology from the University of Chicago. She was a postdoctoral fellow at the University of Michigan.

JESSE ROTHSTEIN is Chancellor's professor of public policy and economics at the University of California, Berkeley (UC Berkeley), with appointments in the Department of Economics and the Goldman School of Public Policy. He is also the co-founder and co-director of the California Policy Lab and is a research associate of the National Bureau of Economic Research and a fellow of the National Education Policy Center, the CESifo Research Network, the Institute for the Study of Labor, and the Learning Policy Institute. He previously served as chief economist at the U.S. Department of Labor, senior economist with the Council of Economic Advisers, Executive Office of the President, and director of the Institute for Research on Labor and Employment at UC Berkeley. Rothstein is a labor economist, with research interests in education policy, tax and transfer policy, and the labor market. His recent work includes studies of teacher quality, school finance, intergenerational economic mobility, take-up of safety net benefits, and the labor market during the Great Recession. He has been named the John T. Dunlop Outstanding Scholar by the Labor and Employment Relations Association. Rothstein holds an M.P.P. and Ph.D. from UC Berkeley.

MICHAEL R. STRAIN is director of Economic Policy Studies and Arthur F. Burns Scholar in Political Economy at the American Enterprise Institute. Much of his recent research has studied the employment effects of public policies, including the minimum wage, Earned Income Tax Credit, Paycheck Protection Program, and unemployment insurance. He is the author of *The American Dream Is Not Dead*, which analyzes longer-term economic outcomes for typical workers and households, and he is the editor or coeditor of four volumes on economic and public policy issues. Strain also writes frequently for popular audiences, and his essays and op-eds have been published by *The New York Times*, *The Wall Street Journal*, and *The Washington Post*, among others. He has testified before Congress and speaks often to a variety of audiences. He is Professor of Practice at Georgetown University, a research fellow with the Institute for the Study of Labor in Bonn, a research affiliate with the Institute for Research on Poverty at the University of Wisconsin, Madison, and a member of the Aspen Economic Strategy Group. He is an elected member of the National Academy of Social Insurance. Previously, he worked at the U.S. Census Bureau and the Federal Reserve Bank of New York. He was appointed to the National Academies committee on measuring alternative work arrangements and is currently serving on the National Academies committee on artificial intelligence and the U.S. workforce. He holds a Ph.D. in economics from Cornell University.

STEPHEN J. TREJO is a professor of economics at the University of Texas at Austin. His research focuses on public policy issues involving labor markets, including overtime pay regulation, the experiences of immigrants, and obstacles to the economic progress of minority groups. Much of Trejo's recent work analyzes patterns of socioeconomic mobility among the U.S.-born descendants of contemporary immigrant groups, and one strand of this work explores how selective intermarriage and ethnic identification bias assessments of intergenerational progress for Hispanics and Asians. He has served as a co-editor for the *Journal of Human Resources*, an associate editor for the *Journal of Human Capital*, and a deputy editor for *Demography*. In addition, he was appointed to National Academies of Sciences, Engineering, and Medicine panels that studied immigrant integration, U.S. Hispanics, and health insurance. Trejo holds a B.A. degree in economics from the University of California, Santa Barbara and both M.A. and Ph.D. degrees in economics from the University of Chicago.

STAFF AND CONSULTANTS

NATACHA BLAIN serves as the senior board director of the Board on Children, Youth, and Families and the Committee on Law and Justice at the National Academies of Sciences, Engineering and Medicine. She has served as a supreme court fellow, chief counsel to senator Dick Durbin on the Senate Judiciary Committee, and lead strategic advisor for the Children's Defense Fund's Cradle to Prison Pipeline Campaign. Prior to joining the National Academies, Blain served as associate director/acting executive director of Grantmakers for Children, Youth and Families. There she played a critical role in helping convene and engage diverse constituencies, fostering leadership, collaboration and innovation-sharing through a network of funders committed to the enduring well-being of children, youth, and families. Blain earned her M.S. and Ph.D. in clinical psychology from Allegheny University of Health Sciences and MCP-Hahnemann University (now Drexel University) respectively, and her J.D. from Villanova School of Law.

EMILY BACKES is deputy board director for the Committee on Law and Justice and Board on Children, Youth, and Families in the Division of Behavioral, Social Sciences, and Education at the National Academies of Sciences, Engineering, and Medicine. She also serves as director of the Societal Experts Action Network, a network of leading individuals and institutions in social sciences fields that provides actionable responses to urgent policy questions related to the COVID-19 pandemic. In her time at the Academies, Backes has served as study director for the reports: *Decarcerating Correctional Facilities during COVID-19: Advancing Health, Equity, and Safety*; *The Promise of Adolescence: Realizing Opportunity for All Youth*; *Birth Settings in America: Outcomes, Quality, Access, and Choice*; and *Transforming the Financing of Early Care and Education*. Backes has also provided analytical and editorial assistance to National Academies projects on juvenile justice reform, policing, forensic science, illicit markets, science literacy, science communication, and science and human rights. She received an M.A. and B.A. in history from the University of Missouri, specializing in U.S. human rights policy and international law, and a J.D. from the University of the District of Columbia, where she represented clients as a student attorney with the Low-income Taxpayer Clinic and the Juvenile and Special Education Law Clinic.

JENNIFER APPLETON GOOTMAN is a senior program officer with the Board on Children, Youth, and Families in the Division of Behavioral, Social Sciences and Education. She most recently served as the executive director of the DC Soccer Club, a non-profit youth sports organization serving thousands of children and youth from across Washington, DC. Previously, Gootman was the project director of the Birth Control Initiative for The National Campaign to Prevent Teen & Unplanned Pregnancy (rebranded as Power to Decide), a series of activities designed to rebuild support for and understanding of the important positive role that birth control plays in the lives of women and men. Gootman has worked as a senior program officer for both the Board on Children, Youth, and Families and the Food and Nutrition Board, directing several studies on topics including adolescent risk behavior, adolescent health, teen driving, food marketing to children and youth, youth development programs, and the impact of work on children and youth in low-income families. Her work has focused on child and family policy for low-income families, including welfare reform, child care, child health, youth development, teen pregnancy prevention, and youth sports. Gootman received a B.A. in education and fine arts from the University of Southern California and a M.A. in urban public policy from The New School University.

RITA HAMAD (*Consultant*) is a social epidemiologist in the Department of Social and Behavioral Sciences at the Harvard T.H. Chan School of Public Health. As the director of the Social Policies for Health Equity Research Program, she leads a research team investigating the pathways linking poverty and education with health disparities across the life course. In particular, Hamad studies the health effects of social and economic policies using interdisciplinary quasi-experimental methods. Current studies address the health effects of the earned income tax credit, school segregation, paid leave, and social policies during the COVID-19 pandemic. Hamad has previously provided consultation to federal and state legislators developing poverty alleviation policies to reduce health inequities. She serves as the co-chair of the Interdisciplinary Association for Population Health Science Communications Committee, working to the increase the visibility and impact of population health research. She is also the 2020–2022 James C. Puffer American Board of Family Medicine/National Academy of Medicine Fellow. Hamad holds an M.D. from the University of California San Francisco and a Ph.D. in epidemiology from Stanford University.

PRIYANKA NALAMADA is a program officer at the National Academies of Sciences, Engineering, and Medicine. She primarily supports the work of the Board on Children, Youth, and Families within the Division of Behavioral and Social Sciences and Education. Nalamada work involves providing critical project management support to National Academies' activities, including consensus studies and convenings focused on the health and wellbeing of children and families. In addition to supporting the Committee on Policies and Programs to Reduce Intergenerational Poverty, Nalamada currently supports the cross-divisional Standing Committee on Reproductive Health, Equity, and Society; and directs the consensus study on Promoting Learning and Development in K-12 Out of School Time Settings for Low Income and Marginalized Children and Youth. Most recently Nalamada served as acting director for the Forum for Children's Well-Being. She previously worked for a number of years within the National Academies' Health and Medicine Division and the Policy and Global Affairs Division, developing and supporting activities within the Board on Global Health and the Board on Higher Education and Workforce including the Committee on Defense Research at Historically Black Colleges and Universities and Other Minority Institutions; Minority Serving Institutions America's Underutilized Resource for Strengthening the STEM Workforce; and Forum on Public-Private Partnerships for Global Health and Safety. Nalamada holds a bachelor's degree in political science from Bryn Mawr College.

BRIANA SMITH is a senior program assistant with the Board on Children, Youth, and Families in the Division of Behavioral, Social Sciences, and Education. She has a background working with families of diverse backgrounds with differing socio economic status while with the Fairfax County Department of Neighborhood and Community Services as well as the U.S. military families with Childcare Aware of America. Previously she worked with the Transportation Research Board as a Senior Program Assistant with National Cooperative Highway Research Program and Behavioral Traffic Safety Cooperative Research Program projects. Currently, she is enrolled at Simmons University in the Library and Information Science Master of Science program with the hopes of becoming a public librarian. Smith earned a B.A. in English at James Madison University and a M.F.A. in writing popular fiction at Seton Hill University.

Appendix B

Perspectives on Intergenerational Poverty

Early in its deliberations, the study committee expressed a desire to build a full picture of not only the populations that are at greatest risk of intergenerational poverty but also of the policies and programs that are working to reduce intergenerational poverty. In response the committee held several information gathering activities to hear from community members, organizational leaders, policy experts, and scholars.

The committee held two public information gathering sessions to increase its understanding of intergenerational poverty within Native American communities[1] and children and families involved with the child welfare and justice systems.[2] The committee also commissioned Ascend at the Aspen Institute to organize a series of listening sessions that were closed to the public to ensure candid discussions. This included two listening sessions with parents and caregivers[3] contending with poverty to hear directly from them about their experiences with programs and systems designed to support their family's financial well-being and improve their children's future; three listening sessions with representatives of community- or state-level organizations serving Latino families, Alaska Native and Native Hawaiian

---

[1] A proceedings and proceedings in brief of this session are available here: https://nap.nationalacademies.org/catalog/26903/intergenerational-poverty-and-mobility-among-native-americans-in-the-united-states

[2] For more information on this session including an agenda and recording: https://www.nationalacademies.org/event/04-14-2022/public-information-gathering-session-policies-and-programs-to-reduce-intergenerational-poverty

[3] The participants in the listening session with parents and caregivers were primarily Black individuals from southern urban areas.

families, and families living in rural communities; and one listening session with public policy experts to gain a better understanding of federal policy levers to promote potential interventions across policy areas delivered at the federal, state, and local levels.

While these sessions were not designed to be representative and do not reflect the full range of perspectives or experiences of those affected by intergenerational poverty, they provided important context for understanding the lived experience of intergenerational poverty.

During these sessions, parents, practitioners, and policy makers discussed their personal and professional experience with policies, programs, research, and data collection that addresses various dimensions of intergenerational poverty in different communities. These conversations served as a backdrop for the committee's review and assessment of the available empirical literature, as well as a reminder of the real-life stories and experiences behind the data.

PUBLIC INFORMATION GATHERING SESSIONS

Perspectives on Native American Communities

This session included three panels to engage with community leaders, researchers, and practitioners on issues surrounding intergenerational poverty and mobility among Native American families in the United States. Representatives from the Oglala Sioux Tribe, the American Indian College Fund, the Native Organizers Alliance, and the American Indian OIC discussed poverty and mobility in their communities and described key barriers and obstacles reducing the chances that Native American children grow up to be happy, healthy, and prosperous adults. They shared Native-led efforts to support upward economic mobility and shed light on the strengths of Native American communities to address intergenerational poverty. Researchers from Johns Hopkins University and Stanford University discussed important historical and structural factors that have shaped economic opportunity and mobility for Native Americans, as well as the current data and research on mobility, gaps in the data, and the challenges in conducting research on this population. Researchers from the Federal Reserve Bank of Minneapolis, Northwestern University, and the University of Washington discussed drivers of intergenerational poverty among Native Americans and interventions that could improve their economic mobility within the domains of health, education, and the labor market.

Perspectives on Children Involved with the Child Welfare and Justice Systems

The committee held this session to (a) better understand structural determinants, especially poverty-related structural determinants, that contribute to involvement with the child welfare and justice systems, (b) identify evidence-based service interventions that reduce the chances that children in these systems are poor as adults, and (c) better understand these systems from a racial/ethnic disparities lens.

Researchers and practitioners with expertise in the child welfare and criminal justice systems—from the University of Maryland, the Juvenile Law Center, the University of California, Berkeley, Arizona State University, Columbia University, University of Notre Dame, and the University of Chicago—discussed how involvement with the justice system and child welfare system affects children's and adolescents' chances of upward mobility in adulthood, how racial disparities and structural factors in the justice system and child welfare system contribute to the causes of intergenerational poverty, and evidence-based programs and policies that target children and their parents and caregivers that are most likely to reduce chances that low-income children will be poor in adulthood. The committee considered these discussions and the research presented in its development of the report, specifically for Chapters 9 and 10.

CLOSED LISTENING SESSIONS

These sessions were held with subsets of committee members and were organized as small group discussions with organizational leaders supporting communities that the committee had identified as not being well represented in its public sessions and in the evidence base. As addressed previously, they do not reflect the full range of perspectives or experiences, but they provided additional valuable context for understanding the lived experience of intergenerational poverty for some.

Parent and Caregiver Perspectives

A group of low-income parents and caregivers shared their stories with vulnerability and candor on their day-to-day struggles to realize their hopes for their children. Many of them worked in low-wage jobs and received public benefits of some sort, yet these sources of income and support were inadequate for making ends meet, unstable, and irregular, and they created a set of bureaucratic challenges and roadblocks that made it difficult to get ahead. These parents' stress levels were palpable and were reflected in poor mental and physical health. Some parents talked about furthering their own educations or making sacrifices to enroll their children in better schools, but the daily financial grind made planning for or investing in children's futures all but impossible. Key themes from these discussions are noted here:

Stability, consistency, and safety are central to parent goals for their children and family:

- *My dream is one neighborhood, one home, one place.*
- *You would be there for your life and your tax dollars go to work for you.*
- *[We need] safe spaces for children to help them grow.*

Other goals that parents mentioned centered around being an agent of change both for their family and their community:

- *I want to try to make a difference.*
- *I want to be a voice to be a change for struggling parents.*
- *Make a difference for the future.*
- *Help other Latinas to get treatment we deserve.*
- *My goal is to provide my daughter with the education she deserves.*

Parents value education and building social skills—both for themselves and their children—as key to achieving those goals. They also believe they have a role in providing that and want parenting skills to help build such skills.

- *Social behavior that is acceptable and social skills that will help them in the real world.*
- *[We need] good learning environments.*
- *Need to have more parent education.*
- *Children need to know laws and rules.*
- *[I am] thankful for programs that help me be in a better position but also want programs that help me be a better parent so that I can raise my child.*

Parents mentioned the stress of the uncertainty of not knowing how you will provide for your family.

- *When I had the extra stimulus, it was this little pink pig of hope. I didn't stress out. Now I am stressed and not sure where I'm going—like my hope is gone.*
- *A lot of stressful nights, after you pay rent, you still have expenses for your child's school and other things. How can you provide for your child and still have a normal life for yourself?*

Parents identified barriers that they and their children face in achieving their goals.

- *Parents need to be aware of benefits so that they can provide for their children.*
- *Parents need to be better educated.*
- *Biggest barrier is mental health; need assistance in finding help to get better. Currently, Medicaid just throws drugs at you.*
- *My Dad was troubled, so I was troubled too.*
- *We have to work longer so that means we aren't spending time with our kids.*
- *I stress that my kids won't have enough food. Do we skip a bill or eat?*
- *To qualify for benefits you have to fit in a box. I don't fit in a box because I am a grandmother and not a traditional caregiver and so don't qualify.*

Several parents highlighted the phasing out of benefits—the cliff effect—as a key barrier:

- *When you are about to get ahead, they cut you off.*
- *[Temporary Assistance for Needy Families] and Section 8 have so many hoops you have to jump through that it is not worth it.*
- *Change income limits so that we don't have a benefits cliff.*
- *When you are trying to help people, help them gradually walk themselves off the program but don't drastically cut them off. Living on these programs wasn't intended to be a way of life but a help to be where you need to be in life.*

Among the responses when asked which government programs helped them personally:

- *Subsidized housing (although a help and hindrance, because they are a help when you don't have a job but a hindrance if you have a job and have earnings and triggers a bureaucratic nightmare as well as new, higher rent.)*
- *[Supplemental Nutrition Assistance Program], important but not enough; disconnect between what a family actually needs and what the government thinks a family needs; doesn't take into account non-traditional parents.*
- *Our children deserve the stars and the moon but we can't give it to them.*

- *Child Tax Credit and the Stimulus checks were helpful as it made it able for me to save as well as meet our needs. Now that it's gone, I had to use all my savings.*

Public Policy Perspectives

Public policy experts shared their perspectives on how federal policy can be used to encourage and support the most effective programs at the federal, state, and local levels. They discussed what the committee needs to know about current mechanisms and processes for designing policy and delivering these potential interventions at the federal, state, and local levels, as well as policy areas that the committee should be considering. They suggested that those living in poverty should be involved in the conversation, that important policy should not be narrow or restrained, and that states and localities offer important contributions to this conversation.

- *We must talk to people who live in intergenerational poverty and see what they want. Start with people and offer dignity back to them.*
- *Siloes at the federal level are harmful.*
- *We need good practices that aren't regionally bound.*
- *Bring states to the table—that is where federal levers can come in and make states act another way.*

Rural Community Perspectives

Representatives from community- and state-level organizations serving rural communities spoke to the committee about the unique challenges of rural poverty and the kinds of programs that are needed to serve these families.

- *In communities impacted by substance abuse disorder, we struggle with how to protect privacy but help humans whose lives are rugged and ragged. There is no anonymity in rural areas. How do we be transparent but still acknowledge families who have these "marks" about them? How do we give families with substance abuse problems stigma-free assistance?*
- *Rural folks are isolated. People believe that poverty is because something is wrong with you. But it is important for folks to understand, No it's the system.*
- *We can't count on anybody to come save us. What we have to do to is to save ourselves. The light bulb comes on when you are exposed to new ideas on how to make stuff happen.*

- *Programs should be designed by families; there is a lot of talent among the families we serve, and we should tap into that.*
- *They should be creating programs that promote social capital.*
- *Best programs are in response to and together with people whose lives show up as not doing well. Mindset shift needs to happen. Programs push us to do better but wish they would also ask us to report on the dreams and aspirations rural families have. We only get info on what's wrong with the family.*
- *Be intentional about families. Identify their aspirations and then help families achieve those aspirations.*

Alaskan Native and Pacific Islander Community Perspectives

Representatives from organizations serving Alaskan Native and Pacific Islander communities noted the need to support social connectedness and a sense of well-being among community (cultural/spiritual wellness), as a key factor in uplifting families out of poverty. Participants also highlighted the positive role of community organizations and called for more "trust-based" philanthropy, which would give these organizations the flexibility to meet the needs of families. They noted they often feel "their hands are tied" with government funding, and they do not have the ability to make real-time decisions to help families. They also expressed the need to create/develop programming with the community. Participants highlighted administrative burden to accessing social safety net programs as a key barrier and suggested more "cross-enrollment" opportunities are needed.

- *Our families often share that our current systems here (education, housing, health) focus on preserving wealth for the already wealthy, even at the expense of others. This reinforces injustices perpetuated against Native Hawaiians, disconnects us from our culture, and limits opportunities for families to thrive.*
- *The most inspiring folks are people in hard situations. They have the best energy as they are most motivated for change but don't know how to make that change. Keeps you inspired.*
- *Our families seek fiscal stability, education, healthy relationships, healthy families and cultural/spiritual wellness.*
- *Common themes that I find among our families: Limited choices for our families, disempowerment, exploitation, and unaccountability of those in power. All as a result of ongoing trauma. In response to those barriers, our people dig into cultural identity, communities and connecting to the collective.*

Latino Community Perspectives

Representatives from organizations serving Latino communities shared their thoughts on the challenges these communities face and what they need most to improve their children's chances for upward mobility.

- *The biggest issue for us is immigration. We have families with mixed status so being able to access various resources may be challenging.*
- *Winter and seasonal work especially for immigrant families is a barrier. Their hours of work go down and with the increase in the cost of living it is harder for families to have a sense of economic stability.*
- *Our families talk all the time about not having access to opportunities, about being turned away, about being fearful of talking to anyone because they don't know if they will speak their language.*
- *Just because resources are available in our community, doesn't mean they are accessible. If there is a child care center even in your neighborhood, if they are not operating from six am to seven pm and they don't have teachers who speak your language, as much as you want access to that child care, it is not going to work for your family.*

Appendix C

Appendices to Chapters

APPENDIX C: CHAPTER 2
A DEMOGRAPHIC PORTRAIT OF
INTERGENERATIONAL POVERTY

This appendix details the methods used to construct Chapter 2's portrait of intergenerational mobility. It first describes the population-level data used to measure mobility for recent generations by subgroup and geographic area and then describes the historical data used to measure trends in economic mobility over time. Finally, it presents distributional data on economic status as measured by adjusted gross income (AGI) and the income concept used in the Supplemental Poverty Measure (SPM).

Contemporary Measures of Mobility by Subgroup and Area Based on Tax Data

Data

Our featured estimates of economic mobility by race, gender, and geography are obtained directly from the Opportunity Atlas data constructed by Chetty et al. (2018, 2020). Here, we briefly summarize their methods as they pertain to the results we summarize in the main text; see Chetty et al. (2018, 2020) for further details.

To measure present-day intergenerational mobility in the United States, Chetty et al. combine three sources of data: (1) the Census 2000 and 2010 short forms; (2) federal income tax returns from 1989, 1994, 1995, and

1998–2015; and (3) the Census 2000 long form and the 2005-2015 American Community Surveys. The target population comprises all children in the 1978–1983 birth cohorts (a) who were born in the United States or are authorized immigrants who came to the United States in childhood and (b) whose parents were also U.S. citizens or authorized immigrants.[1] After excluding children who cannot be linked to parents or have no address information during childhood, the primary analysis sample comprises 20.5 million children, which covers 96% of the target population. When reporting race-specific estimates, an additional 5% of children for whom race data is missing are excluded.

Parental income is defined as the mean of parents' household income over 5 years: 1994, 1995, and 1998–2000. Parents' household income is measured as AGI in years in which a parent files a tax return and is defined as zero otherwise. Children's annual income is defined similarly, except that data from W-2 forms (which are available in more recent years) are used to impute income for non-filers. Children's income is measured as the mean of children's annual incomes in 2014 and 2015 (when they are between ages 31 and 37).

Methods

We use children's and parents' income ranks to measure intergenerational mobility. A child's income rank is measured as his or her percentile in the national distribution of incomes (measured between ages 31 and 37) relative to all others in his birth cohort who are included in our primary analysis sample. Similarly, we measure parents' income rank as their percentile in the national distribution of parental income for their child's birth cohort. For any given parental income percentile, we can then directly calculate the mean income percentile of their children, as shown in Figures 2-1 through 2-5.[2] These relationships provide measures of relative mobility, addressing the question "What are the outcomes of children from low-income families relative to those of children from high-income families?"

---

[1] We construct this sample by identifying all children born between 1978 and 1983 who were claimed as a dependent child on a 1040 tax form at some point between 1994 and 2015 by an adult who appears in the 2016 Numident file and was between ages 15 and 50 at the time of the child's birth. We define a child's parent as the person who first claims the child as a dependent (between 1994 and 2015).

[2] From children's and parent's income ranks, we can also create a summary statistic measure of intergenerational mobility: the correlation between children's and parents' income ranks (rank-rank slope). Chetty et al. (2014a) show that rank-rank slopes provide a more robust measure of relative mobility than another commonly used measure, the elasticity of children's income with respect to parental income.

For the geographic analyses in Figures 2-8 and 2-9, children are assigned to locations based on the location of their parents (when the child was first claimed as a dependent), irrespective of where they live as adults.

Comparisons with Studies Based on the Panel Study of Income Dynamics

Two studies based on data from the Panel Study of Income Dynamics (PSID) provide comparative information on intergenerational poverty persistence and intergenerational income mobility from low economic status in childhood—Parolin et al. (2022) and Fisher and Johnson (2023).

Parolin et al. (2022) estimate intergenerational poverty persistence using data gathered in the 1968–2019 waves of the PSID. Since their income measure includes both cash and two in-kind sources (Supplemental Nutrition Assistance Program [SNAP] and refundable tax credits), it is closer to an SPM-based than an Official Poverty Measure-based measure of total household income. A family is defined as poor if this income measure falls below the Official Poverty Measure threshold for a family of that size. The Parolin et al. sample consists of PSID participants observed in the data for at least 6 years between birth and age 10 and for at least 1 year between ages 25 and 30. Childhood poverty is defined as living in a household with income below the poverty threshold for 50% or more of the years between birth and age 10. Adult poverty is defined using the same income measure, but only in a single year—age 30. The small number of individuals who did not identify as "White" or "Black" are excluded from the calculations, so the "All" columns of Appendix Tables C.2.2 are based only on Black and White PSID families.

Fisher and Johnson (2023) study PSID individuals observed between ages 14 and 18 in childhood and ages 31 and 35 in adulthood. Their birth cohorts span the period from 1954 to 1982, and PSID data are drawn from the 1968 through 2017 waves. Total household income equals the sum of taxable income, cash transfer income, and social security income for the head, spouse/partner, and other family units in the household. Total consumption values are imputed for every PSID household and wave based on reported food expenditures and, beginning in 1999, responses to a more comprehensive set of consumption questions, as well as to the Consumer Expenditure Survey (Fisher & Johnson 2021). Wealth data are available in the PSID for 1984, 1989, 1994, and the period 1999–2017. Wealth is imputed in other waves using information on home value and on interest and dividend income.

We sought PSID counterpart estimates for Figure 2-6, which shows the average adult income ranks for children with household AGI at the 10th and 50th percentiles of childhood income distribution. Special tabulations by Fisher and Johnson using data from their article provided average economic rank in adulthood for children in the 8th to 12th and 48th to 52nd percentiles of the PSID-based distributions of income, consumption, and wealth.

Poverty Transitions

Table C-2-1 shows intergenerational data on low-income rates and transitions in Internal Revenue Service (IRS) data using the bottom decile or quintile of the child or adult distributions to define low-income thresholds. Overall rates of low-income status for the bottom decile and quintile are, by definition, 10% and 20%, respectively. In both cases, rates are three times as high for Black as for White individuals.

Counterpart numbers for the PSID are shown in the first three columns of Table C-2-2. The Parolin et al. (2022) annual measure of poverty—cash plus tax credits and SNAP benefits relative to the official poverty line—yields an average annual poverty rate of 12.3%. In their main analyses, Parolin et al. (2022) consider children to be poor if their household income fell below the poverty threshold in more than half of their birth-to-age-10 years. Despite this unusual definition, their estimate of childhood poverty—11.3%—is very similar to the average of the annual rates, and it is much higher for Black (38.2%) than White (5.4%) children. Their estimate of poverty in adulthood (10.3%) is also similar, although the racial gap for this adult poverty measure is smaller than for its childhood counterpart.

Given the committee's focus on reducing intergenerational poverty, the most relevant estimates from these two data sources are of the fraction of children living in poor or low-income families who are also observed to be poor or low-income in adulthood. These are shown in the "Conditional Poverty Persistence" columns of the two tables. Rates are similar for the 20th percentile threshold in tax data (33.7%; also shown in Figures 2-1 and 2-2) and in the PSID data (28.6%; also shown in Figure 2-1). Lowering the threshold to the 10th percentile produces a considerably lower (19.6%) estimate of conditional mobility out of poverty/low-income status. In both datasets, substantially fewer Black than White children escape poverty/low-income status.

Also of interest is the general prevalence of intergenerational poverty—the fraction of all children who live in low-income families in both childhood and adulthood. This is simply the product of childhood poverty rates and intergenerational persistence. So, if, for example, 12% of children grow up in poor families and one-third of poor children are also poor in adulthood, then the fraction of all children poor in both generations is one-third of 12%—or 4% in all. Estimates of intergenerational poverty/low-income prevalence are highest (6.7%) for the IRS-based 20th-percentile cutoff for

TABLE C-2-1 Intergenerational poverty statistics based on Adjusted Gross Income (AGI) data in tax records

	Poverty defined by 10th percentile (bottom decile)				Poverty defined by 20th percentile (bottom quintile)			
	Average annual child poverty rate (% of children with average AGI in bottom decile in childhood)	Average annual adult poverty rate (% of children with average AGI in bottom decile in adulthood)	Conditional poverty persistence (Among children in bottom decile, % in bottom decile in adulthood)	Intergenerational poverty prevalence (% of children with AGI in bottom decile in both childhood and adulthood)	Average child poverty rate (% of children with average AGI in bottom quintile in childhood)	Adult poverty rate (% of children with average AGI in bottom quintile in adulthood)	Conditional poverty persistence (Among children in bottom quintile, % in bottom quintile in adulthood) (Figure 2-1)	Intergenerational poverty prevalence (% of children with AGI in bottom quintile in both childhood and adulthood)
All	0.100	0.100	0.196	0.020	0.200	0.200	0.337	0.067
White	0.055				0.117	0.151	0.291	0.034
Black	0.192				0.377	0.303	0.373	0.141
Black-White	0.137				0.260	0.152	0.082	0.107
White men					0.117	0.166	0.313	0.037
Black men					0.373	0.394	0.485	0.181
White women					0.117	0.136	0.267	0.031
Black women					0.380	0.217	0.268	0.102

SOURCE: Chetty et al. (2020); see text for more information. No publicly available data are available for the blank cells in the 10th percentile columns.

TABLE C-2-2 Intergenerational poverty statistics based on data from the Panel Study of Income Dynamics

	Average yearly child poverty rate (Fraction of years poor between ages 0 & 10, 1970–2003)	Average yearly adult poverty rate (Fraction of years poor between ages 25 & 30, 1995–2019)	Child poverty (poor more than 50% of years between birth and age 10)	Adult poverty (% poor at age 30)	Conditional poverty persistence (Among poor children, % poor at age 30)	Intergenerational poverty prevalence (% of population poor in both childhood and at age 30
All	0.123	0.102	0.113	0.101	0.286	0.032
White	0.074	0.075	0.054	0.072	0.198	0.011
Black	0.371	0.231	0.382	0.231	0.344	0.130
Black-White	0.297	0.156	0.328	0.159	0.146	0.119
White men	0.072	0.067	0.054	0.068	0.172	0.009
Black men	0.341	0.206	0.359	0.220	0.346	0.122
White women	0.076	0.084	0.054	0.077	0.225	0.012
Black women	0.401	0.254	0.408	0.243	0.346	0.140

SOURCE: Parolin et al. (2022); see text for more information.

low-income status, lowest (2.0%) for the IRS-based 10th-percentile threshold, and in between (3.2%) for the PSID-based poverty measure. In both cases where race-specific estimates are available, the prevalence of persistent poverty/low-income status is higher for Black than for White children.

Income Mobility

Text Figure 2.6 shows adult outcomes for children with household incomes that placed them on the 10th or 50th rung of the childhood economic ladder based on data from tax records. Table C-2-3 and Figure C-2-1 provide data on income, consumption, and wealth from the PSID as described above and in Fisher and Johnson (2023). The two data sources and various measures of economic well-being tell a broadly similar story about intergenerational economic mobility:

- Children starting out on the 10th rung of the economic ladder, on average, climb to considerably higher rungs in adulthood. This is especially true for White children, for whom rungs average between the 36th and 45th, depending on the measure.
- The average adult destinations for Black children are between 11 and 18 rungs lower than for White children.

Translating Percentiles of the Adjusted Gross Income Distribution to Incomes Relative to the Poverty Line

To support the report's data efforts, commissioned consultants were asked to match the AGI of children (based on their families' incomes) to a measure of their families' incomes relative to the poverty line (measured under the SPM). The consultants produced estimates of this correspondence by determining children's position in the AGI percentile distribution and then calculating the average income-to-needs of children within each percentile, with income-to-needs ratios assessed using the SPM. They first describe the steps they took to match the percentiles of the AGI distribution to income-to-needs ratios in greater detail and the challenges encountered in this process. They use the Historical Supplemental Poverty Measure Data Series (Wimer et al., 2022) and the Annual and Social Economic Supplement to the Current Population Survey, retrieved from IPUMS[3]-CPS (Flood et al., 2022) to produce these results.

---

[3] "IPUMS" stands for Integrated Public Use Microdata Series.

TABLE C-2-3 Intergenerational income mobility statistics based on data from the Internal Revenue Service (IRS) and Panel Study of Income Dynamics (PSID)

	Conditional mobility from 10th percentile (Fig. 2-6)		Conditional mobility from 50th percentile (Fig. 2-6)
	Chetty et al., (2020) based on data from the IRS		
	Average percentile rank, based on adjusted gross income (AGI; Fig. 2-6)		Average percentile rank, based on AGI (Fig. 2-6)
All	37.6		50.6
White	40.7		52.6
Black	29.3		38.8
Black-White	−11.4		−13.8
White men	39.7		51.5
Black men	27.0		36.5
White women	41.7		53.7
Black women	31.5		41.0
	Fisher and Johnson (2023), based on PSID		
	Average percentile rank, based on full income	Average percentile rank, based on wealth	Average percentile rank, based on consumption
All	0.301	0.331	0.334
White	0.364	0.449	0.389
Black	0.234	0.269	0.267
Black-White	−0.130	−0.180	−0.122

	Average percentile rank, based on full income	Average percentile rank, based on wealth	Average percentile rank, based on consumption
All	0.583	0.500	0.581
White	0.610	0.528	0.553
Black	0.298	0.373	0.501
Black-White	−0.312	−0.155	−0.052

SOURCE: Data from Chetty et al. (2020) for IRS data; Fisher and Johnson (2023) for PSID data. See text for more information.

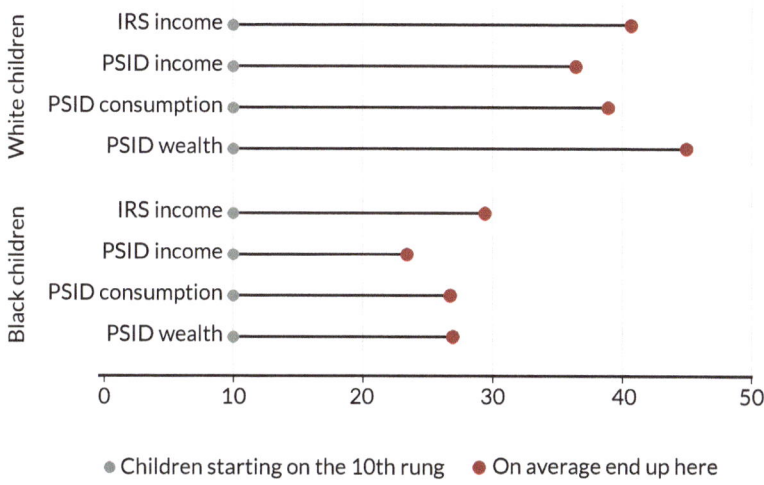

● Children starting on the 10th rung   ● On average end up here

FIGURE C-2-1 Intergenerational mobility based on several measures of economic status, by race/ethnicity.
NOTES: This figure shows the mean percentile of economic status in adulthood for children with parents at the 10th income percentile of that same measure of economic status. Child "IRS" economic status is measured by mean AGI in 1994–2000 for childhood and 2014–2015 for adulthood in IRS tax records. Children were born between 1978 and 1983. All PSID measures are based on individuals observed between ages 14 and 18 in childhood and ages 31 and 35 in adulthood. Children were born between 1954 and 1982. "Income" is pre-tax cash income of household; "consumption" is based on reported and imputed expenditures; and "wealth" is based on reported and imputed wealth. PSID data are based on individuals in the 8th to 12th percentiles of the childhood measure of economic status.
SOURCE: Data from Chetty et al. (2020), based on data from the IRS and Fisher and Johnson (2023), based on data from the PSID.

*Matching Children's Placement in the AGI Distribution
to Income-to-Needs Ratios*

The AGI distribution underlying results presented in Chapter 2 is tabulated at the tax unit level, where children under age 18 are typically dependents within tax units and their parents or guardians are the primary tax filers (see the following section for a discussion of the exceptions to this arrangement). The first step in matching children's placement in the AGI distribution to a measure of their income-to-needs was to determine the total AGI of the tax units in which children were claimed as dependents.

To do so, we first needed to construct tax units in the data from the Annual Social and Economic Supplement to the Current Population Survey (ASEC-CPS) that included primary tax filers and their dependents under age 18 or 24 (the latter in the case of those in school). Note that our objective was to link child dependents to those who claim them as dependents, so we do not discuss linking older dependents to the filers who may have claimed them. The ASEC-CPS microdata made available by IPUMS-CPS includes a variable from the Census Tax Model that identifies individuals as joint filers, heads of household, single filers, or non-filers (see O'Hara, 2004 for a discussion of the Census Bureau's Tax Model). Note that we exclude children under 18 who are identified by the Census Tax Model as primary tax filers from our primary analysis; see the following section for a more detailed discussion of this decision and the sensitivity of our results to it.

We begin by using the tax-filing type variable to identify the universe of individuals who may have filed, and the subset who may have claimed dependents, the latter being heads of household or joint filers. The next step is to identify which of the non-filers are dependents of the tax filers who may have claimed dependents, which we accomplish by taking the following steps:

1. Identify children who could possibly be claimed as dependent; this includes those who were not tax filers and were under age 18 at the time of the March ASEC-CPS survey administration or those under age 24 who were in school at the time the survey was administered.
2. Link those children to the filers in their household unit using the following rules:
   a. If they live with either the mother, father, or both, and their parents were tax filers, they are placed in their parents' tax units.
   b. If their parent(s) are not filers or they do not live with their parents but they live with a relative who is a filer that claims dependents (according to the Census Tax Model), they are placed in the unit of that filer.

c. If their parents are non-filers and the children do not live with any relatives who are filers, a non-filing tax unit is created that links the children to their parents.
  d. If they do not live with their parents, and none of their relatives files taxes, a non-filing tax unit is created that links the children to their eldest relative.

Once we identified these tax units, we calculated the total AGI across all members of the tax unit using the ASEC-CPS AGI variable. The AGI variable was constructed by the Census' Tax Model and is described in the IPUMS-CPS codebook as including "an individual's total gross (pre-tax) income from taxable sources minus certain items, such as individual retirement plan contributions (payments to a Keogh plan or a deductible Individual Retirement Account), alimony paid, medical savings accounts, and non-reimbursed employee business expenses."[4] In the case of joint-filers, we also ensured that income sources were not double-counted when totaling AGI across tax unit members. The total AGI of the tax unit represented the AGI of each child's family and is the primary variable used in the subsequent analyses described below. We produced these estimates for data representative of 1994, 1995, 1998, 1999, and 2000.

Determining Children's Income-to-Needs Ratios

Next, we determine the income-to-needs ratio of all children in the data using variables available in the Historical SPM Data Series (Wimer et al., 2022). As described by Fox et al. (2015) and Wimer et al. (2016), the Historical SPM Data Series includes the necessary inputs for measuring poverty under the SPM from 1967 to 2009 (before the data were available in the ASEC-CPS). We define children's income-to-needs ratio as the total resources for the SPM poverty unit divided by the poverty threshold for their unit, all measured using the SPM and available in the Historical SPM Data Series. See Fox et al. (2015) for a more extensive discussion of the construction of the SPM resources variables, and Nolan et al. (2017) for a discussion of the SPM poverty thresholds construction. Again, we produced these results for data representative of 1994, 1995, 1998, 1999, and 2000.

---

[4] Additional information on this variable is available at https://cps.ipums.org/cps-action/variables/ADJGINC#description_section

*Matching Percentiles of the AGI Distribution
to Income-to-Needs Ratios*

Our final step was to determine the percentiles of the AGI distribution in the data when limiting to children under age 18, and then to find the average income-to-needs of children within these percentiles. We weighted these averages using the person-lev2 weights available in the ASEC-CPS microdata files. Again, we produced these results for data representative of 1994, 1995, 1998, 1999, and 2000. Figure C-2-2 depicts the 5-year averages of these results, while Table C-2-4 presents the results by year.

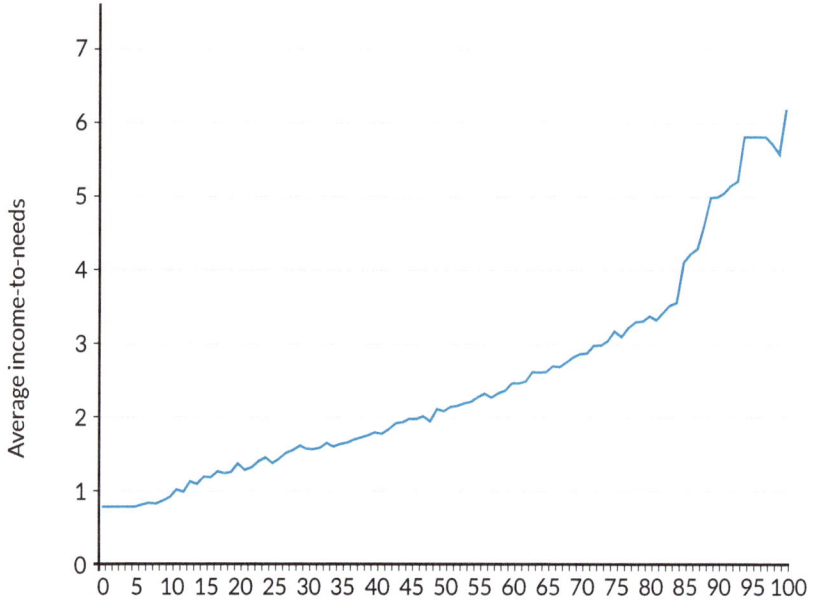

Percentile of the adjusted gross income distribution

FIGURE C-2-2 Average income-to-needs of children by percentile of the AGI income distribution for children under age 18.
NOTES: Figure C-2-2 shows the average income-to-needs of children by their position in the AGI distribution. AGIs are determined based on the total AGI of the tax unit claiming each child in the ASEC-CPS data retrieved from IPUMS-CPS (2022) and matched to income-to-needs ratios based on data from the Historical SPM Data Series (Wimer et al., 2022). Results are produced with data representative of 1994, 1995, 1998, 1999, and 2000. Children identified as independent tax filers (i.e., nondependents) based on the Census Tax Model are not included in these results (see Figure C-2-4 and Table C-2-2 for results inclusive of this population).
SOURCE: Data from the Historical SPM Data Series (Wimer et al., 2022) and the ASEC-CPS data from IPUMS-CPS (2022).

TABLE C-2-4 Average income-to-needs by percentile of the adjusted gross income (AGI) distribution, children under age 18

Percentile AGI	Avg. Income-to-Needs					5-year average	Percentile AGI	Avg. Income-to-Needs					5-year average
	1994	1995	1998	1999	2000			1994	1995	1998	1999	2000	
1	0.77	0.87	0.79	0.76	0.76	0.79	51	1.96	2.04	2.25	2.18	2.27	2.14
2	0.77	0.87	0.79	0.76	0.76	0.79	52	1.97	2.01	2.24	2.20	2.35	2.15
3	0.77	0.87	0.79	0.76	0.76	0.79	53	1.94	2.13	2.31	2.27	2.29	2.19
4	0.77	0.87	0.79	0.76	0.76	0.79	54	2.08	1.99	2.23	2.37	2.38	2.21
5	0.77	0.87	0.79	0.76	0.76	0.79	55	2.24	2.06	2.27	2.33	2.49	2.28
6	0.77	0.87	0.79	0.76	0.91	0.82	56	2.28	2.21	2.16	2.45	2.53	2.33
7	0.77	0.87	0.79	1.02	0.75	0.84	57	2.09	2.22	2.32	2.30	2.44	2.27
8	0.77	0.87	0.86	0.72	0.94	0.83	58	2.11	2.30	2.40	2.27	2.58	2.33
9	0.77	0.85	0.96	0.87	0.90	0.87	59	2.26	2.26	2.43	2.35	2.54	2.37
10	0.71	0.69	1.13	0.98	1.08	0.92	60	2.22	2.41	2.51	2.61	2.58	2.47
11	0.81	0.95	1.00	1.13	1.21	1.02	61	2.29	2.33	2.56	2.50	2.65	2.47
12	0.95	0.89	0.96	1.08	1.08	0.99	62	2.33	2.35	2.54	2.45	2.79	2.49
13	0.89	1.10	1.10	1.26	1.30	1.13	63	2.46	2.53	2.65	2.67	2.78	2.62
14	0.85	1.06	1.11	1.10	1.36	1.10	64	2.39	2.47	2.63	2.73	2.84	2.61
15	1.07	1.31	1.10	1.25	1.25	1.20	65	2.34	2.56	2.73	2.71	2.75	2.62
16	0.99	1.16	1.30	1.17	1.32	1.19	66	2.58	2.56	2.84	2.70	2.81	2.70
17	1.19	1.15	1.14	1.52	1.34	1.27	67	2.52	2.52	2.78	2.70	2.92	2.69

(*continued*)

TABLE C-2-4 Continued

Percentile AGI	Avg. Income-to-Needs						Percentile AGI	Avg. Income-to-Needs					
	1994	1995	1998	1999	2000	5-year average		1994	1995	1998	1999	2000	5-year average
18	1.18	1.18	1.16	1.34	1.37	1.25	68	2.53	2.72	2.76	2.82	2.94	2.75
19	1.07	1.21	1.29	1.27	1.45	1.26	69	2.60	2.62	2.81	3.09	2.97	2.82
20	1.20	1.42	1.46	1.44	1.35	1.37	70	2.67	2.71	2.84	3.01	3.07	2.86
21	1.28	1.30	1.25	1.32	1.28	1.29	71	2.68	2.83	2.94	2.95	2.94	2.87
22	1.12	1.39	1.30	1.45	1.34	1.32	72	2.66	2.89	3.13	3.04	3.16	2.98
23	1.36	1.26	1.48	1.45	1.47	1.40	73	2.68	2.89	3.11	3.12	3.09	2.98
24	1.36	1.35	1.46	1.53	1.58	1.46	74	2.93	2.85	3.18	3.03	3.20	3.04
25	1.31	1.27	1.36	1.43	1.52	1.38	75	3.16	3.05	3.18	3.24	3.23	3.17
26	1.32	1.46	1.45	1.49	1.48	1.44	76	3.01	2.95	3.19	3.15	3.17	3.09
27	1.27	1.57	1.66	1.62	1.47	1.52	77	2.99	3.00	3.30	3.46	3.33	3.22
28	1.43	1.62	1.59	1.49	1.65	1.56	78	3.04	3.18	3.37	3.50	3.38	3.29
29	1.58	1.58	1.70	1.65	1.57	1.62	79	3.10	3.11	3.27	3.66	3.38	3.30
30	1.44	1.48	1.67	1.55	1.72	1.57	80	3.16	3.07	3.43	3.67	3.54	3.37
31	1.54	1.41	1.72	1.55	1.63	1.57	81	3.22	3.15	3.36	3.47	3.40	3.32
32	1.46	1.51	1.61	1.61	1.75	1.59	82	3.30	3.29	3.40	3.54	3.56	3.42
33	1.49	1.56	1.72	1.71	1.77	1.65	83	3.32	3.34	3.68	3.59	3.66	3.52
34	1.53	1.55	1.62	1.58	1.75	1.61	84	3.41	3.48	3.60	3.45	3.83	3.55
35	1.51	1.48	1.63	1.67	1.90	1.64	85	3.48	3.44	3.64	3.96	6.00	4.10
36	1.55	1.65	1.56	1.68	1.85	1.66	86	3.57	3.71	3.87	3.94	6.00	4.22

APPENDIX C

37	1.57	1.68	1.83	1.63	1.80	1.70	87	3.64	3.67	4.16	3.96	6.00	4.29
38	1.60	1.72	1.64	1.75	1.92	1.73	88	3.70	3.75	4.14	5.40	6.00	4.60
39	1.63	1.69	1.82	1.78	1.86	1.76	89	3.78	3.71	6.01	5.40	6.00	4.98
40	1.67	1.73	1.86	1.77	1.94	1.79	90	3.78	3.75	6.01	5.40	6.00	4.99
41	1.65	1.62	1.81	1.90	1.92	1.78	91	3.83	3.97	6.01	5.40	6.00	5.04
42	1.70	1.73	1.88	1.92	1.95	1.84	92	4.01	4.30	6.01	5.40	6.00	5.14
43	1.85	1.90	1.91	1.89	2.06	1.92	93	4.28	4.33	6.01	5.40	6.00	5.20
44	1.94	1.85	1.87	1.99	2.01	1.93	94	4.52	7.07	6.01	5.40	6.00	5.80
45	1.81	1.90	1.97	2.02	2.19	1.98	95	4.52	7.07	6.01	5.40	6.00	5.80
46	1.77	1.91	2.00	1.93	2.28	1.98	96	4.52	7.07	6.01	5.40	6.00	5.80
47	1.84	1.92	2.09	1.97	2.25	2.01	97	4.52	7.07	6.01	5.40	6.00	5.80
48	1.88	1.70	2.06	2.01	2.08	1.95	98	4.52	7.07	5.50	5.87	5.58	5.71
49	2.00	1.97	2.28	2.04	2.27	2.11	99	4.57	6.70	5.54	5.34	5.71	5.57
50	1.95	1.88	2.06	2.28	2.25	2.08	100	4.59	6.70	7.66	5.65	6.32	6.18

NOTES: Table C-2-4 shows the average income-to-needs of children by their position in the AGI distribution. AGIs determined based on the total AGI of the tax unit claiming each child in the ASEC-CPS data retrieved from IPUMS-CPS (2022) and matched to income-to-needs ratios based on data from the Historical SPM Data Series (Wimer et al., 2022). Produced with data representative of 1994, 1995, 1998, 1999, and 2000. Children identified as independent tax filers (i.e., non-dependents) based on the Census Tax Model are not included in these results (see Figure C-2-4 and Table C-2-2 for results inclusive of this population).

SOURCE: Data from the Historical SPM Data Series (Wimer et al., 2022) and ASEC-CPS data from IPUMS-CPS (2022).

*Tax Filers Under Age 18 and Challenges That Arose
When Producing These Estimates*

In producing these results, one issue that arose concerned the assignment of minors with earnings to individual tax units based on the Census Bureau's tax model, a group we call "minor filers." They are teenagers with low levels of earnings (and thus low AGIs) who also live with other family members. The minor filers are predominantly teenagers with very low incomes that the Census Tax Model identifies as needing to file taxes (either on their own return or possibly as dependent tax filers). In the years that we examine, there is no flag for "dependent tax filers," and the Census assigns many teenagers in this group to be single filers. In the weighted 2000 data, there are 28.4 million children ages 11–17, and 10.7% of them (or 3.1 million) are minor filers.[5] Unweighted, this translates to 27,255 children ages 11–17 and 3,235 minor filers. All minor filers are ages 15–17, and the majority (1.7 million weighted) are age 17. The same pattern holds in earlier data years.

The distribution of tax unit AGI associated with these minor filers is also very different from that of other children claimed as dependents (Figure C-2-3, left panel): their median AGI is $2,850, versus $44,000 for children claimed as dependents.[6] At the same time, the distribution of the income-to-needs ratio is more similar between these groups (a bit higher for minor filers; Figure C-2-3, right panel). This is because the minor filers are often living with other family members and are thus part of larger poverty units than their individual tax unit, and the other members of these larger poverty units bring in additional resources. The average poverty rate of minor filers is actually lower than that of children claimed as dependents (4.7% vs 14.2%). On average, when compared with dependent children, the minor filers have lower levels of AGI in their tax unit (because it is just them) but also lower poverty rates.

The minor filers are not evenly distributed across the AGI distribution. Instead, they are concentrated at the bottom end of the distribution (because they have low AGIs) and they introduce more data points in that tail. Thus, when we include them in the analysis, they end up dominating these lower percentiles and they push many children claimed as dependents into higher percentiles of the distribution. Because minor filers dominate these lower percentiles when they are included *and* the distribution of their income-to-needs ratios is relatively higher than for children claimed as dependents (Figure C-2-3, right panel), they make it appear as though

---

[5] The number of teenagers flagged as filers by the Census Tax Model likely does not line up with the tax data, but that is a limitation that we cannot avoid.

[6] When combining minor filers and children claimed as dependents, the median AGI is $38,004.

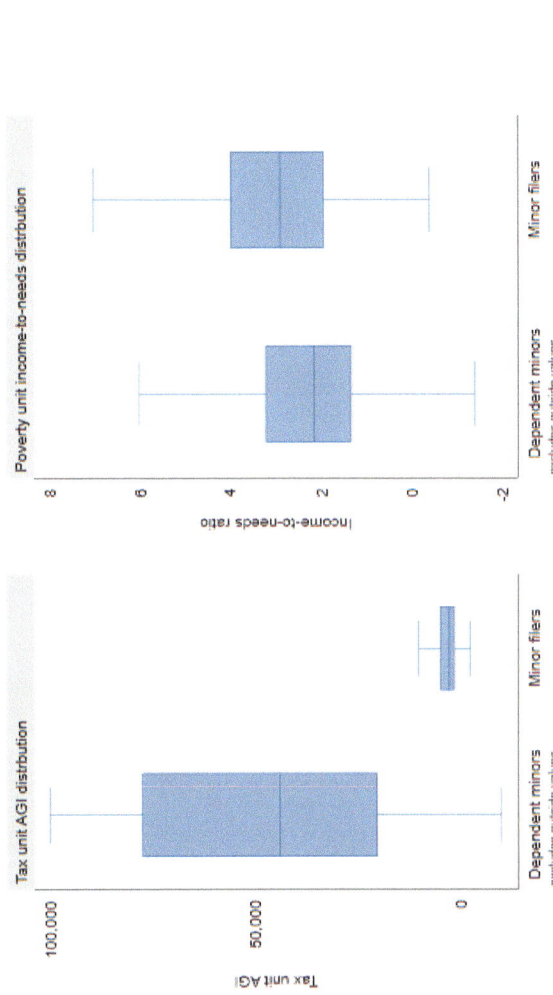

FIGURE C-2-3 Adjusted gross income and income-to-needs distribution of children under age 18 by tax-unit dependency status.
NOTES: Figure C-2-3 shows the AGI distribution and the distribution of income-to-needs ratios among children under 18 in the 2001 ASEC-CPS (representative of 2000) who are identified by the Census Tax Model as dependents versus those identified as independent tax filers. See O'Hara (2004) for a discussion of the Census Bureau's Tax Model.
SOURCE: Data from the Historical SPM Data Series (Wimer et al., 2022) and ASEC-CPS data from IPUMS-CPS (2022). Limited to data representative of the 2000 calendar year.

these bottom percentiles have higher income-to-needs ratios. This pattern is depicted in Figure C-2-4, which plots the income-to-needs from our primary results (also presented in Figure C-2-2), and when we include minor filers in the analysis. We do not include this group of children in our primary estimates but provide supplemental results inclusive of them in Table C-2-5.

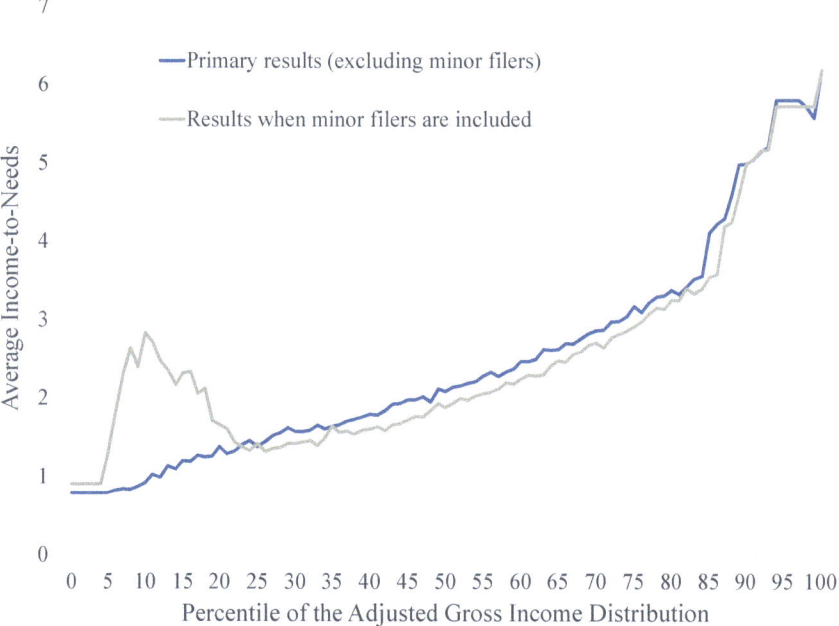

FIGURE C-2-4 Average income-to-needs of children by percentile of the AGI income distribution, including and excluding minor filers.
NOTES: Figure C-2-4 shows the average income-to-needs of children by their position in the AGI distribution and presents results under two scenarios: when including and when excluding children identified as independent tax filers (i.e., non-dependents) based on the Census Tax Model in the dataset. See O'Hara (2004) for a discussion of the Census Bureau's Tax Model. AGIs are determined based on the total AGI of the tax unit claiming each child in the ASEC-CPS data from IPUMS-CPS (2022) and matched to income-to-needs ratios based on data from the Historical SPM Data Series (Wimer et al., 2022).
SOURCE: Data from the Historical SPM Data Series (Wimer et al., 2022) and ASEC-CPS data from IPUMS-CPS (2022).

TABLE C-2-5 Average income-to-needs by percentile of the adjusted gross income (AGI) distribution when minor filers are included

Percentile AGI	Avg. income to needs						Percentile AGI	Avg. income to needs					
	1994	1995	1998	1999	2000	5-year average		1994	1995	1998	1999	2000	5-year average
1	0.84	0.94	0.89	0.90	0.94	0.90	51	1.79	1.87	1.94	1.83	1.96	1.88
2	0.84	0.94	0.89	0.90	0.94	0.90	52	1.80	1.97	1.88	1.96	2.03	1.93
3	0.84	0.94	0.89	0.90	0.94	0.90	53	1.91	1.91	2.05	1.98	2.12	1.99
4	0.84	0.94	0.89	0.90	0.94	0.90	54	1.95	1.85	1.97	1.89	2.22	1.97
5	0.84	0.94	0.89	0.90	0.94	0.90	55	2.07	1.77	2.01	2.07	2.20	2.02
6	0.84	0.94	0.89	3.54	2.85	1.28	56	1.90	2.06	2.22	2.04	2.06	2.05
7	0.84	0.94	0.89	3.17	2.89	1.82	57	1.87	1.97	2.06	2.22	2.24	2.07
8	0.84	0.94	3.35	2.52	3.18	2.30	58	2.00	1.92	2.24	2.13	2.27	2.12
9	0.84	3.89	3.01	2.93	2.91	2.64	59	1.97	2.15	2.24	2.27	2.34	2.19
10	0.84	2.69	2.76	2.56	2.73	2.39	60	2.07	2.00	2.27	2.26	2.28	2.18
11	2.58	3.11	3.20	3.02	2.69	2.83	61	2.31	2.04	2.19	2.30	2.37	2.24
12	2.47	2.39	2.81	2.65	2.87	2.71	62	2.13	2.18	2.18	2.39	2.58	2.29
13	1.88	2.46	2.69	2.43	2.66	2.47	63	2.07	2.32	2.22	2.27	2.51	2.28
14	2.22	2.13	2.17	2.14	2.81	2.35	64	2.25	2.28	2.27	2.23	2.45	2.29
15	1.93	2.20	2.30	1.98	2.26	2.17	65	2.19	2.39	2.49	2.39	2.58	2.41
16	2.24	2.31	2.68	2.53	2.35	2.31	66	2.38	2.37	2.47	2.62	2.54	2.47
17	2.23	2.12	2.35	2.42	2.33		67	2.35	2.30	2.50	2.49	2.65	2.46

(*continued*)

TABLE C-2-5 Continued

Percentile AGI	Avg. income to needs						Percentile AGI	Avg. income to needs					
	1994	1995	1998	1999	2000	5-year average		1994	1995	1998	1999	2000	5-year average
18	1.86	2.09	2.25	1.96	2.11	2.06	68	2.44	2.45	2.58	2.58	2.71	2.55
19	2.27	1.95	2.53	2.02	1.80	2.12	69	2.38	2.41	2.66	2.72	2.76	2.59
20	1.60	1.74	1.69	1.70	1.81	1.71	70	2.50	2.61	2.74	2.77	2.75	2.67
21	1.50	1.90	1.72	1.44	1.73	1.66	71	2.55	2.55	2.83	2.80	2.79	2.70
22	1.58	1.65	1.73	1.49	1.57	1.60	72	2.52	2.56	2.75	2.56	2.82	2.64
23	1.36	1.59	1.44	1.44	1.35	1.44	73	2.57	2.63	2.76	2.91	2.98	2.77
24	1.20	1.41	1.34	1.39	1.51	1.37	74	2.69	2.60	2.80	2.96	3.00	2.81
25	1.29	1.29	1.33	1.28	1.44	1.33	75	2.66	2.83	2.88	2.92	2.96	2.85
26	1.24	1.32	1.29	1.60	1.63	1.42	76	2.69	2.84	3.00	3.03	2.99	2.91
27	1.22	1.37	1.31	1.43	1.24	1.32	77	2.88	2.79	3.06	2.98	3.15	2.97
28	1.26	1.43	1.27	1.45	1.38	1.36	78	3.10	2.87	3.19	3.05	3.17	3.07
29	1.32	1.27	1.52	1.31	1.42	1.37	79	3.01	3.01	3.25	3.32	3.16	3.15
30	1.26	1.52	1.47	1.37	1.48	1.42	80	3.04	3.05	3.16	3.17	3.25	3.13
31	1.42	1.39	1.35	1.51	1.43	1.42	81	3.06	2.97	3.32	3.54	3.33	3.25
32	1.35	1.27	1.62	1.55	1.39	1.44	82	3.04	3.17	3.17	3.52	3.30	3.24
33	1.34	1.48	1.48	1.52	1.48	1.46	83	3.16	3.16	3.47	3.66	3.52	3.39
34	1.27	1.34	1.37	1.52	1.46	1.39	84	3.32	3.09	3.37	3.42	3.44	3.33
35	1.38	1.60	1.44	1.48	1.51	1.48	85	3.28	3.15	3.47	3.57	3.47	3.39
36	1.57	1.60	1.75	1.72	1.55	1.64	86	3.44	3.49	3.60	3.49	3.68	3.54

37	1.45	1.62	1.69	1.54	1.50	1.56	87		3.49	3.44	3.58	3.79	3.57	3.58
38	1.52	1.51	1.62	1.59	1.65	1.58	88	3.59	3.59	3.86	3.87	6.02	4.18
39	1.44	1.45	1.75	1.49	1.59	1.54	89	3.64	3.61	4.05	3.91	6.02	4.24
40	1.51	1.53	1.56	1.62	1.72	1.59	90	3.75	3.70	4.09	5.41	6.02	4.59
41	1.51	1.56	1.62	1.65	1.69	1.60	91	3.77	3.66	6.05	5.41	6.02	4.98
42	1.54	1.52	1.60	1.71	1.79	1.63	92	3.85	3.90	6.05	5.41	6.02	5.05
43	1.55	1.47	1.63	1.54	1.75	1.59	93	4.10	4.20	6.05	5.41	6.02	5.16
44	1.56	1.76	1.58	1.65	1.75	1.66	94	4.15	4.21	6.05	5.41	6.02	5.17
45	1.52	1.59	1.78	1.66	1.82	1.68	95	4.15	7.00	6.05	5.41	6.02	5.72
46	1.71	1.67	1.69	1.72	1.81	1.72	96	4.15	7.00	6.05	5.41	6.02	5.72
47	1.61	1.71	1.82	1.76	1.92	1.76	97	4.15	7.00	6.05	5.41	6.02	5.72
48	1.73	1.62	1.77	1.78	1.87	1.76	98	4.15	7.00	6.05	5.41	6.02	5.72
49	1.79	1.77	1.83	1.79	2.02	1.84	99	4.15	7.00	6.05	5.41	6.02	5.72
50	1.90	1.89	1.94	1.99	1.93	1.93	100	4.15	7.00	6.05	5.41	6.02	5.72

NOTES: Table C-2-2 shows the average income-to-needs of children by their position in the AGI distribution and when including children identified as independent tax filers (i.e., non-dependents) based on the Census Tax Model in the dataset. See O'Hara (2004) for a discussion of the Census Bureau's Tax Model. See Table C-2-1 for results excluding minor filers from this analysis. AGIs are determined based on the total AGI of the tax unit claiming each child in the ASEC-CPS data from IPUMS-CPS (2022) and matched to income-to-needs ratios based on data from the Historical SPM Data Series (Wimer et al., 2022).
SOURCE: Produced with data representative of 1994, 1995, 1998, 1999, and 2000 from the Historical SPM Data Series (Wimer et al., 2022) and ASEC-CPS data from IPUMS-CPS (2022).

Historical Trends in Absolute Mobility

Data

A key challenge in measuring mobility historically is the lack of longitudinal (panel) data that could allow researchers to link children to their parents and construct measures of mobility analogous to those discussed above. Chapter 11, which covers research needs, discusses ongoing efforts to remedy this problem by linking historical census data (the American Opportunity Study). Lacking such data at the time, Chetty et al. (2017) develop a method of estimating absolute mobility—the share of children who earn more than their parents—using currently available cross-sectional historical data on income distributions. Note that their method cannot be used to construct measures of relative mobility historically, nor can it be used to measure mobility across subgroups or areas reliably. We therefore focus here on their analysis of national trends in mobility.

To measure absolute mobility over time in the United States, Chetty et al. (2017) use data from the decennial U.S. Census and CPS to estimate marginal income distributions for children in the 1940 to 1984 birth cohorts and for their parents. Marginal income distributions at age 30 for these children are obtained from the CPS March 1970 to March 2014 samples. The sample of children comprises U.S.-born members of the 1940 to 1984 birth cohorts who, at age 30, were present in the United States and not institutionalized. We compute household income as the sum of spouses' personal pretax income.

Parents' income distributions for children in each of the 1940 to 1984 birth cohorts are constructed by pooling data from census cross sections between 1940 and 2000, using the 1% IPUMS samples, and focusing on individuals who have children between ages 16 and 45. To cover all parents via decennial censuses, parents' incomes are estimated when the highest earner is between ages 25 and 35, a symmetric window around age 30. For example, the income distribution of parents of children in the 1970 birth cohort is estimated as follows. First, the authors use the 1970 census and select parents between ages 25 and 35 who have a child younger than age 1 in 1970. Next, they turn to the 1980 census and select parents between ages 26 and 35 who have 10-year-old children (i.e., individuals who had a child in 1970 when they were between ages 16 and 25). Third, to identify parents between ages 35 and 45 who had children younger than age 1 in 1970, they turn to the 1960 census and select all individuals ages 25–35. This last group receives a weight equal to the fraction of individuals in the 1970 census between ages 35 and 45 who had a child younger than age 1 in

1970.⁷ Income distributions for parents with children in other birth cohorts are estimated analogously.

In their baseline series, which we show in Figure 2-10, Chetty et al. adjust for inflation using the benchmark CPI-U-RS. Choices of the inflation index can affect measures of absolute mobility significantly, as pointed out by Strain (2020) and by others; Chetty et al. demonstrate that the qualitative conclusion of declining absolute mobility is robust to reasonable choices of the inflation index, but the magnitudes of the decline remain debatable.

Methods

Chetty et al. (2017) focus on a measure of *absolute* mobility to address the question: "What fraction of children born in a given year (e.g., 1940, 1970) grow up to have a household income that exceeds that of their parents?" To do so, they combine children's and parent's marginal income distributions constructed as described above with a nonparametric rank-rank copula that measures relative mobility. This copula is a 100 × 100 matrix, where each (i,j) cell in the matrix indicates the probability that a child born to parents with income percentile i will grow up to have income percentile j.

The copula is constructed using modern tax records based on near-population data in Chetty et al. (2014a). The sample used to construct the copula comprises children in the 1980 to 1982 birth cohorts who are linked to parents by being claimed as dependents on federal income tax forms. This comprises more than 10 million parent-child pairs. To construct the copula, children's and parent's income are first measured using concepts similar to those described above. For tax filers, income is defined as adjusted gross income plus the nontaxable portion of Supplemental Security Income and Social Security Disability Income. For non-filers, income is the sum of W-2 wage earnings, Supplemental Security Income, Social Security Disability Income, and unemployment insurance income. If individuals' incomes are missing in these data, they are assigned a value of zero. Children's incomes are mean income in 2011 and 2012 (when they are between the ages of 30 and 32) and parents' incomes are mean taxable income between 1996 and 2000, the first 5 years for which population tax records are available.⁸

To produce their baseline series of absolute mobility—shown in Figure 2-10—Chetty et al. apply the copula estimated for the 1980 to 1982 cohorts

---

⁷ This approach assumes that the income distribution of those who have children after age 35 is representative of the income distribution of the general population. Chetty et al. (2017) show that results are robust to restricting attention to parents who have children between ages 25 and 35.

⁸ Parents are between ages 30 and 60 when we measure their incomes. Since the distribution of income ranks is fairly stable between ages 30 and 60 (Chetty et al., 2014a), this approach provides a reasonable estimate of the copula that one would obtain using income ranks at age 30 for all parents.

to *all* cohorts, effectively assuming that relative mobility did not change across cohorts. Using children's and parent's marginal income distributions, for each child's income percentile r^k and parent's income percentile r^p, they calculate whether children at r^k earn more than parents at r^p. The copula provides the probability that each children-parent rank pair (r^k, r^p) occurs. They then measure absolute mobility as the fraction of cases where children at r^k earn more than parents at r^p, integrating over the copula.

The strong assumption of constant relative mobility over time is based on evidence from Chetty et al. (2014b) that relative mobility has remained stable overall in recent cohorts. Furthermore, Chetty et al. show that their estimates of absolute mobility are insensitive to assumptions about the degree of relative mobility in early cohorts (in the 1940s and 1950s), since virtually all children out-earned virtually all parents in those cohorts, implying that absolute upward mobility rates were close to 100% during that time period irrespective of the degree of relative mobility.[9]

---

[9] Formally, they compute bounds on absolute mobility using linear programming methods to search over all plausible copulas for the maximum and minimum levels of absolute mobility consistent with the marginal income distribution, and show that these bounds are very tight in early cohorts.

APPENDIX C: CHAPTER 3
RACIAL DISPARITIES IN INTERGENERATIONAL POVERTY

This appendix provides a much broader literature review on several of the topics discussed in Chapter 3 of the report. The titles of the sections below correspond to the section titles in the Chapter 3 text; two additional sections discuss gender issues and Black immigrants.

Patterns of Intergenerational Mobility by Race and Gender

As shown in Figures 2-4 and 2-5 in Chapter 2, Black women who grew up in low-income families attain rates of upward mobility that are equal to those of similar White women when measured by individual earnings (roughly 39% for both groups), but they are less upwardly mobile when measured by household income (26% vs. 47%). Meanwhile, Black men have lower rates of upward mobility than similar White men using both measures. (The difference in individual earnings mobility rates relative to White people of the same gender is similar for Native American men and women, whereas it is much larger for Black men than for Black women. Also, individual and household income mobility favors Native American men over Native American women.)

Chetty et al. (2020) find that Black men are less likely to be working, have lower wage rates, have lower educational attainment, and are more likely to be incarcerated than White men from similar family backgrounds. In exploring the correlates of these gaps between Black and White men, Chetty et al. rule out parental characteristics, family wealth, and ability differences as explanations, and instead write: "We conclude that neighborhoods with low poverty rates, high rates of father presence among blacks, and low levels of racial bias among Whites have better outcomes for black boys and smaller racial gaps" (p. 718).

Chetty et al. (2020, p. 747) note two implications of these gender differences. They write:

> It is important to note, however, that this finding does not imply that the unconditional Black-White gap in women's individual incomes will vanish with time. This is because Black women continue to have substantially lower levels of household income than White women, both because they are less likely to be married and because Black men earn less than White men (Online Appendix Figure V). As a result, Black girls grow up in lower-income households than White girls in each generation, leading to a persistent racial disparity in individual income for women even in the absence of an intergenerational gap in their individual incomes.

Nevertheless, the key to closing income disparities for both Black and White women is to close intergenerational gaps in income between Black and White men.... The model predicts that in the absence of intergenerational gaps for women, the steady-state gap for both women and men is proportional to the intergenerational gap in individual incomes for men.

The second statement above suggests a tight focus on policies and programs specifically for Black boys and men, even though the first statement identifies the cycle of intergenerational poverty for females, with Black girls each generation growing up in lower-income households than White girls in each generation. Ignoring investments in Black girls and women would maintain this cycle. The committee also highlights the importance of a relational, historical, intersectional, and (qualified) resilience approach to understanding these gendered patterns of Black-White disparities.

First, as stated in Chapter 2, the fact that Black women exhibit similar individual mobility but not household mobility as White women "is probably due to the fact that Black women are more likely than White women to live in single-parent families, and thus also more likely to be the main breadwinners in their families." Since Black women are more likely to be heads of households than White women, their average socioeconomic position will be more disadvantaged than that of similar White women. Within coupled households (that are same-race and opposite-gender), Black women's earnings act as compensatory for the relatively low earnings of Black men, whereas White men's higher earnings compensate for the lower earnings of White women. Too close of a focus on Black men's outcomes ignores the need for policies that support low-income Black girls and women in their need to generate even greater socioeconomic resources.

Second, the gendered contours of racial discrimination and racism are historically specific and change over time. Black women disproportionately experienced rape during slavery, whereas Black men disproportionately experienced lynching after slavery. The 15th Amendment, ratified in 1870, granted only Black men the right to vote, whereas Black (and White) women were disfranchised until 1920 with the ratification of the 19th Amendment. Black men and women both experienced racism in the labor market in the early- to mid-20th century, but Black women were disproportionately confined to domestic labor whereas Black men were relegated to unskilled blue-collar jobs (outside of agriculture). The historical violence, exclusion, and exploitation explored in this chapter were experienced differently by Black men and women. Similarly, the forms of discrimination and racism today are different and may yield different disparities across race and gender. For example, while low-income Black boys have lower rates of upward mobility than Black girls, Black men on average have substantially higher wealth levels than Black women (Chang et al., 2021).

While attention to Black men may be relevant to the narrow question of intergenerational income mobility, such a focus reflects a presentist bias regarding the changing nature of gendered racism and does not allow for discussions of policies and interventions that can support Black women's mobility while also improving Black men's outcomes.

Third, the comparison by race within genders obscures the fact that both Black and White women trail White men in achieving upward mobility. Roughly 39% of Black and White women who grew up poor rise to the top three quintiles of the individual income distribution as adults, compared with 54% of White men. Gender-based discrimination and what might be called "structural sexism" (Homan, 2019) reduces the socioeconomic mobility and well-being of all women (Ridgeway & Correll, 2004), just as structural racism negatively effects the outcomes of all Black people, with Black men and women showing different outcomes relative to White people in different domains (see, e.g., Kim, 2009; Paul et al., 2022). Only comparing Black women to White women and Black men to White men controls away the workings of racialized gender structures in education, health, housing, families, law, and the labor market. An intersectional approach recognizes that Black women from low-income backgrounds still do not enjoy the same opportunities for upward mobility as similar White men.

Finally, the performance of Black women also reflects their effort and resilience, and individual- and community-level protective factors. This success goes even further in some domains. For example, at every parental income level, Black women have higher college attendance rates than even White men (Chetty, 2020, p. 716). These outcomes are attained in spite of racism and discrimination (and sexism), not because racism and discrimination do not exist. Black girls are more likely than White girls to experience school discipline (Morris, 2016); less likely to be seen by adults as needing nurturing, care, and support (Epstein et al., 2017); and less likely to receive a substance abuse treatment referral in the juvenile justice system (Johnson et al., 2022), to name just a few examples. Yet they show greater achievement in some areas. Upward mobility is also not without its health costs. Research on "skin-deep resilience" has found that the positive mindsets and behaviors of upwardly mobile low-income youth pay off in educational attainment and other outcomes, but also take a toll on physiological health (Chen et al., 2020; Miller et al., 2015). This finding holds across race and gender, but studies have not looked simultaneously at the effortful striving required for upward mobility and experiences of racial (and gender) discrimination. The resilience shown by low-income Black girls who climb the socioeconomic ladder must be qualified by these factors and does not obviate a discussion of the contexts of discrimination and structural racism within which Black girls and boys grow up.

While the situation for Black boys and men merits specific policy interventions where appropriate, it is important that the success of some low-income Black girls and women not exclude them from policy attention. Racial disparities are group-based average differences in outcomes. However, because individual experience varies—often greatly—around the average, group averages by themselves tell us little about the specific characteristics of individuals. Instead, averages offer a way of describing the status of one group compared with another (National Academies, 2022b).

Defining Disparity, Inequality, Discrimination, and Structural Racism

Racial disparities illustrate the differences in rates, trends, or probabilities between White people and Black and Native American people in key life experiences that are relevant for upward mobility. For example, Black babies born to women with a high school diploma or less are 1.5 to 2 times as likely to have low birthweight as White children born to similar mothers (Pollack et al., 2021). Low birthweight is negatively associated with adult educational and labor market outcomes (Black et al., 2007; Conley & Bennett, 2000; Currie, 2009). The homes where infants spend their time are also deeply unequal environments. For example, 5.8% of Native American households lack complete plumbing, compared with only 0.3% of White households. Water access, quality, affordability, and infrastructure are not issues only plaguing low-income countries (Meehan et al., 2020), but instead disproportionately affect low-income Black and Native Americans in the United States (Almond et al., 2018; Deitz & Meehan, 2019; McDonald & Jones, 2017; Mueller & Gasteyer, 2021; Roller et al., 2019; Tanana et al., 2021), and contaminated water increases the incidence of infant low birthweight (Currie et al., 2013).

Furthermore, racial disparities are evident in, for example, exposure to environmental toxins (Lane et al., 2022; Taylor, 2014), proximity to pediatricians and primary care doctors (Gaskin et al., 2012; Kruse et al., 2016), availability of full-service grocery stores and healthy food (Pindus & Hafford, 2019; Walker et al., 2010), access to libraries and broadband internet (Burke, 2007; Dolcini et al., 2021), residence in high-poverty neighborhoods (Erickson et al., 2008; National Equity Atlas, 2019; Sampson et al., 2008), and attendance at schools with college-preparatory curricula (Rose & Betts, 2004; U.S. Department of Education Office for Civil Rights, 2016). It is the cumulative and intersecting nature of these disparate exposures over the life course that partially explains higher rates of intergenerational poverty.

Racial inequality encompasses a broader range of processes than that identified solely based on research on racial disparity. In the context of the criminal justice system, for example, studying race within this larger framework on inequality has several advantages. According to National Academies (2022b, p. 29):

> First, the decomposition of racial disparities into differential offending and differential treatment is placed in a larger social context in which the social structure outside the criminal justice system may influence offending, differential treatment within the system, and criminal justice policy design. Second, in the inequality framework, a reduction in disparity at a particular point may not reduce racial inequality in the broader community. Large racial inequalities in housing, jobs, and quality education can persist even if racial disparities in criminal justice contact are reduced.

In other words, racial inequality is often used to refer to system-level racial gaps whereas racial disparities are used to characterize differences in a single outcome or variable.

Studies of racial discrimination using statistical, audit, and experimental methods (Pager & Shepherd, 2008), as well as several meta-analyses, find clear patterns of racial discrimination against Black Americans in areas such as employment, housing, health and mental health care, criminal prosecution, conviction, and sentencing, consumer markets, and in children's placement into gifted classes (Anwar et al., 2012; Bertrand & Mullainathan, 2004; Besbris et al., 2015; Card & Giuliano, 2016; Faber & Mercier, 2022; Gaddis, 2015; Ge et al., 2020; Kugelmass, 2016; O. Mitchell, 2005; Pager & Shepherd, 2008; Quillian et al., 2020a; Wu, 2016). There is less research on racial discrimination against Native Americans, but audit, self-report, and correlational studies show frequent experiences of discrimination across a range of settings (Abramson et al., 2015; Findling et al., 2019; Hurst, 1997; Puumala et al., 2016; Robert Wood Johnson, 2018; Stepanikova & Oates, 2017; Turner & Ross, 2004; Wilmot & Delone, 2010; Weber et al., 2018; however, see Button & Walker, 2020, which does not find employment discrimination in a large audit study). Discrimination is relevant for intergenerational poverty because it excludes Black people and Native Americans from access to and participation in contexts that enhance opportunities or exposes them to practices that reduce opportunity.

The term "racism" is sometimes used to describe individual dispositions linked to beliefs in racial stereotypes and negative sentiments against a racialized outgroup. Survey researchers have designed scales to measure racism among individual respondents (National Research Council, 2004), and psychologists have designed experiments to detect racial bias among research subjects (see, for example, Eberhardt et al., 2004; Geller et al., 2021). This evidence demonstrates the ways in which belief, sentiment, and cognition operate at the individual level to drive decision making and other behavior in a direction that is harmful to racialized outgroups. Beyond the level of the individual, social organizations and institutions (e.g., neighborhoods, families, markets, health care systems) are often run or structured in a way that is harmful to racialized outgroups, even in the absence of individual-level racism. Scholars have described this configuration of social relations as "structural racism."

Some scholars emphasize the historical character of structural racism, in which "whiteness, a privileged racial category justified by negative racist stereotypes, [is] passed down from generation to generation, so as to become acceptable, normal, and part of the public common sense" (Marable, 2001, p. 13; see also Rucker & Richeson, 2021). Whereas racial inequality describes (perhaps enduring and multidimensional) group-based differences, structural racism attributes such inequality to social organization and institutions. Against this background, structural racism is defined as the operation of race as an organizing social force to enact, codify, or enable the oppression of one or more groups. Once a society becomes racialized, invidious racial distinctions affect "social relations and practices" at "all societal levels" (Bonilla-Silva, 1997). Structural racism is not defined by individual bigotry, prejudice, or discrimination but rather is based on how social, economic, and political institutions of government and civil society are organized by law, policy, practice, and norms. In this way, the argument that posits structural racism as a force contends that inequalities by race occur specifically because of social and institutional factors that perpetuate racial inequality.

Understanding the historical roots of structural racism is crucial to recognizing its effects today and how it has evolved over time (Glenn, 2015; Harris, 1993). Structural racism is reflected in the distribution of political power, economic wealth, material conditions, and equal access to, or fair treatment by, social systems over time, from housing to health care to the criminal justice system (Feagin & Elias, 2013). However, these impacts are neither linear nor constant. Since laws change and social forces are dynamic, shifting with politics, demographics, economics, and social movements, structural racism has evolved over time (see. e.g., Alexander, 2010).

A classic example of structural racism is the passage of voter disenfranchisement laws after the passage of the 15th Amendment. Laws establishing poll taxes, literacy tests, and grandfather clauses disproportionately excluded Black men from registering and casting a vote (Baker, 2022; Manza & Uggen, 2006). They were written without any explicit reference to race in order not to violate the 15th Amendment, which disallowed racial discrimination in voting. Yet their intentions to exclude Black voters were clear, and these laws produced large racial disparities in voter participation between White men and Black men, and often complete Black disenfranchisement. These disparities were the evidence of legally sanctioned second-class citizenship for Black Americans. The 24th Amendment to the Constitution eliminated poll taxes, and the Voting Rights Act of 1965 added enforcement powers to combat the structural racism of ostensibly race-neutral disenfranchisement laws. Yet law and practice are not equivalent, and later policies, such as partisan redistricting, felon disenfranchisement, and voter identification restrictions have continued to disproportionately curtail the franchise for Black citizens. Thus, structural racism encompasses both those neutral policies that are motivated by racist intent and those that reinforce racial hierarchies resulting from past intentional racism, regardless of motivation (Roithmayr, 2014).

Researchers have developed novel measures to study contemporary structural racism, including one that combines indicators of political participation, employment and job status, educational attainment, and judicial treatment (Lukachko et al., 2014). In this study, structural racism is defined by state-level racial disparities across those four domains. Using this measure, the researchers found that Black people living in states with high levels of structural racism were more likely to experience myocardial infarction relative to their counterparts living in states with low levels of structural racism (Lukachko et al., 2014). Another group of researchers developed a measure of state-level structural racism that combines indicators of residential segregation, incarceration rates (though not adjusted for crime), educational attainment, economic indicators, and employment status. This latter study found that higher levels of structural racism were associated with a larger disparity between Black and White victims of fatal police shootings (Mesic et al., 2018; National Academies of Sciences, Engineering, and Medicine [National Academies], 2021).

A final illustration of structural racism is how ostensibly objective artificial intelligence algorithms produce racially disparate outcomes (Benjamin, 2019; Noble, 2018). Obermeyer et al. (2019) document how such algorithms in health care result in doctors providing fewer medical interventions and less care for Black patients. Manifold structures in American society—e.g., the tax code, criminal fines and fees, and the child welfare system (Brown, 2021; Jacobs, 2014; U.S. Commission on Civil Rights, 2017; Williams, 2022)—have built-in, unstated stereotypes, biases, and rules that contribute to the ongoing impoverishment of Black and Native American people.

Contemporary scholars view racial inequality as at least partly structural, cumulatively generated through the mutual and reciprocal interaction of institutions (Powell, 2008; Ray, 2019; Sampson, 2012; Williams & Collins, 2001; Wilson, 1987). The mechanisms of structural racism today can be (although they are not always) found in an array of public policies such as zoning laws and in the pricing of goods and services, as well as in credit risk scoring to limit access to loans or rental housing (using income, zip codes, and arrest records). Still, it is often the case that contemporary forms of structural racism can be traced back to racially exclusive or racially targeted policies and practices of earlier moments in history.

The National Academies noted in a 2017 report on racial health disparities (National Academies, 2017d, p. 104):

> Though inequities may occur on the basis of socioeconomic status, gender and other facts, we illustrate these points through the lens of racism, in part because disparities based on race and ethnicity remain the most persistent and difficult to address. Racial factors play an important role in structuring socioeconomic disparities; therefore, addressing socioeconomic factors without addressing racism is unlikely to remedy these.

Historical Roots of Racial Disparities in Intergenerational Mobility

As noted in the main text, Native Americans and Black Americans stand out as groups subjected to centuries of structural racism rooted in beliefs about White supremacy. The notion of intergenerational poverty has a presentist bias, a narrow time band, and a limited definition of well-being. In other words, we measure only economic status (wages, income, wealth), across at most three generations, in the most recent time period for which we have the best economic data. For example, research on multigenerational poverty finds that 1 in 5 Black families experience poverty across three generations, compared with roughly 1 in 100 White families (Winship et al., 2021; also see Collins & Wanamaker, 2022; Pfeffer & Killewald, 2018). A much longer historical view, however, shows that African and Native American peoples were not "poor" before European contact, but rather sustained themselves and often prospered for millennia in complex societies with functioning governing and economic systems (Carlos et al., 2022; Rodney, 2018).

The plunge into poverty and its persistence across generations in what became the United States is the result of successive waves of theft, destruction, and exploitation of people, land, and property into the present. Among the most glaring forms of historical structural racism that set Black and Native Americans on a course of socioeconomic disadvantage relative to other groups are (a) forced migration and land theft, (b) chattel slavery, labor exploitation, and property theft, (c) scientific racism, and (d) forced assimilation and legalized racial discrimination enforced by racially oppressive institutions. These mechanisms are discussed in detail in the sections that follow.

Forced Migration and Land Theft

The core of European colonialism along the Atlantic coast, and later throughout what would become the United States, was the removal of Native Americans in order to control the land and its riches. Indian wars, removal, and dispossession were the foundations of early policies of land acquisition as European colonizers and later settlers moved westward. Indigenous tribes, whose presence on or possession of land and property lay in the path of White expansion, were often defined as savages or bandits by nature and as criminals by law or custom. Tactics for seizure of Native lands included "threatening genocide, offering bounties for Indian scalps, and exacting massively disproportionate revenge for Indian atrocities" (Kiernan, 2007, p. 310).

Because of incomplete Native land-transfer records, it has proven challenging to fully evaluate the claim that Native Americans lost their land largely through market mechanisms rather than by force (Banner, 2005). However, critics of this contention point to rich documentation of the converse, showing that "Indian nations were forcibly removed, subjected to military containment, deceived by treaties, and defrauded of their landed birthright by unscrupulous non-Indians" (Geisler, 2014, p. 58). Treaties were binding primarily on the Native tribes only, and many were rescinded, unilaterally amended, or annulled without notifying Native leaders. Geisler (2014) concluded that:

> though there were pragmatic moments in which Anglo-Americans found it in their interest to pay Indians for land rather than mount armies against them, the *longue duree* is a different story... Indians in America lost their land through coercion muted by market-like negotiations on some occasions and coercion without pretense on others (pp. 58–59).

Box C-3-1 highlights the experience of the Sauk people.

The practice of impoverishing Native Americans continued through law and force. The Louisiana Purchase (1803), the Indian Removal Act (1830), the Homestead Act (1862), and the Dawes Act (or General Allotment Act, 1887), among many others, authorized through various measures the occupation and expropriation of Native territories.

The Homestead Acts were a series of laws passed between the mid-1800s and the 1930s by which an applicant could acquire ownership of government land, the most well-known (and first) being the Homestead Act of 1862, which accelerated the settlement of western territory. These acts played out on Native lands taken by conquest and coercive pacification, bringing few monetary rewards to Native people (Geisler, 2014). By 1934, some 270 million acres in 160 tracts, nearly 10% of all the land in

> **BOX C-3-1**
> **History of Land Dispossession and the Sauk Tribe**
>
> In the late 18th century, the Sauk, Fox, and Meskwaki people lived in what is now Illinois, Wisconsin, and Iowa. They established migratory cycles of hunting and planting to take advantage of the rich natural resources. According to Rigal (2009, p. 207–208):
>
> During the summer, they lived in multi-family lodges, in large, relatively permanent summer villages situated on river terraces or flood plains along the river. There they harvested corn, squash, and other crops planted in the rich soil of bottomlands replenished by frequent floods. In those days, the Iowa River was lined with marshy sloughs that filled with water whenever the river rose. As a result, the river valleys (unlike the open prairie) gave rise to an abundance of trees and plant cover that could shelter and support large animal populations throughout the year. Every fall, as cold weather approached, Poweshiek's and Wapashashiek's villages broke up into smaller family units that dispersed to winter hunting camps, usually in sheltered creek valleys. There they harvested muskrat, raccoon, otter, deer, and occasionally beaver. In the early spring, these hunting groups reunited, first to make maple sugar in the stands of maple trees that flourished throughout the watershed and then to reconstitute their summer villages along the Iowa River, plant their crops, and begin the cycle anew. Similar seasonal cycles had been followed by Native peoples in the western Great Lakes and Upper Mississippi River Valley for at least 2,000 years.
>
> However, by the 1800s large numbers of White American settlers began to arrive. In the spring of 1829, while the Sauk families were away from their summer villages in Saukenuk in western Illinois, where the Rock and Mississippi rivers converge, White settlers moved in and "enclosed nearly all the Sac Indians [sic] cornfields," wrote a colonial officer at the time. He continued: "The Indians on their arrival were surprised

the United States, had been given away to more than 1.4 million claimants, virtually all of whom were White (approximately 3,500 Black people received land), for a trivial filing fee (Merritt, 2016). Claimants took legal possession of the land after 5 years, conditional on 5 years of continuous residence on the land, building a home, and farming the land. As of 2000, an estimated 46 to 93 million people were descendants of families who took up this "free land" (Shanks, 2005) and the wealth it has generated.

The General Allotment Act (or the Dawes Act) of 1887 aimed to allot federal lands to individual Native American families for private ownership. Its execution, however, resulted in the transfer of roughly 27 million acres of tribal land to non-Native owners (Royster, 1995), a checkerboard ownership pattern frustrating tribal governance and development, and a fractionated pattern of ownership between multiple heirs and the federal government. Comparing a Minnesota reservation that was allotted to one that was not, Akee (2020) found that allotment decreased Native American homeownership and displaced people into wage labor as opposed to

> at this, as also the destruction committed by the settlers, by tearing down many of their lodges" (quoted in Wallace, 1982, p. 270). Sauk leader Black Hawk wrote of the incident in his autobiography describing: "I received information that three families of whites had arrived at our village, and destroyed some of our lodges, and were making fences and dividing our cornfields for their own use… I immediately started for Rock River, a distance of ten day's travel, and on my arrival, found the report to be true. I went to my lodge, and saw a family occupying it" (quoted in Pratt, 2001, p. 116).
>
> This band of Sauk families left for the hunting season and returned to find that White settlers had appropriated their land, fields, and homes. This process was repeated across the territory. By 1832, Black Hawk and the Sauk people were defeated and displaced west of the Mississippi River. Whereas they had once thrived on the richness of the land, "In less than a decade, their ancient way of life was in ruinous decline. Hunger and want had become common, as had drunkenness and debt" (Trask, 2007, p. 3).
>
> Although the tribes were forcibly relocated to Kansas and Oklahoma, dozens of families moved back to Iowa in the 1850s. Today, the Sac and Fox Tribe of the Mississippi in Iowa maintain a settlement of over 8,000 acres and have 1,450 enrolled tribal members (https://www.meskwaki.org/history/). This story of dispossession, impoverishment, despair, and resilience expands the chronology, scope, and relevant variables for a contemporary discussion of intergenerational poverty. The economic productivity of Sauk cornfields and the real property of their lodges were stolen through duplicitous "treaties" and White settler occupation, all enforced by violence. Their poverty ensued, despite ongoing valiant efforts at reconstituting their cultural and economic wealth.
>
> SOURCE: Committee generated.

self-employed farming from 1900 to 1910. Leonard et al. (2020) found in a national study of allotted lands that fractionation was associated with decreased per capita income among Native Americans as recently as 2000. Frye and Parker (2021) show that tribal areas with constrained sovereignty over their lands—one result of the Indian Reorganization Act of 1934—have lower per capita incomes. Contemporary forms of discrimination and dispossession are illustrated in the withholding of loans to Native American (and Black) farmers and ranchers, resulting in disproportionate foreclosure and property loss (Carpenter, 2012), and in the higher prices of mortgage loans to Native American home buyers (Cattaneo & Feir, 2021).

The Indian Appropriations Act of 1851 created the U.S. reservation system, which increased the government's control of Native American people and natural resources and expanded territories for White settlements. In the first of several appropriation acts, funds were allocated to move Native people living in the West onto reservations. Most Native lands today are trust lands, meaning the federal government holds the legal title to the land, and that Native tribes or individual tribal members lack ownership and control over the land.

More recently, in the 1950s and 1960s, Congress passed 12 "termination" bills, which ended federal responsibilities for tribes in several states and turned over governing power to the states. By 1957, 2.5 million acres had been removed from federal trust protection (Philp, 1983, p. 166). However, federal trust protection is itself no protection against dubious practices of extraction (Fixico, 2011), as illustrated by a $3.4 billion settlement with the U.S. government in *Cobell v. Salazar* (2009), which found that the Department of Interior and other agencies had breached their trust obligations with hundreds of thousands of Native American plaintiffs in the class. Overall, roughly 56 million acres are held in federal trust as Native reservations, a mere fraction of the 1.9 billion acres that make up the contemporary United States, once occupied by Native peoples.

In all, Native Americans experienced a 98.9% reduction in their access to land from the period of European arrival to the present. The remaining lands are more susceptible to climate risks and less abundant in mineral resources than the territory on which they historically resided (Farrell et al., 2021). These collective experiences of dispossession remain salient. Whitbeck et al. (2004) report that roughly 42% of a sample of Native American respondents in the U.S. Midwest and Canada think about this loss of land at least monthly, and greater proportions think about the loss of language, spiritual ways, and culture.

Chattel Slavery, Labor Exploitation, and Property Theft

The story for Black Americans begins not with land dispossession but with theft of labor and personhood. The first enslaved Africans arrived to what would become the United States in the early 1500s (Guasco, 2014; Johnson, 1923), prior to the 1619 English settlement at Jamestown, Virginia. The Anglo-centered history records slavery as flourishing in the United States for 244 years until the Emancipation Proclamation of 1863, though the timeline is likely much longer given bondage on U.S. shores decades before 1619 and for 2 years after 1863.

Indentured servitude began in early colonial America in response to the need for labor. Most indentured servants were poor Europeans—Irish, Scots, and English—but some were Africans who had been sold into bondage. Typically, servants worked off their indentures and were freed 4 to 7 years after they began. During the earliest years of settlement, no slave laws were in place. However, with increasing demands for labor, rising costs of indentured servants, and increasing demands for land from newly freed servants, colonists established laws in the mid-1600s to hold Africans and their descendants in perpetual servitude. Statutes decreed slavery as a lifelong

APPENDIX C

and heredity condition and enslaved people as the legal property (i.e., chattel) of their "owners" to be bought, sold, traded, or willed as owners wished (Bridgewater, 2005; Franklin, 1969). This system made labor more profitable and readily renewable across generations. Laws ensured that any children born to an enslaved woman belonged not to the mother but to the White man who owned the mother. Enslavers' biological children—born of the rape of enslaved women—had no legal right to any of the father's property, which was ordinarily granted via paternity (Bridgewater, 2005).

When the 13th Amendment was adopted as part of the U.S. Constitution in 1865, officially abolishing chattel slavery, the newly freed people had no land, capital, or equipment for farming. Ida B. Wells, a well-known Black journalist who lived in the late 19th and early 20th century, aptly summed up the situation, noting that the end of slavery left Black people "homeless, penniless, ignorant, nameless, and friendless… We were turned loose to starvation, destitution, and death" (cited in Darity & Mullen, 2020, p. 9). After leading the Union army to victory over the Confederate states, General Sherman ordered the redistribution of 400,000 acres of land along coastal areas of South Carolina and Georgia (40 acres and a mule per family) to help newly freed Black individuals gain economic independence. Shortly thereafter, President Lincoln's successor Andrew Johnson rescinded the order, and the land remained in White possession (Darity & Mullen, 2020; Saito, 2020). Darity and Mullen (2020) argue that had Sherman's order been carried out, it "would have dramatically reversed black asset poverty and reduce blacks' economic vulnerability across generations" (p. 175).

Just as the economic prosperity stolen from Native Americans through land and people theft is incalculable, so are the profits wrought from slavery, which touched every colonial and U.S. institution, from law to the economy to social mores to universities. Economic historians estimate that the present value for lost wages during the period of slavery range from $2.1 to $4.7 trillion, not accounting for land loss or the opportunity costs of educational and discriminatory practices (Darity & Mullen, 2020; Marketti, 1990). Labor exploitation and the stealing of property, land, and assets from Black Americans continued after the formal dissolution of slavery. Between 1865 and the beginning of World War II, Black Americans in the South experienced widespread labor theft and exploitation reminiscent of slavery that impoverished generations of Black families (e.g., through sharecropping, convict leasing, and peonage; Blackmon, 2008; Carper, 1976; Mancini, 1996). Sharecropping was a system of land tenancy in the South that kept Black people working the land they had worked as enslaved people. With little to no capital of their own, they could not even afford the provisions to plant and were thus forced to buy them on credit from White landowners, with agreements to repay the costs upon harvest. Planters kept Black tenants in perpetual debt through unfair contracts and accounting practices, backed by Jim Crow laws that accorded few to no rights to Black people and by White terrorist violence. Box C-3-2 illustrates the experience of a sharecropper in Florida in the 1920s.

The forced labor of prisoners, overwhelmingly Black men, was also rampant during this period. In southern states in the period after the Civil War—and in compliance with the 13th Amendment that allows for "involuntary servitude" in the case of criminal conviction—southern jurisdictions arrested and convicted hundreds of thousands of Black men and some women (LeFlouria, 2015) and sold their labor to private corporations without pay, or with remuneration going to the local government. To replace the social controls of slavery removed by the Emancipation Proclamation, state legislatures in the south passed an array of interlocking laws referred to as "Black Codes" in 1865–1866 that barred Black citizens from voting, serving on juries, testifying against White people in court, and working in skilled jobs. These laws criminalized many aspects of Black daily life (e.g.,

---

BOX C-3-2
Labor Exploitation Through Sharecropping

Journalist Isabel Wilkerson (2011, p. 54) recounts a story told by George Swanson, whose family sharecropped in Florida in the 1920s. Swanson's uncle tried in vain to negotiate on equal footing. Wilkerson writes:

"During the lull before harvest time, one of George's uncles, Budross, went to the little schoolhouse down in the field and learned to read and count. When it came time to settle up over the tobacco George's grandmother Lena had raised, the uncle stood by while the planter went over the books with her. When they got through, George's uncle spoke up.

"'Ma, Mr. Reshard cheatin' you. He ain't addin' them figures right.'

"The planter jumped up. 'Now you see there, Lena, I told you not to send that boy to school! Now he done learn how to count and now done jumped up and called my wife a lie, 'cause my wife figured up these books.'

"The planter's men came and pistol-whipped the uncle right then and there.

"The family had to get him out that night. 'To call a white woman a lie,' George said, 'they came looking for him that night. They came, fifteen or twenty of them on horseback, wagon.'"

In cases like these, not only was the sharecropping family cheated out of their harvests or wages, but they were also forced to flee their homes, taking as much as they could but losing their property and productive investments in the cultivation of the land. Even greater violence ensued if Black people organized against the theft of the sharecropping system. Two hundred Black people were massacred in Elaine, Arkansas, in 1919, after organizing a union to bargain for fair wages (Stockley, 2004).

SOURCE: Committee generated

unemployment, indigency, and disrespect of White people were made illegal) to provide pretexts for jail terms. Black people were often unable to pay even minor fines and, as a result, were sentenced to labor (Carper, 1976; Mancini, 1996).

In his book, *Slavery by Another Name*, Douglas Blackmon defines convict leasing as "a system in which armies of free men, guilty of no crimes and entitled by law to freedom, were compelled to labor without compensation, were repeatedly bought and sold, and were forced to do the bidding of white masters through the regular application of extraordinary physical coercion" (2008, p. 4). Supposed convicts were sold to work in mines, on railroads, on plantations, and in timber fields. The system was highly profitable for private firms who paid no wages and for the state systems that sold the labor of people convicted of "crimes." One contract to the Walker Coal and Iron Company in Georgia in 1874 "called for the leasing of 100 prisoners for five years at $11 per convict per year" (Mancini, 1978, p. 341), or about 7 cents per day, when the average daily wage for miners in the United States at the time was $1.97 (Abbott, 1905, Table XII).

Convict leasing was used not only to enrich private and public coffers but also to impoverish newly freed Black people. Sociologist Christopher Muller (2018) shows that in Georgia after emancipation, Black imprisonment in the convict lease system for property crimes increased most in parts of the state where Black people were gaining an economic foothold through valuable land ownership and leaving sharecropping through urban residence, while White incarceration remained steady. White southerners used punishment as a method to interrupt this progress and to instead return Black men and some women to the status of unpaid laborers. Not only did disproportionate incapacitation stymie economically productive activities, but convict labor was essential to the South's agricultural production and industrialization, and it enriched the jailers and their jurisdictions.

Even Black Americans who were able to escape this exploitative system had to contend with discriminatory laws and lending practices that largely barred Black people from land ownership, apprenticeship programs for skilled training, trade unions, and other routes to upward mobility (Lancaster, 2000). During Reconstruction (1865–1877), the period after the Civil War when efforts were made to reintegrate Confederate states and redress the inequities of slavery, Black Codes were abolished. However, after Reconstruction ended, many of the provisions of these codes were reenacted in Jim Crow laws. Adopted in southern states in the 1870s and 1880s and enforced until 1965, Jim Crow laws legalized and mandated racial segregation in all public facilities (e.g., schools, transportation, hospitals, prisons, morgues), relegating Black people to inferior treatment, jobs, and facilities (Franklin, 2013; Lancaster, 2000).

Contemporary labor exploitation continues within prisons. While there is some contracting of prisoner labor to private industry, the majority of this labor benefits federal, state, and local governments, lowering the costs of operating prisons and distorting the true costs of mass incarceration. The American Civil Liberties Union (ACLU) and the University of Chicago Law School's Global Human Rights Clinic (2022) estimate that incarcerated people "produce more than $2 billion a year in goods and commodities and over $9 billion a year in services for the maintenance of the prisons where they are warehoused" (p. 6). Yet they are paid nearly nothing. Private companies, on the other hand, extract revenues through negotiated contracts for high-priced services targeted at prisoners, such as food, telephone, and internet communications (Lara-Millan, 2021). This unpaid labor represents resources that are not passed on to children of incarcerated people, most of whom are living in poverty. Using the ACLU/University of Chicago assumption of 6.5-hour workdays (across industry types) for 22 workdays per month, if 400,000 workers were paid the 2022 federal minimum wage of $7.25/hour, and 20% of their wages were passed through to the custodial parents for care of their children, that would be ($[6.5 \times 22 \times 12 \times \$7.25] \times 400,000) \times 0.2 = \$995,280,000$ of income for their families.

One historical example of property theft concerns The Freedmen's Bank, which was established after the Civil War in lieu of land reparations and as a way to integrate Black families into the national economy. Signed as The Freedmen's Bank Act of 1865 by President Abraham Lincoln, it established a bank that served more than 60,000 Black depositors across 34 branches just before its demise in 1874 (Hunter, 2018). The bank's White managers advertised aggressively in Black publications while using the deposits for risky investments in railroads and unsecured loans. Legal scholar Mehrsa Baradaran (2017, p. 29) writes, "As one white observer explained, the white managers, entrusted with guarding the meager savings of the freed slaves, 'looted the bank'." The economic crisis of 1873 was the final straw, and the bank failed in 1874. The deposits were not federally guaranteed, and only 62% of the more than $3 million in deposits (or roughly $76 million in 2022 dollars) was ever repaid (Hunter, 2018). Half of the Black people with holdings in the bank got nothing (Washington, 1997). Stein and Yannelis (2020, p. 5374) show the effects of this asset destruction over the long run, finding that "African Americans in the present day who live in counties that once had a Freedman's Savings Bank branch are more likely to list mistrust of financial institutions as a reason for being unbanked; this association is not present for Whites."

There was also property destruction in places of Black urban settlement. In the late 1890s, Black people made up more than half of Wilmington, North Carolina. They were relatively prosperous and had significant representation in the city government, having been enfranchised during the Reconstruction era. In 1898, White residents staged what historians now label as a violent coup in order to regain power (Zucchino, 2020). Estimates are that between 60 and 250 Black people were killed. The economic effects were evident in Black employment and labor status. All of Wilmington's Black city workers were fired and replaced by White employees. The number of Black business owners declined, and Black businesses were disproportionately displaced from the downtown area (Hamilton & Darity, 2006).

The economic toll is even more quantifiable for the Tulsa massacre of 1921, in which as many as 300 Black people were killed. White mobs—deputized and armed by the local police—destroyed roughly 35 acres of the Greenwood section of the city, called Black Wall Street for its concentration of thriving Black-owned businesses (Messer et al., 2018). The Oklahoma Commission to Study the Tulsa Race Riot of 1921 (2001) reported claims for property damage of $1.8 million, or nearly $30 million in today's dollars. Messer et al. (2018) figure that if the same 1,256 homes were destroyed in Tulsa in 2018, the cost would be roughly $150 million. None of the property claims were ever repaid to Black families.

This historical violence and property loss reverberates in present-day socioeconomic well-being. Albright et al. (2021) show that the Tulsa massacre lowered the occupational status of Black Tulsans into the 1940s and lowered their homeownership rates up to 2000, the last year of observations. Moreover, Black homeownership rates were also lower in Black areas across the country that received significant newspaper coverage of the Tulsa massacre. Just as the failure of the Freedman's Bank made Black people leery of banks (Stein & Yannelis, 2020), the Tulsa massacre "provided a warning of the danger of the accumulation of wealth through home ownership" (Albright et al., 2021, p. 31) that has persisted for decades. In addition to the reverberations from historical forms of expropriation, more recent and contemporary practices of asset extraction are manifest through the racially disparate use of eminent domain (U.S. Commission on Civil Rights, 2014), unfair property tax assessments (Atuahene & Berry, 2018), and Black home loss through foreclosure and institutional purchases (Hwang, 2019), just to name a few.

Scientific Racism

During the mid to late 1600s, race ideology developed as justification for White supremacy, land theft and genocidal wars against Native peoples, and permanent enslavement of Black people. Native people were regarded as fierce, as evil, as savages fated by God for conquest, and Black people as inferior subhumans without capacity for reasoning, imagination, and sentiment (Franklin, 1969; Smedley, 1998; Stannard, 1992). Science played a supporting role in hardening early folk beliefs among White colonists and settlers about "race" and inequality. From the 18th century and well into the 20th century, anthropologists, biologists, and psychologists developed techniques to measure differences in physical characteristics as a basis for racial classification and subordination (Gould, 1996). For example, during slavery, a physician invented the diagnosis of "drapetomania," a mental illness hypothesized to cause enslaved Africans, who were thought to be naturally servile, to flee captivity, for which the prescribed treatment was severe whipping (Opara et al., 2022). "Studies" using these techniques purported to confirm the inferiority of Black and Native people, and to support the belief that "White blood" increased the mental capacity of Black and Native children of mixed racial backgrounds (Guthrie, 1976; Smedley & Smedley, 2005).

Integral to the social construction of race ideology that developed during this period was the valuation of phenotypic traits associated with European ancestry and the devaluation of those associated with non-White people, biases that exist to this day among Black Americans (e.g., Adams et al., 2016; Maddox & Gray, 2002) as well as some Native tribal groups (Brown et al., 2018). Color and phenotypic hierarchies established during slavery also cast a long shadow in establishing practices of anti-Blackness (Franklin, 1969; Frazier, 1957). Studies have found that lighter skin tone among Black people is positively correlated with socioeconomic outcomes (Monk, 2021), higher self-esteem among Black youth (Adams et al., 2020), attribution of more positive traits (Maddox & Gray, 2002), lower rates of school suspension, better physical health, greater upward mobility, and increased odds of full-time employment and college attendance (Han, 2020; Hannon et al., 2013; Hargrove, 2019; Keith & Herring, 1991; Ryabov, 2013). Analyzing archival records of capital murder cases, Eberhardt et al. (2006) showed that defendants whose appearance was perceived as more stereotypically Black were significantly more likely to receive a death sentence than defendants whose appearance was perceived as less stereotypically Black, controlling for numerous factors. Persistent skin tone stratification illustrates the lasting effects of the ideologies created to justify racism and colonialism.

Forced Assimilation and Legalized Racial Discrimination

The original U.S. constitution directed that for purposes of representation and taxes, the population would be determined "excluding Indians not taxed, [and including] three fifths of all other Persons." This separation and erasure of Native Americans and sub-humanization of Black people is built into the fabric of the United States and has clear contemporary manifestations, such as in the "willful blindness toward Native American victimization" by law enforcement (Perry, 2006, p. 412; also see Fryberg & Stephens, 2010), and the digital association of Black people with apes in facial recognition internet searches (Noble, 2018, p. 6).

Anti-Indigeneity undergirded a variety of U.S. government policies that pressured Native Americans to assimilate. The Dawes Act of 1887, for example, authorized a division of tribal lands into individual plots to encourage Natives to farm and ranch like White homesteaders (https://www.nps.gov/articles/000/dawes-act.htm). Laws such as the Civilization Fund Act of 1819 funded schools and forced Native children to attend boarding schools where displays of Native culture and identity were forbidden. By 1925, some 60,000 Native children—about 80% of Native school-age children—had been forced to attend boarding schools. In keeping with the philosophy of assimilation, "Kill the Indian, Save the Man," children in these schools were forbidden to speak their native language, wear traditional clothes (which were replaced by uniforms), or perform tribal practices (replaced by Christian practices). Long hair was cut, braids were prohibited, and tribal names were replaced by English-language names (Adams, 1995; Pember, 2019). Contact with family and community members was discouraged and sometimes forbidden altogether (Adams, 1995; American Indian Relief Council, n.d.; Pember, 2019). Evidence of abuses of students in off-reservation boarding schools led to passage of the Indian Child Welfare Act in 1978, which gave Native parents the legal right to refuse their child's placement in off-reservation schools. Many large Native boarding schools closed in the 1980s and early 1990s. Some located on reservations were taken over by tribes. Still, as of 2021, 15 such boarding schools remain open (Blakemore, 2021; National Native American Boarding School Healing Coalition, 2020).

Forced assimilation is a form of structural racism whose psychological consequences for Native Americans is the focus of a growing number of studies. Compared with all other racial groups, Indigenous youth and adults have higher rates of suicide, substance use disorders, and mental health problems. Research has linked these disparities to both current and historical racial discrimination (Skewes & Blume, 2019) or "historical trauma," conceptualized as "cumulative emotional and psychological wounding over the lifespan and across generations, emanating from massive group trauma experiences" (Yellow Horse Brave Heart, 2003, p. 7). The wounds include the loss of religion, language, and culture—as experienced by Native youth removed from their families to live in boarding schools—as well as loss of ancestral homelands.

Observational work suggests that Native parents who are alienated from Native cultural and spiritual traditions may be less able to provide their children with a supportive, nurturing family environment, putting their children at increased risk for mental and substance abuse disorders (Zimmerman &

Shannon, 2013). Evans-Campbell et al.'s (2012) study of Native Americans found that former boarding school attendees, compared with non-attendees, reported higher rates of current illicit drug use, alcohol use disorder, suicidal ideation, and attempted suicide. In addition, adults raised by former attendees of boarding schools, when compared with their counterparts, were more likely to have an anxiety disorder, PTSD symptoms, and suicidal thoughts in their lifetime. In a similar vein, there is evidence of deleterious multigenerational effects of relocation experiences on Indigenous families. In Walls and Whitbeck's (2012) longitudinal study, grandparent-generation participation in government relocation programs, in which reservation-dwelling Native Americans moved to large urban areas for vocational training and job opportunities, not only harmed the well-being of the grandparent generation (e.g., alcohol and drug problems, depressive symptoms) but also rippled downward to harm the mental health of the parent and youth generations. These studies suggest that historical trauma could contribute to higher rates of intergenerational poverty among Native Americans by undermining the psychological functioning and nurturing capacities in the grandparent and parent generations, in turn increasing substance use and mental health problems in the child generation that ultimately lower educational and occupational attainment and reduce upward mobility.

For Black Americans, slavery and Jim Crow laws throughout the United States continued to shape economic and social opportunity with lasting impacts into the present day. Baker (2022) finds that a composite measure of Black people's state-level exposure to slavery, sharecropping, disenfranchisement, and resistance to desegregation is significantly correlated with contemporary Black poverty and Black-White disparities in poverty. Similarly, Althoff and Reichardt (forthcoming) find that the socioeconomic status of Black families today depends strongly on their historical exposure to racially oppressive institutions. Research (Althoff & Reichardt, 2023) shows that Black people whose ancestors were enslaved up until the Civil War have lower education, income, and wealth today as compared with Black people who were free before the Civil War. While the direct effects of enslavement on these families continued through 1940, the ongoing effects are due to the disproportionate exposure to Jim Crow laws among those families who were enslaved until the Civil War. Thus, state-specific factors perpetuated the socioeconomic disparities that slavery had created among Black families. According to Althoff and Reichardt (forthcoming, pp. 3–4), Black families freed in states with more oppressive regimes experienced significantly lower rates of economic progress starting in the Jim Crow era (1877–1964). For example, consistent with Louisiana's Jim Crow regime being far stricter than Texas's, we find that families freed in Louisiana attained 1.2 fewer years of education by 1940 than families freed only a few miles away in Texas. The magnitudes of those border discontinuities are virtually identical to the general state differences in how families fared after slavery, suggesting that Jim Crow single-handedly shaped the geography of Black economic progress. Althoff and Reichardt (2023, p. 5) conclude: "This result implies that systemic discrimination—the higher exposure to ongoing discrimination because of past discrimination (Bohren et al., 2022)—is at the core of the persisting legacy of racially oppressive institutions in the US."

Contemporary Drivers of Racial Disparities in Intergenerational Poverty

As with the section above, we offer additional discussion and detail about some but not all of the domains covered in the main text, and add an additional section on Black immigrants. The first two subsections here are titled to correspond with their respective section in the main text.

Crime, Victimization, and Criminal Justice

Slavery and colonialism are intertwined systems of racialized economic oppression to benefit those in power. Power is maintained through violence and the threat of violence, often justified under the guise of punishment for supposed wrongdoing or crime (for historical overviews on punishment against Black and Native people, see Ross [2010], Thompson [2019], Ulmer & Bradley [2019], Hinton & Cook [2021]). Early regimes of punishment against Black and Native Americans were manifested in the physical acts of whippings, scalpings, and murders, and also in economic practices of dispossession and indebting. There was punishment for slow work, punishment for speaking one's native language, punishment for playing musical instruments, punishment for leaving or staying on designated lands (territories, plantations, reservations, hunting grounds), punishment for reading or refusing to read, and punishment for using resources from the land for survival (Ross, 2010). Punishment is linked to intergenerational poverty because it limits or eliminates the ability of the parental generation to invest in children economically, socially, psychologically, and culturally. When state punishment is enacted against children, it stifles their educational, psychological, and economic growth.

The historical relationship between punishment and economic disfranchisement has been illustrated above through the example of convict leasing. Punishment was similarly used against Native Americans as a pretext for economic and land dispossession. California Statute Chapter 133 of 1850—very wrongly named "An Act for the Government and Protection of Indians"—deputized White settlers as police, judge, and jury, with the purpose of expropriating labor. The text of the law makes clear the connection between criminal punishment and economic exploitation authorized in the 13th amendment:

> When an Indian is convicted of an offence before a Justice of the Peace, punishable by fine, any white man may, by consent of the justice, give bond for said Indian, conditioned for the payment of said fine and costs, and in such case the Indian shall be compelled to work for the person so bailing, until he has discharged or cancelled the fine assessed against him (quoted in Teran, 2016, p. 24).

Unlike the convict leasing system in the South, individual settlers were enriched by the labor of supposedly criminal Native Americans, who were in turn deprived of the ability to sustain themselves and their families. A frequent grounds for conviction was the "hunger offense of stealing cattle" (p. 26), a crime that resulted from the systematic elimination of Native American food sources (Ross, 2010). In 1861, in Northern California, several hundred Native American men were killed for stealing cattle. In similar cases, the wives and daughters of slain Native American men were taken by White settlers for forced sexual and physical labor.

Law is used strategically to define "crime" in ways that facilitate the maintenance of power and economic hierarchies. Punishment against Black and Native peoples can be exacted to extract labor and land, or for managing periods when their labor was not required (Muller & Schrage, 2021; Western et al., 2006). The "crimes" for which punishment has been levied have been in response to Black and Native people's attempts at bodily, cultural, economic, and spiritual freedom. These historical practices of shaping law and defining crime in anti-Black and anti-Indigenous ways reverberate today in widespread stereotypes about Black and Native lawlessness, disorder, aggression, and criminality (Muhammad, 2019; Ross, 2010), which justify tough-on-crime policies that target Black and Native communities for policing, punishment, and removal from their families and communities, including through supposedly supportive institutions such as schools and the child welfare system (Jacobs, 2014; Roberts, 2022).

This brief history challenges a common starting point when discussing race, crime, and punishment: the notion that Black and Native people commit more crime and therefore experience more punishment. The definition of crime and the accordant punishments are themselves tools of control—from the vagrancy and trespassing laws of the 19th century to the continued 18-to-1 sentencing disparity between crack and cocaine possession. Even using conventional definitions of crime, there appears to be a

APPENDIX C

weak and small relationship between an individual's race and many areas of self-reported offending (Sohoni et al., 2021).

Disparities in incarceration rates between White and Black people are longstanding, dating back to the earliest record keeping in the 1800s. Figure C-3-1 (from Muller, 2012) compares Nonwhite and White incarceration rates from 1880 to 1950 (separate data for Blacks are not available). At the beginning of the time period, the Nonwhite incarceration rate is roughly two times the White rate, while by the end of the time period the gap had widened, with the Nonwhite rate roughly five times the White rate. The ratio (or disparity) of the Black:White incarceration rates peaked at about 7:1 in the early 2000s (National Research Council, 2014), and has declined to roughly 5:1 in the most recent period (Nellis, 2021). In other words,

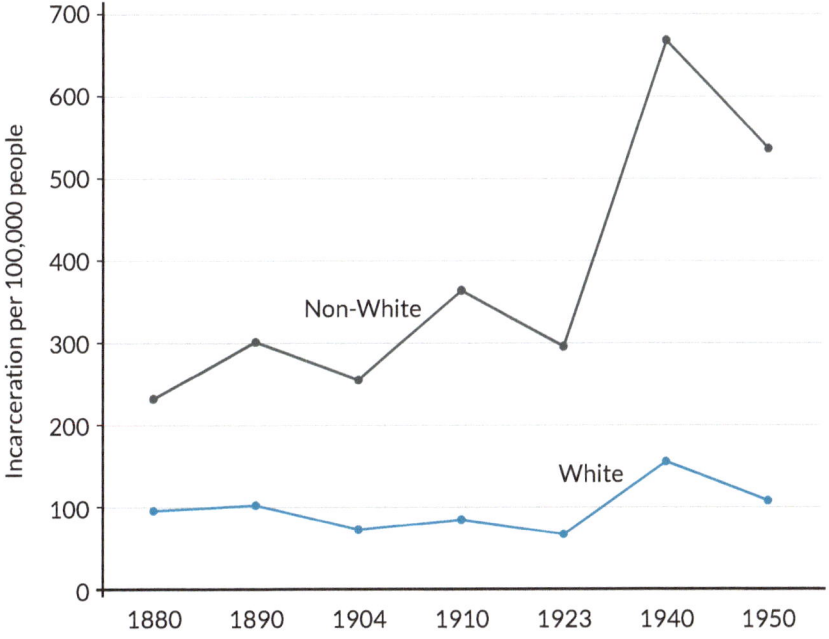

FIGURE C-3-1 Incarceration rates by race from 1880 to 1950.
NOTES: The states included in the analysis are northern and southern U.S. states. Northern states include Connecticut, Illinois, Indiana, Maryland, Massachusetts, Michigan, Missouri, New Jersey, New York, Ohio, Pennsylvania, and Wisconsin. Southern states include Alabama, Arkansas, Florida, Georgia, Kentucky, Louisiana, Mississippi, North Carolina, Oklahoma, South Carolina, Tennessee, and Virginia.
SOURCE: Data from Muller (2012). The underlying data from the graph were obtained using the software WebPlotDigitizer. https://automeris.io/WebPlotDigitizer/

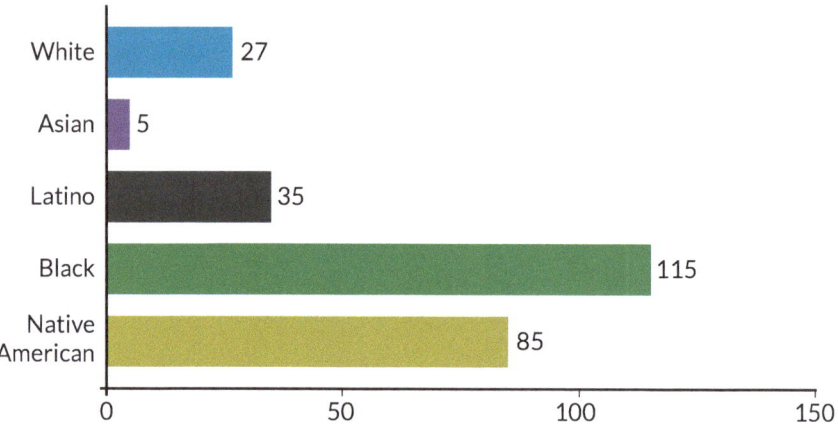

FIGURE C-3-2 Rate of youth confined in juvenile residential placement facilities per 100,000 by race/ethnicity, 2019.
NOTE: Youth are defined as persons 17 years old and younger.
SOURCE: Data from the Prison Policy Initiative (2021).

contemporary Black/White disparities in incarceration are roughly equal to what they were in 1950. Figure C-3-2 shows that contemporary racial disparities in incarceration rates are also evident for juveniles, with Native and Black juveniles experience much higher rates than White, Asian, and Latino youth.

Racial disparities in offending and cumulative disadvantages across multiple domains reverberate through the stages of criminal processing (e.g., policing, arrest, prosecution, sentencing, incarceration) to produce racial inequality in the criminal justice system (Alexander, 2010; National Academies, 2022b). Researchers have discussed three policy changes that have been important for how structural racism has contributed to these racial disparities in the criminal justice system. The first policy change, collectively known as the War on Drugs, intensively criminalized drug use and drug sales disproportionately in Black communities (Provine, 2011; Tonry, 1996; Tonry & Melewski, 2008). The punitive effect of the War on Drugs can be seen in the increasing probability of imprisonment given a drug arrest and the growing share of people in prison convicted of drug crimes (Beck & Blumstein, 2018; Blumstein & Beck, 1999; Tonry & Melewski, 2008). Given the large racial disparity in drug arrests and prison admissions, the growth in drug incarceration also tended to increase the racial disparity in incarceration through the 1980s and 1990s. The second major policy change contributing to racially disparate criminalization was the War on Crime, which encompassed a variety of changes in sentencing policy at the state and federal levels that increased the duration of prison sentences, particularly for violent offenses. Third, policing strategies changed in the final decades of the 20th century to focus more on crime prevention and to allocate resources more intensively to areas and people who were viewed as high risk (National Academies, 2022b).

Involvement in the criminal legal system has long-term economic effects for young people and adults. People with a conviction experience a cumulative loss of roughly $100,000 in earnings, and people who have experienced incarceration experience nearly $500,000 in lost earnings over their lifetime (Craigie et al., 2020). Incarceration and conviction have similar negative effects on wealth (Maroto, 2015; Schneider & Turney, 2015; Sykes & Maroto, 2016). Given the racial disparities in criminal justice processing, the negative effects on employment and earnings exacerbate racial gaps in socioeconomic outcomes (Gordon et al., 2021; Lyons & Pager, 2007; Pettit, 2011; Western & Sirois, 2019). There is little research on the socioeconomic outcomes after incarceration for Native Americans.

Housing and Neighborhood Environments

Racial disparities in housing are driven by the acts of both private citizens and state actors in coordinating efforts to exclude Black people from property ownership and White neighborhoods. For example, the Servicemen's Readjustment Act of 1944, more commonly known as the GI Bill, offered preferred mortgage financing, tuition for college and vocational training, and enhanced unemployment benefits to returning veterans. While it was federal law, it was administered locally. Black veterans returning to the Jim Crow South in the 1940s, 1950s, and 1960s were denied access to mortgages—as well as to the college tuition benefits (Turner & Bound, 2003)—and thus to the wealth-enhancing possibilities of homeownership and education. Black veterans in the North faced less absolute exclusion, but the federally promoted practice of redlining (discussed in Chapter 3) similarly made the GI Bill widely inaccessible for broadly improving Black people's housing situation (Agbai, forthcoming; Cohen, 2003; Delmont, 2022). Using conservative assumptions, Meschede et al. (2022) estimate that "Black veterans received at most 70% of the value that white veterans received," and the gap was greatest for government spending on housing benefits.

Another example is racially restrictive covenants—agreements written into property deeds that prohibited owners from selling or renting to Black people and, in some places, other marginalized groups such as those of Mexican, Jewish, and Asian people (Jones-Correa, 2000). These agreements date from the late 19th century and were driven by antipathy to living near African Americans and by widespread assumptions that Black neighbors provoked falling property values. After racial zoning by municipalities was ruled unconstitutional in 1917 in *Buchanan v. Warley*, proponents read a 1926 Supreme Court decision in *Corrigan v. Buckley* as tacitly supporting *private* restrictive agreements. For example, one house in a White neighborhood in Chicago that abutted a growing Black neighborhood to the west was covered by two restrictive covenants—one in 1937 and another in 1944 (Pattillo, 2007). The covenant created an exclusionary bond and opened up any violators to legal action and damages. Racially restrictive covenants were supported and propagated by real estate boards, private institutions like universities, and federal agencies, even after the Supreme Court ruled them to be unenforceable in *Shelley v. Kraemer* (1948). There is no national accounting of the spread of these restrictive covenants, but Santucci (2020) documents at least 4,000 such agreements covering properties in Philadelphia alone, as just one example.

The federal government began to play a major role in housing policy after the Great Depression, creating a panoply of policies that reflected the racial prejudices and exclusionary biases of the era. The National Industrial Recovery Act (1933), the establishment of the Homeowners Loan Corporation (HOLC; 1933) and the Federal Housing Administration (1934), the U.S. Housing Act (1937), and the Servicemen's Readjustment Act (the GI Bill that established "VA loans," 1944) all set in motion a national building and financing program to stabilize the U.S. housing market and provide shelter for low- and moderate-income families and, later, for veterans returning from World War II.

The new regime of housing finance systematically disadvantaged African Americans. While working-class European-immigrant urban neighborhoods received low ratings in the rating system, their residents could assimilate and move into "White" neighborhoods where mortgage dollars flowed (Guglielmo, 2003). On the other hand, federal government guidelines warned against the presence of non-White residents. Historian Kenneth Jackson (1985) recounts the example of Lincoln Terrace in St. Louis. The development was intended for and marketed to middle-class White families but was unsuccessful in this plan, and Black families moved in. In 1937, even though the structures were only 10 years old, the federal HOLC gave the neighborhood its lowest rating and withheld mortgage financing, stating that it had "little or no value today, having suffered a tremendous decline in values due to the colored element now controlling the district" (p. 200).

While the HOLC may have been relatively fair in some cities in apportioning home loans to Black households (Fishback et al., 2022; Hillier, 2003), the Federal Housing Authority (FHA) was certainly not. In Chicago in 1938, the Chicago Housing Authority created a map of mortgage-lending risk based on the FHA's evaluations. The entirety of the city's Black community was colored in red. The Chicago Housing Authority summarized the message of the map bluntly: "All Negro census tracts fall within the area where loans have not been made by the major loaning agencies, and loans will not be made" (quoted in Pattillo, 2007, p. 331).

Capitalizing on the exclusion of Black people from the conventional housing finance market, private investors created a shadow market selling "on contract" (Satter, 2009). White "sellers" retained the deed and imposed stringent requirements for maintenance and repayment. With the slightest infraction, owners repossessed properties and kept all of the payments made by the Black "buyer." Contract selling extracted an estimated $3 billion (in 2019 dollars) in wealth from Black families in Chicago in the 1960s (Dubois Cook Center, 2019), and has re-emerged in the post-2008 housing collapse period in predominately Black cities like Atlanta (Immergluck, 2018).

The most recent episode of housing discrimination is the subprime and foreclosure crisis (Hwang et al., 2015; Rugh & Massey, 2010). In December of 2011, the U.S. Department of Justice issued a press release with the headline, "Justice Department Reaches $335 Million Settlement to Resolve Allegations of Lending Discrimination by Countrywide Financial Corporation; More than 200,000 African-American and Hispanic Borrowers who Qualified for Loans were Charged Higher Fees or Placed into Subprime Loans." This was just one of many lawsuits and settlements to come.

Subprime loans are characterized by higher interest rates, payment plans that assume upward value trajectories, deferred or "balloon" payments, interest-only payments, prepayment penalties, and other complicated and disadvantageous arrangements that are often not fully disclosed or explained to the homebuyer. Contrary to the exclusionary practices wrought by redlining, predatory inclusion marks the targeting of Black households for financial instruments that prove detrimental to their socioeconomic well-being.

The rash of subprime lending eventually led to the foreclosure crisis. Black and Latino households were roughly twice as likely to be affected by foreclosure through home loss or serious arrears (Bocian et al., 2011), and Black and Latino neighborhoods were also disproportionately affected (Hall et al., 2015). Roughly 8% of Black households (240,000 households) lost their homes between 2005 and 2008 (Bocian et al., 2010). Disparities in foreclosures and steep declines in housing values had a cascading effect on household wealth, since homes represent the major portion of most people's wealth profile. The median net worth of Black Americans in the United States declined by 53% from 2005 to 2009 (and by an even larger 66% for Latino households), but declined by only 16% for White households. This represented a doubling of the racial wealth gap (Pew Research Center, 2011). The foreclosure crisis and recession were particularly pronounced among Black families with children, widening an already large Black-White wealth gap among such households. Percheski and Gibson-Davis (2020, p. 10) report that by 2016, "black child households had 1 cent of median wealth for every dollar of wealth held by non-Hispanic white child households." The targeting of subprime mortgages to Black buyers negatively impacted Black wealth and Black neighborhoods, continuing a cycle of lowering household resources that might promote intergenerational mobility.

Comparisons with Black Immigrants

Although not included in the main text, a discussion of the socioeconomic status and mobility outcomes of Black immigrants offers additional evidence on racism and discrimination as drivers of intergenerational poverty. Black immigrants have been heralded as a "model minority" (Ukpokodu, 2018), and their success is often advanced as a counter-explanation for the poor social position of Black Americans. The logic goes like this: because both Black Americans and Black immigrants share similar phenotypic characteristics, both groups must suffer from similar levels of discrimination. Therefore, if Black immigrants can succeed despite the barriers of racism and discrimination, then cultural differences, rather than racism, must account for observed differences (Patterson, 2006, 2015; Sowell, 1979, 1981). Such arguments, however, omit important factors discussed here that help explain disparities between immigrant and native-born Black people (Hamilton, 2019; Model, 2008).

The Hart-Cellar Immigration Act of 1965 paved the way for large waves of Black immigrants to migrate to the United States (Portes & Rumbaut, 2014). In 1960, Black immigrants accounted for less than 1% of Black people residing in the United States. By 2010, almost 10% of Black people in the United States were foreign-born, a 10-fold increase in 50 years (Hamilton, 2019). When these new waves of Black immigrants arrived, scholars noted that some Black immigrants had better outcomes than Black Americans. For example, data from the 1980 U.S. Census showed that prior to adjusting for relevant human capital characteristics, Black immigrants from the English-speaking Caribbean were more likely to be in the labor force, had greater employment rates, and earned more than Black

Americans, findings that led some to conclude that culture, rather than racism, explained the poor outcomes of Black Americans (Sowell, 1979, 1981).

These early accounts of labor market disparities between Black immigrants and Black Americans severely overstated the advantages of Black immigrants. After controlling for a standard set of human characteristics, most subgroups of Black immigrants have similar or lower employment rates and earnings than Black Americans (Hamilton, 2019; Model, 2008). Black immigrants' labor force participation rates are higher than those of Black and White Americans, which suggests that disparities in labor force participation likely result from different reservation wages between immigrants and natives, in general, rather than differences in cultural practices (Hamilton, 2019).

Early studies of labor market disparities between Black immigrants and Black Americans also ignored selection bias issues (Patterson, 2006; Sowell, 1981). Like other contemporary immigrants, Black immigrants are a self-selected group of movers (Feliciano, 2005; Feliciano & Lanuza, 2017; Hamilton, 2019; Model, 2008). Most Black immigrants are selected on a range of factors that are positively correlated with better labor market outcomes, including age, health, education, and social class position (Hamilton, 2019). For example, Black Jamaican U.S. immigrants have 13.13 mean years of education, compared with 9.64 years among individuals residing in Jamaica. Similarly, Nigerian U.S. immigrants have 15 mean years of education compared with 6 years among adults residing in Nigeria (Hamilton, 2019). Given the dramatic difference in the home country education distribution between the United States and most Black immigrant sending countries, most Black immigrants also occupy a more favorable social class position in their home country than in the United States (Feliciano, 2020; Hamilton, 2019). Studies have consistently found that the outcomes of Black immigrants are more similar to those of Black Americans who have also made a move across states since birth than to those of Black American nonmovers, which suggests that the favorable outcomes of Black immigrants result from unobserved factors associated with migration (both domestic and international) than from cultural differences between Black immigrants and Black Americans (Butcher, 1994; Hamilton, 2019; Model, 2008).

Any advantages experienced by Black immigrants do not apply to all Black immigrants, even those from the same region or country. For example, among Black women from the English-speaking Caribbean, early arrivals tended to have better labor market outcomes than more recent arrivals. Model (2008) argues that when the Hart-Cellar Act passed in 1965, there were relatively few immigrants from the English-speaking Caribbean residing in the United States to sponsor the visas of family members. As a result, immigrants with skills needed in the United States were among the early drivers of migration after 1965. This fact generated a flow of women from the English-speaking Caribbean who were positive-selected on skills and education (many were employed in the health care sector) as well as risk taking and motivation, given that these women arrived in the country with a small or no established co-ethnic community. Over time, however, family reunification drove an increase in migration, which resulted in a less highly selected group of migrants.

Indeed, patterns of intergenerational mobility among immigrants highlight the role of contemporary discrimination in affecting the outcomes of Black immigrants. Using a century of U.S. censuses and contemporary tax records, Abramitzky and Boustan (2022) find that sons of immigrants raised in the bottom 25th percentile of the income distribution were in a more favorable position in the income distribution than the sons of U.S.-born fathers. For the post-1965 immigration era, the only countries of origin whose immigrants' sons were in a lower position than sons of U.S.-born fathers were Haiti, Trinidad and Tobago, and Jamaica. Hence, Black immigrants differ from non-Black immigrants and seem to face similar barriers to upward mobility as Black natives.

TABLE C-3-1 Interventions in Chapters 4 through 10 that have been shown to be effective for Black, Latino, or Native American children and families

Driver	Program or policy example supported by direct evidence	Key reference(s) (and limitations)	Effect on Black people or mostly Black sample?	Effect on Latino people or mostly Latino sample?	Effect on Native American people or mostly Native American sample?
Education					
Early childhood	None identified in recent research				
K–12 education	Increase K–12 school spending in the poorest districts	Rothstein & Schanzenbach, 2022	Significant impacts for Black students	Not assessed	Not assessed
	Increase K–12 school spending	Johnson & Nazaryan, 2019; Johnson, 2011	School funding is a mechanism by which school desegregation improves long-term outcomes for Black students	Not assessed	Not assessed
	Recruit Black teachers	Gershenson et al., 2022	Significant impacts for Black students on high school graduation and college enrollment (for males)	Not assessed	Not assessed

(continued)

319

TABLE C-3-1 Continued

Driver	Program or policy example supported by direct evidence	Key reference(s) (and limitations)	Effect on Black people or mostly Black sample?	Effect on Latino people or mostly Latino sample?	Effect on Native American people or mostly Native American sample?
	Reduce exclusionary school discipline	Bacher-Hicks et al., 2019	Harsh disciplinary practices increase arrest and incarceration and school dropout, and decrease college enrollment, especially for Black and Latino males	Harsh disciplinary practices increase arrest and incarceration and school dropout, and decrease college enrollment, especially for Black and Latino males	Not assessed
	Develop Ethnic Studies courses	Bonilla et al., 2021	Not assessed	Increases high school graduation and strong suggestive results for postsecondary enrollment	Not assessed
Postsecondary education	Expand effective financial aid programs for low-income students and increase campus supports (such as tutoring and case management)	ASAP: Miller and Weiss, 2021; Buffett: Angrist et al. 2017; HAIL: Dynarski, 2022b	Significant impacts of ASAP for Black student attainment; significant impact of HAIL for Black students on application but not admission or enrollment	Significant impacts of ASAP for Latino student attainment; significant impact of HAIL for Latino students on application but not admission or enrollment	Not assessed

Career training	Expand high-quality career and technical education programs in high school and sectoral training programs for adults and youth	Fein et al., 2021 for Year Up; Roder & Elliott, 2019 for Project Quest	Significant impacts of Year-Up and Project Quest on earnings of Black youth	Significant impacts of Year-Up and Project Quest on earnings of Latinos	Not assessed
Child and Maternal Health					
Family planning	Increase funding for Title X family planning programs and ensure that Medicaid beneficiaries have access to family planning services	Bailey, 2013 does not show subgroup results by race/ethnicity	Not assessed	Not assessed	Not assessed
Health insurance	Expand access to Medicaid with continuous 12-month eligibility and 12-month post-partum coverage; expand access to Indian Health Service for all eligible mothers and children	Brown et al., 2020 does not show subgroup results by race/ethnicity	Wherry & Meyer (2016), larger improvements in life expectancy among Black children relative to White children	Not assessed	Not assessed
Pollution reduction	Support EPA to work with local partners to adopt and expand efficient methods of monitoring outdoor and—especially in schools—indoor air quality	Isen et al., 2017 document impacts for Black subsample; Currie et al., 2023 document the CAA disproportionately improved air quality among Black families	Significant impacts of pollution reduction on earnings of Black children; CAA accounts for 60% of the racial convergence in air pollution exposure in the United States since 2000	Not assessed	Not assessed

321

(*continued*)

TABLE C-3-1 Continued

Driver	Program or policy example supported by direct evidence	Key reference(s) (and limitations)	Effect on Black people or mostly Black sample?	Effect on Latino people or mostly Latino sample?	Effect on Native American people or mostly Native American sample?
Nutrition	Expand child access to existing nutrition programs for legal permanent residents and undocumented parents; increase WIC enrollment by extending infant certification, allowing adjunctive eligibility, and increasing remote access services	East, 2020 analysis of second-generation child health based on immigrant eligibility uses an 80% Hispanic sample	Not assessed	Significantly better birth outcomes for the children of women whose own mothers were eligible for WIC benefits when they were in utero	Not assessed
Family Income, Employment, and Wealth					
Work-based income support	Expand the Earned Income Tax Credit by increasing payments along some or all portions of the schedule and possibly by providing a credit to families with no earnings	Bastian and Michelmore, 2018	Generally positive effects of EITC expansions on the educational attainment and earnings of Black children	Not assessed	Not assessed
Family Structure					
	None identified by research to date	NA			

Housing and Neighborhoods

Residential mobility	Expand coverage of the Housing Choice Voucher program and couple it with customized counseling and case management services	Bergman et al., 2019 do not show race/ethnicity-specific results or have majority-minority sample.	Not assessed	Not assessed

Neighborhood Crime and the Criminal Justice System

Juvenile incarceration	Eliminate most or all juvenile detention and incarceration for non-felony offenses and for felony offenses, especially those that are nonviolent	Aizer & Doyle, 2015; Baron et al., 2023	Significant negative effects of juvenile detention on the completed schoolings and adult crime for Black youth	Not assessed	Not assessed
Child investment strategies	Scale up evidence-based therapeutic interventions such as the Becoming a Man program; improve school quality and reduce lead exposure in ways identified in the education and health categories	Heller, 2017 uses a majority Black sample	Significant reduction in crime and increases in high school graduation for Black youth	Not assessed	Not assessed
Strengthen communities to reduce violent crime and victimization	Scale up programs that abate vacant lots and abandoned homes; increase grants to community-based organizations	Branas et al., 2018 sample was majority Black	Significant reductions in crime	Not assessed	Not assessed

(continued)

323

TABLE C-3-1 Continued

Driver	Program or policy example supported by direct evidence	Key reference(s) (and limitations)	Effect on Black people or mostly Black sample?	Effect on Latino people or mostly Latino sample?	Effect on Native American people or mostly Native American sample?
Policing strategies	Expand funding for policing in high-crime neighborhoods and use of effective strategies like community policing	Chalfin et al., 2022	Significant reductions in homicides for Black people	Not assessed	Not assessed
Reduce gun violence	Reduce access to guns in ways that pass constitutional review; promote child access prevention laws, restrictions on right-to-carry laws, limited access of domestic abusers, and sentencing add-ons for violence involving firearms.	DeSimone et al., 2013 do not show subgroup results for child protection laws; nor does Donohue et al., 2022 for right-to-carry laws, though the cities included in the analysis have large Black populations.	Not assessed	Not assessed	Not assessed
Child Maltreatment					
	None identified by research to date				

NOTES: ASAP = Accelerated Study in Associates Program; CAA = Clean Air Act; EITC = Earned Income Tax Credit; EPA = Environmental Protection Agency; HAIL = High Achieving Involved Leader program at the University of Michigan; WIC = Special Supplemental Nutrition Program for Women, Infants, and Children.

APPENDIX C: CHAPTER 4
CHILDREN'S EDUCATION

This appendix provides a broader literature review on several of the drivers discussed in Chapter 4 of the report, as well as on the interventions supported by direct or indirect evidence. In the case of early childhood interventions, we review the literature that led the committee to not propose any interventions.

Early Childhood Interventions

Several home visiting and early care and education programs have demonstrated long-term impacts on adult education, employment, incarceration, and health. In the case of contemporary early childhood programs, however, few rigorous evaluations have shown similar intermediate- or long-term impacts. Moreover, it is not clear how current programs might be changed in ways that would produce longer-term impacts. The committee was therefore unable to identify specific ways in which further investments in these programs, as currently implemented, would reliably reduce intergenerational poverty. This is not to say that all existing programs are ineffective or that additional investments during this childhood period are bound to fail, but simply that the current evidence base does not tell us how to make expansions of them succeed. Below we provide a review of the literature that leads us to our conclusions.

Home Visiting Programs

Home visiting programs typically involve trained professional or paraprofessional visitors who make regular visits to parents and young children. These home visitors coach parents, typically low-income mothers, on parenting during the prenatal period and early childhood years. As a prevention strategy, home visiting is designed to promote infant and child health, foster educational development, and help prevent child abuse and neglect. All 50 states have home visiting programs (Office of Planning, Research, and Evaluation, 2021). Some of these programs, like the Nurse Family Partnership home visiting program, have demonstrated long-term impacts on child outcomes like substance use and academic skills during the school years—impacts likely to reduce intergenerational poverty (Avellar & Paulsell, 2011).

The Patient Protection and Affordable Care Act of 2010 expanded federal funding for home visiting programs but also required that 75% of its funds be used for programs, and that the programs demonstrate their effectiveness in rigorous research studies. The Office of Planning, Research, and Evaluation contracted to conduct a regular systemic review of home visiting research, the Home Visiting Evidence of Effectiveness (HomVee) review, and publish findings on its website (Avellar & Paulsell, 2011).

The 2021 HomVee review (Office of Planning, Research, and Evaluation, 2021) included 22 programs that reported statistically positive outcomes in randomized control trials (RCTs) or rigorous quasi-experimental studies. As of September 2021, the review included evaluations of 53 home visiting models, focusing on the 22 models that met the stringent Office of Planning, Research, and Evaluation criteria for evidence-based models. The impacts of those 22 programs on child outcomes were found to be ineffective much more often than effective: Approximately 130 impacts were "positive," in 600 cases there was "no difference," and in 7 cases the impact was "negative." A broader look at the results shows limited evidence that programs changed parenting or child outcomes. Overall, they suggest that home visiting programs can, but typically do not, increase cognitive stimulation in the home and decrease the use of punitive, harsh punishment. Even when such programs are successful in changing parenting behavior, the size of their impacts is modest—about 0.10 standard deviations (Michalopoulos et al., 2019). In most cases, their positive impacts were limited to shorter-run improvements in birth outcomes, reductions in hospitalization, declines in behavior problems, or increased access to services like Temporary Assistance for Needy Families or Special Supplemental Nutrition Program for Women, Infants, and Children.

Table C-4-1 provides a broader overview of the HomVee results from the most promising home visiting programs that were evaluated between 2019 and 2020. Because the evaluations include so many parenting and child outcomes, we set a statistical significance threshold of $p < 0.10$ and simply count the number of impact coefficients that fall below that threshold. Given the nature of significance testing, we would expect to see 10% of the coefficients below $p < 0.10$ even if there were no true impacts.

Promising evidence of longer-term impacts on problem behaviors was reported for both the Nurse Family Partnership (NFP) and Attachment and Biobehavioral Catch-up–Infant (ABC). The NFP provides one-on-one home visits by nurses who focus on improving maternal and infant health and promoting family economic self-sufficiency during pregnancy and the child's first 2 years. Follow-up studies of the NFP study participants in the early implementations of the programs showed reduced behavior problems at 15 years, reduced substance use at 12 years, and increased vocabulary and academic skills at 1 to 2 years post-intervention (Kitzman et al., 2010; Olds et al., 2002).

But these findings were not replicated in other NFP evaluation studies. As seen in Table C-4-1, a review of child impacts from a broader implementation of NFP found significant results less than 10% of the time—which

TABLE C-4-1 Ratio of statistically significant ($p < 0.10$) treatment impacts to outcomes examined in the HomVee literature review

	Program cost per child per year	Positive parenting practices	Child development and school readiness	Reductions in child maltreatment
Attachment and Biobehavioral Catch-Up	$7,000 to train parent coaches. Families receive 10 1-hour sessions	11/23	8/19	Not measured
Healthy Families America	$4,101[a]	28/131	12/56	20/209
Home Instruction for Parents of Preschool Youngsters	$4,246[b]	1/1	11/49	Not measured
Maternal Infant Health Program	$518[c]	Not measured	Not measured	0/18
Nurse Family Partnership	$6,000 (SC)–$9,600(NY)[d]	7/37	13/142	7/26
Parents as Teachers	$3,841[e]	3/92	7/67	0/4
Play and Learning Strategies (PALS) Infant	$3,206[f]	1/13	6/14	Not measured

NOTES: [a]https://crimesolutions.ojp.gov/ratedprograms/200#programcost; [b]https://www.wsipp.wa.gov/BenefitCost/Program/748; [c]Administration for Children and Families (2023); [d]www.nursefamilypartnership.org/wp-content/uploads/2020/08/NFP-Benefits-and-Costs.pdf; [e]www.wsipp.wa.gov/ReportFile/1020/Wsipp_Evidence-Based-Programs-to-Prevent-Children-from-Entering-and-Remaining-in-the-Child-Welfare-System-Benefits-and-Costs-for-Washington_Report.pdf; [f]https://www.utep.edu/education/cerps/_Files/docs/papers/CERPS_Working_Paper_2016_3.pdf
SOURCE: Adapted from Duncan et al. (2023).

could easily have occurred by chance. ABC–Infant provides trained parent coaches to mothers of infants, many of whom are either foster parents or parents deemed to be abusive. ABC focuses on promoting mutually responsive interactions by having parents and coaches watch videos of interactions together (Office of Planning, Research, and Evaluation, 2021). Follow-up studies of early implementations of ABC–Infant reported higher rates of attachment security at 9 years, higher levels of emotional regulation at 8 years, and higher vocabulary skills at 3 and 5 years (Raby et al., 2018; Zajac et al., 2019). Again, these promising findings were not replicated in other studies. Across all ABC-Infant studies, Table C-4-1 shows significant child impacts less than half of the time (Office of Planning, Research, and Evaluation, 2021).

An independent meta-analysis of home visiting programs, which was limited to randomized control trials (RCTs) and rigorous quasi-experimental studies, also showed mixed results (Fryer, 2016). Fryer (2016) concluded that home visiting, as currently implemented, was not generating statistically significant impacts on children's development, perhaps partly because of problems conducting the regular visits with parents. Consistent with the HomVee review, he pointed out that widely touted programs like the NFP show promise in reducing child abuse and improving child outcomes, but even these programs show inconsistent findings of long-term impacts across follow-up studies (Fryer, 2016).

Some international at-scale programs have shown substantial impacts. For example, the Preparing for Life Program (Doyle, 2020) in Ireland incorporates home visiting, group parenting classes, and baby massage into an intensive 5-year intervention for economically disadvantaged Irish families. An RCT indicated the program raised children's cognitive scores by two-thirds of a standard deviation and socioemotional/behavioral scores by one-quarter of a standard deviation. Earlier analyses indicated Preparing for Life improved parent-child interactions, cognitive stimulation, time use, nutrition, and discipline strategies, and these changes may mediate the cognitive gains but not the socio-emotional goals (Doyle, 2020).

In summary, home visiting is widely implemented in the United States. Careful evaluations of the funded programs in the country have yielded some promising findings but provide little cause for confidence that additional investments in scaled-up programs would consistently improve parenting and child outcomes. Some findings from a few programs in the United States and from programs in other countries provide evidence that home visiting programs can be successful, but further development is needed to develop at-scale home-visiting programs in the United States with sustained positive impacts.

Early Care and Education

Early care and education (ECE) programs are widely viewed as one of the most successful policy levers for promoting the educational success and social mobility of young children living in low-income homes (Heckman, 2011). Based in part on long-run evidence of early care and education programs impacts on adult outcomes, both state and federal governments have invested heavily in these programs to improve opportunities for children raised in poverty. The federal government spends about $9.66 billion annually to serve nearly 1 million infants, toddlers, and preschoolers and their low-income families (Barnett & Friedman-Krauss, 2016), and in 2019 state and local pre-kindergarten programs spent $8.75 billion to serve about

1.9 million preschoolers, most of whom are from low-income families (Friedman-Krauss & Barnett, 2020).

Perry and Abecedarian

The ability of intensive model programs to improve the life chances of disadvantaged children is illustrated by the well-known Perry Preschool and Abecedarian interventions. Perry was implemented in the 1960s in Ypsilanti, Michigan, while Abecedarian ran during the 1970s in Chapel Hill, North Carolina. Perry provided center care and home visiting to 65 3- and 4-year-olds from low-income Black families. The first Perry cohort received one year of program services, and the remaining four cohorts received 2 years. Costs across the five cohorts averaged $23,000 per child (Heckman et al., 2010). Heckman et al. (2010) estimate that the dollar value of benefits generated by the program amounted to between six and nine times the cost of the program, with benefits driven in roughly equal measure by increases in earnings and reductions in crime. When considering that high benefit/cost ratio, however, it is important to recognize that the home environments of the comparison group of children were of much lower quality relative to the home environments of today's children. Only 21% of Perry mothers and 11% of Perry fathers had graduated from high school, and family sizes averaged 6.7—much larger than today (Schweinhart, 1993).[1]

Abecedarian provided considerably more services than Perry and over a much longer period. These included center care and pediatric care for about 100 low-income, predominantly Black children from 3 months of age to kindergarten entry. The per-child cost of this 5-year program has been estimated at $105,000 (García et al., 2021. Even given the program's expense, its long-run benefits have been estimated to total more than six times its costs: More than two-thirds of the benefits were driven by crime reductions, and the remainder reflect differences in adult health and the

---

[1] In the 1960s and 1970s, children from low-income families, especially Black children, faced conditions best described as deplorable. In the mid-1960s, the Food Stamp program and tax credit programs such as the Earned Income Tax Credit had not yet been introduced. Racial discrimination in parts of the country denied Blacks access to quality schools and hospital care, including childbirth in hospitals with a physician present. Parental schooling levels were much lower than they are today, and family sizes were much larger (Duncan & Magnuson, 2013). Today families, including low-income families, are about twice as likely to use child care, especially center-based child care (Duncan & Magnuson, 2013). These factors produced conditions that made it much easier for a Head Start or model program like Perry to demonstrate effectiveness for enrolled children when compared with children experiencing business-as-usual conditions. This explanation probably accounts, at least in part, for the fact that end-of-treatment impacts are substantially smaller in more recent evaluations (Duncan & Magnuson, 2013).

labor income of participants and their parents (the 5 years of full-time child care enabled parents to establish and maintain more continuous and higher-paying careers; García et al., 2020). As in the case of Perry, the low-quality nature of the home environments of children in the Abecedarian evaluation is reflected in the low average levels of mothers' completed schooling (10.2 years), IQ (85.5), and age at their child's enrollment (19.9 years; Ramey et al., 2000).

Both Perry and Abecedarian focused on encouraging adult-child interactions, hands-on learning activities, and frequent conversations between children and teachers (Schweinhart & Weikart, 1980; Ramey et al., 2012). The teachers, their supervisors, and researchers collaborated in developing the interventions and classroom activities that were later incorporated into many early childhood curricula. However, the evaluations were not designed to enable researchers to disentangle the separate contributions of these components to improving children's development, and these programs differ in many ways from today's early care and education programs (as discussed in more detail below).

Results from these two early RCT interventions provide convincing evidence that ECE programs can improve educational attainment, income, and health in adulthood (Heckman, 2011). The key policy and program issue for the committee is whether much larger-scale and less expensive versions of ECE programs—run or supervised by governments rather than researchers, provided to children from families with higher incomes and schooling levels, and living in communities with a much richer set of center-based child care options in programs that do provide the same types of educational experiences as Perry and Abecedarian—can generate impacts comparable to those of Perry and Abecedarian.

Head Start

Head Start began in 1965 as part of the War on Poverty and provided part-time center-based ECE to low-income children (Office of Headstart, 2023). It was offered to thousands of children in its early years, with a focus on promoting health and social skills. Strong quasi-experimental studies have demonstrated long-term benefits for children who attended Head Start during the period from 1965 to 1980 in terms of higher rates of college enrollment (Bailey et al., 2021; see also Johnson, 2011; Ludwig & Miller, 2007). Evidence from cohorts that entered Head Start in the 1980s and 1990s tends to show higher levels of education and reductions in special education and grade retention, even if impacts on academic and social skills fade out during elementary school (Deming, 2009; Garces et al., 2002).

Head Start has changed over time: It now provides longer hours of care, employs more teachers who have completed a bachelor's degree, and includes a focus on promoting early academic skills (Office of Headstart, 2023). Evidence is mixed regarding the effectiveness of its more recent incarnations, which have been offered to low-income children in an environment with many more alternative center-based programs. The Head Start Impact Study (HSIS), a large RCT begun in 2001, was based on a random sampling of Head Start centers that reported waiting lists. HSIS showed consistent end-of-program impacts on language and literacy that faded out by third grade, no consistent impacts on math, and some mixed evidence on reducing problem behaviors (Table C-4-2, based on Puma et al., 2012).

A careful reanalysis of these data revealed larger gains for children who would not otherwise have used center care than for those who would otherwise have enrolled in other ECE centers, as well as for children who did not speak English at home (Feller et al., 2016; Kline & Walters, 2016). Finally, more recent analyses of adult outcomes suggest that the young-adult impacts reported for the earlier cohorts faded in later adulthood. Moreover, later Head Start cohorts did not show the same young-adult impacts as did the earlier cohorts, and there were even some negative impacts (Pages et al., 2023).

Public Pre-Kindergarten Programs

Public pre-K programs are public ECE programs that are typically funded by states or localities and often require local matching funds. Almost all states (44 out of 50, plus DC and Guam) provide pre-K programs. Overall, 34% of four-year-olds and 6% of three-year-olds were enrolled in state-funded preschools in the 2019–2020 school year (Friedman-Krauss et al., 2021). As of 2020, 35 of the 55 state and local programs were targeted to serve children from low-income families, albeit with qualifying incomes that were often twice the qualifying incomes for Head Start (35 state programs have income eligibility requirements; Friedman-Krauss & Barnett, 2020).

TABLE C-4-2 Ratio of statistically significant ($p < 0.10$) treatment impacts averaged over the two cohorts on outcomes examined in the Puma et al., 2012 Head Start Impact Study

	End of Head Start year	End of 3rd grade
Literacy	11 of 16	1 of 6
Math	1 of 4	0 of 4
Problem behaviors	2 of 18	6 of 30

SOURCE: Data from Puma et al. (2012).

Promoting children's school readiness skills, especially early literacy skills, is the primary goal of public pre-K programs (Phillips et al., 2017). Most offer few, if any, support services, such as transportation or health screenings and referrals (Friedman-Krauss et al., 2021). As state or local programs, their performance standards vary widely. Most pre-K programs have standards regarding curricula, teacher education, class sizes, and adult-child ratios. However, only about one-third of the pre-K programs have performance standards that meet or exceed those of Head Start, according to the National Institute for Early Educational Research (NIEER) (Friedman-Krauss et al., 2021). Not surprisingly, given substantial differences in the number of hours per week these programs provide care and in their performance standards, per-child costs to the state range widely, from under $4,000 for programs that meet fewer than half of the quality criteria recommended by NIEER to over $18,000 for programs that meet all those criteria (Friedman-Krauss & Barnett, 2020).

Evaluations of state pre-K programs suggest that children completing the programs show better school-readiness outcomes than similarly-aged children who had not (or not yet) enrolled in a pre-K program. A summary of the findings (Phillips et al., 2017) indicates that pre-K attenders entered kindergarten with much higher math and literacy skills (effects of 0.50 standard deviations or larger). Many evaluations also reported small to moderate impacts on language and executive functioning (effects of between 0.10 and 0.50 standard deviations; Phillips et al., 2017).

However, evaluations of longer-term impacts reveal that the advantages enjoyed by pre-K attenders often fade out or disappear completely as nonattenders catch up. Yet some evaluations show longer-run gains despite shorter-run fade-out. The most rigorous study of longer-term impacts examined Boston's universal pre-K program (Gray-Lobe et al., 2021). It showed that pre-K attenders were more likely to enroll in and graduate from college than those who applied for but lost the attendance lottery. In the context of this report, it is important to note that impacts were generally smaller for participants whose families were in the lowest income categories.

It is striking to note that medium-term impacts shown in the most rigorous evaluations of recent pre-K studies include worrisome negative effects in elementary school. A random-assignment evaluation of the Tennessee pre-K program reported significant negative longer-term pre-K impacts on both academic and social-emotional outcomes in third through sixth grade (Durkin et al., 2022; Lipsey et al., 2018). In sixth grade, the English and math scores of pre-K children were 0.28 and 0.40 standard deviations lower than the scores of children who applied for admission but lost the lottery. Attenders drew significantly more disciplinary actions than non-attenders. An RCT evaluation of the North Carolina pre-K program (Peisner-Feinberg et al., 2020) reported that at the end of kindergarten, pre-K children had lower scores (effect sizes of 0.24 to 0.28 standard deviations in math, executive functioning, and social skills) than non-pre-K children. However, these differences were not statistically significant after adjusting for the large number of comparisons in the study (Peisner-Feinberg et al., 2020).

Less rigorous studies provide inconsistent evidence regarding differences between pre-K attenders and nonattenders.[2] The most promising results are from a follow-up study of children who were eligible in 2005–2006 for the Tulsa Universal Pre-K. Gormley et al. (2023) reports that pre-K attendees were more likely than nonattending children with similar demographic characteristics subsequently to enroll in college (increase of 12 percentage points). In other studies that attempted to match attenders and nonattenders using propensity score methods on school-age demographic characteristics, pre-K attenders in Boston, North Carolina, New Jersey, Maryland (Minervino, 2014) and Georgia (Early et al., 2019) showed slightly higher reading and math scores on state-mandated reading and math tests in third and fifth grade.

ECE programs in other countries provide some evidence of positive impacts on adult outcomes of their at-scale ECE programs. One of the ECE programs showing long-term impacts is the Norwegian program, which requires a college-educated teacher, good adult-child ratios (typically 16 children and 3 adults), and a play-oriented experiential orientation to instruction (Havnes & Mogstad, 2011). Uneven expansion of the Norwegian program during the 1970s allowed for a difference-in-difference analysis that demonstrated that attending preschool between the ages of 3 and 6 led to a substantial increase in completed schooling, labor market attachment, and earnings (Havnes & Mogstad, 2011).

Possible Explanations for Discrepant Findings on Long-Term ECE Impacts

Whereas the two large publicly funded ECE programs, Head Start and public pre-K, have shown positive impacts on school readiness, the evidence for medium- and longer-term impacts is mixed. The earliest ECE programs, like Perry and Abecedarian, were clearly effective at improving earnings, educational attainment, and health, as well as at decreasing crime and incarceration—all of which are factors that tend to lower the rate of intergenerational poverty (Campbell et al., 2012; Heckman et al., 2010). Earlier Head Start and pre-K programs also showed promising long-term impacts on educational attainment and crime (Bailey et al., 2021; Deming,

---

[2] These studies use propensity score matching without having access to pre-treatment assessment of skills. The committee judged that this method was not as rigorous as random assignment or regression discontinuity methods.

2009; Gary-Lobe, 2021). In contrast, the most rigorous evaluations of today's Head Start and pre-K programs suggest that they have null to negative medium-term impacts. It is possible that longer-run follow-up will show the kinds of positive impacts seen in Perry and Abecedarian. However, until the evaluation evidence shows more consistently positive impacts for these programs, the committee cannot, based on the evidence, confidently recommend expansions as an approach that is likely to reduce intergenerational poverty.

Transforming Model Programs into At-Scale Public Programs

Programs like Perry and Abecedarian were small, conducted by developmental researchers and led by trained ECE teachers. Classrooms were carefully monitored to ensure that the program was being implemented successfully and teachers were actively engaged in developing the curriculum. It is naïve to believe that findings from those programs will generalize to large public programs that serve millions of children each year (Tseng, 2017). Even replications like the Infant Health and Development Program, which used the Abecedarian curriculum and included almost 1,000 low-birthweight children, predominantly from low-income families, were led by researchers who continued to monitor the implementation carefully (Ramey et al., 2012). Today's programs rely on performance standards that are less focused, yet more comprehensive. They include substantially less monitoring and supportive collaborative coaching than the early RCT studies (Friedman-Strauss & Barnett, 2020). Again, these factors are probably one reason why today's programs have smaller impacts on the outcomes collected in early RCT studies, although they are unlikely to explain fade-out.

Targeting Recipients of ECE Services

Evidence shows that Head Start impacts were larger and more likely to be sustained when the children who attended Head Start would otherwise have stayed home with their parents or been cared for in a home-based ECE setting (Feller et al., 2016; Kline & Walters, 2016), and this suggests that increasing funding for Head Start might have longer-term impacts and reduce intergenerational poverty if the program could specifically target those children. However, a Head Start expansion could not be designed to exclude children who would otherwise be in other center-based care.

Growing evidence indicates that children who do not speak English at home may gain more and maintain those gains longer when they attend ECE programs (Phillips et al., 2017). In the RCT HSIS, children whose home language was not English showed larger gains in vocabulary skills if they attended Head Start, and those gains remained statistically significant through first grade (Feller et al., 2016). The RCT evaluation of North Carolina pre-K reports statistically significant impacts on kindergarten language skills for children who did not speak English at home, even when those impacts faded in the sample as a whole (Peisner-Feinberg et al., 2020). These impacts were small in both studies (< 0.20 standard deviations), however, raising questions about whether they were sufficiently large to reduce intergenerational poverty even if maintained past first grade.

To What Extent Subsequent Experiences Support Initial Gains

The extent to which communities and schools support and build on the skills children have acquired in ECE programs is clearly important for maintaining the programs' impacts and may play a role in fade-out. Children from low-income families who attend public ECE programs, especially if they are members of racially minoritized groups, tend to transition to lower-quality schools, encounter lower teacher expectations, and experience harsh punitive discipline in schools and by the local police (for details, see the sections on K–12 schools and juvenile justice). A lack of "sustaining environments" after low-income children leave their ECE programs makes it difficult for children to maintain the gains they have made in those programs.

The lack of sustaining environments to maintain ECE short-term impacts has been widely cited as an explanation for the fade-out of those impacts over time (Abenavoli, 2019). Despite some studies reporting that pre-K attenders continued to show higher levels of skills than nonattenders when they transition from pre-K programs into more effective schools or have more effective teachers (Abenavoli, 2019), this conclusion was not supported in a comprehensive meta-analysis of all studies testing the sustaining environment hypothesis published through 2018 (B. Bailey et al., 2020). Others argue that redundancy in instruction between pre-K and kindergarten, especially in literacy and math, accounts for the marked convergence in those skills, but pre-K fade-out did not diminish when pre-K and kindergarten instruction included less redundancy, despite wide-scale evidence of considerable overlap in early reading and math instruction (Burchinal et al., 2022). Thus, findings do not suggest that current "sustaining" elementary schools support learning more effectively for pre-K attenders than nonattenders. Nevertheless, it is logical to assume that there would be less fade-out of pre-K impacts if kindergarten teachers were encouraged to differentiate instruction based on entry skills (Cohen-Vogel et al., 2021).

Changes in Instructional Focus Over Time

Another explanation focuses on changes over time in the instructional content and approach of ECE programs. Abecedarian and Perry focused on strong caregiver-child relationships, with frequent multi-turn conversations, and on hands-on learning activities in which teachers scaffolded learning (Ramey et al., 2012; Weikart & Schweinhart, 1997). Head Start initially focused heavily on promoting health and social skills. Around 2000, ECE programs began to emphasize teaching early literacy and math skills to address kindergarten-entry gaps between low- and middle-income children (Office of Headstart, 2023).

Some have argued that preschool instruction in language, executive functioning, and social skills is more likely to be maintained over time than instruction in basic reading and math skills (McCormick et al., 2021). Early programs like Abecedarian did not teach the basic skills and children entered kindergarten with large treatment impacts on cognitive skills, no treatment impact on reading skills, and small impacts on math skills (Burchinal et al., 2022). Large differences in both reading and math skills emerged in second grade and were maintained through 21 years of age (Campbell et al., 2012). Similar adult impacts for the Abecedarian Project were reported for the Norwegian ECE program, which had a similar instructional focus on experiential learning and frequent teacher-child interactions (Havnes & Mogstad, 2011). In contrast, more recent evaluations of Head Start (Puma et al., 2012) and pre-K (Phillips et al., 2017) consistently show impacts at the end of the program on literacy and math skills that appear to fade out by second grade.

This focus on teaching these basic skills in preschool and the way they are too often taught is likely difficult for children. Teaching early academic skills often involves instruction to the entire class, with preschoolers being expected to sit still for relatively long periods (Bratsch-Hines et al., 2019). Focus on teaching these rote basic skills results in large gains in the pre-K year (Phillips et al., 2017), but these same skills are often taught again in kindergarten, once more typically in large groups (Cohen-Vogel et al., 2021). Sitting still in large group instruction is difficult for all children, especially very young children, and some teachers may become impatient and harsh, which may in turn exacerbate children's problem behaviors (Christopher & Farran, 2020). The combination of redundant instruction and harsh interactions with teachers may cause children to disengage from learning, perhaps setting them on less positive academic trajectories during the early school years. Again, extensive time in whole-group instruction was not part of the Perry, Abecedarian, and Norwegian ECE programs. Those programs focused on hands-on learning, typically through individual or small group activities in centers.

Given all this mixed evidence, and especially given that positive long-term impacts have been largely limited to earlier programs that did not focus heavily on teaching basic reading and math skills (e.g., Campbell et al., 2012; Deming, 2009; Gormley et al., 2023; Heckman et al., 2010), or limited to programs that have made center-based ECE available to children who would otherwise have been cared for by parents or in a home-based setting (Feller et al., 2016), the committee was unable to recommend the expansion of Head Start or pre-K enrollment. However, we hope that these ECE programs will help us identify engaging teaching practices for promoting the skills that appear to be fundamental to subsequent learning, such as language and general knowledge, executive functioning, and social skills (Burchinal et al., 2020; Fuhs et al., 2014; Pace et al., 2019; Welsh et al., 2010), and enable us to coordinate learning experiences that allow children to use the skills they acquired in ECE when they transition to public school.

Quality Improvement Initiatives

Quality Rating and Improvement Systems (QRIS) are a policy initiative that rates the quality of ECE settings, using state-determined performance standards, and incentivizes improvement by making the ratings visible to parents and providing financial incentives for higher-quality programs.[3] These state-level policies promote smaller class sizes, better-credentialed teachers, the high-quality implementation of proven curricula, and professional development programs for teachers. While there is considerable evidence that higher-rated programs do in fact provide higher-quality ECE, it has not been consistently shown that QRIS ratings are related to child outcomes, even by correlational studies based on national data (Sabol et al., 2013) or in state evaluations (Boller et al., 2015; Hong et al., 2015; Sabol & Pianta, 2015). Perhaps even more worrisome is correlational evidence that children do not benefit from attending programs with higher levels of "quality" in terms of most of the QRIS components (Hong et al., 2019).

Child Care Subsidies

Another approach to supporting out-of-home care for young children is through child care subsidies to low-income parents who work or attend school. Studies have shown that such subsidies funded by the Child Care and Development Block Grant increase the likelihood that recipient parents will enter the workforce or enroll in school or training programs (Herbst, 2017; Herbst & Tekin, 2010; Tekin, 2005).

---

[3] For more information, see www.buildinitiative.org

But would subsidies reduce intergenerational poverty? The most direct evidence on child impacts comes from a study linking eligibility for subsidies to indicators of child development (Herbst & Tekin, 2010; see also Johnson & Ryan, 2015). It found a negative effect of subsidy receipt on reading and math test scores and an unfavorable effect on behavior problems, and some of these perverse effects were found to persist until the end of kindergarten. This may be because the original funding provided relatively low subsidies that led to enrollment in low-quality child care settings. Reauthorization addressed this issue, but too recently to allow us to examine impacts. Two Canadian studies reported positive links between subsidies and child outcomes among very-low-income children in Canada overall (Polyzoi et al., 2020) but negative impacts in Quebec among a largely middle-income population (Baker et al., 2019).

Increasing the nation's investment in child care subsidies may benefit low-income families by increasing their resources, promoting parental education and training, and supporting parental work. As in the case of Head Start and pre-K expansions, however, we cannot conclude that the evidence supports subsidy expansions as a reliable way of reducing intergenerational poverty.

K–12 Education

Increase K–12 School Spending in the Poorest Districts

Plausible expansions of federal funding could make a difference at the margin to both between-state and within-state gaps, but only if they are not offset by reductions in state and local funding. Hoxby (2001) argues that many redesigned state funding formulas are poorly conceived, creating incentives for local districts to cut taxes when state funding is available and potentially reducing overall spending in targeted districts. Similarly, Gordon (2004) finds that changes in federal Title I spending are fully offset by reductions in local funding over the next few years. On the other hand, the examination by Lafortune et al. (2018) of more recent state finance reforms indicates 100% "stickiness" of the additional state funding, with no offset via reduced local funding even many years in the future. Thus, the literature does not fully resolve the question of "stickiness" of intergovernmental grants, though it seems likely that some maintenance of effort rules would be required for any federal program to be effective.

While the recent literature is clear that additional funding yields benefits for children that persist into adulthood, it does not provide clear estimates of optimal funding levels. Baker et al. (2021) estimate that the shortfall of education spending from a standard for "adequacy" totals $104 billion per year—substantially more than total current federal spending on

K–12 education of around $60 billion. It seems implausible that the federal role could expand that much.

We explore one potential federal policy change short of closing the entire adequacy gap. We base it on Lafortune et al.'s, (2018) analysis of post-1990 state finance reforms. They estimate that a typical reform raised spending in the lowest-income fifth of districts in the state by $1,377 per pupil (in 2013 dollars), or about 12% of the average of $11,595. Total public-school enrollment is about 50 million, so approximately 10 million students attend schools in the bottom fifth of districts. Thus, increasing spending in these districts by $1,000 per pupil would increase total spending by $10 billion per year.

As noted above, not all federal funding would "stick." If we assume that changes in state and local effort reduce the effectiveness or intended concentration of federal spending by one-third, federal expenditures would need to rise by $15 billion to achieve the above increase in expenditures in low-income districts.

What would be the impact of this? Jackson et al.'s (2016) results indicate that a 12% increase in spending would reduce the adult poverty rates of low-income children growing up in these districts by $0.12 \times 0.61 = 7$ percentage points and increase their adult family incomes by 21%. Using more recent reforms, Rothstein and Schanzenbach (2022) find that exposure to a typical reform for 12 years raises average earnings of students in a state by 4% but note that this combines effects on low- and non-low-income students and on high- and low-income districts.

How many children would be affected? Approximately 17% of public-school students (8.5 million) are in poverty (Digest of Education Statistics, Table 102.70). Lafortune et al., (2018) finds that about one-third of free and reduced-price lunch students (a proxy for student poverty) attend school in the lowest-income fifth of districts. Thus, the above reform would reach approximately 2.8 million children from families below the poverty line. (Though note that above we assumed that states would divert one-third of spending to other districts than the lowest income. These districts have children in poverty as well, so the number of children in poverty who would be affected would be larger.) If this reform reduced their adult poverty rate by 7 percentage points, that would reduce intergenerational poverty by 16,000 students out of each birth cohort.

Promising Approaches Within K–12

As discussed in the report, there is limited evidence about long-term effects of specific programs or practices within the K–12 system, but there are a number of promising approaches that have been shown to have strong shorter-term impacts. If these early impacts are found to persist, these approaches would be candidates for recommended interventions; in the meantime, we see them as promising and worth consideration, but not meeting our evidentiary standards for committee recommendations. We discuss several here, acknowledging that this list is not exhaustive.

High-dosage tutoring for struggling students

Evaluations have demonstrated that programs providing frequent tutoring sessions, individually or in small groups, to students with skills below grade level improves academic skills (Fryer, 2016). Although improved academic skills do not translate directly into lower poverty in adulthood, the evidence on shorter-run improvements from carefully crafted tutoring programs is promising enough to include in our list of profitable ways districts might promote school success among disadvantaged students.

The tutoring programs that appear to be successful involve sessions provided by trained volunteers or educators to struggling students, individually or in groups of six or fewer, for at least 50 hours over the school year (Fryer, 2016). They range from programs like Reading Recovery for early elementary students (D'Agostino et al., 2017) to tutoring sessions for high school students (Guryan et al., 2023). Rigorous evaluations summarized in a meta-analysis indicate that these programs have moderate short-term impacts and, in the studies with longer-term follow-ups, those impacts were maintained for at least a year and translated into higher rates of high school graduation. Tutoring programs that did not meet these two criteria showed neither short- nor long-term impacts (Fryer, 2016).

Based on this evidence, Kraft and Falken (2021) propose creating a national tutoring network that could be adopted by school districts and encouraged by federal funding. In the proposal, tutors could include high school students who tutor in elementary schools as an elective class, college students who tutor in middle schools via the federal work-study program, and full-time 2- and 4-year college graduates who tutor in high schools via AmeriCorps. Their estimates suggests that targeted approaches to scaling schoolwide tutoring nationally, such as focusing on K–8 Title I schools, would cost between $5 and $15 billion annually. They do not provide estimates of the impacts on either the tutors or the students being tutored.

Several large evaluations estimated both long-term impacts and program costs. A meta-analysis examined Reading Recovery, a widely implemented early-grade intervention in which struggling elementary school students receive 20 weeks of individually designed diagnostic teaching by trained professionals (D'Agostino et al., 2017). Synthesizing results from RCTs or high-quality quasi-experimental studies yielded an effect on reading achievement of 0.59 standard deviations at a cost of $2,500 to $9,000 per student. Guryan et al. (2023) report on a multi-study evaluation of the Saga Education tutoring program, which provides similar high-dosage tutoring to 9th and 10th graders at a relatively low cost ($3,500 to $4,300 per participant per year) that yielded higher math test scores and increased grades in math and non-math courses, with estimated impacts of 0.37 standard deviation that persisted several years later.

In sum, high-dosage tutoring for struggling K–12 students that focuses on matching instruction to skills level appears effective at improving skills in the short-term and improving important young adult outcomes such as high school graduation. These programs may be cost-effective when educated young adults serve as the tutors and follow carefully crafted instructional plans.

Improving teacher quality

It has long been known that schools serving low-income students have a more difficult time attracting and retaining high-quality teachers and that students of color do better in school when matched with teachers of color (Gershenson et al., forthcoming, 2016; Lindsay & Hart, 2017). So, the problem is both one of allocating teachers across schools and school districts as well as increasing the supply of high-quality teachers, and in particular high-quality teachers of color.

One promising model for increasing teacher quality is university programs that encourage and facilitate science, technology, engineering, and mathematics (STEM) undergraduate majors to be certified as public-school teachers. The UTeach program at the University of Texas-Austin is an exemplar; as of 2018 programs similar to it are also available at 44 universities in 21 states. As explained in Backes et al. (2018), UTeach recruits math and science majors to pursue careers in teaching and offers free field-based courses that enable interested students to try out teaching before committing their early careers to it. It was funded by grants from, among other places, the nonprofit National Math and Science Initiative, but could presumably be supported in some way with federal money.

The Backes et al. (2018) non-experimental evaluation found that Texas students taught by UTeach graduates perform significantly better on end-of-grade tests in math in middle school and end-of-course tests in math and science in high school by 8% to 15% of a standard deviation on the test, depending on grade and subject. As to teacher diversity, UTeach increased the fraction of Hispanic (but not Black) science and math teachers in the schools they studied.

Other approaches to diversifying the teacher labor forces include urban teacher residency models, such as Alder Graduate School of Education and the Boston Teacher Residency programs. An evaluation of the latter found that program graduates were more diverse than Boston Public School teachers, were more likely to remain teachers and, after several years, outperformed veteran teachers in the district (Papay et al., 2012). Teacher training and certification programs drawing students from community colleges and minority-serving institutions—such as the Department of Education's Center of Educational Excellence for Black Teachers Program at Historically Black Colleges and Universities—are also likely to draw and train minority group teachers than traditional programs, but the evaluation literature on this is thin.

Reducing punitive school discipline

Experimental and correlational evidence reviewed in the main text shows that exposure to harsh discipline in schools leads to worse adult educational and criminal legal outcomes. Given the disproportionate experience of school discipline by low-income and Black, Latino, and Native American children—which is not accounted for by behavioral differences (Skiba et al., 2011)—this experience likely also contributes to these children's lower rates of intergenerational mobility. Teacher-student race matching has been shown in both correlational and experimental studies to reduce punitive discipline for students of color (Lindsay & Hart, 2017; Shirrell et al., 2021). Another promising approach—and one of the few that includes outcomes for Native American students—is restorative justice practices (Anyon et al., 2016; Gregory et al., 2016).

A meta-analysis of RCT interventions to reduce harsh discipline found that students' academic skills, counseling, mentoring programs, and teacher training all showed promising results for reducing in-school or out-of-school suspensions (Valdebenito et al., 2019). For example, Okonofua et al. (2016) tested a brief randomly assigned on-line intervention with math teachers in five middle schools in three school districts that "encouraged teachers to understand and value students' experiences and negative feelings that can cause misbehavior and to sustain positive relationships when students misbehave." This "empathetic mindset" reduced suspension of students of the treated teachers by half during the academic year as compared with the control group. The effect was consistent across racial, gender, and prior-year suspension groups. While this study had a 1-year observation period, Valdebenito et al. (2019) find that the effects of most interventions faded after 6 months, suggesting the importance of ongoing and repeated training and awareness.

A practice known as Positive Behavioral Interventions and Supports (PBIS) has been shown in RCTs to reduce exclusionary discipline (Bradshaw et al., 2010). PBIS is a schoolwide practice in which "schools establish a set of positively stated, schoolwide expectations for student behavior, which are taught to all students and staff" (Bradshaw et al., 2012, p. e1137; also see www.pbis.org). Descriptive studies in Canada and Oregon showed that

PBIS schools showed no Native American-White disparities in punitive discipline (Greflund et al., 2014; Vincent et al., 2015), and an RCT of PBIS with a racial equity focus showed greater reductions in punitive discipline for Black students (McIntosh et al., 2021). PBIS with added school mental health supports shows additional effectiveness. Weist et al. (2022) report RCT results that this "Interconnected Systems Framework" compared with either PBIS or just mental health services showed "reduced office discipline referrals (ODRs) and in-school suspensions, as well as reduced ODRs and out-of-school suspensions for African American students."

There are no studies of the direct effects of discipline practices and interventions on children's later adult outcomes. However, the evidence reviewed here and in the main section establishes a clear indirect relationship between school discipline and intergenerational mobility. There is causal evidence on policies and practices that effectively reduce punitive discipline and causal evidence that children who experience more punitive school discipline are less likely to graduate from high school and attend college and more likely to have criminal legal contact.

Smaller class sizes in the early grades

The well-known STAR evaluation used randomization to study the effect of small classes in K–3 on test scores of low-income students in Tennessee. Assignment to a smaller class had positive effects on test scores through these grades (Krueger 1999, 2003). Although there has been some criticism of the experiment on the grounds that it did not incorporate modern practices like careful collection of baseline data, subsequent reanalysis has shown both that the treatment arms were balanced (supporting the interpretation of the treatment effects as causal) and that the early-grade effects persisted to later grades and even to college enrollment (Chetty et al., 2011; Krueger & Whitmore 2001). There is also suggestive evidence of effects on adult earnings, though the sample was not large enough to measure these precisely (Chetty et al., 2011). In the case of class size reduction, there is little evidence about whether this is more or less effective than alternative ways of spending the same resources.

When California attempted to quickly reduce class sizes in the 1990s, districts had to hire many new, inexperienced teachers to fill the new classrooms, which may have offset the benefits of the small classes (Jepsen & Rivkin, 2009). This appears to be an implementation issue; in the longer run, there is no evidence that a gradual increase in teacher hiring requires bringing in lower-quality teachers.

Expand high-quality ("no excuses") charter schools

Several recent evaluations of a group of charter schools in Boston have used admissions lotteries to identify the causal effect of enrollment in these schools. The schools have in common a "no excuses" model, characterized by high expectations, rigid curricula, and strict discipline, and serve a high-poverty population. The lottery studies find very large positive effects on student test scores (Abdulkadiroğlu et al., 2011). Studies of other schools using similar models elsewhere also indicate large effects (e.g., Dobbie & Fryer, 2011). This stands in stark contrast to estimates of the effect of the average charter school, which is generally near zero (CREDO, 2013). Longer-term follow-ups indicate positive effects of the Boston no-excuses schools on students' eventual 4-year college enrollment and persistence, an outcome that these schools specifically target (Angrist et al., 2016). There is not yet evidence of effects on college completion or adult poverty.

This evidence is strongly suggestive that it would be beneficial to expand the no-excuses charter school sector, though the absence of longer-term evidence prevents us from adopting this as a recommendation. Moreover, the rigorous studies to date examine high-poverty urban populations in a few large cities with struggling public school systems, and it remains unclear how specific the no-excuses effects are to these settings (Angrist et al., 2013).

Increase racial, ethnic, and socioeconomic diversity within schools

Another driver of disparities in educational quality is school segregation. In particular, majority non-White schools tend to have less funding, fewer resources, and less skilled teachers (Bischof & Owens, 2019). In 1954, the Supreme Court passed its landmark *Brown v. Board of Education*, and other subsequent court orders further reinforced it. This resulted in court-ordered desegregation in school districts around the country, which led to slow but substantial racial integration throughout the United States (Orfield et al., 2016; Reardon & Owens, 2014; Reardon et al., 2012). In studies using national data that exploited quasi-random variation in the timing of the initial court orders, the resulting desegregation in the 1960s and 1970s was found to improve educational and occupational attainment among Black adults (Johnson, 2011). Specifically, each additional year of exposure to court-ordered desegregation led to a 1.8 percentage-point increase in the likelihood of high school graduation, and the average effects of a 5-year exposure to court-ordered school desegregation led to about a 15% increase in wages. This study also found effects on potential mechanisms, including increased per-pupil spending and reduced class sizes, and it showed improvements in other downstream outcomes like overall self-reported health (Johnson & Nazaryan, 2019).

In 1991, the Supreme Court ruled in *Board of Education v. Dowell* that earlier court-ordered desegregation plans were not intended to be permanent. Roughly 600 of the nearly 1,000 school districts that were under court-ordered desegregation were subsequently released from oversight.

These more recent court decisions resulted in "resegregation" of the released school districts (Reardon & Yun, 2002; Reardon et al., 2012), and highly segregated schools with less than 10% White enrollment have more than tripled in recent decades to nearly 20% (Orfield et al., 2016). While no studies to our knowledge have examined the effects of these recent changes on adult earnings or poverty, a handful of studies have leveraged the longitudinal and geographic variation in the timing of these local court decisions to demonstrate worsened health among affected children while they are still in school (Wang et al., 2022) as well as negative effects on health as they age into adulthood (Kim et al., 2022; Shen, 2018). Another study examined the end of race-based busing in North Carolina during this period, exploiting changes in maps for school boundaries, and found that attending a more segregated school district resulted in decreased high school exam scores among both White and racial/ethnic minority students, deceased high school graduation and college attendance among White students, and increased crime among minority boys (Billings et al., 2013).

Postsecondary Education

Community college completion provides low-socioeconomic status (SES) students with meaningful economic returns relative to noncompleting students (Mountjoy, 2022), and 4-year degree completion provides low-SES students substantially larger returns (Card, 1999; Zimmerman, 2014). Even for low-SES students, higher education provides relatively greater returns when students enroll at higher-value universities (Black et al., 2023; Bleemer, 2021a, 2022) and in higher-paying fields of study (Bleemer & Mehta, 2021). Federal higher education policy would thus maximally promote economic mobility by increasing aggregate college-going, improving educational quality at institutions and in programs where low-SES students enroll, and shifting low-SES students toward higher-value institutions and programs.

Effective Financial Aid for Low-Income Students

The evidence on the effectiveness of the Pell grant program has been quite mixed (Eng & Matsudaira, 2021), though there is some support for increasing its maximum value while limiting offsets by states and localities by reducing their financial support (Denning et al., 2019). Stronger evidence on the effectiveness of scholarship assistance to low-income students include the HAIL program by the University of Michigan (Dynarski et al., 2021, 2022a) and the Buffett Scholarship in Nebraska (Angrist et al., 2022).

*Direct Federal Support for Colleges and Universities
That Enroll Low-SES Students*

Increasing spending at less-selective colleges and universities has larger positive effects on completion than reducing tuition (Deming & Walters, 2017), and attending universities with greater support for student services to promote college engagement improves retention and degree attainment (Cohodes & Goodman, 2014). Federal funding targeted toward increased academic support at universities with large low-SES enrollment is therefore important. Increases in Pell grants often offset state educational funding instead of improving educational and support services (Turner, 2012, 2017), though there have been cases where such offsets are restricted and where increases in Pell grant generosity have led to higher attainment of credentials (Denning et al., 2019).

University enrollments are responsive to institutional incentives to increase low-SES enrollments (Hoxby & Turner, 2019). The universities that face the excise tax are well funded and likely very high-value for low-SES students (Chetty et al., forthcoming) but enroll relatively few low-SES students (Chetty et al., 2020).

College tutoring and other student services substantially increase retention and completion (Bettinger & Baker, 2014; Canaan et al., 2022a,b; Scrivener et al., 2015). AmeriCorps tutoring programs have also been very successful in improving low-SES student outcomes at younger ages (Markovitz et al., 2022). A range of support programs for low-income students in community college, including the Accelerated Study in Associates Program (ASAP; Azurdia & Galkin, 2020; Miller et al., 2020) and Stay the Course (Evans et al., 2020) have also been successful in raising student persistence and program completion (see also Dawson et al., 2020).

Our cost estimate of $8 to $10 billion a year for institutional supports to improve completion rates among low-income students is based on the facts that ASAP and Stay the Course cost about $10,000 and $6,000 respectively per student over 3 years, and a similar number of students in 4-year institutions with less-intensive supports (like Inside Track or Project STAR—see Dawson et al., 2020).

Minority Serving Institutions and Intergenerational Mobility

The evidence regarding the effects of attending minority serving institutions (MSIs) on graduation rates, earnings, and occupational status shows likely long-term occupational and graduation benefits, but mixed effects on earnings (Boland et al., 2021; Elu et al., 2019; Fryer & Greenstone, 2010; Gordon et al., 2020; Kim & Conrad, 2006; Park et al., 2018; Price et al., 2011; Strayhorn, 2008). However, MSIs enroll more than three times the proportion of students from the lowest income quintiles and exhibit twice the mobility rates—defined as moving students from the lowest to the highest income quintiles by age 30—compared with predominately White institutions, despite having fewer resources (Espinosa et al., 2018). MSIs enroll and graduate a disproportionate number of Black, Hispanic, and Native American students. Chetty et al. (2017) show that five of the top 10 colleges and universities that promote upward intergenerational mobility are Hispanic-serving institutions. Black students who attend historically Black colleges and universities with high proportions of Pell-eligible students are more likely to graduate than Black students at similar but predominately White institutions (Education Trust, 2019). And Native Americans who attended tribal colleges and universities had lower debt loads compared with peers at non-tribal colleges and universities (Gallup, 2019). A National Academies of Sciences report (2019, p. 125) suggested seven steps to improve student success at MSIs, with a particular focus on improving STEM education and increasing STEM majors.

Beyond the upward mobility of their own students, MSIs can serve as important pipelines into professions that can increase the upward mobility of the next generation of low-income youth. Rigorous causal studies show that Black students—especially low-income Black boys—have better educational outcomes when they are taught by Black teachers in elementary school (Gershenson et al., forthcoming, 2016; Lindsay & Hart, 2017), just as racial concordance between patients and doctors has been found to improve health outcomes for adults and children (Alsan et al., 2019; Greenwood et al., 2020; Saha et al., 1999; Shen et al., 2018; Takeshita et al., 2020; Thornton et al., 2011; Traylor et al., 2010).

Adjustments to Federal Financial Aid Formulas and Integrated Postsecondary Education Data (IPEDS) Data Collection

Free Application for Student Aid completion is a substantial barrier to low-SES students' college application and enrollment (Bettinger et al., 2012). Low-SES students become more likely to apply to and enroll in college if universities reveal their expected costs of attendance, net of financial aid, prior to application, at least in circumstances where those costs are low, as is often true for low-SES students (Dynarski et al., 2021, 2022b).

College major attainment is a first-order determinant of the return to higher education, with the relative economic return to certain majors (like economics and computer science) rivaling the baseline return to a college education (Altonji et al., 2016). Many universities restrict access to lucrative college majors on the basis of prior academic preparation and performance, and these restrictions disproportionately exclude low-SES students from lucrative fields of study (Bleemer & Mehta, 2021). Providing information on major restriction policies through Integrated Postsecondary Education Data System (IPEDS) could better inform students about their access to lucrative fields of study and incentivize universities to widen access for low-SES students.

Target Federal Higher Education Funding Toward High-Value-Added College Programs

Information on which universities and university programs provide high-value education to low-SES students is improving over time (e.g. Chetty et al., 2020). It is important that federal support for higher education institutions be increasingly targeted toward high-value programs as such information becomes available. For example, community college nursing programs tend to provide outsized economic returns to relatively low-SES students (Grosz, 2020, 2021).

Career Education

Career and Technical Education Pathways in High School

There is rigorous evidence that high-quality career and technical education (CTE) improves higher education and labor market outcomes for disadvantaged students from a number of studies, all of which are based either on RCTs or lotteries among students who had applied to high school programs that were oversubscribed. For example:

1. *Career academies*—Career Academies are programs within comprehensive high schools that orient CTE and work experience toward specific sectors of the economy—like health care, information technology (IT), or finance. Kemple and Willner (2008) shows that, 8 years after random assignment (and 5 years after the completion of high school), Career Academies raised the earnings of males by 18% and of students overall by 11%. They also improved marriage rates and stable household formation. But they had no lasting impact on educational attainment, either through dropout rates or higher education. But Hemelt and Lenard (2019) show that an IT academy in North Carolina increased high school graduation (by 7–8 percentage points) and postsecondary enrollments 3 to 6 years after entry in the 9th grade.
2. *Technical high schools*—Studies by Dougherty (2018), Ecton and Dougherty (2023), and Brunner et al. (2021) of technical high schools in Massachusetts and Connecticut—the enrollments of which were oversubscribed—show evidence of lower high school

dropout rates and higher earnings for students who did not enroll in college. Seven years after enrollment, low-income students from technical high schools in Massachusetts had annual earnings approximately $3,500 higher than similar students from other high schools, among those who did not attend college (Ecton & Doughtery, 2023); on-time graduation rates were also 7–10 percentage points higher (Doughtery, 2018). Among male technical school attendees in Connecticut, dropout rates were 10 percentage points lower and earnings were $1,600 higher (Brunner et al., 2021).

3. *P-Tech and other pathways*—P-Tech is a program which began as a collaboration in New York between high schools, the City University of New York, and IBM. It is a program covering grades 9–14, where students engage in IT training and work experience along with their academic work. The model is now spreading to other locations and industries. According to Rosen et al. (2020), high school students in P-Tech had passed their New York regents exams and enrolled in postsecondary programs more frequently than students in other high schools. Bonilla (2020), in a study of a competitive grant to build pathways to postsecondary education and work in high-demand industries in California high schools, also found significantly lower rates of dropping out.

If the impacts on dropping out and high school completion persist, then these programs generate large positive impacts. The total social and economic cost of high school dropout, analyzed by Belfield and Levin (2007) and updated to current dollars, suggests social costs of approximately $1 million in present discounted value over the life cycle for each dropout, in terms of lost earnings, higher costs to taxpayers, and higher nonpecuniary costs (with the last two primarily associated with crime and poor health).

Moreover, the costs of these CTE approaches per student are not terribly high. For instance, the marginal costs for each Career Academy student are roughly $1,100–2,400 per year (Hemelt & Lenard, 2018), while the overall costs of technical high schools are $6,000; assuming that the cost of high school without either program is nearly $5,000, the two figures suggest the costs of the two approaches are quite comparable. So, the expected value of a program that raises high school graduation rates by 10 percentage points would be at least $100,000 per person while costing vastly less. Also, while some models of CTE have traditionally produced evidence of lower enrollments in 4-year colleges, the studies above mostly show little evidence of this.

One concern about CTE programs has been that they might "track" students away from 4-year colleges and universities. As indicated, they appear to raise enrollments in 2-year colleges, especially when "career pathways" are created that explicitly link students to programs there. But the studies above show little evidence that high-quality CTE lowers enrollment in 7-year programs or attainment of bachelor of arts degrees.

Postsecondary Sectoral Training Programs

A number of sector-based training program models have been developed in the past 20 years and have been subjected to rigorous random-assignment evaluations. Among the most successful, Per Scholas (one of the WorkAdvance[4] programs), Project Quest,[5] and Year Up[6] generated average earnings gains for participants of approximately $5,000–$8,000 that last for at least 5 to 11 years in RCT evaluations, while direct costs of training and supports (but not employment under Year Up) are about $6,000 to $12,500 (see Table C-4-3).

It is important to note that not all sectoral training programs are as effective as these. For example, Per Scholas is one of four sectoral training programs evaluated by MDRC. Across all four, earnings impacts averaged about $2,500 per year. We do not understand enough about what made

Table C-4-3 Sector-based training program models

	Target population	Description of program	Direct cost per participant	Annual earnings gains
Year Up	Ages 18–24, high school diploma or GED	6 months of classroom training, 6 months of internship plus program-based supports	$23,000 total, of which employers cover all but 40% ($9,200)	Nearly $8,000 per year by year 5
Per Scholas	Ages 18 and above, high school diploma or GED	Training in IT by private providers plus program-based supports	$5,800	$4,800 in year 7
Project Quest	Ages 18 and above, high school diploma or GED	Training primarily in health care certificate programs at community colleges with program-based supports	$12,500	$4,600 in year 11

SOURCE: Committee generated, data from Year Up (2023); Kanengiser and Schaberg (2022); Order and Elliot (2021).

---

[4] For more information see https://www.mdrc.org/publication/employment-and-earnings-effects-workadvance-demonstration-after-seven-years

[5] For more information see https://economicmobilitycorp.org/eleven-year-gains-project-quests-investment-continues-to-pay-dividends/

[6] For more information see https://www.yearup.org/about/newsroom/press/year-announces-significant-sustained-earnings-gains-young-adults-five-year

Per Scholas so effective, so it is important that the process of scaling up the program models we discuss be done in a way that carefully monitors implementation quality and program effectiveness.

Also noteworthy is that these programs have not been proven for general populations of disadvantaged youth. All employed careful screening, with some reporting acceptance rates ranging between 10% and 30% (Kazis & Molina, 2016; Maguire, 2016).

And finally, in addition to the direct costs listed in the table, all of these kinds of training programs carry an opportunity cost of lost earnings during the training period for participants, which can last six months to 2 years.

Details of Our Calculations

In arriving at our aggregate cost estimate, we assume an average direct cost of about $10,000 per trainee.[7] Year Up—which involves about 6 months of classroom training and 6 months of paid internship at a private company for low-income high school graduates—costs a lot more if you include the costs of the internship. Employer payments tend to cover about 60% of its costs and we assume that would also be true for our scaled-up programs. (Year Up is also working on variations of its model, to see whether it can generate lower-cost versions.)

So, comparing benefits to costs, the very best programs can pay for themselves in roughly 3–4 years (if earnings are foregone for 1–2 years), while a somewhat wider range of programs can take more than 5–6 years to pay for themselves. Assuming no further fade-out of impacts, the present discounted values of future earnings streams for program participants generate substantial benefits for them and the public (especially if the earnings gains can reduce crime, poor health, or the need for participants to rely on public benefit programs in the future). Assuming some moderate fade-out can still generate public benefits that clearly exceed costs

At what scale would one need to provide these programs, and at what total cost?

- *Youth*—About 3.2 million students graduated from high school in 2019, and two-thirds of them enrolled right away in college. So just

---

[7] For more information see https://www.mdrc.org/publication/employment-and-earnings-effects-workadvance-demonstration-after-seven-years. We include it in these options for the following reasons: (a) earnings impacts have been estimated over longer time periods than for the other programs; (b) students earn college credentials which might draw returns for longer periods and with greater portability; and (c) as a community college program, it might be easier to scale. And although Year Up is considerably more expensive than Per Scholas, we include the latter because of its exclusive focus on youth, its broad industry range, and its larger impacts to date on youth earnings.

over 1 million had no immediate chance of getting a postsecondary credential. If we add in high school dropouts who might get a GED, plus enrollees who will not complete any credential or earn enough credits to raise their earnings, plus those who obtain very weak credentials, we end up with about 1.5–2.0 million students every year who could benefit. On the other hand, Year Up and the other sectoral programs screen out many students (with poor cognitive skills and other barriers to work), so many of these youth would not be eligible to enter these programs, or might not even apply for other reasons. If we offer Year Up or another program to 1 million of these students per year, it would cost $10 billion annually (not including foregone earnings of the students)—or less if fewer are enrolled.

- *Adults*—In this case, we use a *stock* estimate of the population of potential low-income participants in these programs, rather than a *flow*. We can consider offering something like Project Quest or Per Scholas to adults at ages 25–44 (or perhaps a bit lower) who have moderately young children (perhaps below age 13) and have incomes below 200% of poverty. Roughly 30% or so of such adults meet the income criteria, and we assume that around 60% have children in this age range (though the true number might differ). There are 88 million Americans in that age range, so about 15–16 million fit the additional eligibility criteria. If we offered one million of them entry into Per Scholas or Project Quest each year, that would also cost $10 billion a year.

Scaling Challenges

In all cases, scaling these programs up while maintaining quality would be challenging—so the scaling would need to take place slowly and deliberately. The original sites that have been evaluated to date are fairly small. Each of the programs is now trying to replicate itself, but these efforts will not generate nearly enough scale to achieve our goals. The programs are also exploring ways to achieve more scale while maintaining quality, such as the use of online training to reduce cost, and partnerships with other providers (like community colleges) to expand their reach. The efforts of the city of San Antonio to scale up Project Quest have been described in presentations.[8]

---

[8] For more information see https://www.bexar.org/DocumentCenter/View/30320/Project-QUEST---Bexar-County-SBED-Webinar

APPENDIX C: CHAPTER 5
CHILD AND MATERNAL HEALTH

This appendix provides details on a number of the driver sections and interventions in Chapter 5.

Inadequacy of Funding for the Indian Health Service (IHS)

Not all Native American individuals are eligible for the IHS, a direct provider of health care services for the IHS. Out of 5.7 Native American individuals, 2.7 are eligible. They include those who reside in geographic areas covered by the IHS. However, a recent government report concluded that "[f]unding for IHS addresses only an estimated 48.6% of the health care needs of Native American children and has historically been subject to year-by-year discretionary allocations from Congress, which creates substantial long-term uncertainty in funding and makes it challenging to maintain and modernize needed health care infrastructure" (U.S. Department of Health and Human Services, 2022). The IHS served 64% of the eligible population in 2020.

Per capita spending is considerably lower for the IHS, at $4,078, than it is for Medicaid ($8,109) and for the U.S. population more generally ($10,742). Multiple factors explain this difference. One has to do with the types of services provided, with IHS providing primary and emergency care but not tertiary care. Another is that IHS operates under a global budget, so that if the number of people served increases, per capita spending, by definition, declines. Medicaid and Medicare, in contrast, increase funding with the number of people and services provided. A tribal budget formulation workgroup concluded that nearly $50 billion is needed to adequately fund the IHS in fiscal year 2023. To put this in perspective, funding for the IHS in 2022 was $6.8 billion (IHS budget appropriation), plus an additional $1.26 billion in reimbursements from health insurance providers. This excludes temporary COVID-19 funding. Tribal priorities for IHS funding include mental health, alcohol/substance abuse, and health care facilities construction (U.S. Department of Health and Human Services, 2022).

Mental Health

Youth suicide rates have increased significantly over time for all racial/ethnic groups. In 1980, suicide was the seventh most common cause of death. By 2018, it had risen to the third most common cause. Importantly, the method of suicide has shifted to include more use of firearms, which are deadlier. Suicide by firearm among 10–14-year-olds increased 146% over the past decade and increased by 51% for 15–24-year-olds (Everytown,

2022). Differences in suicide rates by gender, race, and ethnicity underscore the disproportionate burden borne by Native American populations, for whom rates can be more than six times higher than the group with the lowest rate, Latino youth. The group with the next highest rate is White adolescents. While suicides among Black and Latino youth are less frequent, the rate for Black youth has risen more quickly over time.

There is some research showing that mental health treatment can make a difference. Analyses of multiple cognitive behavioral therapy (CBT) interventions, including CBT and interpersonal psychotherapy for adolescents, have found them to be effective for the treatment of adolescent depression (Klein et al., 2007). Research on the effectiveness of pharmacological treatments is more varied, with some of the stronger evidence for selective serotonin reuptake inhibitors (Cipriani et al., 2016; Strawn et al., 2015). Most research on the effectiveness of treatment focuses on mental health outcomes. Given the strong evidence that mental health affects educational attainment and earnings, research linking mental health treatment with future economic outcomes would be very informative.

The Centers for Disease Control and Prevention (CDC) and the Substance Abuse and Mental Health Services Administration (SAMHSA) have each developed evidence-based guidelines and strategies to address gaps in youth mental health care. The CDC has outlined the importance of early identification, providing resources to support families and identifying gaps in workforce development funding. This includes training professionals from fields that are connected to mental health and also integrating mental health care with routine health care. SAMHSA has focused on reducing emergency department utilization for children with mental health issues, reducing criminal justice interactions, and encouraging community-based care coordination.

With research pointing to the importance of location-based policy levers (e.g., So et al., 2019), SAMHSA has prioritized Certified Community Behavioral Health Clinics, which are a central part of the agency's strategy, with 400 grantees nationally, but is also supporting school-based services. Another area where there is growing evidence of effectiveness in addressing both physical and mental health care needs, especially among low-income communities, is in school-based health centers (SBHCs). A review of the evidence on the effectiveness of SBHCs on educational and health outcomes led the Community Preventive Services Task Force to recommend continued implementation and maintenance of SBHCs (Community Preventive Services Task Force, 2016). SBHCs receive funding from multiple sources (50% from the federal government and the rest from local and state sources). From 1996 to 2017, total funds dedicated to SBHCs have increased from $42 to $91 million, and the number of SBHCs has grown from 900 to 2,584. However, this growth masks significant geographic disparities: the number of states with SBHC programs declined over this period from 34 to 17.

Pollution

Federal clean-up of Superfund sites has been linked, causally, with important medium-term outcomes. Using data from 1994 to 2002 on the timing of Superfund site clean-up and comparing the outcomes of siblings born to the same family before and after a clean-up, researchers have linked Superfund site clean-ups with improved cognitive test scores and halving in the rate of children with a cognitive disability (Persico et al., 2020). If one only considers the reduction in special education expenditures associated with the clean-up, the researchers calculate that Superfund clean-ups would pay for themselves within 40 years. Researchers have also linked Superfund Site clean-ups with reduced child blood lead levels and improved infant health (Currie et al., 2011a; Klemick et al., 2020).

Children living in households below the poverty line and Black children are more likely to live near one of the 300,000 facilities that emit toxic chemicals, known as toxic release inventory (TRI) sites (Perlin et al., 1999). There is research linking childhood exposure to toxic chemicals at these sites to short-term, and more recently long-term, outcomes including educational attainment and wages. Researchers address the nonrandom placement of TRI sites in various ways. In the short term, evidence suggests that proximity to TRI sites increases infant mortality and reduces birthweight. In a recent working paper, Persico (2022) exploits variation in exposure across siblings derived from the opening of a plant and/or a family moving. Children exposed to a TRI site in utero complete 1.2 fewer years of school and have nearly 60% lower income in adulthood than their unexposed siblings. It is important to note that the TRI program, managed by the Environmental Protection Agency, tracks the management of 770 toxic chemicals and publishes this information for the public.[1] The TRI program does not set standards for chemical emission levels.

Nutrition and Food Insecurity

For pregnant individuals, accessing healthy nutrition is critical to ensure healthy birth outcomes, such as lowering the risk of low birthweight (da Silva Lopes et al., 2017), as well as developmental outcomes into

---

[1] Facilities that manufacture, process, or otherwise use these chemicals in amounts above established levels must annually report the amount released (i.e., emitted into the air or water) and/or managed through recycling, energy recovery, and treatment. According to Persico (2022), 221 million Americans lived in a zipcode with a TRI as of 2016.

childhood, such as cognition (Borge at al., 2017; Ramakrishnan et al., 2012; Veena et al., 2016). Nutritional status during pregnancy is also associated with overweight and obesity in children. For example, there is a correlation between obesity during pregnancy and poor neonatal outcomes, such as higher risks of having preterm birth, large for gestational age, and perinatal death (Aviram et al., 2011; Marchi et al., 2015). Obesity during pregnancy is also correlated with poor infant and childhood outcomes, including child obesity, and with poor health outcomes into adulthood (Langley-Evans, 2015; Poston et al., 2011).

The federal nutrition programs have been shown to be effective at reducing food insecurity in childhood and improving child health and future economic outcomes. Supplemental Nutrition Assistance Program (SNAP) in particular has been linked to improvements in newborn health, improved child outcomes, reductions in poverty, and improved economic and health outcomes in adulthood (Almond et al., 2011; M. Bailey et al., 2020; Hoynes & Schanzenbach, 2015; Hoynes et al., 2011, 2015, 2016). However, SNAP benefits are often consumed before the end of the month, resulting in increased food insecurity, decreased food consumption and other spending, and impaired dietary quality (Calloway et al., 2015; Franckle et al., 2019; Gregory & Smith, 2019; Hamrick & Andrews, 2016; Todd, 2015; Weinstein et al., 2009; Whiteman et al., 2018), which in turn have negative impacts on academic achievement (Bond et al., 2022; Cotti et al., 2018; Gassman-Pines & Bellows, 2018; Gennetian et al., 2016). Another complication is that SNAP benefits are to a large degree fungible with cash incomes, making it difficult to know to what extend intergenerational impacts are the result of increased food consumption or increased economic resources.

The Special Supplementation Nutrition Program for Women, Infants, and Children (WIC) is associated with positive impacts on nutrition, dietary intake, food security, and health, including birth outcomes, the latter of which is causally associated with educational attainment and later economic outcomes (Black et al., 2007; Royer, 2009). Improvements in 2009 to the nutritional content of WIC food packages—including the addition of a fruit and vegetable voucher and requirements that bread be whole grain and milk be low fat—have been found to improve dietary quality, perinatal outcomes, and early child development (Guan et al., 2021; Hamad et al., 2019a,b; Tester et al., 2016).

Despite these numerous benefits, participation rates among eligible children decline significantly after infancy (> 98%) across 1–4 years of age, (65%, 49%, 44%, 25%, respectively), and only 52% of eligible pregnant individuals participate (USDA, 2022). These numbers increased during the pandemic due to the multiple waivers that existed (remote benefits issuance, physical presence, allowance of uploading electronic certification documents, etc.) that streamlined certification, but quantitative data on national impact does not yet exist. COVID-19 waivers increasing the WIC fruit/vegetable benefit also improved dietary intake, but evidence is still needed to prove its positive impact on health.

Factors contributing to the high numbers of children who are WIC eligible but not enrolled include concerns regarding immigration status, lack of transportation to attend in-person appointments, and administrative barriers that made it more difficult for families to enroll or stay enrolled in WIC (National Academies, 2017e; Vargas & Pirog, 2016). For SNAP, take-up rates are generally high (82% nationally, though they can be as low as 55% in some states). The main barrier to SNAP utilization among children is the ineligibility of many immigrant groups. Among immigrants, only those with permanent residency and those who are refugees can access SNAP benefits. The undocumented and those awaiting permanent residency are not eligible. Having parents or siblings in the latter categories affects the benefit levels of eligible children who are U.S. citizens. As a result, children in immigrant families are at higher risk for food insecurity (Capps et al., 2009; East, 2020; Kaushal et al., 2013; Van Hook & Balistari, 2006).

There is causal evidence that expanding coverage to immigrant families is effective in improving child outcomes. East (2020) examines the experience of U.S.-born children of immigrants whose parents were subject to changes in eligibility for SNAP over time, though the children maintained their eligibility throughout. Eliminating (restoring) parental eligibility for SNAP while maintaining child eligibility effectively reduced (increased) total monthly SNAP benefit payments. East (2020) also explores the impact of having SNAP from infancy through age 5 on health outcomes at ages 6–16, including parent reports of child health. She documents effects of SNAP benefit levels on parent-reported child health that are similar to the effects on self-reported health generated from the roll-out of SNAP as documented by Hoynes et al. (2018). An additional year of eligibility for SNAP reduces the probability of fair/poor health by 5% at ages 6–16 in the more recent study, compared with a 3% reduction in the same measure of self-reported health by adults associated with SNAP roll-out.

Paid Family and Medical Leave

There are some interventions that may be promising avenues for increasing intergenerational mobility through improvement in child and maternal health. These include paid family and medical leave. Only 23% of U.S. civilian workers report having access to paid leave for medical, caregiving, or parental obligations (Beach & Walsh, 2021). Lack of access to paid leave disproportionately impacts low-income and racial/ethnic minority workers (Bartel et al., 2019; Boyens et al., 2022). Paid family and medical leave policies improve neonatal health outcomes, including reductions in rates of low birthweight and the risk of prematurity especially for unmarried and Black mothers (Rossin, 2011; Stearns, 2015), which in turn affect health in childhood (Lichtman-Sadot & Bell, 2017) and educational attainment and earnings later in life.

APPENDIX C: CHAPTER 6
CHILDREN'S FAMILY INCOME, WEALTH, AND PARENTAL EMPLOYMENT

This appendix first details the evidence regarding the likely impacts of expanding the Earned Income Tax Credit (EITC). Next, it describes the distribution of family wealth and reviews the correlational and causal evidence linking wealth to intergenerational outcomes. Finally, it provides more details on income and wealth interventions supported by direct or indirect evidence.

Impacts of the Earned Income Tax Credit on Child Outcomes

Much of the report's discussion of the effects of family income and of income-oriented interventions centers around the EITC, which has been prominent in both policy and research for decades. There is an extensive literature on the EITC and its impacts (Hoynes & Rothstein, 2017; and Nichols & Rothstein, 2016, for reviews). The paper that most directly tackles the specific question of the EITC's impact on intergenerational poverty is a working paper by McInnis et al. (2023). They relate variation in EITC receipt during childhood to the probability of being in poverty as an adult, between ages 25 and 45, and as measured by the Official Poverty Measure. They found that a $1,000 increase in annual EITC exposure during childhood reduces the likelihood of being in poverty as an adult by 9%.

They conclude that this effect is driven by increases in both children's adult employment and earnings. They find that a $1,000 increase in annual EITC exposure during childhood increases adulthood employment by 4 percentage points and increases annual earnings by between 10% and 30%. They do not find evidence that childhood EITC exposure affects adulthood family structure (marrying or having children), which rules out one potential alternative mechanism.

Some papers have studied the effect of the EITC on childhood outcomes that plausibly affect whether children grow up to be in poverty as adults. Dahl and Lochner (2012) found that increases in family income due to EITC expansions raised math and reading test scores by about 0.06 standard deviations per $1,000; Chetty et al. (2011) found slightly larger effects, 0.06–0.09. Bastian and Michelmore (2018; see also Michelmore, 2013) showed that a $1,000 increase in EITC exposure boosts the odds of high-school completion by 1.3%, of college completion by 4.2%, and of young-adult employment by 1%. They suggest that the mechanism is through higher family income. Manoli and Turner (2014) found that an extra $100 of EITC rebate in a student's senior year of high school increases college enrollment by 0.2 to 0.3 percentage points.

There are also studies that show effects of EITC on various aspect of health among recipients' children, which may plausibly reduce later poverty as an adult (e.g., if child health improves subsequent education and employment; see Chapter 5). For example, Hoynes et al. (2015) showed that a $1,000 increase in EITC exposure is associated with a modest decline in low birthweight. Similarly, Klevens et al. (2017) found that state EITCs are associated with a decrease in pediatric abusive head trauma, while Batra and Hamad (2021) found reduced food insecurity in the months after EITC refund receipt, and Hamad and Rehkopf (2016) found reduced behavioral problems with increased EITC refund size.

Studies vary in whether they find that effects are larger for EITC payments received while young or later in childhood. With respect to heterogeneous effects by race, a handful of studies of nonpoverty outcomes have found larger effects for Black recipients. For example, Komro et al. (2019) and Batra et al. (2022) both found larger effects of state and federal EITC benefits, respectively, for birth outcomes among Black mothers.

An ambiguity in all of the work on the EITC's impacts on child outcomes concerns whether the EITC's impact derives from the additional resources available to families, from increased maternal employment in response to the EITC's incentives or from a combination of the two. Although papers often describe their effects as reflecting the impact of $1,000, they all identify this from a policy that encourages greater work among mothers, but they cannot separately identify that effect. Distinguishing these effects is critically important to evaluating the potential impact of policies that might raise income with no or negative effects on employment. What evidence we have on this issue derives from other studies, for example of the effects of winning lotteries (Bulman et al., 2021; Cesarini et al., 2017).

Wealth

This appendix section focuses on the relationship between wealth and intergenerational poverty. We briefly cover trends in wealth and wealth inequality, followed by causes of these trends with a focus on differences by race and ethnicity. We then examine evidence from studies on parental wealth and adult child outcomes, and conclude with our suggested policy intervention, establishing federal child trust accounts or baby bonds.

Wealth-based metrics have become increasingly important for explaining the economic lives of Americans. They serve both as a mechanism of social mobility and as a means of solidifying social, political, and economic status. Studies have shown that differences in familial wealth holdings exist at birth. They persist across the life course and perpetuate intergenerationally; at least 25% of the younger generation's wealth is directly attributable to their parents' level of wealth (Feiveson & Sabelhaus, 2018). As a result, the life chances of children from families at the lower end of the wealth distribution, on average, follow significantly different trajectories from those whose families were at the middle and top end (Pfeffer & Killewald, 2019). Lack of wealth constrains opportunities, inhibits choice, and increases economic vulnerability.

Trends in Wealth and Wealth Inequality

Wealth in the United States is highly skewed. Average household wealth was approximately $748,800 in 2019, while the median value was $121,700.[1] These numbers are explained by two related phenomena. First, most households are concentrated at the lower end of the wealth distribution with a wealthy minority at the top. And second, the share of wealth held by the top 1% of U.S. families was 33.1%, while the top 10% held 71% of U.S. wealth, compared with the 27% and 2% held by the bottom 50–90th percentile and bottom 50% of U.S. households. The wealth distribution has become more unequal in recent decades, with the top 1% owning an increasing share of overall U.S. wealth. From 1989 to 2019 the share owned by the top 1% increased from 25 to 34% (Bricker et al., 2020). The Gini coefficient, a measure ranging from zero for perfect equality to one for maximum inequality captures how evenly distributed wealth is in an economy, provides another way of showing this trend. For the United States, the coefficient peaked in 2016 at 0.86 (last year calculated) yet it remained relatively unchanged between 1950 (0.83) and 2007 (0.82), rising most recently post-Great Recession (Kuhn et al., 2020).

Wealth holdings vary by many of the same group traits that cause income to vary including age, education, household composition, geography, and race/ethnicity. U.S. households with children are less wealthy than households without children. In 2019 they had a median wealth level of $64,050 compared with $114,850 of households with nonresidential children. They are also more unequal than nonchild households, with a Gini coefficient of 0.90 compared with 0.86 for nonchild households (Gibson-Davis & Hill, 2021).

Trends in Wealth and Wealth Inequality By Race/Ethnicity

A focus on wealth reveals extreme economic inequality by race/ethnicity. In 2019, median wealth for White households was $188,200 compared

---

[1] These values do not include defined benefit pension assets. The Federal Reserve estimates that median wealth increases to $172,000 when inclusive of defined benefit reserves (Bricker et al., 2020).

with $24,100 and $36,100 for Black and Latino households, respectively (Bhutta et al., 2020). Few datasets are available that specifically track the wealth of Native Americans, but research from the National Longitudinal Survey of Youth estimated that in 2000, the median wealth for Native Americans in the survey was $5,700, compared with the median wealth of $65,000 for the sample overall (Zagorsky, 2006).

Percheski and Gibson-Davis (2020) found that between 2004 and 2016, Black-White wealth inequality grew faster in households with children than among all households. By 2016, they found, non-Hispanic White child households had a median wealth of $47,250, compared with a median wealth of $294 among Black child households. Pfeffer and Killewald (2019) found that Black children born in the middle 22% of the wealth distribution are 2.5 times more likely to fall into the bottom 20% of the wealth distribution than White children born into the same tier of wealth.

Causes of Wealth Inequality Trends

Kuhn et al. (2020) explored trends in household wealth inequality between 1950 and 2016, and the growing concentration of wealth at the higher end of the distribution. They found that private business revenue explains much of the increase for the wealthy minority. Growth in wealth among households in the middle of the wealth distribution has been driven by increases in homeownership and, more notably, home equity.

Several recent papers have examined the importance of intergenerational wealth on present wealth inequality (Adermon et al., 2018; Pfeffer and Killewald, 2018; Toney, 2022). Pfeffer and Killewald (2018) found that grandparent wealth is an independent predictor of adult grandchildren's wealth using U.S. panel data, and Adermon et al. (2018) found the same with Swedish data. Pfeffer and Killewald (2018) found that for both White and Black families, education explains more of the intergenerational wealth gaps and social-class persistence than homeownership, bequests or inheritances, business ownership, or marriage. Toney (2022) showed that the composition of assets within wealth portfolios is static across generations, although the relationship is weaker among Black households.

Causes of Wealth Inequality By Race and Ethnicity

Racial/ethnic wealth gaps reflect historical and contemporary processes and policies that have predominantly supported wealth accumulation for White Americans and impeded or exploited wealth opportunities for Black Americans from slavery and sharecropping and debt traps to more recent evidence of biased home appraisal practices and targeted subprime mortgage lending (Bayer et al., 2016; Berger, 2018; Faber, 2013; O'Connell, 2012; Perry et al., 2018; Reece, 2020). Black and Hispanic homeowners had much higher rates of delinquency and default in the downturn. These estimated differences are especially pronounced for loans originated near the peak of the housing boom. These findings suggest that black and Hispanic homeowners drawn into the market near the peak were especially vulnerable to adverse economic shocks and raise concerns about homeownership as a mechanism for reducing racial disparities in wealth. Racial differences in wealth accumulation and growing wealth gaps over time have been also attributed to differences in asset holdings and returns on those investments. In recent decades, greater amounts of financial asset ownership among White households and appreciation in stock equity have rewarded them over time. Returns to housing, where Black households hold much of their wealth, have appreciated less due to longstanding patterns of residential racial segregation (Boulware & Kuttner, 2020; Derenoncourt et al., 2022). Other contributing factors include differences in the incidence and size of inheritances (Bhutta et al., 2020). Not only are White households more likely to receive financial inheritances, but they are also more likely to expect them (Addo & Darity, 2021).

Obstacles to wealth accumulation have also operated partly through disparities in income throughout the life course, as income from employment and capital are the primary ways households are able to set aside money to save and build wealth via investments, educational attainment, and asset purchases (Elmi & Lopez, 2021). Derenoncourt et al. (2022) showed that Black-White differences in savings rates are explained by initial wealth levels, age, and education, and Gittleman and Wolff (2004) found no differences in savings after accounting for income.

Background Section for Interventions

EITC Proposal

Graphs depicting the three examples of modifications to the EITC are shown in text Figure 6-7. In the panels for Options 1-3, the 2022 EITC payment for a single parent with two children is shown as a solid line. The phase-in and phase-out rates (the slopes of the two lines), the maximum credit, and the exact locations of the earnings thresholds all vary with family size, but the general pattern is similar. The final graph shows only the incremental credit payments associated with each one.

Taking the example of Option 1, the solid line in the figure shows the current (2022) value of the credit as a function of family earned income. Families with zero earnings are not eligible for any EITC benefits. As family earnings increase up to $15,410 (the "phase-in" portion of the schedule), EITC payments increase as well—up to a maximum payment in 2022 of $6,164. Between $15,410 and $20,130 (the "flat" portion), this maximum payment is constant. Once earnings exceed $20,130, the credit payment is gradually reduced, so that when earned income reaches about $50,000, EITC payments fall to zero. The dashed line shows how much higher tax credit payments would be if all payment amounts from the 2022 schedule were increased by 40%.

Combining the EITC with Other Programs to Increase Income Stability

The committee considered expansions along the lines of the 2021 Child Tax Credit, which made credits available to families without earnings without increasing the incentive to work. On the plus side, it would provide resources to more low-income families with children than the EITC alone, but it would probably lead to a reduction in maternal employment relative to the status quo. Option 3 in Figure 6-7 combines the addition of credits for families without earnings with an increase in the credit for those with earnings, in order to preserve (and indeed increase) the incentive to work relative to current policy.

The EITC's annual payments are typically distributed as tax refunds 1 or 2 months after the end of the year in which the income is earned, which may limit the credit's usefulness in financing recurrent monthly expenses, like child care. Prior work has shown that the lump-sum annual nature of the EITC leads to fluctuations in spending and food security across the year (Batra & Hamad, 2021; McGranahan & Schanzenbach, 2013). It also could limit the work-promoting effects insofar as this annual structure restricts the ability of new mothers to use the credit to finance child care during their first year as new parents. At the same time, the annual structure of the EITC makes it a form of involuntary savings, which people use to help purchase durable goods that are likely to increase workforce participation, such as vehicles (Goodman-Bacon & McGranahan, 2008). The temporary, 6-month-long expansion of the Child Tax Credit (CTC) in 2021 was implemented as a monthly advance payment, and early quasi-experimental evidence indicates that the 2021 expanded CTC improved household food sufficiency and parental mental health (Batra et al., 2023; Shafer et al., 2022). This indirect evidence suggests that more regular payments could help to provide more income stability, though there is no rigorous evidence of the effect of a monthly payment structure on employment, earnings, or multiyear poverty.

The report discusses several combinations of the EITC proposals with other programs that might help increase income stability. Here are more details for the three possible options listed in the text:

- Combine an expansion of the EITC with expanded coverage of the Child Care and Development Fund block grant. Evidence reviewed in the report suggests that the Child Care and Development Fund child care subsidies have raised maternal employment, especially in low-income families. Because these subsidies are paid when child care services are received, they help to address the mis-timing problem that arises between child care expenses and EITC receipt during a child's first year of life.
- Combine an expansion of the EITC with a restructuring of the Child and Dependent Care Tax Credit (CDCTC) to provide more generous and timely reimbursement for the child care expenses of low-income parents. Following Ziliak (2014), the National Academies (2019a) report proposed making the CDCTC fully refundable and, for low-income families with children under age 6, reimbursing up to $4,000 per year in child care costs for the first child and a total of $6,000 for two or more children under age 6.
- Combine an expansion of the EITC with a monthly refundable CTC. An expanded CTC was also recommended in the 2019 National Academies report and was temporarily implemented for the 2021 tax year. This would be most feasible for an expansion such as EITC expansion Option 3. Past efforts to provide the EITC as a monthly payment have encountered resistance from recipients who were concerned that they might have to repay the credit if their earnings turned out to be lower than expected. Thus, this combination would be most feasible for expanding Option 3, which guarantees at least $1,000 per child for all families with earnings lower than $43,560.

The Minimum Wage

In theory, minimum wages have offsetting effects: They raise wages for some workers, but by increasing the cost to businesses of employing workers, they reduce employment. Thus, their impact on poverty is theoretically ambiguous.

It is worth noting that even the employment effect is itself ambiguous. While competitive models of the labor market yield an unambiguous prediction of negative effects on employment, in other models that allow for employer market power, job search, or other deviations from perfect competition, modest minimum wages can have small or even positive effects on employment. Even in these models, though, sufficiently large minimum wage increases will reduce employment. These models are well reviewed by Dube (2019a) and Belman and Wolfson (2014).

It is thus an empirical question whether increases in the minimum wage will reduce employment, and by how much. There is no consensus in the economics literature about the exact amount, with high-quality studies reaching opposite conclusions. Neumark and Shirley (2021) observe that the minimum wage is an unusual research topic in that the state of the literature itself is under fierce debate.

Neumark and Shirley assemble the entire set of published minimum wage studies from the past three decades. They identify the "core estimates" from each study, in most cases identified by the authors of the studies. They find that 79.2% of estimated employment elasticities are negative, and that the evidence of negative employment effects is even stronger for teens and young adults, lesser-educated workers, and workers directly affected by the minimum wage. This is surprisingly consistent with other literature reviews. For example, among the 36 papers he considers, Dube (2019a) obtains a median estimate of the own-wage elasticity (the percentage employment reduction induced by a 1% increase in average wages induced by a higher minimum wage) of –0.17. Of those 36 studies, 26 are based on "narrow subgroups," including teens, restaurant or retail workers, and lower-educated immigrants. Among those 26 studies, Dube reports a median own-wage elasticity of –0.19.

This negative average effect reflects a number of estimates indicating positive or zero effects. One prominent recent study (Cengiz et al., 2019) finds that each 1% increase in average wages induced by increases in the minimum wage actually raises employment by 0.41%, though the confidence interval includes some negative effects, as large as –0.45%. This implies that employment reductions offset no more than half of the effect of wage increases. Other studies come to similar conclusions as Dube's (2019a) review. Clemens and Strain (2021) estimate own-wage elasticities of –0.26 for less-educated workers and –0.23 for younger workers.

In the committee's view, the evidence supports an own-wage elasticity in a range that includes near-zero, that is centered around –0.2, and that includes larger magnitudes for certain subgroups of workers.

Some studies find that larger minimum wage increases are associated with relatively larger employment reductions—that is, the employment elasticity is nonlinear. The average minimum wage increase in the 138 state-level changes studied by Cengiz et al. (2019) was around eight log points. Clemens and Strain (2018, 2021) studied the last decade of minimum wage increases and found little evidence that "small" increases of under $1 are associated with disemployment effects. For "small" increases, Clemens and Strain's results are qualitatively similar to the results in Cengiz et al. Dube

(2019a, p. 3) concludes that "the best evidence suggests that the employment effects are small up to around 59% of the median wage."

However, Clemens and Strain find larger disemployment effects of "large" increases of over $1. Among individuals ages 16–25 with less education than a high-school degree, they find that a one percent increase in wages induced by a higher minimum wage reduces employment by around one percent. For workers ages 16–21, they find a reduction in employment of –0.4%.

Jardim et al. (2017, 2018, 2022) studied Seattle's path to a $15-per-hour minimum wage, which reached as high as $11 in 2015 and $13 in 2016. Using administrative data from Washington State, Jardim (2022) found larger employment effects than are typically found. However, their point estimates have wide confidence intervals, and their results are also consistent with a selection effect deriving from the booming Seattle economy, or even spillovers from the minimum wage itself (Rothstein & Schanzenbach, 2017).

A contrasting result comes from Godoy and Reich (2021), who studied low-wage counties where minimum wages reached as high as 82% of the median wage. They did not find adverse effects of minimum wage increases on employment, hours, or annual weeks of work.

Another outstanding question is whether the long-run effects of minimum wage increases differ from the short-run effects that have been more studied. Clemens and Strain (2021) found that the medium-run disemployment effects of relatively large minimum wage increases are larger than the short-run effects. Meer and West (2016) argue that minimum wage increases affect employment by reducing its growth over time rather than by quickly reducing its level. Adjustment costs—driven in part by firm entries and exits within an industry—might help explain larger longer-term disemployment effects (Aaronson et al., 2015; Sorkin, 2015). Brummund and Strain (2020) found larger disemployment effects from the practice of indexing minimum wage increases to inflation, and speculate that modest, nominal increases are easier for firms to absorb without adjusting headcount than longer-lasting increases.

A minimum wage increase could reduce poverty even if it also reduces employment, if the benefits to the still-employed workers are larger than the costs to those who lose employment. (Note that for any own-wage elasticity above –1, the aggregate earnings of near-minimum-wage workers rise; the literature is clear that employment responses are much smaller than this threshold.) The picture is clearer here; studies generally find at least some poverty reduction (as measured by the Official Poverty Measure) from minimum wage increases, though there is disagreement about the magnitude. Dube (2019b) found that over three or more years, each 10% increase in the minimum wage reduces poverty by between 2.2% and 4.6%, a large effect. Godoy and Reich (2021) found substantial declines in both household and child poverty.

Other studies suggest much smaller effects. Using Survey of Income and Program Participation data from 1996 to 2007, Sabia and Nielsen (2015) found little evidence that federal or state minimum wage increases reduce poverty, material hardship, or receipt of public program benefits among workers, younger individuals without high school degrees, or younger black individuals. Neumark and Wascher (2002) concluded that the minimum wage redistributes income among low-income families. They found that minimum wage increases make it more likely that poor families escape poverty, but also more likely that families above the poverty line fall into poverty. These effects roughly offset one another.

As with employment effects, the best available option is to try to aggregate these disparate findings. The Congressional Budget Office (2019) concluded that the weight of the evidence points to modest effects on poverty. Using the TRIM3 model and the Supplemental Poverty Measure, the National Academies' *Roadmap to Reducing Child Poverty* (2019a) estimated modest poverty reductions from minimum wage increases, as well.

Union-related Interventions

The Chapter 6 text discusses the contribution that the decline in unionization has made to low wages and poverty, particularly for non-college workers. An expansion of union representation in the U.S. labor market would lift the wage distribution and reduce both parents' and children's poverty. Policies to accomplish this are a perennial topic of discussion. Advocates for unions argue that the legal framework created by the National Labor Relations Act no longer works well, and that it is too easy for employers to prevent union recognition through both legal and extra-legal methods.

Proposals include changes in the union recognition process, changes in the rules governing union behavior, and changes in the way that union bargaining units are funded. In the former category are proposals like "card check" recognition, whereby unions can be recognized based on a majority of workers signing cards in support, outside of a formal election. Another proposal, contained in the Protecting the Right to Organize (PRO) Act introduced in 2021, would prohibit employers from holding mandatory meetings from which union representatives are barred, to argue against the union. The PRO Act also includes provisions that would permit secondary strikes to place pressure on employers to recognize or bargain with unions, increase fines for employers who violate labor law, and weaken state "right to work" laws. The evidence base for these proposals is limited, and the report does not include specific recommendations regarding unions or labor law.

Assisting and Incentivizing the Creation of More Good Jobs

Besides increasing union membership or raising the minimum wage, other proposals to help or incentivize employers to create more "good jobs"—jobs with atypically high pay relative to the skills of workers (Andersson et al., 2005)—have already been implemented or proposed and are under discussion.

For instance, the Biden Administration has created a Good Jobs Challenge at the U.S. Department of Commerce and a Good Jobs Initiative at the U.S. Department of Labor. The former is a competitive grants program to fund training explicitly linked to "good jobs," using $500 million allocated to the Department of Commerce from the American Relief Plan Act of 2021.[2] The latter seeks to improve worker awareness of ways to improve job quality, and also to form partnerships between the department and employers or various government agencies (with appropriate technical assistance) to help create more good jobs.[3]

Regarding incentives and assistance to firms, the idea of rewarding firms for creating good jobs is embodied in a legislative proposal called the Patriot Employer Tax Credit, proposed by Senators Brown (D-OH) and Durbin (D-IL) in 2021.[4] Another approach is to provide tax credits to publicly owned firms that set themselves up as "B-corporations" (or "Benefit" corporations) rather than the more traditional "C-corporations"; the former allows firms to explicitly consider benefits conferred on workers and society among its goals, while the latter allows firms only to maximize shareholder value. Kim (2018) has called for encouraging the formation of more B-corporations through explicit corporate tax cuts.

Regarding assistance to state, local, and regional government agencies and their partners, Rodrik (2022) calls for assistance at the local level to economic development partnerships that will create more "good jobs," while calling for federal creation of a new entity (which he calls the Advanced Research Partner Agency for Workers) to fund technological innovation that is worker-friendly and would therefore create more good jobs as firms automate. In addition, Congressman Ro Khanna (D-CA; 2022) has proposed a range of such efforts, though they are focused on smaller cities and rural areas that have suffered job and income loss in recent decades.

Of course, while these kinds of ideas have some broad support, we have virtually no rigorous evidence to date on their cost-effectiveness. Further

---

[2] https://eda.gov/arpa/good-jobs-challenge

[3] https://www.dol.gov/newsroom/releases/osec/osec20220121#:~:text=The%20%E2%80%9CGood%20Jobs%E2%80%9D%20initiative%2C,all%20workers%20and%20job%20seekers

[4] https://www.congress.gov/bill/116th-congress/senate-bill/223/text?q=%7B%22search%22%3A%5B%22S.+524%22%5D%7D

experimentation with and rigorous evaluation of such efforts is justified and needed.

Improving Access of Disadvantaged Workers to Better Jobs

Proposed or actual efforts to improve employment opportunities for the most disadvantaged workers—such as returning citizens (people released to life in the community after incarceration) or those with particular disabilities, especially among people of color—take a variety of approaches. These include:

1. Strengthening enforcement of federal Equal Employment Opportunity (EEO) law provisions that forbid broad discrimination against returning citizens;
2. Providing direct assistance to workers who face employment barriers;
3. Offering incentives or assistance to employers who hire such workers or are located in impoverished locales, where many such workers live; and
4. Issuing federal "Second Chance" grants to states and localities or other partnerships that provide job training and other assistance to returning citizens or other hard-to-employ groups.

EEO law forbids employers to explicitly deny employment to anyone with a felony conviction or criminal record—since it creates a disparate impact on less-educated men of color—unless the decision to deny is explicitly tied to the requirements of a job, the offense committed by the job applicant, whether he or she has reoffended since that time, and the duration of time that has elapsed since the last conviction (U.S. Equal Employment Opportunity Commission, 2012). The Equal Employment Opportunity Commission has also brought some high-profile cases against major private firms that appeared to violate such rules (such as BMW and Dollar General) and obtained convictions against them.

Still, it is almost certainly true that many employers, especially in small- and medium-sized companies, violate these rules. There are also literally thousands of federal and state rules that explicitly bar returning citizens from particular occupations where they are perceived as being high-risk (especially those involving children or very elderly populations that are regarded as more vulnerable), and from obtaining occupational licensure. Scholars in this area understand that some of these restrictions are sensible, while others might be less so (Bushway et al., 2022). Thus, efforts to both increase enforcement of existing law and periodically review other barriers created by various federal or state rules might constitute a reasonable way to reduce such barriers and hardships.

Direct assistance to workers who face these barriers to employment includes subsidized or transitional jobs, in which a public or nonprofit entity funds temporary jobs for these workers—usually for 6 to 9 months in duration—with a public or private employer, in the hope that the worker's employability grows over time and might eventually be sustainable without any public assistance. The primary goal is therefore to raise employment and earnings during the time of the subsidy as well as afterwards, and to reduce long-term dependence on government benefits or incarceration. But, except for a few well-known success stories (like the Center for Employment Opportunity in New York or Recycle Force in Indiana), short-term employment improvements usually dissipate fairly quickly once the subsidy expires, and other outcomes, like recidivism, are not broadly improved except for specific populations (Cummings & Bloom, 2020).

Another approach involves efforts to allow more offenders to participate in work release programs while they are still incarcerated (Berk, 2008) or to facilitate their hiring through the issuance of "certificates of rehabilitation" or "certificates of relief" (Leasure & Anderson, 2016). Evidence suggests positive and cost-effective impacts of both approaches, though only small efforts have been rigorously evaluated to date.

Direct assistance to employers who hire returning citizens or others facing such barriers are provided by the Work Opportunity Tax Credit. This is a federal tax credit to companies that hire from a list of workers facing such barriers, including "returning citizens;" but take-up by employers is usually low, and evidence of its cost-effectiveness in expanding employment and earnings is quite limited (Hamersma, 2008).

Another body of policies includes incentives, like tax credits, to employers who locate in low-income parts of cities and want their concerns validated. Neumark (2018) reviewed the evidence to date on "enterprise zones" and other tax credits associated with location in or near neighborhoods, finding that such programs are generally not effective or cost a great deal of funding per net job created for the low-income adults. He also includes his own proposals for subsidies to firms that hire low-income local residents.

Finally, the federal government has funded some "second chance" programs with grants to states or to partnerships of employers and other community-based organizations. Examples include the Reentry Employment Opportunities (REO) program and Pathways Home, both administered by the U.S. Department of Labor. Rigorous evaluations of these efforts are in progress, though such evidence is not yet available to date.

Overall, more experimentation with and evaluation of a wide range of such policy efforts is encouraged, including attempts to scale programs like REO that appear successful.

Steps to Increase the Wealth of Low-Income Households

Attempts to increase the wealth of low-income households and improve short-term outcomes for their families and longer-term outcomes for their children have focused on building financial savings in preparation for paying for college. This is unsurprising given that a college degree remains one of the key engines of social mobility in the United States (Hout, 2012). Thus, intergenerational poverty is reduced through the educational attainment of one's children. More specifically, in obtaining a college degree, that wealth is a necessary component for enrolling in, persisting through, and completing one's degree. Proposals include expanding college savings plans (i.e., 529 plans), encouraging child development accounts (CDAs), and obtaining assets, such as by becoming a homeowner. Although promoting homeownership was not its original intent, the mortgage interest deduction is the main federal program associated with promoting homeownership. This tax benefit for homeowners with a mortgage is regressive, disproportionately benefits White households, and is not associated with reducing costs of entry for low-income households (Meschede et al., 2021; Sommer & Sullivan, 2018). Therefore, efforts to increase wealth through financial savings program are the focus.

Unlike 529 college savings plans, CDAs are savings plans primarily targeted at low- and moderate-income families. They are designed to reduce the barriers to long-term household savings by eliminating transaction costs while decreasing cognitive burdens. CDAs have been associated with college retention (Elliott & Beverly, 2011) and reduced college debt (Elliott et al., 2014). Evidence from national CDA studies on low-income households found that parents in the treatment group were more likely to open 529 plans and accumulate higher average balances. Except for the initial seed deposit, these initiatives rely on policy levers such as matching funds and the motivations of the parents to build savings. They draw upon the already limited resources of these households rather than increasing the inflow of assets into them. When initial seed money was provided, it was found to be low ($500–1000) and did not increase the average amount of personal savings held (Grinstein-Weiss et al., 2014).

To raise wealth among low-income households, especially those of Black and Native American families, the committee considered proposals to create Baby Bonds for children born in the United States, with the value of the bonds determined by the family's income and net worth at the time of the child's birth and targeting families with incomes below the SPM thresholds and total net worth less than one fourth of the federal poverty line.

Baby Bonds would address the intergenerational perpetuation of wealth inequality via familial inheritance and *inter vivo* wealth transfers (Darity & Hamilton, 2012; Hamilton & Darity, 2010). The approach recognizes that a substantial wealth endowment is necessary for social and economic prosperity. Similar to CDAs, these funds would be earmarked for the child's college costs, homeownership, or business investments, so they would not be accessible until young adulthood; in contrast to CDAs, the initial investment funds would be means-tested and require no additional monies from the households.

In the United States, the idea of Baby Bonds has captured the interest of scholars and politicians for many years. The idea is currently being tested in Washington, DC, and Connecticut. In fall 2007, as part of her 2008 presidential bid, Hillary Clinton proposed a $5,000-at-birth baby bond, which she mentioned again on the presidential campaign trail in the fall of 2016 (Matthews, 2019). In the 2020 presidential election, candidate and U.S. senator Cory Booker leveraged the research of economists Darrick Hamilton and William Darity (2010) to announce his new Baby Bond bill, American Opportunity Accounts (Kliff, 2018). Notably, the American Opportunity Accounts legislation calibrates the amount of the endowment based on parental income, although the original version of the proposal calibrates the amount based on parental wealth. The proposal had an estimated cost of 2% of federal expenditures.

There has been limited research conducted on the impact that Baby Bonds could have at a national level. Zewde (2020) used longitudinal data from the Panel Study of Income Dynamics to simulate wealth accumulation among young adults (18–25-year-olds in 2015) if they would have received Baby Bonds when they were newborns. Individuals were divided into five quintiles of household wealth at birth, with initial bond values defined categorically and tied inversely to household wealth at birth (from $200 for the top 20% of households to $50,000 for the bottom 20%). Bond values were assumed to grow at 2% annually through 2015. The estimated cost of this proposal is $82 billion per year.

The American Opportunity Accounts proposal is like Zewde's with the exception that means-testing would be based on household income, not wealth. Households would receive $1,000 at birth and up to $2,000 every year through age 18, with 2% to 3% annual returns.

Baby Bonds are a universal wealth intervention program that could yield a disproportionate benefit for Black and Native American families, because their wealth (and income) levels are so low. However, even if the assumptions in Zewde's simulation are basically sound, a Baby Bond program that markedly narrows the racial gap in wealth by early adulthood still leaves other drivers of the racial wealth gap in operation as youth move through adulthood (e.g., differential incomes, differential savings, differential rates of return on real estate, differential inheritances; Bruenig, 2019). This argues for considering Baby Bonds as part of a package of strategies to reduce racial/ethnic disparities in wealth (Cassidy et al., 2019).

APPENDIX C: CHAPTER 8
CHILDREN'S HOUSING AND
NEIGHBORHOOD ENVIRONMENTS

This appendix provides details on a number of intervention areas mentioned in Chapter 8.

Evidence on Housing Assistance for Intergenerational Mobility

Housing assistance comes in many forms, including rapid housing services, housing choice vouchers (HCVs), public housing, project-based vouchers, tax credits, and other state and local programs for both renters and homeowners. In various ways, these means-tested programs reduce the cost of housing for low-income families. Currently, the largest federal housing subsidy is the mortgage interest deduction for homeowners, which mostly benefits middle- and high-income households. For low-income households, the Low-Income Housing Tax Credit program (LIHTC) is the largest housing subsidy program. LIHTC provides funding to investors for the costs of developing low-income rental housing.

It is possible that housing subsidies alone—without requirements about where recipients use them—might decrease intergenerational poverty; however, the evidence on this is mixed and limited. As an income subsidy alone, housing assistance lifted roughly three million people out of poverty in 2019, including 936,000 children (Fischer et al., 2021). This intervention interrupts child poverty and thus makes it more likely that children will remain out of poverty as adults. Furthermore, housing assistance is not merely an income subsidy, but may also improve housing quality, promote stability, and reduce parental stress (Gubits et al., 2018; Schapiro et al., 2022; Warren & Font, 2015; Wood et al., 2008).

Correlational studies of the effects of housing assistance on children's outcomes show positive results, such as reduced blood lead levels (Ahrens et al., 2016), less overcrowding and grade retention (Currie & Yelowitz, 2000), and improved performance on standardized tests (Schwartz et al., 2020). Longitudinal studies find positive effects of growing up in various kinds of subsidized housing on educational attainment, employment, and earnings (Kucheva, 2018; Newman & Harkness, 2002). Using national data on over 1.7 million children eligible for or receiving housing assistance and using a between-sibling analytical model, Pollakowski et al. (2022) found that growing up in public or HCV housing increases earnings for all groups, and reduces adult incarceration at age 26, especially for Black women. In addition, a handful of quasi-experimental studies comparing families receiving Department of Housing and Urban Development assistance with families on a waiting list have consistently found improved health outcomes, including better child mental health, and fewer missed school days and better physical and mental health among adults, a reduction in the uninsured rate, and fewer unmet medical needs (Fenelon et al., 2017, 2018, 2021; Simon et al., 2017).

However, the evidence from randomized trials or natural experiments regarding the long-term effects of housing subsidies on children does not show uniformly positive effects. The Welfare to Work Voucher Experiment offered vouchers to families receiving welfare in six cities. It reduced poverty, homelessness, crowding, and residential moves, but it showed no consistent direct effects on children's educational or socioemotional outcomes (Wood et al., 2008). The authors of that study suggest that longer-term tracking of outcomes for children is warranted by the short-term housing impacts. A study of an HCV lottery in Chicago found no statistically significant effects of receiving a housing choice voucher for children's long-run educational, criminal, or health outcomes up to 14 years after the lottery (Jacob et al., 2015).

On the other hand, the Family Options Study—which was a randomized controlled trial at 12 sites that offered permanent housing subsidies to families experiencing homelessness—reduced homelessness, food insecurity, the number of schools that children attended, school absences, and behavior problems among children by the 3-year follow-up. Other experimental and quasi-experimental research, such as studies of the Moving to Opportunity (MTO) experiment (discussed in Chapter 8) or public housing demolitions, cannot compare the effects of receiving or not receiving housing subsidies, since all participants were in either voucher or public housing at baseline. While MTO gave vouchers without restrictions on where they could be used, all families already had housing assistance by virtue of living in public housing. Although correlational and longitudinal evidence is available on the positive long-term effects of housing subsidies, there are few randomized studies. It is also important to note that although the LIHTC program has surpassed the HCV program in the number of households served, there is no correlational or causal evidence on the long-term effects of tax credit units.

There are many proposals for increasing housing subsidies for low-income families. Collinson et al. (2019) discuss a range of considerations in making the current policy landscape more effective. They believe that the variation in local markets renders a one-size-fits-all housing policy less effective. They also discuss the possibility of broadening the reach of current subsidy dollars by providing more "shallow" subsidies and possibly time limits, instead of the long and deep subsidies that the HCV, LIHTC, and public housing currently offer. Finally, they point out the need to address locational challenges with the disproportionate siting of public housing and LIHTC units and the disproportionate concentration of HCVs in high-poverty neighborhoods, both of which contribute to intergenerational poverty.

In another proposal, Collyer et al. (2020) focus less on how housing subsidy programs function and more on expanding their reach. They propose combining a universal entitlement to housing assistance with increased Earned Income Tax Credit (EITC) and Child Tax Credit funding. They estimate that the expansion of the HCV alone would cut the national poverty rate by 9%. Overall, housing assistance is an area that needs a stronger causal evidence base. Several experts we consulted suspected there was promise for housing subsidies to improve long-term outcomes, but lacked the strong evidence to support that view without uncertainty.

Evidence on Improving the Housing Supply

It is important to complement efforts to increase *demand* for housing in high-opportunity neighborhoods by expanding the *supply* of housing overall, which could increase supply in neighborhoods that are good for children's long-term outcomes. Researchers agree that there is a supply problem in the United States, but there is debate about the reasons for low supply and the consequences for affordability (Been et al., 2019; Schuetz, 2022). Boosting supply using existing policy might be achieved by incentivizing development through a targeting of LIHTC projects in opportunity-rich areas, as well as by relaxing zoning restrictions (i.e., "upzoning") in high-opportunity neighborhoods. While we do not have direct evidence on the efficacy of such interventions, research shows that the price of opportunity—that is, the ratio of average levels of upward mobility to average rent—is currently much higher in metro areas that have stricter land use regulations (Chetty et al., 2016).

Evidence on Improving Neighborhood Characteristics

While the best evidence to date on the intergenerational mobility effects of improving housing and neighborhoods for children focuses on moving to higher opportunity neighborhoods, it is equally important to consider how to bring better opportunities to neighborhoods that currently do not offer good prospects for upward mobility. There is a growing body of strong experimental evidence that remediating vacant lots and abandoned buildings reduces crime and violence (Branas et al., 2018), and there is correlational evidence that increasing the density of community organizations and increasing community investments (e.g., through mortgage dollars) also reduces crime (Sharkey et al., 2017; Velez et al., 2012). This literature is reviewed in Chapter 9. There is also evidence that desegregating neighborhoods, improving the quality of schools, reducing pollution, and focusing on factors such as social capital may help to promote intergenerational mobility (Ananat, 2011; Card & Krueger et al., 1992; Hohl et al., 2019; Isen et al., 2017; see Chyn & Daruich, 2022, for a simulation analysis).

Evidence on Improving Housing for Native Americans

Native American families face distinct housing-related barriers to intergenerational mobility. Overcrowding, poor housing quality, homelessness, infrastructural deficits, complex land ownership, and limited mortgage availability are acute issues for Native Americans, especially on reservation lands (Kunesh, 2021; Pindus et al., 2017). Advocacy organizations, such as the National American Indian Housing Council, call for the reauthorization of the Native American Housing Assistance and Self-Determination Act of 1996, which expired in 2013. Congress has continued to fund its programs every year, in any case, but continued appropriations have not kept up with housing needs (Walters, 2022). Moreover, self-determination and community control are important prerequisites for Native American housing justice (Kunesh, 2021). We could identify no studies on the short- or long-term effects of targeted housing interventions on Native American children.

APPENDIX C: CHAPTER 9
NEIGHBORHOOD CRIME AND CRIMINAL JUSTICE SYSTEM

This appendix discusses the nature and causes of trends in crime and incarceration, as well as racial/ethnic differences in those trends. It then provides details on a number of the intervention areas mentioned in Chapter 9.

Trends in Crime and Incarceration: Causes and Policy Implications

Declines in Crime Over Time

After peaking in the early to mid-1990s, crime in the United States fell dramatically to levels not observed since the 1960s (see Figure C-9-1). Between 1993 and 2019, violent crime per 100,000 declined from 747 to 379 and property crimes fell by a similar proportion, from 4,740 to 2,109

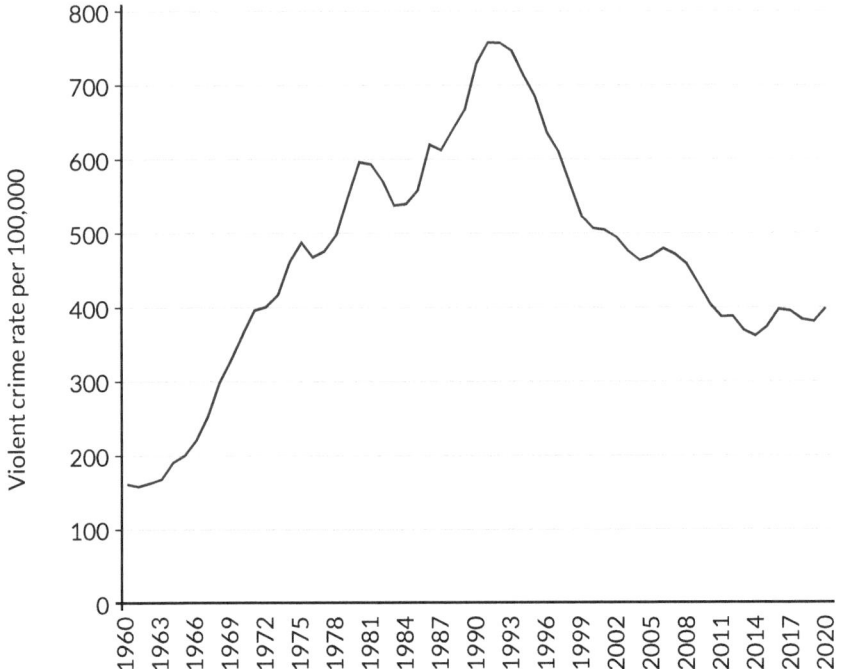

FIGURE C-9-1 U.S. violent crime rate per 100,000, 1960–2021.
NOTE: The violent crime rate is the sum of reported homicides, rapes, robberies, and aggravated assaults per 100,000 people in the United States.
SOURCE: Figure adapted from James (2018) for years 1960–2016 and using data from the Federal Bureau of Investigation's (2022) Crime Data Explorer for violent crimes for years 2017–2021.

(Gramlich, 2020). Violent crime has again risen somewhat since 2014 (FBI, 2019a, Table 1), and homicides have spiked since 2019, although those rates remain well below their peak in the early 1990s. Nearly 80% of all recent homicide victims are killed with guns (Johns Hopkins Center for Gun Violence Solutions, 2022), and new "right-to-carry" laws in many states have contributed substantially to the surge in gun violence (Donohue et al., 2022). One aspect of violent crime that has not declined over time is school shootings, which increased over the past 50 years more than tenfold, from 19 in 1970 to 240 in 2021 (Naval Postgraduate School, 2023)

Concurrent with the decline in crime has been unprecedented growth in incarceration in the United States, which increased by a factor of three or four between 1980 and 2013 (Figure 9-5). While crime began to fall starting in the early to mid-1990s, incarceration rates continued to increase through 2009, peaking at 1.61 million individuals in U.S. state and federal prisons. Some of the persistently high rates of incarceration in the United States can be traced to those cohorts coming of age in the 1980s and 1990s, when the punitiveness of the criminal justice system increased, resulting in high incarceration rates for these cohorts. Researchers have shown that even though current punitiveness has declined, because the current sentencing structure escalates punishment for those with prior offences, those who came of age in the 1980s and 90s have continued to be incarcerated at high rates for many years after (Shen et al., 2020).

The population of adults in prison is largely male, with low levels of formal education (the majority have less than a high school degree) and disproportionately Black, and to a lesser extent Latino (Raphael & Stoll, 2013; see Figure C-9-2). The increase in incarceration is explained in large part by tougher sentencing laws. Lofstrom and Raphael (2016, p. 123) conclude that "the vast expansions occurring during the 1990s and during the first few years of the new century have bought little in terms of crime reduction but imposed substantial costs on the sanctioned, their families, and their communities." This suggests that most of the decline in U.S. crime over this period can be explained by other factors, such as the aging of the population, the waning of the crack-cocaine epidemic, a decline in blood-lead levels in children following the elimination of lead from gasoline, and policing practices (Lofstrom & Raphael, 2016).

Juvenile Crime and Confinement

Like adult crime, juvenile crime has been declining over time from a high in the mid-1990s through 2019. Unlike adult incarceration, however, juvenile confinement has decreased by 60% since 2000. This decline is primarily attributed to falling crime rates, though increasing reliance on

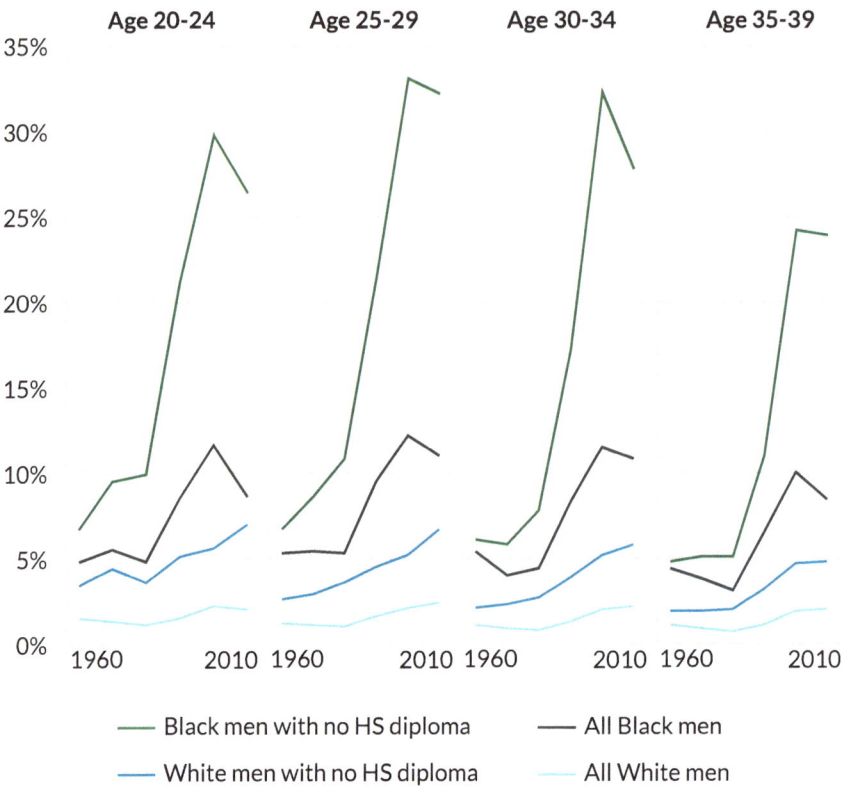

FIGURE C-9-2 Incarceration rates by race, age, and education from 1960 to 2010.
NOTES: Data represent the percentage of each group experiencing incarceration in a given year. Percentages were calculated using cohorts of births in 5-year increments. Data on incarceration come from 1960 to 2000 U.S. Census data and the 2010 American Community Survey from IPUMS.
SOURCE: Data from Neal and Rick (2014).

diversion and other alternatives to detention, as well as capping juvenile sentences, may have played a secondary role.

It is important to note that despite the decline in juvenile detention, youth are still incarcerated in the United States at rates far higher than in nearly all other countries (Nowak, 2019). Moreover, while for all young people involvement in the criminal justice system has fallen, Black, Latino and Native American youths are still significantly more likely than their White counterparts to be arrested, referred to court, and placed in out-of-home facilities after adjudication (Office of Juvenile Justice and Delinquency Prevention, 2022; see Figure C-9-3).

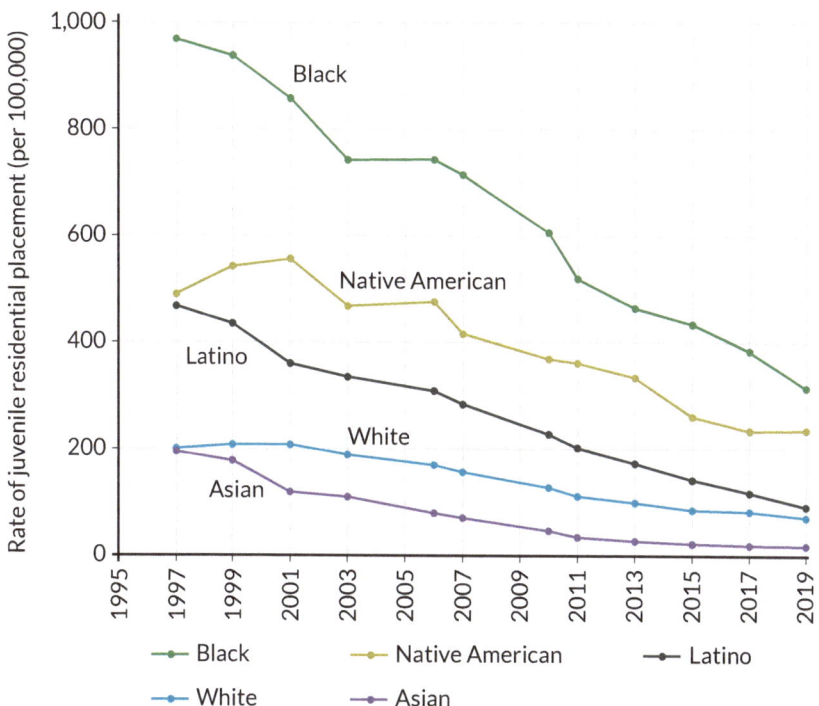

FIGURE C-9-3 Rate of juvenile confinement by race/ethnicity, 1997–2019.
SOURCE: Data from Office of Juvenile Justice and Delinquency Prevention Statistical Briefing Book. https://www.ojjdp.gov/ojstatbb/special_topics/ qa11801.asp?qaDate=2019

Disproportionate Impact on Communities of Color

The declines in crime experienced since the mid-1990s were felt most profoundly in poor communities and Black and Latino neighborhoods (Kneebone & Raphael, 2011). Cities with larger shares of households under the poverty line and of Black and Latino families experienced sharper declines in crime than did higher-income cities. This pattern is observed within cities as well; high-poverty, high-minority neighborhoods have experienced the sharpest declines in crime since the mid-1990s (Sharkey, 2018a). Individual victimization rates by income are not available, but rates by race can be found in the National Crime Victimization Survey. Between 1993 and 2013, the largest declines in violent and nonviolent victimization were experienced by Black and Latino individuals.

But declines in crime have also come at a cost to low-income communities. Incarceration rates tripled between 1980 and 2008, and the share of the adult population under criminal justice monitoring more generally (probation, parole, prison, or jail) also tripled, with the result that three percent of the adult population in 2013 was being monitored or supervised. It is therefore estimated that 9% of children born between 1999 and 2005 had a caregiver in prison at some point during their childhoods (Finlay et al., 2022). Policing has become more aggressive in many cities. While some policing tactics appear to have reduced crime, not all have had that effect. Policing tactics such as stop-and-frisk, for example, do not appear to have reduced crime in New York City; instead, it appears that they have reduced the educational attainment of young people most likely to be affected by frequent police stops (Bacher-Hicks & de la Campa, 2020; Cullen & Grawert, 2016).

Overall, the increase in criminal sanctioning in the United States has been borne largely by poor, Black, Latino, and Native American families. This has imposed substantial costs on poor families, causing an increase in household debt from fines (Harris et al., 2010) as well as a decline in earnings and household resources owing to incarceration (Comfort et al., 2016; Johnson, 2009; Mueller-Smith, 2015). Research has documented strong correlations between parental incarceration and children's problematic behavior and depression (Wakefield & Wildeman, 2013), leading to worse health, lower levels of education, and greater reliance on public assistance later in life (Miller & Barnes, 2015). Causal evidence on the intergenerational transmission of criminal justice involvement is mixed; some studies have found that children whose parents were incarcerated are more likely to be incarcerated themselves (Dobbie et al., 2018; Wildeman, 2020), while others have found that parental incarceration actually reduces the probability of child incarceration (Norris et al., 2021).

Underlying Causes

What's behind recent trends in crime and incarceration for adults and juveniles? The divergence in those trends beginning in the early to mid-1990s, as crime fell but incarceration continued to rise, suggests that the increase in incarceration is driven not by rising crime rates, but by changes in criminal justice policy. Specifically, increasing bail amounts, mandatory minimum sentencing, three-strikes laws, truth-in-sentencing laws, increased plea bargaining, and longer sentencing more generally have all played a role in increasing rates of incarceration. State and local expenditures on jails and corrections rose from $5 billion in 1977 to $30 billion in 2017, with an average annual cost per person in jail of $34,000 (Pew, 2021). Spending on jails as a percentage of local spending is uncorrelated with state crime rates.

While incarceration during the 1980s may have played an important role in reducing the crime that peaked in the early 1990s, research suggests that while crime rates also dropped during the period that followed, that cannot be attributed to the increased incarceration that occurred at the same time. Canada and Western European nations experienced similar declines in crime beginning in the mid-1990s without increases in incarceration, and California, forced to dramatically reduce the number of people imprisoned in the state, saw crime continue to fall (Sundt et al., 2016). In addition to the studies reviewed in the main text, research has identified other strategies to reduce neighborhood crime and violence:

- Mello (2018) reports that adding one police officer prevents four violent crimes and 15 property crimes.
- Reductions in lead pollution have been shown to have a causal impact on crime and disciplinary infractions in school (Aizer & Currie, 2019; Grönqvist et al., 2020; Reyes, 2007).
- Evidence on "proactive policing" methods like "focused deterrence" and "hot spots policing" is analyzed in Braga et al. (2019b); and a review of the cost-effectiveness of these and other tactics (like community policing) as well as negative evidence on "stop-and-frisk" can be found in the National Academies report on policing (National Academies, 2018).
- Braga et al. (2019a) argue that more effective and targeted policing could reduce gun violence and that more community policing might help repair frayed relationships between the police and residents of color in poor neighborhoods.
- Community efforts to reduce violence appear to be successful, according to Webster et al. (2012), who evaluated the Safe Streets program in Baltimore and showed the benefits of training local leaders to de-escalate situations where violence is likely.
- Safe lighting and environmental design has been shown to lower crime (Chalfin et al., 2021; Cozens et al., 2005).

Direct-Evidence Interventions

Reducing Juvenile Detention

The committee's policy idea to reduce most or all juvenile detentions and incarceration is based on several bodies of evidence. Most importantly, juvenile detention and incarceration, even for short periods of time and for both nonviolent and violent crimes, is likely to increase the intergenerational persistence of poverty. Detention and incarceration have been shown to reduce the likelihood that a young person will complete high school by about 10 percentage points and increase the likelihood of incarceration in adulthood (Aizer & Doyle, 2015; Baron et al., 2023). Additional evidence shows that youth build "criminal capital" when they are detained; that is, their arrests after detention or incarceration are influenced by the types of crime committed by the detained or incarcerated youth they interacted with (Bayer et al., 2009).

Furthermore, although impacts on public disorder are a very important issue, the committee knows of no strong research showing that the incarceration of juveniles for low-level offenses promotes public order. Causal studies show that the threat of juvenile detention or incarceration has little deterrent effect. Since more severe sanctions do not appear to significantly deter juvenile offending, it is likely that reducing reliance on prison for juveniles will not increase crime, but may well reduce it (Cullen et al., 2011; Lee & McCrary, 2017; Mulvey & Schubert, 2011).

It should also be noted that if incapacitation is the goal, there are many much cheaper ways to achieve it. Diversion programs for low-risk offenders in adult courts have been shown to reduce incarceration, increase future earnings, and reduce future recidivism (Mueller-Smith & Schnepel, 2021). These results are based on a sample of offenders over age 18, but roughly one-quarter of the sample is aged 18–22, and the impacts are largest for the youngest offenders. Nationally, 25% of juveniles are diverted. National Institute of Justice's Office of Justice Programs rates juvenile diversion programs as "promising" based on two meta-analyses of evaluation studies that find negative effects on reoffending, although one meta-analysis finds no results (Schwalbe et al., 2012; U.S. Department of Justice, 2015; Wilson & Hoge, 2013). The Adolescent Diversion Program has shown statistically significant reductions in youth reoffending over multiple replication studies (Smith et al., 2004). The program relies on community-based interventions with families and working with young people to identify their goals. Given the high numbers of juveniles detained or incarcerated for nonviolent offenses, there is scope for expanded diversion.

However, diversion for juveniles must accord with best practices for supporting young people who are diverted. According to Schlesinger (2018, p. 60), "current eligibility rules and program requirements often lead to the de facto exclusion of youth of color from formal diversion programs, while punitive responses to small rule violations produce sometimes shockingly low completion rates." High-needs youth, in particular, have struggled to complete diversion programs. Research suggests that diversion programs for youth should provide needed services in community and home-based settings free of charge and include only youth at high risk of detention or incarceration (and exclude low-risk youth who would otherwise be released on their own).

The Office of Juvenile Justice and Delinquency Prevention (OJJDP) provides grants to state and local agencies to support efforts to improve their juvenile justice system and support delinquency prevention programs. To receive grants, states must demonstrate that they are in compliance with the core requirements of the OJJDP, which include deinstitutionalizing status offenders, reducing racial/ethnic disparities, and removing or separating all juveniles from adults. However, funding for the OJJDP has declined significantly over time, from $565 million in 2002 to $360 million in 2022. With less funding available to states, but significant monitoring and compliance costs, some states have chosen to forgo OJJDP funding altogether. As of 2019, 48,000 youth were still detained, often for nonviolent offenses or before they had had a hearing, which suggests that there is room for additional declines that would be unlikely to jeopardize public safety. The reduction in OJJDP funding will probably stall progress in this regard. Eliminating the detention of juveniles committing status offenses, technical violations, public order offenses, and nonviolent offenses would reduce juvenile detention rates by 45% (for as many as 13,380 of the 27,635 youth currently in such facilities).[1]

The committee disagreed about the precise implications of its recommendation. It agreed that the evidence indicates positive impacts on juvenile offenders of moving from detention and incarceration to proven monitoring, supervision, service, and programing strategies, but disagreed about the potential for possible impacts on crime and disorder (McCarthy et al., 2016; Shem-Tov et al., 2022). Thus, most committee members believed that the above principle would eliminate *all* detention of juveniles for non-felony and nonviolent offenses (and most detention for felony offenses), while others believed that it would merely eliminate *most* such detention, and less for serious offending.

Reducing Offending Through Human Capital Investments Such as Becoming a Man (BAM)

The committee identifies funding BAM so that it can eventually serve more of the population of at-risk adolescent boys, which is estimated to range between 300,000 and 500,000 annually. This range is based on those at risk of not graduating from high school and/or of arrest. The number of male high school dropouts (excluding those who had obtained GEDs) as of 2018 was approximately 300,000, based on a male graduation rate of 82% (Reeves et al., 2021). Half a million male juveniles were arrested in 2019, the last full year before the onset of the COVID-19 pandemic (Puzzanchera, 2021).

Scaling the intervention to serve this population will likely be challenging, given the need to identify appropriate partners for implementation, and

---

[1] The remaining youth are in residential treatment (10,256), group homes (3,375), and adult prisons and jails (4,535; Sawyer, 2019).

must be done incrementally. It is important that funding be made available and provided gradually, as the program scales up appropriately over time.

Grants to Remediate Vacant Lots and Abandoned Homes

A possible grant program for neighborhood physical improvements would require cities to use funds to clean up, improve, and erect welcoming fencing around vacant lots or stabilize and treat the facades of abandoned or unsafe and deteriorating homes. Funds must be used in high-poverty (defined, for example, by a Census-based poverty rate of 20% or more) neighborhoods with above-city-average rates of violent crime. Jurisdictions would be allowed to partner with community-based organizations or provide grants for low-income property owners.

Grants to Community-Based Organizations

The American Rescue Plan Act (ARPA) allocated $350 billion to state, local, and tribal governments to support recovery from the global COVID-19 pandemic (U.S. Department of Treasury, 2023). Many cities have partnered with local organizations to address violence, but nonprofit growth in general (not just focused on violence) can decrease community violence (Sharkey et al., 2017). The National Council of Nonprofits has developed principles for distributing these funds, which include recommendations for appropriate (not prohibitive) application, monitoring, and reporting requirements that allow smaller organizations to compete. Existing ARPA money must be spent by 2024. Maintaining the level of funding to nonprofits achieved through ARPA would avoid a contraction of nonprofit capacity and a vacuum in services after this date.

Adopting Proven Policing Strategies

Although policing has been shown to lower crime, especially homicides, and can be an effective means of reducing premature death and victimization, any efforts to increase or enhance policing to reduce crime must consider the potential for strong negative impacts of aggressive policing and frequent stops and searches of low-income and particularly minority youth.

In the case of hiring additional police officers, the cost of each additional police officer in the United States is about $170,000 (in 2022 dollars; Chalfin & McCrary, 2018); every extra $1 billion spent will generate approximately 6,000 officers and save 600 lives (Chalfin et al., 2022), assuming that the crime-reducing returns to new officers do not diminish. Of course, the costs of policing vary greatly across geographic areas, so the homicide-prevention gains would also be greater in areas where the police cost less.

Reducing Firearms-Related Deaths Among Children and Youth

The rise in firearm-related injuries has occurred against a backdrop of loosened gun restrictions and increased gun ownership: Between 2007 and 2017, the number of guns owned in the United States increased by one-third and now stands at 393 million (Ingraham, 2018).

Indirect-Evidence Interventions

A number of interventions that may be promising avenues for increasing intergenerational mobility by reducing crime and the footprint of the criminal justice system still lack strong evidence of their effectiveness. One set of interventions addresses parental and caregiver interaction with the criminal justice system, which can negatively impact child development through multiple channels, including, but not limited to, a reduction in household resources available for child investment. Another set of interventions provides additional supports to at-risk youth that have the potential to reduce offending and/or the negative impact of interaction with the criminal justice system. More research is needed to establish whether these interventions can increase intergenerational mobility.

Reducing the Negative Impact of Caregiver Involvement in the Criminal Justice System

The high level of caregiver involvement in the criminal justice system among low-income and especially minority children has implications for child well-being. Not only does incarceration reduce earnings during and after detention, but also court fees and fines increase household debt, further reducing the resources available for investing in children. While there is no evidence estimating the direct impact of fines and fees on children, and evidence of the impact of parental incarceration on children is mixed, the committee considered policy proposals that have the potential to increase intergenerational mobility by reducing the disruptions in resources caused by parental involvement with the criminal justice system. Policy proposals explored:

- **Courts could consider the best interest of the child in pretrial detention and sentencing decisions.**[2] Illinois, for example, has recently

---

[2] Lerer (2013) makes the legal case for why and how such considerations can be codified in law.

amended its state law to mandate that courts consider how a decision to detain or incarcerate a defendant will affect a dependent child. This "Best Interests of the Child Act" became effective in 2020 and has not yet been evaluated.[3]

- **Courts could consider financial obligations to children in setting court fees and fines.** Correlational research shows that low-income defendants are less able to pay their court fines and fees (Bing et al., 2022; Sykes et al., 2022), and that legal financial obligations are associated with prolonged contact with the criminal justice system and an increased likelihood of technical violations for people on probation (Link, 2021; Pager et al., 2022; Ruhland et al., 2020). O'Neill et al. (2022) show that fines and fees are concentrated among residents of high-poverty and non-White neighborhoods, and that higher per-capita fines and fees in a neighborhood are associated with a higher neighborhood poverty rate in the future. Relief for parents with criminal legal debt would reduce families' financial stress and free up resources for investments in children.

Programs to Support At-Risk Youth: Mentorship, Community-Based Support, Restorative Justice, Reduction of Financial Hardship, Reduction in School Shootings

- **Choose to Change**[4] targets at-risk youth and provides them with community-based, individualized support as well as cognitive behavioral therapy to help them process trauma and develop healthy decision-making tools.
- **Mentoring.** Mentoring relationships provided through programs or occurring naturally have a well-established potential to help reduce delinquent behavior and juvenile justice system involvement among youth. A recent comprehensive review of mentoring programs found evidence of potential benefits, but no evidence yet of reducing juvenile justice system involvement (Hawkins et al., 2020).
- **Restorative justice in the juvenile justice system and schools.** Restorative justice is defined as a system of justice that focuses on the rehabilitation of offenders through reconciliation with victims and the community at large. Restorative justice has been implemented

---

[3] The law, Illinois Public Act 101-0471, can be found here: https://ilga.gov/legislation/publicacts/101/PDF/101-0471.pdf

[4] https://urbanlabs.uchicago.edu/attachments/dd47d0bf9f85c9543e871d03b25fa1dcc8ee779f/store/cf2bff02b6f54df79d84cd3c2b20d7bd0ec398cdd7a4de0744e6e8860d6f/Choose+to+Change+Research+Brief.pdf

within the criminal justice system and in school disciplinary settings (Shem-Tov et al., 2022).
- *Restorative justice in the criminal justice system.* Meta-reviews (Kimbrell et al., 2022; Wilson et al., 2017) of the evidence on the overall efficacy of restorative justice in the juvenile justice system concluded that overall, it appears to lead to a "moderate reduction in future delinquent behavior relative to more traditional juvenile court processing"; however, there are large variations depending on the type of study and setting. The most promising programs seem to be those that incorporate victim-offender conferencing, arbitration/mediation, and circle sentencing programs. It is important to note that not all restorative justice programs aim to reduce juvenile detention; for some, the program offers an opportunity to remove a conviction from a juvenile's record among those at no risk of detention. One such study is Make It Right, evaluated by a randomized controlled trial by Shem-Tov et al. (2022), which has been shown to reduce re-arrest after 6 months by 44% and after 4 years by 30%.
- *Restorative justice in schools.* Restorative justice is also being implemented in schools as an alternative to suspension, again with significant variation in effectiveness across programs and settings. A 2019 review (Fronius et al., 2019) of the evidence suggests that restorative justice does in fact dramatically reduce suspension (note that only one RCT was carried out [Augustine et al., 2018]). Few studies evaluate impacts on other domains.
- **Eliminating fines and fees for juveniles.** In 2016, Santa Clara County, California, spent nearly $450,000 to collect $400,000 in fines and fees assessed against juvenile defendants (Shapiro, 2019). In 2018, the State of California abolished all new juvenile fees (but not fines). Eliminating juvenile fines and fees has the potential to reduce the financial burden on low-income families (Chambers et al., 2021) and decrease recidivism. Given the high costs of collection, efforts are likely to be revenue-neutral in the short run and have the potential to lower costs in the long run if they reduce recidivism.
- **Reducing school shootings.** School shootings are the result of suicidal thoughts, despair, and access to guns, specifically assault weapons (Gius, 2017). Addressing mental health (see Chapter 5) and gun safety is key to reducing school shootings. Research is needed on the most effective ways to address both issues, and findings should be distributed widely to state and local governments.

APPENDIX C: CHAPTER 10
CHILD MALTREATMENT

This appendix presents details on the descriptive literatures on the causes and possible consequences of involvement in the child protective services (CPS).

Descriptive Studies of the Possible Consequences of CPS Involvement

Many, but not all, children who are maltreated are referred to CPS, also known as child welfare services. Font and Maguire-Jack (2020a) compared children who were reported to CPS—90% of whose families received Supplemental Nutrition Assistance Program (SNAP)—to children whose families received SNAP but were not reported to CPS. They excluded the relatively small subset of children who were reported to CPS and placed into foster care or group care. They found that children and youth reported to CPS had lower rates of high school graduation and employment, and higher rates of teen parenthood and incarceration, than youth without maltreatment allegations (see also Casanueva et al., 2014). Although correlational, their study confirms that low-income children involved with the child welfare system are at elevated risk of poor mobility-related outcomes in young adulthood, making them a group at high risk of intergenerational poverty. Using similar data and methods, Font et al. (2021) showed that child welfare involvement persists across generations.

Mental health is likely an important mechanism linking child maltreatment with intergenerational transmission of poverty (Chapter 5; Jones Harden & Slopen, 2022; Yoshikawa et al., 2012). Moreover, substantial literature links a child's history of maltreatment with mental health challenges when they are older (Edwards et al., 2003; Jaffee & Maikovich-Fong, 2013; Negriff, 2020; Southerland et al., 2009). For example, Jonson-Reid et al. (2009) found that, even after controlling for family poverty, maltreated children were more likely to receive mental health services than their nonmaltreated counterparts.

The research literature provides conflicting evidence on whether associations between maltreatment or child welfare involvement and both time in the system and later outcomes vary by race and ethnicity. In their review of outcomes for children in the child welfare system and differences by race, Barth et al. (2020, 2022) found that, once socioeconomic status and related risk factors are controlled, Black children's trajectories through the child welfare system are similar to those of other racial/ethnic groups. An exception is Black children's duration in foster care, which has been found to be about 25% longer than that of children from other groups, potentially attributable to their reduced likelihood of experiencing reunification and adoption as permanency outcomes (Wulczyn, 2020).

In a large study of children in Mississippi, Yoon et al. (2021) documented that children involved in the child welfare system had worse educational outcomes than those who were not, specifically with respect to grade retention and chronic absenteeism. Further, they found that Black male children who were involved in the child welfare system had worse educational outcomes than either White males or Black or White females who were involved in the system.

Mersky and Topitzes (2010) analyzed data from the Chicago Longitudinal Study, which included 1,539 racial/ethnic minority children (93% Black; 7% Latino) from economically disadvantaged backgrounds. They found that children with substantiated reports of maltreatment had an increased likelihood of adverse education and employment outcomes during early adulthood. Jonson-Reid et al. (2009) found that, even after controlling for family poverty, Black youth who were maltreated were less likely to have obtained mental health services than White youth who were maltreated, suggesting racial disparities in mental health service receipt that may have implications for intergenerational poverty among Black children.

Descriptive Studies of the Possible Consequences of Foster Care Placement

Foster Care

Research using the National Survey of Child and Adolescent Well-being to examine outcomes of young adults who had been in foster care as adolescents indicates that greater than 40% lived as adults in households with incomes below the poverty line, which exceeds the proportion of youth living in poverty in the general population (Administration for Children and Families, 2008). Further, while the authors found no differences in adult poverty by race and ethnicity, they did find that young adult females who had been in foster care were more likely to be living in poverty than males. On the other hand, employment levels (approximately 58% working full- or part-time) of young adults who had been in foster care were similar to those of the larger population of young adults.

A recent meta-analysis by Kennedy et al. (2022) found that associations between having been in foster care and lower employment and financial stability in adulthood in the descriptive literature tend to be larger for Black youth than for White youth, although the reverse is true for associations with poor mental health; associations between foster care and educational achievement tend not to differ by race.

In a study comparing economic outcomes for Black, White, Latino, and Native American youth who had been in foster care, which used data from the National Youth in Transition Database, Watt and Kim (2019) found more educational attainment but less employment among Black than White youth who had been in foster care. White and Latino youth had similar educational outcomes, while Native American youth displayed worse educational outcomes than youth from other racial/ethnic groups. Native American youth also exhibited a higher likelihood of homelessness and incarceration after emancipating from foster care than other racial/ethnic groups.

Kinship Care

Kinship care refers to foster care by a relative, such as a grandmother, aunt, or uncle. The correlational evidence on the long-term poverty-associated outcomes for youth who have experienced kinship care is limited and ambiguous. Some studies document increased mental health challenges (Bramlett et al., 2017; Rufa & Fowler, 2016), whereas others point to enhanced mental health outcomes (Ehrle & Geen, 2002; Gleeson, 2012; Winokur et al., 2018). Similarly, some research suggests that kinship care is associated with criminal justice involvement for youth (e.g., Ryan et al., 2010), while other research documents that kinship care may protect youth from criminal justice involvement (e.g., Cutuli et al., 2016; Winokur et al., 2008). Noteworthy in this literature is that Black youth who have been in foster care have a much higher likelihood of involvement in the criminal justice system than White youth in similar circumstances (Barth et al., 2010; Boyd, 2014; DeFina & Hannon, 2013; Jonson-Reid et al., 2009; Ryan et al., 2016; Watt & Kim, 2019). And while Black and White male youth who had been in kinship care have been found to be at increased risk of delinquency, Latino males in kinship care were at reduced risk of delinquency (Ryan et al., 2010).

Apart from criminal justice involvement, some studies suggest that placement in kinship care (rather than placement with unrelated foster parents) confers benefits for children from racial/ethnic minority backgrounds that include increased placement stability, safety, and child well-being (Gleeson, 2012; Winokur et al., 2018). At the same time, however, other research suggests that the lower socioeconomic status of kinship care parents (e.g., poverty, food insecurity, reduced receipt of foster care payments; Fuller-Thomson & Minkler, 2000; Miller-Cribbs & Farber, 2008; Taylor et al., 2020) potentially contributes to the poverty rates found among young adults who have been in the foster/kinship care system (Harris & Skyles, 2008; Miller-Cribbs & Farber, 2008). Research is clearly needed in these areas, particularly regarding the family factors (e.g., poverty, service utilization) that contribute to these conflicting outcomes (Coleman & Wu, 2016; Xu et al., 2021).

Background Sections for Interventions

Economic Support Policies

Theory suggests that parental income may impact maltreatment and child welfare involvement through the two primary mechanisms discussed in Chapter 6. The resource and investment model, which is rooted in economic theory (Becker, 1991), emphasizes the detrimental consequences of material resource deprivation. Such limited resources may directly constitute child neglect or may produce circumstances that prompt child welfare involvement, such as insufficient resources to provide safe child care. The family stress model described in Chapter 6 offers psychological and sociological perspectives (Elder, 1974; Masarick & Conger, 2017), highlighting the effects of stress produced by economic deprivation on parental and child behavior and mental health. Family stress may lead to parental maltreatment behaviors or produce mental health challenges that pose maltreatment risks or prompt child welfare involvement.

Evidence presented in the text on the impacts of economic support policies on child maltreatment was limited to areas with the strongest evidence—a child support experiment, the Earned Income Tax Credit program, Medicaid, and food and nutrition programs. Here we review evidence based on other economic support programs.

Studies of the Aid to Families with Dependent Children (AFDC) and Temporary Assistance to Needy Families Programs

A handful of studies (and many correlational studies, which are not reviewed here) have assessed the effects of the AFDC and Temporary Assistance to Needy Families (TANF) programs on child maltreatment. (Welfare reforms enacted in 1996 replaced the AFDC program with the TANF program.) For example, Paxson and Waldfogel (2002) leveraged state-level variation in combined AFDC/TANF and food stamps benefit generosity from 1990–1996, as well as a host of other state-level factors, to examine the association of benefit generosity with child maltreatment. They found that a 10% increase in a state's maximum combined benefit was associated with a 24% reduction in its foster care caseload. However, they found nonsignificant associations of benefit generosity with both child maltreatment reports and substantiations.

Some AFDC-related studies have found welfare-related work requirements to be associated with fewer physical abuse investigations and foster care entries, work incentives to be associated with reductions in overall and neglect substantiations, and time limits to be associated with increased substantiations. Ginther and Johnson-Motoyama (2017) used state-level variation data from 2004 to 2015 to examine the effects of TANF behavioral requirements on child welfare caseloads. They found that severe sanctions (e.g., loss of benefits if a household does not meet work requirements) are associated with greater maltreatment substantiations and foster care caseloads, and that time limits of less than 5 years are associated with greater substantiations. Consistent with this finding, Slack et al. (2007), using individual-level data from Illinois and fixed-effects models, found that welfare sanctions without income supplementation from other sources are associated with increased risk of a child neglect investigation.

Paxson and Waldfogel (2003) examined the impacts of the 1996 welfare reform on child maltreatment caseloads using data from 1990 to 1998. They found consistent evidence that more generous benefits are associated with large reductions in the foster care caseload, as well as some evidence that strict time limits and sanction policies are associated with greater rates of maltreatment substantiation.

Finally, in an individual-level analysis of Delaware's randomized welfare reform experiment, in which families were assigned to either the AFDC program (unconditional cash benefit for families with children) or the TANF-like welfare program that included work requirements, a family cap, and a 24-month time limit on cash benefits, Fein and Lee (2003) found that participants assigned to the TANF-like program were more likely to experience sanctions, have their case closed due to sanctions, and reach the 24-month time limit. This group also experienced a large increase (on the order of 50%) in substantiated child neglect reports. Notably, however, this study did not directly examine the effect of income or benefit level on child maltreatment.

Minimum Wage Policy

The committee identified two studies that examined the link between minimum wage policy and child maltreatment. Raissian and Bullinger's (2017) state-level regression analyses of change over time in the state minimum wage and in child maltreatment rates found that a $1 per hour increase in the state minimum wage (an increase of 16% on average) is associated with a 9% decrease in child maltreatment investigation rates (marginally significant at $p < 0.10$) and a significant decrease in neglect investigations of 10%. However, Schneider et al. (2022), using survey data from the Fragile Families and Child Wellbeing Study and behaviorally approximated measures of child maltreatment (parental physical aggression, psychological aggression, physical neglect, supervisory neglect) to examine the effect of a $1 per hour increase in the local (city) minimum wage, found inconsistent results in terms of magnitude, direction, and significance of the estimates depending on model specification (lagged dependent variable, city fixed effects, individual fixed effects). While the two studies provide inconsistent evidence regarding the relation between the minimum wage and child maltreatment, Raissian and Bullinger's findings employ a stronger and more representative approach and also analyze the impact of the minimum wage on child maltreatment rates rather than solely on self-reported parental behaviors.

Employment Conditions

Some rigorous evidence points to the importance of contextual economic factors in driving maltreatment and child welfare involvement. For instance, Raissian (2015) used variation in unemployment rates caused by the economic recessions and recoveries in the United States between 2000 and 2010 to examine the effects of county-level unemployment on county-level maltreatment and child welfare involvement rates. She found that a 1 percentage point higher unemployment rate was associated with a reduction in child maltreatment reports of just over 4%. She argues that these results may reflect unemployed parents' increased ability to invest time in caring for children and to the context and stress of low-wage work. Additionally, Lindo et al. (2018) found differences in the relationships between county-level employment factors, including employment rates and mass layoff rates, and child maltreatment rates, suggesting that increased unemployment among men predicts greater child maltreatment while increased unemployment among women predicts lower rates of child maltreatment. Some data limitations, particularly around the sex of child maltreatment perpetrators, which is frequently missing in available data, complicate the interpretation of such findings.

Early Home Visiting Programs

As reviewed in the appendix to Chapter 4, early home visiting programs have gained popularity as a possible means of family intervention. It is important to recognize, however, that individual programs differ substantially in terms of target population, program quality and intensity, staff qualifications, and curriculum. As such, home visiting should be viewed as a catch-all category of intervention, and it is not possible to determine whether home visiting, in general, serves to reduce child maltreatment. Rather the focus must be on the effects of specific programs.

The Chapter 4 review reached mixed conclusion regarding the overall efficacy of these programs. Here the focus is on their possible impacts on child maltreatment. Two recent reviews of home visitation programs (Duffee et al., 2017; Sama-Miller et al., 2019) and three recent meta-analyses (Casillas et al., 2016; Gubbels et al., 2021; van der Put, 2017) yield several general conclusions. First, eight early home visiting programs have demonstrated meaningful reductions in child maltreatment through a rigorous randomized evaluation in at least one sample. These include Child First, Early Head Start Home Visiting, Early Start (New Zealand), Health Access Nurturing Development Services (HANDS), Healthy Families America, Nurse-Family Partnership, Parents as Teachers, and SafeCare Augmented. Second, average effect sizes are relatively modest. The mean effect sizes estimated in recent meta-analyses are 0.14^1 (Gubbels et al., 2021; program range: 0.01–0.68), 0.21 (van der Put, 2017; program range: 0.07–0.34), and 0.22 (Castillas et al., 2016; no program range provided). Third, effects tend to be larger for programs that serve a larger proportion of racial/ethnic minority families (Gubbels et al., 2021). Fourth, replication is relatively uncommon: many programs have demonstrated positive effects in some sites or samples that have not been replicated in other sites or samples (Sama-Miller et al., 2019). Note, also, that in addition to the programs included in these reviews, a recent randomized evaluation of the Family Connects universal (communitywide) nurse home visiting program for newborns in Durham County, North Carolina, using a sample of approximately 5,000 families randomized at birth to program eligibility or a status quo control group, found that treatment-group children had 39% fewer child welfare investigations than control-group children (Goodman et al., 2021).

These optimistic findings are not consistent with those from the rigorous U.S. HomeVee review of the effects of early home visiting models. The HomeVee review focuses on substantiated reports of child maltreatment (in contrast with other evaluations that have a lower bar for maltreatment measures), child welfare measures such as custody loss and placement outside the home, health care encounters that may occur specifically as a result of child maltreatment, such as treatment for injuries or ingestions, and indicators of child maltreatment on the Conflict Tactics Scale-Parent Child measure.[2] Of particular note, unsubstantiated child maltreatment investigations were excluded as a potential outcome. Evaluations from 10

---

[1] If the rate of child maltreatment reports in the comparison group is 15%, then an effect size of 0.14 translates into a 10% rate (a 5 percentage point reduction) for the group receiving home visitation services.

[2] For more information see https://homvee.acf.hhs.gov/outcomes/reductions%20in%20child%20maltreatment/In%20Brief

of the program models provided information on impacts of at least some of these elements of child maltreatment.[3]

In contrast to results from the published reviews and meta-analyses cited above, the HOMVEE review found more favorable than null effects in only 2 of the 10 cases—Early Start (New Zealand) and the HANDS Program. For the most frequently evaluated programs, the number of favorable and null results were 20/188 for Healthy Families America (HFA)® and 7/19 for the Nurse-Family Partnership (NFP)® program.

Early Childhood Education and Care Programs

A relatively small literature has rigorously examined whether early childhood education and care program participation—including child care subsidies, prekindergarten programs, Early Head Start, and Head Start—may serve to reduce child maltreatment.[4] Such programs have the potential to reduce maltreatment by providing access to consistent child care when parents may be working, reducing the time children spend with (potentially maltreating) parents (both of which may reduce parental stress) and, in some cases, intervening directly with parents around developmentally appropriate expectations and parenting strategies. At the same time, however, teachers and child care providers are mandatory child maltreatment reporters, such that exposure thereto has the potential to increase reporting.

On the whole, findings from studies examining the impact of such programs on child maltreatment have been inconsistent. Pac (2021), for example, in a state-level study leveraging exogenous variation across states and over time in access to early childhood education and care programs (child care subsidies, Head Start, Early Head Start, state prekindergarten programs) on child welfare investigations, found little evidence of the effects of these programs on investigations overall or for abuse or neglect. Nevertheless, correlational studies of several specific programs have yielded

---

[3] The programs were Early Head Start Home-Based Option, Early Start (New Zealand), HANDS Program, HFA®, Healthy Steps (National Evaluation 1996 Protocol), Maternal Infant Health Program (MIHP), NFP®, Parents as Teachers®, Promoting First Relationships® - Home Visiting Intervention Model, and SafeCare Augmented.

[4] There are also a handful of descriptive studies in this area. For example, Maguire-Jack et al. (2019) found an association of child care subsidy receipt with decreased supervisory (but not other forms of) neglect. Klein et al., (2017), using a sample of child welfare-involved children, find that whereas participation in an early childhood education and care program, in general, was not associated with the probability of a subsequent foster care placement, Head Start participating children were 93% less likely to be placed in foster care, and children experiencing multiple types of child care were seven times more likely to be placed in foster care, than children who were not participating in an early childhood education and care program. Ha et al. (2015) find associations of unstable child care arrangements with self-reported measures of maltreatment.

promising results. Zhai et al. (2013), for instance, used data from the Fragile Families and Child Wellbeing Study and propensity score matching to compare child maltreatment outcomes for children participating in Head Start with those for otherwise similar children. They found that Head Start-participating children were 45% less likely than those in parental care to be investigated for child maltreatment by age 5 but that the likelihood of investigation did not differ between children enrolled in Head Start and those enrolled in other (nonparental) forms of care.

The most rigorous evidence to date comes from evaluations of Early Head Start and the Chicago Parent-Child Centers early education programs. Green et al. (2014) linked child-level data on a subsample of children participating in the randomized Early Head Start Evaluation (those in seven of 17 sites) to state child welfare administrative data. Initial analyses found that, between ages 5 and 9, Early Head Start participants were approximately 36% less likely than control group members to have been involved with the child welfare system and had 38% fewer total child welfare system encounters. These differences were largely driven by reductions in physical and sexual abuse investigations, whereas neglect investigations were more likely among the treatment than control group. Effects were uneven across sites, however, perhaps reflecting differences in program structure or geographic factors. Moreover, follow-up analyses at age 15 found no treatment-control group differences in child welfare investigations, substantiations, or foster care placements, perhaps reflecting fade-out of the initial effects.

The randomized evaluation of the Chicago Parent-Child Centers program (Reynolds & Robertson, 2003) demonstrated long-term reductions in child welfare involvement. The Parent Child Centers provide both preschool and comprehensive family support to low-income families for up to 6 years. The evaluation found that between birth and age 17, participants were about 50% less likely to experience a child maltreatment investigation or substantiation than control group members, with similar effects for abuse and neglect. The study authors note that key elements of the program's effectiveness include a focus on literacy, intensive parental involvement and well-trained staff. Notably, some 93% of the sample in the Chicago Parent-Child Center evaluation were Black children.

APPENDIX C: CHAPTER 11
RESEARCH AND DATA NEEDS FOR UNDERSTANDING AND AMELIORATING INTERGENERATIONAL POVERTY

This appendix includes the following: (a) a listing of all of the committee's conclusions about drivers of intergenerational poverty in Chapters 2-10, organized by chapter; (b) a listing of the committee's conclusions about research and data needs in Chapter 11; Table C-11-1, which lists tax return data available to the Census Bureau and not available but needed for linkage for statistical purposes, including research; and (c) Table C-11-2, which lists program records of nontaxable benefits for accurate measurement of family income over time available to the Census Bureau and not available but needed. The committee's list of program and policy ideas, supported by direct evidence, for interventions to reduce intergenerational poverty is provided in Table 11-1 in the body of Chapter 11.

Report Conclusions About Drivers of Intergenerational Poverty

Chapter 2: A Demographic Portrait of Intergenerational Poverty

Conclusion 2-1: As measured by household income, rates of intergenerational persistence in low-income status in the United States differ starkly by race/ethnicity. The lowest rates are found for Asian children, followed by White and Latino children. In contrast, persistence rates are very high for Black and Native American children. When adult economic success is measured using individual earnings rather than household income, mobility patterns are generally similar. Black women who grew up in low-income households are an exception; their earnings in adulthood are just as high, on average, as those of White women who grew up in similar economic circumstances. This reflects the greater likelihood that they are the primary earners in their families.

Conclusion 2-2: Racial/ethnic disparities are an enduring feature of the intergenerational trajectories of children, with Black and Native American children experiencing much less upward mobility than White children growing up in the same economic circumstances.

Conclusion 2-3: Children of immigrants from almost every country of origin—rich and poor nations alike—experience greater intergenerational mobility than children of U.S.-born parents. This immigrant advantage is larger for children from lower-income households, and to a large extent it reflects the fact that immigrants are more likely to *settle in areas that offer their children better opportunities for upward mobility.*

Conclusion 2-4: Children's chances of growing up and escaping low-income status vary substantially depending on where they live. At both a broad regional level and within community boundaries, there are areas where low-income children tend to grow up and join the middle class, as well as areas where generations are more likely to remain mired in poverty. The spatial patterns of economic mobility vary by racial/ethnic group; nonetheless, disparities in economic mobility between Black and White children persist even within neighborhoods.

Conclusion 2-5: After declining over the past 75 years, the fraction of children doing better than their parents is now lower in the United States than in most other industrialized countries. The most likely cause is that gains from economic growth have been disproportionately enjoyed by higher-income families, which has made it even more difficult for those at the bottom rungs of the income distribution to work their way up.

Chapter 3: Racial Disparities in Intergenerational Poverty

Conclusion 3-1: The challenges that Black and Native American families face in propelling their children into socioeconomic security result from contemporary and historical disparities, discrimination, and structural racism. Behaviors and choices can also have major causal impacts on intergenerational mobility. Many factors influence the behaviors and choices of Black and Native Americans, including the experiences of historical violence, oppression, and marginalization manifested through mechanisms of contemporary structural racism. These factors are crucial in shaping the relevant determinants of poverty over generations.

Chapter 4: Children's Education

Conclusion 4-1: By imparting skills and other capacities valued by employers, the education system is a key driver of upward intergenerational mobility for low-income children. Large gaps in school achievement and completed schooling persist across socioeconomic, racial, and ethnic subgroups, pose a key challenge for policy makers seeking to reduce intergenerational poverty, and underscore the importance of education-related interventions.

Conclusion 4-2: The vast U.S. education system is a potentially important factor in enabling individuals to escape from poverty. However, it fails to equalize educational opportunities for students across socioeconomic and racial/ethnic groups. Research points to many possible ways to improve the quality of educational experiences offered to students in K–12 and postsecondary school settings, to create high-quality job training programs, and to prepare young people for the labor market.

Chapter 5: Child and Maternal Health

Conclusion 5-1: Improving the health of children experiencing poverty has been shown to improve economic status in adulthood as measured by future educational attainment, employment, earnings, and reduced reliance on public assistance. Two important mechanisms include access to family planning services and health insurance coverage in pregnancy and childhood, both of which are key to improving the short- and long-term health and economic outcomes of children. Yet many low-income families are still without health insurance coverage or access to family planning services. This is due in part to administrative barriers that reduce child Medicaid enrollment, the fact that Medicaid coverage for pregnancy often ends 2 months post-partum, an Indian Health Service that serves only half the eligible population, and declines in funding for Title X over time. For access to mental health, additional barriers include lack of providers.

Conclusion 5-2: A child's environment (pollution, stress, and violence) exerts a strong influence on child health and development, with long-term economic consequences. Federal regulation of pollution has led to significant improvements in infant and child health and, ultimately, adult income. Due in large part to federal action, disparities in exposure to pollution by income, race, and ethnicity have declined significantly over time. While child mortality has been falling over time, firearm-related violence is on the rise and is now the leading cause of death among all children in the United States, with significant disparities by income, race, and ethnicity. Direct exposure to violence or victimization resulting in premature death and disability, as well as indirect exposure resulting in increased stress, anxiety, and depression with long-term consequences, both contribute to the intergenerational persistence of poverty.

Conclusion 5-3: Today, children living in poverty are still more likely to reside in households that experience food and nutrition insecurity than their better-off counterparts. Evidence from the introduction of the Supplemental Nutrition Assistance Program program in the 1960s and 1970s suggests that food supplements for children in low-income families, both in utero and during childhood, can contribute to intergenerational mobility, improving child health and ultimately future adult health and earnings. Evidence on the impact of SNAP from a more recent period shows similar effects on child health, at least in the short to medium term, suggesting that long-term outcomes of enhancing child nutrition today may be similarly effective in promoting intergenerational mobility. Barriers to take-up in Special Supplemental Nutrition Program for Women, Infants, and Children and reduced eligibility among immigrant families limit the ability of children in the United States to benefit from federal nutrition programs.

Chapter 6: Children's Family Income, Wealth, and Parental Employment

Conclusion 6-1: When tax credits, Supplemental Nutrition Assistance Program benefits, and other noncash sources are counted as part of income, the family incomes of children on the bottom rungs of the income distribution have nearly doubled over the past 40 years, and rates of child poverty have been cut in half. The family incomes of children on the middle rungs have grown a bit faster, while those of children on the top rungs have grown much faster. Child poverty in the United States is considerably higher than in other Anglophone countries when poverty is measured by relative income position.

Conclusion 6-2: Low wages among less-educated workers (including lower-skilled workers who are parents) over the last several decades in the United States can be attributed largely to three factors: competitive market forces, such as technological change and globalization, which have increased skill requirements for middle-class jobs; structural problems, as limited information for employees and the costs associated with changing jobs have strengthened the bargaining power of employers and reduced the power of employees; and weakening laws and institutions, such as federal minimum wages and unionization.

Conclusion 6-3: Earnings and employment gaps by gender, especially among less-educated women, can probably be attributed in part to difficulties securing affordable and high-quality child care. Gaps by race, especially between Black and other groups of men, reflect differences in skill and experience, but also reflect discrimination and other barriers to employment. Discriminatory barriers appear to be especially severe for previously incarcerated men, particularly Black men.

Conclusion 6-4: Evidence suggests that income transfer programs during childhood and adolescence have the potential to improve children's educational and labor market attainment, as well as their physical health, in adulthood. Studies examining policy changes over the past 30 years provide the strongest evidence for intergenerational impacts of expansions of the Earned Income Tax Credit, which increases both employment and income.

Conclusion 6-5: Higher parental earnings and employment among low-income families can potentially reduce intergenerational poverty by raising family income, increasing access to the Earned Income Tax Credit and other safety-net benefits, and—at both the family and neighborhood levels—providing positive role models and access to good jobs through social networks. Interventions such as the EITC that promote employment and increase income improve children's long-run outcomes; interventions that promote employment in the absence of increased income do not appear to improve child outcomes; and evidence on whether income supplementation alone improves long-term child outcomes is inconclusive, with some studies showing positive effects and others showing no improvement.

Conclusion 6-6: Controlling for income, family wealth is strongly correlated with children's adult outcomes. There is mixed evidence on the causal impact of wealth transfers on children's long-run outcomes. Black families, having significantly less wealth than White families, are more likely to be both income- and wealth-poor, and more likely to experience downward intergenerational wealth mobility. No causal studies have examined differential wealth impacts by race.

Chapter 7: Children's Family Structure

Conclusion 7-1: Single-parent families have become much more prevalent over the past 50 years, though largely among parents who lack community college or 4-year college degrees. Rising rates of incarceration account for some but not most of these trends. There is a strong association between growing up in a single-parent family and low-income status in adulthood. Evidence on causal links between growing up in a single-parent family and being poor as an adult is strongly suggestive.

Conclusion 7-2: While it appears that married, two-parent family structures may, in fact, reduce intergenerational poverty, we lack direct evidence of policies and programs that are capable of promoting such structures.

Chapter 8: Children's Housing and Neighborhood Environments

Conclusion 8-1: The evidence on the effects of housing on intergenerational poverty is nearly all correlational or drawn from longitudinal panel surveys. The most consistent correlational evidence is on the effects of housing quality on children's short-term outcomes, with the strongest evidence on the long-term effects of lead exposure. There is also correlational evidence on the negative effects of homelessness, overcrowding, residential mobility, and very low or high housing costs on children's short and long-term outcomes.

Conclusion 8-2: Strong evidence shows improvements in low-income children's long-term economic, educational, and health outcomes when they move to less disadvantaged neighborhoods. Less is known regarding which characteristics of neighborhoods foster upward mobility.

Chapter 9: Neighborhood Crime and the Criminal Justice System

Conclusion 9-1: Crime victimization and exposure have negative consequences for children's development and long-term economic outcomes. Gun violence is now the leading cause of death among American children. Low-income, Black, and Native American youth are more likely to have these exposures. Rigorous research shows that neighborhood violent crime can be reduced through community investments and engagement, certain kinds of policing, and gun safety regulations.

Conclusion 9-2: While reductions in crime and victimization clearly benefit children, some efforts to reduce crime also have the potential to harm them. Aggressive policing has been linked to worse educational outcomes for youth, especially Black and Latino youth. Juvenile detention lowers the rate of high school completion and increases the likelihood of incarceration in adulthood. Declines in juvenile offending, stemming in part from increased investment in children's education and health, have lowered juvenile detention rates, although significant disparities by race and income remain. Finally, the rise in adult incarceration has increased the number of low-income children with parents/caregivers under supervision, reducing household earnings and increasing household debt. As a result, fewer resources are available to invest in children.

Chapter 10: Child Maltreatment

Conclusion 10-1: Children who have been maltreated and (or) involved with child welfare are at elevated risk of intergenerational poverty.

APPENDIX C   405

However, high-quality research provides mixed evidence on the effects of foster care (occurring in only 3% of all child welfare cases) on subsequent outcomes in adolescence and adulthood and almost no evidence regarding the impact of child protective services more generally.

Conclusion 10-2: *Causal evidence on factors leading to maltreatment and child welfare involvement is limited, although most evidence points to household economic hardship as elevating the risk of child welfare involvement and to income support and income-support policies reducing risk for child welfare involvement. Evidence on the likely favorable impacts of Medicaid and food and nutrition program eligibility is also relatively strong.*

Chapter 11: Research and Data Needs for Understanding and Ameliorating Intergenerational Poverty

Conclusion 11-1: *In many domains, such as education, there is a lack of strong causal evidence about the effects of policies and programs on intergenerational poverty at the needed scale. Sometimes this is because careful research has failed to establish long-term effects. More often, the issue is a lack of data that would support estimates of long-run program impacts.*

Conclusion 11-2: *For many reasons, it is difficult to conduct research on intergenerational poverty and effective policies and programs to reduce it. Owing to the scale of effort required, it is suggested that funding organizations (public and private) consider joint grantmaking and the adoption of the following funding principles and research best practices to maximize the likelihood of achieving valid results:*
- *Funding principles: (a) prioritize strong research designs that provide causal estimates of program impacts, (b) set aside funding, not only for rigorous, small-scale experiments, but also for replications and long-term follow-ups of promising programs, and (c) fund research arms for specific communities that are at highest risk of intergenerational poverty (e.g., American Indians on tribal lands, rural Black people).*
- *Evaluation research can often be enhanced by (a) the use of mixed research methods (qualitative, quantitative including rigorous controlled experiments) to ensure to the extent possible that all relevant attitudes, behaviors, and outcomes are addressed; (b) multidisciplinary and diverse research and implementation teams to facilitate communication with the communities being studied and ensure that experiments include*

important control variables; and (c) the incorporation of community input through long-term, two-way dialogue to gain informed participation of community members throughout the life of a study and to tailor the research design for maximum effectiveness in the particular setting.

Conclusion 11-3: Existing census, survey, and administrative data linked for families over time and across subject domains—income, wealth, demographics, health, education, and others—can facilitate cost-effective research and evidence building on intergenerational poverty and socioeconomic mobility, looking both backward and forward in time. The research and policy analysis community needs timely, cost-efficient access to linked datasets with appropriate confidentiality protection.

Conclusion 11-4: At present, data for studying intergenerational poverty and related topics are controlled by a variety of federal and state agencies and are difficult to link or use for research or policy evaluation. Recent developments designed to ameliorate this situation include the Foundations for Evidence-based Policymaking Act of 2018, which presumes access to federal data by statistical agencies for evidence-building and calls for a streamlined process for researcher access to such data; supportive reports of the Commission on Evidence-based Policymaking and other organizations; and innovative projects at the Census Bureau and other agencies aimed at building linked datasets.

Conclusion 11-5: Significant challenges remain for access to linked datasets for analysis of intergenerational poverty and related topics. They include technical issues related to constructing and evaluating linked datasets; technical and policy issues regarding new methods of privacy protection and their effects on data accuracy; making access feasible in terms of cost, timeliness, and adequate budgets for the agencies linking the data; and legal barriers (e.g., research and evaluation must be justified in terms of agency benefits).

TABLE C-11-1 Internal Revenue Service (IRS)/Social Security Administration (SSA) income tax data for accurate measurement of family income over time: items available to the Census Bureau and additional items needed for data linkage

IRS or SSA Form/ Years Covered	Items Currently Available to Census Bureau	Additional Data Elements Needed
IRS W-2 Forms (feed into SSA Detailed Earnings Record [DER]—see below), 1999–present	Wages, tips and other compensation; Social Security wages; Deferred wages—2005 to present	Information back to 1999 (from IRS) and 1978 (from SSA); employee deductions (e.g., for health insurance); employer contributions to health insurance; other employer benefits (e.g., moving expenses)
SSA DER, 1978–present	Wages and salaries, including deferred wage contributions to 401(k), 403(b), 408(k), 457(b), and 501(c) plans Self-employment earnings (sole proprietor/ independent contractor, covered earnings only)	Information needed for the Current Population Survey Annual Social and Economic Supplement (CPS ASEC) for 1980, 1992, 1993, 1995; for the American Community Survey for 2005–2018; for the Survey of Income and Program Participation (SIPP) for 1985–1989; for the decennial census for 1980–2020
IRS 1040 Form, 1999–present	Marital status Number/type of exemptions Wage and salary income (taxable) Dividend income Interest income Gross rent and royalty income (no expenses) *Total* of wages, interest, dividends, alimony, business income, pensions and annuities, rents and royalties, farm income, unemployment compensation, and total Social Security benefits Adjusted gross income Number of Earned Income Tax Credit-qualifying children Whether filed Schedules, A, C, D, E, F, or self employment (SE) or Form 8814 (children's income)—2000–present	Rental expenses Unemployment compensation Pensions and annuities Capital gains/losses Deductions Credits Total tax owed Occupation (text field)
IRS 1040 Form, Schedule SE, 1999–present	Net earnings from farming Net earnings from nonfarming activities Taxable self-employment	

(continued)

TABLE C-11-1 Continued

IRS or SSA Form/ Years Covered	Items Currently Available to Census Bureau	Additional Data Elements Needed
IRS 1099 Forms, 1999 (or year form initiated)–present	Retirement, disability, survivors (except Social Security, Veterans Administration) (1099-R)—limited information Miscellaneous—receipt but not amounts	Capital gains (1099-B) Dividends (1099-DIV) Government payments (e.g., state tax refunds) (1099-G) Interest (1099-INT) Credit card and 3rd party network transactions (1099-K) Miscellaneous (1099-MISC) Tax-deferred educational accounts spending (529, Coverdell) (1099-Q) Retirement, disability, survivors (1099-R)—additional information Unemployment compensation (1099-U) 1098-T (educational financial aid)
IRS—Other Common Forms	Not available	Form 1098 (mortgage interest payments) Form 5498 (Individual Retirement Account contributions)
SSA Payment History Update System	Social Security Payments (for use in CPS ASEC and SIPP only)	Approval for use in all surveys and linkage projects
SSA Supplemental Security Income (SSI) Record	SSI payments (for use in CPS ASEC and SIPP only—not taxable, so not on any IRS form)	Approval for use in all surveys and linkage projects

SOURCE: Bee and Rothbaum (2019, Table 1) for items available to the Census Bureau (see also Code of Federal Regulations, Title 26, Chapter F, Section 301.6103(j)(1)); the committee determined the need for additional items.

TABLE C-11-2 Nontaxable benefit records for accurate measurement of family income over time: Records available to the Census Bureau and additional records needed for data linkage

Program—Custodian	Currently Available to Census Bureau	Additional Records Needed
Public Assistance—States	Some states, some cash assistance	All states, all types of cash assistance
Veteran's Benefits—Veterans Administration	Some benefit data available for limited uses	All benefit data for all approved linkage projects
Supplemental Nutrition Assistance Program—States	Available for some states for some years	All states, all years
Women, Infant, and Children Supplemental Nutrition Program—States	Available for some states for some years	All states, all years
National School Lunch Program—States	Not available	All states, all years
Low Income Home Energy Assistance Program—States	1 state for some years	All states, all years
Medicare/Medicaid—Department of Health and Human Services/Centers for Medicare & Medicaid Services	Available	
Housing Assistance—Department of Housing and Urban Development	Some housing programs available	All programs
Educational Loans—Department of Education	Not available	National Student Loan Data System information

SOURCE: Bee and Rothbaum (2019, Table 1) for records available to the Census Bureau; the committee determined the need for additional records.

References

Aarland, K., Santiago, A. M., Galster, G. C., & Nordvik, V. (2021). Childhood housing tenure and young adult educational outcomes: Evidence from sibling comparisons in Norway. *Journal of Housing Economics, 54*, 101772.

Aaronson, D., Hartley, D., & Mazumder, B. (2021a). The effects of the 1930s HOLC "redlining" maps. *American Economic Journal: Economic Policy, 13*(4), 355–392.

Aaronson, D., Faber, J., Hartley, D., Mazumder, B., & Sharkey, P. (2021b). The long-run effects of the 1930s HOLC "redlining" maps on place-based measures of economic opportunity and socioeconomic success. *Regional Science and Urban Economics, 86*, 103622.

Aaronson, D., French, E., Sorkin, I., & To, T. (2018). Industry dynamics and the minimum wage: A putty-clay approach. *International Economic Review, 59*(1), 51–84.

Abbott, E. (1905). The wages of unskilled labor in the United States 1850–1900. *Journal of Political Economy, 13*(3), 321–367.

Abdulkadiroğlu, A., Angrist, J. D., Dynarski, S. M., Kane, T. J., & Pathak, P. A. (2011). Accountability and flexibility in public schools: Evidence from Boston's charters and pilots. *The Quarterly Journal of Economics, 126*(2), 699–748.

Abenavoli, R. (2019). The mechanisms and moderators of "fade-out": Towards understanding why the skills of early childhood program participants converge over time with the skills of other children. *Psychological Bulletin 145*(12), 1103–1127. https://dx.doi.org/10.1037/bul0000212

Abramitzky, R., Boustan, L., Jácome, E., & Pérez, S. (2021). Intergenerational mobility of immigrants in the United States over two centuries. *American Economic Review, 111*(2), 580–608.

Abramson, C. M., Hashemi, M., & Sánchez-Jankowski, M. (2015). Perceived discrimination in U.S. healthcare: Charting the effects of key social characteristics within and across racial groups. *Preventive Medicine Reports 2*, 615–662.

Acosta, S., & Gartland, E. (2021). *Families wait years for housing vouchers due to inadequate funding*. Center for Budget and Policy Priorities. https://www.cbpp.org/research/housing/families-wait-years-for-housing-vouchers-due-to-inadequate-funding

Adamkiewicz, G., Zota, A. R., Fabian, M. P., Chahine, T., Julien, R., Spengler, J. D., & Levy, J. I. (2011). Moving environmental justice indoors: Understanding structural influences on residential exposure patterns in low-income communities. *American Journal of Public Health, 101*(S1), S238–S245.

Adams, D. W. (1995). *Education for extinction: American Indians and the boarding school experience, 1875–1928*. University Press of Kansas.

Adams, E., Kurtz-Costes, B., & Hoffman, A. (2016). Skin tone bias among African Americans: Antecedents and consequences across the life span. *Developmental Review, 40*, 93–116.

Addo, F. R., & Darity, W. A. Jr. (2021). Disparate recoveries: Wealth, race, and the working class after the Great Recession. *The ANNALS of the American Academy of Political and Social Science, 695*(1), 173–192.

Addo, F. R., Houle, J. N., & Simon, D. (2016). Young, Black, and (still) in the red: Parental wealth, race, and student loan debt. *Race and Social Problems, 8*, 64–76.

Adermon, A., Lindahl, M., & Waldenström, D. (2018). Intergenerational wealth mobility and the role of inheritance: Evidence from multiple generations. *The Economic Journal, 128*(612), F482–F513.

Administration for Children and Families. (2008). *Adolescents involved with child welfare: A transition to adulthood*. NSCAW Report prepared by Research Triangle Institute. U.S. Department of Health and Human Services.

___. (2022). *Child maltreatment, 2020*. U.S. Department of Health and Human Services.

___. (2023). *Home visiting evidence of effectiveness, models eligible for Maternal, Infant, and Early Childhood Home Visiting (MIECHV) funding*. U.S. Department of Health and Human Services. https://homvee.acf.hhs.gov/HRSA-Models-Eligible-MIECHV-Grantees

Admon, L. K., Daw, J. R., Winkelman, T. N., Kozhimannil, K. B., Zivin, K., Heisler, M., & Dalton, V. K. (2021). Insurance coverage and perinatal health care use among low-income women in the U.S., 2015–2017. *JAMA Network Open, 4*(1), e2034549.

Advisory Committee on Data for Evidence Building (ACDEB). (2021). *Advisory Committee on Data for Evidence Building: Year 1 report*. U.S. Bureau of Economic Analysis. https://www.bea.gov/system/files/2021-10/acdeb-year-1-report.pdf

___. (2022). *Advisory Committee on Data for Evidence Building: Year 2 report*. U.S. Bureau of Economic Analysis. https://www.bea.gov/system/files/2022-10/acdeb-year-2-report.pdf

Agan, A., & Starr, S. (2018). Ban the box, criminal records, and racial discrimination: A field experiment. *The Quarterly Journal of Economics, 133*(1), 191–235.

Agbai, C. O. (forthcoming). *Wealth begins at home: The housing benefits of the 1944 GI Bill and the making of the racial wealth gap in homeownership and home value*. https://osf.io/preprints/socarxiv/t5xby/

Ahrens, K. A., Haley, B. A., Rossen, L. M., Lloyd, P. C., & Aoki, Y. (2016). Housing assistance and blood lead levels: Children in the United States, 2005–2012. *American Journal of Public Health, 106*(11), 2049–2056.

Aizer, A. (2007). Public health insurance, program take-up, and child health. *The Review of Economics and Statistics, 89*(3), 400–415.

Aizer, A., & Currie, J. (2019). Lead and juvenile delinquency: New evidence from linked birth, school, and juvenile detention records. *Review of Economics and Statistics, 101*(4), 575–587.

Aizer, A., Currie, J., Simon, P., & Vivier, P. (2018). Do low levels of blood lead reduce children's future test scores? *American Economic Journal: Applied Economics, 10*(1), 307–341.

Aizer, A., Devereux, P., & Salvanes, K. (2022). Grandparents, moms, or dads? Why children of teen mothers do worse in life. *Journal of Human Resources, 57*(6), 2012–2047.

Aizer, A., & Doyle, J. J. Jr. (2015). Juvenile incarceration, human capital, and future crime: Evidence from randomly assigned judges. *The Quarterly Journal of Economics, 130*(2), 759–803.

Aizer, A., Eli, S., Ferrie, J., & Lleras-Muney, A. (2016a). The long-run impact of cash transfers to poor families. *American Economic Review*, 106(4), 935–971.
Aizer, A., Stroud, L., & Buka, S. (2016b). Maternal stress and child outcomes: Evidence from siblings. *Journal of Human Resources*, 51(3), 523–555.
Akee, R. (2020). Land titles and dispossession: Allotment on American Indian reservations. *Journal of Economics, Race, and Policy*, 3(2), 123–143
Akee, R., Copeland, W., Costello, E. J., & Simeonova, E. (2018). How does household income affect child personality traits and behaviors? *American Economic Review*, 108(3), 775–827.
Akee, R. K. Q., Copeland, W. E., Keeler, G., Angold, A., & Costello, E. J. (2010). Parents' incomes and children's outcomes: A quasi-experiment. *American Economic Journal: Applied Economics*, 2(1), 86–115.
Akee, R., & Taylor, J. B. (2014) *Social and economic change on American Indian reservations: A databook of the U.S. Censuses and American Community Survey, 1990–2010*. Taylor Policy Group, Inc. http://taylorpolicy.com/s/AkeeTaylorUSDatabook2014-05-15.pdf
Albright, A., Cook, J. A., Feigenbaum, J. J., Kincaide, L., Long, J., & Nunn, N. (2021). *After the burning: The economic effects of the 1921 Tulsa race massacre* (NBER Working Paper No. 28985). National Bureau of Economic Research.
Alesina, A., & Ferrara, E. L. (2011). *A test of racial bias in capital sentencing* (NBER Working Paper No. 16981). National Bureau of Economic Research. https://doi.org/10.3386/w16981
Alesina, A., Sacerdote, B., & Glaeser, E. (2001). *Why doesn't the United States have a European-style welfare state?* (NBER Working Paper No. 8524). National Bureau of Economic Research. https://doi.org/10.3386/w8524
Alexander, D., & Currie, J. (2017). Is it who you are or where you live? Residential segregation and racial gaps in childhood asthma. *Journal of Health Economics*, 55, 186–200.
Alexander, M. (2010). *The new Jim Crow mass incarceration in the age of colorblindness*. New Press.
Allcott, H., Diamond, R., Dubé, J. P., Handbury, J., Rahkovsky, I., & Schnell, M. (2019). Food deserts and the causes of nutritional inequality. *The Quarterly Journal of Economics*, 134(4), 1793–1844.
Allen, H., Eliason, E. Zewde, N., & Gross, T. (2019). Can Medicaid expansion prevent housing evictions? *Health Affairs*, 38(9), 1451–1457.
Almond, D., Chay, K., & Greenstone, M. (2006). *Civil rights, the War on Poverty, and Black-White convergence in infant mortality in the rural South and Mississippi* (MIT Working Paper No. 07-04). Massachusetts Institute of Technology Departments of Economics. https://dspace.mit.edu/bitstream/handle/1721.1/63330/civilrightswaron00almo.pdf?sequence=1
Almond, D., Currie, J., & Duque, V. (2018). Childhood circumstances and adult outcomes: Act II. *Journal of Economic Literature*, 56(4), 1360–1446.
Almond, D., Hoynes, H. W., & Schanzenbach, D. W. (2011). Inside the war on poverty: The impact of food stamps on birth outcomes. *The Review of Economics and Statistics*, 93(2), 387–403.
Alsan, M., Garrick, O., & Graziani, G. (2019). Does diversity matter for health? Experimental evidence from Oakland. *American Economic Review*, 109(12), 4071–4111.
Alsan, M., & Wanamaker, M. (2018). Tuskegee and the health of Black men. *The Quarterly Journal of Economics*, 133(1), 407–455.
Althoff, L., & Reichardt, H. (2023). *Jim Crow and Black economic progress after slavery* (The Long-Run Prosperity Working Paper No. 23005). Hoover Institution. https://www.hoover.org/sites/default/files/2023-05/LRP%20WP%2023005.pdf

Altonji, J. G., Kahn, L. B., & Speer, J. D. (2016). Cashier or consultant? Entry labor market conditions, field of study, and career success. *Journal of Labor Economics, 34*(S1), S361-S401.

American Civil Liberties Union & the University of Chicago Law School Global Human Rights Clinic. (2022). *Captive labor: Exploitation of incarcerated workers.* https://www.aclu.org/sites/default/files/field_document/2022-06-15-captivelaborresearchreport.pdf

American Indian Relief Council. (n.d.). History and culture: Boarding schools. http://www.nativepartnership.org/site/PageServer?pagename=airc_hist_boardingschools

An, B. P., & Gamoran, A. (2009). Trends in school racial composition in the era of unitary status. In C. E. Smrekar & E. B. Goldring (Eds.), *From the courtroom to the classroom: The shifting landscape of school desegregation* (pp. 19–48). Harvard University Press.

Ananat, E. O. (2011). The wrong side(s) of the tracks: The causal effects of racial segregation on urban poverty and inequality. *American Economic Journal: Applied Economics, 3*(2), 34–66.

Ananat, E., Glasner, B., Hamilton, C., & Parolin, Z. (2022). *Effects of the expanded Child Tax Credit on employment outcomes: Evidence from real-world data from April to December 2021* (NBER Working Paper No. 29823). National Bureau of Economic Research.

Anders, J., Barr, A. C., & Smith, A. A. (2023). The effect of early childhood education on adult criminality: Evidence from the 1960s through 1990s. *American Economic Journal: Economic Policy, 15*(1), 37–69.

Andersson, F., Holzer, H. J., & Lane, J. I. (2005). *Moving up or moving on: Who gets ahead in the low-wage labor market?* Russell Sage Foundation.

Andrews, R., Casey, M., Hardy, B. L., & Logan, T. D. (2017). Location matters: Historical racial segregation and intergenerational mobility. *Economics Letters, 158*, 67–72.

Ang, D. (2021). The effects of police violence on inner-city students. *The Quarterly Journal of Economics, 136*(1), 115–168.

Angrist, J., Autor, D., Hudson, S., & Pallais, A. (2017). *Evaluating post-secondary aid: Enrollment, persistence, and projected completion effects* (NBER Working Paper No. 23015). National Bureau of Economic Research.

Angrist, J., Autor, D., & Pallais, A. (2022). Marginal effects of merit aid for low-income students. *The Quarterly Journal of Economics, 137*(2), 1039–1090.

Angrist, J. D., Cohodes, S. R., Dynarski, S. M., Pathak, P. A., & Walters, C. R. (2016). Stand and deliver: Effects of Boston's charter high schools on college preparation, entry, and choice. *Journal of Labor Economics, 34*(2), 275–318.

Angrist, J. D., Pathak, P. A., & Walters, C. R. (2013). Explaining charter school effectiveness. *American Economic Journal: Applied Economics, 5*(4), 1–27.

The Annie E. Casey Foundation. (2019a). *Data snapshot: Kids count. Children living in high-poverty, low-opportunity neighborhoods.* https://assets.aecf.org/m/resourcedoc/aecf-childrenlivinginhighpoverty-2019.pdf

___. (2019b). *Data snapshot: Kids in concentrated poverty.* https://www.aecf.org/blog/percentage-of-kids-in-concentrated-poverty-worsens-in-10-states-and-puerto

___. (2021). *Youth incarceration in the United States.* https://www.aecf.org/resources/youth-incarceration-in-the-united-states

Anwar, S., Bayer, P., & Hjalmarsson, R. (2012). The impact of jury race in criminal trials. *The Quarterly Journal of Economics, 127*(2), 1017–1055.

Anyon, Y., Gregory, A., Stone, S., Farrar, J., Jenson, J. M., McQueen, J., Downing, B., Greer, E., & Simmons, J. (2016). Restorative interventions and school discipline sanctions in a large urban school district. *American Educational Research Journal, 53*(6), 1663–1697. https://doi.org/10.3102/0002831216675719

Arbogast, I., Chorniy, A. & Currie, J. (2022). *Administrative burdens and child Medicaid enrollments* (NBER Working Paper No. 30580). National Bureau of Economic Research. https://doi.org/10.3386/w30580

Ards, S. D., & Myers, S. L. Jr. (2001). The color of money: Bad credit, wealth, and race. *American Behavioral Scientist*, 45(2), 223–239.

Arnold, D., Dobbie, W., & Yang. C. S. (2018). Racial bias in bail decisions. *The Quarterly Journal of Economics*, 133(4), 1885–1932.

Artiga, S., Orgera, K., & Damico, A. (2020). *Changes in health coverage by race and ethnicity since the ACA, 2010–2018* [Issue Brief]. Kaiser Family Foundation. https://files.kff.org/attachment/Issue-Brief-Changes-in-Health-Coverage-by-Race-and-Ethnicity-since-the-ACA-2010-2018.pdf

Arya, N., & Rolnick, A. C. (2008). *A tangled web of justice: American Indian and Alaska Native youth in federal, state, and tribal justice systems*. Scholarly Works. https://scholars.law.unlv.edu/facpub/981

Atherton, O. E., Conger, R. D., Ferrer, E., & Robins, R. W. (2016). Risk and protective factors for early substance use initiation: A longitudinal study of Mexican-Origin youth. *Journal of Research on Adolescence*, 26(4), 864–879.

Athey, S., Chetty, R., Imbens, G. W., & Kang, H. (2019). *The surrogate index: Combining short-term proxies to estimate long-term treatment effects more rapidly and precisely* (NBER Working Paper No. 26463). National Bureau of Economic Research.

Atuahene, B., & Berry, C. (2018). Taxed out: Illegal property tax assessments and the epidemic of tax foreclosures in Detroit. *UC Irvine Law Review*, 9(4).

Augustine, C. H., Engberg, J., Grimm, G. E., Lee, E., Wang, E. L., Christianson, K., & Joseph, A. A. (2018). *Can restorative practices improve school climate and curb suspensions? An evaluation of the impact of restorative practices in a mid-sized urban school district*. RAND Corporation.

Autor, D. (2014). Skills, education, and the rise of earnings inequality among the "other 99 percent." *Science*, 344(6186), 843–851.

———. (2022). *The labor market impacts of technological change: From unbridled enthusiasm to qualified optimism to vast uncertainty* (NBER Working Paper No. 30074). National Bureau of Economic Research.

Autor, D., Dorn, D., & Hanson, G. (2019). When work disappears: Manufacturing decline and the falling marriage market value of young men. *American Economic Review: Insights*, 1(2), 161–178.

Autor, D., Figlio, D., Karbownik, K., Roth, J., & Wasserman, M. (2016). School quality and the gender gap in educational achievement. *American Economic Review*, 106(5), 289–295.

Autor, D. H., Katz, L. F., & Kearney, M. S. (2008). Trends in US wage inequality: Revising the revisionists. *The Review of Economics and Statistics*, 90(2), 300–323.

Avellar, S., & Paulsell, D. (2011). *Lessons learned from the home visiting evidence of effectiveness review*. Office of Planning, Research and Evaluation, Administration for Children and Families, U.S. Department of Health and Human Services.

Avenancio-León, C., & Howard, T. (2022). The assessment gap: Racial inequalities in property taxation. *The Quarterly Journal of Economics*, 137(3), 1383–1434.

Aviram, A., Hod, M., & Yogev, Y. (2011). Maternal obesity: Implications for pregnancy outcome and long-term risks–a link to maternal nutrition. *International Journal of Gynecology & Obstetrics*, 115, S6–S10.

Azurdia, G., & Galkin, K. (2020). *An eight-year cost analysis from a randomized controlled trial of CUNY's accelerated study in associate programs* (Working Paper). MDRC. https://www.mdrc.org/publication/eight-year-cost-analysis-randomized-controlled-trial-cuny-s-accelerated-study-associate

Bacher-Hicks, A., Billings, S. B., & Deming, D. J. (2019). *The school to prison pipeline: Long-run impacts of school suspensions on adult crime* (NBER Working Paper No. 26257). National Bureau of Economic Research. https://doi.org/10.3386/w26257

Bacher-Hicks, A., & de la Campa, E. (2020). *Social costs of proactive policing: The impact of NYC's stop and frisk program on educational attainment*. John F. Kennedy School of Government, Harvard University. https://drive.google.com/file/d/1sSxhfmDY3N1VAN5XwyRObE65tmAZzhTj/view

Backes, B., Goldhaber, D., Cade, W., Sullivan, K., & Dodson, M. (2018). Can UTeach? Assessing the relative effectiveness of STEM teachers. *Economics of Education Review*, 64, 184–198.

Backes, B., Holzer, H. J., & Velez, E. D. (2015). Is it worth it? Postsecondary education and labor market outcomes for the disadvantaged. *IZA Journal of Labor Policy*, 4(1), 1–30.

Baicker, K., Taubman, S., Allen, H., Bernstein, M., Gruber, J., Newhouse, J.P., Schneider, E., Wright, B., Zaslavsky, A., Finkelstein, A., & the Oregon Health Study Group (2013). The Oregon Experiment—Effects of Medicaid on clinical outcomes. *New England Journal of Medicine*, 368(18), 1713–1722.

Bailey, D. H., Jenkins, J. M., & Alvarez-Vargas, D. (2020). Complementarities between early educational intervention and later educational quality? A systematic review of the sustaining environments hypothesis. *Developmental Review*, 56, 100910.

Bailey, M. J. (2013). *Fifty years of family planning: New evidence on the long-run effects of increasing access to contraception* (NBER Working Paper No. 19493). National Bureau of Economic Research. https://doi.org/10.3386/w19493

Bailey, M. J., Hershbein, B., & Miller, A. R. (2012). The opt-in revolution? Contraception and the gender gap in wages. *American Economic Journal: Applied Economics*, 4(3), 225–254.

Bailey, M. J., Hoynes, H. W., Rossin-Slater, M., & Walker, R. (2020). *Is the social safety net a long-term investment? Large-scale evidence from the food stamps program* (NBER Working Paper No. 26942). National Bureau of Economic Research. https://doi.org/10.3386/w26942

Bailey, M. J., Malkova, O., & McLaren, Z. M. (2019). Does access to family planning increase children's opportunities? Evidence from the war on poverty and the early years of Title X. *Journal of Human Resources*, 54(4), 825–856.

Bailey, M. J., Sun, S., & Timpe, B. (2021). Prep school for poor kids: The long-run impacts of Head Start on Human capital and economic self-sufficiency. *American Economic Review*, 111(12), 3963–4001.

Bailey, T. R., Jaggars, S. S., & Jenkins, D. (2015). *Redesigning America's community colleges: A clearer path to student success*. Harvard University Press.

Baker, B. D., Di Carlo, M., & Weber, M. (2021, March). *The adequacy of school district spending in the U.S.* [Research Brief No. 02-2021]. School Finance Indicators Database, Albert Shanker Institute, Rutgers Graduate School of Education. https://files.eric.ed.gov/fulltext/ED613513.pdf

Baker, M., Gruber, J., & Milligan, K. (2019). The long-run impacts of a Universal Child Care Program. *American Economic Journal: Economic Policy*, 11(3), 1–26.

Baker, M., Messacar, D., & Stabile, M. (2021). *The effects of child tax benefits on poverty and labor supply: Evidence from the Canada Child Benefit and Universal Child Care Benefit* (NBER Working Paper No. 28556). National Bureau of Economic Research. https://doi.org/10.3386/w28556

Baker, R. S. (2022). The historical racial regime and racial inequality in poverty in the American south. *American Journal of Sociology*, 127(6), 1721–1781.

Bald, A., Chyn, E., Hastings, J., & Machelett, M. (2022). The causal impact of removing children from abusive and neglectful homes. *Journal of Political Economy*, 130(7), 1919–1962.

Balko, R. (2020, June 10). There's overwhelming evidence that the criminal justice system is racist. Here's the proof. The Washington Post. https://www.washingtonpost.com/graphics/2020/opinions/systemic-racism-police-evidence-criminal-justice-system/

Banks, N. (2019, February 19). Black women's labor market history reveals deep-seated race and gender discrimination. Working Economics Blog. https://www.epi.org/blog/black-womens-labor-market-history-reveals-deep-seated-race-and-gender-discrimination/

Banner, S. (2005). *How the Indians lost their land: Law and power on the frontier*. Harvard University Press.

Baradaran, M. (2017). *The color of money: Black banks and the racial wealth gap*. Harvard University Press.

Barnert, E. S., Perry, R., & Morris, R. E. (2016). Juvenile incarceration and health. *Academic Pediatrics, 16*(2), 99–109.

Barnett, W. S., & Friedman-Krauss, A. H. (2016). State(s) of Head Start. National Institute for Early Education Research. http:// nieer.org/headstart

Baron, E. J., & Gross, M. (2022a). *Is there a foster care to prison pipeline? Evidence from quasi-randomly assigned investigators* (NBER Working Paper No. 29922). National Bureau of Economic Research. https://doi.org/10.3386/w29922

Baron, E. J., Hyman, J. M., & Vasquez, B. N. (2022b). *Public school funding, school quality, and adult crime* (NBER Working Paper No. 29855). National Bureau of Economic Research. https://doi.org/10.3386/w29855

Baron, E. J., Jacob, B., & Ryan, J. (2023). Pretrial juvenile detention. *Journal of Public Economics, 217*, 104798.

Barr, A., Eggleston, J., & Smith, A. A. (2022). *Investing in infants: The lasting effects of cash transfers to new families* (NBER Working Paper No. 30373). Natural Bureau of Economic Research. https://doi.org/10.3386/w30373

Barr, A., & Smith, A. (2023). Fighting crime in the cradle: The effects of early childhood access to nutritional assistance. *Journal of Human Resources, 58*(1), 43–73.

Barrett, J. T., Lee, L. K., Monuteaux, M. C., Farrell, C. A., Hoffmann, J. A., & Fleegler, E. W. (2022). Association of county-level poverty and inequities with firearm-related mortality in U.S. youth. *JAMA Pediatrics, 176*(2), e214822.

Barros, N., Tulve, N. S., Heggem, D. T., & Bailey, K. (2018). Review of built and natural environment stressors impacting American-Indian/Alaska-Native children. *Reviews on Environmental Health, 33*(4), 349–381.

Bartel, A. P., Kim, S., & Nam, J. (2019). Racial and ethnic disparities in access to and use of paid family and medical leave: Evidence from four nationally representative datasets. *Monthly Laboratory Review, 142*, 1.

Barth, R. P., Berrick, J. D., Garcia, A. R., Drake, B., Jonson-Reid, M., Gyourko, J. R., & Greeson, J. K. (2022). Research to consider while effectively re-designing child welfare services. *Research on Social Work Practice, 32*(5), 483–498.

Barth, R. P., Duncan, D. F., Hodorowicz, M. T., & Kum, H. C. (2010). Felonious arrests of former foster care and TANF-involved youth. *Journal of the Society for Social Work and Research, 1*(2), 104–123.

Barth, R. P., Jonson-Reid, M., Greeson, J. K., Drake, B., Berrick, J. D., Garcia, A. R., Shaw, T. V., & Gyourko, J. R. (2020). Outcomes following child welfare services: What are they and do they differ for Black children? *Journal of Public Child Welfare, 14*(5), 477–499.

Bassok, D., Finch, J. E., Lee, R., Reardon, S. F., & Waldfogel, J. (2016). Socioeconomic gaps in early childhood experiences: 1998 to 2010. *AERA Open, 2*(3).

Bassuk, E. L., DeCandia, C. J., Beach, C. A., & Berman, F. (2014). *America's youngest outcasts: A report card on child homelessness*. The National Center on Family Homelessness, American Institutes for Research.

Bastian, J., & Michelmore, K. (2018). The long-term impact of the earned income tax credit on children's education and employment outcomes. *Journal of Labor Economics, 36*(4), 1127–1163.

Batra, A., & Hamad, R. (2021). Short-term effects of the earned income tax credit on children's physical and mental health. *Annals of Epidemiology, 58*, 15–21.

Batra, A., Jackson, K., & Hamad, R. (2023). Effects of the 2021 Expanded Child Tax Credit on adults' mental health: A quasi-experimental study: Study examines the effects of the expanded Child Tax Credit on mental health among low-income adults with children and racial and ethnic subgroups. *Health Affairs, 42*(1), 74–82.

Batra, A., Karasek, D., & Hamad, R. (2022). Racial differences in the association between the U.S. Earned Income Tax Credit and birthweight. *Women's Health Issues, 32*(1), 26–32.

Baum, S., Holzer, H. J., & Luetmer, G. (2020). *Should the federal government fund short-term postsecondary certificate programs?* Urban Institute. https://files.eric.ed.gov/fulltext/ED610038.pdf

Baum, S., & McPherson, M. (2022). *Can college level the playing field? Higher education in an unequal society.* Princeton University Press.

Bayer, P., & Charles, K. K. (2018). Divergent paths: A new perspective on earnings differences between Black and White men since 1940. *The Quarterly Journal of Economics, 133*(3), 1459–1501.

Bayer, P., Ferreira, F., & Ross, S. L. (2016). The vulnerability of minority homeowners in the housing boom and bust. *American Economic Journal: Economic Policy, 8*(1), 1–27.

Bayer, P., Ferreira, F., & Ross, S. L. (2018). What drives racial and ethnic differences in high-cost mortgages? The role of high-risk lenders. *The Review of Financial Studies, 31*(1), 175–205.

Bayer, P., Hjalmarsson, R., & Pozen, D. (2009). Building criminal capital behind bars: Peer effects in juvenile corrections. *The Quarterly Journal of Economics, 124*(1), 105–147.

Beach, W. W., & Walsh, M. J. (2021). National Compensation Survey: Employee Benefits in the United States, March 2021, Tables 17 and 33. U.S. Department of Labor, U.S. Bureau of Labor Statistics. https://www.bls.gov/ncs/ebs/benefits/2021/employee-benefits-in-the-united-states-march-2021.pdf

Beck, A. J., & Blumstein, A. (2018). Racial disproportionality in U.S. state prisons: Accounting for the effects of racial and ethnic differences in criminal involvement, arrests, sentencing, and time served. *Journal of Quantitative Criminology, 34*, 853–883.

Becker, G. S. (1991). *A treatise on the family: Enlarged edition.* Harvard University Press.

Bee, A., & Rothbaum, J. (2019, October 2). *The Administrative Income Statistics (AIS) project: Research on the use of administrative records to improve income and resource estimates* (Working Paper No. SEHSD-WP2019-36). U.S. Census Bureau.

Beland, L. P., & Kim, D. (2016). The effect of high school shootings on schools and student performance. *Educational Evaluation and Policy Analysis, 38*(1), 113–126.

Belfield, C. R., & Levin, H. M. (2007). *The economic losses from high school dropouts in California* (Vol. 1). California Dropout Research Project.

Bell, M. L., & Ebisu, K. (2012). Environmental inequality in exposures to airborne particulate matter components in the United States. *Environmental Health Perspectives, 120*(12), 1699–1704.

Belman, D., & Wolfson, P. J. (2014). *What does the minimum wage do?* Upjohn Press. https://www.upjohn.org/what-does-minimum-wage-do

Benjamin, R. (2019). *Race after technology: Abolitionist tools for the new Jim Code.* Polity Books.

Berger, L. M., & Font, S. A. (2015). The role of the family and family-centered programs and policies. *The Future of Children, 25*, 155.

Berger, L. M., & Waldfogel, J. (2011). *Economic determinants and consequences of child maltreatment* (Social, Employment, and Migration Working Paper No. 111). Organisation for Economic Co-operation and Development. https://doi.org/10.1787/5kgf09zj7h9t-en

Bergman, P., Chetty, R., DeLuca, S., Hendren, N., Katz, L., & Palmer, C. (2019). *Creating moves to opportunity: Experimental evidence on barriers to neighborhood choice* (NBER Working Paper No. 26164). National Bureau of Economic Research. http://www.nber.org/papers/w26164

Berk, J. (2008). *Does work release work?* [Unpublished Manuscript]. Brown University. https://citeseerx.ist.psu.edu/document?repid=rep1&type=pdf&doi=ec5f557cc5b792681ce8c7f21ed50e7c249b4107

Bernardo, C. D. O., Bastos, J. L., González-Chica, D. A., Peres, M. A., & Paradies, Y. C. (2017). Interpersonal discrimination and markers of adiposity in longitudinal studies: a systematic review. *Obesity Reviews*, 18(9), 1040–1049.

Bertrand, M., & Mullainathan, S. (2004). Are Emily and Greg more employable than Lakisha and Jamal? A field experiment on labor market discrimination. *American Economic Review*, 94(4), 991–1013.

Bettinger, E. P., & Baker, R. B. (2014). The effects of student coaching: An evaluation of a randomized experiment in student advising. *Educational Evaluation and Policy Analysis*, 36(1), 3–19.

Bettinger, E. P., Long, B. T., Oreopoulos, P., & Sanbonmatsu, L. (2012). The role of application assistance and information in college decisions: Results from the H&R Block FAFSA experiment. *The Quarterly Journal of Economics*, 127(3), 1205–1242.

Bhutta, N., Chang, A., Dettling, L. & Hsu, J. (2020, September 28). Disparities in wealth by race and ethnicity in the 2019 survey of consumer finances. *FEDS Notes*. Board of Governors of the Federal Reserve System. https://doi.org/10.17016/2380-7172.2797

Billings, S. B., Deming, D. J., Rockoff, J. (2013). School segregation, educational attainment, and crime: Evidence from the end of busing in Charlotte-Mecklenburg. *The Quarterly Journal of Economics*, 129(1), 435–476.

Billings, S. B., & Schnepel, K. T. (2017). The value of a healthy home: Lead paint remediation and housing values. *Journal of Public Economics*, 153(C), 69–81.

Binder, A. J., & Bound, J. (2019). The declining labor market prospects of less-educated men. *Journal of Economic Perspectives*, 33(2), 163–190

Bing, L., Pettit, B., & Slavinski, I. (2022). Incomparable punishments: How economic inequality contributes to the disparate impact of legal fines and fees. *The Russell Sage Foundation Journal of the Social Sciences*, 8(2), 118–136.

Birckhead, T. R. (2012). Delinquent by reason of poverty. *Washington University Journal of Law & policy*, 38, 53.

Bischoff, K., & Owens, A. (2019). The segregation of opportunity: Social and financial resources in the educational contexts of lower-and higher-income children, 1990–2014. *Demography*, 56(5), 1635–1664.

Black, J. E. (2002). The "mascotting" of Native America: Construction, commodity, and assimilation. *American Indian Quarterly*, 605–622.

Black, R., & Huelsman, M. (2012). *Overcoming obstacles to college attendance and degree completion: Toward a pro-college savings agenda*. New America Foundation. https://www.newamerica.org/asset-building/policy-papers/overcoming-obstacles-to-college-attendance-and-degree-completion/

Black, S. E., Devereux, P. J., & Salvanes, K. G. (2007). From the cradle to the labor market? The effect of birth weight on adult outcomes. *The Quarterly Journal of Economics*, 122(1), 409–439.

———. (2016). Does grief transfer across generations? Bereavements during pregnancy and child outcomes. *American Economic Journal: Applied Economics*, 8(1), 193–223.

Black, S. E., Schanzenbach, D. W., & Breitwieser, A. (2017). The recent decline in women's labor force participation. *The 51% Driving Growth through Women's Economic Participation*, 5–17. Brookings Institution.

Blackmon, D. (2008). *Slavery by another name: The re-enslavement of Black Americans from the Civil War to World War II.* Doubleday

Black, S. E., Denning, J. T., & Rothstein, J. (2023). Winners and losers? The effect of gaining and losing access to selective colleges on education and labor market outcomes. *American Economic Journal: Applied Economics, 15*(1), 26–67.

Blake, K. S., Kellerson, R. L., & Simic, A. (2007). *Measuring overcrowding in housing.* U.S. Department of Housing and Urban Development, Office of Policy Development and Research. https://www.huduser.gov/Publications/pdf/Measuring_Overcrowding_in_Hsg.pdf

Blakemore, E. (2021, July 9). A century of trauma at U.S. boarding schools for Native American children. *National Geographic.* https://www.nationalgeographic.com/history/article/a-century-of-trauma-at-boarding-schools-for-native-american-children-in-the-united-states

Blanchflower, D. G., Levine, P. B., & Zimmerman, D. J. (2003). Discrimination in the small-business credit market. *Review of Economics and Statistics, 85*(4), 930–43.

Blau, D. M., Haskell, N. L., & Haurin, D. R. (2019). Are housing characteristics experienced by children associated with their outcomes as young adults? *Journal of Housing Economics, 46*, 101631.

Blau, F. D., & Kahn, L. M. (2017). The gender wage gap: Extent, trends, and explanations. *Journal of Economic Literature, 55*(3), 789–865.

Bleakley, H., & Chin, A. (2004). Language skills and earnings: Evidence from childhood immigrants. *Review of Economics and statistics, 86*(2), 481–496.

___. (2008). What holds back the second generation? The intergenerational transmission of language human capital among immigrants. *Journal of Human Resources, 43*(2), 267–298.

___. (2010). Age at arrival, English proficiency, and social assimilation among US immigrants. *American Economic Journal: Applied Economics, 2*(1), 165–192.

Bleemer, Z. (2021). Top percent policies and the return to postsecondary selectivity. CSHE Research Paper Series (CSHE No. 1.2021). Center for Studies in Higher Education. https://economics.princeton.edu/wp-content/uploads/2021/01/BleemerZachary-JMP.pdf

___. (2022). Affirmative action, mismatch, and economic mobility after California's Proposition 209. *The Quarterly Journal of Economics, 137*(1), 115–160.

Bleemer, Z., & Mehta, A. (2021). *College major restrictions and student stratification* Research & Occasional Paper Series (CSHE No. 14.2021). Center for Studies in Higher Education.

Blumstein, A., & Beck, A. J. (1999). Population growth in U.S. prisons, 1980–1996. *Crime and Justice, 26*, 17–61.

Bocian, D. G., Li, W., & Ernst, K. S. (2010). *Foreclosures by race and ethnicity: The demographics of a Crisis CRL Research Report.* Center for Responsible Lending. https://www.responsiblelending.org/mortgage-lending/research-analysis/foreclosures-by-race-and-ethnicity.pdf

Bocian, D. G., Li, W., Reid, C., & Quercia, R. (2011). *Lost ground, 2011: Disparities in mortgage lending and foreclosures.* Center for Responsible Lending. http://www.responsiblelending.org/mortgage-lending/research-analysis/Lost-Ground-2011.pdf.

Bohren, M. A., Vazquez Corona, M., Odiase, O. J., Wilson, A. N., Sudhinaraset, M., Diamond-Smith, N., Berryman, J., Tunçalp, Ö., & Afulani, P. A. (2022). Strategies to reduce stigma and discrimination in sexual and reproductive healthcare settings: A mixed-methods systematic review. *PLOS Global Public Health, 2*(6), e0000582.

Boland, W. C., Gasman, M., Samayoa, A. C., & Bennett, D. (2021). The effect of enrolling in minority serving institutions on earnings compared to non-minority serving institutions: A college scorecard analysis. *Research in Higher Education, 62*(2), 121–150.

Boller, K., Paulsell, D., Del Grosso, P., Blair, R., Lundquist, E., Kassow, D.Z., Kim, R. & Raikes, A. (2015). Impacts of a child care quality rating and improvement system on child care quality. *Early Childhood Research Quarterly, 30*, 306–315.

Bona, K., Li, Y., Winestone, L. E., Getz, K. D., Huang, Y. S., Fisher, B. T., Desai, A. V., Richardson, T., Hall, M., Naranjo, A., Henderson, T. O., Aplenc, R., & Bagatell, R. (2021). Poverty and targeted immunotherapy: Survival in children's oncology group clinical trials for high-risk neuroblastoma. *Journal of the National Cancer Institute, 113*(3), 282–291.

Bond, T. N., Carr, J. B., Packham, A., & Smith, J. (2022). Hungry for success? SNAP timing, high-stakes exam performance, and college attendance. *American Economic Journal: Economic Policy, 14*(4), 51–79.

Bonilla, S. (2020). The dropout effects of career pathways: Evidence from California. *Economics of Education Review, 75*, 101972.

Bonilla, S., Dee, T. S., & Penner, E. K. (2021). Ethnic studies increases longer-run academic engagement and attainment. *Proceedings of the National Academy of Sciences, 118*(37), e2026386118.

Bönke, T., Harnack, A., & Luthen, H. (2019). *Are children better off? Intergenerational mobility of living standards* (NBER Working Paper No. 15889). National Bureau of Economic Research. http://www.nber.org/papers/w15889

Bor, J., Venkataramani, A., Williams, D., & Tsai, A. (2018). Police killings and their spillover effects on the mental health of Black Americans: A population-based, quasi-experimental study. *The Lancet, 392*(10144), 302–310

Borge, T. C., Aase, H., Brantsæter, A. L., & Biele, G. (2017). The importance of maternal diet quality during pregnancy on cognitive and behavioural outcomes in children: A systematic review and meta-analysis. *BMJ Open, 7*(9), e016777.

Borman, G. D., Pyne, J., Rozek, C. S., & Schmidt, A. (2022). A replicable identity-based intervention reduces the Black-White suspension gap at scale. *American Educational Research Journal, 59*(2), 284–314.

Borowsky, J., Brown, J. H., Davis, E. E., Gibbs, C., Herbst, C. M., Sojourner, A., Tekin, E. & Wiswall, M. J. (2022). *An equilibrium model of the impact of increased public investment in early childhood education* (NBER Working Paper No. 30140). National Bureau of Economic Research.

Bostic, R. W., & Lee, K. O. (2008). Mortgages, risk, and homeownership among low-and moderate-income families. *American Economic Review, 98*(2), 310–314.

Boulware, K. D., & Kuttner, K. N. (2020, May). Wealth stratification and portfolio choice. *American Economic Association Papers and Proceedings, 110*, 411–415.

Bourguignon, F. (2022). Digitalization and inequality. In Z. Qureshi & C. Woo (Eds.) *Shifting paradigms: Growth, finance, jobs, and inequality in the digital economy*, 177. Bookings Institution Press.

Boustan, L. P. (2010). Was postwar suburbanization "White Flight"? Evidence from the Black Migration, *The Quarterly Journal of Economics, 125*(1), 417–443. https://doi.org/10.1162/qjec.2010.125.1.417

Boyce, W. T., Levitt, P., Martinez, F. D., McEwen, B. S., & Shonkoff, J. P. (2021). Genes, environments, and time: The biology of adversity and resilience. *Pediatrics, 147*(2).

Boyens, C., Karpman, M., & Smalligan, J. (2022). *Access to paid leave is lowest among workers with the greatest needs*. Urban Institute.

Boyd, R. (2014). African American disproportionality and disparity in child welfare: Toward a comprehensive conceptual framework. *Children and Youth Services Review, 37*, 15–27.

Boyle, J., Yeter, D., Aschner, M., & Wheeler, D. C. (2021). Estimated IQ points and lifetime earnings lost to early childhood blood lead levels in the United States. *Science of the Total Environment, 778*, 146307.

Bradshaw, C. P., Mitchell, M. M., & Leaf, P. J. (2010). Examining the effects of school-wide positive behavioral interventions and supports on student outcomes. *Journal of Positive Behavior Interventions, 12*, 133–148.

Bradshaw, C. P., Waasdorp, T. E., & Leaf, P. J. (2012). Effects of school-wide positive behavioral interventions and supports on child behavior problems. *Pediatrics, 130*(5), e1136–e1145.

Braga, A. A., Brunson, R. K., & Drakulich, K. M. (2019a). Race, place, and effective policing. *Annual Review of Sociology, 45*, 535–55.

Braga, A. A., Turchan, B., Papachristos, A. V., & Hureau, D. M. (2019b). Hot spots policing of small geographic areas effects on crime. *Campbell Systematic Reviews, 15*(3), e1046.

Bramlett, M. D., Radel, L. F., & Chow, K. (2017). Health and well-being of children in kinship care: Findings from the National Survey of Children in Nonparental Care. *Child Welfare, 95*(3), 41.

Branas, C. C., South, E., Kondo, M. C., Hohl, B. C., Bourgois, P., Wiebe, D. J., & MacDonald, J. M. (2018). Citywide cluster randomized trial to restore blighted vacant land and its effects on violence, crime, and fear. *Proceedings of the National Academy of Sciences, 115*(12), 2946–2951.

Branas, C. C., Rubin, D., & Guo, W. (2012). Vacant properties and violence in neighborhoods. *Cartographic Modeling Lab Papers*. https://doi.org/10.5402/2012/246142

Bratsch-Hines, M. E., Burchinal, M., Peisner-Feinberg, E., & Franco, X. (2019). Frequency of instructional practices in rural prekindergarten classrooms and associations with child language and literacy skills. *Early Childhood Research Quarterly, 47*, 74–88.

Braveman, P., Burke, W., Dolan, S., Stevenson, D., Jackson, F., Collins, J., Driscoll, D., Haley, T., Acker, J., Shaw, G., McCabe, E., Hay, W., Thornburg, K., Acevedo-Garcia, D., Cordero, J., Wise, P., Legaz, G., Rashied-Henry, K. & Waddell, L. (2021). Explaining the Black-White disparity in preterm birth: A consensus statement from a multi-disciplinary scientific work group convened by the March of Dimes. *Frontiers in Reproductive Health, 3*. https://doi.org/10.3389/frph.2021.684207

Braveman, P. A., Cubbin, C., Egerter, S., Williams, D. R., & Pamuk, E. (2010). Socioeconomic disparities in health in the United States: What the patterns tell us. *American Journal of Public Health, 100*(S1), S186–S196.

Brazil, N. (2020). The unequal spatial distribution of city government fines: The case of parking tickets in Los Angeles. *Urban Affairs Review, 56*(3), 823–856.

Bricker, J., Goodman, S., Moore, K. B., & Henriques Volz, A. (2020, September 28). Wealth and income concentration in the SCF: 1989–2019. *FEDS Notes*. Board of Governors of the Federal Reserve. https://doi.org/10.17016/2380-7172.2795

Bridgewater, P. D. (2005). Ain't I a slave: Slavery, reproductive abuse, and reparations. *UCLA Women's Law Journal, 14*, 89–161.

Brody, G. H., Stoneman, Z., Flor, D., McCrary, C., Hastings, L., & Conyers, O. (1994). Financial resources, parent psychological functioning, parent co-caregiving, and early adolescent competence in rural two-parent African-American families. *Child Development, 65*(2), 590–605.

Brown, C. C., & Hamermesh, D. S. (2019). Wages and hours laws: What do we know? What can be done? *The Russell Sage Foundation Journal of the Social Sciences, 5*(5), 68–87.

Brown, D. A. (2021). *The whiteness of wealth: How the tax system impoverishes Black Americans—and how we can fix it*. Crown Publishing Group.

Brown, D., Branden, K., & Hall, R. (2018). Native American colorism: From historical manifestations to the current era. *American Behavioral Scientist, 62*(14), 2023–2036.

Brown, D. W., Kowalski, A. E., & Lurie, I. Z. (2020). Long-term impacts of childhood Medicaid expansions on outcomes in adulthood. *The Review of Economic Studies, 87*(2), 792–821.

Bruenig, M. (2019). Baby bonds only modestly reduce the racial wealth gap. *People's Policy Project*. https://www.peoplespolicyproject.org/2019/01/22/baby-bonds-only-modestly-reduce-the-racial-wealth-gap/

Brummund, P., & Strain, M. R. (2020). Does employment respond differently to minimum wage increases in the presence of inflation indexing? *Journal of Human Resources*, 55(3), 999–1024.

Brunner, E. J., Dougherty, S. M., & Ross, S. L. (2021). The effects of career and technical education: Evidence from the Connecticut Technical High School System. *Review of Economics and Statistics*, 1–46.

Buckner, J. C. (2008). Understanding the impact of homelessness on children: Challenges and future research directions. *American Behavioral Scientist*, 51(6), 721–36.

Budman, A., Tamir, C., Mora, L., & Noe-Bustamante, L. (2020). *Facts on U.S. immigrants, 2018: Statistical portrait of the foreign-born population in the United States*. Pew Research Center. https://www.pewresearch.org/hispanic/2020/08/20/facts-on-u-s-immigrants-current-data/

Bulman, G., Fairlie, R., Goodman, S., & Isen, A. (2021). Parental resources and college attendance: Evidence from lottery wins. *American Economic Review*, 111(4), 1201–1240.

Bullinger, L. R., Fleckman, J. M., & Fong, K. (2021). Proximity to SNAP-authorized retailers and child maltreatment reports. *Economics & Human Biology*, 42, 101015.

Bullinger, L. R., & Fong, K. (2021). Evictions and neighborhood child maltreatment reports. *Housing Policy Debate*, 31(3-5), 490–515.

Bullinger, L. R., Raissian, K. M., & Schneider, W. (2022). The power of the future: Intergenerational income mobility and child maltreatment in the United States. *Child Abuse & Neglect*, 130, 105175.

Bunting, L., Davidson, G., McCartan, C., Hanratty, J., Bywaters, P., Mason, W., & Steils, N. (2018). The association between child maltreatment and adult poverty—A systematic review of longitudinal research. *Child Abuse & Neglect*, 77, 121–133.

Burchinal, M. R., Foster, T. J., Bezdek, K. G., Bratsch-Hines, M., Blair, C., & Vernon-Feagans, L. (2020). School-entry skills predicting school-age academic and social-emotional trajectories. *Early Childhood Research Quarterly*, 51(1), 67–80. https://doi.org/10.1016/j.ecresq.2019.08.004

Burchinal, M., Foster, T., Garber, K., Cohen-Vogel, L., Bratsch-Hines, M., & Peisner-Feinberg, E. (2022). Examining three hypotheses for pre-kindergarten fade-out. *Developmental Psychology*.

Burdick-Will, J., Nerenberg, K. M., Grigg, J. A., & Connolly, F. (2021). Student mobility and violent crime exposure at Baltimore City public elementary schools. *American Educational Research Journal*, 58(3), 602–634.

Burkhauser, R. V., Corinth, K., Elwell, J., & Larrimore, J. (2023). Evaluating the success of the War on Poverty since 1963 using an absolute full-income poverty measure. *Journal of Political Economy*, 131(9). https://doi.org/10.1086/725705

Busch, S. H., Golberstein, E., & Meara, E. (2014). The FDA and ABCs unintended consequences of antidepressant warnings on human capital. *Journal of Human Resources*, 49(3), 540–571.

Bushway, S., Cabreros, I., Paige, J. W., Schwam, D., & Wenger, J. B. (2022). Barred from employment: More than half of unemployed men in their 30s had a criminal history of arrest. *Science Advances*, 8(7), eabj6992.

Butcher, K. F. (1994). Black immigrants in the United States: A comparison with native Blacks and other immigrants. *Industrial and Labor Review*, 47(2), 265–284.

Button, P., & Walker, B. (2020). Employment discrimination against Indigenous Peoples in the United States: Evidence from a field experiment. *Labour Economics*, 65, 101851.

Butz, A. M., Matsui, E. C., Breysse, P., Curtin-Brosnan, J., Eggleston, P., Diette, G., Williams, D. A., Yuan, J., Bernert, J. T., & Rand, C. (2011). A randomized trial of air cleaners and a health coach to improve indoor air quality for inner-city children with asthma and secondhand smoke exposure. *Archives of Pediatrics & Adolescent Medicine*, 165(8), 741–748.

Cabral, M., Kim, B., Rossin-Slater, M., Schnell, M., & Schwandt, H. (2021). *Trauma at school: The impacts of shootings on students' human capital and economic outcomes* (NBER Working Paper No. 28311). National Bureau of Economic Research.

Cajner, T., Radler, T., Ratner, D. & Vidangos, I. (2017). *Racial gaps in labor market outcomes in the last four decades and over the business cycle* (Working Paper No. 2017-071). Finance and Economics Discussion Series. Board of Governors of the Federal Reserve System, https://doi.org/10.17016/FEDS.2017.071

Calloway, E. E., Fricke, H. E., Pinard, C. A., Smith, T. M., & Yaroch, A. L. (2015). Monthly SNAP benefit duration and its association with food security, hunger-coping, and physiological hunger symptoms among low-income families. *Journal of Applied Research on Children, 6*(2), 5.

Campbell, F. A., Pungello, E., Burchinal, M. R., Kainz, K., Pan, Y., Wasik, B. H., Barbarin, O. A., Sparling, J. J., & Ramey, C. T. (2012). Adult outcomes as a function of an early childhood educational program: An Abecedarian Project follow-up. *Developmental Psychology, 48*(4), 1033–1043. https://doi.org/10.1037/a0026644

Canaan, S., Deeb, A., & Mouganie, P. (2022a). Adviser value added and student outcomes: Evidence from randomly assigned college advisers. *American Economic Journal: Economic Policy, 14*(4), 151–191.

Canaan, S., Fischer, S., Mouganie, P., & Schnorr, G. (2022b). Keep me in, coach: The short- and long-term effects of targeted academic coaching. *Upjohn Institute Working Papers, 22*(370).

Cancian, M., Yang, M.-Y., & Slack, K. S. (2013). The effect of additional child support income on the risk of child maltreatment. *Social Service Review, 87*(3), 417–437.

Caplan, B. (2018). *The case against education: Why the education system is a waste of time and money*. Princeton University Press.

Capps, R., Horowitz, A., Fortuny, K., Bronte-Tinkew, J., & Zaslow, M. (2009). *Young children in immigrant families face higher risk of food insecurity* (Vol. 7). Child Trends Research Brief Publication.

Card, D. (2022). Who set your wage? *American Economic Review, 112*(4), 1075–1090.

Card, D., & Giuliano, L. (1999). The causal effect of education on earnings. *Handbook of Labor Economics, 3*, 1801–1863.

___. (2005). Is the new immigration really so bad? *The Economic Journal, 115*(507), F300–F323.

___. (2016). Universal screening increases the representation of low-income and minority students in gifted education. *Proceedings of the National Academy of Sciences, 113*(48), 13678–13683.

Card, D., & Krueger, A. B. (1992). School quality and Black-White relative earnings: A direct assessment. *The Quarterly Journal of Economics, 107*(1), 151–200.

Card, D., Mas, A., & Rothstein, J. (2008). Tipping and the dynamics of segregation. *The Quarterly Journal of Economics, 123*(1), 177–218.

Carlos, A. M., Feir, D. L., & Redish, A. (2022). Indigenous nations and the development of the US economy: Land, resources, and dispossession. *The Journal of Economic History, 82*(2), 516–555.

Carneiro, P., Heckman, J. J., & Masterov, D. V. (2005). Labor market discrimination and racial differences in premarket factors. *The Journal of Law and Economics, 48*(1), 1–39.

Carson, A. E. (2021). *Prisoners in 2020—Statistical tables* (NCJ 302776). Office of Justice Programs, Bureau of Justice Statistics, U.S. Department of Justice. https://bjs.ojp.gov/content/pub/pdf/p20st.pdf

Carpenter, S. (2012). The USDA discrimination cases: Pigford, in re Black farmers, Keepseagle, Garcia, and Love. *Drake Journal of Agricultural Law, 17*(1). https://aglawjournal.wp.drake.edu/wp-content/uploads/sites/66/2016/09/agVol17No1-Carpenter.pdf

Carper, N. G. (1976). Slavery revisited: Peonage in the South. *Phylon, 37*(1), 85–99.

Casanueva, C., Dolan, M., & Smith, K. R. (2014). *National Survey of Child and Adolescent Well-Being, No. 21: Disconnected youth involved in child welfare*. (Report No. 2014-63). Office of Planning, Research and Evaluation, Administration for Children and Families, U.S. Department of Health and Human Services.

Case, A., Lubotsky, D., & Paxson, C. (2002). Economic status and health in childhood: The origins of the gradient. *American Economic Review*, 92(5), 1308–1334.

Casillas, K. L., Fauchier, A., Derkash, B. T. & Garrido, E. F. (2016). Implementation of evidence-based home visiting programs aimed at reducing child maltreatment: A meta-analytic review. *Child Abuse & Neglect*, 53, 64–80.

Cassidy, C., Heydemann, R., Price, A., Unah, N., & Darity Jr, W. (2019). *Baby bonds: A universal path to ensure the next generation has the capital to thrive*. The Samuel DuBois Cook Center on Social Equity. https://insightcced.org/wp-content/uploads/2019/12/ICCED-Duke_BabyBonds_December2019-Linked.pdf

Cattaneo, L., Feir, D. (2021). The price of mortgage financing for Native Americans. *Journal of Economics, Race, and Policy*, 4, 302–319. https://doi-org.turing.library.northwestern.edu/10.1007/s41996-020-00069-8

Cavalluzzo, K., & Wolken, J. (2005). Small business loan turndowns, personal wealth, and discrimination. *The Journal of Business*, 78(6), 2153–2178.

Cellini, S. R., & Turner, N. (2019). Gainfully employed? Assessing the employment and earnings of for-profit college students using administrative data. *Journal of Human Resources*, 54(2), 342–370.

Cengiz, D., Dube, A., Lindner, A., & Zipperer, B. (2019). The effect of minimum wages on low-wage jobs. *The Quarterly Journal of Economics*, 134(3), 1405–1454.

Center for Research on Education Outcomes (CREDO). (2013). *National charter school study: 2013*. https://credo.stanford.edu/wp-content/uploads/2021/08/ncss_2013_final_draft.pdf

Centers for Disease Control and Prevention. (n.d.). About underlying cause of death, 1999—2022. *CDC Wonder*. U.S. Department of Health and Human Services. https://wonder.cdc.gov/ucd-icd10.html

Centers for Disease Control and Prevention. (2023). Data and statistics (WISQARS). Injury Prevention & Control. U.S. Department of Health and Human Services. https://www.cdc.gov/injury/wisqars/index.html

Cesarini, D., Lindqvist, E., Notowidigdo, M. J., & Östling, R. (2017). The effect of wealth on individual and household labor supply: Evidence from Swedish lotteries. *American Economic Review*, 107(12), 3917–3946.

Chalfin, A., Hansen, B., Lerner, J., & Parker, L. (2021). Reducing crime through environmental design: Evidence from a randomized experiment of street lighting in New York City. *Journal of Quantitative Criminology*, 1–31.

Chalfin, A., Hansen, B., Weisburst, E. K., & Williams, M. C. Jr. (2022). Police force size and civilian race. *American Economic Review: Insights*, 4(2), 139–158.

Chalfin, A., & McCrary, J. (2017). Criminal deterrence: A review of the literature. *Journal of Economic Literature*, 55(1), 5–48.

___. (2018). Are U.S. cities underpoliced? Theory and evidence. *Review of Economics and Statistics*, 100(1), 167–186.

Chambers, J. E., Martin, K. D., & Skeem, J. L. (2021). Policy brief: Eliminating fees in the Alameda County juvenile justice system meaningfully reduced financial burdens on families. *California Policy Lab*. https://www.capolicylab.org/wp-content/uploads/2021/11/Eliminating-fees-in-the-Alameda-County-Juvenile-Justice-System.pdf

Chang, M., Hernández Kent, A., & McCulloch, H. (2021). Understanding the gender wealth gap, and why it matters. *The future of building wealth: Brief essays on the best ideas to build wealth—for everyone*. Aspen Institute Financial Security Program, Federal Reserve Bank of St. Louis. https://futureofwealth.org/the-book/

Charles, C. Z., Roscigno, V. J., & Torres, K. C. (2007). Racial inequality and college attendance: The mediating role of parental investments. *Social Science Research*, *36*(1), 329–352.

Charles, K. K., & Guryan, J. (2008). Prejudice and wages: An empirical assessment of Becker's The Economics of Discrimination. *Journal of Political Economy*, *116*(5), 773–809.

Chaturvedi, R., & Gabriel, R. A. (2020). Coronavirus disease health care delivery impact on African Americans. *Disaster Medicine and Public Health Preparedness*, *14*(6), 756–758.

Chay, K., & Greenstone, M. (2003a). *Air quality, infant mortality, and the Clean Air Act of 1970* (NBER Working Paper No. 10053). National Bureau of Economic Research. http://www.nber.org/papers/w10053

———. (2003b). The impact of air pollution on infant mortality: Evidence from geographic variation in pollution shocks induced by a recession. *The Quarterly Journal of Economics*, *118*(3), 1121–1167.

Chen, A., Oster, E., & Williams, H. (2016). Why is infant mortality higher in the United States than in Europe? *American Economic Journal: Economic Policy*, *8*(2), 89–124.

Chen, E., Yu, T., Siliezar, R., Drage, J. N., Dezil, J., Miller, G. E., & Brody, G. H. (2020). Evidence for skin-deep resilience using a co-twin control design: Effects on low-grade inflammation in a longitudinal study of youth. *Brain, Behavior, and Immunity*, *88*, 661–667.

Chen, H., Hill, C. J., & Holzer, H. J. (2009). *Against the tide: Household structure, opportunities, and outcomes among White and minority youth*. W. E. Upjohn Institute for Employment Research.

Chen, X., & Rafail, P. (2022). Physical disorder and crime revisited: New evidence from intensive longitudinal data. *Social Science Research*, *102*, 102637.

Chetty, R., Deming, D. J., & Friedman, J. N. (2023). *Diversifying society's leaders? The determinants and causal effects of admission to highly selective private colleges* (NBER Working Paper No. 31492). National Bureau of Economic Research. https://doi.org/10.3386/w31492

Chetty, R., Friedman, J. N., Hendren, N., Jones, M. R., & Porter, S. R. (2018). *The opportunity atlas: Mapping the childhood roots of social mobility* (NBER Working Paper No. 25147). National Bureau of Economic Research. http://www.nber.org/papers/w25147

Chetty, R., Friedman, J. N., Hilger, N., Saez, E., Schanzenbach, D. W., & Yagan, D. (2011). How does your kindergarten classroom affect your earnings? Evidence from Project STAR. *The Quarterly Journal of Economics*, *126*(4), 1593–660.

Chetty, R., Grusky, D., Hell, M., Hendren, N., Manduca, R., & Narang, J. (2017). The fading American Dream: Trends in absolute income mobility since 1940. *Science*, *356*(6336), 398–406.

Chetty, R., & Hendren, N. (2015). *The impacts of neighborhoods on intergenerational mobility: Childhood exposure effects and county-level estimates*. Harvard University and National Bureau of Economic Research. https://scholar.harvard.edu/files/hendren/files/nbhds_paper.pdf

———. (2018a). The impacts of neighborhoods on intergenerational mobility I: Childhood exposure effects. *The Quarterly Journal of Economics*, *133*(3), 1107–1162.

———. (2018b). The impacts of neighborhoods on intergenerational mobility II: County-level estimates. *Quarterly Journal of Economics*, *133*(3), 1163–1228.

Chetty, R., Hendren, N., Jones, M. R., & Porter, S. R. (2020). Race and economic opportunity in the United States: An intergenerational perspective. *The Quarterly Journal of Economics*, *135*(2), 711–783.

Chetty, R., Hendren, N., & Katz, L. F. (2016). The effects of exposure to better neighborhoods on children: New evidence from the moving to opportunity experiment. *American Economic Review*, *106*(4), 855–902.

Chetty, R., Hendren, N., Kline, P., & Saez, E. (2014a). Where is the land of opportunity? The geography of intergenerational mobility in the United States. *The Quarterly Journal of Economics, 129*(4), 1553–1623.

Chetty, R., Hendren, N., Kline, P., Saez, E., & Turner, N. (2014b). Is the United States still a land of opportunity? Recent trends in intergenerational mobility. *American Economic Review 104*(5), 141–147.

Chetty, R., Jackson, M. O., Kuchler, T., Stroebel, J., Hendren, N., Fluegge, R. B., Gong, S., Gonzalez, F., Grondin, A., Jacob, M., & Johnston, D. (2022). Social capital I: Measurement and associations with economic mobility. *Nature, 608*(7921), 108–121.

Chetty, R., Stepner, M., Abraham, S., Lin, S., Scuderi, B., Turner, N., Bergeron, A., & Culter, D. (2016). The association between income and life expectancy in the United States, 2001–2014. *JAMA, 315*(16), 1750–1766. https://doi.org/10.1001/jama.2016.4226

Child Welfare Information Gateway. (2019). *Long-term consequences of child abuse and neglect.* U.S. Department of Health and Human Services, Administration for Children and Families, Children's Bureau. https://www.childwelfare.gov/pubpdfs/long_term_consequences.pdf

Christensen, P., Sarmiento-Barbieri, I., & Timmins, C. (2021). *Racial discrimination and housing outcomes in the United States rental market* (NBER Working Paper No. 29516). National Bureau of Economic Research. https://doi.org/10.3386/w29516

Christensen, P., & Timmins, C. (2022). Sorting or steering: The effects of housing discrimination on neighborhood choice. *Journal of Political Economy, 130*(8), 2110–2163.

Christopher, C., & Farran, D. (2020). Academic gains in kindergarten related to eight classroom practices. *Early Childhood Research Quarterly, 53*, 638–649.

Chu, E. M., & Ready, D. D. (2018). Exclusion and urban public high schools: Short-and long-term consequences of school suspensions. *American Journal of Education, 124*(4), 479–509.

Chyn, E. (2018). Moved to opportunity: The long-run effects of public housing demolition on children. *American Economic Review, 108*(10), 3028–3056.

Chyn, E., & Daruich, D. (2022). *An equilibrium analysis of the effects of neighborhood-based interventions on children* (NBER Working Paper No. 29927). National Bureau of Economic Research. https://doi.org/ 10.3386/w29927

Chyn, E., Collinson, R., & Sandler, D. (2023). *The long-run effects of residential desegregation programs: Evidence from Gautreaux* (Working Paper). University of Texas-Austin, National Bureau of Economic Research, University of Notre Dame, U.S. Census Bureau. https://robcollinson.github.io/RobWebsite/CCS_Gautreaux.pdf

Chyn, E., Haggag, K., & Stuart, B. A. (2022). *The effects of racial segregation on intergenerational mobility: Evidence from historical railroad placement* (NBER Working Paper No. 30563). National Bureau of Economic Research. https://doi.org/10.3386/w30563

Ciocca Eller, C., & DiPrete, T. A. (2018). The paradox of persistence: Explaining the Black-White gap in bachelor's degree completion. *American Sociological Review, 83*(6), 1171–1214.

Cipriani, A., Zhou, X., Del Giovane, C., Hetrick, S.E., Qin, B., Whittington, C., Coghill, D., Zhang, Y., Hazell, P., Leucht, S., & Cuijpers, P. (2016). Comparative efficacy and tolerability of antidepressants for major depressive disorder in children and adolescents: A network meta-analysis. *The Lancet, 388*(10047), 881–890.

Clay, K., Muller, N. Z., & Wang, X. (2021). Recent increases in air pollution: Evidence and implications for mortality. *Review of Environmental Economics and Policy, 15*(1), 154–162.

Clemens, J., & Strain, M. R. (2018). The short-run employment effects of recent minimum wage changes: Evidence from the American Community Survey. *Contemporary Economic Policy, 36*(4), 711–722.

___. (2021). *The heterogeneous effects of large and small minimum wage changes: Evidence over the short and medium run using a pre-analysis plan* (NBER Working Paper No. 29264). National Bureau of Economic Research. https://doi.org/10.3386/w29264

Cobb-Clark, D. A., & Zhu, A. (2017). Childhood homelessness and adult employment: The role of education, incarceration, and welfare receipt. *Journal of Population Economics, 30*(3), 893–924.

Cobell v. Salazar, et al., 1285 U.S. (D.D.C. 2009). Class Action Settlement Agreement. https://www.justice.gov/archive/civil/cases/cobell/docs/pdf/settlement_12082009.pdf

Cohen, L. (2003) *A consumers' republic: The politics of mass consumption in postwar America*. Random House Inc.

Cohen-Vogel, L., Little, M., Jang, W., Burchinal, M., & Bratsch-Hines, M. (2021). A missed opportunity? Instructional content redundancy in pre-K and kindergarten. *AERA Open, 7,* 23328584211006163.

Cohodes, S. R., & Goodman, J. S. (2014). Merit aid, college quality, and college completion: Massachusetts' Adams scholarship as an in-kind subsidy. *American Economic Journal: Applied Economics, 6*(4), 251–285.

Coleman, K. L., & Wu, Q. (2016). Kinship care and service utilization: A review of predisposing, enabling, and need factors. *Children and Youth Services Review, 61,* 201–210.

Coleman, M. G. (2003). Job skill and Black male wage discrimination. *Social Science Quarterly, 84*(4), 892–906.

Coleman-Jensen, A., Rabbitt, M. P., Gregory, C. A., & Singh, A. (2022). Household food security in the United States. *Economic Research Report, 155.*

Coley, R. L., Leventhal, T., Lynch, A. D., & Kull, M. (2013). Relations between housing characteristics and the well-being of low-income children and adolescents. *Developmental Psychology, 49*(9).

Collins, P. H. (2002). *Black feminist thought: Knowledge, consciousness, and the politics of empowerment.* Routledge.

Collins, W. J., & Wanamaker, M. H. (2022). African American intergenerational economic mobility since 1880. *American Economic Journal: Applied Economics, 14*(3), 84–117.

Collinson, R., Ellen, I. G., & Ludwig, J. (2019). Reforming housing assistance. *The ANNALS of the American Academy of Political and Social Science, 686*(1), 250–285.

Collinson, R., Humphries, J. E., Mader, N. S., Reed, D. K., Tannenbaum, D. I., & Van Dijk, W. (2022). *Eviction and poverty in American cities* (NBER Working Paper No. 30382). National Bureau of Economic Research. https://doi.org/10.3386/w30382

Collyer, S., Wimer, C., Curran, M., Friedman, K., Hartley, R.P., Harris, D. & Hinton, A. (2020). Housing vouchers and tax credits: Pairing the proposal to transform section 8 with expansions to the EITC and the child tax credit could cut the National Child Poverty rate by half. *Poverty & Social Policy Brief, 4*(9).

Colmer, J., & Voorheis, J. (2022). *The grandkids aren't alright: The intergenerational effects of prenatal pollution exposure* (Working Paper CES 20-36). U.S. Census Bureau, Center for Economic Studies. https://www2.census.gov/ces/wp/2020/CES-WP-20-36.pdf

Colmer, J., Voorheis, J., & Williams, B. (2022). *Air pollution and economic opportunity in the United States.* U.S. Census Bureau. https://www.colorado.edu/economics/sites/default/files/attached-files/colmer.pdf

Comfort, M., McKay, T., Landwehr, J., Kennedy, E., Lindquist, C., & Bir, A. (2016). The costs of incarceration for families of prisoners. *International Review of the Red Cross, 98*(903), 783–798.

Commission on Evidence-Based Policymaking. (2017). *The promise evidence-based policymaking: Report of the Commission on Evidence-Based Policymaking.* https://bipartisanpolicy.org/wp-content/uploads/2019/03/Appendices-e-h-The-Promise-of-Evidence-Based-Policymaking-Report-of-the-Comission-on-Evidence-based-Policymaking.pdf

Community Preventive Services Task Force. (2016). School-based health centers to promote health equity: Recommendation of the Community Preventive Services Task Force. *American Journal of Preventive Medicine*, 51(1), 127–128.

Confidentiality and disclosure of returns and return information, 26 U.S. Code § 6103. (1979). https://www.law.cornell.edu/uscode/text/26/6103

Conger, R. D., Ge, X., Elder Jr, G. H., Lorenz, F. O., & Simons, R. L. (1994). Economic stress, coercive family process, and developmental problems of adolescents. *Child Development*, 65(2), 541–561.

Conger, R. D., Wallace, L. E., Sun, Y., Simons, R. L., McLoyd, V. C., & Brody, G. H. (2002). Economic pressure in African American families: A replication and extension of the family stress model. *Developmental Psychology*, 38(2), 179.

Congressional Budget Office. (2019). The effects on employment and family income of raising the minimum wage.

___. (2020). Table 1: Estimated effect on the Deficit of Rules Committee Print 116-56, the Patient Protection and Affordable Care Enhancement Act, as Amended by Amendment Number 6 (Pallone, Neal, Scott). https://www.cbo.gov/system/files/2020-06/Combined%20Tables.pdf

Conley, D. (1999). *Being Black, living in the red: Race, wealth, and social policy in America*. University of California Press.

___. (2001a). Capital for college: Parental assets and postsecondary schooling. *Sociology of Education*, 59–72.

___. (2001b). A room with a view or a room of one's own? Housing and social stratification. *Sociological forum*, 16(2), 263–280.

Conley, D., & Bennett, N. (2000) Is biology destiny? Birth weight and life chances. *American Sociological Review*, 65(3), 458–467. https://doi.org/10.2307/2657467

___. (2001). Birthweight and income: Interactions across generations. *Journal of Health and Social Behavior*, 42(4), 450–465.

Cook, P. J., & Donohue, J. J. (2017). Saving lives by regulating guns: Evidence for policy. *Science*, 358(6368), 1259–1261.

Cook, B. L., Trinh, N. H., Li, Z., Hou, S. S. Y., & Progovac, A. M. (2016). Trends in racial-ethnic disparities in access to mental health care, 2004–2012. *Psychiatric Services*, 68(1), 9–16.

Cook, T. D., Shadish, W. R., & Wong, V. C. (2008). Three conditions under which experiments and observational studies produce comparable causal estimates: New findings from within-study comparisons. *Journal of Policy Analysis and Management*, 27(4), 724–750.

Cooper, D., & Luengo-Prado, M. J. (2015). House price growth when children are teenagers: A path to higher earnings? *Journal of Urban Economics*, 86, 54–72.

Coopersmith, J. (2009). Characteristics of public, private, and Bureau of Indian Education Elementary and Secondary School teachers in the United States: Results From the 2007-08 schools and staffing survey. First Look (NCES 2009-324). *National Center for Education Statistics*.

Cordes, S. A., Schwartz, A. E., & Elbel, B. (2023). The effects of owner-occupied housing on student outcomes: Evidence from NYC. *Regional Science and Urban Economics*, 98, 103857.

Cordoba, J. C., Isojärvi, A. T., & Li, H. (2021). *Equilibrium unemployment: The role of discrimination*. Finance and Economics Discussion Series 2021-080. Board of Governors of the Federal Reserve System. https://doi.org/10.17016/FEDS.2021.080

Corinth, K., Meyer, B., Stadnicki, M., & Wu, D. (2021). *The anti-poverty, targeting, and labor supply effects of the proposed Child Tax Credit expansion* (Working Paper No. 2021-115). University of Chicago, Becker Friedman Institute for Economics. https://dx.doi.org/10.2139/ssrn.3938983

Cotti, C., Gordanier, J., & Ozturk, O. (2018). When does it count? The timing of food stamp receipt and educational performance. *Economics of Education Review, 66*, 40-50.

Coulton, C., Crampton, D., Irwin, M., Spilsbury, J., & Korbin, J. (2007). How neighborhoods influence child maltreatment: A review of the literature and alternative pathways. *Child Abuse & Neglect, 31*(11-12), 1117–42.

Cox, R., Cunningham, J. P., Ortega, A., & Whaley, K. (2022). *Black lives: The high cost of segregation* (Working Paper Series). Washington Center for Equitable Growth. https://equitablegrowth.org/working-papers/black-lives-the-high-cost-of-segregation/

Cozens, P. M., Saville, G., & Hillier, D. (2005). Crime prevention through environmental design (CPTED): A review and modern bibliography. *Property Management, 23*(5), 328–356.

Craigie, T.-A., Grawert, A. C., & Kimble, C. (2020). *Conviction, imprisonment, and lost earnings: How involvement with the criminal justice system deepens inequality.* Brennan Center for Justice at New York University School of Law. https://www.brennancenter.org/media/6676/download

Crenshaw, K. W., Ocen, P., & Nanda, J. (2015). *Black girls matter: Pushed out, overpoliced and underprotected.* Columbia Law School. https://scholarship.law.columbia.edu/faculty_scholarship/3227

Cross, C. J. (2018). Extended family households among children in the United States: Differences by race/ethnicity and socio-economic status. *Population Studies, 72*(2), 235–251.

Cullen, F. T., Jonson, C. L., & Nagin, D. S. (2011). Prisons do not reduce recidivism: The high cost of ignoring science. *The Prison Journal, 91*(3 Suppl), 48S–65S. https://doi.org/10.1177/0032885511415224

Cullen, J., & Grawert, A. (2016). *Fact Sheet: Stop and Frisk's Effect on Crime in New York City.* Brennan Center. https://www.brennancenter.org/our-work/research-reports/fact-sheet-stop-and-frisks-effect-crime-new-york-city

Cummings, D., & Bloom, D. (2020). Can subsidized employment programs help disadvantaged job seekers? A synthesis of findings from evaluations of 13 programs. *OPRE Report, 23*.

Currie, J. (2009). Healthy, wealthy, and wise: Socioeconomic status, poor health in childhood, and human capital development. *Journal of Economic Literature, 47*(1), 87–122.

Currie, J., Greenstone, M., & Moretti, E. (2011a). Superfund cleanups and infant health. *American Economic Review, 101*(3), 435–441.

Currie, J., Heep, S., & Neidell, M. (2011b). Quasi-experimental approaches to evaluating the impact of air pollution on children's health. *Health affairs (Project Hope), 30*(12), 2391.

Currie, J., & Gruber, J. (1996a). Saving babies: The efficacy and cost of recent changes in the Medicaid eligibility of pregnant women. *Journal of Political Economy, 104*(6), 1263–1296.

___. (1996b). Health insurance eligibility, utilization of medical care, and child health. *The Quarterly Journal of Economics, 111*(2), 431–466.

___. (1997). *The technology of birth: Health insurance, medical interventions, and infant health* (NBER Working Paper No. 5985). National Bureau of Economic Research. https://doi.org/10.3386/w5985

Currie, J., & Moretti, E. (2003). Mother's education and the intergenerational transmission of human capital: Evidence from college openings. *The Quarterly Journal of Economics, 118*(4), 1495–532.

Currie, J., & Rajani, I. (2015). Within-mother estimates of the effects of WIC on birth outcomes in New York City. *Economic Inquiry, 53*(4), 1691–1701.

Currie, J., & Schwandt, H. (2016). Mortality inequality: The good news from a county-level approach. *Journal of Economic Perspectives, 30*(2), 29–52.

Currie, J., & Stabile, M. (2003). Socioeconomic status and child health: Why is the relationship stronger for older children? *American Economic Review, 93*(5), 1813–1823.

___. (2006). Child mental health and human capital accumulation: The case of ADHD. *Journal of Health Economics*, 25(6), 1094–1118.
Currie, J., Stabile, M., Manivong, P., & Roos, L. L. (2010). Child health and young adult outcomes. *Journal of Human resources*, 45(3), 517–548.
Currie, J., & Tekin, E. (2012). Understanding the cycle: Childhood maltreatment and future crime. *Journal of Human Resources*, 47(2), 509–549.
Currie, J., Voorheis, J., & Walker, R. (2023). What caused racial disparities in particulate exposure to fall? New evidence from the Clean Air Act and satellite-based measures of air quality. *American Economic Review*, 113(1), 71–97.
Currie, J., & Walker, R. (2011). Traffic congestion and infant health: Evidence from E-ZPass. *American Economic Journal: Applied Economics*, 3(1), 65–90.
Currie, J., & Widom, C. (2010). Long-term consequences of child abuse and neglect on adult economic well-being. *Child Maltreatment*, 15(2), 111–120.
Currie, J., & Yelowitz, A. (2000). Are public housing projects good for kids? *Journal of Public Economics*, 75(1), 99–124.
Currie, J., Zivin, J. G., Meckel, K., Neidell, M., & Schlenker, W. (2013). Something in the water: Contaminated drinking water and infant health. *Canadian Journal of Economics/Revue Canadienne D'Économique*, 46(3), 791–810.
Currie, J., Zivin, J. G., Mullins, J., & Neidell, M. (2014). *What do we know about short-and long-term effects of early-life exposure to pollution?* (NBER Working Paper No. 19571). National Bureau of Economic Research. https://doi.org/10.3386/w19571
Cutuli, J. J., Goerge, R. M., Coulton, C., Schretzman, M., Crampton, D., Charvat, B. J., Lalich, N., Raithel, J. A., Gacitua, C., & Lee, E. L. (2016). From foster care to juvenile justice: Exploring characteristics of youth in three cities. *Children and Youth Services Review*, 67, 84–94.
D'Agostino, J. V., Lose, M. K., & Kelly, R. H. (2017). Examining the sustained effects of Reading Recovery. *Journal of Education for Students Placed at Risk*, 22(2), 116–127.
da Silva Lopes, K., Ota, E., Shakya, P., Dagvadorj, A., Balogun, O. O., Peña-Rosas, J. P., De-Regil, L. M. & Mori, R. (2017). Effects of nutrition interventions during pregnancy on low birth weight: An overview of systematic reviews. *BMJ Global Health*, 2(3), e000389.
Dahl, G. B., & Lochner, L. (2012). The impact of family income on child achievement: Evidence from the Earned Income Tax Credit. *American Economic Review*, 102(5), 1927–1956.
Danilo, T., & Saenz, M. (2021). *Economic security programs reduce overall poverty, racial and ethnic inequities*. Center on Budget and Policy Priorities. https://www.cbpp.org/sites/default/files/atoms/files/1-28-21pov.pdf
Darity Jr, W., & Hamilton, D. (2012). Bold policies for economic justice. *The Review of Black Political Economy*, 39(1), 79–85.
Darity, W. A. Jr., & Mullen, A. K. (2020). *From here to equality: Reparations for Black Americans in the twenty-first century*. UNC Press Books.
Davis, J. M., & Heller, S. B. (2020). Rethinking the benefits of youth employment programs: The heterogeneous effects of summer jobs. *Review of Economics and Statistics*, 102(4), 664–677.
Davis, J., & Mazumder, B. (2022). *The decline in intergenerational mobility after 1980* (Working Paper No. WP-2017-5). Federal Reserve Bank of Chicago. https://ssrn.com/abstract=2944584
Davis, M. A., Lee, K. A., Harris, M., Ha, J., Langa, K. M., Bynum, J. P., & Hoffman, G. J. (2022). Time to dementia diagnosis by race: A retrospective cohort study. *Journal of the American Geriatrics Society*, 70(11), 3250–3259.
Davison, M., Penner, A. M., Penner, E. K., Pharris-Ciurej, N., Porter, S. R., Rose, E. K., Shem-Tov, Y., & Yoo, P. (2022). School discipline and racial disparities in early adulthood. *Educational Researcher*, 51(3), 231–234.

Dawson, R. F., Kearney, M. S., & Sullivan, J. X. (2020). *Comprehensive approaches to increasing student completion in higher education: A survey of the landscape* (NBER No. w28046). National Bureau of Economic Research.

De Brey, C., Snyder, T. D., Zhang, A., & Dillow, S.A. (2021). Digest of Education Statistics 2019 (NCES 2021-009). National Center for Education Statistics, Institute of Education Sciences, U.S. Department of Education.

de Zeeuw, M. (2019). *Report on minority-owned firms: Small Business Credit Survey*. Federal Reserve Bank of Atlanta. https://www.fedsmallbusiness.org/medialibrary/fedsmallbusiness/files/2019/20191211-ced-minority-owned-firms-report.pdf

DeFina, R., & Hannon, L. (2013). The impact of mass incarceration on poverty. *Crime & Delinquency, 59*(4), 562–586.

Deitz, S., & Meehan, K. (2019). Plumbing poverty: Mapping hot spots of racial and geographic inequality in US household water insecurity. *Annals of the American Association of Geographers, 109*(4), 1092–1109.

Delmont, M. (2022). *Half American: The epic story of African Americans fighting World War II at home and abroad*. Viking.

Deloria, V. (1999). *Spirit & reason: The Vine Deloria, Jr., reader*. Fulcrum Publishing.

Deming, D. (2009). Early childhood intervention and life-cycle skill development: Evidence from Head Start. *American Economic Journal: Applied Economics, 1*(3), 111–134.

Deming, D. J., & Walters, C. R. (2017). *The impact of price caps and spending cuts on US postsecondary attainment* (NBER Working Paper No. 23736). National Bureau of Economic Research.

Denning, J. T., Marx, B. M., & Turner, L. J. (2019). ProPelled: The effects of grants on graduation, earnings, and welfare. *American Economic Journal: Applied Economics, 11*(3), 193–224.

Derenoncourt, E. (2022). Can you move to opportunity? Evidence from the Great Migration. *American Economic Review, 112*(2), 369–408.

Derenoncourt, E., Kim, C. H., Kuhn, M., & Schularick, M. (2022). *Wealth of two nations: The U.S. racial wealth gap, 1860–2020* (NBER Working Paper No. 30101). National Bureau of Economic Research.

Derenoncourt, E., & Montialoux, C. (2021). Minimum wages and racial inequality. *The Quarterly Journal of Economics, 136*(1), 169–228.

Desmond, M. (2014). *Policy Research Brief: Poor Black women are evicted at alarming rates, setting off a chain of hardship*. John D. and Catherine T. MacArthur Foundation. https://www.macfound.org/media/files/hhm_research_brief_-_poor_black_women_are_evicted_at_alarming_rates.pdf

___. (2021). Capitalism. *The 1619 Project: A new origin story*, 165–185. One World.

Desmond, M., An, W., Winkler, R., & Ferriss, T. (2013). Evicting children. *Social Forces, 92*(1), 303–327.

Desmond, M., & Gershenson, C. (2017). Who gets evicted? Assessing individual, neighborhood, and network factors. *Social Science Research, 62*, 362–377.

Deshpande, M., & Mueller-Smith, M. (2022). Does welfare prevent crime? The criminal justice outcomes of youth removed from SSI. *The Quarterly Journal of Economics, 137*(4), 2263–2307.

DeSimone, J., Markowitz, S., & Xu, J. (2013). Child access prevention laws and nonfatal gun injuries. *Southern Economic Journal, 80*(1), 5–25.

Dettlaff, A. J., & Boyd, R. (2022). The causes and consequences of racial disproportionality and disparities. *Handbook of Child Maltreatment*, 221–237.

Dettlaff, A. J., Rivaux, S. L., Baumann, D. J., Fluke, J. D., Rycraft, J. R., & James, J. (2011). Disentangling substantiation: The influence of race, income, and risk on the substantiation decision in child welfare. *Children and Youth Services Review, 33*(9), 1630–1637.

Deutscher, N. (2020). Place, peers, and the teenage years: Long-run neighborhood effects in Australia. *American Economic Journal: Applied Economics*, 12(2), 220–249.
Development Services Group, Inc. (2016). *Tribal youth in the juvenile justice system: Literature review*. Office of Juvenile Justice and Delinquency Prevention. https://www.ojjdp.gov/mpg/litreviews/Tribal-youth-in-the-Juvenile-Justice-System.pdf
DeVoe, J. F., & Darling-Churchill, K. E. (2008). Status and trends in the education of American Indians and Alaska Natives: 2008 (NCES No. 2008-084). *National Center for Education Statistics*.
Deyhle, D., & Swisher, K. (1997). Chapter 3: Research in American Indian and Alaska Native education: From assimilation to self-determination. *Review of Research in Education*, 22(1), 113–194.
Dobbie, W., & Fryer, R. G., Jr. (2011). Are high-quality schools enough to increase achievement among the poor? Evidence from the Harlem Children's Zone. *American Economic Journal: Applied Economics*, 3(3), 158–187.
Dobbie, W., Grönqvist, H., Niknami, S., Palme, M., & Priks, M. (2018). *The intergenerational effects of parental incarceration* (NBER Working Paper No. 24186). National Bureau of Economic Research.
Dolezsar, C. M., McGrath, J. J., Herzig, A. J., & Miller, S. B. (2014). Perceived racial discrimination and hypertension: A comprehensive systematic review. *Health Psychology*, 33(1), 20–34.
Donohue, J. J., Cai, S. V., Bondy, M. V., & Cook, P. J. (2022). *More guns, more unintended consequences: The effects of right-to-carry on criminal behavior and policing in U.S. cities* (NBER Working Paper No. 30190). National Bureau of Economic Research. https://doi.org/10.3386/w30190
Doren, C., & Grodsky, E. (2016). What skills can buy: Transmission of advantage through cognitive and noncognitive skills. *Sociology of Education*, 89(4), 321–342.
Dougherty S. M. (2018). The effect of career and technical education on human capital accumulation: Causal evidence from Massachusetts. *Education Finance and Policy*, 13(2), 119–148.
Doyle, J. J. (2007). Child protection and child outcomes: Measuring the effects of foster care. *American Economic Review*, 97(5), 1583–1610.
Doyle, J. J., Jr. (2008). Child protection and adult crime: Using investigator assignment to estimate causal effects of foster care. *Journal of Political Economy*, 116(4), 746–770.
Doyle, O. (2020). The first 2,000 days and child skills. *Journal of Political Economy*, 128(6), 2067–2122.
Doyle, O., Harmon, C., & Walker, I. (2007). *The impact of parental income and education on child health: Further evidence for England* (IZA DP No. 1832). IZA Discussion Paper Series. https://www.researchgate.net/publication/37144215_The_impact_of_parental_income_and_education_on_child_health_Further_evidence_for_England
Drake, B., Jolley, J. M., Lanier, P., Fluke, J., Barth, R. P., & Jonson-Reid, M. (2011). Racial bias in child protection? A comparison of competing explanations using national data. *Pediatrics*, 127(3), 471–478.
Du, Y. (2021). Racial bias still exists in criminal justice system? A review of recent empirical research. *Touro Law Review*, 37.
Dubay, L., & Kenney, G. (2003, October 7). Expanding public health insurance to parents: Effects on children's coverage under Medicaid. *Health Services Research*, 38(5), 1283–1302. https://doi.org/10.1111%2F1475-6773.00177
Dube, A. (2019a). *Impacts of minimum wages: Review of the international evidence*. National Bureau of Economic Research, IZA Institute of Labor Economics. https://assets.publishing.service.gov.uk/media/5dc0312940f0b637a03ffa96/impacts_of_minimum_wages_review_of_the_international_evidence_Arindrajit_Dube_web.pdf

___. (2019b). Minimum wages and the distribution of family incomes. *American Economic Journal: Applied Economics, 11*(4), 268–304.
DuBois, W. E. B. (1998). *Black Reconstruction in America, 1860–1880*. Free Press.
Duffee, J. H., Mendelsohn, A. L., Kuo, A. A., Legano, L. A., Earls, M. F., Council on Committee Pediatrics, Council on Early Childhood, Committee on Child Abuse and Neglect, Chilton, L. A., Flanagan, P. J., Dilley, K. J., Green, A. E., Gutierrez, J. R., Keane, V. A., Krugman, S. D., Linton, J. M., McKelvey, C. D., Nelson, J. L., Flaherty, E. G., ... & Williams, P. G. (2017). Early childhood home visiting. *Pediatrics, 140*(3). https://doi.org/10.1542/peds.2017-2150
Duncan, B., & Trejo, S. J. (2012). Low-skilled immigrants and the U.S. labor market. *The Oxford Handbook of the economics of poverty*, 203–248. Oxford University Press.
Duncan, G. J., Kalil, A., Mogstad, M., & Rege, M. (2023). Investing in early childhood development in preschool and at home. In E. A. Hanushek, L. Woessmann, & S. J. Machin *Handbook of the Economics of education*. Elsevier. https://www.sciencedirect.com/science/article/abs/pii/S1574069222000058
Duncan, G. J., & Magnuson, K. (2013). Investing in preschool programs. *Journal of Economic Perspectives, 27*(2), 109–132.
Duncan, G. J., Magnuson, K., & Votruba-Drzal, E. (2014). Boosting family income to promote child development. *The Future of Children, 24*(1), 99–120. https://doi.org/10.1353/foc.2014.0008
Duncan, G. J., Morris, P. A., & Rodrigues, C. (2011). Does money really matter? Estimating impacts of family income on young children's achievement with data from random-assignment experiments. *Developmental Psychology, 47*(5), 1263.
Duncan, G. J., & Murnane, R. J. (2014). *Restoring opportunity: The crisis of inequality and the challenge for American education*. Harvard Education Press.
Duncombe, W., & Yinger, J. (2005). How much more does a disadvantaged student cost? *Economics of Education Review, 24*(5), 513–532.
Dunn, J. R. (2020). Housing and healthy child development: Known and potential impacts of interventions. *Annual Review of Public Health, 41*(1), 381–396.
Durkin, K., Lipsey, M. W., Farran, D. C., & Wiesen, S. E. (2022). Effects of a statewide prekindergarten program on children's achievement and behavior through sixth grade. *Developmental Psychology, 58*(3), 470–484. https://doi.org/10.1037/dev0001301
Dynarski, S., Libassi, C. J., Michelmore, K., & Owen, S. (2021). Closing the gap: The effect of reducing complexity and uncertainty in college pricing on the choices of low-income students. *American Economic Review, 111*(6), 1721–1756.
Dynarski, S., Nurshatayeva, A., Page, L. C., & Scott-Clayton, J. (2022a). *Addressing nonfinancial barriers to college access and success: Evidence and policy implications* (NBER Work Paper No. 30054). National Bureau of Economic Research.
Dynarski, S., Page, L. C., & Scott-Clayton, J. (2022b). *College costs, financial aid, and student decisions.* (NBER Working Paper No. 30275). National Bureau of Economic Research. https://doi.org/10.3386/w30275
Early, D. M., Li, W., Maxwell, K. L., & Ponder, B. D. (2019). Participation in Georgia's pre-K as a predictor of third-grade standardized test scores. *AERA Open, 5*(2), 2332858419848687.
East, C. N. (2020). The effect of food stamps on children's health: Evidence from immigrants' changing eligibility. *Journal of Human Resources, 55*(2), 387–427.
East, C. N., Miller, S., Page, M., & Wherry, L. R. (2017). *Multi-generational impacts of childhood access to the safety net: Early life exposure to Medicaid and the next generation's health* (NBER Working Paper No. 23810). National Bureau of Economic Research. https://doi.org/10.3386/w23810

Eberhardt, J. L., Davies, P. G., Purdie-Vaughns, V. J., & Johnson, S. L. (2006). Looking deathworthy: Perceived stereotypicality of Black defendants predicts capital-sentencing outcomes. *Psychological Science, 17*(5), 383–386.

Eberhardt, J. L., Goff, P. A., Purdie, V. J., & Davies, P. G. (2004). Seeing Black: Race, crime, and visual processing. *Journal of Personality and Social Psychology, 87*(6), 876.

Eberstadt, N. (2016). *Men without work: America's invisible crisis*. Templeton Foundation Press.

Eckenrode, J., Smith, E. G., McCarthy, M. E., & Dineen, M. (2014). Income inequality and child maltreatment in the United States. *Pediatrics, 133*(3), 454–461.

Economic Policy Institute. (2022a). Wages by percentile and wage ratios. *State of Working America Data Library*. https://www.epi.org/data/#?subject=wage-percentiles

___. (2022b). Employment-to-population ratio. *State of Working America Data Library*. https://www.epi.org/data/#?subject=epop

Ecton, W. G., & Dougherty, S. M. (2023). Heterogeneity in high school career and technical education outcomes. *Educational Evaluation and Policy Analysis, 45*(1), 157–181.

Education Trust. (2019). *A look at Black student success: Identifying top- and bottom-performing institutions*. https://edtrust.org/wp-content/uploads/2014/09/A-Look-at-Black-Student-Success.pdf

Edwards, V. J., Holden, G. W., Felitti, V. J., & Anda, R. F. (2003). Relationship between multiple forms of childhood maltreatment and adult mental health in community respondents: Results from the adverse childhood experiences study. *American Journal of Psychiatry, 160*(8), 1453–1460.

Ehrle, J., & Geen, R. (2002). Kin and non-kin foster care—Findings from a national survey. *Children and Youth Services Review, 24*(1-2), 15–35.

Eitle, D., & Turner, R. J. (2002). Exposure to community violence and young adult crime: The effects of witnessing violence, traumatic victimization, and other stressful life events. *Journal of Research in Crime and Delinquency, 39*(2), 214–237.

Elder, G. H. (1974). *Children of the Great Depression*. University of Chicago Press.

Elder, T. E., Figlio, D. N., Imberman, S. A., & Persico, C. L. (2021). School segregation and racial gaps in special education identification. *Journal of Labor Economics, 39*(S1), S151–S197.

Elder, T., & Zhou, Y. (2021). The Black-White gap in noncognitive skills among elementary school children. *American Economic Journal: Applied Economics, 13*(1), 105–132.

Eliason, E. L. (2020). Adoption of Medicaid expansion is associated with lower maternal mortality. *Women's Health Issues, 30*(3), 147–152.

Elliott, III, W., & Beverly, S. G. (2011). The role of savings and wealth in reducing 'wilt' between expectations and college attendance. *Journal of Children and Poverty, 17*(2), 165–185.

Elliott, W., Lewis, M., Grinstein-Weiss, M., & Nam, I. (2014). Student loan debt: Can parental college savings help. *Federal Reserve Bank of St. Louis Review, 96*(4), 331–357.

Elliott-Groves, E., & Fryberg, S. A. (2019). A future denied" for young Indigenous people: From social disruption to possible futures. In E. A. McKinley & L. T. Smith (Eds.), *Handbook of Indigenous Education*, (pp. 631–649).

Elmi, S., & Lopez, B. (2021). *Foundations of a New Wealth Agenda*. Aspen Institute.

Eng, A., & Matsudaira, J. (2021). Pell grants and student success: Evidence from the universe of federal aid recipients. *Journal of Labor Economics, 39*(S2), S413–S454.

Epstein, R., Blake, J., & González, T. (2017). *Girlhood interrupted: The erasure of Black girls' childhood*. Center on Poverty and Inequality, Georgetown Law School. https://genderjusticeandopportunity.georgetown.edu/wp-content/uploads/2020/06/girlhood-interrupted.pdf

Equitable Data Working Group. (2022). *A vision for equitable data recommendations from the Equitable Data Working Group.* https://www.whitehouse.gov/wp-content/uploads/2022/04/eo13985-vision-for-equitable-data.pdf

Espinosa, L. L., Kelchen, R., & Taylor, M. (2018). *Minority Serving Institutions as engines of upward mobility.* American Council on Education. https://www.acenet.edu/Documents/MSIs-as-Engines-of-Upward-Mobility.pdf

Elu, J. U., Ireland, J., Jeffries, D., Johnson, I., Jones, E., Long, D., Price, G. N., Sam, O., Simons, T., Slaughter, F., & Trotman, J. (2019). The earnings and income mobility consequences of attending a Historically Black College/University: Matching estimates from 2015 U.S. department of education college scorecard data. *The Review of Black Political Economy*, 46(3), 171–192.

Evans, W. N., & Garthwaite, C. L. (2014). Giving mom a break: The impact of higher EITC payments on maternal health. *American Economic Journal: Economic Policy*, 6(2), 258–290.

Evans, W. N., Kearney, M. S., Perry, B., & Sullivan, J. X. (2020). Increasing community college completion rates among low-income students: Evidence from a randomized controlled trial evaluation of a case-management intervention. *Journal of Policy Analysis and Management*, 39(4), 930–965.

Evans, W. N., & Owens, E. G. (2007). Cops and crime. *Journal of Public Economics*, 91(1-2), 181–201.

Evans-Campbell, T., Walters, K., Pearson, C., & Campbell, C. (2012). Indian boarding school experience, substance use, and mental health among urban two-spirit American Indian/Alaska Natives. *American Journal of Drug and Alcohol Abuse*, 38(5), 421–427.

Everytown. (2022). *The rise of firearm suicide among young Americans.* https://everytownresearch.org/report/the-rise-of-firearm-suicide-among-young-americans/

The Eviction Lab. (2018). *National estimates: Eviction in America.* Princeton University. https://evictionlab.org/national-estimates/

Faber, J. W. (2013). Racial dynamics of subprime mortgage lending at the peak. *Housing Policy Debate*, 23(2), 328–349.

Faber, J. W., & Mercier, M.-D. (2022). Multidimensional discrimination in the online rental housing market: Implications for families with young children. *Housing Policy Debate*, 1–24.

FAIR Health. (2021). *The impact of COVID-19 on pediatric mental health: A study of private healthcare claims.* A FAIR Health White Paper.

Faircloth, S. C., & Tippeconnic III, J. W. (2010). The dropout/graduation crisis among American Indian and Alaska Native Students: UCLA. Civil Rights Project/Proyecto Derechos Civiles. https://www.civilrightsproject.ucla.edu/research/k-12-education/school-dropouts/the-dropout-graduation-crisis-among-american-indian-and-alaska-native-students-failure-to-respond-places-the-future-of-native-peoples-at-risk/faircloth-tippeconnic-native-american-dropouts.pdf

Fairlie, R. W., Couch, K. A., & Xu, H. (2021, September 28). *Racial disparities in unemployment during the COVID-19 pandemic and recovery.* Prepared for the Federal Reserve Bank of Boston's 64th Economic Conference. https://www.bostonfed.org/-/media/Documents/events/2021/racial-disparities-in-todays-economy/Racial-Disparities-in-Unemployment-during-the-COVID-19-Pandemic-and-Recovery.pdf?la=en

Fairlie, R. W., & Robb, A. M. (2010). *Disparities in capital access between minority and non-minority-owned businesses: The troubling reality of capital limitations faced by MBEs.* U.S. Department of Commerce, Minority Business Development Agency. https://www.mbda.gov/sites/default/files/migrated/files-attachments/DisparitiesinCapitalAccessReport.pdf

Farber, H. S., Herbst, D., Kuziemko I., & Naidu, S. (2018). *Unions and inequality over the twentieth century: New evidence from survey data* (NBER Working Papers No. 24587). National Bureau of Economic Research. https://doi.org/10.3386/w24587

Farrell, J., Burow, P. B., McConnell, K., Bayham, J., Whyte, K., & Koss, G. (2021). Effects of land dispossession and forced migration on Indigenous peoples in North America. *Science, 374*(6567), eabe4943.

Faurschou, E. (2018). Quasi-experimental evidence of neighbourhood exposure effects in Denmark [Master's thesis]. University of Copenhagen.

Feagin, J., & Elias, S. (2013). Rethinking racial formation theory: A systemic racism critique. *Ethnic and Racial Studies, 36*(6), 931–960.

Federal Bureau of Investigation. (2019a). Table 1: Crime in the United States by volume and rate per 100,000 inhabitants, 2000–2019. 2019 Crime in the United States, Expanded Homicide Data. https://ucr.fbi.gov/crime-in-the-u.s/2019/crime-in-the-u.s.-2019/tables/table-1

___. (2019b). Table 3: Murder offenders by age, sex, race, and ethnicity. 2019 Crime in the United States, Expanded Homicide Data. https://ucr.fbi.gov/crime-in-the-u.s/2019/crime-in-the-u.s.-2019/topic-pages/tables/expanded-homicide-data-table-3.xls

___. (2022). Federal Bureau of Investigation Crime Data Explorer. Crime Data Explorer for violent crimes for years 2017–2021. https://cde.ucr.cjis.gov/LATEST/webapp/#/pages/home

Feierman, J., Goldstein, N., Haney-Caron, E., & Columbo. J. F. (2016). *Debtors' prison for kids? The high cost of fines and fees in the juvenile justice system.* Juvenile Law Center. http://debtorsprison.jlc.org/documents/jlc-debtors-prison.pdf

Feigenberg, B., & Miller, C. (2021). Racial divisions and criminal justice: Evidence from southern state courts. *American Economic Journal: Economic Policy, 13*(2), 207–240.

Fein, D., Dastrup, S., & Burnett, K. (2021). *Still bridging the opportunity divide for low-income youth: Year Up's longer-term impacts* (OPRE Report 2021-56). Office of Planning, Research, and Evaluation, Administration for Children and Families, U.S. Department of Health and Human Services.

Fein, D. J., & Lee, W. S. (2003). The impacts of welfare reform on child maltreatment in Delaware. *Children and Youth Services Review, 25*(1–2), 83–111.

Feiveson, L., & Sabelhaus, J. (2018). How does intergenerational wealth transmission affect wealth concentration? FEDS Notes. Board of Governors of the Federal Reserve System. https://doi.org/10.17016/2380-7172.2209

Feliciano, C. (2005). Educational selectivity in US immigration: How do immigrants compare to those left behind? *Demography, 42*(1), 131–152.

Feliciano, C., & Lanuza, Y. R. (2017). An immigrant paradox? Contextual attainment and intergenerational educational mobility. *American Sociological Review, 82*(1), 211–241.

Feller, A., Grindal, T., Miratrix, L., & Page, L. C. (2016). Compared to what? Variation in the impacts of early childhood education by alternative care type. *ANNALS of Applied Statistics, 10*(3), 1245–1285. https://doi.org/10.1214/16-AOAS910

Fenelon, A., Boudreaux, M., Slopen, N., & Newman, S. J. (2021). The benefits of rental assistance for children's health and school attendance in the United States. *Demography, 58*(4), 1171–1195.

Fenelon, A., Mayne, P., Simon, A. E., Rossen, L. M., Helms, V., Lloyd, P., Sperling, J. & Steffen, B. L. (2017). Housing assistance programs and adult health in the United States. *American Journal of Public Health, 107*(4), 571–578.

Fenelon, A., Slopen, N., Boudreaux, M., & Newman, S. J. (2018). The impact of housing assistance on the mental health of children in the United States. *Journal of Health and Social Behavior, 59*(3), 447–63.

Ferguson, R. F. (2016). Aiming higher together: Strategizing better educational outcomes for boys and young men of color. *Urban Institute.* https://www.urban.org/sites/default/files/publication/80481/2000784-Aiming-Higher-Together-Strategizing-Better-Educational-Outcomes-for-Boys-and-Young-Men-of-Color.pdf

Fertig, A. (2019). *The long-term health consequences of childhood food insecurity* (Research Discussion Paper Series No. 2012-03). University of Kentucky Center for Poverty.

Findling, M. G., Casey, L. S., Fryberg, S. A., Hafner, S., Blendon, R. J., Benson, J. M., Sayde, J. M., & Miller, C. (2019). Discrimination in the United States: Experiences of Native Americans. *Health Services Research*, *54*, 1431–1441.

Finlay, K., Mueller-Smith, M., & Street, B. (2022). *Measuring intergenerational exposure to the US justice system: Evidence from longitudinal links between survey and administrative data* (Working Paper No. 2211). Department of Economics, University of Missouri.

Fischer, W., Acosta, S., & Gartland, E. (2021). *More housing vouchers: Most important step to help more people afford stable homes*. Center on Budget and Policy Priorities. https://www.cbpp.org/research/housing/more-housing-vouchers-most-important-step-to-help-more-people-afford-stable-homes

Fishback, P., Rose, J., Snowden, K., & Storrs, T. (2022). *New evidence on redlining by federal housing programs in the 1930s* (Working Paper No. 2022-01). Federal Reserve Bank of Chicago. https://doi.org/10.21033/wp-2022-01

Fisher, J., & Johnson, D. (2023). *Intergenerational mobility using income, consumption, and wealth*. The Washington Center for Equitable Growth. https://equitablegrowth.org/working-papers/intergenerational-mobility-using-incomeconsumption-and-wealth/

FitzGerald, C., & Hurst, S. (2017). Implicit bias in healthcare professionals: A systematic review. *BMC Medical Ethics*, *18*(1), 1–18.

Fitzsimons, E., Goodman, A., Kelly, E., & Smith, J. P. (2017). Poverty dynamics and parental mental health: Determinants of childhood mental health in the UK. *Social Science & Medicine*, *175*, 43–51.

Fixico, D. L. (2011). *The invasion of Indian country in the twentieth century*. University Press of Colorado.

Flage, A. (2018). Ethnic and gender discrimination in the rental housing market: Evidence from a meta-analysis of correspondence tests, 2006–2017. *Journal of Housing Economics*, *41*, 251–273.

Fletcher, J. (2014). The effects of childhood ADHD on adult labor market outcomes. *Health Economics*, *23*(2), 159–181.

Flood, S., King, M., Rodgers, R., Ruggles, S., Warren, J. R., Westberry, M. (2022) Integrated Public Use Microdata Series, Current Population Survey: Version 10.0. IPUMS, The University of Minnesota. https://doi.org/10.18128/D030.V10.0

Font, S. A., Berger, L. M., & Slack, K. S. (2012). Examining racial disproportionality in child protective services case decisions. *Children and Youth Services Review*, *34*(11), 2188–2200.

Font, S. A., Cancian, M., Berger, L. M., & DiGiovanni, A. (2021). Patterns of intergenerational child protective services involvement. *Child Abuse & Neglect*, *99*, 104247.

Font, S. A., & Maguire-Jack, K. (2020a). It's not "just poverty": Educational, social, and economic functioning among young adults exposed to childhood neglect, abuse, and poverty. *Child Abuse & Neglect*, *101*, 104356.

___. (2020b). The scope, nature, and causes of child abuse and neglect. *The ANNALS of the American Academy of Political and Social Science*, *692*, 26–49.

Foverskov, E., White, J. S., Froslev, T., Sorensen, H. T., & Hamad, R. (2022a). Risk of psychiatric disorders for refugee children and adolescents living in disadvantaged neighborhoods: A quasi-experimental study. *JAMA Pediatrics*, *176*(11), 1107–1114.

Foverskov, E., White, J. S., Norredam, M., Frøslev, T., Kim, M. H., Glymour, M. M., Pedersen, L., Sørensen, H. T., & Hamad, R. (2022b). Neighbourhood socioeconomic disadvantage and psychiatric disorders among refugees: A population-based, quasi-experimental study in Denmark. *Social Psychiatry and Psychiatric Epidemiology*, *58*(5), 771–721.

Fox, C. (2012). *Three worlds of relief*. Princeton University Press.

Fox, L. E. (2016). Parental wealth and the Black–White mobility gap in the U.S. *Review of Income and Wealth*, *62*(4), 706–723.

Fox, L., & Burns, K. (2021). The Supplemental Poverty Measure: 2020. *Current Population Reports*. U.S. Census Bureau.

Franckle, R. L., Thorndike, A. N., Moran, A. J., Hou, T., Blue, D., Greene, J. C., Bleich, S. N., Block, J. P., Polacsek, M., & Rimm, E. B. (2019). Supermarket purchases over the supplemental nutrition assistance program benefit month: A comparison between participants and nonparticipants. *American Journal of Preventive Medicine, 57*(6), 800–807.

Franklin, J. H. (1969). *From slavery to freedom: A history of Negro Americans*. Vintage Books.

———. (2013). *Reconstruction after the Civil War* (3rd ed.). University of Chicago Press.

Franklin, T. W. (2013). Sentencing Native Americans in US federal courts: An examination of disparity. *Justice Quarterly, 30*(2), 310–39.

Frazier, E. F. (1957). *Black bourgeoisie*. Free Press.

Freddie Mac. (2022). *Racial and ethnic valuation gaps in home purchase appraisals*. Freddie Mac. https://www.freddiemac.com/research/pdf/202205-Note-Appraisals-09.pdf

Frederiksen, B., Ranji, U., Salganicoff, A., & Long, M. (2021). *Women's sexual and reproductive health services: Key findings from the 2020 KFF Women's Health Survey*. Kaiser Family Foundation. https://www.kff.org/womens-health-policy/issue-brief/womens-sexual-and-reproductive-health-services-key-findings-from-the-2020-kff-womens-health-survey/

Freedman, A. A., Papachristos, A. V., Smart, B. P., Keenan-Devlin, L. S., Khan, S. S., Borders, A., Kershaw, K. N., & Miller, G. E. (2022). Complaints about excessive use of police force in women's neighborhoods and subsequent perinatal and cardiovascular health. *Science Advances, 8*(3), eabl5417.

Friedman, B., & Pattillo, M. (2019). Statutory inequality: The logics of monetary sanctions in state law. *RSF: The Russell Sage Foundation Journal of the Social Sciences, 5*(1), 174–196. https://www.rsfjournal.org/content/rsfjss/5/1/174.full.pdf

Friedman-Krauss, A., & Barnett, S. (2020). *Access to high-quality early education and racial equity*. National Institute for Early Education Research, Rutgers Graduate School of Education. https://nieer.org/wp-content/uploads/2021/02/Special-Report-Access-to-High-Quality-Early-Education-and-Racial-Equity.pdf

Friedman-Krauss, A., Barnett, W. S., Garver, K. A., Hodges, K. S., Weisenfeld, G. G., & Gardiner, B. A. (2021). *The state of preschool 2020: State preschool yearbook*. National Institute for Early Education Research

Fronius, T., Darling-Hammond, S., Persson, H., Guckenburg, S., Hurley, N., & Petrosino, A. (2019). *Restorative justice in U.S. schools: An updated research review*. WestEd. https://www.wested.org/wp-content/uploads/2019/04/resource-restorative-justice-in-u-s-schools-an-updated-research-review.pdf

Frost, R. (2020). *Are Americans stuck in place? Declining residential mobility in the U.S.* The Joint Center for Housing Studies. https://www.jchs.harvard.edu/sites/default/files/harvard_jchs_are_americans_stuck_in_place_frost_2020.pdf

Fryberg, S. A., Covarrubias, R., & Burack, J. A. (2013). Cultural models of education and academic performance for Native American and European American students. *School Psychology International, 34*(4), 439–452.

Fryberg, S. A., Covarrubias, R., & Burack, J. A. (2018). The ongoing psychological colonization of North American indigenous people: Using social psychological theories to promote social justice. *The Oxford Handbook of Social Psychology and Social Justice*, 113–128.

Fryberg, S. A., & Eason, A. E. (2017). Making the invisible visible: Acts of commission and omission. *Current Directions in Psychological Science, 26*(6), 554–559.

Fryberg, S. A., & Leavitt, P. A. (2014). A sociocultural analysis of high-risk Native American children in schools. *Cultural and Contextual Perspectives on Developmental Risk and Well-Being, 39*, 57–80.

Fryberg, S. A., & Markus, H. R. (2007). Cultural models of education in American Indian, Asian American and European American contexts. *Social Psychology of Education, 10*, 213–246.

Fryberg, S. A., Markus, H. R., Oyserman, D., & Stone, J. M. (2008). Of warrior Chiefs and Indian princesses: The psychological consequences of American Indian mascots. *Basic and Applied Social Psychology, 30*(3), 208–218.

Fryberg, S. A., & Stephens, N. M. (2010). When the world is colorblind, American Indians are invisible: A diversity science approach. *Psychological Inquiry, 21*(2), 115–119.

Fryberg, S. A., & Townsend, S. S. M. (2008). The psychology of invisibility. In G. Adams, M. Biernat, N. R. Branscombe, C. S. Crandall, & L. S. Wrightsman (Eds.), *Commemorating Brown: The social psychology of racism and discrimination*, 173–193. American Psychological Association.

Frye, D., & Parker, D. P. (2021). Indigenous self-governance and development on American Indian Reservations. *American Economic Association Papers & Proceedings, 111*, 233–237.

Fryer Jr., R. G. (2016). *The production of human capital in developed countries: Evidence from 196 randomized field experiments* (NBER Working Paper No. 22130). National Bureau of Economic Research.

Fuhs, M. W., Nesbitt, K. T., Farran, D. C., & Dong, N. (2014). Longitudinal associations between executive functioning and academic skills across content areas. *Developmental Psychology, 50*(6), 1698. https://doi.org/10.1037/a0036633

Fuller-Thomson, E., & Minkler, M. (2000). African American grandparents raising grandchildren: A national profile of demographic and health characteristics. *Health & Social Work, 25*(2), 109–118.

Gaddis, S. M. (2015). Discrimination in the credential society: An audit study of race and college selectivity in the labor market. *Social Forces, 93*, 1451–1479.

Galama, T., Lleras-Muney, A., & van Kippersluis, H. (2018). *The effect of education on health and mortality: A review of experimental and quasi-experimental evidence* (NBER Working Paper No. 24225). National Bureau of Economic Research. https://doi.org/10.3386/w24225

Galster, G., Marcotte, D. E., Mandell, M. B., Wolman, H., & Augustine, N. (2007). The impact of parental homeownership on children's outcomes during early adulthood. *Housing Policy Debate, 18*(4), 785–827.

Garces, E., Thomas, D., & Currie, J. (2002). Longer-term effects of Head Start. *American Economic Review, 92*(4), 999–1012.

García, J. L., Heckman, J. J., Leaf, D. E., & Prados, M. J. (2020). Quantifying the life-cycle benefits of an influential early-childhood program. *Journal of Political Economy, 128*(7), 2502–2541.

García, J. L., Heckman, J. J., & Ronda, V. (2021). *The lasting effects of early childhood education on promoting the skills and social mobility of disadvantaged African Americans* (Working Paper No. 2021-83). Becker Friedman Institute for Economics at University of Chicago.

Gartland, E. (2022). *Chart book: Funding limitations create widespread unmet need for rental assistance*. Center for Budget and Policy Priorities. https://www.cbpp.org/research/housing/funding-limitations-create-widespread-unmet-need-for-rental-assistance

Gassman-Pines, A., & Bellows, L. (2018). Food instability and academic achievement: A quasi-experiment using SNAP benefit timing. *American Educational Research Journal, 55*(5), 897–927.

Gay, G., & Howard, T. C. (2000). Multicultural teacher education for the 21st century. *The Teacher Educator, 36*(1), 1–16.

Ge, Y., Knittel, C. R., MacKenzie, D., & Zoepf, S. (2020). Racial discrimination in transportation network companies. *Journal of Public Economics, 190*, 104205.

Geisler, C. (2014). Disowned by the ownership society: How Native Americans lost their land. *Rural Sociology*, 79(1), 56–78.
Geller, A., Goff, P. A., Lloyd, T., Haviland, A., Obermark, D., & Glaser, J. (2021). Measuring racial disparities in police use of force: Methods matter. *Journal of Quantitative Criminology*, 37, 1083–1113.
Gennetian, L. A., Seshadri, R., Hess, N. D., Winn, A. N., & Goerge, R. M. (2016). Supplemental Nutrition Assistance Program (SNAP) benefit cycles and student disciplinary infractions. *Social Service Review*, 90(3), 403–433.
Geronimus, A. T., Hicken, M., Keene, D., & Bound, J. (2006). "Weathering" and age patterns of allostatic load scores among Blacks and Whites in the United States. *American Journal of Public Health*, 96(5), 826–833.
Gershenson, S., Hart, C. M., Hyman, J., Lindsay, C. A., & Papageorge, N. W. (2022). The long-run impacts of same-race teachers. *American Economic Journal: Economic Policy*, 14(4), 300–342.
Gershenson, S., Holt, S. B., & Papageorge, N. W. (2016). Who believes in me? The effect of student–teacher demographic match on teacher expectations. *Economics of Education Review*, 52, 209–224.
Gibson-Davis, C., & Hill, H. D. (2021). Childhood wealth inequality in the United States: Implications for social stratification and well-being. *The Russell Sage Foundation Journal of the Social Sciences*, 7(3), 1–26.
Gibson-Davis, C., Keister, L. A., & Gennetian, L. A. (2021). Net worth poverty in child households by race and ethnicity, 1989–2019. *Journal of Marriage and Family*, 83(3), 667–682.
Gill, C., Weisburd, D., Telep, C. W., Vitter, Z., & Bennett, T. (2014). Community-oriented policing to reduce crime, disorder and fear and increase satisfaction and legitimacy among citizens: A systematic review. *Journal of Experimental Criminology*, 10(4), 399–428.
Gilliam, W. S., Maupin, A. N., Reyes, C. R., Accavitti, M., & Shic, F. (2016). Do early educators' implicit biases regarding sex and race relate to behavior expectations and recommendations of preschool expulsions and suspensions? *Yale University Child Study Center*, 9(28), 1–16.
Gilraine, M. (2023). Air filters, pollution and student achievement. *Journal of Human Resources*. https://doi.org/10.3368/jhr.0421-11642R2
Gilraine, M., & Zheng, A. (2022). *Air pollution and student performance in the U.S* (NBER Working Paper No. 30061). National Bureau of Economic Research.
Ginther, D. K., & Johnson-Motoyama, M. (2017). Do state TANF policies affect child abuse and neglect? Paper presented at the APPAM 9th Annual Fall Research Conference: Chicago, IL. https://www.econ.iastate.edu/files/events/files/gintherjohnsonmotoyama_appam.pdf
Giscombé, C. L., & Lobel, M. (2005). Explaining disproportionately high rates of adverse birth outcomes among African Americans: The impact of stress, racism, and related factors in pregnancy. *Psychological Bulletin*, 131(5), 662.
Gittleman, M., & Wolff, E. N. (2004). Racial differences in patterns of wealth accumulation. *Journal of Human Resources*, 39(1), 193–227.
Gius, M. (2017). The effects of state and federal gun control laws on school shootings. *Applied Economics Letters*, 25(5), 317–320.
Gleeson, J. (2012). What works in kinship care? *What Works in Child Welfare?*, 193–216. Child Welfare League of America.
Glenn, E. N. (2015). Settler colonialism as structure: A framework for comparative studies of U.S. race and gender formation. *Sociology of Race and Ethnicity*, 1(1), 52–72.
Godoey, A., & Reich, M. (2021). Are minimum wage effects greater in low-wage areas? *Industrial Relations: A Journal of Economy and Society*, 60(1), 36–83.

Goe, L. (2007). *The link between teacher quality and student outcomes: A research synthesis*. National Comprehensive Center for Teacher Quality. http://files.eric.ed.gov/fulltext/ED521219.pdf

Goff, P. A., Jackson, M. C., Di Leone, B. A., Culotta, C. M., & DiTomasso, N. A. (2014). The essence of innocence: Consequences of dehumanizing Black children. *Journal of Personality and Social Psychology, 106*(4), 526–545. https://doi.org/10.1037/a0035663

Goldin, C. (2021). *Career and family*. Princeton University Press.

Goodman, A., Joyce, R., & Smith, J. P. (2011). The long shadow cast by childhood physical and mental problems on adult life. *Proceedings of the National Academy of Sciences, 108*(15), 6032–6037.

Goodman-Bacon, A. (2021). The long-run effects of childhood insurance coverage: Medicaid implementation, adult health, and labor market outcomes. *American Economic Review, 111*(8), 2550–2593.

Goodman-Bacon, A., & McGranahan, L. (2008). How do EITC recipients spend their refunds? *Economic Perspectives, 32*(2).

Goodman, W. B., Dodge, K. A., Bai, Y., Murphy, R. A., & O'Donnell, K. (2021). Effect of a universal postpartum nurse home visiting program on child maltreatment and emergency medical care at 5 years of age: A randomized clinical trial. *JAMA Network Open, 4*(7), e2116024.

Gordon, E. K., Hawley, Z. B., Kobler, R. C., & Rork, J. C. (2020). The paradox of HBCU graduation rates. *Research in Higher Education, 62*(3), 332–358.

Gordon, G., Jones, J. B., Neelakantan, U., & Athreya, K. (2021). *Incarceration, earnings, and race* (Working Paper No. 21-11). Federal Reserve Bank of Richmond. https://www.richmondfed.org/-/media/richmondfedorg/publications/research/working_papers/2021/wp21-11.pdf

Gordon, N. (2004). Do federal grants boost school spending? Evidence from Title I. *Journal of Public Economics, 88*(9-10), 1771–1792.

Gormley Jr, W. T., Amadon, S., Magnuson, K., Claessens, A., & Hummel-Price, D. (2023). Universal pre-K and college enrollment: Is there a link? *AERA Open, 9*, 23328584221147893.

Gould, S. J. (1996). *The mismeasure of man*. W.W. Norton & Company.

Goyer, J. P., Cohen, G. L., Cook, J. E., Master, A., Apfel, N., Lee, W., Henderson, A. G., Reeves, S. L., Okonofua, J. A. & Walton, G. M. (2019). Targeted identity-safety interventions cause lasting reductions in discipline citations among negatively stereotyped boys. *Journal of Personality and Social Psychology, 117*(2), 229.

Gramlich, J. (2020). *What the data says (and doesn't say) about crime in the United States*. Pew Research Center. https://www.pewresearch.org/fact-tank/2020/11/20/facts-about-crime-in-the-u-s/

Gray-Lobe, G., Pathak, P. A., & Walters, C. R. (2021). *The long-term effects of universal preschool in Boston* (NBER Working Paper No. 28756). National Bureau of Economic Research.

Green, B. L., Ayoub, C., Bartlett, J. D., Von Ende, A., Furrer, C., Chazan-Cohen, R., Vallotton, C., & Klevens, J. (2014). The effect of Early Head Start on child welfare system involvement: A first look at longitudinal child maltreatment outcomes. *Children & Youth Services Review, 42*, 127–135.

Greenwood, B. N., Hardeman, R. R., Huang, L., & Sojourner, A. (2020). Physician–patient racial concordance and disparities in birthing mortality for newborns. *Proceedings of the National Academy of Sciences, 117*(35), 21194–21200.

Greflund, S., McIntosh, K., Mercer, S. H., & May, S. L. (2014). Examining disproportionality in school discipline for Aboriginal students in schools implementing PBIS. *Canadian Journal of School Psychology, 29*(3), 213–235.

Gregory, A., Clawson, K., Davis, A., & Gerewitz, J. (2016). The promise of restorative practices to transform teacher-student relationships and achieve equity in school discipline. *Journal of Educational and Psychological Consultation, 26*(4), 325–353. https://doi.org/10.1080/10474412.2014.929950

Gregory, A., Skiba, R. J., & Mediratta, K. (2017). Eliminating disparities in school discipline: A framework for intervention. *Review of Research in Education, 41*(1), 253–278.

Gregory, C. A., & Smith, T. A. (2019). Salience, food security, and SNAP receipt. *Journal of Policy Analysis and Management, 38*(1), 124–154.

Grinstein-Weiss, M., Shanks, T. R. W., & Beverly, S. G. (2014). Family assets and child outcomes: Evidence and directions. *The Future of Children*, 147–170.

Grönqvist, H., Nilsson, J. P., & Robling, P. O. (2020). Understanding how low levels of early lead exposure affect children's life trajectories. *Journal of Political Economy, 128*(9), 3376–3433.

Grosz, M. (2020). The returns to a large community college program: Evidence from admissions lotteries. *American Economic Journal: Economic Policy, 12*(1), 1–29.

___. (2021). Admissions policies, cohort composition, and academic success: Evidence from California. *Journal of Human Resources*.

Gruber, J. (2004). Is making divorce easier bad for children? The long-run implications of unilateral divorce. *Journal of Labor Economics, 22*(4), 799–833.

Guan, A., Hamad, R., Batra, A., Bush, N. R., Tylavsky, F. A., & LeWinn, K. Z. (2021). The revised WIC food package and child development: A quasi-experimental study. *Pediatrics, 147*(2).

Guasco, M. (2014). *Slaves and Englishmen: Human bondage in the early modern Atlantic world*. University of Pennsylvania Press.

Gubbels, J., van der Put, C. E., Stams, G. J. M., Prinzie, P. J., & Assink, M. (2021). Components associated with the effect of home visiting programs on child maltreatment: A meta-analytic review. *Child Abuse & Neglect, 114*, 104981. https://doi.org/10.1016/j.chiabu.2021.104981

Gubits, D., Shinn, M., Wood, M., Brown, S. R., Dastrup, S. R., & Bell, S. H. (2018). What interventions work best for families who experience homelessness? Impact estimates from the family options study. *Journal of Policy Analysis and Management, 37*(4), 835–866.

Guglielmo, T. A. (2003). *White on arrival: Italians, race, color, and power in Chicago, 1890–1945*. Oxford University Press.

Gundersen, C., & Kreider, B. (2009). Bounding the effects of food insecurity on children's health outcomes. *Journal of Health Economics, 28*(5), 971–983.

Guryan, J., Ludwig, J., Bhatt, M. P., Cook, P. J., Davis, J. M., Dodge, K., Farkas, G., Fryer Jr, R. G., Mayer, S., Pollack, H. & Steinberg, L. (2023). Not too late: Improving academic outcomes among adolescents. *American Economic Review, 113*(3), 738–765.

Guthrie, R. (1976). *Even the rat was white: A historical view of psychology*. Harper & Row.

Ha, Y., Collins, M. E., & Martino, D. (2015). Child care burden and the risk of child maltreatment among low-income working families. *Children and Youth Services Review, 59*, 19–27.

Haider, S., Stoffel, C., Donenberg, G., & Geller, S. (2013). Reproductive health disparities: A focus on family planning and prevention among minority women and adolescents. *Global Advances in Health and Medicine, 2*(5), 94–99.

Hall, H., & Nielsen, E. (2020). *How do children spend their time? Time use and skill development in the PSID*. Board of Governors of the Federal Reserve System. https://doi.org/10.17016/2380-7172.2577

Hall, M., Crowder, K., & Spring, A. (2015). Variations in housing foreclosures by race and place, 2005–2012. *ANNALS of the American Academy of Political and Social Science, 660*(1), 217–237.

Hällsten, M., & Pfeffer, F. T. (2017). Grand advantage: Family wealth and grandchildren's educational achievement in Sweden. *American Sociological Review*, 82(2), 328–360.

Hamad, R., Batra, A., Karasek, D., LeWinn, K. Z., Bush, N. R., Davis, R. L., & Tylavsky, F. A. (2019a). The impact of the revised WIC food package on maternal nutrition during pregnancy and postpartum. *American Journal of Epidemiology*, 188(8), 1493–1502.

Hamad, R., Collin, D. F., Baer, R. J., & Jelliffe-Pawlowski, L. L. (2019b). Association of revised WIC food package with perinatal and birth outcomes: A quasi-experimental study. *JAMA Pediatrics*, 173(9), 845–852.

Hamad, R., Elser, H., Tran, D. C., Rehkopf, D. H., & Goodman, S. N. (2018). How and why studies disagree about the effects of education on health: A systematic review and meta-analysis of studies of compulsory schooling laws. *Social Science & Medicine*, 212, 168–178.

Hamad, R., Öztürk, B., Foverskov, E., Pedersen, L., Sørensen, H. T., Bøtker, H. E., & White, J. S. (2020). Association of neighborhood disadvantage with cardiovascular risk factors and events among refugees in Denmark. *JAMA Network Open*, 3(8), e2014196.

Hamad, R., & Rehkopf, D. H. (2016). Poverty and child development: A longitudinal study of the impact of the earned income tax credit. *American Journal of Epidemiology*, 183(9), 775–784.

Hamermesh, D. S. (2021). Moms' time—Married or not. *Mothers in the Labor Market*, 1–27. Springer International Publishing.

Hamersma, S. (2008). The effects of an employer subsidy on employment outcomes: A study of the work opportunity and welfare-to-work tax credits. *Journal of Policy Analysis and Management: The Journal of the Association for Public Policy Analysis and Management*, 27(3), 498–520.

Hamilton, D., & Darity, W., Jr. (2010). Can 'baby bonds' eliminate the racial wealth gap in putative post-racial America? *The Review of Black Political Economy* 37(3-4), 207–216.

Hamilton, T. G. (2019). *Immigration and the remaking of Black America*. Russell Sage Foundation.

Hamilton, T., & Darity, D. (2006). Appendix O: An interpretation of the economic impact of the Wilmington riot of 1897 summary of preliminary findings. *1898 Wilmington Race Riot Report*, 437–464. https://digital.ncdcr.gov/digital/collection/p249901coll22/id/5842

Hamre, B. K., & Pianta, R. C. (2010). Classroom environments and developmental processes: Conceptualization and measurement. *Handbook of Research on Schools, Schooling, and Human Development*, 25–41. Routledge.

Hamrick, K. S., & Andrews, M. (2016). SNAP participants' eating patterns over the benefit month: A time use perspective. *PloS One*, 11(7), e0158422.

Han, J. (2020). Does skin tone matter? Immigrant mobility in the U.S. labor market. *Demography*, 57(2), 705–726.

Hanchett, T. W. (2000). The other 'subsidized housing': Federal aid to suburbanization, 1940s–1960s. *From tenements to the Taylor homes: In search of an urban housing policy in twentieth-century America*, 163–179.

Hannon, L., DeFina, R., & Bruch, S. (2013). The relationship between skin tone and school suspension for African Americans. *Race and Social Problems*, 5, 281–295.

Hardy, B. L., & Logan, T. D. (2020). *Racial economic inequality amid the COVID-19 crisis*. The Hamilton Project.

Hargrove, T. W. (2019). Light privilege? Skin tone stratification in health among African Americans. *Sociology of Race and Ethnicity*, 5(3), 370–387.

Harkness, J., & Newman, S. (2003). Differential effects of homeownership on children from higher-and lower-income families. *Journal of Housing Research*, 14(1), 1–19.

Harris, A., Evans, H., & Beckett, K. (2000). Equal treatment and the reproduction of inequality. *Fordham Law Review*, 69, 1753.

___. (2010). Drawing blood from stones: Legal debt and social inequality in the contemporary United States. *American Journal of Sociology*, 115(6), 1753–1799.

Harris, A., Pattillo, M. & Sykes, B. (2022). Studying the system of monetary sanctions. *The Russell Sage Foundation Journal of the Social Sciences*, 8(2), 1–34.

Harris, A., & Seckl, J. (2011). Glucocorticoids, prenatal stress and the programming of disease. *Hormones and Behavior*, 59(3), 279–289.

Harris, C. I. (1993). Whiteness as property. *Harvard Law Review*, 106(8), 1707–1791.

Harvey, H. (2020). Cumulative effects of doubling up in childhood on young adult outcomes. *Demography*, 57(2), 501–528.

Hashim, S. A., Kane, T. J., Kelley-Kemple, T., Laski, M. E., & Staiger, D. O. (2020). *Have income-based achievement gaps widened or narrowed?* (NBER Working Paper No. 27714). National Bureau of Economic Research.

Haskins, A. R., Amorim, M., & Mingo, M. (2018). Parental incarceration and child outcomes: Those at risk, evidence of impacts, methodological insights, and areas of future work. *Sociology Compass*, 12(3), e12562.

Haskins, R. (2015). The family is here to stay—or not. *The Future of Children*, 129–153.

Hastings, O. P., & Schneider, D. (2021). Family structure and inequalities in parents' financial investments in children. *Journal of Marriage and Family*, 83(3), 717–736.

Hauptman, M., Niles, J. K., Gudin, J., & Kaufman, H. W. (2021). Individual-and community-level factors associated with detectable and elevated blood lead levels in U.S. children: Results from a national clinical laboratory. *JAMA Pediatrics*, 175(12), 1252–1260.

Haurin, D. R., Parcel, T. L., & Haurin, R. J. (2002). Does homeownership affect child outcomes? *Real Estate Economics*, 30(4), 635–666.

Havnes, T., & Mogstad, M. (2011). No child left behind: Subsidized child care and children's long-run outcomes. *American Economic Journal: Economic Policy*, 3(2), 97–129.

Hawkins, A. J., Hokanson, S., Loveridge, E., Milius, E., Duncan, M., Booth, M., & Pollard, B. (2022). How effective are ACF-funded couple relationship education programs? A meta-analytic study. *Family Process*, 61(3), 970–985.

Hayes, T. O. N., & Barnhorst, M. (2020). *Incarceration and poverty in the United States*. American Action Forum.

Heard-Garris, N., Winkelman, T. N. A., Choi, H., Miller, A. K., Kan, K., Shlafer, R., & Davis, M. M. (2018). Health care use and health behaviors among young adults with history of parental incarceration. *Pediatrics*, 142(3), e20174314. https://doi.org/10.1542/peds.2017-4314

Heckman, J. J. (2011). The economics of inequality: The value of early childhood education. *American Educator*, 35(1), 31.

Heckman, J. J., LaLonde, R. J., & Smith, J. A. (1999). The economics and econometrics of active labor market programs. *Handbook of Labor Economics*, 3, 1865–2097.

Heckman, J. J., Moon, S. H., Pinto, R., Savelyev, P. A., & Yavitz, A. (2010). The rate of return to the HighScope Perry Preschool Program. *Journal of Public Economics*, 94(1), 114–128.

Heissel, J. A., Sharkey, P. T., Torrats-Espinosa, G., Grant, K., & Adam, E. K. (2018). Violence and vigilance: The acute effects of community violent crime on sleep and cortisol. *Child Development*, 89(4), e323–e331.

Heller, S. B., Shah, A. K., Guryan, J., Ludwig, J., Mullainathan, S., & Pollack, H. A. (2017). Thinking, fast and slow? Some field experiments to reduce crime and dropout in Chicago. *The Quarterly Journal of Economics*, 132(1), 1–54.

Hemelt, S. W., Ladd, H. F., & Clifton, C. R. (2021). Do teacher assistants improve student outcomes? Evidence from school funding cutbacks in North Carolina. *Educational Evaluation and Policy Analysis, 43*(2), 280–304.

Hemelt, S., & Lenard, M. (2018). Career Academies and the Resurgence in Career and Technical Education in the United States [CALDER Policy Brief No. 8-0918-1].

Hemelt, S. W., Lenard, M. A., & Paeplow, C. G. (2019). Building bridges to life after high school: Contemporary career academies and student outcomes. *Economics of Education Review, 68*, 161–178.

Herbers, J., Reynolds, A., & Chen, C. (2013). School mobility and developmental outcomes in young adulthood. *Development and Psychopathology, 25*(2), 501–515.

Herbert, C. E., & Belsky, E. S. (2008). The homeownership experience of low-income and minority households: A review and synthesis of the literature. *Cityscape: A Journal of Policy Development and Research, 10*(2), 5–59.

Herbst, C. M. (2017). Universal child care, maternal employment, and children's long-run outcomes: Evidence from the US Lanham Act of 1940. *Journal of Labor Economics, 35*(2), 519–564.

Herbst, C. M., & Tekin, E. (2010). Child care subsidies and child development. *Economics of Education Review, 29*(4), 618–638.

Herd, P., & Moynihan, D. P. (2019). *Administrative burden: Policymaking by other means.* Russell Sage Foundation.

Herz, D., Lee, P. Lutz, L., Stewart, M., Tuell, J., & Wiig, J. (2012). *Addressing the needs of multi-system youth: Strengthening the connection between child welfare and juvenile justice.* The Center for Juvenile Justice Reform and Robert F. Kennedy Children's Action Corps.

Hill, J. L., Waldfogel, J., Brooks-Gunn, J., & Han, W. J. (2005). Maternal employment and child development: A fresh look using newer methods. *Developmental Psychology, 41*(6), 833.

Hillier, A. E. (2003). Who received loans? Home Owners' Loan Corporation lending and discrimination in Philadelphia in the 1930s. *Journal of Planning History, 2*(1), 3–24.

Hinton, E. (2016). *From the war on poverty to the war on crime: The making of mass incarceration in America.* Harvard University Press.

Hinton, E., & Cook, D. (2021). The mass criminalization of Black Americans: A historical overview. *Annual Review of Criminology, 4*, 261–286.

Hinton, E., Henderson, L., & Reed, C. (2018). An unjust burden: The disparate treatment of Black Americans in the criminal justice system. *Vera Institute of Justice*, 1–20.

Hirsch, B. T. (1980). The determinants of unionization: An analysis of interarea differences. *ILR Review, 33*(2), 147–161.

Hirsch, R. A., Dierkhising, C. B., & Herz, D. C. (2018). Educational risk, recidivism, and service access among youth involved in both the child welfare and juvenile justice systems. *Children and Youth Services Review, 85*, 72–80. https://doi.org/10.1016/j.childyouth.2017.12.001

Hoffman, J. S., Shandas, V., & Pendleton, N. (2020). The effects of historical housing policies on resident exposure to intra-urban heat: A study of 108 US urban areas. *Climate, 8*(1), 12.

Hohl, B. C., Kondo, M. C., Kajeepeta, S., MacDonald, J. M., Theall, K. P., Zimmerman, M. A., & Branas, C. C. (2019). Creating safe and healthy neighborhoods with place-based violence interventions. *Health Affairs, 38*(10), 1687–1694.

Holme, J. J. (2022). Growing up as rents rise: How housing affordability impacts children. *Review of Educational Research, 92*(6), 953–995.

Holupka, S., & Newman, S. J. (2012). The effects of homeownership on children's outcomes: Real effects or self-selection? *Real Estate Economics, 40*(3), 566–602.

Holzer, H. (2015). *Job market polarization and worker skills: A tale of two middles*. Brookings Institution.
___. (2021). *Why are the employment rates of Black men so low?* Brookings Institution. https://www.brookings.edu/articles/why-are-employment-rates-so-low-among-black-men/
Holzer, H. J., & Baum, S. (2017). *Making college work: Pathways to success for disadvantaged students*. Brookings Institution.
Holzer, H., & Neumark, D. (2000). Assessing Affirmative Action. *Journal of Economic Literature*.
Holzer, H. J., Raphael, S., & Stoll, M. A. (2003). *Employment dimensions of reentry: Understanding the nexus between prisoner reentry and work*. New York University Law School.
___. (2006). Employers in the boom: How did the hiring of less-skilled workers change in the 1990s? *Review of Economics and Statistics*, 88(2), 283–299.
Holzer, H. J., & Xu, Z. (2021). Community college pathways for disadvantaged students. *Community College Review*, 49(4), 351–388.
Homan, P. (2019). Structural sexism and health in the United States: A new perspective on health inequality and the gender system. *American Sociological Review*, 84(3), 486–516.
Hong, S. L. S., Howes, C., Marcella, J., Zucker, E., & Huang, Y. (2015). Quality Rating and Improvement Systems: Validation of a local implementation in LA County and children's school-readiness. *Early Childhood Research Quarterly*, 30, 227–240.
Hong, S. L. S., Sabol, T. J., Burchinal, M. R., Tarullo, L., Zaslow, M., & Peisner-Feinberg, E. S. (2019). ECE quality indicators and child outcomes: Analyses of large child care studies. *Early Childhood Research Quarterly*, 49, 202–217.
Hotz, V. J., Bollinger, C. R., Komarova, T., Manski, C. F., Moffitt, R. A., Nekipelov, D., Sojourner, A., & Spencer, B. D. (2022). Balancing data privacy and usability in the federal statistical system. *Proceedings of the National Academy of Sciences*. Balancing data privacy and usability in the federal statistical system | PNAS
Hotz, V. J., Wiemers, E., Rasmussen, J., & Koegel, K. M. (2021). *The role of parental wealth and income in financing children's college attendance and its consequences* (NBER Working Paper No. 25144). National Bureau of Economic Research. https://doi.org/10.3386/w25144
Howell, J., & Korver-Glenn, E. (2021). The increasing effect of neighborhood racial composition on housing values, 1980–2015. *Social Problems*, 68(4), 1051–1071.
Hoxby, C. M. (2001). All school finance equalizations are not created equal. *The Quarterly Journal of Economics*, 116(4), 1189–1231.
Hoynes, H., Miller, D., & Simon, D. (2015). Income, the earned income tax credit, and infant health. *American Economic Journal: Economic Policy*, 7(1), 172–211.
Hoynes, H., Page, M., & Stevens, A. H. (2011). Can targeted transfers improve birth outcomes?: Evidence from the introduction of the WIC program. *Journal of Public Economics*, 95(7-8), 813–827.
Hoynes, H., & Rothstein, J. (2017). Tax policy toward low income families. In A. Auerbach & K. Smetters, *Economics of tax policy*, 183–225. Oxford University Press.
Hoynes, H., & Schanzenbach, D. W. (2015). U.S. food and nutrition programs. In R. A. Moffitt (Eds.), *Economics of means-tested transfer programs in the United States*, 1, 219–301. University of Chicago Press.
Hoynes, H., Schanzenbach, D. W., & Almond, D. (2016). Long-run impacts of childhood access to the safety net. *American Economic Review*, 106(4), 903–934.
Hu, L., Kaestner, R., Mazumder, B., Miller, S., & Wong, A. (2018). The effect of the affordable care act Medicaid expansions on financial wellbeing. *Journal of Public Economics*, 163, 99–112.
Huang, M., Chen, J., Yang, Y., Yuan, H., Huang, Z., & Lu, Y. (2021). Effects of ambient air pollution on blood pressure among children and adolescents: A systematic review and meta-analysis. *Journal of the American Heart Association*, 10(10), e017734.

Hullenaar, K., & Ruback, R. B. (2020). *Juvenile violent victimization, 1995–2018*. Office of Juvenile Justice and Delinquency Prevention. https://ojjdp.ojp.gov/juvenile-violent-victimization.pdf

Hunter, M. A. (2018). Seven billion reasons for reparations. *Souls, 20*(4), 420–432.

Hurst, E., Rubinstein, Y., & Shimizu, K. (2021). *Task-based discrimination* (NBER Working Paper No. 29022). National Bureau of Economic Research. https://doi.org/10.3386/w29022

Hurst, M. (1997). The determinants of earnings differentials for Indigenous Americans: Human capital, location, or discrimination? *The Quarterly Review of Economics and Finance, 37*(4), 787–807. https://doi.org/10.1016/S1062-9769(97)90004-1

Hwang, J. (2019). Racialized recovery: Postforeclosure pathways in Boston neighborhoods. *City & Community, 18*(4), 1287–1313. https://doi.org/10.1111/cico.12472.

Hwang, J., Hankinson, M., & Brown, K. S. (2015). Racial and spatial targeting: Segregation and subprime lending within and across metropolitan areas. *Social Forces, 93*(3), 1081–1108.

Immergluck, D. (2018). Old wine in private equity bottles? The resurgence of contract-for-deed home sales in US urban neighborhoods. *International Journal of Urban and Regional Research, 42*(4), 651–665.

Immergluck, D., Ernsthausen, J., Earl, S., & Powell, A. (2020). Evictions, large owners, and serial filings: findings from Atlanta. *Housing Studies, 35*(5), 903–924.

Ingraham, C. (2018, June 19). There are more guns than people in the United States, according to a new study of global firearm ownership. Washington Post. https://www.washingtonpost.com/news/wonk/wp/2018/06/19/there-are-more-guns-than-people-in-the-united-states-according-to-a-new-study-of-global-firearm-ownership/?noredirect=on

Institute of Medicine. (2003). *Unequal treatment: Confronting racial and ethnic disparities in health care*. The National Academies Press. https://doi.org/10.17226/12875

Institute on Race and Poverty. (2009). *Communities in crisis: Race and mortgage lending in the Twin Cities*. University of Minnesota Law School. http://www.irpumn.org/uls/resources/projects/IRP_mortgage_study_Feb._11th.pdf

Isen, A., Rossin-Slater, M., & Walker, W. R. (2017). Every breath you take—every dollar you'll make: The long-term consequences of the clean air act of 1970. *Journal of Political Economy, 125*(3), 848–902.

Jackson, B. A., & Reynolds, J. R. (2013). The price of opportunity: Race, student loan debt, and college achievement. *Sociological Inquiry, 83*, 335–368.

Jackson, C. K., Johnson, R.C., & Persico, C. (2016). The effects of school spending on educational and economic outcomes: Evidence from school finance reforms. *The Quarterly Journal of Economics, 131*(1), 157–218.

Jackson, C. K., & Mackevicius, C. (2021). *The distribution of school spending impacts* (NBER Working Paper No. 28517). National Bureau of Economic Research.

Jackson, K. T. (1985). *Crabgrass frontier: The suburbanization of the United States*. Oxford University Press.

Jacob, B. A., Kapustin, M., & Ludwig, J. (2015). The impact of housing assistance on child outcomes: Evidence from a randomized housing lottery. *The Quarterly Journal of Economics, 130*(1), 465–506.

Jacobs, M. D. (2014). *A generation removed: The fostering and adoption of Indigenous children in the postwar world*. University of Nebraska Press.

Jácome, E., Kuziemko, I., & Naidu, S. (2021). *Mobility for all: Representative intergenerational mobility estimates over the 20th century* (NBER Working Paper No. 29289). National Bureau of Economic Research.

Jaffee, S. & Maikovich-Fong A. (2013). Child maltreatment and risk for psychopathology. In Beauchaine, T. P., & S. P. Hinshaw, *Child and adolescent psychopathology* (2nd ed.), 171–196. Wiley.

James, N. (2018). Recent violent crime trends in the United States. *Congressional Research Service*, 45236.

Jardim, E., Long, M.C., Plotnick, R., Van Inwegen, E., Vigdor, J., & Wething, H. (2017). *Minimum wage increases, wages, and low-wage employment: Evidence from Seattle* (NBER Working Paper No. 23532). National Bureau of Economic Research.

Jardim, E, Long, M. C., Plotnick, R., Van Inwegen, E., Vigdor, J. & Wething, H. (2018). *Minimum wage increases and individual employment trajectories* (NBER Working Paper No. 25182). National Bureau of Economic Research.

Jardim, E., Long, M. C., Plotnick, R., Van Inwegen, E., Vigdor, J. & Wething, H. (2022). Minimum-wage increases and low-wage employment: Evidence from Seattle. *American Economic Journal: Economic Policy*, 14(2), 263–314.

Jbaily, A., Zhou, X., Liu, J., Lee, T. H., Kamareddine, L., Verguet, S., & Dominici, F. (2022). Air pollution exposure disparities across US population and income groups. *Nature*, 601(7892), 228–233.

Jepsen, C., & Rivkin, S. (2009). Class size reduction and student achievement the potential tradeoff between teacher quality and class size. *Journal of Human Resources*, 44(1), 223–250.

Jez, S. J. (2014). The differential impact of wealth versus income in the college-going process. *Research in Higher Education*, 55(7), 710–34.

Johns Hopkins Center for Gun Violence Solutions. (2022). *A year in review: 2020 gun deaths in the U.S.* Johns Hopkins Center for Gun Violence Solutions. https://publichealth.jhu.edu/gun-violence-solutions.

Johnson, A. D., & Ryan, R. M. (2015). The role of child-care subsidies in the lives of low-income children. *Child Development Perspectives*, 9(4), 227–232.

Johnson, J. G. (1923). A Spanish settlement in Carolina, 1526. *The Georgia Historical Quarterly*, 7(4), 339–345.

Johnson, M. E., Lloyd, S. L., Bristol, S. C., Elliott, A. L., & Cottler, L. B. (2022). Black girls and referrals: Racial and gender disparities in self-reported referral to substance use disorder assessment among justice-involved children. *Substance Abuse Treatment, Prevention, and Policy*, 17(1), 1–10.

Johnson, R. (2009). Ever-increasing levels of parental incarceration and the consequences for children. *Do prisons make us safer*, 177–206.

Johnson, R. C. (2011). *Long-run impacts of school desegregation & school quality on adult attainments* (NBER Working Paper No. 16664). National Bureau of Economic Research.

Johnson, R., & Nazaryan, A. (2019). *Children of the dream: Why school integration works*. Basic Books.

Johnson-Motoyama, M., Ginther, D. K., Oslund, P., Jorgenson, L., Chung, Y., Phillips, R., Beer, O. W. J., Davis, S., & Sattler, P. L. (2022). Association between state Supplemental Nutrition Assistance Program policies, child protective services involvement, and foster care in the US, 2004–2016. *JAMA Network Open*, 5(7), e2221509.

Johnston, E. M., McMorrow, S., Alvarez Caraveo, C., & Dubay, L. (2021). Post-ACA, more than one-third of women with prenatal medicaid remained uninsured before or after pregnancy: Study examines insurance coverage and access to care before, during, and after pregnancy for women with prenatal Medicaid coverage. *Health Affairs*, 40(4), 571–578.

Joint Center for Housing Studies of Harvard University. (2022). *The state of the nation's housing 2022*. Joint Center for Housing Studies of Harvard University, Harvard Graduate School of Design, Harvard Kennedy School. https://www.jchs.harvard.edu/sites/default/files/reports/files/Harvard_JCHS_State_Nations_Housing_2022.pdf

Jones, C. P. (2002). Confronting institutionalized racism. *Phylon, 50*(1/2), 7–22

Jones-Correa, M. (2000). The origins and diffusion of racial restrictive covenants. *Political Science Quarterly, 115*(4), 541–568.

Jones Harden, B., & Slopen, N. (2022). Inequitable experiences and outcomes in young children: Addressing racial and social-economic disparities in physical and mental health. *Annual Review of Developmental Psychology, 4*.

Jonson-Reid, M., Drake, B., & Kohl, P. L. (2009). Is the overrepresentation of the poor in child welfare caseloads due to bias or need? *Children and Youth Services Review, 31*(3), 422–427.

Jussim, L., & Harber, K. D. (2005). Teacher expectations and self-fulfilling prophecies: Knowns and unknowns, resolved and unresolved controversies. *Personality and Social Psychology Review, 9*(2), 131–155.

Kaiser Family Foundation. (2022). The impact of gun violence on children and adolescents. https://www.kff.org/mental-health/issue-brief/the-impact-of-gun-violence-on-children-and-adolescents/

___. (2023). Key data on health and health care by race and ethnicity. https://www.kff.org/racial-equity-and-health-policy/report/key-data-on-health-and-health-care-by-race-and-ethnicity/#top

___. (2024). Medicaid postpartum coverage extension tracker. https://www.kff.org/medicaid/issue-brief/medicaid-postpartum-coverage-extension-tracker/

Kanengiser, H., & Schaberg, K. (2022). *Employment and earnings effects of the WorkAdvance demonstration after seven years*. MDRC. https://www.mdrc.org/publication/employment-and-earnings-effects-workadvance-demonstration-after-seven-years

Karagiannaki, E. (2017). The effect of parental wealth on children's outcomes in early adulthood. *The Journal of Economic Inequality, 15*(3), 217–243.

Katz, L. F., Roth, J., Hendra, R., & Schaberg, K. (2022). Why do sectoral employment programs work? Lessons from WorkAdvance. *Journal of Labor Economics, 40*(S1), S249–S291.

Katznelson, I. (2005). *When affirmative action was White: An untold history of racial inequality in twentieth-century America*. W.W. Norton & Company.

Kaushal, N., Magnuson, K., & Waldfogel, J. (2011). Parents supplement children's in-school educational activities and promote children's learning through a wide variety of investments. For preschool-age children, family income may be invested in early care and education programs as well as enrichment activities and items such. *Whither Opportunity?: Rising Inequality, Schools, and Children's Life Chances, 187*.

Kaushal, N., Waldfogel, J., & Wight, V. R. (2014). Food insecurity and SNAP participation in Mexican immigrant families: The impact of the outreach initiative. *The BE Journal Of Economic Analysis & Policy, 14*(1), 203–240.

Kazis, R. & Molina, F. (2016). *Implementing the WorkAdvance model*. MDRC.

Kearney, M. S. (2022). *The "college gap" in marriage and children's family structure* (NBER Working Paper No. 30078). National Bureau of Economic Research.

Kearney, M. S., & Levine, P. B. (2017). The economics of nonmarital childbearing and the marriage premium for children. *Annual Review of Economics, 9*, 327–352.

Kearney, M. S., Harris, B. H., Jácome, E., & Parker, L. (2014). *Ten economic facts about crime and incarceration in the United States*. The Hamilton Project.

Keith, V., & Herring, C. (1991). Skin tone stratification in the Black community. *American Journal of Sociology, 97*(3), 760–778.

Kemple, J. J., & Willner, C. J. (2008). *Career academies: Long-term impacts on labor market outcomes, educational attainment, and transitions to adulthood*. MDRC.

Kennedy, R., Potter, M. H., & Font, S. A. (2022). A meta-regression of racial disparities in wellbeing outcomes during and after foster care. *Journal of Violence, Trauma, & Abuse*. https://doi.org/10.1177/15248380221111481

Kermani, A., & Wong, F. (2021). *Racial disparities in housing returns* (NBER Working Paper No. 29306). National Bureau of Economic Research.
Khadka, A., Fink, G., Gromis, A., & McConnell, M. (2020). In utero exposure to threat of evictions and preterm birth: Evidence from the United States. *Health Services Research, 55*, 823–832.
Khanna, R. (2022). *Dignity in the digital age: How to make tech work for all of the US*. Simon and Schuster.
Kids Count Data Center. (2023). *Children living in high-poverty areas by race and ethnicity in the United States*. https://datacenter.kidscount.org/data/bar/7753-children-living-in-high-poverty-areas-by-race-and-ethnicity?loc=1&loct=1#1/any/false/2026/10,11,9,12,1,185,13/14942
Kiernan, B. (2007). *Blood and soil: A world history of genocide and extermination from Sparta to Darfur*. Yale University Press.
Kilpatrick, D. G., & Acierno, R. (2003). Mental health needs of crime victims: Epidemiology and outcomes. *Journal of Traumatic Stress, 16*(2), 119–132.
Kim, A. (2018). *Tax cuts for the companies that deserve them*. Progressive Policy Institute.
Kim, H., & Drake, B. (2018). Child maltreatment risk as a function of poverty and race/ethnicity in the USA. *International journal of epidemiology, 47*(3), 780–787.
Kim, H., Wildeman, C., Jonson-Reid, M., & Drake, B. (2017). Lifetime prevalence of investigating child maltreatment among US children. *American Journal of Public Health, 107*(2), 274–280.
Kim, M. (2009). Race and gender differences in the earnings of Black workers. *Industrial Relations: A Journal of Economy and Society, 48*(3), 466–488.
Kim, M. M., & Conrad, C. F. (2006). The impact of historically Black colleges and universities on the academic success of African-American students. *Research in Higher Education, 47*, 399–427.
Kim, M. J., Mason, W. A., Herrenkohl, T. I., Catalano, R. F., Toumbourou, J. W., & Hemphill, S. A. (2017). Influence of early onset of alcohol use on the development of adolescent alcohol problems: A longitudinal binational study. *Prevention Science, 18*(1), 1–11.
Kim, M. H., Schwartz, G. L., White, J. S., Glymour, M. M., Reardon, S. F., Kershaw, K. N., Gomez, S. L., Collin, D. F., Inamdar, P. P., Wang, G. & Hamad, R. (2022). School racial segregation and long-term cardiovascular health among Black adults in the US: A quasi-experimental study. *PLoS Medicine, 19*(6), e1004031.
Kimbrell, C.S., Wilson, D.B. & Olaghere, A. (2022). Restorative justice programs and practices in juvenile justice: An updated systematic review and meta-analysis for effectiveness. *Criminology & Public Policy, 22*(1), 161–195. https://doi.org/10.1111/1745-9133.12613
Kitzman, H. J., Olds, D. L., Cole, R. E., Hanks, C. A., Anson, E. A., Arcoleo, K. J., Luckey, D. W., Knudtson, M. D., Henderson, C. R., Jr. & Holmberg, J. R. (2010). Enduring effects of prenatal and infancy home visiting by nurses on children: Follow-up of a randomized trial among children at age 12 years. *Archives of Pediatrics & Adolescent Medicine, 164*(5), 412–418.
Klein, J. B., Jacobs, R. H., & Reinecke, M. A. (2007). Cognitive-behavioral therapy for adolescent depression: A meta-analytic investigation of changes in effect-size estimates. *Journal of the American Academy of Child & Adolescent Psychiatry, 46*(11), 1403–1413.
Klein, S., Fries, L., & Emmons, M. M. (2017). Early care and education arrangements and young children's risk of foster placement: Findings from a National Child Welfare Sample. *Children & Youth Services Review, 83*, 168–178.
Klevens, J., Schmidt, B., Luo, F., Xu, L., Ports, K.A., & Lee, R.D. (2017). Effect of the Earned Income Tax Credit on hospital admissions for pediatric abusive head trauma, 1995–2013. *Public Health Reports, 132*(4), 505–511.

Kliff, S (2018). An exclusive look at Cory Booker's plan to fight wealth inequality: Give poor kids money. Vox. https://www.vox.com/policy-and-politics/2018/10/22/17999558/cory-booker-baby-bonds

Kline, P., & Walters, C. R. (2016). Evaluating public programs with close substitutes: The case of Head Start. *The Quarterly Journal of Economics, 131*(4), 1795–1848.

Kling, J. R., Liebman, J. R., & Katz, L. F. (2001). Bullets don't got no name: Consequences of fear in the ghetto [Unpublished Paper]. National Bureau of Economic Research.

Kneebone, E., & Raphael, S. (2011). *City and suburban crime trends in metropolitan America.* Brookings Institution Metropolitan Policy Program.

Knudsen, E. I., Heckman, J. J., Cameron, J. L., & Shonkoff, J. P. (2006). Economic, neurobiological, and behavioral perspectives on building America's future workforce. *Proceedings of the National Academy of Sciences, 103*(27), 10155–10162.

Kodros, J. K., Bell, M. L., Dominici, F., L'Orange, C., Godri Pollitt, K. J., Weichenthal, S., Wu, X., & Volckens, J. (2022). Unequal airborne exposure to toxic metals associated with race, ethnicity, and segregation in the USA. *Nature Communications, 13*(1), 1–10.

Komro, K. A., Markowitz, S., Livingston, M. D., & Wagenaar, A. C. (2019). Effects of state-level earned income tax credit laws on birth outcomes by race and ethnicity. *Health Equity, 3*(1), 61–67.

Kondo, M., Hohl, B., Han, S., & Branas, C. (2016). Effects of greening and community reuse of vacant lots on crime. *Urban Studies, 53*(15), 3279–3295.

Kovski, N. L., Hill, H. D., Mooney, S. J., Rivara, F. P., & Rowhani-Rahbar, A. (2022). Short-term effects of tax credits on rates of child maltreatment reports in the United States. *Pediatrics, 150*(1), e2021054939.

Kraft, M. A., & Falken, G. T. (2021). A blueprint for scaling tutoring and mentoring across public schools. *AERA Open, 7*, 23328584211042858.

Kravitz-Wirtz, N., Bruns, A., Aubel, A. J., Zhang, X., & Buggs, S. A. (2022). Inequities in community exposure to deadly gun violence by race/ethnicity, poverty, and neighborhood disadvantage among youth in large U.S. cities. *Journal of Urban Health, 99*(4), 610–625

Krieger, N., & Smith, G. D. (2016). The tale wagged by the DAG: Broadening the scope of causal inference and explanation for epidemiology. *International Journal of Epidemiology, 45*(6), 1787–1808.

Krieger, N., Van Wye, G., Huynh, M., Waterman, P. D., Maduro, G., Li, W., Gwynn, R. C., Barbot, O., & Bassett, M. T. (2020). Structural racism, historical redlining, and risk of preterm birth in New York City, 2013–2017. *American Journal of Public Health, 110*(7), 1046–1053.

Krueger, A. B. (1999). Experimental estimates of education production functions. *The Quarterly Journal of Economics, 114*(2), 497–532.

———. (2003). Economic considerations and class size. *The Economic Journal, 113*(485), F34–F63.

Krueger, A. B., & Whitmore, D. M. (2001). The effect of attending a small class in the early grades on college-test taking and middle school test results: Evidence from Project STAR. *The Economic Journal, 111*(468), 1–28.

Krysan, M., & Crowder, K. (2017). *Cycle of segregation: Social processes and residential stratification.* Russell Sage Foundation.

Kucheva, Y. (2018). Subsidized housing and the transition to adulthood. *Demography, 55*(2), 617–642.

Kuebler, M. (2012). Lending in the modern era: Does racial composition of neighborhoods matter when individuals seek home financing? A pilot study in New England. *City & Community, 11*(1), 31–50.

Kugelmass, H. (2016). "Sorry, I'm not accepting new patients" an audit study of access to mental health care. *Journal of Health and Social Behavior, 57*(2), 168–183.

Kuhfeld, M., Soland, J., Pitts, C., & Burchinal, M. (2020). Trends in children's academic skills at school entry: 2010 to 2017. *Educational Researcher*, 49(6), 403–414.

Kuhn, M., Schularick, M., & Steins, U. I. (2020). Income and wealth inequality in America, 1949–2016. *Journal of Political Economy*, 128(9), 3469–3519.

Kull, M. A., Coley, R. L., & Lynch, A. D. (2016). The roles of instability and housing in low-income families' residential mobility. *Journal of Family and Economic Issues*, 37(3), 422–434.

Kunesh, P. H. (2021). The significance of belonging for Indigenous peoples: The power of place and people—Creating a vision for community in Indian country through self-governance and self-determination. *Journal of Affordable Housing and Community Development Law*, 30, 23–46.

Kurlychek, M. C., & Johnson, B. D. (2019). Cumulative disadvantage in the American criminal justice system. *Annual Review of Criminology*, 2(1), 291–319.

Kvangraven, I. H. (2020). Nobel rebels in disguise—Assessing the rise and rule of the randomistas. *Review of Political Economy*, 32(3), 305–341.

Lacey, N., Soskice, D., & Hope, D. (2018). Understanding the determinants of penal policy: Crime, culture, and comparative political economy. *Annual Review of Criminology*, 1, 195–217.

Lacey, N., & Zedner, L. (2017). Criminalization: Historical, legal, and criminological perspectives. *Oxford Handbook of Criminology*, 57–76.

Ladson-Billings, G. (1995). But that's just good teaching! The case for culturally relevant pedagogy. *Theory into Practice*, 34(3), 159–165.

Lafortune, J., Rothstein, J., & Schanzenbach, D. W. (2018). School finance reform and the distribution of student achievement. *American Economic Journal: Applied Economics*, 10(2), 1–26.

Lafortune, J., & Schönholzer, D. (2022). The impact of school facility investments on students and homeowners: Evidence from Los Angeles. *American Economic Journal: Applied Economics*, 14(3), 254–289.

Laliberté, J.-W. (2021). Long-term contextual effects in education: Schools and neighborhoods. *American Economic Journal: Economic Policy*, 13(2), 336–377.

LaLonde, R. J. (1986). Evaluating the econometric evaluations of training programs with experimental data. *The American Economic Review*, 604–620.

Lancaster, D. (2000). The alchemy and legacy of the United States of America's sanction of slavery and segregation: Property law and equitable remedy analysis of African American reparations. *Howard Law Journal*, 43(2), 171–212.

Lane, H. M., Morello-Frosch, R., Marshall, J. D., & Apte, J. S. (2022). Historical redlining is associated with present-day air pollution disparities in US cities. *Environmental Science & Technology Letters*, 9(4), 345–350.

Langley-Evans, S. C. (2015). Nutrition in early life and the programming of adult disease: A review. *Journal of Human Nutrition and Dietetics*, 28, 1–14.

Lankford, H., Loeb, S., & Wyckoff, J. (2002). Teacher sorting and the plight of urban schools: A descriptive analysis. *Educational Evaluation and Policy Analysis*, 24(1), 37–62.

Lanning, J. A. (2013). Opportunities denied, wages diminished: Using search theory to translate audit-pair study findings into wage differentials. *The BE Journal of Economic Analysis & Policy*, 13(2), 921–958.

Lara-Millan, A. (2021). Theorizing financial extraction: The curious case of telephone profits in the Los Angeles county jails. *Punishment & Society*, 23(1), 107–126.

Larson, K., & Halfon, N. (2010). Family income gradients in the health and health care access of U.S. children. *Maternal and Child Health Journal*, 14(3), 332–342.

Laws, M. B., Lee, Y., Rogers, W. H., Beach, M. C., Saha, S., Korthuis, P. T., Sharp, V., Cohn, J., Moore, R. & Wilson, I. B. (2014). Provider–patient communication about adherence to anti-retroviral regimens differs by patient race and ethnicity. *AIDS and Behavior*, 18, 1279–1287.

Leasure, P., & Andersen, T. S. (2016). The effectiveness of certificates of relief as collateral consequence relief mechanisms: An experimental study. *Yale Law & Policy Review*, 35, 11.

Lebrun-Harris, L. A., Ghandour, R. M., Kogan, M. D., & Warren, M. D. (2022). Five-year trends in US children's health and well-being, 2016–2020. *JAMA Pediatrics*.

Lee, B. J., & Mackey-Bilaver, L. (2007). Effects of WIC and food stamp program participation on child outcomes. *Children & Youth Services Review*, 29(4), 501–517.

Lee, B. R., Bright, C. L., Svoboda, D. V., Fakunmoju, S., & Barth, R. P. (2011). Outcomes of group care for youth: A review of comparative studies. *Research on Social Work Practice*, 21(2), 177–189. https://doi.org/10.1177/1049731510386243

Lee, D. S., & McCrary, J. (2017). The deterrence effect of prison: Dynamic theory and evidence. *Regression discontinuity designs*, 38, 73–146. Emerald Publishing Limited.

Lee, F. S., Heimer, H., Giedd, J. N., Lein, E. S., Šestan, N., Weinberger, D. R., & Casey, B. J. (2014). Adolescent mental health—Opportunity and obligation. *Science*, 346(6209), 547–549.

LeFlouria, T. L. (2015). *Chained in silence: Black women and convict labor in the New South*. UNC Press Books.

Legewie, J., & Fagan, J. (2019). Aggressive policing and the educational performance of minority youth. *American Sociological Review*, 84(2), 220–247.

Leifheit, K. M., Pollack, C. E., Raifman, J., Schwartz, G. L., Koehler, R. D., Bronico, J. V. R., Benfer, E. A., Zimmerman, F. J., & Linton, S. L. (2021). Variation in state-level eviction moratorium protections and mental health among US adults during the COVID-19 pandemic. *JAMA Network Open*, 4(12), e2139585.

Leonard, B., Parker, D. P., & Anderson, T. L. (2020). Land quality, land rights, and indigenous poverty. *Journal of Development Economics*, 143, 102435.

Lerer, T. (2013). Sentencing the family: Recognizing the needs of dependent children in the administration of the criminal justice system. *Northwestern Journal of Law & Social Policy*, 9(1). http://scholarlycommons.law.northwestern.edu/njlsp/vol9/iss1/2

Leventhal, T., & Newman, S. (2010). Housing and child development. *Children and Youth Services Review*, 32(9), 1165–1174.

Lew, I. (2016). *Housing inadequacy remains a problem for the lowest-income renters*. Joint Center for Housing Studies. https://www.jchs.harvard.edu/blog/housing-inadequacy-remains-a-problem-for-the-lowest-income-renters

Lewis, T. T., Williams, D. R., Tamene, M., & Clark, C. R. (2014). Self-reported experiences of discrimination and cardiovascular disease. *Current Cardiovascular Risk Reports*, 8(1), 365.

Lichtman-Sadot, S., & Bell, N. P. (2017). Child health in elementary school following California's paid family leave program. *Journal of Policy Analysis and Management*, 36(4), 790–827.

Lindo, J. M., Schaller, J., & Hansen, B. (2013). Caution! Men not at work: Gender-specific labor market conditions and child maltreatment. *Journal of Public Economics*, 163, 77–98.

Lindsay, C. A., & Hart, C. M. (2017). Teacher race and school discipline: Are students suspended less often when they have a teacher of the same race? *Education Next*, 17(1), 72–9.

Link, N. W. (2021). Paid your debt to society? Court-related financial obligations and community supervision during the first year after release from prison. *Corrections*, 1–17.

Lipsey, M. W., Farran, D. C., & Durkin, K. (2018). Effects of the Tennessee Prekindergarten Program on children's achievement and behavior through third grade. *Early Childhood Research Quarterly*, 45(1), 155–176. http://doi.org/10.1016/j.ecresq.2018.03.005

Liss, E., Korpi, M., & Wennberg, K. (2019). *The American Dream lives in Sweden: Trends in intergenerational absolute income mobility* (Ratio Working Papers No. 325). The Ratio Institute.

Lochner, L. (2020). Education and crime. *The Economics of Education* (2nd ed.). Academic Press.
Lochner, L., & Moretti, E. (2004). The effect of education on crime: Evidence from prison inmates, arrests, and self-reports. *American Economic Review*, 94(1), 155–189.
Lofstrom, M., & Raphael, S. (2016). Crime, the criminal justice system, and socioeconomic inequality. *Journal of Economic Perspectives*, 30(2), 103–126.
Logan, J., & Stults, B. (2022). *Metropolitan segregation: No breakthrough in sight* (Working Papers No. 22-14). Center for Economic Studies, U.S. Census Bureau.
Logan, J. R. (2013). The persistence of segregation in the 21st century metropolis. *City & Community*, 12(2), 160–168
Logan, J. R., Foster, A., Xu, H., & Zhang, W. (2020). Income segregation: Up or down, and for whom? *Demography*, 57(5), 1951–1974.
Lomawaima, K. T., & McCarty, T. L. (2006). *"To remain an Indian": Lessons in democracy from a century of Native American education*. Teachers College Press.
Long, M. C., & Bateman, N. A. (2020). Long run changes in underrepresentation after affirmative action bans in public universities. *Educational Evaluation and Policy Analysis*, 42(2), 199–207.
Looney, A., & Turner, N. (2018). *Work and opportunity before and after incarceration*. Brookings Institution.
Lopoo, L. M., & DeLeire, T. (2014). Family structure and the economic wellbeing of children in youth and adulthood. *Social Science Research*, 43, 30–44.
Lopoo, L. M., & London, A. S. (2016). Household crowding during childhood and long-term education outcomes. *Demography*, 53(3), 699–721.
Lopoo, L. M., & Western, B. (2005). Incarceration and the formation and stability of marital unions. *Journal of Marriage and Family*, 67(3), 721–734.
Losen, D. J., & Martinez, P. (2020). *Lost opportunities: How disparate school discipline continues to drive differences in the opportunity to learn*. Learning Policy Institute. https://learningpolicyinstitute.org/media/508/download?inline&file=CRDC_School_Discipline_REPORT.pdf
Lou, C., Hahn, H., Maag, E., Daly, H., Casas, M., & Steuerle, C. E. (2022). *Kids' Share 2022: Report on federal expenditures on children through 2021 and future projections*. Urban Institute. https://www.urban.org/sites/default/files/2022-09/kids-share-2022-spreads.pdf
Love, H. (2021). *Want to reduce violence? Invest in place*. Brookings. https://www.brookings.edu/research/want-to-reduce-violence-invest-in-place/
Lovenheim, M. F. (2011). The effect of liquid housing wealth on college enrollment. *Journal of Labor Economics*, 29(4), 741–771.
Lovenheim, M. F., & Reynolds, C. L. (2013). The effect of housing wealth on college choice: Evidence from the housing boom. *Journal of Human Resources*, 48(1), 1–35.
Ludwig, J., & Miller, D. L. (2007). Does Head Start improve children's life chances? Evidence from a regression discontinuity design. *The Quarterly Journal of Economics*, 122(1), 159–208.
Ludwig, J., Sanbonmatsu, L., Gennetian, L., Adam, E., Duncan, G. J., Katz, L. F., Kessler, R. C., Kling, J. R., Lindau, S. T., Whitaker, R. C., & McDade, T. W. (2011). Neighborhoods, obesity, and diabetes—A randomized social experiment. *New England Journal of Medicine*, 365(16), 1509–1519.
Lukachko, A., Hatzenbuehler, M. L., & Keyes, K. M. (2014). Structural racism and myocardial infarction in the United States. *Social Science and Medicine*, 103, 42–50.
Lundberg, S., & Pollak, R. A. (2014). The uneven retreat from marriage in the U.S., 1950–2010. In *Human capital and history: The American record*, 241–272. University of Chicago Press
Lyons, C. J., & Pettit, B. (2011). Compounded disadvantage: Race, incarceration, and wage growth. *Social Problems*, 58(2), 257–280.

M'Balou Camara, K. Z., Hamilton, D., & Darity Jr, W. (2019). *Entering entrepreneurship: Racial disparities in the pathways into business ownership*. The Samuel DuBois Cook Center on Social Equity, Duke University. https://drive.google.com/file/d/1PKPONU9 Wwglun8OOtSlbAaf8BtSan_C5/view?usp=sharing

MacDonald, J., Fagan, J., & Geller, A. (2016). The effects of local police surges on crime and arrests in New York City. *PLoS One, 11*(6), e0157223.

Machin, S., Marie, O., & Vujić, S. (2011). The crime reducing effect of education. *The Economic Journal, 121*(552), 463–84.

Maciag, M. C., & Phipatanakul, W. (2022). Update on indoor allergens and their impact on pediatric asthma. *Annals of Allergy, Asthma & Immunology, 128*(6), 652–658.

Macpherson, D. A., & Hirsch, B. T. (2021). *Five decades of union wages, nonunion wages, and union wage gaps at unionstats.com* (IZA Discussion Paper No. 14398). Institute for the Study of Labor. https://ssrn.com/abstract=3855962

Maddox, K., & Gray, S. (2002). Cognitive representations of Black Americans: Reexploring the role of skin tone. *Personality and Social Psychology Bulletin, 28*(2), 250–259.

Maguire, S. (2016). *Optimizing talent: The promise and perils of adapting sectoral training models for young workers*. Workforce Strategies Initiative, The Aspen Institute.

Maguire-Jack, K., Purtell, K. M., Showalter, K., Barnhart, S., & Yang, M. Y. (2019). Preventive benefits of US childcare subsidies in supervisory child neglect. *Children & Society, 33*(2), 185–194.

Maguire-Jack, K., Yoon, S., & Hong, S. (2022). Social cohesion and informal social control as mediators between neighborhood poverty and child maltreatment. *Child Maltreatment, 27*(3), 334–343.

Maier, A., Daniel, J., Oakes, J., & Lam, L. (2017). *Community schools as an effective school improvement strategy: A review of the evidence*. Learning Policy Institute.

Mancini, M. (1996). *One dies, get another: Convict leasing in the American South, 1866–1928*. University of South Carolina Press.

Manduca, R., & Sampson, R. J. (2019). Punishing and toxic neighborhood environments independently predict the intergenerational social mobility of Black and White children. *Proceedings of The National Academy of Sciences, 116*(16), 7772–7777.

———. (2021). Childhood exposure to polluted neighborhood environments and intergenerational income mobility, teenage birth, and incarceration in the USA. *Population and Environment, 42*(4), 501–523.

Manduca, R., Hell, M., Adermon, A., Blanden, J., Bratberg, E., Gielen, A. C., Van Kippersluis, H., Lee, K. B., Machin, S. J., Munk, M., & Nybom, M. (2020). *Trends in absolute income mobility in north America and Europe* (Discussion Paper No. 13456). Institute of Labor Economics. https://docs.iza.org/dp13456.pdf

Manoli, D., & Turner, N. (2014). *Cash-on-hand and college enrollment: Evidence from population tax data and policy nonlinearities* (NBER Working Paper No. 19836). National Bureau of Economic Research.

Manza, J., & Uggen, C. (2006). *Locked out: Felon disenfranchisement and American democracy*. Oxford University Press.

Marable, M. (2001). Structural racism and American democracy: Historical and theoretical perspectives. *Souls, 3*(1), 6–24.

Marchi, J., Berg, M., Dencker, A., Olander, E. K., & Begley, C. J. O. R. (2015). Risks associated with obesity in pregnancy, for the mother and baby: A systematic review of reviews. *Obesity Reviews, 16*(8), 621–638.

Marketti, J. (1990). Estimated present value of income diverted during slavery. In *The wealth of races: The present value of benefits from past injustices*, 107–123.

Markovitz, C. E., Hernandez, M. W., Hedberg, E. C., & Whitmore, H. W. (2022). Evaluating the effectiveness of a volunteer one-on-one tutoring model for early elementary reading intervention: A randomized controlled trial replication study. *American Educational Research Journal, 59*(4), 788–819.

Markowitz, A. J., & Ansari, A. (2020). Changes in academic instructional experiences in Head Start classrooms from 2001–2015. *Early Childhood Research Quarterly, 53,* 534–550.

Maroto, M. L. (2015). The absorbing status of incarceration and its relationship with wealth accumulation. *Journal of Quantitative Criminology, 31*(2), 207–236.

Marshall, A. T., Betts, S., Kan, E. C., McConnell, R., Lanphear, B. P., & Sowell, E. R. (2020). Association of lead-exposure risk and family income with childhood brain outcomes. *Nature Medicine, 26*(1), 91–97.

Masarik, A. S., & Conger, R. D. (2017). Stress and child development: A review of the Family Stress Model. *Current Opinion in Psychology, 13,* 85–90.

Massey, D. S., & Denton, N. A. (1993). *American apartheid: Segregation and the making of the underclass.* Harvard University Press.

Massey, D. S., & Lundy, G. (2001). Use of Black English and racial discrimination in urban housing markets: New methods and findings. *Urban Affairs Review, 36*(4), 452–469.

Massey, D. S., Rugh, J. S., Steil, J. P., & Albright, L. (2016). Riding the stagecoach to hell: A qualitative analysis of racial discrimination in mortgage lending. *City & Community, 15*(2), 118–136.

Mateyka, P. (2015). *Desire to move and residential mobility: 2010–2011.* U.S. Census Bureau, U.S. Department of Commerce. https://www.census.gov/content/dam/Census/library/publications/2015/demo/p70-140.pdf

Matthews, D. (2019). Study: Cory Booker's baby bonds nearly close the racial wealth gap for young adults. *Vox.* https://www.vox.com/future-perfect/2019/1/21/18185536/cory-booker-news-today-2020-presidential-election-baby-bonds

Mayne, S. L., Hannan, C., Davis, M., Young, J. F., Kelly, M. K., Powell, M., Dalembert, G., McPeak, K. E., Jenssen, B.P., & Fiks, A. G. (2021). COVID-19 and adolescent depression and suicide risk screening outcomes. *Pediatrics, 148*(3).

Mazzara, A., & Knudsen, B. (2019). *Where families with children use housing vouchers: A comparative look at the 50 largest metropolitan areas.* Center on Budget and Policy Priorities. https://www.cbpp.org/research/housing/where-families-with-childrenuse-housing-vouchers

McCarthy, P., Schiraldi, V., & Shark, M. (2016). The future of youth justice: A community-based alternative to the youth prison model. *New Thinking in Community Corrections Bulletin* (NCJ 250142). U.S. Department of Justice, National Institute of Justice.

McCormick, M., Weiland, C., Hsueh, J., Pralica, M., Weissman, A. K., Moffett, L., Snow, C., & Sachs, J. (2021). Is skill type the key to the PreK fadeout puzzle? Differential associations between enrollment in PreK and constrained and unconstrained skills across kindergarten. *Child Development, 92*(4), e599–e620.

McDonald, Y. J., & Jones, N. E. (2018). Drinking water violations and environmental justice in the United States, 2011–2015. *American Journal of Public Health, 108*(10), 1401–1407.

McEwen, B. S., & Seeman, T. (1999). Protective and damaging effects of mediators of stress. Elaborating and testing the concepts of allostasis and allostatic load. *Annals of the New York Academy of Sciences, 896,* 30–47. https://doi.org/10.1111/j.1749-6632.1999.tb08103.x

McEwen, B., & Stellar, E. (1993). Stress and the individual: Mechanisms leading to disease. *Archives of Internal Medicine, 153*(18), 2093–2101.

McGinty, E. E., Nair, R., Assini-Meytin, L. C., Stuart, E. A., & Letourneau, E. J. (2022). Impact of Medicaid expansion on reported incidents of child neglect and physical abuse. *American Journal of Preventive Medicine, 62*(1), e11–e20. https://www.sciencedirect.com/science/article/abs/pii/S0749379721004049

McGranahan, L., & Schanzenbach, D. W. (2013). *The Earned Income Tax Credit and food consumption patterns* (Working Paper No. 2013-14). Federal Reserve Bank of Chicago. https://ssrn.com/abstract=2366846

McInnis, N. S., Michelmore, K., & Pilkauskas, N. (2023). *The Intergenerational transmission of poverty and public assistance: Evidence from the Earned Income Tax Credit* (NBER Working Paper No. 31429). National Bureau of Economic Research.

McIntosh, K., Girvan, E. J., Fairbanks Falcon, S., McDaniel, S. C., Smolkowski, K., Bastable, E., Santiago-Rosario, M. R., Izzard, S., Austin, S. C., Nese, R. N. & Baldy, T. S. (2021). Equity-focused PBIS approach reduces racial inequities in school discipline: A randomized controlled trial. *School Psychology*, 36(6), 433.

McIntyre, L., Williams, J. V., Lavorato, D. H., & Patten, S. (2013). Depression and suicide ideation in late adolescence and early adulthood are an outcome of child hunger. *Journal of affective Disorders*, 150(1), 123–129.

McLanahan, S., Tach, L., & Schneider, D. (2013). The causal effects of father absence. *Annual Review of Sociology*, 39, 399–427.

McLoyd, V. C. (1990). The impact of economic hardship on Black families and children: Psychological distress, parenting, and socioemotional development. *Child Development*, 61(2), 311–346.

———. (1997). The impact of poverty and low socioeconomic status on the socioemotional functioning of African-American children and adolescents: Mediating effects. *Social and Emotional Adjustment and Family Relations in Ethnic Minority Families*, 7, 34.

McMillan, A., & Chakraborty, A. (2016). Who buys foreclosed homes? How neighborhood characteristics influence real estate-owned home sales to investors and households. *Housing Policy Debate*, 26(4-5), 766–784.

Meehan, K., Jepson, W., Harris, L. M., Wutich, A., Beresford, M., Fencl, A., London, J., Pierce, G., Radonic, L., Wells, C. & Wilson, N. J. (2020). Exposing the myths of household water insecurity in the global north: A critical review. *Wiley Interdisciplinary Reviews: Water*, 7(6), e1486.

Meer, J., & West, J. (2016). Effects of the minimum wage on employment dynamics. *Journal of Human Resources*, 51(2), 500–522.

Mehranbod, C. A., Gobaud, A. N., Jacoby, S. F., Uzzi, M., Bushover, B. R., & Morrison, C. N. (2022). Historical redlining and the epidemiology of present-day firearm violence in the United States: A multi-city analysis. *Preventive Medicine*, 165, 107207.

Mehta, N. K., Lee, H., & Ylitalo, K. R. (2013). Child health in the United States: Recent trends in racial/ethnic disparities. *Social Science & Medicine*, 95, 6–15.

Mello, S. (2018). More COPS, less crime. *Journal of Public Economics*, 172, 174–200.

Merritt, K. (2016). Land and the roots of African American poverty. aeon. https://aeon.co/ideas/land-and-the-roots-of-african-american-poverty

Mersky, J. P., & Topitzes, J. (2010). Comparing early adult outcomes of maltreated and non-maltreated children: A prospective longitudinal investigation. *Children and Youth Services Review*, 32(8), 1086–1096.

Meschede, T., Eden, M., Jain, S., Jee, E., Miles, B., Martinez, M., Stewart, S., Jacob, J., & Madison, M. (2022). *Final Report from our GI Bill study* [IERE Research Brief]. Brandeis University. https://heller.brandeis.edu/iere/pdfs/racial-wealth-equity/racial-wealth-gap/gi_bill_may_2022.pdf

Meschede, T., Morgan, J., Aurand, A., & Threet, D. (2021). *Misdirected housing supports: Why the mortgage interest deduction unjustly subsidizes high-income households and expands racial disparities*. National Low Income Housing Coalition. https://nlihc.org/sites/default/files/NLIHC-IERE_MID-Report.pdf

Meschede, T., Sullivan, L., Shapiro, T. M., Kroeger, T., & Escobar, F. (2019). *Not only unequal paychecks: Occupational segregation, benefits, and the racial wealth gap*. Institute on Assets and Social Policy, The Heller School for Social Policy and Management, Brandeis University.

Mesic, A., Franklin, L., Cansever, A., Potter, F., Sharma, A., Knopov, A. & Siegel, M. (2018). The relationship between structural racism and Black-White disparities in fatal police shootings at the state level. *Journal of the National Medical Association, 110*(2), 106–116.

Messer, C. M., Shriver, T. E., & Adams, A. E. (2018). The destruction of Black Wall Street: Tulsa's 1921 riot and the eradication of accumulated wealth. *American Journal of Economics and Sociology, 77*(3-4), 789–819.

Metzger, M. W. (2014). The reconcentration of poverty: Patterns of housing voucher use, 2000 to 2008. *Housing Policy Debate, 24*(3), 544–567.

Metzger, M. W., Fowler, P. J., Anderson, C. L., & Lindsay, C. A. (2015). Residential mobility during adolescence: Do even "upward" moves predict dropout risk? *Social Science Research, 53*, 218–230.

Metzler, M., Merrick, M. T., Klevens, J., Ports, K. A., & Ford, D. C. (2017). Adverse childhood experiences and life opportunities: Shifting the narrative. *Children and Youth Services Review, 72*, 141–149.

Michalopoulos, C., Faucetta, K., Hill, C. J., Portilla, X. A., Burrell, L., Lee, H., Duggan, A., & Knox, V. (2019). *Impacts on family outcomes of evidence-based early childhood home visiting: Results from the mother and infant home visiting program evaluation* [OPRE Report 2019-07]. Office of Planning, Research, and Evaluation, Administration for Children and Families, U.S. Department of Health and Human Services

Michelmore, K. (2013). *The effect of income on educational attainment: Evidence from state earned income tax credit expansions.* http://dx.doi.org/10.2139/ssrn.2356444

Miller, C., Headlam, C., Manno, M., & Cullinan, D. (2020). Increasing Community College Graduation Rates with a Proven Model: Three-Year Results from the Accelerated Study in Associate Programs (ASAP) Ohio Demonstration. *MDRC*.

Miller, C., & Weiss, M. (2021). *Increasing community college graduation rates. A synthesis of findings on the ASAP model from six colleges across two states* (Working Paper). mdrc. https://www.mdrc.org/work/publications/increasing-community-college-graduation-rates

Miller, G. E., Yu, T., Chen, E., & Brody, G. H. (2015). Self-control forecasts better psychosocial outcomes but faster epigenetic aging in low-SES youth. *Proceedings of the National Academy of Sciences, 112*(33), 10325–10330.

Miller, H. V., & Barnes, J. C. (2015). The association between parental incarceration and health, education, and economic outcomes in young adulthood. *American Journal of Criminal Justice, 40*, 765–784.

Miller, S., Wherry, L. R., & Greene Foster, D. (2023). The economic consequences of being denied an abortion. *American Economic Journal: Economic Policy, 15*(1), 394–437.

Miller, S., & Wherry, L. R. (2019). The long-term effects of early life Medicaid coverage. *Journal of Human Resources, 54*(3), 785–824.

Miller-Cribbs, J. E., & Farber, N. B. (2008). Kin networks and poverty among African Americans: Past and present. *Social Work, 53*(1), 43–51.

Minervino, J. (2014). *Lessons from research and the classroom: Implementing high-quality pre-k that makes a difference for young children.* Bill & Melinda Gates Foundation. https://docs.gatesfoundation.org/documents/lessons%20from%20research%20and%20the%20classroom_september%202014.pdf

Mitchell, O. (2005). A meta-analysis of race and sentencing research: Explaining the inconsistencies. *Journal of Quantitative Criminology, 21*(4), 439–466.

Mitchell, T. W. (2005). Destabilizing the normalization of rural Black land loss: A critical role for legal empiricism. *Wisconsin Law Review*, 557.

Mittleman, J. (2018). A downward spiral? Childhood suspension and the path to juvenile arrest. *Sociology of Education, 91*(3), 183–204.

Model, S. (2008). *West Indian immigrants: A Black success story?* Russell Sage Foundation.

Molina, K. M., Alegría, M., & Chen, C. N. (2012). Neighborhood context and substance use disorders: A comparative analysis of racial and ethnic groups in the United States. *Drug and Alcohol Dependence, 125,* S35–S43.

Monarrez, T., & Chien, C. (2021). Dividing lines: Racially unequal school boundaries in us public school systems: Research report. *Urban Institute.*

Monk, E. P. (2021). The unceasing significance of colorism: Skin tone stratification in the United States. *Daedalus, 150*(2), 76–90. https://doi.org/10.1162/DAED_a_01847

Morgan, R., & Thompson, A. (2022). Criminal victimization, 2020—Supplemental statistical tables. Office of Justice Programs, Bureau of Justice Statistics, U.S. Department of Justice. https://bjs.ojp.gov/content/pub/pdf/cv20sst.pdf

Morgan, W. J., Crain, E. F., Gruchalla, R. S., O'Connor, G. T., Kattan, M., Evans III, R., Stout, J., Malindzak, G., Smartt, E., Plaut, M. & Walter, M. (2004). Results of a home-based environmental intervention among urban children with asthma. *New England Journal of Medicine, 351*(11), 1068–1080.

Morris, M. (2016). *Pushout: The criminalization of Black girls in schools.* New Press.

Moss, H. B., Chen, C. M., & Yi, H. Y. (2014). Early adolescent patterns of alcohol, cigarettes, and marijuana polysubstance use and young adult substance use outcomes in a nationally representative sample. *Drug and Alcohol Dependence, 136,* 51–62.

Moulton, V., Goodman, A., Nasim, B., Ploubidis, G. B., & Gambaro, L. Parental wealth and children's cognitive ability, mental, and physical health: Evidence from the UK millennium cohort study. *Child Development, 92*(1), 115–123.

Mountjoy, J. (2022). Community colleges and upward mobility. *American Economic Review, 112*(8), 2580–2630.

Mueller, J. T., & Gasteyer, S. (2021). The widespread and unjust drinking water and clean water crisis in the United States. *Natural Communications, 12,* 3544. https://doi.org/10.1038/s41467-021-23898-z

Mueller-Smith, M. (2015). The criminal and labor market impacts of incarceration [Unpublished Working Paper]. University of Michigan. https://sites.lsa.umich.edu/mgms/wp-content/uploads/sites/283/2015/09/incar.pdf

Mueller-Smith, M., & Schnepel, K. T. (2021). Diversion in the criminal justice system. *The Review of Economic Studies, 88*(2), 883–936.

Muhammad, K. G. (2019). *The condemnation of Blackness: Race, crime, and the making of modern urban America, with a new preface.* Harvard University Press.

Muller, C. (2012). Northward migration and the rise of racial disparity in American incarceration, 1880–1950. *American Journal of Sociology, 118*(2), 281–326.

___. (2018). Freedom and convict leasing in the postbellum south. *American Journal of Sociology, 124*(2), 367–405.

Muller, C., & Schrage, D. (2021). The political economy of incarceration in the cotton south, 1910–1925. *American Journal of Sociology, 127*(3), 828–866.

Mulvey, E. P., & Schubert, C. A. (2011). Youth in prison and beyond. In D. M. Bischop & B. C. Feld (Eds.), *The Oxford handbook of juvenile crime and justice.* https://doi.org/10.1093/oxfordhb/9780195385106.013.0033

Musu-Gillette, L., de Brey, C., McFarland, J., Hussar, W., Sonnenberg, W., & Wilkinson-Flicker, S. (2017) Status and Trends in the Education of Racial and Ethnic Groups 2017 (NCES 2017-051). U.S. Department of Education, National Center for Education Statistics. Washington, DC.

Nader, K., Pynoos, R., Fairbanks, L., & Frederick, C. (1990). Children's PTSD reactions one year after a sniper attack at their school. *The American Journal of Psychiatry, 147*(11), 1526–1530. https://doi.org/10.1176/ajp.147.11.1526Eitle

Nagaraj, A., & Tranchero, M. (2023). *How Does Data Access Shape Science? Evidence from the Impact of U.S. Census's Research Data Centers on Economics Research.* University of California, Berkeley. U_FSRDC_paper.pdf (squarespace.com)

Nam, Y., & Huang, J. (2009). Equal opportunity for all? Parental economic resources and children's educational attainment. *Children and Youth Services Review, 31*(6), 625–634.

Nam, S., Jeon, S., Lee, S. J., Ash, G., Nelson, L. E., & Granger, D. A. (2022). Real-time racial discrimination, affective states, salivary cortisol and alpha-amylase in Black adults. *PloS One, 17*(9), e0273081.

Nanda, J. (2019). The construction and criminalization of disability in school incarceration. *Columbia Journal of Race and Law, 9*.

Nardone, A., Casey, J. A., Morello-Frosch, R., Mujahid, M., Balmes, J. R., & Thakur, N. (2020). Associations between historical residential redlining and current age-adjusted rates of emergency department visits due to asthma across eight cities in California: an ecological study. *The Lancet Planetary Health, 4*(1), e24–e31.

Nardone, A., Rudolph, K. E., Morello-Frosch, R., & Casey, J. A. (2021). Redlines and greenspace: The relationship between historical redlining and 2010 greenspace across the United States. *Environmental Health Perspectives, 129*(1), 017006.

National Academies of Sciences, Engineering, and Medicine (National Academies). (2017a). *Federal statistics, multiple data sources, and privacy protection: Next steps*. The National Academies Press. https://doi.org/10.17226/24893

___. (2017b). *Improving collection of indicators of criminal justice system involvement in population health data programs: Proceedings of a workshop*. The National Academies Press. https://doi.org/10.17226/24633

___. (2017c). *Innovations in federal statistics: Combining data sources while protecting privacy*. The National Academies Press. https://doi.org/10.17226/24652

___. (2017d). *Communities in action: Pathways to health equity*. The National Academies Press.

___. (2017e). *Review of WIC food packages: Improving balance and choice: Final report*. The National Academies Press. https://doi.org/10.17226/23655

___. (2018). *Proactive policing: Effects on crime and communities*. The National Academies Press. https://doi.org/10.17226/24928

___. (2019a). *A roadmap to reducing child poverty*. The National Academies Press. https://doi.org/10.17226/25246

___. (2019b). *Minority Serving Institutions: America's underutilized resource for strengthening the STEM workforce*. The National Academies Press. https://doi.org/10.17226/25257

___. (2021). *The future of nursing 2020–2030: Charting a path to achieve health equity*. The National Academies Press.

___. (2022a). *Toward a 21st century national data infrastructure: Mobilizing information for the common good*. The National Academies Press. https://doi.org/10.17226/26688

___. (2022b). *Reducing racial inequality in crime and justice: Science, practice, and policy*. The National Academies Press.

___. (2023). *Advancing antiracism, diversity, and equity inclusion in STEMM organizations: Beyond broadening participation*. The National Academies Press. https://doi.org/10.17226/26803

National Center for Education Statistics (NCES). (2019). *Profile of very low- and low-income undergraduates in 2015–2016* (Report No. NCES 2020460REV). https://nces.ed.gov/pubs2020/2020460rev.pdf

___. (2019). Indicator 23: Postsecondary Graduation Rates. https://nces.ed.gov/programs/raceindicators/indicator_red.asp

National Center for Healthy Housing. (2009). *Housing interventions and health: A review of the evidence*. National Center for Healthy Housing. https://nchh.org/resource-library/report_housing-interventions-and-health_a-review-of-the-evidence.pdf

National Community Reinvestment Coalition. (2020). *Redlining and neighborhood health*. https://ncrc.org/holc-health/

National Native American Boarding School Healing Coalition. (2020). *American Indian boarding schools by state*. https://boardingschoolhealing.org/wp-content/uploads/2021/06/NABS-Boarding-school-list-2021-acc.pdf

National Research Council. (2004). *Measuring racial discrimination*. The National Academies Press. https://doi.org/10.17226/10887

___. (2009). *Protecting student records and facilitating education research: A workshop summary*. The National Academies Press. https://doi.org/10.17226/12514

___. (2012). *Education for life and work: Developing transferable knowledge and skills in the 21st century*. The National Academies Press. https://doi.org/10.17226/13398

___. (2013). *Reforming juvenile justice: A developmental approach. committee on assessing juvenile justice reform*. The National Academies Press.

___. (2014). *The growth of incarceration in the United States: Exploring causes and consequences*. The National Academies Press.

Naval Postgraduate School. (2023). CHDS School Shooting Safety Compendium. Shooting Incidents at K-12 Schools (Jan 1970–Jun 2022). Center for Homeland Defense and Security. https://www.chds.us/ssdb/charts-graphs/

Neal, D. A., & Johnson, W. R. (1996). The role of premarket factors in Black-White wage differences. *Journal of Political Economy, 104*(5), 869–895.

Neal, D., & Rick, A. (2014). *The prison boom and the lack of Black progress after Smith and Welch*. National Bureau of Economic Research. https://doi.org/10.3386/w20283

Negriff, S. (2020). ACEs are not equal: Examining the relative impact of household dysfunction versus childhood maltreatment on mental health in adolescence. *Social Science & Medicine, 245*, 112696.

Nellis, A. (2021). *The color of justice: Racial and ethnic disparity in state prisons*. The Sentencing Project. https://www.sentencingproject.org/wp-content/uploads/2016/06/The-Color-of-Justice-Racial-and-Ethnic-Disparity-in-State-Prisons.pdf

Neumark, D. (2012). Detecting discrimination in audit and correspondence studies. *Journal of Human Resources, 47*(4), 1128–1157. www.muse.jhu.edu/article/488623

___. (2018). Experimental research on labor market discrimination. *Journal of Economic Literature, 56*(3), 799–866.

Neumark, D., & Shirley, P. (2021). *Myth or measurement: What does the new minimum wage research say about minimum wages and job loss in the United States?* (NBER Working Paper No. 28388). National Bureau of Economic Research.

Neumark, D., & Wascher, W. (2002). Do minimum wages fight poverty? *Economic Inquiry, 40*(3), 315–333.

New York Civil Liberties Union. (2013). Analysis finds racial disparities, ineffectiveness in NYPD Stop-And-Frisk Program; Links tactic to soaring marijuana arrest rate. https://www.nyclu.org/en/press-releases/analysis-finds-racial-disparities-ineffectiveness-nypd-stop-and-frisk-program-links

Newman, S. J., & Harkness, J. M. (2002). The long-term effects of public housing on self-sufficiency. *Journal of Policy Analysis and Management, 21*(1), 21–43.

Newman, S. J., & Holupka, C. S. (2014). Housing affordability and investments in children. *Journal of Housing Economics, 24*, 89–100.

___. (2015). Housing affordability and child well-being. *Housing Policy Debate, 25*(1), 116–151.

Nichols, A., & Rothstein, J. (2016). Chapter 2. The Earned Income Tax Credit. In R. A. Moffitts (Eds.) *Economics of Means-Tested Transfer Programs in the United States, Volume I*, 137–218. University of Chicago Press. https://doi.org/10.7208/9780226370507-004

Nielsen, M. O., & Silverman, R. A. (Eds.). (2009). *Criminal justice in Native America*. University of Arizona Press.

Noble, S. (2018). *Algorithms of oppression: How search engines reinforce racism*. NYU Press.

Norris, S., Pecenco, M., & Weaver, J. (2021). The effects of parental and sibling incarceration: Evidence from Ohio. *American Economic Review, 111*(9), 2926–2963.

Nowak, M. (2019). *The United Nations global study on children deprived of liberty*. United Nations. https://omnibook.com/view/e0623280-5656-42f8-9edf-5872f8f08562/page/294

Nowicki, J. M. (2018). *K–12 education: Discipline disparities for Black students, boys, and students with disabilities*. (GAO-18-258). U.S. Government Accountability Office.

Nowicki, J. M. (2020). *K–12 education: Characteristics of school shootings*. (GAO-20-455). U.S. Government Accountability Office.

Nunn, R., & Hunt, J. (2021). How labor market institutions matter for worker compensation. *The ANNALS of the American Academy of Political and Social Science, 695*(1), 225–241.

Nuru-Jeter, A., Dominguez, T. P., Hammond, W. P., Leu, J., Skaff, M., Egerter, S., Jones, C. P. & Braveman, P. (2009). It's the skin you're in: African-American women talk about their experiences of racism: An exploratory study to develop measures of racism for birth outcome studies. *Maternal and Child Health Journal, 13*(1), 29–39.

Obermeyer, Z., Powers, B., Vogeli, C., & Mullainathan, S. (2019). Dissecting racial bias in an algorithm used to manage the health of populations. *Science, 366*(6464), 447–453.

O'Connell, H. A. (2012). The impact of slavery on racial inequality in poverty in the contemporary U.S. South. *Social Forces, 90*(3), 713–734.

Office of the Assistant Secretary for Planning and Evaluation (ASPE), U.S. Department of Health and Human Services. (2021). *Health insurance coverage and access to care for American Indians and Alaska Natives: Current trends and key challenges* [Issue Brief No. HP-2021-18]. Office of the Assistant Secretary for Planning and Evaluation, U.S. Department of Health and Human Services. https://aspe.hhs.gov/reports/healthinsurance-coverage-changes-aian

Office of the Assistant Secretary for Planning and Evaluation & U.S. Department of Health and Human Services. (2022). *How Increased Funding Can Advance the Mission of the Indian Health Service to Improve Health Outcomes for American Indians and Alaska Natives* (Report No. HP-2022-21). U.S. Department of Health and Human Services. https://aspe.hhs.gov/sites/default/files/documents/1b5d32824c31e113a2df43170c45ac15/aspe-ihs-funding-disparities-report.pdf

Office of Head Start. (2023). *Head Start History*. Administration for Children, Youth, and Families. https://www.acf.hhs.gov/ohs/about/history-head-start

Office of Juvenile Justice and Delinquency Prevention (OJJDP). (2016). *Tribal Youth in the Juvenile Justice System*. https://ojjdp.ojp.gov/model-programs-guide/literature reviews/tribal_youth_in_the_juvenile_justice_system.pdf

___. (2022). *Racial and ethnic disparity in juvenile justice processing: Literature review: A product of the Model Programs Guide*. https://ojjdp.ojp.gov/model-programs-guide/literature-reviews/racial-and-ethnic-disparity

Ogbu, J. U., & Davis, A. (2003). *Black American students in an affluent suburb: A student of academic disengagement*. Garland.

Oklahoma Commission to Study the Tulsa Race Riot of 1921. (2001). *Tulsa Race Riot*. https://www.okhistory.org/research/forms/freport.pdf

Okonofua, J. A., & Eberhardt, J. L. (2015). Two strikes race and the disciplining of young students. *Psychological Science, 26*(5), 617–624.

Okonofua, J. A., Paunesku, D., & Walton, G. M. (2016). Brief intervention to encourage empathic discipline cuts suspension rates in half among adolescents. *Proceedings of the National Academy of Sciences, 113*(19), 5221–5226.

Okonofua, J. A., Walton, G. M., & Eberhardt, J. L. (2016). A vicious cycle: A social–psychological account of extreme racial disparities in school discipline. *Perspectives on Psychological Science, 11*(3), 381–398.

Olds, D. L., Eckenrode, J., Henderson, C. R., Kitzman, H., Powers, J., Cole, R., Sidora, K., Morris, P., Pettitt, L. M. & Luckey, D. (1997). Long-term effects of home visitation on maternal life course and child abuse and neglect: Fifteen-year follow-up of a randomized trial. *JAMA, 278*(8), 637–643.

Olds, D., Henderson Jr, C.R., Cole, R., Eckenrode, J., Kitzman, H., Luckey, D., Pettitt, L., Sidora, K., Morris, P. & Powers, J. (1998). Long-term effects of nurse home visitation on children's criminal and antisocial behavior: 15-year follow-up of a randomized controlled trial. *JAMA, 280*(14), 1238–1244.

Olds, D. L., Robinson, J., O'Brien, R., Luckey, D. W., Pettitt, L. M., Henderson, C. R., Jr, Ng, R. K., Sheff, K. L., Korfmacher, J., Hiatt, S., & Talmi, A. (2002). Home visiting by paraprofessionals and by nurses: A randomized, controlled trial. *Pediatrics, 110*(3), 486–496. https://doi.org/10.1542/peds.110.3.486

Oliver, M. L., & Shapiro, T. M. (1997). *Black Wealth/White Wealth: A new perspective on racial inequality*. Routledge.

O'Neill, K. K., Kennedy, I., & Harris, A. (2022). Debtors' blocks: How monetary sanctions make between-neighborhood racial and economic inequalities worse. *Sociology of Race and Ethnicity, 8*(1), 43–61.

Opara, I. N., Riddle-Jones, L., & Allen, N. (2022). Modern day Drapetomania: Calling out scientific racism. *Journal of General Internal Medicine, 37*(1), 225–226.

Orfield, G, Jongyeon, E., Frankenberg E., & Siegel-Hawley G. (2016). *"Brown" at 62: School segregation by race, poverty and state*. University of California Los Angeles Civil Rights Project.

Organisation for Economic Co-operation and Development. (2019). *Negotiating our way up: Collective bargaining in a changing world of work*. OECD Publishing. https://doi.org/10.1787/1fd2da34-en

Orr, A. J. (2003). Black-White differences in achievement: The importance of wealth. *Sociology of Education, 76*(6), 281–304.

Orrell, B. (Ed.). (2021). *Minding our workforce: The role of noncognitive skills in career success*. American Enterprise Institute. https://www.aei.org/wp-content/uploads/2021/05/Minding-our-Workforce.pdf?x91208

O'Shea, T. C. (2006). Physical deterioration, disorder, and crime. *Criminal Justice Policy Review, 17*(2), 173–187

Osofsky, J. D. (1999). The impact of violence on children. *The Future of Children, 9*(3), 33–49.

Osterman, P. (2018). In search of the high road: Meaning and evidence. *ILR Review, 71*(1), 3–34.

Ostrovsky, Y. (2017). *Doing as well as one's parents? Tracking recent changes in absolute income mobility in Canada*. Statistics Canada. http://www.statcan.gc.ca/pub/11-626-x/11-626-x2017073-eng.htm

Ouss, A. (2020). Misaligned incentives and the scale of incarceration in the United States. *Journal of Public Economics, 191*, 104285.

Owens, A. (2016). Inequality in children's contexts: Income segregation of households with and without children. *American Sociological Review, 81*(3), 549–574

Owens, J., & McLanahan, S. S. (2020). Unpacking the drivers of racial disparities in school suspension and expulsion. *Social Forces, 98*(4), 1548–1577.

O'Hara, A. (2004). *New methods for simulating CPS taxes*. U.S. Census Bureau. https://www.census.gov/library/working-papers/2004/demo/oharataxmodel.html

Pac, J. (2019). *Three essays on child maltreatment prevention* [Doctoral Dissertation]. Columbia University. https://www.proquest.com/docview/2235352545?pq-origsite=gscholar&fromopenview=true

___. (2021). Early childhood education and care programs in the United States: Does access improve child safety? *Social Service Review, 95*, 66–109.

Pac, J., Collyer, S., Berger, L. M., O'Brien, K., Parker, E., Pecora, P., Rostad, W., Waldfogel, J., & Wimer, C. (2023). The effects of child poverty reductions on child protective services involvement. *Social Service Review, 97*(1).

Pace, A., Alper, R., Burchinal, M. R., Golinkoff, R. M., & Hirsh-Pasek, K. (2019). Measuring success: Within and cross-domain predictors of academic and social trajectories in elementary school. *Early Childhood Research Quarterly, 46*, 112–125.

Packham, A. (2017). Family planning funding cuts and teen childbearing. *Journal of Health Economics, 55*, 168–185.

Pager, D. (2003). The mark of a criminal record. *American Journal of Sociology, 108*(5), 937–975.

Pager, D. (2007). *Marked: Race, crime, and finding work in an era of mass incarceration.* University of Chicago Press,

Pager, D., Goldstein, R., Ho, H., & Western, B. (2022). Criminalizing poverty: The consequences of court fees in a randomized experiment. *American Sociological Review, 87*(3), 529–553.

Pager, D., & Shepherd, H. (2008). The sociology of discrimination: Racial discrimination in employment, housing, credit, and consumer markets. *Annual Review of Sociology, 34*, 181.

Pager, D., Western, B., & Sugie, N. (2009). Sequencing disadvantage: Barriers to employment facing young Black and White men with criminal records. *The ANNALS of the American Academy of Political and Social Science, 623*(1), 195–213.

Pages, R., Bailey, D. H., & Duncan, G. J. (2023). The impacts of Abecedarian and Head Start on educational attainment: Reasoning about unobserved mechanisms from temporal patterns of indirect effects. *Early Childhood Research Quarterly, 65*, 261–274.

Paik, L., & Packard, C. (2019). *Impact of juvenile justice fines and fees on family life: Case study in Dane County, WI.* Arnold Ventures. http://debtorsprison. jlc. org/documents/JLC-Debtors-Prison-dane-county.pdf

Papageorge, N. W., Gershenson, S., & Kang, K. M. (2020). Teacher expectations matter. *Review of Economics and Statistics, 102*(2), 234–251.

Papay, J. P., & Kraft, M. A. (2015). Productivity returns to experience in the teacher labor market: Methodological challenges and new evidence on long-term career improvement. *Journal of Public Economics, 130*, 105–119.

Papay, J. P., West, M. R., Fullerton, J. B., & Kane, T. J. (2012). Does an urban teacher residency increase student achievement? Early evidence from Boston. *Educational Evaluation and Policy Analysis, 34*(4), 413–434.

Paradies, Y., Ben, J., Denson, N., Elias, A., Priest, N., Pieterse, A., Gupta, A., Kelaher, M. & Gee, G. (2015). Racism as a determinant of health: A systematic review and meta-analysis. *PloS One, 10*(9), e0138511.

Park, T. J., Flores, S. M., & Ryan, C. J. (2018). Labor market returns for graduates of Hispanic-serving institutions. *Research in Higher Education, 59*(1), 29–53.

Parolin, Z., Matsudaira, J., Waldfogel, J., & Wimer, C. (2022). Exposure to childhood poverty and racial differences in economic opportunity in young adulthood. *Demography, 59*(6), 2295–2319.

Parpouchi, M., Moniruzzaman, A., & Somers, J. M. (2021). The association between experiencing homelessness in childhood or youth and adult housing stability in Housing First. *BMC Psychiatry, 21*(1), 1–14.

Paschall, K. W., Gershoff, E. T., & Kuhfeld, M. (2018). A two decade examination of historical race/ethnicity disparities in academic achievement by poverty status. *Journal of Youth and Adolescence, 47*, 1164–1177.

Patterson, O. (2006). A poverty of the mind. *New York Times.* https://www.nytimes.com/2006/03/26/opinion/a-poverty-of-the-mind.html

___. (2015). The social and cultural matrix of Black Youth. In O. Patterson & E. Fosse (Eds.), *The Cultural matrix*, 45–136. Harvard University Press.

Pattillo, M. (2007). *Black on the block: The politics of race and class in the city*. University of Chicago Press.

Paul, M., Zaw, K., & Darity, W. (2022). Returns in the labor market: A nuanced view of penalties at the intersection of race and gender in the US. *Feminist Economics*, 28(2), 1–31.

Paxson, C., & Waldfogel, J. (2002). Work, welfare, and child maltreatment. *Journal of Labor Economics*, 20, 435–474.

___. (2003). Welfare reforms, family resources, and child maltreatment. *Journal of Policy Analysis and Management*, 22, 85–113.

Peisner-Feinberg, E., Kuhn, L., Zadrozny, S., Foster, T., & Burchinal, M. (2020). *Kindergarten follow-up findings from a small-scale RCT study of the North Carolina Pre-Kindergarten Program*. The University of North Carolina, School of Education.

Pelton, L. H. (2015). The continuing role of material factors in child maltreatment and placement. *Child Abuse & Neglect*, 41, 30–39.

Pember, M. A. (2019, March 8). Death by civilization. The Atlantic. https://www.theatlantic.com/education/archive/2019/03/traumatic-legacy-indian-boarding-schools/584293/

Percheski, C., & Gibson-Davis, C. (2020). A penny on the dollar: Racial inequalities in wealth among households with children. *Socius*, 6, 2378023120916616.

Perlin, S., Sexton, K., & Wong, D. W. S. (1999). An examination of race and poverty for populations living near industrial sources of air pollution. *Journal of Exposure Analysis and Environmental Epidemiology*, 9, 29–48.

Perlman, S., & Fantuzzo, J. (2010). Timing and influence of early experiences of child maltreatment and homelessness on children's educational well-being. *Children and Youth Services Review*, 32(6), 874–883.

Perry, A. M., Rothwell, J., & Harshbarger, D. (2018). *The devaluation of assets in Black neighborhoods: The case of residential property*. The Brookings Institute. https://www.brookings.edu/wp-content/uploads/2018/11/2018.11_Brookings-Metro_Devaluation-Assets-Black-Neighborhoods_final.pdf

Perry, B. (2006). Nobody trusts them! Under-and over-policing Native American communities. *Critical Criminology*, 14(4), 411–444.

Persico, C. (2022). *Can pollution cause poverty? The effects of pollution on educational, health and economic outcomes* (NBER Working Paper No. 30559). National Bureau of Economic Research.

Persico, C., Figlio, D., & Roth, J. (2020). The developmental consequences of superfund sites. *Journal of Labor Economics*, 38(4), 1055–1097.

Persson, P., & Rossin-Slater, M. (2018). Family ruptures, stress, and the mental health of the next generation: Reply. *American Economic Review*, 108(4-5), 1256–1263.

Peterson, R. D., & Krivo, L. J. (2010). *Divergent social worlds: Neighborhood crime and the racial-spatial divide*. Russell Sage Foundation.

Pettit, B. (2014). *Invisible men: Mass incarceration and the myth of Black progress*. Russell Sage Foundation.

Pew Research Center. (2011). *Twenty-to-one: Wealth gaps rise to record highs between Whites, Blacks and Hispanics*. https://www.pewresearch.org/wp-content/uploads/sites/3/2011/07/SDT-Wealth-Report_7-26-11_FINAL.pdf

___. (2021). *Local spending on jails tops $25 billion in latest nationwide data. Costs increased despite falling crime and fewer people being admitted to jail*. https://www.pewtrusts.org/en/research-and-analysis/issue-briefs/2021/01/local-spending-on-jails-tops-$25-billion-in-latest-nationwide-data

Pfeffer, F. (2011). Status attainment and wealth in the United States and Germany. In T. M. Smeeding, R. Erikson, M. J̈antti (Eds.) *Persistence, privilege, and parenting: The comparative study of intergenerational mobility*, pp. 109–37. Russell Sage Found.

Pfeffer, F. T., & Killewald, A. (2018). Generations of advantage. Multigenerational correlations in family wealth. *Social Forces, 96*(4),1411–1442.

___. (2019). Intergenerational wealth mobility and racial inequality. *Socius.*

Phillips, D., Lipsey, M. W., Dodge, K. A., Haskins, R., Bassok, D., Burchinal, M. R., Duncan, G. J., Dynarski, M., Magnuson, K. A., & Weiland, C. (2017). *Puzzling it out: The current state of scientific knowledge on pre-kindergarten effects: A consensus statement.* The Brookings Institution. https://www.brookings.edu/research/puzzling-it-out-the-currentstate-of-scientific-knowledge-on-pre-kindergarten-effects/

Phillips, M., Brooks-Gunn, J., Duncan, G. J., Klebanov, P., & Crane, J. (1998). *Family background, parenting practices, and the Black–White test score gap.* Brookings Institution Press.

Philp, K. R. (1983). Termination: a legacy of the Indian New Deal. *The Western Historical Quarterly, 14*(2), 165–180.

Pindus, N., Kingsley, T., Biess, J., Levy, D., Simington, J., & Hayes, C. (2017). *Housing needs of American Indians and Alaska Natives in tribal areas: A report from the assessment of American Indian, Alaska Native, and Native Hawaiian housing needs: Executive summary.* U.S. Department of Housing and Urban Development, Office of Policy Development and Research. https://www.huduser.gov/portal/sites/default/files/pdf/HNAI-HousingNeeds.pdf

Piquero, A. R., & Jennings, W. G. (2017). Research note: Justice system–imposed financial penalties increase the likelihood of recidivism in a sample of adolescent offenders. *Youth Violence and Juvenile Justice, 15*(3), 325–340.

Policy Advocacy Clinic. (2017). *Making families pay: The harmful, unlawful, and costly practice of charging juvenile administrative fees in California.* Berkeley Law, University of California. https://www.law.berkeley.edu/wp-content/uploads/2015/12/Making-Families-Pay.pdf

Pollack, C. E., Bozzi, D. G., Blackford, A. L., DeLuca, S., Thornton, R. L., & Herring, B. (2021). Using the moving to opportunity experiment to investigate the long-term impact of neighborhoods on healthcare use by specific clinical conditions and type of service. *Housing Policy Debate*, 1–21.

Pollakowski, H. O., Weinberg, D. H., Andersson, F., Haltiwanger, J. C., Palloni, G., & Kutzbach, M. J. (2022). Childhood housing and adult outcomes: A between-siblings analysis of housing vouchers and public housing. *American Economic Journal: Economic Policy, 14*(3), 235–272.

Polyzoi, E., Acar, E., Babb, J., Skwarchuk, S. L., Brownell, M., Kinnear, R., & Cliteur, K. (2020). Children facing deep poverty in Manitoba, Canada: Subsidized licensed childcare and school readiness for children with and without special needs. *Journal of Research in Childhood Education, 34*(2), 306–329.

Pope, N. G., Johnston, A., & Jones, M. (forthcoming). *Divorce, family arrangement, and children's adult outcomes* (Working Paper).

Portes, A., & Rumbaut, R. G. (2014). *Immigrant America: A portrait, updated, and expanded* (4th ed.). https://doi.org/10.1525/9780520959156

Poston, L., Harthoorn, L. F., & Van Der Beek, E. M. (2011). Obesity in pregnancy: Implications for the mother and lifelong health of the child: A consensus statement. *Pediatric Research, 69*(2), 175–180.

Powell, J. A. (2008). Structural racism: Building upon the insights of John Calmore. *North Carolina Law Review*, 86

Pratt, S. L. (2001). The given land: Black Hawk's conception of place. *Philosophy & Geography, 4*(1), 109–125.

Price, G. N., Spriggs, W., & Swinton, O.H. (2011). The relative returns to graduating from a historically Black college/university: Propensity score matching estimates from the national survey of Black Americans. *The Review of Black Political Economy*, 38(2), 103–130.

Prince, J. D., & Wald, C. (2018). Risk of criminal justice system involvement among people with co-occurring severe mental illness and substance use disorder. *International Journal of Law and Psychiatry*, 58, 1–8.

Prinz, R. J., Sanders, M. R., Shapiro, C. J., Whitaker, D. J., & Lutzker, J. R. (2009). Population-based prevention of child maltreatment: The US Triple P system population trial. *Prevention Science*, 10, 1–12.

Provine, D. M. (2011). Race and inequality in the war on drugs. *Annual Review of Law and Social Science*, 7, 41–60.

Puma, M., Bell, S., Cook, R., Heid, C., Broene, P., Jenkins, F., Mashburn, A., & Downer, J. (2012). *Third grade follow-up to the Head Start Impact Study: Final report* (OPRE Report No. 2012-45). Administration for Children & Families.

Putnam-Hornstein, E., Ahn, E., Prindle, J., Magruder, J., Webster, D., & Wildeman, C. (2021). Cumulative rates of child protection involvement and terminations of parental rights in a California birth cohort, 1999–2017. *American Journal of Public Health*, 111(6), 1157–1163.

Putnam-Hornstein, E., Needell, B., King, B., & Johnson-Motoyama, M. (2013). Racial and ethnic disparities: A population-based examination of risk factors for involvement with child protective services. *Child Abuse & Neglect*, 37(1), 33–46.

Puumala, S. E., Burgess, K. M., Kharbanda, A. B, Zook, H. G., Castille, D. M., Pickner, W. J., & Payne, N. R. (2016). The role of bias by emergency department providers in care for American Indian children. *Medical Care*, 54(6), 562.

Puzzanchera, C. (2021). *Juvenile Justice Statistics. National Report Series Bulletin: Juvenile Arrests, 2019*. Office of Justice Programs, U.S. Department of Justice. https://ojjdp.ojp.gov/publications/juvenile-arrests-2019.pdf

Quillian, L. (2012). Segregation and poverty concentration: The role of three segregations. *American Sociological Review*, 77(3), 354–379.

Quillian, L., Lee, J. J., & Honoré, B. (2020a). Racial discrimination in the U.S. housing and mortgage lending markets: A quantitative review of trends, 1976–2016. *Race and Social Problems*, 12(1), 13–28.

Quillian, L., Lee, J. J., & Oliver, M. (2020b). Evidence from field experiments in hiring shows substantial additional racial discrimination after the callback. *Social Forces*, 99(2), 732–759. https://doi.org/10.1093/sf/soaa026

Quillian, L., Pager, D., Hexel, O., & Midtbøen, A. H. (2017). Meta-analysis of field experiments shows no change in racial discrimination in hiring over time. *Proceedings of the National Academy of Sciences*, 114(41), 10870–10875.

Raby, K. L., Freedman, E., Yarger, H. A., Lind, T., & Dozier, M. (2018). Enhancing the language development of toddlers in foster care by promoting foster parents' sensitivity: Results from a randomized control trial. *Developmental Science*. https://doi.org/10.1111/desc.12753

Radez, J., Reardon, T., Creswell, C., Lawrence, P. J., Evdoka-Burton, G., & Waite, P. (2021). Why do children and adolescents (not) seek and access professional help for their mental health problems? A systematic review of quantitative and qualitative studies. *European Child & Adolescent Psychiatry*, 30(2), 183–211.

Radford, G. (2008). *Modern housing for America: Policy struggles in the New Deal era*. University of Chicago Press.

Raffaele Mendez, L. M. (2003). Predictors of suspension and negative school outcomes: A longitudinal investigation. *New Directions for Youth Development*, 2003(99), 17–33.

Raissian, K. M. (2015). Does unemployment affect child abuse rates? Evidence from New York State. *Child Abuse & Neglect, 48*, 1–12.

Raissian, K. M., & Bullinger, L. R. (2017). Money matters: Does the minimum wage affect child maltreatment rates? *Children and Youth Services Review, 72*, 60–70.

Ramakrishnan, U., Grant, F., Goldenberg, T., Zongrone, A., & Martorell, R. (2012). Effect of women's nutrition before and during early pregnancy on maternal and infant outcomes: A systematic review. *Paediatric and Perinatal Epidemiology, 26*, 285–301.

Ramey, C. T., Campbell, F. A., Burchinal, M., Skinner, M. L., Gardner, D. M., & Ramey, S. L. (2000). Persistent effects of early childhood education on high-risk children and their mothers. *Applied Developmental Science, 4*(1), 2–14.

Ramey, C. T., Sparling, J. J., & Ramey, S. L. (2012). *Abecedarian: The ideas, the approach, and the findings*. Sociometrics Corporation.

Raphael, S., & Stoll, M. A. (2013). *Why are so many Americans in prison?* Russell Sage Foundation.

Ray, V. (2019). A theory of racialized organizations. *American Sociological Review, 84*(1), 26–53.

Reardon, S. F. (2011). The widening academic achievement gap between the rich and the poor: New evidence and possible explanations. In G. J. Duncan & R. J. Murnane (Eds.) *Whither opportunity?: Rising inequality, schools, and children's life chances*, 91–116. Russell Sage Foundation.

___. (2021). *The economic achievement gap in the U.S., 1960–2020: Reconciling recent empirical findings* (CEPA Working Paper No. 21.09). Stanford Center for Education Policy Analysis. https://cepa.stanford.edu/wp21-09

Reardon, S., & Bischoff, K. (2011). Income inequality and income segregation. *American Journal of Sociology, 116*(4), 1092–1153.

Reardon, S. F., Bischoff, K., Owens, A., & Townsend, J. B. (2018). Has income segregation really increased? Bias and bias correction in sample-based segregation estimates. *Demography, 55*(6), 2129–2160.

Reardon, S. F., Grewal, E. T., Kalogrides, D., & Greenberg, E. (2012). Brown fades: The end of court-ordered school desegregation and the resegregation of American public schools. *Journal of Policy Analysis and Management, 31*(4), 876–904.

Reardon, S. F., & Portilla, X. A. (2016). Recent trends in income, racial, and ethnic school readiness gaps at kindergarten entry. *Aera Open, 2*(3), 2332858416657343.

Reardon, S. F., & Owens, A. (2014). 60 years after Brown: Trends and consequences of school segregation. *Annual Review of Sociology, 40*, 199–218.

Reardon, S. F., & Yun, J. T. (2002). Integrating neighborhoods, segregating schools: The retreat from school desegregation in the South, 1990–2000. *North Carolina Review, 81*, 1563.

Redding, R. (2010). *Juvenile justice bulletin: Juvenile transfer laws: An effective deterrent to delinquency*. Office of Juvenile Justice and Delinquency Prevention. https://www.ojp.gov/pdffiles1/ojjdp/220595.pdf

Reddy, A. L., Gomez, M., & Dixon, S. L. (2017). The New York State Healthy Neighborhoods Program: Findings from an evaluation of a large-scale, multisite, state-funded healthy homes program. *Journal of Public Health Management and Practice, 23*(2), 210–218.

Redner-Vera, E., & Wang, X. (2022). Examining cumulative disadvantage against American Indian defendants in federal courts. *Justice Quarterly*, 1–28.

Reece, R. L. (2020). Whitewashing slavery: Legacy of slavery and White social outcomes. *Social Problems, 67*(2), 304–323.

Reeves, A. N. (2014). *Written in Black & White: Exploring confirmation bias in racialized perceptions of writing skills*. [Yellow Paper Series]. Nextions LLC. https://www.ncada.org/resources/CLE/WW17/Materials/Wegner%20_%20Wilson--Confirmation%20Bias%20in%20Writing.pdf

Reeves, R. (2022). *Of boys and men: Why the modern male is struggling, why it matters, and what to do about it.* Brookings Institution Press.

Reeves, R., Buckner, E., & Smith, E. (2021). *The unreported gender gap in high school graduation rates.* Brookings Institution. https://www.brookings.edu/blog/up-front/2021/01/12/the-unreported-gender-gap-in-high-school-graduation-rates/

Reséndez, A. (2016). *The other slavery: The uncovered story of Indian enslavement in America.* Houghton Mifflin Harcourt.

Reuben, A., Caspi, A., Belsky, D. W., Broadbent, J., Harrington, H., Sugden, K., Houts, R. M., Ramrakha, S., Poulton, R., & Moffitt, T. E. (2017). Association of childhood blood lead levels with cognitive function and socioeconomic status at age 38 years and with IQ change and socioeconomic mobility between childhood and adulthood. *JAMA, 317*(12), 1244–1251.

Reyes, J. W. (2007). Environmental policy as social policy? The impact of childhood lead exposure on crime. *The BE Journal of Economic Analysis & Policy, 7*(1).

Reynolds, A. J., & Robertson, D. L. (2003). School–based early intervention and later child maltreatment in the Chicago longitudinal study. *Child Development, 74*(1), 3–26.

Ribar, D. C. (2015). Why marriage matters for child wellbeing. *The Future of Children*, 11–27.

Riddle, T., & Sinclair, S. (2019). Racial disparities in school-based disciplinary actions are associated with county-level rates of racial bias. *Proceedings of the National Academy of Sciences, 116*(17), 8255–8260.

Ridgeway, C. L., & Correll, S. J. (2004). Unpacking the gender system: A theoretical perspective on gender beliefs and social relations. *Gender & Society, 18*(4), 510–531.

Rigal, L. (2009). Watershed days on the Treaty Line, 1836-1839. *The Iowa Review, 39*(2), 202–223.

Rivara, F., Adhia, A., Lyons, V., Massey, A., Mills, B., Morgan, E., Simckes, M., & Rowhani-Rahbar, A. (2019). The effects of violence on health. *Health Affairs, 38*(10), 1622–1629.

Robert Wood Johnson Foundation. (2018). *Discrimination in America: Final summary.* https://cdn1.sph.harvard.edu/wp-content/uploads/sites/94/2018/01/NPR-RWJF-HSPH-Discrimination-Final-Summary.pdf

Roberts, D. (2022). *Torn apart: How the child welfare system destroys Black families—and how abolition can build a safer world.* Basic Books.

___. (2019). *Nine year gains: Project QUEST's continuing impact.* Economic Mobility Corporation.

Rodgers III, W. M., & Spriggs, W. E. (1996). What does the AFQT really measure: Race, wages, schooling and the AFQT score. *The Review of Black Political Economy, 24*(4), 13–46.

Rodney, W. (2018). *How Europe underdeveloped Africa.* Verso Books.

Rodrik, D. (2022). *An industrial policy for good jobs.* Hamilton Project, Brookings Institution.

Rogoff, B. (2003). *The cultural nature of human development.* Oxford University Press.

Roithmayr, D. (2014). *Reproducing racism: How everyday choices lock in White advantage.* New York University Press

Roller, Z., Gasteyer, S., Nelson, N., Lai, W., & Shingne, M. (2019). *Closing the water access gap in the United States: A national action plan.* Dig Deep and U.S. Water Alliance. http://uswateralliance.org/sites/uswateralliance.org/files/Closing%20the%20Water%20Access%20Gap%20in%20the%20United%20States_DIGITAL.pdf

Romm, K. F., Patterson, B., Crawford, N. D., Posner, H., West, C. D., Wedding, D., Horn, K., & Berg, C. J. (2022). Changes in young adult substance use during COVID-19 as a function of ACEs, depression, prior substance use and resilience. *Substance Abuse, 43*(1), 212–221.

Rose, E. K., Schellenberg, J. T., & Shem-Tov, Y. (2022). *The effects of teacher quality on adult criminal justice contact* (NBER Working Paper No. 30274). National Bureau of Economic Research.

Rosen, R., Byndloss, D., Parise, L., Alterman, E., & Dixon, M. (2020). *Bridging the School-to-Work Divide: Interim Implementation and Impact Findings from New York City's P-TECH 9-14 Schools*. MDRC.

Rosenbaum, J. (2022). Educational and criminal justice outcomes 12 years after school suspension. *Youth & Society*, 52(4), 515–547.

Ross, L. (2010). *Inventing the savage: The social construction of Native American criminality*. University of Texas Press.

Rossin, M. (2011). The effects of maternity leave on children's birth and infant health outcomes in the United States. *Journal of Health Economics*, 30(2), 221–239.

Rossin-Slater, M., Schnell, M., Schwandt, H., Trejo, S., & Uniat, L. (2020). Local exposure to school shootings and youth antidepressant use. *Proceedings of the National Academy of Sciences*, 117(38), 23484–23489.

Rostad, W. L., Ports, K. A., & Tang, S. (2019). Mothers' homeownership and children's economic success 20 years later among a sample of U.S. citizens. *Children and Youth Services Review*, 99, 355–359.

Rothstein, J., & Schanzenbach, D. W. (2022). Does money still matter? Attainment and earnings effects of post-1990 school finance reforms. *Journal of Labor Economics*, 40(S1), S141–S178.

Rothstein, J., & Schanzenbach, D. W. (2017). What does the Seattle experience teach us about minimum wages? Econofact, Tufts University. https://econofact.org/what-does-the-seattle-experience-teach-us-about-minimum-wages

Rothstein, R. (2004). *Class and schools: Using social, economic, and educational reform to close the Black-White achievement gap*. Teachers College Press.

Rothstein, R. (2017). *The color of law: A forgotten history of how our government segregated America*. Liveright Publishing.

Rovner, J. (2016). *Racial disparities in youth commitments and arrests*. The Sentencing Project. https://www.sentencingproject.org/publications/racial-disparities-in-youth-commitments-and-arrests/

Royer, H. (2009). Separated at girth: U.S. twin estimates of the effects of birth weight. *American Economic Journal: Applied Economics*, 1(1), 49–85.

Roygardner, L., Schneider, A., & Steiger, D. (2019). *Promoting health coverage of American Indian and Alaska Native Children*. Georgetown University Center for Children and Families.

Royster, J. V. (1995). The legacy of allotment. *Arizona State Law Journal*, 27, 1–78.

Rucker, J. M., & Richeson, J. A. (2021). Toward an understanding of structural racism: Implications for criminal justice. *Science*, 374(6565), 286–290

Rufa, A. K., & Fowler, P. J. (2016). Kinship foster care among African American youth: Interaction effects at multiple contextual levels. *Journal of Social Service Research*, 42(1), 26–40.

Rugh, J. S., & Massey, D. S. (2010). Racial segregation and the American foreclosure crisis. *American Sociological Review*, 75(5), 629–651.

___. (2014). Segregation in post-civil rights America: Stalled integration or end of the segregated century? *Du Bois Review: Social Science Research on Race*, 11(2), 205–232.

Ruhland, E., Holmes, B., & Petkus, A. (2020). The role of fines and fees on probation outcomes. *Criminal Justice and Behavior*, 47(10), 1244–1263.

Ryabov, I. (2013). Colorism and school-to-work and school-to-college transitions of African American adolescents. *Race and Social Problems*, 5(1), 15–27.

Ryan, J. P., Hong, J. S., Herz, D., & Hernandez, P. M. (2010). Kinship foster care and the risk of juvenile delinquency. *Children and Youth Services Review*, 32(12), 1823–1830.

Ryan, J. P., Perron, B. E., & Huang, H. (2016). Child welfare and the transition to adulthood: Investigating placement status and subsequent arrests. *Journal of Youth and Adolescence*, 45(1), 172–182.

Sabia, J. J., & Nielsen, R. B. (2015). Minimum wages, poverty, and material hardship: New evidence from the SIPP. *Review of Economics of the Household*, 13, 95–134.

Sabol, T. J., Kessler, C. L. Rogers, L. O., Petitclerc, A., Silver, J., Briggs-Gowan, M., & Wakschlag, L. S. (2022). A window into racial and socioeconomic status disparities in preschool disciplinary action using developmental methodology. *ANNALS of the New York Academy of Sciences, 1508*(1), 123–136.

Sabol, T. J., & Pianta, R. C. (2015). Validating Virginia's quality rating and improvement system among state-funded pre-kindergarten programs. *Early Childhood Research Quarterly, 30,* 183–198.

Sabol, T. J., Soliday Hong, S. L., Pianta, R. C., & Burchinal, M. R. (2013). Can rating pre-K programs predict children's learning? *Science, 341*(6148), 845–846.

Saha, S., Komaromy, M., Koepsell, T. D., & Bindman, A. B. (1999). Patient-physician racial concordance and the perceived quality and use of health care. *Archives of internal medicine, 159*(9), 997–1004.

Saito, N. T. (2020). *Settler colonialism, race, and the law: Why structural racism persists.* New York University Press.

Sama-Miller, E., Akers, L., Mraz-Esposito, A., Coughlin, R., & Zukiewicz, M. (2017). *Home visiting evidence of effectiveness review: Executive summary.* Mathematica Policy Research. https://econpapers.repec.org/paper/mprmprres/ab92c1547bc142a6815d64f332358eb3.htm

Sampson, R. J. (2012). *Great American city: Chicago and the enduring neighborhood effect.* University of Chicago Press.

Sampson, R. J., Sharkey, P., & Raudenbush, S. W. (2008). Durable effects of concentrated disadvantage on verbal ability among African-American children. *Proceedings of the National Academy of Sciences, 105*(3), 845–852.

The Samuel Dubois Cook Center on Social Equity. (2019). *The plunder of Black wealth in Chicago: New findings on the lasting toll of predatory housing contracts.* Duke University. https://socialequity.duke.edu/wp-content/uploads/2019/10/Plunder-of-Black-Wealth-in-Chicago.pdf

Sanchez Cumming, C., & Kopparam, R. (2021, April 1). What the U.S. Census Household Pulse Survey reveals about the first year of the coronavirus recession, in six charts. Equitable Growth. https://equitablegrowth.org/what-the-u-s-census-household-pulse-survey-reveals-about-the-first-year-of-the-coronavirus-recession-in-six-charts/

Sandel, M., Sheward, R., Ettinger de Cuba, S., Coleman, S., Heeren, T., Black, M. M., Casey, P. H., Chilton, M., Cook, J., Cutts, D. B., & Rose-Jacobs, R. (2018). Timing and duration of pre-and postnatal homelessness and the health of young children. *Pediatrics, 142*(4).

Santucci, L. (2020). Documenting racially restrictive covenants in 20th century Philadelphia. *Cityscape, 22*(3), 241–268.

Satter, B. (2009). *Family properties: Race, real estate, and the exploitation of Black urban America.* Macmillan.

Sawyer, P. J., Major, B., Casad, B. J., Townsend, S. S., & Mendes, W. B. (2012). Discrimination and the stress response: Psychological and physiological consequences of anticipating prejudice in interethnic interactions. *American Journal of Public Health, 102*(5), 1020–1026.

Sawyer, W. (2019). *Youth confinement: The whole pie 2019.* Prison Policy Initiative. https://www.prisonpolicy.org/reports/youth2019.html

Schapiro, R., Blankenship, K., Rosenberg, A., & Keene, D. (2022). The effects of rental assistance on housing stability, quality, autonomy, and affordability. *Housing Policy Debate, 32*(3), 456–472.

Schanzenbach, D., & Strain, M. R. (2021). Employment effects of the Earned Income Tax Credit: Taking the long view. *Tax Policy and the Economy, 35*(1), 87–129.

Schildberg-Hörisch, H. (2016). Parental employment and children's academic achievement. *IZA World of Labor, 231.* https://doi.org/10.15185/izawol.231

Schilling, S., Lanier, P., Rose, R. A., Shanahan, M., & Zolotor, A. J. (2020). A quasi-experimental effectiveness study of Triple P on child maltreatment. *Journal of Family Violence*, 35, 373–383.

Schinasi, L. H., Kanungo, C., Christman, Z., Barber, S., Tabb, L., & Headen, I. (2022). Associations between historical redlining and present-day heat vulnerability housing and land cover characteristics in Philadelphia, PA. *Journal of Urban Health*, 99(1), 134–145.

Schlesinger, T. (2018). Decriminalizing racialized youth through juvenile diversion. *The Future of Children*, 28(1), 59–82.

Schmidt, N. M., Krohn, M. D., & Osypuk, T. L. (2018). Modification of housing mobility experimental effects on delinquency and educational problems: Middle adolescence as a sensitive period. *Journal of Youth and Adolescence*, 47(10), 2009–2026.

Schneider, D., Harknett, K., & Stimpson, M. (2018). What explains the decline in first marriage in the United States? Evidence from the panel study of income dynamics, 1969 to 2013. *Journal of Marriage and Family*, 80(4), 791–811.

Schneider, D., & Turney, K. (2015). Incarceration and Black–White inequality in homeownership: A state-level analysis. *Social Science Research*, 53, 403–414.

Schneider, W., Bullinger, L. R., & Raissian, K. M. (2022). How does the minimum wage affect child maltreatment and parenting behaviors? An analysis of the mechanisms. *Review of Economics of the Household*, 20, 1119–1154.

Schuetz, J. (2022). *Dysfunctional policies have broken Americas housing supply chain*, Brookings Institution. United States of America. https://policycommons.net/artifacts/4142186/dysfunctional-policies-have-broken-americas-housing-supply-chain/4950950/

Schwalbe, C. S., Gearing, R. E., MacKenzie, M. J., Brewer, K. B., & Ibrahim, R. (2012). A metaanalysis of experimental studies of diversion programs for juvenile offenders. *Clinical Psychology Review*, 32(1), 26–33.

Schwartz, A. E., Horn, K. M., Ellen, I. G., & Cordes, S. A. (2020). Do housing vouchers improve academic performance? Evidence from New York City. *Journal of Policy Analysis and Management*, 39(1), 131–158.

Schwartz, A. E., Laurito, A., Lacoe, J., Sharkey, P., & Ellen, I. G. (2022). The academic effects of chronic exposure to neighbourhood violence. *Urban Studies*, 59(14), 3005–3021.

Schwartz, G. L., Feldman, J. M., Wang, S. S., and Glied, S. A. (2022). Eviction, healthcare utilization, and disenrollment among New York City Medicaid patients. *American Journal of Preventive Medicine*, 62(2), 157–164.

Schwartz, G. L., Leifheit, K. M., Berkman, L. F., Chen, J. T., & Arcaya, M. C. (2021). Health selection into eviction: Adverse birth outcomes and children's risk of eviction through age 5 years. *American Journal of Epidemiology*, 190(7), 1260–1269.

Schwarzenberg, S. J., Georgieff, M. K., Daniels, S., Corkins, M., Golden, N. H., Kim, J. H., Lindsey, C., & Magge, S. N. (2018). Advocacy for improving nutrition in the first 1000 days to support childhood development and adult health. *Pediatrics*, 141(2).

Schweinhart, L. J. (1993). *Significant benefits: The High/Scope Perry Preschool Study through age 27. Monographs of the high/scope educational research foundation, No. 10.* High/Scope Educational Research Foundation.

Schweinhart, L. J., & Weikart, D. P. (1980). *Young children grow up: Effects of the Perry preschool program on youths through age 15. (Monographs of the HighScope educational research foundation, 7)*. HighScope Press.

Scott-Clayton, J. (2011). *The shapeless river: Does a lack of structure inhibit students' progress at community colleges?* (CCRC Working Paper No. 25). Assessment of Evidence Series. Community College Research Center, Columbia University.

Scrivener, S., Weiss, M. J., Ratledge, A., Rudd, T., Sommo, C., & Fresques, H. (2015). *Doubling graduation rates: Three-year effects of CUNY's Accelerated Study in Associate Programs (ASAP) for developmental education students*. MDRC.

Sedlak, A. J., Mettenburg, J., Basena, M., Petta, I., McPherson, K., Greene, A., & Li, S. (2010). *Fourth National Incidence Study of Child Abuse and Neglect (NIS–4): Report to Congress*. U.S. Department of Health and Human Services, Administration for Children and Families. https://www.acf.hhs.gov/sites/default/files/documents/opre/nis4_report_congress_full_pdf_jan2010.pdf

Seeman, T. E., & Crimmins, E. (2001). Social environment effects on health and aging: Integrating epidemiologic and demographic approaches and perspectives. *ANNALS of the New York Academy of Sciences, 954*(1), 88–117.

Seeman, M., Merkin, S. S., Karlamangla, A., Koretz, B. & Seeman, T. (2014). Social status and biological dysregulation: The "status syndrome" and allostatic load. *Social Science & Medicine, 118*, 143–151.

Seirawan, H., Faust, S., & Mulligan, R. (2012). The impact of oral health on the academic performance of disadvantaged children. *American Journal of Public Health, 102*(9), 1729–1734.

Semega, J., & Kollar, M. (2022) *U.S. Census Bureau, Current Population Reports, P60-276, Income in the United States: 2021*. U.S. Government Publishing Office.

Shafer, P. R., Gutiérrez, K. M., De Cuba, S. E., Bovell-Ammon, A., & Raifman, J. (2022). Association of the implementation of child tax credit advance payments with food insufficiency in US households. *JAMA Network Open, 5*(1), e2143296–e2143296.

Shambaugh, J. C., & Strain, M. R. (2021). The recovery from the Great Recession: A long, evolving expansion. *The ANNALS of the American Academy of Political and Social Science, 695*(1), 28–48.

Shanks, T. W. (2005). The Homestead Act: A major asset-building policy in American History. In Sherraden, M. (Eds.) *Inclusion in the American Dream: Assets, poverty, and public policy*. Oxford University Press.

Shapiro, L. R. (2019). The crippling costs of the juvenile justice system: A Legal and policy argument for eliminating fines and fees for youth offenders. *Emory, 69*, 1305.

Sharkey, P. (2010). The acute effect of local homicides on children's cognitive performance. *Proceedings of the National Academy of Sciences, 107*(26), 11733–11738.

Sharkey, P. (2013). *Stuck in place: Urban neighborhoods and the end of progress toward racial equality*. University of Chicago Press.

___. (2018a). *Uneasy peace: The great crime decline, the renewal of city life, and the next war on violence*. WW Norton & Company.

___. (2018b). The long reach of violence: A broader perspective on data, theory, and evidence on the prevalence and consequences of exposure to violence. *Annual Review of Criminology, 1*, 85–102.

Sharkey, P., Schwartz, A. E., Ellen, I. G., & Lacoe, J. (2014). High stakes in the classroom, high stakes on the street: The effects of community violence on student's standardized test performance. *Sociological Science, 1*, 199.

Sharkey, P. T., Tirado-Strayer, N., Papachristos, A. V., & Raver, C. C. (2012). The effect of local violence on children's attention and impulse control. *American Journal of Public Health, 102*(12), 2287–2293.

Sharkey, P., & Torrats-Espinosa, G. (2017). The effect of violent crime on economic mobility. *Journal of Urban Economics, 102*, 22–33.

Sharkey, P., Torrats-Espinosa, G., & Takyar, D. (2017). Community and the crime decline: The causal effect of local nonprofits on violent crime. *American Sociological Review, 82*(6), 1214–1240.

Shaw, M. (2019). The reproduction of social disadvantage through educational demobilization: A critical analysis of parental incarceration. *Critical Criminology, 27*(2), 275–290.

Shear, S. B., Knowles, R. T., Soden, G. J., & Castro, A. J. (2015). Manifesting destiny: Re/presentations of Indigenous Peoples in K–12 U.S. history standards. *Theory & Research in Social Education, 43*(1), 68–101.

Shem-Tov, Y., Raphael, S., & Skog, A. (2021). *Can restorative justice conferencing reduce recidivism? Evidence from the make-it-right program* (NBER Working Paper No. 29150). National Bureau of Economic Research.

Shen, M. (2018). The association between the end of court-ordered school desegregation and preterm births among Black women. *PloS One, 13*(8), e0201372.

Shen, Y., Bushway, S. D., Sorensen, L. C., Smith, H. L. (2020). Locking up my generation: Cohort differences in prison spells over the life course. *Criminology, 58*, 645–677. https://doi.org/10.1111/1745-9125.12256

Shirrell, M., Bristol, T. J., & Britton, T. A. (2021). *The effects of student-teacher ethnoracial matching on exclusionary discipline for Asian American, Black, and Latinx Students: Evidence from New York City* (EdWorkingPaper No. 21-475). https://www.edworkingpapers.com/sites/default/files/ai21-475.pdf

Shonkoff, J. P. (2010). Building a new biodevelopmental framework to guide the future of early childhood policy. *Child Development, 81*(1), 357–367.

Shonkoff, J. P., Boyce, W. T., & McEwen, B. S. (2009). Neuroscience, molecular biology, and the childhood roots of health disparities: Building a new framework for health promotion and disease prevention. *JAMA, 301*(21), 2252–2259.

Shonkoff, J. P., & Garner, A. S., Committee on Psychosocial Aspects of Child and Family Health, Committee on Early Childhood, Adoption, and Dependent Care, & Section on Developmental and Behavioral Pediatrics. (2012). The lifelong effects of early childhood adversity and toxic stress. *Pediatrics, 129*(1), e232–e246.

Shoub, K., Christiani, L., Baumgartner, F. R., Epp, D. A., & Roach, K. (2021). Fines, fees, forfeitures, and disparities: A link between municipal reliance on fines and racial disparities in policing. *Policy Studies Journal, 49*(3), 835–859.

Shrider, E. A., & Creamer, J. (2023). *Current Population Reports, P60-280, Poverty in the United States: 2022*. U.S. Census Bureau, U.S. Government Publishing Office.

Shrider, E. A., & Ramey, D. M. (2018). Priming the pump: Public investment, private mortgage investment, and violent crime. *City & Community, 17*(4), 996–1014.

Simon, A. E., Fenelon, A., Helms, V., Lloyd, P. C., & Rossen, L. M. (2017). HUD housing assistance associated with lower uninsurance rates and unmet medical need. *Health Affairs, 36*(6), 1016–1023.

Simons, R. L., Murry, V., McLoyd, V., Lin, K. H., Cutrona, C., & Conger, R. D. (2002). Discrimination, crime, ethnic identity, and parenting as correlates of depressive symptoms among African American children: A multilevel analysis. *Development and Psychopathology, 14*(2), 371–393.

Simsek, M., Costa, R., & de Valk, H. A. (2021). Childhood residential mobility and health outcomes: A meta-analysis. *Health & Place, 71*, 102650.

Skewes, M., & Blume, A. (2019). Understanding the link between racial trauma and substance use among American Indians. *American Psychologist, 74*(1), 88–100.

Skiba, R. J., Chung, C.-G., Trachok, M., Backer, T. L., Sheya, A., & Hughes, R. (2014). Parsing disciplinary disproportionality: Contributions of infraction, student, and school characteristics to out-of-school suspension and expulsion. *American Educational Research Journal, 51*(4), 640–670.

Slack, K. S., Lee, B. J., & Berger, L. M. (2007). Do welfare sanctions increase child protection system involvement? A cautious answer. *Social Service Review, 81*, 207–228.

Slopen, N., Lewis, T. T., & Williams, D. R. (2016). Discrimination and sleep: A systematic review. *Sleep medicine, 18*, 88–95.

Smedley, A. (1998). "Race" and the construction of human identity. *American Anthropologist, 100*(3), 690–702.

Smedley, A., & Smedley, B. (2005). Race as biology is fiction, racism as a social problem is real. *American Psychologist, 60*(1), 16–26.

Smith, A. (2007). Soul wound: The legacy of Native American schools. Amnesty International Magazine.

Smith, E. P., Wolf, A. M., Cantillon, D. M., Thomas, O., & Davidson, W. S. (2004). The Adolescent Diversion Project: 25 years of research on an ecological model of intervention. *Journal of Prevention & Intervention in the Community, 27*(2), 29–47.

Smith, J. P. (2007). The impact of socioeconomic status on health over the life-course. *Journal of Human Resources, 42*(4), 739–764.

Smith, J. P. (2009). The impact of childhood health on adult labor market outcomes. *The review of economics and statistics, 91*(3), 478–489.

Smith, J., & Smith, G. (2010). Long-term economic costs of psychological problems during childhood. *Social Science and Medicine, 71*(1), 110–115.

Smith, L. E., Mozaffar, N. S., Feierman, J., Center, J. L., Parker, L., NeMoyer, A. J.D., Goldstein, N.E., Spence, J. M. H., Thompson, M. C., & Jenkins, V. L. (2022). *Reimagining restitution: New approaches to support youth and communities.* Juvenile Law Center. https://debtorsprison.jlc.org/documents/JLC-Reimagining-Restitution.pdf

Smith, R. A. (2002). Race, gender, and authority in the workplace: Theory and research. *Annual Review of Sociology, 28*, 509–542.

Snyder, T. D., & Dillow, S. A. (2011). *Digest of Education Statistics, 2010* (NCES 2011-015). National Center for Education Statistics.

Snyder, T. D., Dillow, S. A., & Hoffman, C. M. (2009). *Digest of education statistics, 2008* (NCES 2009-020). National Center for Education Statistics.

So, M., McCord, R. F., & Kaminski, J. W. (2019). Policy levers to promote access to and utilization of children's mental health services: A systematic review. *Administration and Policy in Mental Health and Mental Health Services Research, 46*(3), 334–351.

Sohoni, T. W. P., Ousey, G. C., Bower, E., & Mehdi, A. (2021). Understanding the gap in self-reported offending by race: A meta-analysis. *American Journal of Criminal Justice, 46*(5), 770–792.

Solari, C. D., & Mare, R. D. (2012). Housing crowding effects on children's wellbeing. *Social Science Research, 41*(2), 464–476.

Sommer, K., & Sullivan, P. (2018). Implications of U.S. tax policy for house prices, rents, and homeownership. *American Economic Review, 108*(2), 241–274.

Sorkin, I. (2015). Are there long-run effects of the minimum wage? *Review of Economic Dynamics, 18*(2), 306–333.

South, E. C., MacDonald, J., & Reina, V. (2021). Association between structural housing repairs for low-income homeowners and neighborhood crime. *JAMA Network Open, 4*(7), e2117067–e2117067.

Southerland, D., Casanueva, C. E., & Ringeisen, H. (2009). Young adult outcomes and mental health problems among transition age youth investigated for maltreatment during adolescence. *Children and Youth Services Review, 31*(9), 947–956.

Sowell, T. (1979). Three Black histories. *Wilson Quarterly,* 6–106.

___. (1981). *Ethnic America: A history.* Basic Books.

St. Pierre, C., Ver Ploeg, M., Dietz, W. H., Pryor, S., Jakazi, C. S., Layman, E., Noymer, D., Coughtrey-Davenport, T., & Sacheck, J. M. (2022). Food insecurity and childhood obesity: A systematic review. *Pediatrics, 150*(1).

Stannard, D. (1992). *American holocaust: The conquest of the New World.* Oxford University Press.

Stansbury, A. M., & Summers, L. H. (2017). *Productivity and pay: Is the link broken?* (NBER Working Paper No. 24165). National Bureau of Economic Research.

Stearns, J. (2015). The effects of paid maternity leave: Evidence from Temporary Disability Insurance. *Journal of Health Economics, 43*, 85–102.

Steil, J. P., Albright, L., Rugh, J. S., & Massey, D. S. (2018). The social structure of mortgage discrimination. *Housing Studies, 33*(5), 759–776.

Stein, L. C., & Yannelis, C. (2020). Financial inclusion, human capital, and wealth accumulation: Evidence from the freedman's savings bank. *The Review of Financial Studies, 33*(11), 5333–5377.

Steinman, K. J., Shoben, A. B., Dembe, A. E., & Kelleher, K. J. (2015). How long do adolescents wait for psychiatry appointments? *Community Mental Health Journal*, 51(7), 782–789.

Stepanikova, I., & Oates, G. R. (2017). Perceived discrimination and privilege in health care: The role of socioeconomic status and race. *American Journal of Preventive Medicine*, 52(1), S86–S94.

Stephens, M., Jr., & Toohey, D. (2022). The impact of health on labor market outcomes: Evidence from a large-scale health experiment. *American Economic Journal: Applied Economics*, 14(3), 367–399.

Stewart, R., Watters, B., Horowitz, V., Larson, R. P., Sargent, B., & Uggen, C. (2022). Native Americans and Monetary Sanctions. *The Russell Sage Foundation Journal of the Social Sciences*, 8(2), 137–156.

Stockhausen, M. (2018). *Like father, like son?—A comparison of absolute and relative intergenerational labour income mobility in Germany and the U.S.* (SOEPaper No. 989). https://ssrn.com/abstract=3269209 or http://dx.doi.org/10.2139/ssrn.3269209

Stockley, G. (2004). *Blood in their eyes: The Elaine race massacres of 1919*. University of Arkansas Press.

Strain, M. (2020). *The American dream is not dead (but populism could kill it)*. American Enterprise Institute.

Strain, M. R., Schanzenbach, D. W., Streeter, R., & Wilcox, W. B. B. (2022). *Rebalancing: Children first*. AEI Brookings.

Stratford, B. (2018). American Indian and Alaska Native communities face unique challenges when it comes to public health data. Child Trends. https://www.childtrends.org/blog/american-indian-alaska-native-communities-face-unique-challenges-comes-public-health-data

Strawn, J. R., Welge, J. A., Wehry, A. M., Keeshin, B., & Rynn, M. A. (2015). Efficacy and tolerability of antidepressants in pediatric anxiety disorders: A systematic review and meta-analysis. *Depression and Anxiety*, 32(3), 149–157.

Strayhorn, T. L. (2008). Influences on labor market outcomes of African American college graduates: A national study. *The Journal of Higher Education*, 79(1), 28–57.

Sugar, S., C. Peters, N. De Lew, & B. Sommers. (2021, April 12). *Medicaid churning and continuity of care: Evidence and policy considerations before and after the COVID-19 pandemic*. U.S. Department of Health and Human Services, Assistant Secretary for Planning and Evaluation. https://aspe.hhs.gov/reports/medicaid-churningcontinuity-care

Sullivan, M. L. (1989). *"Getting paid": Youth crime and work in the inner city*. Cornell University Press.

Sundt, J., Salisbury, E. J., & Harmon, M. G. (2016). Is downsizing prisons dangerous? The effect of California's Realignment Act on public safety. *Criminology & Public Policy*, 15(2), 315–341.

Sykes, B. L., & Maroto, M. (2016). A wealth of inequalities: Mass incarceration, employment, and racial disparities in US household wealth, 1996 to 2011. *The Russell Sage Foundation Journal of the Social Sciences*, 2(6), 129–152.

Sykes, B. L., Ballard, M., Giuffre, A., Goodsell, R., Kaiser, D., Mata, V. C., & Sola, J. (2022). Robbing Peter to pay Paul: Public assistance, monetary sanctions, and financial doubledealing in America. *The Russell Sage Foundation Journal of the Social Sciences*, 8(1), 148–178.

Sykes, J., Križ, K., Edin, K., & Halpern-Meekin, S. (2015). Dignity and dreams: What the Earned Income Tax Credit (EITC) means to low-income families. *American Sociological Review*, 80(2), 243–267.

Takeshita, J., Wang, S., Loren, A. W., Mitra, N., Shults, J., Shin, D. B., & Sawinski, D. L. (2020). Association of racial/ethnic and gender concordance between patients and physicians with patient experience ratings. *JAMA Network Open*, 3(11), e2024583–e2024583.

Tanana, H., Garcia, J., Olaya, A., Colwyn, C., Larsen, H., Williams, R., & King, J. (2021). *Universal access to clean water for tribes in the Colorado River Basin* [Research Paper]. University of Utah College of Law.

Taylor, J., & Meschede, T. (2018). Inherited prospects: The importance of financial transfers for White and Black college-educated households' wealth trajectories. *American Journal of Economics and Sociology*, 77(3-4), 1049–1076.

Taylor, K.-Y. (2019). *Race for profit: How banks and the real estate industry undermined Black homeownership*. UNC Press Books.

Taylor, S. E., Repetti, R. L., & Seeman, T. (1997). Health psychology: What is an unhealthy environment and how does it get under the skin? *Annual Review of Psychology*, 48.

Taylor, S. E., & Seeman, T. E. (1999). Psychosocial resources and the SES-health relationship. *ANNALS of the New York Academy of Sciences*, 896(1), 210–225.

Tekin, E. (2005). Child care subsidy receipt, employment, and child care choices of single mothers. *Economics Letters*, 89(1), 1–6. https://doi.org/http://dx.doi.org/10.1016/j.econlet.2005.03.005

Teran, J. (2016). The violent legacies of the California missions: Mapping the origins of Native women's mass incarceration. *American Indian Culture and Research Journal*, 40(1), 19–32.

Tester, J. M., Leung, C. W., & Crawford, P. B. (2016). Revised WIC food package and children's diet quality. *Pediatrics*, 137(5).

Teye, S. O., Yanosky, J. D., Cuffee, Y., Weng, X., Luquis, R., Farace, E., & Wang, L. (2021). Exploring persistent racial/ethnic disparities in lead exposure among American children aged 1–5 years: Results from NHANES 1999–2016. *International Archives of Occupational and Environmental Health*, 94(4), 723–730.

Thiede, B. C., Brooks, M. M., & Jensen, L. (2021). Unequal from the start? Poverty across immigrant generations of Hispanic children. *Demography*, 58(6), 2139–2167.

Thomas, M., Miller, D. P., & Morrissey, T. W. (2019). Food insecurity and child health. *Pediatrics*, 144(4).

Thomas, M. M., & Waldfogel, J. (2022). What kind of "poverty" predicts CPS contact: Income, material hardship, and differences among racialized groups. *Children and Youth Services Review*, 136, 106400.

Thompson, H. A. (2019). The racial history of criminal justice in America. *Du Bois Review: Social Science Research on Race*, 16(1), 221–241.

Thompson, O. (2021). *Human capital and Black-White earnings gaps, 1966–2017* (NBER Working Paper No. 28586). National Bureau of Economic Research.

Thornton, R. L. J., Powe, N. R., Roter, D., & Cooper, L. A. (2011). Patient–physician social concordance, medical visit communication and patients' perceptions of health care quality. *Patient Education and Counseling*, 85(3), e201–e208.

Tillman, K. H. (2007). Family structure pathways and academic disadvantage among adolescents in stepfamilies. *Sociological Inquiry*, 77(3), 383–424.

Todd, J. E. (2015). Revisiting the Supplemental Nutrition Assistance Program cycle of food intake: Investigating heterogeneity, diet quality, and a large boost in benefit amounts. *Applied Economic Perspectives and Policy*, 37(3), 437–458.

Tomaskovic-Devey, D., Thomas, M., & Johnson, K. (2005). Race and the accumulation of human capital across the career: A theoretical model and fixed-effects application. *American Journal of Sociology*, 111(1), 58–89. https://doi.org/10.1086/431779

Ton, Z. (2014). *The good jobs strategy: How the smartest companies invest in employees to lower costs and boost profits*. Houghton Mifflin Harcourt.

Toney, J. (2022). Is there wealth stability across generations in the U.S.? Evidence from panel study, 1984–2017. *Contemporary Economic Policy*, 40(4), 551–567.

Toney, J., and Robertson, C. L. (2021, May). Intergenerational Economic Mobility and the Racial Wealth Gap. *AEA Papers and Proceedings*, 3, 206–210.

Tønnessen, M., Telle, K., & Syse, A. (2016). Childhood residential mobility and long-term outcomes. *Acta Sociologica*, 59(2), 113–129.
Tonry, M. (1996). The effects of American drug policy on Black Americans, 1980-1996. *European Journal on Criminal Policy & Research*, 4, 36.
Tonry, M., & Melewski, M. (2008). The malign effects of drug and crime control policies on Black Americans. *Crime and Justice*, 37(1), 1–44.
Torche, F. (2018). Prenatal exposure to an acute stressor and children's cognitive outcomes. *Demography*, 55(5), 1611–1639.
Trafzer, C. E., & Hyer, J. R. (Eds.). (1999). *Exterminate them: Written accounts of the murder, rape, and enslavement of Native Americans during the California gold rush*. MSU Press.
Trask, K. A. (2007). *Black Hawk: The battle for the heart of America*. Macmillan.
Traylor, A. H., Schmittdiel, J. A., Uratsu, C. S., Mangione, C. M., & Subramanian, U. (2010). Adherence to cardiovascular disease medications: Does patient-provider race/ethnicity and language concordance matter? *Journal of General Internal Medicine*, 25, 1172–1177.
Tseng, V., Easton, J. Q., & Supplee, L. H. (2017). Practice partnerships: Building two-way streets of engagement. *Social Policy Report*, 30(4). Society for Research in Child Development.
Turner, L. J. (2017). *The economic incidence of Federal Student Grant Aid* [Unpublished Manuscript]. http://econweb.umd.edu/~turner/Turner_FedAidIncidence_Jan2017.pdf
Turner, M. A., & Ross, S. L. (2004). *Discrimination in metropolitan housing markets: Phase 3—Native Americans*. U.S. Department of Housing and Urban Development.
Turner, M. A., Santos, R., Levy, D.K., Wissoker, D., Aranda, C., & Pitingolo, R. (2013). *Housing discrimination against racial and ethnic minorities 2012*. U.S. Department of Housing and Urban Development, Office of Policy Development and Research.
Turner, N. (2012). Who benefits from student aid? The economic incidence of tax-based federal student aid. *Economics of Education Review*, 31(4), 463–481.
Turner, S., & Bound, J. (2003). Closing the gap or widening the divide: The effects of the GI Bill and World War II on the educational outcomes of Black Americans. *The Journal of Economic History*, 63(1), 145–177.
Tyuse, S. W., and Birkenmaier, J. (2006). Promoting homeownership for the poor: Proceed with caution. *Race, Gender & Class*, 295–310.
Ukpokodu, O. N. (2018). African immigrants, the "New Model Minority": Examining the reality in U.S. K–12 schools. *The Urban Review*, 50(1), 69–96.
Ulmer, J. T., & Bradley, M. S. (2019). Criminal justice in Indian country: A theoretical and empirical agenda. *Annual Review of Criminology*, 2(1), 337–357.
U.S. Bureau of Labor Statistics. (2010, August). *Labor force characteristics by race and ethnicity, 2009* (BLS Report No. 1026). https://www.bls.gov/opub/reports/race-and-ethnicity/archive/race_ethnicity_2009.pdf
___. (2021, November). *Labor force characteristics by race and ethnicity, 2020* (BLS Report No. 1095). https://www.bls.gov/opub/reports/race-and-ethnicity/2020/pdf/home.pdf
___. (2023, January). *Labor force characteristics by race and ethnicity, 2021* (BLS Report No. 1100). https://www.bls.gov/opub/reports/race-and-ethnicity/2021/home.htm
U.S. Census Bureau. (2012). *2012 American Community Survey*. http://www.factfinder2.census.gov
___. (2022). *Health insurance coverage by race and Hispanic origin: 2021*. https://www.census.gov/content/dam/Census/library/publications/2022/acs/acsbr-012.pdf
___. (2023). *QuickFacts United States* [Data file]. https://www.census.gov/quickfacts/fact/table/US/PST045221#qf-headnote-b
U.S. Commission on Civils Rights. (2014). *The civil rights implications of eminent domain abuse*. https://www.usccr.gov/files/pubs/docs/FINAL_FY14_Eminent-Domain-Report.pdf
___. (2017). *Targeted fines and fees against communities of color*. https://www.usccr.gov/files/pubs/2017/Statutory_Enforcement_Report2017.pdf

U.S. Department of Agriculture (USDA). (2021). *SNAP—Fiscal year 2022 cost-of-living adjustments.* https://fns-prod.azureedge.us/sites/default/files/resource-files/2022-SNAP-COLA-%20Maximum-Allotments.pdf

___. (2022). *National and state level estimates of WIC eligibility and program reach in 2019.* https://www.fns.usda.gov/wic/national-state-level-estimates-eligibility-program-reach-2019

U.S. Department of Education Office for Civil Rights. (2014, March). *Data snapshot: College and career readiness* [Issue Brief No. 3]. https://www2.ed.gov/about/offices/list/ocr/docs/crdc-college-and-career-readiness-snapshot.pdf

___. (2016). *A first look: Key data highlights on equity and opportunity gaps in our nation's public schools.* https://ocrdata.ed.gov/assets/downloads/2013-14-first-look.pdf

___. (2021). *An overview of exclusionary discipline practices in public schools for the 2017–2018 school year.* https://www2.ed.gov/about/offices/list/ocr/docs/crdc-exclusionary-school-discipline.pdf

___. (2021). *Discipline practices in pre-school.* https://www2.ed.gov/about/offices/list/ocr/docs/crdc-DOE-Discipline-Practices-in-Preschool-part1.pdf

U.S. Department of Housing and Urban Development. (2014). *Evidence matters.* Office of Policy Development and Research. https://www.huduser.gov/portal/periodicals/em/EM_Newsletter_fall_2014.pdf

___. (2017). *Housing needs of American Indians and Alaska Natives in tribal areas: A report from the assessment of American Indian, Alaska Native, and Native Hawaiian housing needs.* https://www.huduser.gov/portal/sites/default/files/pdf/HousingNeedsAmerIndians-ExecSumm.pdf

___. (2021). *2020 Annual Homeless Assessment Report (AHAR): Part 1.* https://www.huduser.gov/portal/sites/default/files/pdf/2020-AHAR-Part-1.pdf

U.S. Department of Justice. (2015). *Practice profile: Juvenile diversion programs.* https://crimesolutions.ojp.gov/ratedpractices/37#mao

U.S. Department of Treasury. (2021). Advancing equity analysis in tax policy. https://home.treasury.gov/news/featured-stories/advancing-equity-analysis-in-tax-policy

___. (2023). Coronavirus state and local fiscal recovery funds. https://home.treasury.gov/policy-issues/coronavirus/assistance-for-state-local-and-tribal-governments/state-and-local-fiscal-recovery-funds

U.S. Environmental Protection Agency (EPA). (1996). *The benefits and costs of the Clean Air Act 1970–1990.* https://nepis.epa.gov/Exe/ZyPDF.cgi/40001KCG.PDF?Dockey=40001KCG.PDF

___. (2020). *Population surrounding 1,857 superfund remedial sites.* Office of Land and Emergency Management. https://www.epa.gov/sites/default/files/2015-09/documents/webpopulationrsuperfundsites9.28.15.pdf

___. (2022). *Air pollution: Current and future challenges.* https://www.epa.gov/clean-air-act-overview/air-pollution-current-and-future-challenges#_edn9

U.S. Equal Employment Opportunity Commission. (2012). *Enforcement guidance on the consideration of arrest and conviction records in employment decisions under Title VII of the Civil Rights Act.* https://www.eeoc.gov/laws/guidance/enforcement-guidance-consideration-arrest-and-conviction-records-employment-decisions

Valdebenito, S., Eisner, M., Farrington, D., Ttofi, M., & Sutherland, A. (2019). What can we do to reduce disciplinary school exclusion? A systematic review and meta-analysis. *Journal of Experimental Criminology, 15.* 10.1007/s11292-018-09351-0

van der Put, C. E., Assink, M., Gubbels, J., & Boekhout van Solinge, N. F. (2018). Identifying effective components of child maltreatment interventions: A meta-analysis. *Clinical Child and Family Psychology Review, 21*(2), 171–202. https://doi.org/10.1007/s10567-017-0250-5

Van Hook, J., & Balistreri, K. S. (2006). Ineligible parents, eligible children: Food stamps receipt, allotments, and food insecurity among children of immigrants. *Social Science Research, 35*(1), 228–251.

Van Ryn, M., & Burke, J. (2000). The effect of patient race and socio-economic status on physicians' perceptions of patients. *Social Science & Medicine, 50*(6), 813–828.

Vargas, E. D., & Pirog, M. A. (2016). Mixed-status families and WIC uptake: The effects of risk of deportation on program use. *Social Science Quarterly, 97*(3), 555–572.

Veena, S. R., Gale, C. R., Krishnaveni, G. V., Kehoe, S. H., Srinivasan, K., & Fall, C. H. (2016). Association between maternal nutritional status in pregnancy and offspring cognitive function during childhood and adolescence: A systematic review. *BMC Pregnancy and Childbirth, 16*(1), 1–24.

Velez, M. B., Lyons, C. J., & Boursaw, B. (2012). Neighborhood housing investments and violent crime in Seattle, 1981–2007. *Criminology, 50*(4), 1025–1056.

Vivier, P. M., Hauptman, M., Weitzen, S. H., Bell, S., Quilliam, D. N., & Logan, J. R. (2011). The important health impact of where a child lives: Neighborhood characteristics and the burden of lead poisoning. *Maternal and Child Health Journal, 15*(8), 1195–1202.

Wadsworth, M. E., & Achenbach, T. M. (2005). Explaining the link between low socioeconomic status and psychopathology: Testing two mechanisms of the social causation hypothesis. *Journal of Consulting and Clinical Psychology, 73*(6), 1146–1153. https://doi.org/10.1037/0022-006X.73.6.1146

Wadsworth, M. E., Evans, G. W., Grant, K., Carter, J. S., & Duffy, S. (2016). Poverty and the development of psychopathology. In D. Cicchetti (Ed.), *Developmental psychopathology: Risk, resilience, and intervention* (pp. 136–179). John Wiley & Sons, Inc. https://doi.org/10.1002/9781119125556.devpsy404

Wainer, A., & Zabel, J. (2020). Homeownership and wealth accumulation for low-income households. *Journal of Housing Economics, 47,* 101624.

Wakefield, S., & Wildeman, C. (2013). *Children of the prison boom: Mass incarceration and the future of American inequality.* Oxford University Press.

Wallace, A. F. C. (1982). Prelude to disaster: The course of Indian-White relations which led to the Black Hawk War of 1832. *The Wisconsin Magazine of History, 65*(4), 247–288.

Walls, M., & Whitbeck, L. (2012). The intergenerational effects of relocation policies on Indigenous families. *Journal of Family Issues, 33*(9), 1272–1293.

Walters, A. (2022). *Native American, Alaska Native, and Native Hawaiian housing programs: 2022 advocates' guide.* National Low Income Housing Coalition. https://nlihc.org/sites/default/files/2022-03/2022AG_5-05_Native-American-Alaska-Native-Native-Hawaiian-Housing-Programs.pdf

Wang, L. (2021, October). The U.S. criminal justice system disproportionately hurts Native people: The data, visualized. PrisonPolicy.org. https://www.prisonpolicy.org/blog/2021/10/08/indigenouspeoplesday/

Wang X., Pengetnze, Y. M., Eckert, E., Keever, G., & Chowdhry, V. (2022). Extending postpartum Medicaid beyond 60 days improves care access and uncovers unmet needs in a Texas Medicaid health maintenance organization. *Front Public Health, 10,* 841832. https://doi.org/10.3389/fpubh.2022.841832

Warren, E. J., & Font, S. A. (2015). Housing insecurity, maternal stress, and child maltreatment: An application of the family stress model. *Social Service Review, 89*(1), 9–39.

Washington, R. (1997). The Freedman's Savings and Trust Company and African American genealogical research. *Federal Records and African American History, 29*(2). https://www.archives.gov/publications/prologue/1997/summer/freedmans-savings-and-trust.html

Watt, T., & Kim, S. (2019). Race/ethnicity and foster youth outcomes: An examination of disproportionality using the national youth in transition database. *Children and Youth Services Review, 102,* 251–258.

Watts, T. W. (2020). Academic achievement and economic attainment: Reexamining associations between test scores and long-run earnings. *AERA Open, 6*(2), 2332858420928985.

Weaver, V. M., Papachristos, A., & Zanger-Tishler, M. (2019). The great decoupling: The disconnection between criminal offending and experience of arrest across two cohorts. *The Russell Sage Foundation Journal of the Social Sciences, 5*(1), 89–123.

Weber, T. L., Ziegler, K. M., Kharbanda, A. B., Payne, N. R., Birger, C., & Puumala, S. E. (2018). Leaving the emergency department without complete care: Disparities in American Indian children. *BMC Health Services Research, 18*(1), 267. https://doi.org/10.1186/s12913-018-3092-z

Webster, D. W., Whitehill, J. M., Vernick, J. S., & Parker, E. M. (2012). *Evaluation of Baltimore's Safe Streets Program: Effects on attitudes, participants' experiences, and gun violence.* Johns Hopkins Center for the Prevention of Youth Violence.

Wei, E., Hipwell, A., Pardini, D., Beyers, J. M., & Loeber, R. (2005). Block observations of neighbourhood physical disorder are associated with neighbourhood crime, firearm injuries and deaths, and teen births. *Journal of Epidemiology & Community Health, 59*(10), 904–908.

Weikart, D. P., & Schweinhart, L. J. (1997). High/Scope Perry Preschool Program. In G. W. Albee & T. P. Gullotta (Eds.), *Primary prevention works*, 146–166. Sage Publications. https://doi.org/10.4135/9781452243801.n7

Weinstein, J. L., Martin, K. S., & Ferris, A. M. (2009). Household food security varies within month and is related to childhood anemia. *Journal of Hunger & Environmental Nutrition, 4*(1), 48–61.

Weisner, T. S. (Ed.). (2005). *Discovering successful pathways in children's development: Mixed methods in the study of childhood and family life.* University of Chicago Press.

Weist, M. D., Splett, J. W., Halliday, C. A., Gage, N. A., Seaman, M. A., Perkins, K. A., Perales, K., Miller, E., Collins, D., & DiStefano, C. (2022). A randomized controlled trial on the interconnected systems framework for school mental health and PBIS: Focus on proximal variables and school discipline. *Journal of School Psychology, 94,* 49–65. https://doi.org/10.1016/j.jsp.2022.08.002

Welsh, J. A., Nix, R. L., Blair, C., Bierman, K. L., & Nelson, K. E. (2010). The development of cognitive skills and gains in academic school readiness for children from low-income families. *Journal of Educational Psychology, 102*(1), 43.

Western, B., & Sirois, C. (2019). Racialized re-entry: Labor market inequality after incarceration. *Social Forces, 97*(4), 1517–1542.

Western, B., Kleykamp, M., & Rosenfeld, J. (2006). Did falling wages and employment increase U.S. imprisonment? *Social Forces, 84*(4), 2291–2311.

Wherry, L. R., & Meyer, B. D. (2016). Saving teens: Using a policy discontinuity to estimate the effects of Medicaid eligibility. *Journal of Human Resources, 51*(3), 556–588.

Wherry L. R., Miller, S., Kaestner, R., & Meyer, B. D. (2018). Childhood Medicaid coverage and later-life health care utilization. *The Review of Economics and Statistics, 100*(2), 287–302.

Whitbeck, L. B., Adams, G. W., Hoyt, D. R., & Chen, X. (2004). Conceptualizing and measuring historical trauma among American Indian people. *American Journal of Community Psychology, 33*(3-4), 119–130.

The White House. (2021). *Executive Order on advancing racial equity and support for underserved communities through the federal government* [Policy Brief]. https://www.whitehouse.gov/briefing-room/presidential-actions/2021/01/20/executive-order-advancing-racial-equity-and-support-for-underserved-communities-through-the-federal-government/

White, J. S., Hamad, R., Li, X., Basu, S., Ohlsson, H., Sundquist, J., & Sundquist, K. (2016). Long-term effects of neighbourhood deprivation on diabetes risk: Quasi-experimental evidence from a refugee dispersal policy in Sweden. *The Lancet Diabetes & Endocrinology*, *4*(6), 517–524.

Whiteman, E. D., Chrisinger, B. W., & Hillier, A. (2018). Diet quality over the monthly Supplemental Nutrition Assistance Program cycle. *American Journal of Preventive Medicine*, *55*(2), 205–212.

Whitney, D. G., & Peterson, M. D. (2019). U.S. national and state-level prevalence of mental health disorders and disparities of mental health care use in children. *JAMA Pediatrics*, *173*(4), 389–391.

Wildeman, C. (2020). The intergenerational transmission of criminal justice contact. *Annual Review of Criminology*, *3*, 217–244.

Wildeman, C., Emanuel, N., Leventhal, J. M., Putnam-Hornstein, E., Waldfogel, J., & Lee, H. (2014). The prevalence of confirmed maltreatment among US children, 2004 to 2011. *JAMA Pediatrics*, *168*(8), 706–713.

Wilkerson, I. (2011). *The warmth of other suns: The epic story of America's great migration*. Vintage.

Williams, D. R., & Collins, C. (2001). Racial residential segregation: A fundamental cause of racial disparities in health. *Public Health Reports*, *116*(5), 404–416.

Williams, R. B. (2022). Federal wealth policy and the perpetuation of White supremacy. *The Review of Black Political Economy*, *49*(2), 130–151.

Williams Shanks, T. R., & Destin, M. (2009). Parental expectations and educational outcomes for young African American adults: Do household assets matter? *Race and Social Problems*, *1*, 27–35.

Wilmot, K. A., & Delone, M. A. (2010). Sentencing of Native Americans: A multistage analysis under the Minnesota sentencing guidelines. *Journal of Ethnicity in Criminal Justice*, *8*(3), 151–180.

Wilson, D. B., Olaghere, A., & Kimbrell, C. S. (2017). *Effectiveness of restorative justice principles in juvenile justice: A meta-analysis*. Inter-university Consortium for Political and Social Research.

Wilson, H. A., & Hoge, R. D. (2013). The effect of youth diversion programs on recidivism: A meta-analytic review. *Criminal Justice and Behavior*, *40*(5), 497–518.

Wilson, V. (2020, November 27). *Racism and the economy: Focus on employment* [Webinar] Federal Reserve Bank of Minneapolis. https://www.minneapolisfed.org/events/2020/racism-and-the-economy-focus-on-employment

Wilson, W. J. (1987). *The truly disadvantaged: The inner city, the underclass, and public policy*. University of Chicago Press.

Wilson, W. J. (1996). *When work disappears. The world of the new urban poor*. Alfred A. Knopf.

Wilson, W. J., & Neckerman, K. M. (1986). Poverty and family structure: The widening gap between evidence and public policy issues. In S. Danziger & D. Weinberg (Eds.), *Fighting poverty: What works and what doesn't*, 232–259. Harvard University Press.

Wimer, C., Fox, L., Garfinkel, I., Kaushal, N., Laird, J., Nam, J., Nolan, L., Pac, J., & Waldfogel, J. (2022). *Historical Supplemental Poverty Measure data 1967–2020*. Center on Poverty and Social Policy, Columbia University. https://www.povertycenter.columbia.edu/

Windle, M., & Zucker, R. A. (2010). Reducing underage and young adult drinking: How to address critical drinking problems during this developmental period. *Alcohol Research & Health*, *33*(1-2), 29–44.

Winokur, M. A., Crawford, G. A., Longobardi, R. C., & Valentine, D. P. (2008). Matched comparison of children in kinship care and foster care on child welfare outcomes. *Families in society*, *89*(3), 338–346.

Winokur, M. A., Holtan, A., & Batchelder, K. E. (2018). Systematic review of kinship care effects on safety, permanency, and well-being outcomes. *Research on Social Work Practice*, 28(1), 19–32.

Winship, S. Pulliam, C., Shiro, A. G., Reeves, R. V. & Deambrosi, S. (2021). *Long shadows: The Black-White gap in multigenerational poverty*. American Enterprise Institute and The Brookings Institution. https://www.brookings.edu/wp-content/uploads/2021/06/Long-Shadows_Final.pdf

Wolf, K. C., & Kupchik, A. (2017). School suspensions and adverse experiences in adulthood. *Justice Quarterly*, 34(3), 407–430.

Woo, B., Kravitz-Wirtz, N., Sass, V., Crowder, K., Teixeira, S., & Takeuchi, D. T. (2019). Residential segregation and racial/ethnic disparities in ambient air pollution. *Race and Social Problems*, 11(1), 60–67. https://doi.org/10.1007/s12552-018-9254-0

Wood, D. (2003). Effect of child and family poverty on child health in the United States. *Pediatrics*, 112(Suppl 3), 707–711.

Wood, M., Turnham, J., & Mills, G. (2008). Housing affordability and family well-being: Results from the housing voucher evaluation. *Housing Policy Debate*, 19(2), 367–412.

Wright, J. P., Dietrich, K. N., Ris, M. D., Hornung, R. W., Wessel, S. D., Lanphear, B. P., Ho, M., & Rae, M. N. (2008). Association of prenatal and childhood blood lead concentrations with criminal arrests in early adulthood. *PLoS Medicine*, 5(5), e101.

Wu, J. (2016). Racial/ethnic discrimination and prosecution: A meta-analysis. *Criminal Justice and Behavior*, 43(4), 437–458.

Wulczyn, F. (2020). Foster care in a life course perspective. *The ANNALS of the American Academy of Political and Social Science*, 692(1), 227–252.

Xu, W. (2022). Legacies of institutionalized redlining: A comparison between speculative and implemented mortgage risk maps in Chicago, Illinois. *Housing Policy Debate*, 32(2), 249–274.

Xu, Y., Bright, C. L., Barth, R. P., & Ahn, H. (2021). Poverty and economic pressure, financial assistance, and children's behavioral health in kinship care. *Child Maltreatment*, 26(1), 28–39.

Year Up. (2023, October 10). Year Up announces significant, sustained earnings gains for young adults in five-year study. https://www.yearup.org/about/newsroom/press/year-announces-significant-sustained-earnings-gains-young-adults-five-year

Yellow Horse Brave Heart, M. (2003). Historical trauma response among Natives and its relationship with substance abuse: A Lakota illustration. *Journal of Psychoactive Drugs*, 35(1), 7–13.

Yeung, W. J., & Conley, D. (2008). Black–White achievement gap and family wealth. *Child Development*, 79(2), 303–324.

Yinger, J. (1995). *Closed doors, opportunities lost: The continuing costs of housing discrimination*. Russell Sage Foundation.

Yoon, S., Quinn, C. R., Shockley McCarthy, K., & Robertson, A. A. (2021). The effects of child protective services and juvenile justice system involvement on academic outcomes: Gender and racial differences. *Youth & Society*, 53(1), 131–152.

Yoshikawa, H., Aber, J. L., & Beardslee, W. R. (2012). The effects of poverty on the mental, emotional, and behavioral health of children and youth: Implications for prevention. *American Psychologist*, 67(4), 272.

Zagorsky, J. L. (2006). Native Americans' Wealth. In J. G. Nembhard & N. Chiteji (Eds). *Wealth accumulation and communities of color in the United States: Current issues*, Ann Arbor, MI, 132–154. The University of Michigan Press.

Zajac, L., Raby, K. L., & Dozier, M. (2019). Sustained effects on attachment security in middle childhood: Results from a randomized clinical trial of the Attachment and Biobehavioral Catch-up (ABC) intervention. *Journal of Child Psychology and Psychiatry*, 61(4), 417–424.

Zewde, N. (2020). Universal baby bonds reduce Black-White wealth inequality, progressively raise net worth of all young adults. *The Review of Black Political Economy*, 47(1), 3–19.

Zhai, F., Waldfogel, J., & Brooks-Gunn, J. (2013). Estimating the effects of Head Start on parenting and child maltreatment. *Children and Youth Services Review*, 35, 1119–1129.

Zhan, M., & Sherraden, M. (2011). Assets and liabilities, educational expectations, and children's college degree attainment. *Children and Youth Services Review*, 33(6), 846–854.

Zhang, N., Baker, H. W., Tufts, M., Raymond, R. E., Salihu, H., & Elliott, M. R. (2013). Early childhood lead exposure and academic achievement: Evidence from Detroit public schools, 2008–2010. *American Journal of Public Health*, 103(3), e72–e77.

Zhong, R., & Popovitch, N. (2022). How air pollution across America reflects racist policy from the 1930s. The New York Times. https://www.nytimes.com/2022/03/09/climate/redlining-racism-air-pollution.html

Zielinski, D. S. (2009). Child maltreatment and adult socioeconomic well-being. *Child Abuse and Neglect*, 33(10), 666–678.

Zigler, E., & Styfco, S. J. (2010). *The hidden history of Head Start*. Oxford University Press.

Ziliak, J. P. (2014). Proposal 10: Supporting low-income workers through the refundable child-care credits. In M.S. Kearney and B.H. Harris (Eds.), *Policies to Address Poverty in America*. The Brookings Institution, The Hamilton Project.

Zimmerman, M., & Shannon, P. (2013, Winter). Native families impacted by historical trauma and the role of the child welfare worker. *CW360o Trauma-Informed Child Welfare Practice*, 30.

Ziol-Guest, K. M., Duncan, G. J., Kalil, A., & Boyce, W. T. (2012). Early childhood poverty, immune-mediated disease processes, and adult productivity. *Proceedings of the National Academy of Sciences*, 109(Supp 2), 17289–17293. https://doi.org/10.1073/pnas.1203167109

Zuberi, T. (2001). *Thicker than blood: How racial statistics lie*. University of Minnesota Press.

Zuberi, T., & Bonilla-Silva, E. (Eds.). (2008). *White logic, White methods: Racism and methodology*. Rowman & Littlefield Publishers.

Zucchino, D. (2020). *Wilmington's lie: The murderous coup of 1898 and the rise of White supremacy*. Atlantic Monthly Press.